Library of Congress Cataloging-in-Publication Data

Ballantine, Jeanne H.
  The sociology of education : a systematic analysis / Jeanne H. Ballantine.—5th ed.
    p. cm.
  Includes bibliographical references (p.) and index.
  ISBN 0-13-025974-8
  1. Educational sociology.. I. Title.

LC191 .B254 2001
  306.43—dc21

                          00-045304

VP/Editorial Director: Laura Pearson
AVP: Nancy Roberts
Managing Editor: Sharon Chambliss
Editorial Assistant: Lee Peterson
AVP, Director of Manufacturing
  and Production: Barbara Kittle
Exec. Managing Editor: Ann Marie McCarthy
Production Liaison: Fran Russello
Project Manager: Linda B. Pawelchak
Manufacturing Manager: Nick Sklitsis
Prepress and Manufacturing Buyer: Mary Ann Gloriande
Cover Director: Jayne Conte
Cover Photo: Alan McEvoy/Wittenberg University
Marketing Manager: Beth Gillett Mejia
Copy Editing: Katherine Evancie
Proofreading: Ellen Denning

This book was set in 10/12 Palatino by DM Cradle Associates
and was printed and bound by The Courier Companies.
The cover was printed by Phoenix Color Corp.

© 2001, 1997, 1993, 1989, 1983 by Prentice-Hall, Inc.
A Division of Pearson Education
Upper Saddle River, New Jersey 07458

Printed in the United States of America

10 9 8 7 6 5 4 3 2 1

ISBN 0-13-025974-8

Prentice-Hall International (UK) Limited, *London*
Prentice-Hall of Australia Pty. Limited, *Sydney*
Prentice-Hall Canada Inc., *Toronto*
Prentice-Hall Hispanoamericana, S.A., *Mexico*
Prentice-Hall of India Private Limited, *New Delhi*
Prentice-Hall of Japan, Inc., *Tokyo*
Pearson Education Asia Pte. Ltd., *Singapore*
Editora Prentice-Hall do Brasil, Ltda., *Rio de Janeiro*

EDITION 5

The Sociology of Educatio

A Systematic Analysis

JEANNE H. BALLANTINE
Wright State University

Prentice
Hall

Upper Saddle River, New Jersey 07458

Contents

CHAPTER 4

*Race, Class, and Gender: Attempts to Achieve Equality
of Educational Opportunity*   *89*

CHAPTER 7

Preface

Integrating the important and diverse topics in the field of sociology of education by showing how they are related is the main goal of this text. It emphasizes the diversity of theoretical approaches and issues in the field and the application of this knowledge to the understanding of education and schooling. Education is changing rapidly; it is no easy task to present the excitement of a dynamic field with diverse and disparate topics. To present the material to students in a meaningful way, a unifying framework—an open systems approach—is used. It is meant to provide coherent structure, not to detract from the theory and empirical content of sociology of education. In the fifth edition of the text, several changes are noted. There are three new chapters. One is on students in the educational system, including factors affecting achievement, in particular family and peers. The former chapter on schools around the world has been divided and expanded into two chapters: one dealing with theories of varying educational systems, the other providing case studies of educational systems within a framework representing several different types of societies, from core to periphery and developed to developing, with different political-economic systems. In addition, extensive updating of findings on educational problems and additional updated data have been included.

After teaching sociology of education to many undergraduate and graduate students and using a variety of materials, I was concerned that the materials available, though excellent in quality, were not reaching undergraduate students who were from sociology, education, and other majors. The level of many texts is quite advanced, the themes of some books make their coverage or approach limited, or the books present research in such depth that they are beyond the grasp of undergraduates. During my work with the Project on Teaching Undergraduate Sociology, I focused on presentation of materials to undergraduates, and I have attempted to translate the ideas developed there to this text. The book is best suited for sociology of education and social foundations of education courses at the undergraduate or beginning graduate level.

Several goals guided the writing:

1. *To make the book comprehensible and useful to students.* Realizing that most students are interested in how the field can help them deal with issues they will face, I emphasize the usefulness of research findings. Choices had to be made concerning which studies and topics to cover. Those chosen should have high interest for students and help them as they interact with school systems.

2. *To present material in a coherent framework.* The instructor has leeway within the open systems approach to add topics, exclude sections of the text, and rearrange the order of topics without losing the continuity and integration present in this framework.

3. *To present diverse theoretical approaches in sociology of education.* Several valuable perspectives exist today; the book gives examples throughout of theories and how they approach issues in the field.

4. *To include as major sections several topics that have not been singled out by many authors but are important current or emerging topics and are of interest to students.* Separate chapters are devoted to higher education, informal education ("climate" and the "hidden curriculum"), the school environment, education around the world, and educational movements and alternatives.

5. *To indicate how change takes place and what role sociologists play.* With the increasing emphasis on applied sociology, more courses are including information on applied aspects of topics covered. This is the focus of the final chapter but is covered throughout the text.

6. *To stimulate students to become involved with educational systems where they can put to use the knowledge available in textbooks.* This text can be used to stimulate discussion and encourage other topics of interest to be introduced into the course in a logical way. Useful features of the book to enhance teaching effectiveness include projects at the end of each chapter; the coverage of issues; and the Instructor's Manual complete with classroom teaching aids, techniques, and test questions.

The book does not attempt to use one theoretical approach to the exclusion of others. Rather, it focuses on the value of several approaches and their different emphases in dealing with the same issue. Because the book is meant as an overview, it surveys the field rather than providing comprehensive coverage of a few topics. This allows instructors flexibility to expand where desired.

The fifth edition provides an update of issues and data, as well as revisions in theories when new trends or developments have occurred.

Thanks go to many people for suggestions on early drafts of the first edition: Peggy Hazen, Paul Klohr, Alan McEvoy, Reece McGee, Matthew Melko, Darryl Poole, Ted Wagenaar, and colleagues at Bulmershe College of Higher Education in England. For reviews of the manuscript of the fifth edition, I am grateful to Edythe M. Krampe, University of California–Irvine; James P. Marshall, University of North Colorado; and Lewis A. Mennerick, University of Kansas. Thanks for help on the research go to Jeffrey Dixon, graduate student at Indiana University, and Harden Ballantine, Ed.D., for the section on alternatives in education. For providing the materials and atmosphere for producing the end product, thanks go to Antioch University Library, University of Reading (England) Library, and the University of London and Bodleian libraries. A special thanks go to the supportive group at Prentice Hall, especially Nancy Roberts and Sharon Chambliss who provided expert editorial assistance.

Finally, my interest in this field is constantly stimulated by the diverse and everchanging experiences of my children as they pass through the stages of schooling and share their experiences, and by Hardy, whose knowledge and creative ideas in the field of education gave original impetus and continuing support and encouragement to this work.

Jeanne H. Ballantine

CHAPTER 1

Sociology of Education

A Unique Perspective on Schools

Education is a lifelong process. It begins the day we are born and ends the day we die. Found in every society, it comes in many forms, ranging from the "school of hard knocks" or learning by experience to formal institutional learning, from postindustrial to nonindustrial communities, from rural to urban settings, and from youth to older persons.

Remember your first day in the formal school setting? You anticipated that day for some time. You met the teacher who would serve as a surrogate parent for the year, and children you would get to know whether you liked them or not. Education was a given, a compulsory part of growing up, and going to college may have been "what people do after high school." But in many areas of the world, education is a privilege available only to a select group. More than 885 million people in the world—49 percent of the adult population in developing countries—are illiterate, and the dropout rate at the primary level is as high as 100 percent in some poor areas. Though primary and secondary school enrollments have increased worldwide during the past several decades, many primary-age children in the world are not even in school, and 54 percent of young women in Africa and 37 percent in southern and western Asia are illiterate (Population Action International, 1998; UNESCO, 1995).

Sociologists are interested in learning experiences of all types, formal and informal, because they fit into the broader focus on group life. The purpose of this introductory chapter is to acquaint you with the unique perspective of the sociology of education: the questions it addresses, the theoretical approaches it uses, the methods used to study educational systems, and the open systems approach used in this book.

THE FIELD OF SOCIOLOGY OF EDUCATION

As students, parents, and members of a community, educational issues face us constantly. Consider the following examples.

Are Our Children Safe in Schools? The most serious school problems according to surveys of the American public are lack of discipline, followed by fighting, violence, and gangs (Rose and Gallup, 1999). Yet, even with the recent shootings in Columbine High School and other schools, 86 percent of the public believes their schools are "very safe and orderly" or "somewhat safe and orderly" (Rose and Gallup, 1999, pp. 41-56).

Should Minimum Competency in Key Subjects Such as Reading and Math Be Required for High School Graduation? In many countries and some cities and states in the United States, students are required to take reading exams in order to enter high school and be graduated from it. Some educators argue that required competency tests force teachers to teach for the tests; others believe that schools should be held responsible for the academic competence of students who move through the system, and tests are one way to hold schools accountable. What are some implications of requiring tests?

How Should Education Be Funded? Many countries have centralized funding and decision making. Across the United States, however, taxpayers are voting on local school levies, and some schools are being forced to curtail programs because there is no money. Is failure of school levies a protest against the job schools are doing? Is it a demand for the development of other funding sources? Is it a bid for more community control?

What Type of Teachers and Classroom Environments Provide the Best Learning Experience for Children? Educators debate lecture versus experiential learning, and cooperative learning versus individualized instruction. Studies (e.g., Pescosolido and Aminzade, 1999) of effective teaching strategies provide information to help educators carry out their roles effectively.

Sociological research knowledge sheds light on educational issues, and thus helps teachers, citizens, and policymakers with the decision-making process. The first step in understanding the institution of education is to understand its meaning and lay the theoretical groundwork.

What Sociologists Study

Sociologists study people in group situations. Within this broad framework are many specialties; these can be divided into studies of institutions in society, studies of processes, and studies of other group-related situations. The structure of society is represented by six major institutions that constitute subject areas in sociology: family, religion, education, politics, economics, and health. Formal, complex organizations, such as schools, are part of the institutional structure of society, and they are often the structures through which institutions carry out their work.

Processes, the action part of society, bring the structure alive. Through the process of socialization, people learn what roles are expected of them. The process of stratification determines where people fit into the social structure and their resultant lifestyle; change is an ever-present process that constantly forces schools and other organizations to adjust to new demands. All of us are educated both formally in school settings and informally by our family, peers, media, and other influences in our lives. Not all children in the world receive a formal school education, but they all experience processes that prepare them in some way for adult roles.

The institution of education interacts and is interdependent with each of the other institutions. For instance, the family's attitudes toward education will affect the child's response to school. Other examples throughout the book will make this apparent, as will the open systems model diagrammed later in this chapter.

Why Study Sociology of Education?

There are several answers to the question of why people study the sociology of education. Someday you may be a professional in the field of education or in a related field; you will be a taxpayer, if you aren't already; or you may be a parent with children in the school system. Right now you are a student involved in higher or continuing education. Why are you taking this class? If you are a sociology major, you are studying education as one of the major institutions of society; if you are an education major, sociology may give you a different perspective on your field. You may be at college in pursuit of knowledge; or this course may be required, or you may need the credit, or, perhaps, the teacher is supposed to be good, or it simply may fit into your schedule. Let's consider some of these reasons further.

Teachers and Other Professionals. In 1996, more than 9 percent of all college graduates, or 105,509 people, were graduated in the field of education (*The Chronicle of Higher Education Almanac*, 1999-2000, p. 32), and many went on to hold teaching positions. Other college graduates teach in their respective academic fields or become involved with policy matters in the schools. Professionals in such fields as social work and business have regular contact with schools when dealing with clients and employees.

Taxpayers. Taxpayers finance schools at the elementary, secondary, and higher-education levels. Almost 100 percent of the money used to pay for physical plants, materials, salaries, and other essentials in the U. S. educational system comes from taxes. Revenues for schools come from three main sources: local, state, and federal funds from sales, income, and property taxes. Considering variations in U.S. school districts with high and low parental incomes and differences among states, in districts with median-income households, the local contribution ranges from 28 to 56 percent, and the federal contribution from 3 to 12 percent. Per pupil expenditure averages $6,028 in low-income areas and averages up to $7,504 in high-income areas (National Center for Educational Statistics, *Condition of Education*, 1999, p. 108). In districts where 25 percent or more of the people are living in poverty, the local contribution averages 27 percent; state, 60 percent; and federal, 13 percent (National Center for Education Statistics, 1991). Sociology helps taxpayers understand the school system.

Parents. A large percentage of adults in the United States are parents; 43 percent of the population are in the primary parenting years from 18 to 44 (U.S. Department of Commerce, 1993); the average size of a household in 1996 was 2.62 members (U.S. Bureau of the Census, 1997, p. 9). According to the Gallup polls on adult attitudes toward education, adults expect schools to teach basic skills, discipline children, and instill values and a sense of responsibility. The concerns of the American public regarding schools have shown a high level of consistency from year to year (see Table 1-1). Fighting, violence, and gangs was the number three concern in 1995 and the number two concern in 1999. Parents need to make decisions regarding their children's education; an understanding of school systems can be gained from a study of the sociology of education.

Students. College attracts a wide variety of students with numerous incentives and goals for their educational experience. Understanding your own and others' goals will help you get the most from your education.

For sociology majors, sociology of education provides a unique look at educational systems and their interdependence among other major institutions in society. For education majors, new insights can be gained by looking into the dynamic interactions both within educational settings and among the institution of education and other institutions in society. These insights should give education majors the ability to deal with complex organizational and interpersonal issues that confront teachers and administrators.

Other Reasons. Knowledge for the sake of knowledge—learning what there is to learn—is another reason to study sociology of education.

TABLE 1-1   Concerns Regarding Schools

1991	*1995*	*1999*
1. Use of drugs	1. Lack of discipline	1. Lack of discipline/more control
2. Lack of discipline	2. Lack of financial support	2. Fighting/violence/gangs
3. Lack of proper financial support	3. Fighting/violence/gangs	3. Lack of financial support/funding/money
4. Difficulty getting good teachers	4. Drug abuse	4. Use of drugs/dope
5. Poor curriculum/poor standards	5. Standards/quality of education	5. Overcrowded schools
6. Large schools/overcrowding	6. Overcrowded schools	6. Crime/vandalism
7. Parents' lack of interest	7. Lack of respect	7. Difficulty getting good teachers/quality teachers
8. Pupils' lack of interest/truancy	8. Lack of family structure/problem of home life	8. Parents' lack of support/interest
9. Integration/busing	9. Crime/vandalism	9. Concern about standards/quality
10. Low teacher pay	10. Integration/segration/racial discrimination	10. Low pay for teachers

Source: Elam, Stanley M., Lowell C. Rose, and Alec M. Gallup, "The 23rd Annual Gallup Poll of the Public's Attitudes Toward the Public Schools," *Phi Delta Kappan*, September 1991, p. 55; "The 27th Annual Gallup Poll," September 1995, p. 53; Rose, Lowell C., and Alec M. Gallup. "The 31st Annual Phi Delta Kappan Poll of the Public's Attitudes Toward the Public Schools." *Phi Delta Kappan*, September 1999, pp. 41-56.

Kinds of Questions Asked by Sociologists of Education

Look through this book and other sociology of education resources to find the kinds of questions asked by sociologists of education. The following sampling of questions that have been considered recently by researchers in the field will give an idea of the wide range of possible subject matter:

1. Are children of parents who are involved in their schooling more successful in school?
2. How effective are different teaching techniques, styles of learning, and classroom organizations in teaching students of various types and abilities?
3. What are some community influences on the school, and how do these affect decision making in schools, especially as it relates to socialization of the young?
4. How does professionalization of teachers affect the school system? Do teacher proficiency exams increase teaching quality?
5. How do issues such as equal opportunity and integration affect schools? Can minority students learn better in an integrated school?
6. Are some students overeducated for the employment opportunities that are available to them?
7. How does education affect income potential?

Multitudes of questions arise, and many of them are being studied around the world. Sociology of education books and courses are organized around the key topics discussed throughout this text.

> **A**pplying Sociology to Education: From what you have read so far, what topic in sociology of education interests you? ◆

THEORETICAL APPROACHES AND THE DEVELOPMENT OF SOCIOLOGY OF EDUCATION

Sociology of education is a fairly new field of inquiry. In the past half-century, emphasis has been given to education as a unique institution and an objective field of study. During this period, studies have focused on social issues in which education plays a part, such as the role of schools in providing opportunities for the poor to raise their economic status, the conflicting value systems over what should be taught in schools, the assimilation of immigrants, and the role of education in promoting equality.

In the twenty-first century, work in the sociology of education can be divided into different *levels of analysis,* from the large-scale *macrolevels* such as education as a societal institution, to small-scale *microlevel* studies of classroom interactions. Scientists use theoretical perspectives to provide logical explanations for why things happen the way they do. Starting the study of a subject with a theoretical perspective provides a guide, or a particular conception of how the social world works. Of course, a point of view also influences what the researcher sees and how it is interpreted.

Just as we have various interpretations of events in our everyday lives, so too there are several sociological perspectives on why things happen the way they do in society. These theories sometimes result in different emphases or interpretations of the same information or data. Just as each individual interprets situations differently depending on his or her background, theorists focus on different key aspects of a research problem.

A theoretical approach helps to determine the questions to be asked by researchers and the way to organize research in order to get answers. Sometimes elements of several theories are combined. The history and key aspects of three important theories are discussed in the following sections. These are followed by recent theoretical approaches attempting to explain the acquisition of knowledge and implications for classrooms. Sociologists using each theoretical approach have made major contributions in the field of sociology of education, and we will discuss many of them throughout the text.

The first two approaches focus on differing views of the way society works. The third deals with interactions in social situations. These three approaches also focus on different levels of analysis: The functional and conflict approaches tend to deal with macrolevel views of social relations and the culture of the school (that is, large-scale societal and cultural systems), whereas the interaction approach focuses on small-scale interaction between individuals and small groups. The open systems approach, which is the framework for this book, is explained at the end of this chapter.

Functionalist Theory

One major theoretical approach in sociology is *functionalism*; it is also referred to as structural-functionalism, consensus, or equilibrium theory. A sociologist using this approach starts with the assumption that society and institutions within society, such as education, are made up of interdependent parts all working together, each contributing some necessary activity to the functioning of the whole society. This approach is often likened to the biological functioning of the human body: Each part plays a role in the total system and all are dependent on each other for survival. Just as the heart or brain is necessary for the survival of a human being, an educational system is necessary for the survival of society.

Reviewing past work in sociology of education helps us formulate a theoretical and practical base on which to build; it also helps provide an historical perspective on the field. Although many philosophers, educators, and social scientists contributed their insights on education to sociological knowledge, early sociologists provided the first scientific treatments of education as a social institution.

Durkheim's Contributions to Functionalism. Émile Durkheim (1858–1917) set the stage for the conservative functional approach to education. As professor of pedagogy at the Sorbonne in Paris before sociology was "admitted" as a major field, he is generally considered to be the first person to recommend that a sociological approach be used in the study of education. He was awarded the Sorbonne's professorship of sociology combined with education in 1906 and held that post for most of the following years until his death. Thus, sociology came into France as a part of education. Because Durkheim taught all students graduating in education, many were exposed to his ideas.

Durkheim was employed to lecture primarily in education, but his sociological approach was his unique contribution. His ideas centered on the relationship between society and its institutions, all of which he believed were interdependent. He was concerned with the breakdown of community, and with solidarity and cohesion in the move from traditional to modern societies. Many of the issues about which Durkheim spoke in the late 1800s are as real today as they were then: the needs of different segments of society in relation to education, discipline in the schools, and the role of schools in preparing young people for society. Most importantly, Durkheim attempted to understand why education took the forms it did, rather than judging those forms, as had been done so often.

Durkheim's major works in the field of sociology of education were published in collections titled *Moral Education* (1961), *The Evolution of Educational Thought* (1977), and *Education and Sociology* (1956). In these works, he outlined a definition of education and the concerns of sociology as he saw them, the importance of education in creating moral values as the foundation of society, and a definition of the field for future sociologists. He wrote

> Education is the influence exercised by adult generations on those that are not yet ready for social life. Its object is to arouse and to develop in the child a certain number of physical, intellectual and moral states which are demanded of him by both the political society as a whole and the special milieu for which he is specifically destined. (1956, p. 28)

Durkheim observed that education takes different forms at different times and places and revealed that we cannot separate the educational system from the society for they reflect each other. In *The Evolution of Educational Thought*, he described the history of education in France, combining ideas from some of his other works in a historical, sociological analysis of the institution of education. Always he stressed that in every time and place education is closely related to other institutions and to current values and beliefs of the society.

In *Moral Education*, Durkheim outlined his beliefs about the function of schools and their relationship to society. Moral values are, for Durkheim, the foundation of the social order, and society is perpetuated through its educational institutions, which help instill values in children. Any change in society reflects a change in education and vice versa. In fact, education is an active part of the process of change. In this work, he analyzed classrooms as "small societies," or agents of socialization. The school serves as an intermediary between the affective morality of the family and the rigorous morality of life in society. Discipline, he contended, is the morality of the classroom, and without it the class is like a mob.

Some aspects of education that are of great concern today—the function of selection and allocation of adult roles and the gap between societal expectations of schools and actual school performance—were not dealt with by Durkheim. He was concerned primarily with value transmission for stability of society and did not consider the possible conflict between this stable view and the values and skills necessary for changing, emerging industrial societies. He argued also that education should be under the control of the state, free from special-interest groups; yet most governments are subject to influence from interest groups and to trends and pressures affecting society. Pressures from the school's environment in the areas of curriculum content, for instance, are very real.

Durkheim outlined certain areas that he believed were important for sociologists as researchers to address, including the functions of education, the relationships of education to societal change, cross-cultural research, and the social system of the school and classroom (Brookover and Erickson, 1975, pp. 4–5). His writings and guidelines for further research provide a useful beginning for the field; they also serve as a measuring stick for how far we have come. Durkheim set the stage for the current functionalist theoretical approach to education. Themes of his general writing are reflected in his concerns about consensus, conflict, and structure in education.

Functional Theory Today. A primary function of schools is the passing on of the knowledge and behaviors necessary to maintain order in society. Because children learn to be social beings and develop appropriate social values through contact with others, schools are an important training ground. Following Durkheim, sociologists see the transmission of moral and occupational education, discipline, and values as necessary for the survival of society.

Functional theorists conceive of institutions as parts of total societies or social systems. The parts of the system are discussed in terms of their *functions*, or purposes, in the whole system. The degree of interdependence among parts in the system relates to the degree of *integration* among these parts; all parts complement each other, and the assumption is that a smooth-running, stable system is well integrated. Shared values, or consensus, among members are important components of the system, as these help keep it in balance.

Functional theorists tend to focus their research on questions concerning the structure and functioning of organizations. For instance, sociologists using this theoretical approach to study educational systems would be likely to focus attention on the structural parts of the organization, such as subsystems and positions within the structure, and on how they are functioning to achieve certain goals. Sociologists who research and interpret events from this theoretical perspective see as central the functions of education for society.

The problem, according to critics of the functionalist approach, is that it fails to recognize the number of divergent interests, ideologies, and conflicting interest groups. Instead, functionalists view schools as supporting the interests of the dominant groups. In addition, the relationships among schooling, skills, and jobs is not necessarily rational or fair, according to some critics (Hurn, 1993, pp. 50–55). In heterogeneous societies, each subgroup may have its own agenda for the schools—an agenda to further its own interests.

A second problem that is often pointed out is the difficulty of analyzing interactions, such as the classroom dynamics of teacher-student or student-student relationships, from this perspective. A related criticism is that the functionalist approach does not deal with the "content" of the educational process (Karabel and Halsey, 1977, p. 11): what is taught and how it is taught. Individuals do not perform roles only within the structure; they create and modify the roles.

In addition, there is a built-in assumption in functional theory that change, when it does occur, is slow and deliberate and does not upset the balance of the system—which simply is not true in all situations. The assumption of change as a "chain reaction" is implied, but it does not necessarily reflect the reality of stable societies or rapidly changing societies.

In a now-classic analysis, Jean Floud and A. H. Halsey (1958) suggest that little progress has been made in the field since the studies of Durkheim and Max Weber (whose theories are discussed in the next section). Floud and Halsey argue that the dominant theoretical approach of structural-functionalism has not been capable of moving the field ahead because of its status quo orientation in a society faced with constant change. "The structural-functionalist is preoccupied with social integration based on shared values . . . therefore education is a means of motivating individuals to behave in ways appropriate to maintain society in a state of equilibrium. This preoccupation tends to play down problems of social change, and is therefore . . . unsuitable for the analysis of modern industrial societies" (Floud and Halsey, 1958, p. 171). In part as a reaction to these shortcomings of structural-functionalism, conflict theory began to play a prominent role in the field. It is important to keep in mind that both functional and conflict theories attempt to explain how education contributes to the maintenance of the status quo in society.

Conflict Theory

In contrast to functional theory is *conflict theory*, which assumes a tension in society and its parts created by the competing interests of individuals and groups. Variations of this approach stem from the writings of Karl Marx and Max Weber. Marx laid down the foundations for conflict theory based on his outrage over the social conditions of the exploited workers in the class system resulting from capitalism. He contended that society's competing groups, the "haves" and the "have-nots," were in a constant state of tension, which could lead to the possibility of struggle. The "haves" control power, wealth, material goods, privilege (including access to the best education), and influence; the "have-nots" present a constant challenge as they seek a larger share of society's wealth. This struggle for power helps determine the structure and functioning of organizations and the hierarchy that evolves as a result of power relations. The "haves" often use coercive power and manipulation to hold society together (Sadovnik, 2001), but this theory recognizes that change is inevitable and sometimes rapid, as the conflicts of interest lead to the overthrow of existing power structures.

Weber's Contributions to the Sociology of Education. Max Weber (1864–1920) presented a particular brand of conflict theory. He believed that power relationships between groups form the basic structure of societies and that a person's status identifies his or her position in the group. Weber contributed less directly than Durkheim to the sociology of education and provided a less systematic treatment of education. His work in related fields of sociology, however, has contributed to our understanding of many aspects of education. He is noted for his work on bureaucracy and for the concept of *status group relationships*. In fact, he writes that the primary activity of schools is to teach particular "status cultures." Power relationships and the conflicting interests of individuals and groups in society influence educational systems, for it is the interests and purposes of the dominant groups in society that shape the schools. Weber's unique approach combined the study of the macroschool organization with an interpretive view of what brings about a situation and how we interpret or define that situation.

Within the school there are "insiders," whose status culture, Weber believes, is reinforced through the school experience, and "outsiders," who face barriers to success in school. Transfer these ideas to school systems today as they deal with poor and minority students and the relevance of Weber's brand of conflict theory becomes evident. His theory deals with conflict, domination, and groups struggling for wealth, power, and status in society. These groups differ in property ownership; cultural status, such as ethnic group; or power derived from positions in government or other organizations. Education is used as one means to attain desired ends. Relating this to Karl Marx's writings on conflict theory, education produces a disciplined labor force for military, political, or other areas of control and exploitation by the elite.

Weber's writings, using cross-cultural examples and exploring preindustrial and modern times, shed light on the role of education in different societies at various time periods (Weber, 1958). In preindustrial times, education served the primary purpose of a differentiating agency that trained people to fit into a way of life and a particular "station" in society. With industrialism, however, new pressures faced education from upwardly mobile members of society vying for higher positions in the economic system. Educational institutions became increasingly important in training people for new roles in society.

Weber described a trend toward the rational organization of bureaucracy in modern society, noting that one characteristic of modern bureaucratic organization is its rational-expert leadership. The leaders are selected on the basis of examinations that single out those who best fit jobs at different levels of the bureaucracy. Today, charismatic leaders and those born into positions of power are less dominant in many institutions, including educational institutions, than are competent, professional experts whose merit is measured by examination (Weber, 1961).

In his essay "The Rationalization of Education and Training" (Gerth and Mills, 1946), Weber points out that rational education develops the "specialist type of man" versus the older type of "cultivated man," described in his discussion of educational systems in early China. Again we see the relevance of

Weber's writings: Today's institutions of higher education are debating the value of vocationally oriented education versus education for the well-rounded person.

Conflict Theory Today. Weber and Marx set the stage for branches of conflict theory held by theorists today. Research from the conflict theorists' perspective tends to focus on those tensions created by power and conflict that ultimately cause change. Some conflict theorists see mass education as a tool of capitalist society, controlling the entrance into higher levels of education through the selection and allocation function and manipulating the public. Another conflict theorist following in Weber's tradition is Randall Collins. He focuses on "credentialism," which is a technique of increased requirements for higher-level positions used by more advantaged individuals to further their status (Collins, 1978). Many conflict theorists believe that until society's economic and political systems are changed, school reform providing equal access will be impossible (Bowles and Gintis, 1976)

Applying conflict theory to the school and classroom level of analysis, Willard Waller believes that schools are in a state of constant potential disequilibrium; teachers are threatened with the loss of their jobs because of lack of student discipline; academic authority is constantly threatened by students, parents, school boards, and alumni who represent other, often competing, interest groups in the system; and students are forced to go to schools, which they may consider oppressive and demeaning (Waller, 1965, pp. 8–9).

Another branch of conflict theory called *cultural reproduction and resistance theories* argues, very generally, that those who dominate capitalistic systems mold individuals to suit their own purposes. Beginning in the 1960s in Europe, these theorists considered how forms of culture are passed on by families and schools (Sadovnik, 2001; Bourdieu and Passeron, 1977). The amount of "cultural capital" one has is an indicator of one's status, and families and schools differ in the amount of cultural capital they provide to children. For instance, an elite, preparatory school provides more cultural capital than a poor, urban school. Reproduction theorists study the cultural processes by which students learn knowledge and what knowledge is transmitted. Resistance to school control has also been the topic of many recent studies. These theories are discussed in some detail in later chapters.

The conflict theory approach implies a volatile system and the ever-present possibility of major disruption because of the unequal distribution of status, cultural capital, opportunity, and other resources. The approach can be useful in attempting to explain situations where conflict exists; however, critics argue that the connection between curriculum and capitalism has not been laid out clearly and that little empirical data has been presented to substantiate the claims (Anyon, 1981). Also, this theory does not offer useful explanations concerning the balance or equilibrium that does exist between segments of a system or the interactions between members of the system. Neither conflict theory nor functional theory focuses on the individual, the individual's "definition of the situation," or interactions in the educational system, as does the third theory, which is discussed in the next section.

Interaction and Interpretive Theories

A third theoretical approach in sociology focuses on individuals' interaction with each other. Individuals sharing a culture are likely to interpret and define many social situations in similar ways because of their similar socialization, experiences, and expectations. Hence, common norms evolve to guide behavior. Differences also exist, however, based on individual experiences, social class, and status. This theory stems from the work of G. H. Mead and C. H. Cooley on the development of self through social interaction, whether in school or other situations.

The *interaction theory* approach has been used increasingly since World War II and emphasizes social-psychological questions. Interaction theories grew from reactions to the macrolevel focus of structural-functional and conflict theories, which focused on structure and process of organizations. These approaches miss the dynamics of everyday school life that shape children's futures. Interactionists ask questions about the most common, ordinary interactions between school participants. Sociologists of education using this approach are likely to focus on interactions between groups of peers, between teachers and students, or between teachers and principals on student attitudes and achievements; on student values; on students' self-concepts and their effect on aspirations; and on socioeconomic status as it relates to student achievement. From this approach have come studies of the effects of teacher expectations of student performance and achievement; studies of the results of ability grouping of students; and studies of schools as total institutions (e.g., Mehan, 2001).

Two interaction theories useful in sociology of education are labeling theory and exchange theory. If Johnny is told repeatedly that he is dumb and will amount to little, he may incorporate this label as part of his self-concept and behave as the label suggests. There is evidence that students behave well or badly depending on teacher expectations. *Labeling theory* is discussed further in other sections of the book.

Exchange theory is based on the assumption that there are costs and rewards involved in our interactions. Reciprocal interactions bind individuals and groups with obligations; for example, students learn and teachers are rewarded. Rewarded behavior is likely to continue. These interaction theories are useful to us in understanding the dynamics of the classroom.

Some theorists have attempted to synthesize micro- and macrolevel theories, arguing that both must be considered if we are to understand educational systems (Bernstein, 1990), which is a view that is consistent with the open systems approach that underlies this book.

Recent Theories in the Sociology of Education

A "new" sociology of education has been the focus of attention for many British sociologists since the early 1970s and has supporters in the United States and elsewhere. In reaction to "macrocosmic" approaches, which put little emphasis on interaction, these theorists base their ideas on symbolic interaction, ethnomethodology, and phenomenology, arguing that an alternative approach to sociology of education is needed if we are to understand educational systems. They stress the need to understand our commonsense views of reality—how we come to view the events and situations around us and react to them as we do. As they are applied to education, these theories have taken the form of studying interaction processes in classrooms, the management and use of knowledge, the question of what it is to be "educated," curriculum content, and so forth. (Some examples of work using this approach are cited in Chapter 6.)

The work of two proponents of this approach, Basil Bernstein and Pierre Bourdieu (Sadovnik, 2001; Karabel and Halsey, 1977, p. 60), seems to show a synthesis of macro- and microcosmic approaches rather than a totally new approach (Bernstein, 1975; Bourdieu, 1973). Bernstein's goal for his life work is to "prevent the wastage of working-class educational potential" (Bernstein, 1961, p. 308). He provides an analysis of the relations among society, schools, and the individual and explains how these reproduce social inequality (Sadovnik, 2001). Bernstein argues that the structural class and power relations of the system (the macrocosmic levels of analysis) and the interactional educational processes of the school (the microcosmic levels) need to be integrated in order to gain an understanding of educational systems (Bernstein, 1974). One effort at integration is seen in his work on the speech patterns that, he argues, perpetuate one's social class. One's family class position determines speech patterns, which, in turn, affect one's position in society—as exemplified by the poorer academic performance of working-class children. He also points out the need to evaluate the effect of class bias in teaching and educational ideology on students' performance.

Bernstein's later work focuses on curriculum and the pedagogy used to transmit knowledge. Curriculum—what is taught—defines "valid knowledge," and how it is transmitted has consequences for different groups of students based on social class and power relations. His attempts to link the societal, institutional, interactional, and intrapsychic realms have moved the field closer to an integration. However, more empirical testing of his theories is necessary, and applications to educational practice and policy need to be carried out (Sadovnik, 2001; Bernstein, 1990).

The central concept in Pierre Bourdieu's work is *cultural capital*. Children from higher social classes have more cultural capital (e.g., proper language; knowledge of art, music, theater, and literature; and knowledge of ideas important in the world), a commodity that can be traded in for higher status in school and later in the workforce. Thus, cultural capital allows students to reproduce their social class through family and schooling.

Several recent proposals for reform of schools are based on educational theories. *Modernism*, largely a Western perspective on education, includes "modern" ideas of rational thought, progress through science and technology, humanism, democracy (equality, justice, and liberty), and the primacy of individualism over established authority (Elkind, 1994, p. 6). It replaced the idea of the divine right of kings and the church with the ideas of progress, universality, and regularity, which led to modern education. Many of the proposed systemic changes in education, such as government goals for uniform national standards (as in *Goals 2000*) and reforms of teacher education training, fall into the modernism category (Darling-Hammond and McLaughlin, 1995).

Postmodernism moves beyond the modernist thought relevant in the industrial era, which attempted all-encompassing explanations of the world. Instead, postmodernists stress the importance of theories relevant to local situations; the connection between theory and practice; and democratic, antitotalitarian, antiracist ideas. They call for respect and understanding of differences. Sometimes called "critical education theory" (Sadovnik, 2001, p. 32), many modern writers including Paolo Freire (1987, 1970) and Henry Giroux (1991) are following the lead of early theorists.

Postmodernism honors human diversity and the variations and ambiguity in the way different people view situations and learning. It also recognizes the political setting in which education occurs. Education results from choices that cannot be made without reference to sets of values and interests in the community, which is entangled in power structures (Cherryholmes, 1988). "Postmodernism is not a rejection of regularity, just a demand that irregularity be accepted as well" (Elkind, 1994, p. 12). This means for education that curriculum should be integrated and interdisciplinary, that universal skills such as critical thinking should be stressed, and that individual children can reach a common goal by different paths. The locus of control in this model is at the individual school level, and children's achievements would be measured in many ways: tests, portfolios, performances, and projects—whatever works best for the children in that school (Bernstein, 1993; Sizer, 1992).

We have made the point that a number of approaches are useful in the sociology of education, depending on the questions one is asking. These theories help us understand and work with educational systems.

Applying Sociology to Education: Which of these approaches would be useful in studying a topic of interest to you? ◆

American Sociology of Education

In American sociology of education there was an early motivation to reform society. Lester Frank Ward, one of the six founding fathers of American sociology and the first president of the American Sociological Association, argued in 1883 that education is a principal source of human progress and an agent of change that can foster moral commitment and cognitive development to better society (Bidwell, 1979). The field was referred to as *educational sociology,* and it focused on practical issues and the formulation of policy and recommendations. The name *sociology of education* was introduced in the late 1920s by Robert Angell (1928). Angell and others believed educational institutions were sources for scientific data; they felt that sociology could not and should not promise to produce answers or suggest changes to solve school problems. Today, however, there is a need for sociologists with both emphases: one group to carry out objective research and one to work with schools in interpreting and implementing scientific findings. The latter group needs to have special training in scientific methodology, as well as practical knowledge of how schools work.

This book deals both with theoretical studies of schools and with the practical application of theory in schools and classrooms. The latter aspect is important because most of you will be using this knowledge in your roles as parents or professionals. Sociology can have practical applications and an impact on policy rather than remaining abstract and theoretical.

THE OPEN SYSTEMS APPROACH

By now it is clear that a number of theoretical approaches are used to study the institution of education. Each provides valuable insights into a complex system. How are we to order this complexity and make it understandable?

Some sociologists favor one theoretical approach for all of their work; others select an approach to fit the problem. Our goal is to understand the educational system and the contribution that each approach can make to that understanding. For this reason, this book is organized around a systems model of education. Using this model, we can break this complex system into its component parts for study. One theoretical approach may be more applicable than another for the study of certain parts of the system or of educational problems that arise in the system. The model enables us to see the interconnections between parts and theories. Let us now move to an explanation of the model.

One-room schoolhouse.

If we want to understand an educational system as a whole, integrated, dynamic entity, we are faced with a problem. Most research studies focus on parts of the whole system, and most theoretical approaches have specific foci. An open systems approach is not a panacea for all the problems we face when trying to get the total picture, but it can help us conceptualize a whole system and understand how the small pieces fit together, and which pieces do not fit. A model provides a useful way of visualizing the many elements in the system; it helps order observations and data and represents a generalized picture of complex interacting elements and sets of relationships (Griffiths, 1965, p. 24). The following model does not refer to one particular organization or theoretical approach, but rather, it gives us a framework to consider the common characteristics of many educational settings.

Although this model indicates the component parts of a total system, it does not imply that one theory is better than another for explaining situations or events in the system. Neither does it suggest which is the best methodology to use in studying any part of the system. It does allow us to visualize the parts we may read about or study in relation to the whole system to see where they fit and what relationship they bear to the whole.

In describing a systems model, Marvin Olsen (1978) has said

It is not a particular kind of social organization. It is an analytical model that can be applied to any instance of the process of social organization, from families to

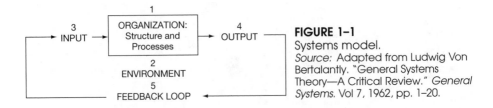

FIGURE 1-1
Systems model.
Source: Adapted from Ludwig Von Bertalantly. "General Systems Theory—A Critical Review." *General Systems.* Vol 7, 1962, pp. 1–20.

nation. . . . Nor is [it] a substantive theory—though it is sometimes spoken of as a theory in sociological literature. This model is a highly general, content-free conceptual framework within which any number of different substantive theories of social organization can be constructed. (p. 228)

Figure 1-1 shows the basic components of any social system. We discuss the parts in a five-step process. An example for each step, taken from an educational setting (see Figure 1-2), is included to help clarify the content of each part of the system.

FIGURE 1-2 Systems model of education.

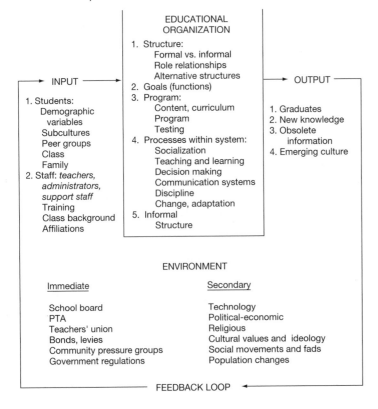

Step 1. Focus your attention on the center box, the *organization*. This refers to the center of activity and the central concern for the researcher. This box can represent a society (such as the United States), an institution (such as education or family), an organization (such as a particular school or church), or a sub-system (such as a classroom). For purposes of discussion, we shall refer to this as "the organization." It is in the organization that action takes place, illustrating that the organization is more than structure, positions, roles, and functions. Within the organizational boundaries is a structure consisting of parts and subparts, positions and roles. Although we speak of the organization as though it were a living entity, we are really referring to the personnel who carry out the activities of the organization and make decisions about organizational action. The processes in the system bring the organization alive. Decision making by key personnel, communication among members of the organization, and socialization into positions in the organization are among the many activities that are constantly taking place.

Some theoretical approaches emphasize only this internal organization analysis, but these processes do not take place in a vacuum. The decision makers holding positions and performing roles in the organization are constantly responding to demands from both inside and outside the organization. The boundaries of the organization are not solid, but remain flexible and pliable in most systems to allow system needs to be met. We call this "open boundaries" or an *open system*.

The formal relationships within educational organizations are only part of the picture. Capturing the informal relationships in the school—who eats lunch with whom, who cuts classes, the subtle cues teachers transmit to students, the gossip in the teachers' lounge—can tell us as much about its functioning as observing formal roles and structure.

Step 2. An open system implies that there is interaction between the organization and the environment outside the organization.

Focus now on the *environment*. This includes everything that surrounds the organization and influences it in some way. Typically, the environment includes other surrounding systems. For a country, these would be all other countries of the world; for an organization, they would be other competing or cooperating organizations. In addition, there is the technological environment, with new developments that affect the operation of the system; the political environment, which affects the system through legal controls; the economic environment, from which the system gets its financing; the surrounding community and its prevailing attitudes; the values, norms, and changes in society, which are often reflected in social movements or fads; population changes; and so forth.

For each organization, the crucial environment will differ and can change over time, depending on issues facing the school. The importance of environment, however, does not change. The organization depends on the environment for meeting many of its resource requirements and for obtaining information.

Each school and school district faces a different set of challenges from the environment. There are necessary and desired interactions with the environment, and some are not so pleasant. The interaction of the school with the environment takes place in our systems model in the form of inputs and outputs.

Step 3. The organization receives *input* from the environment in such forms as information, raw materials, students, personnel, finances, and new ideas. Furthermore, the persons who are members of an organization belong to other organizations in the environment and bring into the organization influences from the outside environment.

Some of the environmental inputs are mandatory for the organization's survival; others vary in degree of importance. For most organizations, some inputs are undesirable, but unavoidable, such as new legal restrictions, competition, or financial pressures. The organization can exert some control over the inputs. For instance, schools have selection processes for new teachers, textbooks, and other curricular materials. Certain positions in the organization are held by personnel who act as *buffers* or liaisons between the organization and its environment. The secretary who answers the phone, for example, has a major protecting and controlling function, and the social worker and counselor are links with the environment.

Step 4. *Output* refers to the material items and the nonmaterial ideas that leave the organization, for example, completed products, such as research findings; graduates; wastes; information; evolving culture; and new technology. There may be personnel in boundary-spanning positions bridging the gap between the organization and the environment. Personnel with responsibility for selling the organization's product, whether they work in a manufacturing organization or in a placement office for college graduates, serve this function.

Step 5. A key aspect of a systems model is the process of *feedback*. This step implies an organization constantly adapting to changes and demands in the environment as a result of new information it receives. For instance, the organizational personnel compare the current state of affairs with desired goals and environmental feedback to determine new courses of action. The positive or negative feedback requires different responses. The basic model (Figure 1–2) can serve us in many ways. It is used as a framework for organizing content in this book. But, as conceived by some of its early proponents, it is more inclusive and flexible, and it can help promote interdisciplinary study. Consider, for example, Kenneth Boulding's (1956) statement:

> [A]n interdisciplinary movement has been abroad for some time. The first signs of this are usually the development of hybrid disciplines. . . . It is one of the main

objectives of General Systems Theory to develop these generalized areas, and by developing a framework of general theory to enable one specialist to catch relevant communications from others. (p. 197)

Sociology of education cannot be discussed within the fields of education and sociology alone. Examples of related fields are numerous: economics and school financing; political science, power, and policy issues; the family and the child; church-state separation controversies; health fields and medical care for children; humanities and the arts; and the school's role in early childhood training.

Several social scientists have pointed to the value of an open systems approach in organizational analysis. David Easton, for example, writes: "A systems analysis promises a more expansive, more inclusive, and more flexible theoretical structure than is available even in a thoroughly self-conscious and well-developed equilibrium approach" (Easton, 1965, p. 20). For our book, this approach not only serves the purposes noted but also helps give unity to a complex field. Each chapter in this book describes some part or process in the educational system.

RESEARCH METHODS IN SOCIOLOGY OF EDUCATION

A theory is used to give direction to research studies, determine data and materials to be collected, and guide interpretations of data. However, a theory is only a guideline. Content must be added. Using scientific and objective techniques, data must be collected in order to test the usefulness and accuracy of theoretical explanations of events.

A sociologist is a scientist and, therefore, employs the scientific method in studying issues and problems. Some sociologists focus their attention on the institution of education and issues related to it. Their research techniques are essentially the same as those used by sociologists studying other areas.

Prior to 1950, few studies of education used objective standards and measures. Most frequently, anecdotes and value judgments were used to illustrate and support arguments. Gradually, the emphasis in published literature moved to empirical studies. Several research methods are now used in sociology of education: participant observation, surveys, secondary analysis, controlled laboratory studies, and case studies. To decide which technique to use, the researcher must define the problem to be studied and determine the level of analysis and possible sources of information related to the problem. Then the researcher selects the population or group to be studied and determines whether to study all or part of the population. The researcher may want to talk directly with the persons in the group to be studied, observe them at some task, obtain statistical information such as test scores, or use a combination of these and other techniques.

Several well-known works rely heavily on observation in schools (Lubeck, 1985; Willis, 1979; Metz, 1978; Jackson, 1968). In each, observation in schools and classrooms produced data to study research questions. Researchers consider how students and teachers construct the classroom social situation. For instance, in a study of similarities and differences among American high schools based on social class differences of students served, Mary Haywood Metz studied teachers' work by observing their classrooms, interviewing them, and reviewing documents about each school. What Metz found was a "common script." The roles and plots were similar, but the setting and actors' lines were recognizable but different based on the social class composition of the school (Metz, 1990).

Another famous study used controlled classroom settings. Robert Rosenthal and Lenore Jacobson studied the effects of teacher expectations on student performance by manipulating the classroom situation. They assigned some children to a special treatment group, and others remained in the regular classroom (Rosenthal and Jacobson, 1968). This experiment comes close to being a controlled laboratory experiment with a minimum of influence from external sources, yet it is difficult to rule out all of the influences from outside the classroom that might have affected the study results.

In yet another well-known study, James Coleman and others (1966) surveyed approximately 5 percent of the schools in the United States to ascertain the degree of equality of educational opportunity. In this massive study, students at five grade levels were given standardized tests. Additional information about the students and schools was collected by survey and secondary analysis. These are several examples of different data collection methods. Other examples of research techniques are considered as we discuss various studies.

At times it is useful to combine methodological techniques in order to obtain the most accurate picture of what we are studying. Coleman, for instance, was criticized for not using observation or other techniques to describe the operations that went on in the schools he surveyed. Using multiple methods to collect data is called *triangulation*.

SOCIOLOGY OF EDUCATION IN THE TWENTY-FIRST CENTURY

When several prominent sociologists of education were asked about their predictions for the field in the years ahead, most predicted that the problems facing American schools would see little improvement in the near future. The problems facing our schools reflect the problems in our society. The sociologists interviewed suggested that sociological theories and methods will make a major contribution to understanding the societal forces and school dynamics that underlie the problems schools will face; this knowledge is essential to tackle the problems of the twenty-first century. The number of children living in poverty and "at risk" educationally is increasing rapidly, especially in urban areas. Books such as Kozol's *Savage Inequalities* (1991) and MacLeod's *Ain't No Makin' It* (1996) document the inequalities between rich and poor school districts and life in poor neighborhoods and schools.

The student population is changing dramatically. Thus, U.S. schools soon will be dealing with the most diverse group of students ever. In 1996, 17 percent of students in grades 1 to 12 were African American and 14.3 percent were Hispanic (National Center for Educational Statistics, *Conditon*, 1999, p.126).

> By 2000, more than 10 states will have [a majority of their] student populations who trace their ancestry to Africa, the Hispanic world, the Pacific Islands, Arabia, or somewhere other than white Europe. The Los Angeles public schools already teach children who speak at least 81 languages other than English at home. Economic inequalities in our society are widening. (*Sociology of Education Newsletter*, 1992, pp. 4–6; see also Natriello, McDill, and Pallas, 1990)

Schools are often expected to be the unifiers of a fragmented society and to produce competent adults who can perform their roles well. To understand how and to what extent this is possible, sociologists of education can contribute knowledge on school, classroom, and family social systems; on the factors contributing to inequality; on nonacademic factors that affect children's learning and achievement; and on many other areas of concern to educational systems. For instance, it is difficult to produce competent adults from abused or neglected children. Longitudinal research (research conducted on a group of students over time), ethnographies, and statistical data sets are among the major methods that will provide the data for analysis of schools (*Sociology of Education Newsletter*, 1992).

ORGANIZATION OF THE BOOK

Each chapter in the book describes some part of the system of education. As you read, be aware of which part is being discussed, and by the end of the book you should have a fairly complete picture of the total educational system. The chapters can be studied out of order and still present the total model. Theoretical approaches discussed in this chapter are related to practical issues throughout the book. In addition, you can enhance your effectiveness in dealing with schools by learning to "do" sociology, learning about the methodology used, and becoming knowledgeable producers and consumers. At the end of each chapter you will find a chapter summary and suggested projects related to each topic. You are encouraged to try to make the subject more useful to yourself by doing these projects. For instance, after reading this chapter, ask yourself what questions you feel sociology of education should address. Keep these in mind as you read. You might also consider doing further research on the questions you raise.

We are now ready to enter the school. The scene is an active, dynamic one. Let us take a close look at some of the processes taking place.

◆ Summary

In this chapter we have discussed the perspective of sociology of education.

I. The Field of Sociology of Education

Sociologists study group life. One of the social institutions that make up society is education: As a part of group life, it is of interest to sociologists. All of us are involved with educational systems during our lives, and education interacts with and is interdependent with other institutions in society.

We study sociology of education because it is or will be relevant to roles we play as taxpayers, parents, professionals, and students.

Researchers in sociology of education have focused on numerous areas of study: the socialization process, the relationship between education and stratification, control of education, and so forth.

The functions or purposes of education are the same in each society but are carried out differently. They include learning to be a productive member of society; passing on culture; selecting, training, and placement of individuals in society; change and innovation; and social and personal development. These functions are not always carried out smoothly and may be points of conflict in school policies.

II. Theoretical Approaches and the Development of Sociology of Education

Sociology of education is a fairly new field; much of the literature has been developed in the past half-century. It has its roots, however, in the works of European sociologists including Durkheim, Marx, and Weber.

In recent years, the field has moved from practical to more theoretical emphases, although both are still used. Three types of theory and research dominate sociology of education: large systems, specific institutions, and interaction in educational settings. Each focuses on a different level of analysis and uses different methods for research:

◆ *Functionalist theory* views the educational system as an integral, interrelated part of the whole societal system, carrying out certain necessary functions for the survival of society. Systems are held together by shared values. Durkheim first applied the sociological perspective and methods to the study of education.

◆ *Conflict theory* assumes that tension exists in society because of competing interest groups. The "haves" control the power and resources, and thus the educational systems including access to higher levels of education. There is the ever-present possibility of struggle. Weber's contributions, less directly in the field of education than Durkheim's, were in the areas of organization and training members for society.

◆ *Interaction theory* focuses on individuals and how they form interpretations of the world around them. Labeling and exchange theory are two types of interaction theory. Recent perspectives include the "new" sociology of education, which is related to interaction theory and claims to be an alternative approach to the macrocosmic theories.

III. The Open Systems Approach

This book is organized around the open systems model presented in Figure 1–1. Each part of the educational system is discussed: the organization, its environment, inputs and outputs, and feedback. Using this approach allows us to visualize the whole system, each subpart in relation to the whole, and the environment surrounding the system. Models help us visualize the relationship between parts.

IV. Research Methods in Sociology of Education

Sociological methods used to study educational systems include observations, surveys, the use of existing data such as test scores, controlled laboratory experiments, and case studies. Any of these methods, or a combination of methods, can be used—depending on the theory and level of analysis used—to collect data to help answer questions within a theoretical framework.

V. Sociology of Education in the Twenty-First Century

Two major changes will affect educational systems in the United States and around the world. One is the changing constituency of education, including large groups of students demanding quality education. In the United States this means more minority students in schools. The second major change for schools involves providing access to technological training for all students.

◆ *Sample Study Questions in Sociology of Education*

The following are examples of research questions that have been asked in recent studies:

◆ Is college a route for getting ahead in society?
◆ How are social class and school achievement related?
◆ Why do girls take fewer math and science courses than boys?

◆ Do schools make a difference in our earning power?

◆ What teaching styles are most effective?

◆ Should non-native-language speakers learn in their own language or in English?

◆ What differences do teacher expectations of students make in students' performance?

◆ What is the importance of the "informal" system of schools?

◆ What affects does TV watching have on educational achievement?

◆ *Putting Sociology to Work*

1. Evaluate your own motive for going to college and for taking this course. Understanding your goals can help you get the most from this course and help you meet your educational needs (refer to pp. 3 and 4).

2. Write down some questions you have concerning schools and relate them to questions asked by functionalists (indicated on pp. 7–10).

3. From the brief descriptions of contributions made by Emile Durkheim and Max Weber, describe those issues facing education today that relate to aspects of their writings.

4. What are some questions concerning education that come to mind when using functional theory? conflict theory? interaction theory?

5. View the film *High School*. Diagram this school using the elements of a systems model. Indicate roles people play and processes being performed. Compare this with your own high school experience (refer to p. 18).

6. Citing an example, explain how the open systems approach can help us conceptualize a whole working organization.

7. Consider the questions asked in relation to each theoretical perspective (project 4). What method(s) could be used to help you answer each question?

8. The projects in this chapter give you the framework for developing a research project of your own: a theoretical perspective, a research question, or a methodology. Plan a research project based on a question of interest to you.

CHAPTER 2

Conflicting Functions and Processes in Education

What Makes the System Work

This chapter is about controversies in schools. Surrounding each function, or purpose, of education are debates about power, access, and knowledge. Schools exist within the larger framework of society. The dynamics of the economic, political, and cultural spheres interact in everyday activities in schools (Apple and Weis, 1986). Therefore, controversies in society at large become controversies within the schools. After a general introduction to the conflicting nature of functions and the importance of processes in educational systems, we examine selected issues and controversies related to each function of education.

CONFLICTING FUNCTIONS OF EDUCATION

In any society, children must be taught the ways of the group and skills necessary for society and the individual to prosper. The basic functions, or purposes, of education are the same in most societies, but the importance of these functions and the means of achieving them vary greatly among societies and even among groups or social classes within each society. For instance, the degree of industrialization of the society will affect the content and the form of the educational process. The form of the political system will affect the content and control of the educational process. The expectations of the family in socializing the child to be a productive member of society will affect the type of educational content. These provide examples of the interdependence of parts in society.

Function 1. Socialization: Learning to Be Productive Members of Society and the Passing On of Culture. Each new generation of children learns the rights and wrongs, values and roles of the society into which they are born. In learning their role, children are socialized, or taught, how to meet the expectations placed on them. Educational systems socialize students to become members of society, to play meaningful roles in the complex network of interdependent positions. Some critics, however, argue that students have different experiences in the school system, depending on their social class, racial or ethnic background, neighborhood in which they live, and other variables that influence their education.

Function 2. Transmission of Culture. Similarly, the transmission of culture is often controversial, each group wanting its programs, curricula, or values promulgated. In addition, different groups of students are taught different norms, skills, values, and knowledge. Thus, a student destined for a leadership or elite position may acquire a different set of skills and knowledge base than one who will enter the blue-collar workforce.

Function 3. Social Control and Personal Development. Social control is, similarly, controversial. Discipline differs by social class, racial-ethnic group, and sex, even though the offense may be the same. Controversies, for instance, surround search and seizure. Do school officials have the right to "protect students" by testing for drugs or searching for weapons or drugs, especially when these searches may affect some groups of students disproportionately?

Function 4. Selecting, Training, and Placement of Individuals in Society. Probably the most controversial function of schools is the selection, training, and placement of individuals in society. Critics argue that we are "reproducing" social classes and maintaining the social hierarchy with educational policies and practices that select some students for higher tracks. Yet some policies, such as testing, give the "appearance" of equality.

The access that students have to technology influences their chances to compete in the future. Experience with computers and other high-tech machines gives some students an edge on leadership positions because these students will gain the skills needed in the future. Thus, the question of balance between ascribed and achieved characteristics in the determination of someone's future educational and occupational success is sometimes raised (Apple and Weis, 1986, p. 14). Chapters 3 and 4 focus on this function.

Function 5. Change and Innovation. Change and innovation are expected functions of education. New technologies challenge students and teachers of all ages as they change the way work is done. Yet, institutions often resist change that affects routine work tasks, and education is no exception.

THE IMPORTANCE OF PROCESSES IN EDUCATIONAL SYSTEMS

Have you ever tried to describe your day using action verbs? Today I *got up*, *dressed*, *ate* my breakfast, *put on* my coat, *walked* to school, *entered* the classroom, *sat* at my desk, *opened* my book, *read* it, *took* notes as the teacher *communicated*, and *learned* about educational systems. The italicized verbs describe *processes*, the action part of your day. Learning, teaching, socializing, disciplining, selecting, innovating, decision making, and changing are only a few of the processes that make up the action part of the system of education. The educational system is a stable and relatively permanent structure. Processes are the action part: what is happening.

Nothing is ever fixed or final. People, things, and organizations are always becoming something new through the process of change. Always we grow older, learn new behaviors, and adjust to changes in the world around us. Educational systems affect our change process, and, in turn, are affected by processes in their environment, or surroundings.

Structure refers to parts of the educational system that can be described and diagrammed: roles, social classes, organizations, institutions, societies. People in the structure act. They bring the structure alive, making it move. Their acts are processes. People bring their own personalities and interpretations to situations and act accordingly. Structure and action cannot be separated; there would be no processes without structure, and structure would be meaningless without processes. We are not simply social classes or roles; we are what results from those structural parts and the processes that make them work.

Implicit in an open systems approach are the processes that make any system a dynamic, working unit. Some processes are found in almost every organization—interaction, decision making, conflict, cooperation. Others are predominant in particular systems. In addition to making the system work and giving it life, processes can produce controversy, as we shall see.

Processes also provide links for the organization, such as between an educational system and the environment. The process of communication, for instance, links the school with parents, community leaders, and state legislators.

THE FUNCTION OF SOCIALIZATION: WHAT WE LEARN AND HOW WE LEARN IT

According to functional theory, a society, in order to prosper, must train its members to be productive and to perform required roles. However, there is disagreement on how, when, and for whom training should take place. Criticisms of the process of socialization include a range of topics. Here we focus on two: early childhood education and the role of the media in socialization.

The Early Childhood Education Controversy

From the moment we are born, the socialization process becomes part of our lives; its influence is felt through the family, school, religious institution, and workplace. Learning to become a member of society has both formal, planned components and informal aspects.

Early childhood education takes on special significance because children are developing their self-concept and social awareness. From studies of mental and physical development, we know that infants show learning at two-and-a-half months, if not earlier (Raymond, 1991, p. A5). In fact, 50 percent of general intelligence develops between birth and age 4 (Begley, 1996). Issues that surround early socialization include where cognitive development should take place (at home or school); at what age children should begin formal schooling; the benefits of preschool for children of working parents or for those living in poverty; and the role of preschool and kindergarten programs in the socialization of children.

The family is the primary context within which the child receives initial socialization. Variations in the process of early childhood socialization are tremendous; they depend on society, social class, and family background. As

"Ready to Learn" initiatives prepare many young children for school.

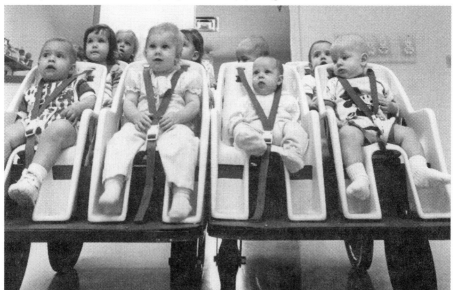

children grow, they come into contact with socialization agents outside the home: relatives, neighbors, church, nursery school, playmates. But there is little preparation for the major transition to the formal institution of the school.

More than half the nations of the world have some formal early childhood education for 3- to 5-year-olds. In some countries, such as China and Israel, care begins shortly after birth and is sometimes mandatory, and in others, such as Sweden and the United Kingdom, legislation addresses the need and funding for day care and nursery schools (Swedish Institute, 1994; Feeney, 1992; "Under Five," 1992, p. 19). In the United States, 43 percent of 3-year-olds, 64 percent of 4-year-olds, and 92 percent of 5-year-olds are enrolled in center-based programs (National Center for Educational Statistics, 1999, p. 122).

For years, bills have been introduced in the U.S. Congress proposing legislation to support early childhood education, reflecting pressure on government and work institutions from women's groups. The federal government's *Goals 2000* included "ready to learn" initiatives for preschoolers. Though the government does fund "model" programs such as Head Start, so far most of the legislation for early childhood education has been defeated, despite the growing number of working mothers with children under age 5 needing day care.

The movement against day care comes mainly from those who consider it a threat to the family and to the maternal role. In addition, early childhood education is distrusted by some because many programs are aimed at particular classes and minority groups such as African Americans. Although stated intentions are to give these children advantages, this "special attention" has been interpreted by some theorists as a technique to perpetuate a class structure and train compliant members of society. Yet, the greatest return on investment, according to one assessment of early childhood education, comes from providing preschool education for 3- and 4-year-olds from low-income families, children who are at special risk of failure. Risk factors cited for children include low household income, minority group status, non-English-speaking homes, single parents, large households, a disabling condition, a mother who became pregnant as a teen and who did not finish high school (Hofferth et al., 1994, p. iii). A substantial number of 3-year-olds from poor families are 9 months or more behind in language and intellectual development by the time they start nursery school. To prevent these losses, some propose training programs for new parents to get children off to a good start in life and promote responsible and effective parenthood (Russell, 1994; Reynolds, 1991; White, 1991).

Those favoring early childhood education pose several arguments:

1. Early childhood education provides valuable learning experiences not available at home.
2. Young children need to interact with children and with adults other than their parents.

3. Parents and siblings are not always the best or most capable handlers of children.
4. For many families, day care is necessary because both parents must work; in the case of single-parent families, the only alternative may be child care.
5. A good day-care center is often preferable to leaving a child with relatives or neighbors.

Early childhood education is not a substitute for home care, but it can provide children with experiences that go beyond those received at home (Ochiltree, 1994).

Studies of access to and quality of preschool programs for at-risk children indicate that the quality of preschool programs such as Head Start is comparable to those for high-income children, but access is reduced (National Center for Education Statistics, 1994). Another study showed that for 3,000 children, most of whom were African American and poor, the lasting effects of preschool education were manifested primarily in five areas:

1. [T]he beneficiaries are less likely to be assigned later to special or remedial classes.
2. There has been the same lasting effect with respect to dropout from school and ... retention in grade (fewer being held back to repeat a year's work because of poor performance).
3. Achievement in mathematics at age 10 (fourth grade) is significantly improved by preschooling. The evidence also suggests a trend toward better scores on reading tests at the same age.
4. Children from poor families who went to preschool programs scored higher than the "control" children on the Stanford Binet IQ test for up to three years afterward. In some projects, this superiority was maintained.
5. Preschool children retain more "achievement orientation," and their mothers tend to develop higher vocational aspirations for them than mothers have for themselves (Halsey, 1980, pp. 172–73).

Though the debate over early childhood education is likely to continue, the need for care will not diminish as more parents work outside the home.

> *A*pplying Sociology to Education: What impact can early childhood education have on different children? Should some or all children be removed from home for part of the day? ◆

Role of the Media and Commercials in Socialization

Many socialization agencies complement or compete with schools for the attention of students. Commercial ventures and the media are two such agencies. Walk into schools and classrooms across the nation and witness big business advertising on school book covers, in texts, and on TV monitors. Tune into the free Internet access sponsored by an advertising agency that provides special offers to students watching the screens. The equipment may have been provided free by marketing research firms who then have access to students for focus group research. And Coke or Pepsi may be the "official drink" of the school in exchange for providing technology and equipment (Labi, 1999, pp. 44–45).

Big business has a vested interest in promoting and supporting education to prepare a trained and competent workforce. It also wants to sell products. Controversies continue over the increasing influence of businesses that have money, and schools that don't, but that need money to buy equipment and supplies. What is undue influence on schools? Are businesses and other interest groups affecting what is taught and how it is taught? These are some of the concerns raised by school districts about the impact of business inside schools.

Television is another controversial agent of socialization. Channel One, started in the spring of 1990 by Whittle Communications, promised to bring video technology and innovative news programming to U.S. classrooms for grades 6 to 12. Currently, more than 12,000 schools and 8 million teens—that is, 40 percent of 12- to 18-year-olds in the United States—receive the ten-minute news programs and two minutes of commercials (Hays, 1999).

Those two minutes of advertising for such products as snack foods, personal care products, movies, clothes, and electronics have created controversy in many school districts. Although the ads help pay for the equipment given to each school—satellite dish, TV in every classroom, videotape recorders, instructional videos, and public service announcements to stay in school and stay off drugs—some argue that it is inappropriate for schools to be involved in influencing students to buy certain products.

Evaluation studies of Channel One programming showed that students liked the news stories and that they had already seen most of the ads on TV (Tiene and Whitmore, 1995). Teachers approve of the programs, rating them A–/B+, and 61 percent of principals believe their schools are better because of Channel One (Johnston, 1995). Yet not everyone agrees that Channel One is a valuable informational resource; critics argue that it promotes commercialism, wastes class time, and ultimately costs taxpayers $1.8 billion in lost teaching time (Hayes, 1999; Sawicky and Molnar, 1998).

When TV first became widespread in the 1950s, many thought that it would solve educational problems and bring education to millions around the world. To some extent this has been realized. TV satellites and distance education beam a variety of programs to many nations, ranging from basic literacy training to advanced college courses; to cite just one example, the European Broadcasting Union has planned a multilingual educational satellite channel for multinational audiences (Couglan, 1995). Thus, education became accessible to a wide population and spread culture and ideas. However, the controversy is this: Do the educational benefits of TV outweigh the negative outcomes? Concerns focus on school achievement and the amount of TV watched; TV's possible distortion of information; and TV's effects on negative behaviors, such as aggression and suicidal tendencies.

The evidence regarding TV watching and school achievement is mixed; more TV means less time for other activities, such as reading and homework. On average, TV watching lowers achievement if it is excessive. The highest achievement has been found among those who watch up to ten hours of TV per week, and the lowest among those watching 30 to 40 hours a week. Thus, limited TV watching, depending on the type of shows watched, can positively affect the way we think and learn. Although TV viewing may be satisfying different needs than those satisfied by reading and other activities, reading for pleasure is more beneficial to achievement. Newspaper reading has declined, and there has been a decline in vocabulary (Glenn, 1994). Interestingly, a survey of students indicates that 40 percent prefer reading to TV, yet most spend twice as much time watching TV as they do reading.

Other variables, such as race, sex, parental education level, educational resources, and intelligence, also play a role in behavior regarding TV. For those concerned about the amount of viewing, it may be encouraging to know that the national poll on "TV watching as the favorite pastime of Americans" was down from 46 percent in 1966 and 1974, to 33 percent in 1986, and 31 percent in 1999. Reading was the favorite evening recreation for 18 percent of adults (Newport, 1999).

Teachers complain that the TV generation expects to be entertained in school or they turn off. There is some support for the "distraction hypothesis," which contends that exposure to TV leads to intolerance for the "slow" pace of schooling. The concern that we become mesmerized by the tube has led some critics to question whether we are critical enough in our TV watching and, whether we accept simplistic explanations without careful consideration.

Perhaps the most serious controversy centers on the behavioral effects of TV watching. The concern is that TV socializes children into antisocial, aggressive behaviors. What kind of teacher is TV? Violence for entertainment teaches that violence is "legitimate, justified, rewarded, effective, clean, heroic, manly" (Slaby, 1994, p. 81). The sights and sounds on video games, films, and TV cartoons influence children. By the time the average child (one who watches two to four hours of television daily) leaves elementary school, he or she will have seen more than 26 violent acts per hour (Smith, 1993), with several possible outcomes:

◆ The *aggressor effect* occurs when children display what they see. A recent example occurred when a popular film depicted a fire in a subway token booth, an act that was repeated in an actual subway by several teens. There is some evidence from studies of TV shows concerning suicides that there is an increase in suicidal behavior in the week or two weeks following the shows. These "copycat" suicides are generally among students who are already at risk.

In a review of research conducted in the past 25 years on media violence, findings indicate that dramatic violence can exert both short- and long-term effects on behavior (Huesmann and Miller, 1994).

◆ The *victim effect* occurs when children identify with the victim; they are fearful, mistrust others, and may carry guns.

◆ The *bystander effect* refers to a callous attitude toward violence; the viewer becomes desensitized (Molitor and Hirsch, 1994).

Despite criticisms from citizens' groups, TV executives say they are "giving people what they want." Yet a poll conducted in the wake of the Columbine massacre found that many Americans believed that media-portrayed violence leads to real-life violence (Newport, 1999) and that as a nation we have become desensitized to violence (Smith, 1993). Congress responded to Americans' concerns by requiring that all TV sets 13 inches or larger and manufactured after January 1, 2000, be equipped with a V-chip. The V-chip, or violence chip, allows parents to control what their children watch based on program ratings provided by the networks (Newport, 1999; Federal Communications Commission, 1999).

Clear evidence regarding the impact of TV on socialization and learning comes from two areas. First, parental involvement in children's TV watching has a powerful effect on its impact. Concerning elementary school children, the child's cognitive and behavioral tendencies are correlated with several aspects of family patterns, two of which are especially relevant to TV watching: parents who play an active role in helping children understand the world around them, including what they see on TV, and parents who watch a limited amount of television. The second source of evidence comes from studies of children's educational television, such as *Sesame Street*, which generally show positive outcomes for children (Biagi, 1998).

In 1990, Congress passed the Children's Television Act with the goal of making TV programming more educational and discouraging commercial TV. Pressure from lobbying groups, such as Action for Children's Television (ACT), has led to some changes, but more regulations are being considered to enforce compliance (Kunkel and Canepa, 1994).

Some schools offer programs to educate children about the effects of TV and about how to be sophisticated viewers (Walker, 1995, pp. 66–67). The Children's Television Workshop (the producers of *Sesame Street*) and CNN Newsroom are making specific episodes available to teachers through an index system. Educational video games are also being developed.

Additionally, with computer games and the Internet, children are constantly bombarded by new exciting stimuli. The battle for the minds of children will continue.

*A*pplying *Sociology to Education:* What issues do you see in the commercial use of TV in schools? Should parents be able to control what children watch on TV? ◆

THE FUNCTION OF CULTURAL TRANSMISSION AND PROCESS OF PASSING ON CULTURE

"The educational foundations of our society are presently being eroded by a rising tide of mediocrity that threatens our very future as a Nation and a people. What was unimaginable a generation ago has begun to occur—others are matching and surpassing our educational attainments. . . . [W]e have, in effect, been committing an act of unthinking, unilateral educational disarmament" (Bell, 1983, p. 5). This statement from the 1983 U.S. report *A Nation at Risk* opened a floodgate of questioning and self-criticism.

With these hard words to the American people came concern about the "cultural literacy" and illiteracy of the United States. Are young people learning the very core of knowledge that holds a nation together with a common thread—information that is understood and shared by all? Some argue that this knowledge core has slipped in several ways (Hirsch, 1987, p. 152). For instance, they argue that we no longer teach many of the classics in Western literature that they argue form the core.

Imagine going into a store and not being able to read the labels on the cans. Illiteracy among young people and adults is a problem that many of those affected try to hide, yet anywhere from 20.8 to 23.6 percent of adults in the United States score in the lowest group on literacy tests (National Center for Education Statistics, *Condition*, 1999, p. 16). It is estimated that there are 27 million functionally illiterate adults in the United States who cannot read simple instructions, and 47 million more who cannot read well. Six percent of U.S. citizens in their early twenties read below the fourth-grade level, and 5 percent cannot perform such routine and uncomplicated tasks as filling out a job application or totaling two entries on a bank-deposit slip (Otto, 1990, p. 360). Illiteracy affects women in poverty disproportionately.

Educators are examining why nine out of ten children who start first grade in the bottom reading group stay there throughout elementary school. Currently, there is a hodgepodge of programs for teaching reading. For some children, new and coordinated approaches to reading may be key. Some advocate a return to phonics-based reading for low-income children instead of the whole-language approach, which works better with at-home support. Others argue that the money spent on intensive, personalized education early in a child's education more than pays off later. For older students, educators are trying everything from tying drivers' licenses to academic performance and staying in school, to offering literacy training in alternative locations such as work settings.

The number of first-year college students who are unprepared for college-level work is also alarming. Data show that 13 percent are in remedial reading, 17 percent are in remedial writing, and 24 percent are in remedial mathematics courses. Studies also show that scientific illiteracy is widespread (National Center for Education Statistics, *Condition*, 1999).

Some Factors Affecting Learning

Learning as a process is influenced not only by the teacher, the techniques used, the classroom setting, and the formal or informal material being taught, but also by the child's ability, motivation, interest in the subject matter, readiness to learn, retentiveness, values and attitudes, relationship with the teacher, feelings about self, relationships with peers, background experiences, and a myriad of other factors. Also of importance are the environmental pressures for learning, the time allotted for learning, family support for learning, and the atmosphere of the school and classroom. Children's learning experiences differ as a result of such variables as race, gender, and class. Thus, it is superficial to explain learning differences among children by one primary factor, such as intelligence.

Because of the back-to-basics movement and concerns about declining achievement-test scores, high school curricula have undergone some significant changes. There has been particular emphasis in the areas of math and science, where educators believed that the United States was losing whatever competitive edge it may have had, especially in high-tech areas. "The low level of scientific and technological literacy in our society is deplorable, and the trickle of talent flowing into careers in engineering, mathematics, and the sciences . . . is deeply disturbing" (National Science Foundation, 1992, p. 1). So begins the National Science Foundation's evaluation of science and math curricula in the United States.

The report *A Nation at Risk* advocated tougher high school requirements, and the response has been positive, resulting in high school graduates taking more academic courses, especially in math and science. Achievement results have also risen, with proficiency scores on the National Assessment of Educational Progress (NAEP) math and science tests increasing nine points from 1990 to 1996 (National Center for Education Statistics, *Condition*, 1999; Carnegie Commission on Science, Technology, and Government, 1991).

Many factors affect math and science education. Some universities are providing special programs for younger students, especially women and minorities, to encourage them in math and science. Some businesses are even promising high school graduates free college educations for staying in school.

Other reports have followed *A Nation at Risk*, some of which are discussed throughout this text; some are sponsored by foundations, others by government agencies or academicians. Some suggest tighter control over curriculum and requirements, and changes in teacher education so that teachers specialize in an area of teaching expertise.

Whatever the recommendations, some positive trends in achievement are beginning to emerge in the United States. For instance, the achievement levels of students are where they were in the 1950s and 1960s, and the majority-minority dispareties are declining and are much smaller than in previous decades (Alexander, 1997).

How to Pass On Culture

The debate over *how* to pass on culture covers issues from what materials, textbooks, and technology to use, to the philosophy of education. This section focuses on two issues related to passing on culture: what teaching techniques are most effective in producing learning outcomes and what role critical thinking plays in education.

Arguments about philosophy of education pit the "back-to-basics" advocates, who stress basic skills, against the "progressive" educators, who argue that education must be relevant to the surrounding environment and future social participation of students. For much of the history of formal education, children have been taught those things that were regarded as important for the community and for the children's prosperity in it. John Dewey (1916) made a great impact on education with the idea that learning could be more effective if it were relevant to the lives of children. Dewey's progressivism contended that schools were irrelevant to the daily lives of most children, and, therefore, an alienating experience; techniques of memorization and authoritarian atmospheres were not conducive to learning. He proposed using the children's experience and involving them actively in the learning process. His extensive writings have been interpreted, misinterpreted, and modified, but they have influenced all movements in education since the turn of the twentieth century, including current postmodern and constructivist movements. Going beyond Dewey's ideas are child-centered curricula that focus on learner needs and interests, are highly flexible, provide many options to the learner, and involve learners in planning their own curricula around their needs. Free, alternative, and charter schools have adopted some of these ideas.

Recent movements to improve the passing on of culture have included "writing-across-the-curriculum," computers in the classroom, accountability and assessment, stricter discipline and increased homework assignments, and critical thinking—that is, reflective and reasonable thinking that is focused on deciding what to believe or do. Some of these ideas result from social forces—achievement test scores, criticisms of schools, and the lack of correspondence between demands to think more maturely and what the school program teaches. The idea of critical thinking contrasts with educational styles that concentrate only on facts. Related to Bloom's (1976) taxonomy and "higher order thinking skills," critical thinking requires one to evaluate evidence and support conclusions before making decisions.

Some teachers do include elements of critical thinking in their teaching, but it is more often found in classrooms of college-bound or brighter students, not in classrooms for children who are most likely to hold working class jobs and where such thought processes would lead to change in the system through which minority children are taught. All students need to be able to express their thoughts cogently in oral and written form, and to evaluate their value stances on issues. Training in critical thinking aids in these processes, but it is not equally available to all.

Recent reports (Chaddock et al., 1999; Borman et al., 1996) on the status of education in the United States have recommended longer school days and year-round school, tougher graduation standards, proficiency exams for promotion, and more homework; as a result, changes are taking place in districts across the country.

What Culture to Pass On

Another debate related to cultural transmission focuses on *what is taught* in schools. What culture is transmitted and what should be transmitted? Who should decide these difficult questions? What should be the goals of the curriculum? In every society there are expectations, usually unwritten, concerning what a successful adult should be able to do, and related ideas about the "products" of schools. An assumption built into the curriculum is that there are desired changes to be made in the students' existing knowledge by the introduction of new ideas, by the correction of misconceptions, or by additions to existing knowledge. The curriculum provides for instruction in areas seen as desirable through "planned experiences."

Who Should Make Decisions Concerning Curriculum Content? Many groups vie for decision-making responsibility, and many have an influence on decisions. We have mentioned environmental influences on curricular decisions. Because educators have been professionally trained to deal with matters related to education and the curriculum, they naturally prefer to keep decision making in the schools, removed from external politics and other pressures. Educators have used various techniques to maintain control of educational decisions and to keep schools independent of external influences; controlling information about what is going on within the school, releasing selected positive information, and assigning sympathetic community members to committees are examples.

"Academic freedom" refers to attempts by schools and colleges to minimize control and influence, primarily from the external environment. Schools can maintain this autonomy to the extent that their program and staff remain uncontroversial. Should controversy arise, however, autonomy may be threatened. Education is an open system and, therefore, subject to pressures and scrutiny from the environment.

In heterogeneous societies without centrally run educational systems, curriculum planners face pressures from many diverse individuals and groups. In centrally run state systems, decisions are more protected from public scrutiny and challenges. The United States is an example of a heterogeneous society and a federally decentralized system.

What Should Be Taught? What is being taught in the formal curriculum can be fairly easily and accurately determined, though the range is great. Examining curriculum plans and textbooks provides a start. Generally, curriculum plans in primary schools focus on developing basic skills; secondary schools refine these skills and add content. Math, language skills, science, art and music, social science, physical education, and history are common components of secondary school curricula. The transmission of specific content, such as sex education, has been the subject of controversy in many communities because of questions of responsibility and control of knowledge by family or educational systems.

Functional theorists see schools as transmitting those parts of the culture necessary to perform successfully in the adult world. Schools provide a transition from the warm, protective, accepting environment of the home to the competitive, performance-oriented atmosphere of the work world. Children learn that the same rules are supposed to apply to all. In this way schools are believed to serve the crucial function of preparing young people for society (Dreeben, 1968; Parsons, 1959).

Conflict theorists view the cultural transmission of these values and norms as serving the needs of a capitalist society rather than those of individuals, who are dehumanized and alienated by the process (Bowles and Gintis, 1976). Schools are seldom completely effective in transmitting these cultural values, however, as exemplified by the disruptions and rebellions in many schools. Jackson, Bootstrom, and Hansen (1993) evaluate the many ways, formal and informal, that values are taught in schools; some of these values become part of the hidden curriculum.

What is being taught reflects forces both inside and outside the school. Internal educational forces are those that have a direct influence on the curriculum and processes of the school. For example, teachers and principals may express preferences for certain materials and classroom organization and reject others, and the structure, composition, hierarchy, philosophy, and architecture of any one school influences the curriculum content within that school.

In addition to the internal educational forces affecting curriculum, there are many environmental factors outside the school. Recall the systems model. The environment includes all those factors outside the school that influence what happens within it. Consider the following:

1. Local, state, and federal regulations stipulate certain curricular requirements. For instance, a state board of education may require that a certain amount of state history be taken before students can graduate. The federal government may require that a certain curricular content be included as a stipulation for receiving federal money.
2. Accrediting agencies reflect state or regional decision making concerning school standards, and they may specify required aspects of curriculum.
3. Testing services that develop achievement tests for different grade levels and for college entrance do much to influence knowledge material taught. Some states require skills tests for graduation from high school.
4. National studies, reports, and reform plans include recommendations for change in the curriculum (Anderson, 1995).

Curriculum content is influenced by certain concerns and trends in society. Career education, women's studies, minority studies (African American, Chicano, Native American, Appalachian, Chinese), multicultural and bilingual education, environmental studies, urban studies, drug and sex education, technology literacy, and community service are among the subjects that have been introduced into curricula as a result of societal trends.

The call for curricula that fairly represent the history and current status of minorities in the United States has led to the multicultural educational movement. Teaching race, class, and gender issues is receiving increasing attention (King, 1999, 1990). Some advocate courses and programs on specific minorities; others push for an accurate portrayal within the existing curriculum of minority history and contributions. Still others advocate global studies to familiarize students with the broader world issues that affect them. Sociologists are uniquely qualified to develop cross-cultural models for curricula that take into consideration micro- and macroexplanations of societies and change. Attempts to pluralize the curriculum have also met with criticism from those who oppose reducing or eliminating teaching of traditional Western culture, which has been at the core of most courses of study in U.S. high schools and colleges. Recommendations to change minority education stress the need for reform from preschool to graduate school (The Carnegie Corporation, 1990). These ideas may prove passing fads, or they may be integrated into the curriculum, or they may remain distinct fields of study. Whatever the case, those with power in society generally make educational decisions.

We now discuss briefly three areas of curriculum decision making that have created heated controversy in many communities and that reflect the diversity in U.S. society: sex and drug education, creationism, and censorship of textbooks.

Applying Sociology to Education: What should be taught in schools, and who should make the decision(s)? What factors are you taking into account in answering these questions? ◆

Sex and Drug Abuse and Education. Schools as condom dispensaries? A few years ago this idea was unthinkable, but with the threat of AIDS confronting more and more teens, "condom sense is common sense." School boards across the country debate the issue of "what culture should be taught," while a growing number of urban school systems, including New York, Philadelphia, and Los Angeles, are making condoms available in attempts to prevent teen pregnancy, venereal disease, and AIDS. The former Surgeon General of the United States, Dr. Jocelyn Elders, was dismissed because of her controversial frank speech on the topic of teenage sex.

Sex and AIDS education are increasing, despite objections from a few vocal parents and community groups that argue that discussion of these topics belongs in the home. They feel schools should discourage sexual activity, not encourage it through classes and the distribution of condoms. Others argue that, if sex and AIDS education are part of the curriculum, moral education should be as well. Estimates indicate that 80 percent of U.S. adults do favor school-based sexuality education (Kyman, 1998).

The fact is that American teens are sexually active at increasingly younger ages. The number of women younger than age 19 having premarital sex has surpassed the 60 percent mark, and by age 15, 30 percent have engaged in sex. Women who see little future opportunity in school or work tend to become sexually active earlier than those who feel in control of their futures. Other high-risk activities such as using drugs, participating in criminal activities, and engaging with multiple partners are associated with early sex. Despite the general increase in contraceptive use, studies show that teenage girls are less likely than older partners to be protected. Thus, more school programs are stressing concerns about transmission of diseases (Hess, Markson, and Stein, 1996, p. 174).

One of the public's top concerns about schools, rated number four in a nationwide poll in 1999 (Gallup, 1999), is drug use. This concern is justified considering the fluctuation in drug use among teens in the past several years. The problem of drug abuse among students as well as others was brought into the limelight with the death of several prominent figures in the sports and entertainment world and reports of extensive misuse among athletes. Each federal administration has proposed programs to fight abuse. In some school districts, programs have included searches and urine tests for drug use, practices that have met with court challenges.

The most successful programs seem to be well-publicized, no-drugs policies that offer help to students in trouble and that involve student leaders; these programs begin drug education as early as kindergarten and involve the whole community in working against drugs. The most promising strategy is comprehensive–encompassing peer groups, families, schools, media, community organizations, and a wide variety of approaches that provide information, develop life skills, use peer facilitators, and change community policies and norms (U.S. Department of Education, "Reaching the Goals," 1993). D.A.R.E. is one such program; it begins in elementary school and ends with a pledge by students to stay off drugs. In fact, D.A.R.E. has become an international movement.

For many teens, the preferred drug is alcohol (see Figure 2–1 for at-school usage), though reported usage has decreased slowly since 1979 from 88 percent of high school seniors reporting use in the past year to 74 percent in 1998 ("Monitoring the Future Study," 1999, p. 41). Messages are passed on through our culture about usage from parents, advertising, and peers. Many underage drinkers are children of alcoholic parents, estimated at up to 15 million persons under age 18 in the United States (McEvoy, 1990). Drug use decreased also: marijuana use declined from a high of 51 percent usage among seniors in 1979 to a low of 22 percent in 1993, but climbed back to 38 percent in 1998 ("Monitoring the Future Study," 1999, p. 41). Factors that increase the probability of drug use include a history of family crime, drug use, or alcoholism; poor child-rearing patterns; low investment in education, delinquent behavior, or academic failure; and early use of drugs. These children are at higher risk for being abused, attempting suicide, running away, delinquency, and poor school

FIGURE 2–1 Percentage of high school seniors who reported using alcohol or drugs at school during the previous year, by type of drug: 1976–98.

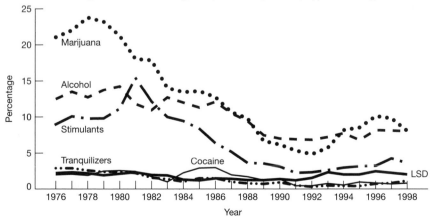

Source: University of Michigan, Survey Reserch Center, *Condition* 1999, p. 83.

achievement. Programs that deal with both the abuse and the causes of abuse are most effective in fighting the problems.

Substance abuse and other problems point again to the controversy—the role of schools versus families in educating students. Should the schools offer drug and alcohol counseling and rehabilitation; sex and AIDS education; pregnancy counseling and testing; contraceptives; and suicide-prevention programs? Or should these personal and moral matters be left to families? The Surgeon General of the United States under the Clinton administration left no doubt as to that office's position: Explicit sex education in schools is essential to prevent the spread of AIDS.

Applying Sociology to Education: What should be the school's role in teaching about moral issues? Who should make these decisions? ◆

Censorship of Textbooks and Library Books. Obscenity, sex, nudity, political or economic "bias," profanity, slang or questionable English, racism or racial hatred, antireligious or anti-American ideas all have been cited as reasons for censoring text and library books in schools. Such books as *Rumplestiltskin, Madame Bovary, Soul on Ice, The Grapes of Wrath,* Shakespeare's *Hamlet,* Chaucer's *The Miller's Tale,* and Aristophanes' *Lysistrata* have been on the "hit list" of organizations attempting to ban books. Some of the books that have been controversial and most frequently censored in recent years include Sophocles' *Antigone,* Huxley's *Brave New World,* Salinger's *The Catcher in the Rye,* Heller's *Catch-22,* Steinbeck's *The Grapes of Wrath,* Shakespeare's *The Merchant of Venice,* Orwell's *1984,* Vonnegut's *Slaughterhouse-Five,* and Lee's *To Kill a Mockingbird* (Simmons, 1994). The most frequently mentioned objections to these books are their vulgar language, profanity, and sexual content. Other targeted books and the reasons given for the challenge include *The Diary of Anne Frank* (a passage suggests that all religions are equally valuable); *Cinderella, The Wizard of Oz,* and *Macbeth* (depictions of good witches and references to the occult); *Romeo and Juliet* (romanticization of suicide); *Ordinary People* by Judith Guest (depressing and obscene); and Alice Walker's *The Color Purple* (troubling ideas about race relations and human sexuality); and *Adventures of Huckleberry Finn* (for offensive language and the portrayal of African Americans) (Hodges, 1995, p. 16; Foerstel, 1994; Bjorklun, 1990, pp. 37–38). Box 2-1 lists the ten most frequently challenged books in 1999 (American Library Association, 2000). The issue is whether concerned parents have the right to have certain material removed from classes and school libraries, especially if they represent only a small percentage of the parents, but are organized and supported by national groups giving them disproportionate influence in their communities. The Supreme Court ruled that school "boards may not remove books from school library shelves simply because they dislike

---

❖❖Box 2–1   *Most Frequently Challenged Books in 1999*

Between 1990 and 1998, of the 5,246 challenges reported to or recorded by the Office for Intellectual Freedom, 1,299 were challenges to "sexually explicit" material, 1,134 to material considered to use "offensive language," 1,062 to material considered "unsuited to age group," 744 to material with an "occult theme or promoting the occult or Satanism," and 474 to material with a homosexual theme or "promoting homosexuality." Other specific challenges were to material that dealt with religious viewpoint (373), nudity (276), racism (219), and sex education (190), or were thought to be antifamily (186). Almost 70 percent of the challenges were to material in schools or school libraries. Another 26 percent were to material in public libraries. Sixty percent of the challenges were brought by parents, 16 percent by patrons, and almost 10 percent by administrators. (The Office for Intellectual Freedom does not claim comprehensiveness in recording challenges. Research suggests there are as many as four or five that go unreported, for every one reported.) The following books were the most frequently challenged in 1999:

1. Harry Potter series, by J. K. Rowling, for its focus on wizardry and magic.
2. Alice series, by Phyllis Reynolds Naylor, for using offensive language and being unsuited to age group.
3. *The Chocolate War*, by Robert Cormier (the most challenged fiction book of 1998), for using offensive language and being unsuited to age group.
4. *Blubber*, by Judy Blume, for offensive language and being unsuited to age group.
5. *Fallen Angels*, by Walter Dean Myers, for offensive language and being unsuited to age group.
6. *Of Mice and Men*, by John Steinbeck, for offensive language and being unsuited to age group.
7. *I Know Why the Caged Bird Sings*, by Maya Angelou, for being too explicit in the book's portrayal of rape and other sexual abuse.
8. *The Handmaid's Tale*, by Margaret Atwood, for its sexual content.
9. *The Color Purple*, by Alice Walker, for sexual content and offensive language.
10. *Snow Falling on Cedars*, by David Guterson, for sexual content and offensive language.

Source: American Library Association (copyright 2000). "The Most Frequently Challenged Books of 1999." Available: http://www.ala.org/bbooks/challeng.html#mfcb (Access Date: March 1, 2000).

---

the ideas contained in these books." Rather, they must establish and follow reasonable procedures before removing controversial books (*Board of Education* v. *Pico*, 1982).

Controversies over library books and class texts have torn communities apart; no community is immune from censorship (Brinkley, 1999). In an analysis of one of the early challenges to books, sociologists Page and Clelland studied the Kanawha County, West Virginia, controversy, describing it as rooted in the "politics of lifestyle" (Page and Clelland, 1978, p. 265). Groups that feel disenfranchized or lack power find a legal way to vent their ideas and frustrations through book banning. For example, the ultrafundamentalists (fundamentalists with a political agenda) "seek to have prayer included in the curriculum of the public schools, because it is a symbolic reaffirmation of their religious values and belief system" (Provenzo, 1990, p. 88). Banned books provide symbolic victories in status politics and in the struggle to regain what was lost in the social revolution of the 1960s. As the religious right has gained political power, censorship cases have risen in public schools and libraries. More than 300 cases occurred between the mid-1970s and the mid-1990s (Jenkinson, 1994).

Most educators claim that censorship threatens academic freedom; groups calling for removal argue that they are protecting their children from secularism, obscenity, and other negative influences. Court rulings have varied, but the balance of cases are coming down on the side of academic freedom, and some districts are retaining controversial books but providing alternatives to children whose parents disapprove (Brinkley, 1999).

Cultural politics is also involved in text selections. State-level text selection involving citizens and interest groups allows the public's competing interests to be represented, but the pressure on school professionals, many of whom are turning toward texts with packaged materials, is somewhat limited (Wong, 1991). Texas and California, the largest buyers of texts, have a major influence on what types of textbooks are produced. The two states constitute about one-fifth of the textbook publisher's market, giving them major influence in what texts will cover, including controversial topics such as evolution and creationism ("California," 1991, p. 11). Even the way historical topics are covered in books is subject to censorship, a practice that is perpetuated by groups with special interests and status politics (Loewen, 1996).

Schools are one place where individuals and communities can dig in and take a stand; events in other institutions may seem uncontrollable. The point is that decision making about curriculum content represents broader issues about power and control of people's lives, what happens to their children, and changes in their communities. Much of the impetus for resisting change in curricula comes from rural and small-town areas, where residents feel pressure from a rapidly changing, urbanized world threatening many of their long-held beliefs and values.

Interest Groups and the Curriculum. Cultural transmission is not a straightforward process but one that reflects the dynamic and heterogeneous viewpoints of a pluralistic society. Consider the issue of creationism versus secular humanism, an issue that also reflects the separation of church and state provided for in the Constitution. Several state Supreme Courts have considered the issue, and the 2000 presidential contenders both took stances favoring the teaching of creationism in schools. Most Americans favor teaching both ideas.

> Americans' support for teaching both creationism and evolution could reflect their divergent views on how the human species came into existence. According to the most recent Gallup poll, 47 percent of Americans believe that God created human beings at one time within the last 10,000 years pretty much in their present form, while 49 percent believe that human beings have developed over millions of years from less advanced forms of life. (Moore, 1999)

The views on this controversial issue vary by age and education, with 56 percent of younger and more educated Americans accepting some form of evolution, and 60 percent of Americans age 65 and older rejecting it. Forty-one percent of noncollege-educated Americans reject evolution as an explanation, whereas 58 percent of college graduates and 66 percent of those with postgraduate education accept evolution (Moore, 1999). This controversial issue is yet another example of the conflicts that can occur in school systems about what information children should learn and how to teach it.

*A*pplying Sociology to Education: How can school districts deal with the competing demands from interest groups? ◆

THE FUNCTION OF SOCIAL CONTROL AND PERSONAL DEVELOPMENT

Community members expect students to learn the skills necessary to become productive, law-abiding citizens. According to functional theory, students learn, through formal or informal means, such values as discipline, respect, obedience, punctuality, and perseverance. These are believed to be essential to survival in the workforce and in school. Schools are expected to instill values related to social control and individual development. In this way, society's problems can be reduced because individuals will be trained to fit into society in acceptable ways. Conflict theorists have a different view of social control, however. They contend that schools are the tool of capitalist societies—controlling training, sorting human beings for places in the societal system, and perpetuating unequal class systems. We will consider each of these theoretical views in the following examples of social control in schools.

Schools have varying ways of passing on the skills of social control, ranging from authoritarian to humanistic methods. The process of discipline is the major method of enforcing control in schools. The means for achieving social control within the school and for preparing disciplined workers creates dilemmas and controversies for schools as well as for society. Three interrelated issues illustrate this point: violence, discipline, and gangs in schools.

Violence and Discipline in Schools

The chance that a white male between the ages of 15 and 19 will die from a gunshot wound now surpasses the chance of dying from natural causes. One-half of the deaths of African American teen males are caused by firearms (Steinberg, 1994). Though schools are fairly safe compared with some other settings in society, and the victimization rates for high school seniors had changed little between 1976 and 1997 ("Monitoring the Future Study," 1999), "violence in and around schools directly affects educators and students by reducing school effectiveness and inhibiting students' learning. Additionally, unsafe school environments may place students who are already at risk of school failure for other reasons in further jeopardy" (National Center for Education Statistics, 1995, p. 134).

The 1998 School Crime and Safety study found that 9 percent of seniors carried a weapon to school at least one day in the four weeks prior to the study, compared to 14 percent in 1993; 3 percent of the weapons were guns. Male students, especially African Americans, are far more likely to carry weapons, with 15 percent carrying a weapon at least once a month compared to 8 percent for white youths (National Center for Education Statistics and U.S. Department of Justice, 1998). Sometimes serious crimes and injuries occur; therefore, some urban schools have installed metal detectors and have regular guards and police patrols in the halls. Perhaps it is these more serious incidents that lead the public to perceive "lack of discipline" and "fighting, violence, and gangs," and "drug abuse" as among the most serious problems facing schools in the United States, locally and nationally (Rose and Gallup, 1999, p. 46).

Though the total number of crimes committed against students did not rise between 1976 and 1997, the number of street gangs present in schools did (National Center for Education Statistics and U.S. Department of Justice, 1998, p. 13). In 1990 approximately 15 percent of students reported gangs present in their schools, and by 1995 that number was 28 percent (School Crime and Safety, 1998, p. viii). This raises questions concerning the rights of students to wear gang insignia or colors to school, and the security of all students in schools with gang members present. Should the schools become guarded fortresses, or less coercive and punitive? Should potential troublemakers be removed to more secure environments, or can they be taught to behave according to school rules?

This brings up the controversial issue of what type of discipline should be used in schools. The use of authoritarian techniques with corporal punishment and suspensions is favored by recent U.S. federal administrations to protect the rights of teachers and students in safe educational environments. Some research indicates that strict discipline is a key component for achievement in low-income city schools. In New York City, former Chancellor Ramon Cortines proposed a policy to suspend for one year any student caught with a gun and possibly to send the student to a special discipline school (Hodges, 1995, p. 17). Some schools have become repressive places with strict discipline and guards in the halls, at times resembling armed camps, and students in high schools and middle schools in some localities are angry and defiant as a result of the atmosphere.

Others argue a positive school climate is necessary to encourage achievement. Some sociologists believe discipline problems represent power struggles between students and adults in a system where students are powerless and often rebel against the authoritarian rules restricting their thoughts and behaviors. These sociologists contend that unless the coercive, alienating power structure surrounding students is radically altered, discipline will always remain a problem. Pedro Noguera (1995) suggests that school actions may encourage a culture of violence, as discussed in Box 2–2.

Various studies present the results of physical punishment as ranging from ineffective as a control mechanism to a breeder of violence. Psychologists point to the ineffectiveness of negative reinforcement, such as corporal punishment, in bringing about desired changes in behavior. Some educators indicate that corporal punishment dehumanizes the school, that it is inappropriate for the school environment, and that it increases disruptive, rebellious behavior and hinders learning. Schools with an emphasis on strict social control may produce prisonlike atmospheres that do not improve the situation (Noguera, 1995). The students who receive the most corporal punishment are those who are already disenchanted with school. Punishment, critics claim, not only discourages students from making an effort to succeed but also labels them negatively among teachers. The point is that teachers and schools can teach violence by condoning and using physical force.

Schools have turned to a number of alternative techniques to deal with problems, including single-sex classes, forced parental involvement, and uniformed police officers in the halls to name a few (Elias, 1995, pp. 54, 56). Evaluation of one policy, school suspension, shows that African American male students in the United States are in many cases disproportionately suspended. The recent case of several African American students fighting at a football game in Decatur, Illinois, drew national attention from the news media when Jesse Jackson argued that their two-year suspension punishment (later reduced) was too severe for the offense. Although suspension may solve the immediate goals of removing the problem and punishing the students, it can create long-term problems that cost society, for example, by reducing suspended students' chances for productive lives, limiting educational opportunities, increasing dropout rates (Bowditch, 1993), causing

◆◆Box 2-2 *Preventing Violence in Schools: Creating a Positive Climate*

The pervasive dysfunction that characterizes social relations in urban public schools is not accidental but is caused by the severity of social and economic conditions in the inner city. However, it is also not unavoidable. There are a few important exceptions to this norm, schools where teachers and students support each other in pursuit of higher personal and collective goals. Such schools, however, are not typical or common. Rather, the average urban school tends to be large, impersonal, and foreboding, a place where bells and security guards attempt to govern the movements of students, and where students more often than not have lost sight of the fact that education and personal growth are ostensibly the reasons why they are required to attend this anonymous institution five days a week.

I have visited urban schools that have found ways to address effectively the problem of violence, ways that do not rely on coercion or excessive forms of control. At one such school, rather than hiring security guards, a grandmother from the surrounding community was hired to monitor students. Instead of using physical intimidation to carry out her duties, this woman greets children with hugs, and when some form of punishment is needed she admonishes them to behave themselves, saying that she expects better behavior from them. I have also visited a continuation high school, where the principal was able to close the campus, not permitting the students to leave at lunch time, without installing a fence or some other security apparatus, but simply by communicating with students about other alternatives for purchasing food so that they no longer felt it necessary to leave for meals. Now the students operate a campus store that both teachers and students patronize. Such measures are effective because they make it possible for children and adults to relate to one another as human beings, rather than as anonymous actors playing out roles.

Improving the aesthetic character of schools by including art in the design of schools, or by making space available within schools for students to create gardens or greenhouses, can make schools more pleasant and attractive. Similarly, by overcoming the divide that separates urban schools from the communities in which schools are located, the lack of adults who have authority and respect in the eyes of children can be addressed. Adults who live within the community can be encouraged to volunteer or, if possible, be paid to tutor, teach, mentor, coach, perform, or just plain help out with a variety of school activities.

The goal of maintaining social control through the use of force and discipline has persisted for too long. Most urban youth today are neither passive nor compliant. The rewards dangled before them of a decent job and material wealth for those who do well in school are seen by too many as either undesirable or unattainable. New strategies for providing an education that is perceived as meaningful and relevant, and that begins to tap into the intrinsic desire of all individuals to obtain greater personal fulfillment, must be devised and supported. Anything short of this will leave us mired in a situation that grows increasingly depressing and dangerous every day.

Many urban schools that feel safe don't have metal detectors or armed security guards, and their principals don't carry baseball bats. What these schools do have is a strong sense of community and collective responsibility. Such schools are seen by students as sacred territory, too special to be spoiled by crime and violence, and too important to risk one's being excluded. Such schools are few, but their existence serves as tangible proof that there are alternatives to chaotic schools plagued by violence, and controlled institutions that aim at producing docile bodies.

Source: Adapted from the original article by Pedro A. Noguera, "Preventing and Producing Violence: A Critical Analysis of Responses to School Violence." *Harvard Educational Review*, 65(2), Summer 1995, pp. 189–212. Copyright © 1995 by the President and Fellows of Harvard College. All rights reserved.

reliance on welfare services, being incarcerated in prisons, and being committed to mental hospitals. Thus, the technique used in a classroom and school affects the atmosphere and student–teacher interactions. More systematic research into power structures, discipline techniques, and their results is needed.

All human beings have certain basic needs—food, shelter, love and affection, respect, trust, knowledge, and truth (Maslow, 1962). If basic underlying needs are not met, children may exhibit disruptive behavior. For instance, if children come to school hungry or lacking affection at home, they are likely to be disruptive in school. Teachers do not always have the time, energy, or interest to deal with these problems directly and instead resort to techniques of discipline or control such as corporal punishment, expulsion (ten days or more) or suspension (ten days or less), detention, transfer to another class or school, loss of privileges, drugs to calm children, or special education classes. There are no easy answers to problems in schools, especially because they reflect problems in the society at large.

Applying *Sociology to Education:* In what situations might authoritarian discipline be most effective? humanistic discipline? Should suspensions be used, and if so, under what circumstances? ◆

THE FUNCTION OF SELECTION AND ALLOCATION: THE SORTING PROCESS

What is the best way to determine whether you or the next person gets the best college placement, admission into your field, and the highest-paying and most prestigious job? This issue is discussed in detail in Chapters 3 and 4; here we consider one method used by most industrial countries—testing. The controversy lies in the role that exams play in placement and whether they are fair to all students.

The Testing Game

Many modern industrial societies emphasize achievement and merit. In these test-oriented societies, it is beneficial to be skilled at test-taking. Most of us are faced with intelligence quotient (IQ) tests, aptitude tests, achievement tests, career-interest inventories, psychological tests, civil service tests, SATs, ACTs, Miller's Analogy test, Graduate Record Examination, job-aptitude tests, and so on. Schools use exams at various checkpoints to track or stream students and to ensure that students are achieving at grade level, because schools are held accountable by the community for their activities. Many states now require students to pass examinations in order to graduate from high school, and students must take the Scholastic Aptitude Test (SAT) or American College Test (ACT) for college entrance. Tests are a part of our lives, helping educators and others to select and allocate according to ability. Do some groups have an advantage in the testing process?

The use of IQ test scores has been controversial for years. Alfred Binet first developed intelligence tests in France to diagnose mental retardation and areas of individual difficulty or weakness. Binet felt that an individual's intelligence was not a fixed quality but could be increased with expert training. It was not his idea to use the test for mass placements, but this soon became common. U.S. Army recruits were given intelligence tests and were classified as alpha (literate) or beta (illiterate) in order to sort and select them for various roles in the armed service. Concerns about IQ testing intensified when schools also began to use the tests for sorting purposes. This practice has come under attack, but many school districts still use IQ tests to help with general placement of children. Since the 1970s, debate intensified with the publication of several books and articles on the nature and use of IQ tests, and concerns have been raised about the nature of intelligence tests:

1. What are we really measuring?
2. To what extent do genetic or environmental factors influence test results?
3. Can we develop a culture-free test?

*A*pplying Sociology to Education: Jot down some characteristics that make someone you know seem intelligent. Compare your ideas of intelligence with someone else's. Probably you have some overlap and some differences in your definitions. Why? ◆

The first problem deals with the nature of intelligence: Social scientists try to pinpoint what we really mean by intelligence; there is not complete agreement on what innate qualities to look for or how to find them and to what extent environmental factors influence intelligence.

As many as 23 different mental abilities have been included in definitions of intelligence—including verbal fluency, spatial perception, analogical reasoning, series and sequence manipulation, memory, and creativity. In attempting to define intelligence, we are not referring to a simple quantity but to a complex system of reasoning. Howard Gardner (1987) refers to the many areas of human functioning as "multiple intelligences"—including practical, social, musical, and spatial abilities. Since he proposed the concept of multiple intelligences in 1983, Gardner has added to the list of intelligences, most recently "naturalist intelligence, a person's ability to identify plants and animals in the surrounding environment" (Gardner, 1999). Others believe intelligence is an information processing framework, which involves the processing of information from the time we perceive it until the time we act on it. The implication is that some people are more adept at processing certain kinds of information than others.

The second problem deals with the controversy over genetic and environmental determinants of intelligence. In 1969, Arthur Jensen stated that what IQ tests measure is 80 percent inherited and 20 percent cultural factors. This statement and the general content of his article in the *Harvard Educational Review* generated a controversy that continues to this day. Jensen and others, such as Richard J. Herrnstein (1980), theorized that IQ differences between socioeconomic, social, and ethnic groups primarily are caused by genetic factors.

Herrnstein and Murray (1994) created a firestorm in the scientific community with their book *The Bell Curve,* arguing that there is a direct link between low IQ, inherited genes, social class placement, and social ills. They implied that race, IQ, and social hierarchy fit together, and that the poor are blameworthy for their position. Their thesis assumes that intelligence is understood, definable, and testable, and that we have a test that can measure intelligence accurately. If one could assume IQ tests to be valid and intelligence to be inherited, some feel that the distribution of positions in society could be justified on the basis of intelligence groups—the argument being that some are more capable than others. Some individuals indeed may be more capable, but we must be sure that we can determine this accurately before pigeonholing the population on the basis of a test. These factors are all questionable and have not held up under scrutiny.

Scientists have critiqued this work on the basis of everything from its underlying assumptions to its methodology. One major critique uses alternative explanations of data, showing that economic success depends more on social class than on IQ, and that we must look beyond individual characteristics to the structure of society to find causes of inequality. Factors ranging from the wealth of individuals' parents to national policies on labor laws, education, and tax deductions serve to distribute rewards unequally. Racial differences are a result of, not a cause of, social inequalities. The authors propose adopting policies to provide more opportunity (Fischer et al., 1996).

The third problem with using intelligence tests to classify members of society deals with whether it is possible to devise tests that are free of cultural bias—class, ethnicity, regionalism, and the other variables that make our nation and school systems so diverse. Consider the following question: Children are asked to draw a horse. Who do you think would draw the "best" horse? Native American children living in rural areas do best at this task because of their familiarity with the subject.

Another environmental factor that affects intelligence tests is the region of the country from which a person comes. In IQ tests administered to army recruits after World War I, researchers noted that army recruits did not follow the stereotypic pattern of African Americans scoring lower than whites, but that region made a significant difference in their scores. Northern whites scored highest, followed in descending order by northern African Americans, southern whites, and southern African Americans. Studies showing the rise in IQ scores of children placed in enrichment programs also point to the importance of environmental factors in IQ. Several other variables affect test scores: the race of the person in charge of the testing situation, the sex of the test-taker, the motivation of the test-taker, how the test-taker feels on the day of the test—even whether the individual had a good breakfast. You probably remember feeling nervous on test days. Some children do better under stress, some do worse, and some just give up in the face of a threatening or difficult situation. Individual factors of this type can affect test scores significantly.

All of the studies point to the problem of ranking or classifying people on the basis of scores that are unreliable or changeable and that are influenced by environmental circumstances. They also suggest that intelligence—as typically measured—is not a fixed, inherited attribute but a variable depending on stimulation and on cultural and environmental factors.

Achievement Tests

The scene of a student waiting by the mailbox in anticipation, dreading to open "the envelope," is familiar around the world. That envelope holds the key to the future of many young people—scores on achievement tests. Because of limited space in university systems, most countries rely on entrance examinations for placement in universities. Those numbers determine for many students their entrance to or rejection by universities. The scores are important—and controversial—because they tap the core of how we evaluate and place people in society.

In the United States, two national achievement tests are given to college-bound high school students: the ACT and the SAT. SAT scores rose 14 points overall between 1994 and 1998, and ACT scores stayed almost constant over the same time period (U.S. Department of Education, 2000). However, scores of African American students are still significantly lower than those of whites and of some other minorities. Some educators criticize the tests, arguing that they do not test classroom reality, but that they tend to shape what happens in the classroom. The Educational Testing Service, authors of the SAT and achievement tests, have developed revised tests that they say are more closely tied to classroom experiences.

Test-makers will continue to improve the validity of their tests; educators will continue to question the relationship between curricular materials and test items; parents and students will share concerns about the meaning of tests for life chances; and minority advocates will keep a watchful eye on tests for bias. However, in meritocracies some forms of testing, however imperfect, are likely to continue.

THE FUNCTION OF CHANGE AND INNOVATION: THE PROCESS OF LOOKING TO THE FUTURE*

Schools provide a link with the future; it is through research and teaching the next generation new knowledge that societies move forward. Universities are generally on the cutting edge of research, passing this knowledge on to students. Although few deny the inevitability of change, questions arise as to how change takes place and who controls change.

One thing we know is that those who possess technological skills and knowledge in the twenty-first century, and who know how to get information important to functioning in the future, will rise in the hierarchy. Can schools teach and implement new technology? Are these tools equally available to all?

The proliferation of computer technology is dramatically changing the process by which educators at all levels disseminate information to students. Whereas students in "traditional classrooms" listen to lectures, instructors in "postmodern classrooms" enhance their lectures with high-resolution computer graphics, virtual sounds, and popular multimedia platforms such as PowerPoint, Astound, and Hyper Studio. Students in traditional classrooms learn about remote cultures by reading a packaged text, but students in postmodern classrooms interact and communicate with people of different cultural backgrounds via the Internet.

In a postindustrial society, access to technology at all educational levels is increasingly important. As part of *Goals 2000*, President Clinton and Congress developed a strategy to make effective use of computer technology in all classrooms (U.S. Department of Education, 1995). Though nationwide access to computer technology and the Internet has not yet been fully realized, there is evidence that the postmodern classroom is quickly replacing the traditional classroom.

The number of computers owned by public schools and the proportion of public schools that have Internet access is on the rise. The average public school had 75 computers in 1997. From 1994 to 1998, the proportion of schools with

*Written with Jeffrey Dixon, Indiana University.

Internet access increased rapidly from 35 percent to 89 percent (National Center for Education Statistics, 1999). There has also been an upsurge in the percentage of instructional rooms with Internet access. Sixty-three percent of instructional rooms had access to the Internet in 1999 compared to only 3 percent in 1994 ("State of American Education Address," 1999).

Reliance on computer technology is equally prevalent in institutions of higher education. Especially prominent is distance learning, a low-cost method of educating large numbers of students. Via two-way interactive video connections and the Internet, students can earn credit for on-line courses (Dunn, 2000). One-third of higher-education institutions offered distance learning courses in 1995, with another 25 percent saying they planned to offer courses in the next three years (National Center for Educational Statistics, 1999). Many colleges followed through with their plans; 44 percent offered distance learning courses in 1998 (Department of Education, 1999).

Although data are still coming in, preliminary research suggests that computer technology has a positive impact on student achievement. At the secretary of education's conference on educational technology in 1999, educators evaluated the relationship between access to computer technology and standardized test scores. Extensively connected, or "postmodern," schools in West Virginia and Idaho boasted gains approaching 15 percent on the Iowa Test of Basic Skills (ITBS), the Test of Academic Proficiency (TAP), and other standardized tests. However, some educators criticize these findings on methodological grounds, arguing that it is difficult to isolate access to computer technology as a variable that either promotes or impedes academic achievement (McNabb, Hawkes, and Rouk, 1999). Whatever the case, preliminary research raises poignant issues regarding the distribution of technology and its educational implications.

With the proliferation of technology comes problems, some old and some new. Most important among them is the fact that access to technology is not equitably distributed. In 1998, schools with few children from poverty backgrounds had Internet access in 62 percent of their classrooms compared to only 39 percent of classrooms in high-poverty schools ("State of American Education Address," 1999). (See Figure 2–2.) Likewise, disparities exist between "high-minority-enrollment schools" and "low-minority-enrollment schools." High-minority-enrollment schools, defined as 50 percent or more minority enrollment, are less likely to have instructional rooms with Internet access (National Center for Education Statistics, 1999). Moreover, computer and Internet access at home is limited to students whose parents can affort it. "About 13 percent of students in the $25,000 to $29,999 household income group used computers at home for schoolwork, compared to 45 percent of students in the $75,000 and over income group" (National Center for Education Statistics, 1999, p. 472).

Educators and policymakers face a formidable challenge in the twenty-first century. In a society dominated by computer technology, they must decide

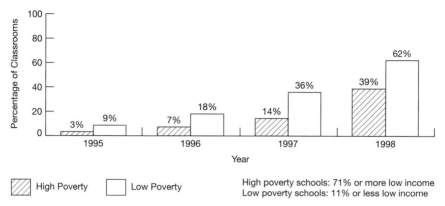

FIGURE 2-2 Percentage of classrooms in high- and low-poverty schools with Internet access.

Source: U.S. Department of Education, National Center for Education Statistics, Internet Access in Public Schools, February 1998; Internet Access in U.S. Public Schools and Classrooms, February 2000. Limitations of Data: Poverty measures are based on free and reduced-price school lunch data, which may underestimate school poverty levels, particularly for older students and immigrant students.

how to make effective use of computers and the Internet in classrooms and how to equitably distribute technology. If such issues are not addressed, some students may be left in the twentieth century.

A*pplying Sociology to Education:* How can educators prepare students for the future? ◆

Any educational issue we choose to investigate is likely to fall under one of the functions of education. Those discussed here provide a few examples. We move now to a discussion of the school function of selection and allocation, which takes place through the process of stratification.

◆ Summary

In this chapter we considered the five primary functions of education and processes that make the system function.

I. Conflicting Functions of Education

To illustrate the dynamic nature of educational systems, examples of controversies surrounding each function are discussed.

II. The Importance of Processes in Educational Systems

Processes are the action part of systems; they link the system parts and the system with the environment. Each function discussed involves processes of education.

III. The Function of Socialization: What We Learn and How We Learn It

Two controversies are discussed:

1. *The early childhood education controversy.* Controversies surround who should provide early care and the long-term results of early care. Research finds that there are some long-term positive effects of programs on poor children, especially if the efforts continue, and no deleterious effects of early childhood education on other children.
2. *Role of the media and commercials in socialization.* Controversies surround the role of media in education or entertaining, and the possible negative results of television watching. Excessive TV watching lowers achievement, and TV violence may increase aggression. There is clear evidence regarding the effect of parental involvement in TV decisions and the positive effects of educational TV for children. Recent industry ratings and V-chips allow more control over TV viewing.

IV. The Function of Cultural Transmission and Process of Passing On Culture

Concern has risen over poor skills of students, as shown by low standardized test scores and cultural illiteracy. Some advocate a strict core curricula to correct deficiencies. What to teach and who should decide are also controversial questions, especially in heterogeneous societies. Two areas exemplify the controversies: (1) drug and sex education and (2) censorship of textbooks and library books, especially concerning issues such as evolution versus creationism.

V. The Function of Social Control and Personal Development

Two issues that point to the conflicting attempts by schools to maintain social control are discipline and gangs. Controversies center on what type of discipline to use, the role of gangs in competing for students' attention, and how to deal with gangs and violence in schools.

VI. The Function of Selection and Allocation: The Sorting Process

How individuals are placed in society is the key controversy here. Because testing is used extensively for placement in schooling and jobs, the fairness of this procedure is discussed. (This function is discussed further in Chapters 3 and 4.)

VII. The Function of Change and Innovation: The Process of Looking to the Future

Who has access to the technological training necessary to advance in society is one issue raised here. To the extent that certain students have more access than others, they may have an edge in future placements and success.

 Putting Sociology to Work

1. Discuss the main processes involved in your role as a student.
2. What controversy over curriculum content has been present in a town with which you are familiar? What sociological factors underlie this controversy?
3. Visit a nursery school and observe. What types of socialization experiences are the children having that might differ from home experiences?
4. Discuss with some parents of young children and with teachers of young children their feelings about early childhood education.
5. Interview fundamentalist religious leaders about their views concerning the school curriculum. What changes or additions, if any, would they like to see? If there are fundamentalist church schools in your area, try to visit, observe, and learn about their programs.
6. Discuss with school board members and school administrators the pressure groups that influence their decision making, on what issues, and using what tactics.
7. Discuss with several teachers the techniques they feel are most effective in helping children learn and the discipline techniques they use in the classroom.
8. What are the biggest discipline problems facing schools in your area? Visit a school in a different type of community and find out the same information. What are the reasons for the similarities or differences in discipline problems? This may involve learning how the school deals with discipline.
9. Interview students of different ages to learn their views about discipline and students' rights.

CHAPTER 3

Education and the Process of Stratification

THE CRISIS IN SCHOOLING

Within the schools lie the keys to our futures; most people believe that schooling is directly linked to occupational and financial success. Because schools are accessible targets for criticism, anger, and hostility, parents, educators, students, and policymakers voice their concerns in public forums and at the ballot box.

There is general agreement that schools should produce individuals who can function in society, but how and why is controversial. Schools still carry out their tasks of transmitting basic skills, but most people around the world have higher expectations of what schools can and should do. In this chapter we consider several issues related to selection and placement of students and to the process of stratification. One of those issues is the very meaning of the phrase *equality of educational opportunity*. Other issues relate to variables that cause different school outcomes for children and adults, public or private schools, ability grouping, home and community environments, teacher and student expectations, and other variables.

Education and Stratification in America

There is a crisis, according to a number of educational critics (Young, 1990), because of changes in the educational environment, and hopes for schools that are not being met. The old Horatio Alger success stories just do not seem to be coming true any more, and the image of the "land of opportunity" is fading. Until recently, Americans believed that with education a person could do anything. Immigrants could come from societies where poverty and caste were inherited, rise in the social structure, and have a chance to reach their full potential. In 1848, Horace Mann, father of public education in the United States, wrote: "Education, beyond all other devices of human origin, is the great equalizer of the conditions of men—the balance wheel of the social machinery" (Mann, 1891). But things have not worked out quite that way.

In the early history of the United States, essential skills were passed from generation to generation through the family. With the growth of industry, new and more formal mechanisms to transmit knowledge were necessary, and this function was gradually transferred from family to school. Schools had the responsibility of preparing workers for industry and assimilating immigrant subcultures into the mainstream. Some early schools, including those for children working in factories, used the "monitorial system"; minimal learning was provided in reading, writing, math, and citizenship by monitors trained under teachers. These schools gave way to the "common schools," espoused by Mann, in an attempt to create a common identity and unifying force in the United States. At first they were open to all white children; later, segregated schools were provided for African Americans. Some children rose in the social structure as a result of education, but others, including Native Americans and freed slaves, fell further behind. Some immigrant groups, not satisfied with the public school education, formed their own schools to serve their own needs.

As industry and formal schooling expanded, the division of labor between those who controlled capital and decision making and those who were controlled began to be formalized and to result in inequalities. Private schools were established for elites, ensuring a continuation of their privileged positions. Mass education was encouraged to provide workers with necessary skills, including punctuality, obedience to authority, and accountability. Many felt that education for factory workers provided hope for a better life, and indeed, that hope was realized for many. However, education also served to perpetuate class distinctions between capitalists and the working class. Such practices as tracking generally favored advantaged students.

Society requires a cadre of trained workers to "keep the wheels of industry turning." Many levels and types of training are necessary, requiring a selection and allocation process that begins at school. The school system is thus expected to raise everyone's chances for a better life, to provide equality of opportunity, and to identify those who are most qualified for the most powerful and prestigious positions in society. The inherent contradiction inevitably leads to some dissatisfaction. Schooling helps some children move up; it locks others into low-level positions in society (Kozol, 1991; *Learning to Fail*, 1991).

Many subcultural groups today wish to maintain their ethnic identities; minority-group pressures have changed the emphasis over time from assimilationist goals to respect for and preservation of minority identities while providing access to social, economic, and political institutions. As we shall see, this model has met with mixed results and the controversies over access continue.

Education and Stratification Around the World

Some argue that improvements in the educational standing of various groups in the United States would lead to social equality; in fact, there has been a reduction in equality of income even though most groups are completing more schooling. In 1996, 19.8 percent of, or 13.8 million, children in the United States lived in poverty—40 percent of African American children, 40 percent of Hispanics, and 16 percent of whites (U.S. Bureau of the Census, 1996).

Mass education has spread around the world in the past two centuries; today about 60 percent of primary-age children in least-developed countries are enrolled in some type of formal schooling (Human Development Report, 1997, p. 179). Worldwide access to secondary education has also increased, but small numbers attend. Similarities in the curricula at both the primary and secondary levels show standard world models, though some countries are providing specialized tracks at the secondary level (Kamens, Meyer, and Benavot, 1996, p. 824).

Around the world, demographic factors such as sex, race, and family status affect individuals' chances for an education and have substantial effects on their future occupations, incomes, and prospects for poverty. A controversial thesis presented by Herrnstein and Murray in *The Bell Curve* (1994) essentially argues that individual placements in society are largely genetically determined. According to this idea, money for education or policies such as affirmative action will have little effect on people's place in society. Social scientists have criticized the book on many grounds, including manipulation of data, limited definitions of terms such as *IQ*, and faulty assumptions. Most point out that social factors in the United States and around the world are the root causes of inequality, and it is these factors that we need to understand and correct (Fraser, 1995; Hauser, 1995).

In order to deal with the complex relationships between the process of stratification and education, we need to address a number of interrelated topics. Several key questions will provide the underlying framework for this chapter and Chapter 4:

1. What role does stratification play in the societal system?
2. What role does education play in social stratification?
3. What are some key variables, both in and outside the schools, that affect stratification?
4. Can education lead to equal opportunity for members of society?

THE PROCESS OF STRATIFICATION: IS INEQUALITY INEVITABLE?

Most of us have a general idea about the meaning of stratification: It refers to a position in society. In the United States, an "open class" system predominates. The majority of us would probably answer "middle class" if asked our position in society. "Middle class" implies an "average" lifestyle—a house, a car, a white-collar wage earner. This contrasts with caste or estate systems, in which structured inequality is built into the society—individuals are born into their permanent, ascribed positions.

From our open class system perspective, stratification is perceived as an interwoven part of the whole societal fabric or system. We cannot isolate one institution, such as education, from the whole system and understand the phenomenon of stratification. Although our focus will be on education, we will bring aspects of family, politics, and economics into our discussion. Figure 3–1 indicates the interrelationships between the process of stratification and the educational system. Note the stratification of groups within the school, among those who enter the school as teachers and students, and in the community.

FIGURE 3–1 Stratification and the educational system.

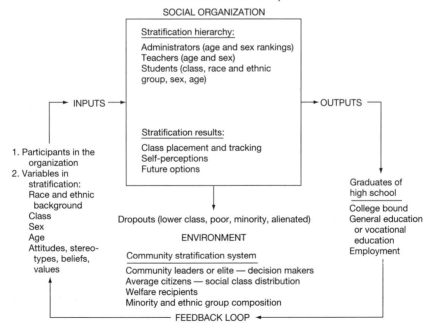

Determinants of Social Class

Sociologists study stratification, defining the meaning of *social class* and discussing its significance and implications for individuals in society. *Class* has been described by Weber (Gerth and Mills, 1946) as a multidimensional concept that is determined by three major variables: wealth, power, and prestige. *Wealth* refers to one's property, capital, and income. The striking fact about the United States is that 80 percent of the wealth is owned by one-twentieth of the population, and the top 5 percent own more than half of all property, leaving a tremendous gulf between rich and poor. Most segments of society have raised their standard of living in recent years, but the relative distribution of wealth has remained nearly the same. The small group at the top of the hierarchy generally perpetuates itself through inherited wealth or high-paying positions.

Power implies the ability to make major decisions or to influence others to act on behalf of one's benefit. Much power has become concentrated in the upper levels of government and business. C. Wright Mills (1956) argues that the "power elite" that dominates society and controls decision making is composed of members of the economic, political, and military elite. Others argue that interest groups such as unions vie with each other for power (e.g., Dye and Zeigler, 1997). In either case, the average person has little power in decision making.

Occupation is a main factor in one's *prestige*. Education affects occupational status, and income is closely associated with one's occupation. Various occupations have different amounts of prestige, including the ability to influence others.

The class system in the United States has been described by many different sociologists. In the 1920s, the Lynds (1929) were among the first to study the relationship between social class and educational achievement. Through an in-depth analysis of a small Midwestern city in the United States referred to as "Middletown," the Lynds concluded that working-class children do not have many of the verbal and behavioral skills and traits that are prerequisite to success in the classroom. In a number of community studies conducted by Warner, Havighurst, and Loeb (1944) in the United States, schools sorted students based on their potential for upward mobility. Lower-class children are often regarded as not capable. Other studies have replicated the social class–educational achievement relationship and confirmed these findings.

Table 3–1 shows one of the many typologies of social class in the United States, indicating the relationship between class and education. Thus, educational achievement is highly correlated with social class; students from lower classes have a much lower likelihood of going on to college than those of higher classes, even though they may have high ability.

One's position in the class stratification system implies a certain lifestyle, membership in certain groups, political affiliations, attitudes toward life chances, health, child-rearing patterns, and many other aspects of life.

TABLE 3–1 Social Class Typology

Class and Percentage of Total Population	Education	Education of Children
Upper class (1–3%)	Liberal arts at elite schools	College education by right for both sexes
Upper-middle (10–15%)	Graduate training	Educational system biased in their favor
Lower-middle (30–35%)	High school Some college	Greater chance of college than working-class child
Working (40–45%)	Grade school Some high school	Educational system biased against them; tendency toward vocational programs
Lower (20–25%)	Illiteracy, especially functional illiteracy	Little interest in education, high dropout rates

Source: Daniel W. Rossides, *Social Stratification: The American Class System in Comparative Perspective* (Englewood Cliffs, NJ: Prentice Hall, 1990), pp. 406–8.

From an early age, we are socialized to be members of a social class and to develop strong loyalties to the values of our class, including its attitudes toward education.

In the United States, the expectation is that we can improve our life position with good education and hard work, that all members of society have an equal opportunity to experience upward mobility. Those with higher levels of education have more chances at better jobs and salaries, but the question remains: Who gets the higher levels of education?

The median earnings of wage and salary workers varies dramatically by amount of schooling completed. In 1994 constant dollars, men more than 25 years old with eight years or less of education received approximate median earnings of $17,555 a year; women received approximately $8,000. With four years of high school, these figures jumped to $22,000 for men and $14,000 for women. With four years of college the figures were $38,565 for men and $26,709 for women (U.S. Department of Commerce, 1998).

Additional degrees command higher incomes (National Center for Education Statistics, 1995, p. vi). "The earnings disadvantage of not finishing high school was about 27 percent for white and black males between 25 and 34 years old" (National Center for Education Statistics, 1991, Tables 357–58). For females it was 39 and 42 percent, respectively (National Center for Education Statistics, 1992, p. 84). Education plays a role in sorting people into occupational categories according to abilities. Many less tangible factors, however, enter into this sorting process, including the following:

1. Differences in the level and quality of education available in the country, region, or community in which one lives.

2. Differential access to educational facilities according to one's social class status, religion, race, and ethnic origins.
3. Differences in one's motivations, values, and attitudes; differences in the willingness and ability of one's parents and significant others to provide the financial and psychological supports necessary for the maximization of talent potentials (Sewell and Shah, 1967).

The status attainment model (see Figure 3–2) shows six major ascribed and achieved variables that affect one's educational and occupational positions:

1. Father's and mother's education, father's occupation, family income
2. Ability, measured by achievement or IQ test (academic aptitude)
3. Academic performance
4. Significant others' encouragement
5. Educational/occupational aspirations
6. Educational attainment's direct influence on occupational attainment

As the arrows imply, these factors with additional influences from external sources interact to determine one's position in society.

If we do not have other favorable factors in our lives, schooling alone is likely to make little difference to our economic and social success in society,

FIGURE 3–2 The process of status attainment in the United States.

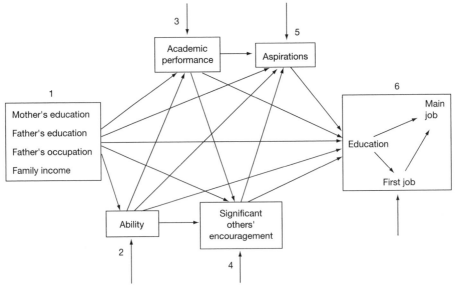

Source: From Beeghley, Leonard, *The Structure of Social Stratification in the United States,* 2/e. Copyright © 1996 by Allyn and Bacon. Reprinted with permission.

though some recent programs in schools that involve one-on-one tutoring, more academic classes, and high expectations have proven successful in increasing the academic achievement of students.

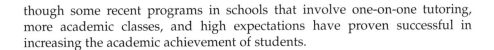

Applying *Sociology to Education:* Think of cases in which the positions of individuals in the stratification system have influenced their educational attainment. ◆

Major Explanations of Stratification

We all have ideas about how society should work and why some people succeed in society whereas others do not. Social scientists have explanations as well. From our systems perspective, we get a general framework for viewing stratification. Schools alone cannot cause or cure problems resulting from the stratification system, because they are but one part of a total, integrated system. Thus, to understand the role of schools in the process of stratification one must view interrelationships among schools, family, politics, religion, economics, and other integral parts of society. This will be the major emphasis of our discussion of stratification, as presented by classical theorists in sociology.

Two opposing theories of stratification are most often used to explain the unequal class system in our society: the functionalist (consensus) theory and the conflict theory. Our discussion here cannot do justice to the volumes of detailed analyses related to these complex theories; however, we can present some of the important issues surrounding these and related theories of stratification.

Functionalist (Consensus) Theory of Stratification. According to the functionalist perspective, each part of society is related to each other part in the total society. In order to maintain a working balance between the parts, the system has certain requirements and agreed-on rules. From this starting point, functional theorists explain the inevitability of inequality and the role education plays in the process of stratification. A major function of schools is to develop, sort, and select individuals by ability levels to fill hierarchical positions; functionalists argue that this is a rational process based on the merit of individuals. By following the argument of Kingsley Davis and Wilbert Moore (1945) in a classic article on stratification, the role of education in the stratification process becomes clearer:

1. People are induced to do what society needs done, motivated to fulfill roles by extrinsic rewards (money, prestige).
2. The importance of a particular role and scarcity of qualified persons to fill the role determine the prestige ranking of positions. For instance, doctors are believed to be more important than bartenders and have more prestige and higher pay.

3. Those positions that are most complex and important and require the most talent and training—that is, education—are the most highly rewarded.

Presumably, then, the more schooling one has completed, the more productive and valuable one is to society. Hence, a stratification system evolves, with some inevitably attaining more education and higher positions than others.

Another well-known theorist, Talcott Parsons, has laid the groundwork for much of functionalist theory. Parsons argues that society has shared norms and values by which to judge or evaluate its members. Those who come closest to meeting the established needs and values of society are likely to have higher status and occupational prestige (Parsons, 1970). Inequality, then, is inevitable, according to Parsons. Some will always be at the top because of their value to society; others will fall to the bottom. The question for Parsons becomes not whether inequality needs to exist, but rather how much inequality is justifiable. There is no easy answer to such a question, although he contends that some inequality is useful in motivating members of society to work hard, get ahead, and fill the positions necessary to keep society running (Sadovnik, 2001).

The selection process that will eventually determine occupational status begins in school, where functionalists argue that students are placed more according to individual abilities than to group differences such as race and sex. Some functionalists point out opportunities that exist for working-class students to achieve mobility through school achievement. They argue that the system is flexible, allowing opportunity for most American students to attend college. They stress the improvements in educational achievement levels of the poor, minorities, and women as evidence that abilities are taking precedence over race and sex. Robert Hauser and David Featherman (1976), in a classic analysis of male students, found that members of minority groups were completing more years of schooling; this, they believe, indicates that inequality in education is declining.

The functionalist view of society has not only many proponents, but also many critics. Criticisms fall into several categories, but of primary concern to us are the ideological critiques:

1. Functional or consensus theory presents a conservative view; many argue that it supports existing systems and the dominant power group, whether good or bad, and preserves the social order. Rather than finding a way out of wars, inequality, and scarcity, it is committed to making things work within existing systems (Hurn, 1993; Gouldner, 1971).

2. The implication that people must meet the needs of the system, rather than vice versa, is believed by some critics to be false and misleading. Similarly, functions of education may represent powerful individuals or groups pursuing their own interests (Hurn, 1993; Levitas, 1974, p. 165).

3. To assume that we can locate the most talented and motivated individuals through the schools or other institutions is questionable, especially when we look

at statistics as to who is successful in society. The socioeconomic status of the student is an important determinant of college graduation. Consistently, higher-status students complete college at a greater rate than lower-status students (Sewell and Shah, 1967).

4. To assume that extrinsic rewards, such as wealth and prestige, are primary motivators for individuals to train for certain occupations may be false. Individuals may have other motivations, such as humanitarian goals, for entering certain occupations. In addition, not all talented individuals who wish to become doctors or lawyers may have the opportunity to pursue those careers.

We turn now to contrasting views of the education system.

Conflict, Neo-Marxist, and Reproduction Theories of Stratification.
Conflict theorists see the stratification system and equality of opportunity from a different perspective. They believe that problems in the educational system stem from the conflicts in the society as a whole. Education is but one part of a system that is based on "haves" and "have-nots." Karl Marx, the father of conflict theory, believed that educational systems perpetuate the existing class structure. When the type of education and knowledge available to various groups of people is controlled, their access to positions in society is controlled. Thus, the educational system is doing its part to perpetuate the existing class system—to prepare children for their roles in the capitalistic, technological society, controlled by the dominant groups in society.

Members of social classes share socialization, which leads to traits such as common language, values, lifestyle, manners, and interests. These "status groups" distinguish themselves from others in terms of categories of moral evaluation—honor, taste, breeding, respectability, propriety, cultivation, good fellows, plain folk. Each group struggles for a greater share of those parts of society that make up "the good life"—wealth, power, and prestige—and it is because of this competition that conflicts exist. Some look to education to reduce inequalities, but according to conflict theorists, education, in fact, serves to reproduce the inequalities based on power, income, and social status (Carnoy, 1974). The values, rules, and institutions of society reflect the interests of the dominant groups, the ruling class; this is evident in the institution of education in the way resources are distributed (Scheurich and Imber, 1991). Thus, education is no exception.

Samuel Bowles, outlining the role of education from the conflict perspective, contends

> (1) that schools have evolved in the U.S. not as part of a pursuit of equality, but rather to meet the needs of capitalist employers for a disciplined and skilled labor force, and to provide a mechanism for social control in the interests of political stability; (2) that as the economic importance of skilled and well-educated labor has grown, inequalities in the school system have become increasingly important in reproducing the class structure from one generation to the next; (3) that the U.S.

school system is pervaded by class inequalities, which have shown little sign of diminishing over the last half-century; and (4) that the evidently unequal control over school boards and other decision-making bodies in education does not provide a sufficient explanation of the persistence and pervasiveness of inequalities in the school system. (Bowles, 1977, p. 137)

Origins of inequality are found in the class structure, capitalism, and modernity, and education reflects this. Inequality is part of the capitalist system, likely to persist as long as capitalism itself persists. Conflict theorists argue that although statistics show a narrowing of the educational gap between groups, this has not been translated into a more equal sharing of society's wealth. The characteristics of workers, such as their age, gender, race, and social class, influence the dollar value attached to education. The characteristics of the particular urban community and the economic structure in which individuals live, however, also affects their job opportunities and, thus, the value of their education. For instance, white male college graduates benefit in types of economic sectors that disadvantage equally educated females (Young, 1990).

Schools have come under increasing attack by frustrated minority groups hoping to improve their lot. A great variety of new approaches and special programs to improve opportunities have been initiated through educational systems. Conflict theorists argue that more extensive alterations in the fabric of societal order will be necessary to attack the underlying causes of inequality.

A new group called "critical theorists" question the availability of chances for low-status individuals to find opportunities. Reproductionists, revisionists, and neo-Marxists have developed explanations of stratification stemming from the idea that the upper-middle class "conspires" to perpetuate their own class interests by limiting access to educational opportunities for other groups. These theorists argue that the underclasses are channeled into poor secondary schools, community colleges, vocational schools, and lower-level jobs. In the process, schools give knowledge to poor and minority children that make them accept failure in school, poor occupational status, and the dominant culture (Giroux, 1994; Apple, 1993, p. 215).

Bowles and Gintis (1976) argue that schools are agencies for "reproducing" the social relations of production necessary to keep capitalistic systems working. Schooling and family are like economic production; some students gain more "cultural capital" for success, while others do not, thus reproducing the social class structure. This is referred to as the *correspondence principle*.

There is some empirical evidence to support the idea that classes are reproduced. In a study of American educational structures and reproduction of the "mental-manual" division of labor (or intellectual, white-collar class versus the working class), Colclough and Beck (1986) found that between 56 and 76 percent of male students reproduced their class status when looking at three key determinants of reproduction: public versus private schooling, socioeconomic community of the schools, and curriculum tracking within the schools. "Curriculum tracking was shown to be the critical determinant of reproduction." The authors found that "students from manual class backgrounds are over twice as likely to be placed in a vocational track" and from there are channeled into manual class jobs (Colclough and Beck, 1986, pp. 172–73).

In the late 1960s and early 1970s sociologists in Europe were exploring the effect that the cultural form and content inside schools had on stratification and reproduction. Young's *Knowledge and Control* (1971), followed by works of Bernstein, Bourdieu, Passeron, and others (1977), argued that "the organization of knowledge, the form of its transmission, and the assessment of its acquisition are crucial factors in the cultural reproduction of class relationships in industrial societies" (Sadovnik, Cookson, and Semel, 2000; Apple and Weis, 1986, pp. 19–20).

Some lower-class students do resist the tendencies toward class reproduction and learn to think independently, even to recognize their disadvantages. Willis describes the school counterculture of working-class boys in England, who rejected the dominant values and norms of the educational process (Willis, 1979). However, Willis's counterculture boys are only a few; many working-class students conform to the norms and try to make the system work for them. The lower and upper extremes of the stratification system are mostly locked into class positions; some individuals in the middle classes are mobile. Providing students with the knowledge needed to get ahead in a way they understand could help provide opportunities (Giroux, 1994).

Viewed from an international perspective, some have argued that schooling in the United States has a limited degree of stratification compared with other countries, especially in Europe. Rubinson points out that political forces in the United States have acted to limit the extent to which political decisions influence schools. Thus, according to this view, class analysis is important but does not necessarily determine schooling (Rubinson, 1986).

Lower-class, minority, and female students in the United States fall disproportionately at the bottom of the economic hierarchy. These three groups—class, race, and sex—are those on which we focus throughout our discussion of equal educational opportunity here and in the next chapter. Sex and race are discussed extensively in the next chapter.

Social-class background can aid or hinder students. Schools have a middle-class "bias" and are more closely aligned with the values and behavior patterns of middle-class children. A student's social class is determined by the home environment and is reflected in school grades, achievement, intelligence test scores, course failure, truancy, suspension, the high school curriculum pursued, and future educational plans. Class is not the only variable affecting achievement, and within each class there is wide variation, but there is definitely a significant relationship between class and achievement.

The sex difference favors girls initially, but this reverses later. Girls achieve grades as high as and higher than those of boys throughout high school. On standardized achievement tests, boys score higher than girls in some areas, such as math and science, and girls score higher in reading and writing. More girls graduate from high school, but about equal numbers of males and females go on to postsecondary education. It is there that males move ahead, obtaining more years of schooling and higher degrees.

Other discussions of inequalities in education and society concern who has *access* to education, the *content* of education, and the *outcomes* of the educational process in terms of power, prestige, and income. These "new left" conflict theorists argue that it is the long-term results of education that in part determine class structure. Other modern theorists argue that *power* and *coercion* are more important determinants of inequality than economics and social class. An altogether different approach to inequality, phenomenology, is concerned with the *content* of the educational process and the passing on of information that can perpetuate the class system. Clearly, many factors contribute to the stratification into unequal class systems. One's theoretical perspective influences policy decisions, which in turn affect school reforms and allocation of resources, benefiting students unequally whether they are gifted, at risk, require special education, belong to a low- or high-socioeconomic level, are minority, or live in an urban or rural community. Our task in the remainder of this chapter is to explore in more detail the role of education in the stratification process.

Applying *Sociology to Education:* Consider students who are at the bottom of the school achievement hierarchy. What factors do you think contribute to their position in the system? ◆

STRATIFICATION AND EQUALITY OF EDUCATIONAL OPPORTUNITY

Equal opportunity exists when all people, even those without status, wealth, or membership in a privileged group, have an equal chance of achieving a high-socioeconomic status in society regardless of their sex, minority status, or social class. This requires removing obstacles to individual achievement, such as prejudice, ignorance, and treatable impairments (Gardner, 1984, p. 46).

The Meaning of "Equality of Educational Opportunity"

James Coleman (1990) explored the concepts of equality and inequality, considering two opposing theories. One states that inequalities are justified only if they provide advantage to the unprivileged in society or if they benefit all. The other states that each person is entitled to what she or he has justly earned. Contrasting these two extremes reveals the dilemma of two sets of values in American society—equal access or individual freedom, the state's right to impose equality versus the individual's right to choose his or her own school. This conflict is exemplified in the disputes over busing. Over time, the equality of educational opportunity has changed in meaning from equal school resources to equal outputs.

In practice, each society places before its children the opportunities deemed appropriate and valuable in that society, and it attempts to give children an equal chance to compete within that framework. Some children's talents may go unappreciated in any particular society. In the United States and other heterogeneous societies there are many competing value systems; those who feel underrepresented argue that the schools are not giving them a fair shot at success within their framework of values.

Conflicts arise over differential treatment in school and unequal outcomes of the educational process in terms of wealth, occupational status, and opportunities. Given that students have different abilities and needs, can some type of equality of outcome be expected? What if unequal outcomes break down along racial, ethnic, social class, or gender lines? Even more controversial are proposals that argue that life chances are unfair to some, and that to ensure "equality of results," society should distribute jobs and wealth. These proposals range from progressive income taxes to curb extreme poverty and wealth to total restructuring of the economic system of society (Apple, 1993). Coleman (1990) concludes that equal treatment of students alone cannot produce equal outcomes.

Social Class Reproduction: The Debate over Public versus Private Schools

Students who get the best educations are more likely to be selected for the preferred jobs in society. What are the "best" educations and how to get them are the questions. Those who can afford to go to elite private schools pay for the special "status rights" and social networks that allow for the "passage of privilege," and hope that this will maintain their privileged position or help them obtain a better position. Studies of women's elite boarding schools, for instance, show higher education attainment and major differences in postsecondary outcomes (Persell, 1992; Persell and Cookson, 1985). Elite secondary schools socialize students into elite peer groups that form their adult primary groups and perpetuate status (Cookson and Persell, 1985). The selection of single-sex or religious private schooling is based largely on family tradition and preference (Lee, 1992).

A major research question, and one that has caused heated debate, is whether private schools produce significantly higher achieving students than public schools. If so, questions arise about the role of public schools, funding for private schools through vouchers, and charter schools. In 1982, Coleman and colleagues published a controversial study, *Public and Private Schools* (Coleman, Hoffer, and Kilgore, 1981). In the study, 58,728 sophomores and seniors in 1,016 public, private, and parochial high schools around the country were tested. Major findings, which have stimulated controversies surrounding the study, indicated that, controlling for family background, students in private schools (mostly Catholic) achieved at a higher level than those in public schools; private schools tended to have smaller classes and more student involvement; private schools provided more disciplined, orderly, and safe environments and have school climates more conducive to achievement; more homework is required in private schools, and they have better attendance records. All of these findings combine to produce higher academic achievement (Hoffer, 1985).

Coleman states "The evidence is strong that the Catholic schools function much closer to the American ideal of the 'common school,' educating children from different backgrounds alike, than do the public schools" (Coleman, 1990, p. 242). Additional findings show that Catholic schools produce positive effects on verbal and math achievement from grades 10 to 12 in high school, with an advantage of one-half to one year over other students. These findings are greatest for minority and low-socioeconomic-group students.

Catholic schools do well in the inner city: Students there achieve higher test scores than do students in public inner-city high schools, have less gang involvement and fewer discipline and dropout problems, take more advanced courses, and receive more value training and character building (MacFarlane, 1994, pp. 10–12), and have more parental involvement. Students in private schools for African Americans receive more college preparatory courses and achieve better test scores (Walsh, 1991).

The main criticisms of Coleman's study fall into three categories: methodological problems, accuracy of interpretations and alternative findings, and policy implications of the findings. Reanalysis of data by a number of researchers has challenged the major finding—that Catholic private schools are superior. Controlling for background variables such as class and race, and considering curriculum and teacher qualifications, critics argue that there is not a significant difference between good public schools and Catholic or other private schools in academic achievement (Topolnicki, 1994).

Just what is a significant difference in achievement is also in question. Some argue that findings that show a one-half-year to one-year difference are not large enough to claim that private schools are significantly superior (Alexander and Pallas, 1985, 1984, 1983).

Advocates of federal support for private education in the form of vouchers, tuition tax credits, or other federal aid are using Coleman's findings and recommendations to bolster their claims. Others, however, contend that federal support would increase religious and racial segregation of schools.

Alternative interpretations suggest other policies. James McPartland and Edward McDill (1982, pp. 77–78), arguing that student body composition accounts for school effectiveness, suggest that policy should be concerned with "allocation practices determining student body enrollments"; busing has been one such practice.

Despite the controversies over Coleman's findings on academic achievement and access to the best educations, research reveals the characteristics that make for effective schools, public or private. Some of these characteristics are high standards and achievement expectations, committed staff, high self-concept in students, effective leadership, appropriate rewards, and flexible heterogeneous grouping (Brookover, Erickson, and McEvoy, 1996). The debate over how to provide all students equal opportunity will continue.

The Controversial Issue of "Choice"

If public schools are found to be wanting, or if private schools receive federal funding, are we undermining a basic institution in society, the mass public school? In response to arguments that we weaken public schools, some politicians and educational leaders are advocating "choice"—allowing parents to select from among schools. Choice is a strategy for reform and restructuring. Most often the plans involve giving families a voucher for each student and allowing them to select from among schools, including private schools.

When a 1999 Gallup poll asked for public attitudes toward public school choice, it found "support for public funding for attendance at private schools has slipped slightly, but the public remains divided on the issue." Asked, "Do you favor or oppose allowing students and parents to choose a private school to attend at public expense?," 55 percent oppose making such choice available, up from 50 percent in 1998. Even Catholic and other private school parents were not in favor of public funds paying for private schooling (Rose and Gallup, 1999). Proponents argue that competition among schools for students will improve school quality. Choice helps increase accountability and gives parents and students more sense of ownership over schools. In fact, choice seems to have worked in some districts, and several states such as Massachucetts (Viadero, 1995), Minnesota, and Texas; and cities such as Milwaukee, White Plains, and parts of Harlem in New York City are experimenting with choice plans. More than half the states have forms of choice plans (Cookson, 1994).

In a controversial discussion of the choice issue, Chubb and Moe question whether school systems should be subjected to individual choice and market forces. The researchers focused on school practices and achievement differences between public and private school students, and their results support the side of choice (Chubb and Moe, 1990). They argue that most school systems have become so politically and bureaucratically complex that elements that encourage high achievement, including autonomy and professionalism of school staff, are limited. Under a free market system, educators could design any programs they think could compete successfully for students. This, in fact, is the idea behind many charter or community schools.

Opponents of choice decry the potential decline in numbers and quality of the common school, or public school, pointing out that only the least capable students will be left, accentuating the problem for ill-prepared students, and the best teachers will go to the better schools. School choice would likely increase religious and social segregation along race and class lines, though some studies show that African American and Hispanic parents, even those with lower levels of education, were more likely than white and Asian Americans to take advantage of school choice options (Schneider et al., 1996). Critics also point out disparities between public and private school students now and argue that little will change without fundamental restructuring of the system. The percentage of children enrolled at each level of schooling by family income is shown in Figure 3–3. Note the differences in the high- and low-income categories (National Center for Education Statistics, *Condition*, 1999).

In an analysis that examined the debate across the political spectrum and did case studies of cities and states with choice programs, Cookson (1994) argues that student achievement and school improvement and equity cannot be better than the reforms put in place by districts to achieve equality and excellence. For instance, there is little evidence at this time that the Milwaukee or Harlem experiments are improving school achievement (Tashman, 1992). His conclusion is that large bureaucratic educational systems are not meeting the needs of communities (Cookson, 1994).

Recent court rulings in Florida, Maine, Vermont, Ohio, and Pennsylvania against school vouchers raise questions about the constitutionality of voucher systems. For instance, Florida courts threw out the nation's first statewide school voucher system, ruling that the Florida Constitution forbids public money to be spent on private education. In 2000, more than 20 states were considering voucher systems, but most are unlikely to pass given the previous rulings. Thus, concerns about public funding of private schools and the effects on the stratification system may be reduced because of legal rulings.

*A*pplying Sociology to Education: What are some advantages and disadvantages of school choice programs for your district? ◆

Ability Grouping and Teacher Expectations

Most highly industrialized societies claim to be meritocracies, societies that attempt to place and advance individuals based on their merits. Yet few achieve a perfect match between abilities and responsibilities. Testing, discussed in

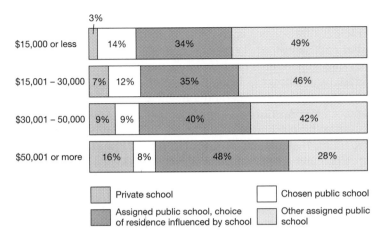

FIGURE 3–3 Distribution of public and private elementary and secondary students, by family income, October 1990.

Source: U.S. Department of Commerce. Bureau of the Census. Reprinted in National Center for Education Statistics, *The Condition of Education 1994,* p. 3.

Chapter 2, is one method used to determine education and job placement, yet many hold strong sentiments against the use of standardized tests for placement and perceive poor, minority, disabled, and female students to be at a disadvantage. In the rush to make schools and teachers accountable, many states and districts instituted placement exams, one outcome of which is ability grouping.

Ability Grouping. The basic question is how best to educate large numbers of students whose backgrounds and abilities differ widely without limiting the instructional opportunities of lower-track students. This is a reasonable question. Efforts to deal with it, however, have often found low-income and minority students at the bottom of the ability grouping system (Burnett, 1995). Therein lies the problem.

Ability grouping is a common practice in schools because most teachers believe that it is easier to teach a group of students with similar ability. Different grouping patterns emerge under different organizational structures, depending on the structural constraints and the school's atmosphere, or "culture." An example of a structural constraint would be students demanding to be placed in a particular track (Kilgore, 1991, pp. 201–202). Groupings are usually based on reading and math levels of students.

Most U.S. schools studied using national data sets have similar tracking systems and sequencing of courses in math (Hoffer and Kamens, 1992); there is more variation in science sequencing, though placement in math and science often go together. Studies show that as early as eighth grade, students' science grouping affects their future science curriculum and their chances to excel in the sciences (Schiller and Stevenson, 1992).

Unfortunately, not all students are placed on the basis of careful evaluation of their interests and abilities. Testing has been a primary method of placing students in tracks, but this method can increase social stratification (Darling-Hammond, 1994). A study of inner-city urban schools found that many factors operate in the placement of students—filling study halls or low-enrollment classes, filling remedial courses so that funding would continue at the school, and staff preferences for course assignments (Riehl, Natriello, and Pallas, 1992). Movement from one track to another is usually downward, based primarily on achievement. A student's socioeconomic level, however, does affect assignments, with higher-socioeconomic-level students disproportionately in college tracks (Lucas, 1992).

Schools in the United States rely more heavily on tracking than schools in any other nation (Oakes, 1990). However, national sequencing of courses, that is a common sequencing across a country, is less common in the United States than in many other countries because of local control of schools and no national governing bodies or tests. Standards set by teachers' organizations and college entrance requirements have some influence on national sequencing of courses and tracking of students in the United States (Schiller and Stevenson, 1992).

Japan, which values group conformity, is an example of a society with heterogeneous grouping in schools, treating all students alike by age cohorts. Though tracking within schools is rare, tracking occurs across schools in Japan, with some schools considered elite. Japanese parents and teachers believe the philosophy that each child is expected to achieve in school, and they believe that all can, although some may need to work harder than others. An underlying assumption in American education, despite the efforts toward equality, is that some will fail.

Conflict theorists argue that elites in the United States are unlikely to change basic structures that work for their class interests (Oakes, 1995, 1987). Thus, reforms in education have benefited some but have not changed their relative educational and economic position. Ability grouping often begins in elementary school and continues through high school as students are "tracked" into curricular models. The problem is to determine who gets placed where; too often, according to conflict theorists, placement correlates directly with the child's background, language skills, appearance, and other socioeconomic variables (Oakes, 1986).

The Supreme Court's 1967 ruling in *Hobson* v. *Hansen* in Washington, DC, stated that separation of students into fast and slow tracks resulted in unconstitutional segregation of minority and nonminority students. Yet, 86 percent of public secondary schools still offer core courses tailored to differences in student ability (National Center for Education Statistics, 1993). Many teachers argue that finding the best "fit" between students and teachers increases classroom effectiveness and that ability grouping of students makes it possible to teach them more effectively at their own levels (National Center for Education Statistics, 1993, p. 47).

Students in different ability groupings have quite different school experiences. For instance, in average to low-ability classrooms there is a more disruptive learning enviroment (Mekosh-Rosenbaum, 1996), whereas students in honors classes participate more (Gamoran et al., 1995). These learning environments affect student life chances, self-concepts, motivations, IQ and achievement levels, and other aspects of school and work experiences. Of the three major ways in which reproduction theorists argue that classes are reproduced (public versus private schooling, socioeconomic class composition of school communities, and ability grouping of students), research shows tracking to be the most important mechanism in the reproduction process. Colclough and Beck (1986, p. 469) show that students from "manual class" (working class) backgrounds are more than twice as likely to be placed in a vocational track as are other students. Table 3–2 illustrates the importance of each of these factors in the reproduction of class.

Thus, we know that ability is not a perfect predictor of placement in ability groupings. Characteristics of schools such as "electivity" (how students are assigned to tracks), inclusiveness, and other school policies, plus student characteristics (socioeconomic status [SES] of students and community, race, percentage of minority students in the school, the proportion of students in the school in an academic track, and the methods for assigning tracks—self-selection versus assignment) are influential in a student's placement. The higher the SES, the more likely students will be in academic tracks (Jones, Vanfossen, and Ensminger, 1995). Placements tend to be fairly stable over the year. We know that students placed in high-ability groups are taught more and at a faster pace than are those in low-ability groups, making it more difficult for students in lower tracks to move up.

Studying the socioeconomic composition of students in different schools is also revealing. Anyon (1980) compared the socioeconomic composition of schools with the work tasks of students, studying five elementary schools with very different compositions based on parents' occupations: two working-class, one mixed (middle-class), one "affluent professional," and one executive elite. The school patterns train students for their respective social classes. In working-class schools, children follow procedures—usually mechanical, rote behavior. In the middle-class school, getting the right answer and following directions is important, but some choice is possible. In the "affluent professional" school, the emphasis is on independent creative activity in which students express and apply ideas and concepts. In the executive elite school, developing analytical intellectual ability, learning to reason, and producing quality academic products are important. Conceptualizing rules by which elements fit together is a key goal.

TABLE 3–2 Social Class and Schooling Structures

Schooling Structure	Mental Class	Manual Class	Overall
I. School Type			
Public schools			
Percent students recruited from	33.37	66.63	—
Percent class membership reproduced	52.92	70.85	64.87
Private schools			
Percent students recruited from	43.93	56.07	—
Percent class membership reproduced	62.02	53.94	57.49
II. School Community			
High-minority communities			
Percent students recruited from	26.59	73.41	—
Percent class membership reproduced	45.27	71.13	64.25
Low-minority communities			
Percent students recruited from	36.29	63.71	—
Percent class membership reproduced	55.33	70.72	65.14
III. Curriculum Track			
General track			
Percent students recruited from	26.96	73.04	—
Percent class membership reproduced	33.41	81.91	68.83
Vocational track			
Percent students recruited from	19.70	80.30	—
Percent class membership reproduced	16.67	90.27	75.77
College-bound track			
Percent students recruited from	45.63	54.37	—
Percent class membership reproduced	69.32	44.95	56.07

Source: "The American Educational Structure and the Reproduction of Social Class: Table 3, Social Class and School Structures" by Glenna Colclough and E. M. Beck from *Sociological Inquiry* 56:4, p. 469. Copyright © 1986 by the University of Texas Press. All rights reserved.

Tracking has other consequences for students who develop "student cultures" within each track. These cultures add to the perpetuation of attitudes and behaviors that reproduce social class. In Israel, a multiethnic society, students from the same ethnic groups have tended to group together. Vocational education has come under question because it reproduces the same class of students in the same occupations (Yogev and Avalon, 1987). Many writers have commented on the effects of grouping. A summary of findings follows.

1. Lower-ability groupings tend to include a disproportionate number of lower-class and minority children; this stratification influences educational attainment and is likely to affect students' later job attainments and earnings.

2. Children from low-socioeconomic backgrounds are more likely to be placed in low-ability groups because of low test scores, which some argue do not measure ability accurately. In addition, they are often stigmatized, and scores keep falling in relation to other groups.

3. Each school has its own stratification system, depending on students coming into the system, but children in any given grouping tend to be more homogeneous in terms of socioeconomic status and race than are children in the school as a whole. In other words, groupings within the school are highly related to the background of the students. Once students are labeled and grouped, there is less chance of their moving from one category to another. Schools in different neighborhoods have different outcomes. For instance, in higher social class districts with excellent schools, students have more college preparatory courses from which to choose (Jones, 1996, p. 21; Spade, 1994, 1997).

4. Students in upper-ability groupings are disproportionately of higher socioeconomic status, are more motivated, and have higher achievement, class rank, and test scores, all of which give them a better start after high school. Teachers give more feedback and praise to high-ability groups and plan more creative activities for them. For the lower-ability groupings, the opposite is true. This same distinction by class status holds at junior and community colleges in the vocational versus academic tracks.

5. Summaries of research on the effects of ability grouping indicate that the practice benefits gifted students and those placed in high tracks. Lower-ability groups receive less teacher attention and poorer instruction, setting them further behind in the quest for equal opportunity. Ability groups often reinforce race and class segregation and stereotypes, and they lower the aspirations and self-esteem of lower-group students.

6. Most problematic is the conflicting evidence on the effects of grouping. In a review of 29 studies on the effects of ability grouping, Slavin (1990) finds little evidence of beneficial effects. He does not address institutional and curricular differences in students' experiences, but mainly uses test scores.

Not only do some studies show no justification for the use of tracking, but they also question programs such as Chapter I that "pull out" students from regular classes (Oakes, 1990). Most damning was a study showing minority students' disproportionate placement in low-ability math and science classes with the least-qualified teachers and insufficient access to computers, science equipment, and quality textbooks. Students in low-ability groups lose ground and perform poorly on reading and math achievement tests (Hallinan, 1990). Grouping can start as early as first grade and can have an impact for several years thereafter (Pallas et al., 1994).

Those in favor of heterogeneous grouping of students believe that tracking on the basis of presumed ability level harms students who are placed in the lower tracks and fails to help those placed in higher tracks. Proponents of untracking students also assert that tracking results in a lack of equity, is a violation of democratic values, produces low self-conceptions of learning ability, and causes a devaluing of self by those placed in lower tracks. Many argue that tracking programs based on presumed ability result in two unfortunate consequences: "more academic failure, and heightened racial and social class animosity" (Brookover et al., 1996, p. 116).

Are there solutions to the problem of homogeneous versus heterogeneous grouping? Most suggestions focus on restructuring classroom groupings: Students work together in many subjects but are grouped in reading, language arts, and math. Low achievers are not stigmatized or made to feel they are "dummies." Low achievers are few in the class, so that the teacher can give them needed help. Success, experts argue, depends on small student-to-teacher ratios, high expectations by teachers, extensive oral communication in class, and experienced, effective teachers (Levine and Stark, 1993).

Some elementary schools in Britain and the United States have attempted alternatives to grouping, making constructive use of the diverse abilities and backgrounds of the students. In these schools, children work at their own levels of ability in reading and math. The teacher gives the class lessons on particular topics suitable for the range of abilities and works with individual children or with small groups, sometimes with the help of an aide. Cooperative relationships between children are encouraged—for example, children who understand a math concept may be assigned to help teach other students. This fosters not only cooperation but also feelings of self-worth because each child's particular talents are recognized. It also prevents some of the problems associated with labeling.

Teacher Expectations and Student Achievement. What difference do teacher expectations of students make in student performance? In a pioneering study, Robert Rosenthal and Lenore Jacobson (1968) tested the effects of teacher expectations on interactions, achievement levels, and intelligence of students. A follow-up study in a San Francisco elementary school with a high percentage of lower-class and Mexican American students gave support to their hypothesis that once a child is labeled by the teacher and others, a "self-fulfilling prophecy" operates: The teacher expects certain behaviors from the child and the child responds to the expectations. Once this pattern is established, it is hard to alter (Bonetari, 1994).

Criticisms of their study have focused on its methodological weaknesses and have pointed out that their findings apply mainly to lower grades. Multiple factors enter into teacher interactions with students; nonetheless, they pioneered in an important area of research that continues to provide valuable insights on teacher–student dynamics. The body of literature that has developed since their study has shown that teacher expectations play a significant role in determining how much and how well students learn (Bamburg,

The way teachers interact with students affects student achievement.

1994). The focus of more recent studies has been on teacher expectations of their class and how this affects their teaching methods and the atmosphere in the class. What difference do teacher expectations of students make in student learning?

Teacher expectations are influenced by various factors, including records of the student's previous work and test scores; the student's dress, name, physical appearance, attractiveness, race, sex, language, and accent; the parents' occupations; single-parent and motherhood status (Cooper, 1995); and the way the student responds to the teacher (see Box 3–1). A study of Mexican American student achievement was shown to be related to teacher attitudes and expectations; teachers viewed the Mexican American students as different from Anglo students. Underachieving Mexican American students valued their cultural traditions more than the high-achieving Mexican American and Anglo students and became resistant to learning when these traditions were marginalized. Achievement was also related to their compliance, appearance, styles of communication, and willingness to support Anglo norms (Pena, 1997).

Teacher expectations are manifested in the teachers' behavior toward and treatment of individual children and their grouping of the children in classroom situations. Children pick up the subtle cues; the "self-fulfilling prophecy" can cause them to believe that they have certain abilities and can influence future behaviors. Many teachers in schools with low-achieving students

We need to guard against using the following factors to impose lower expectations on undeserving students:

> *Sex.* Young boys and older girls are sometimes the recipients of prejudicial low academic expectations. This often is a function of mistaken beliefs about the relevance of boys' maturation and sex-role discrimination, which harms females.
>
> *Socioeconomic status level.* Low expectations are typically held for children of families with low-level income and education. Status based on the jobs held and the place of residence of the parents often are used to prejudge students.
>
> *Race and ethnic identifiers.* African American, Hispanic, and Native American students receive lower expectations than other students. Asian students receive high expectations.
>
> *Negative comments about students.* Negative comments by other teachers or principals often result in lower expectations.
>
> *The status of the school.* Rural and inner-city schools often are associated with lower expectations than suburban schools. The racial, ethnic, and income level of the school is often a factor in such prejudice.
>
> *Appearance.* Lower expectations are associated with clothes and grooming that are out of style, made of cheaper material, not brand name, or purchased at thrift or discount stores.
>
> *Oral language patterns.* Nonstandard English often is the basis for holding lower expectations for students.
>
> *Neatness.* Lower expectations are associated with general disorganization, poor handwriting, or other indicators.
>
> *Halo effect.* There is a tendency to label a student's current achievement based upon past performance evaluations of a child.
>
> *Readiness.* There are negative effects when teachers assume that maturation rates or prior lack of knowledge or experience are unchanging phenomena, thus precluding improvement.
>
> *Seating position.* Lower expectations are typically transmitted to students who sit on the sides and in the back of a classroom.
>
> *Socialization by experienced teachers.* Experienced teachers have a tendency to stress the limitations of certain students for new teachers rather than the need to work on improving the performances of students.
>
> *Student behavior.* Students with poor, nonacademic behavior also tend to receive lower academic expectations from teachers.
>
> *Teacher training institutions.* Some faculty within colleges of education perpetuate myths and ideologies of individual limitations of students. This results in prejudicially low expectations for large numbers of students.
>
> *Teacher education textbooks.* Some textbooks also perpetuate myths and ideologies that individual students have limitations, which reinforce prejudicially low expectations for students.
>
> *Tracking or grouping.* Students in a lower academic track are mistakenly presumed to have been placed there for good reason (i.e., they have limited capacities and can never be expected to learn critical knowledge and skills).

Source: Brookover, Wilbur, et al. *Creating Effective Schools: An In-Service Program.* Holmes Beach, FL: Learning Publications, Inc., 1996, pp. 75–76.

become discouraged about the children's ability to learn. Their expectations for student learning are reduced, creating that self-fulfilling prophecy in which teachers expect less and students give less. Students are influenced by their teachers' expectations, and they internalize those expectations. Even though some students have given up on education, they dislike teachers who do not carry out the illusion of believing in education.

Teachers manipulate the classroom situation so as to affect student performance through ability grouping and creating other groups within the classroom. An example of this is revealed in an experiment conducted by a classroom teacher in Iowa. She was concerned that her students really understand the impact of discrimination, so she set up an experiment, the results of which surprised even her. She divided the children in her all-white class into two groups: blue-eyed and brown-eyed. For the first day, one group was given privileges and made to feel superior. The situation was reversed the next day. The children took their roles very seriously, with the superior ones taking delight in putting down the inferior ones and in excelling in their own work. The inferior for the day were outperformed. The importance of this example is that labels can affect the self-concept of students and their treatment by others, even in such a short-term experiment (Peters, 1971). The major policy recommendation coming from studies of teacher expectations is that positive teacher attitudes and approaches toward learning are necessary if students are to believe that they can achieve; some inner-city schools that have rigorous expectations have raised levels of achievement significantly.

*A*pplying Sociology to Education: How can teachers affect classroom interactions and student self-perceptions? ◆

Financing Schools in the United States

Wealthy school districts attract the best-educated and more experienced teachers. They can offer higher salaries, superior facilities and materials, support staff to handle problems, and a potentially achievement-oriented group of students. Poorer and minority schools get new, inexperienced teachers. There is also a tendency for minority teachers to be placed in schools with heavy concentrations of minority students, depriving all districts of an integrated teaching staff. These are some of the factors that indirectly affect student achievement (Elliott, 1998).

This imbalance has stimulated several court cases concerning equal financing of education. In the 1974 landmark *Serrano* v. *Priest* case, the California Supreme Court ruled that forcing school districts to rely heavily on local property taxes created sharp inequalities between school districts in the state. In 1976, California was ordered to substantially reduce the gap between districts by 1980. Many other state courts considered cases on finances, one of which was heard by the Supreme Court. In *San Antonio Independent School District* v. *Rodriguez*, the Supreme Court left decisions regarding property tax funding of schools up to each state. Property tax is still a part of local school funding, but often it is not the most equitable way of collecting funds for education. School spending per student can be up to four times greater in wealthy districts than in poor ones. Property taxes are highest in cities, causing middle classes to leave and businesses to locate elsewhere, resulting in a small tax base. Urban students often require different types of programs—bilingual, vocational, compensatory, or special education—all of which cost additional money. On average, local districts with high percentages of students in poverty receive a higher percentage of school revenues from the state and federal government, though most federal support is for special programs, such as compensatory education (National Center for Education Statistics, 1995, p. 151; 1992, p. 335).

States help support education through income tax, sales tax, and lotteries. Local districts use primarily property taxes to fund close to 50 percent of local school budgets. And this is where the conflict arises; some districts bring in significantly more tax dollars than others and can afford better education for their children. The federal government holds a big stick over local and state education by threatening to withdraw funding for special programs if districts do not comply with federal laws barring racial bias in programs of instruction such as Title IV of the Civil Rights Act of 1964.

Educators will continue to struggle over ways to involve all children fully in the educational process. For some, this means finding ways to alter the disadvantages of "cultural capital" brought to school by lower-class children. For others, it means restructuring the system so that all children have a place, regardless of family background and financing factors. In the next chapter, we discuss the effect of educational policies and attempts at equality of educational opportunity on specific groups of students.

◆ Summary

Schools are the target for the frustrations of many groups; they represent at the same time a means to get ahead and an institution that is holding some students back.

I. The Crisis in Schooling

According to many experts, there is a crisis in schooling. Both the public and the educators are concerned about evidence indicating the failure of schools to meet expectations. It is also true, however, that we expect schools to solve some problems that have their roots in the structure of societal institutions. This chapter addressed the stratification system, its role in education and society, and equality of educational opportunity.

II. The Process of Stratification: Is Inequality Inevitable?

Stratification, a process that is interlaced through the whole societal structure, refers to our position in society. Our social class, the structure of American stratification, is determined by several variables, including wealth, power, and prestige. Educational attainment is closely associated with these variables. In addition, education is used to sort people into future societal roles. Thus, people look to education to improve their status in society.

There are two major theoretical explanations of stratification systems. Functional theorists see inequality as inevitable, and education as playing a role in selecting and training people for unequal positions in society. The question is this: How much inequality should be tolerated? Among the criticisms of functional theory is the charge that, by assuming inequality, it assumes perpetuation of the status quo.

Conflict theorists disagree with the assumption that inequality is inevitable. They argue that it is perpetuated by those in power, the "haves." We are distinguished by status groups, with the dominant group controlling. Conflict theorists hold that education alone cannot solve the problems of inequality in society, but that it will take a restructuring of the whole society to bring about change.

III. Stratification and Equality of Educational Opportunity

Equality of opportunity refers to all people having an equal chance of achieving a high-socioeconomic status in society, regardless of sex, race, or class. Related to schools, it refers to equal facilities, financing, and availability. Problems arise over different treatment and outcomes—the fact that certain groups come out consistently on the bottom.

Social classes are "reproduced" through several mechanisms, such as elite and private schools, tracking and ability grouping, and teacher expectations. For instance, certain school policies can influence groups negatively. Testing tends to favor middle-class, white students; ability grouping falls along race and class lines. Teacher behaviors and expectations can also affect student achievement. All of these factors can influence the child's achievement and attainment in school.

Many ideas have been proposed to bring about change, including legislation, changing the financing of schools, and compensatory education.

◆ *Putting Sociology to Work*

1. What evidence, if any, do you see in your community for "the crisis in schooling"?
2. Do you have evidence that your social class, race, subculture, or sex has affected your educational experience? Document. Talk with others about their experiences.

3. Describe examples of differences in educational achievement by race, sex, or class from data available for your community or for other communities. How would a structural-functionalist explain these differences? a conflict theorist?
4. Talk to teachers or school officials about school policies that influence stratification: testing, ability grouping, teacher expectations

CHAPTER 4

Race, Class, and Gender

Attempts to Achieve Equality of Educational Opportunity

African American and white, female and male, Hindu and Muslim, rich and poor—such dichotomies in our ascribed status also imply different points on the continuum of educational experiences and outcomes. The positions that individuals hold in the societal and educational systems are influenced by their race, sex, cultural background, and social class. These background factors affect the stratification within educational systems and society as a whole; the dynamics of systems cannot be understood without regard for such factors. In this chapter we focus first on the experiences of females and males in the educational system and on how this influences the status and roles of men and women in society. [A distinction is made in most discussions between "sex," which generally refers to biological aspects of an individual, and "gender," which refers to sociocultural aspects that determine appropriate behavior patterns (Rothenberg, 1995, p. 8). Here we use the terms *sex* and *sex roles* to refer to both biological and sociocultural aspects.] In the second section we look at some attempts to rectify the unequal treatment of racial, ethnic, and other minorities in the educational system and examine the results of these attempts.

GENDER AND EQUALITY
OF EDUCATIONAL OPPORTUNITY

A flyer distributed at Yale Law School rating five women as "Total Packages" (described in sexual terms) (Fox-Genovese, 1995, p. C7). A scandal created by a group of Cornell men who composed a sexually graphic list of the "Top 75 Reasons Why Women Shouldn't Have the Freedom of Speech," a list that got widespread coverage on the Internet, and included such comments as "If she can talk, all she'll do is complain," "She doesn't need to talk to get me a beer," "Highway fatalities would decrease by over 90 percent," and 72 more, many so obscene they are unfit to print anywhere. A study that found sexist humor associated with hostility toward women, with men's enjoyment of sexist humor positively correlated with rape-related attitudes and beliefs and sexual aggression (Ryan and Kanjorski, 1998). These are just three indicators that sexism is alive on many college campuses. Such incidents are revitalizing debates about bias against women in academia; they help explain why it is that girls and boys who go into the same schools and classroom systems come out with different experiences, interests, achievement levels, and expectations (Renzetti and Curran, 1999). Theoretical explanations and scientific research on the different educational experiences focus on socialization, the role of education in societies, and "biological destiny."

Sex-Role Socialization

The socialization process begins the day we are born and ends the day we die. Informal education is a continuous process throughout life; formal education is restricted to certain periods. Girls and boys have different socialization experiences from birth, and by the time they enter nursery school, most children already have a good idea of their gender identity from parents, siblings, TV, and other "socialization agents."

The socialization function takes place in schools, where students spend more than six hours a day in classes and school-related activities. Teachers and schools become important sources of information on sex-appropriate behavior; children learn by observing and imitating adult roles, including the roles of teachers and administrators. They observe the ratio of males to females and the authority structure in the educational hierarchy. They learn their own sex-appropriate behavior through positive and negative sanctions, as well as through textbooks.

Children's toys play a major role in sex socialization as well. "Boys' toys"—chemistry sets, doctor kits, telescopes, microscopes—encourage manipulation of the environment and are generally more career-oriented and more expensive than "girls' toys" (Richmond-Abbott, 1992, p. 87). Parents are generally very conscious of buying sex-appropriate toys for their children. Toy choices carry over to children's play, and by the time young children reach nursery school, they have already learned to play with sex-appropriate toys. Popular video games also portray traditional gender role stereotypes, women as sex objects, and violence against women; in a study of 33 popular video games, no female characters were included in 41 percent, and women were seen as sex objects in 28 percent (Dietz, 1998).

Sexism in textbooks has received a great deal of attention. Books are a major source of messages about sex roles. Among the best known of the many studies done on readers and storybooks are those by a group based in Princeton, New Jersey, called *Women on Words and Images* (1988). They evaluated gender portrayal in children's readers and have updated their findings as new editions from 18 major textbook companies were released. Content analysis of texts examines the sex of the main character, illustrations, positive and negative images of men and women, stereotypes, and many other factors related to the portrayal of sex roles in the societal system. Recent analyses show improvements, but imbalances still favor males in rate of portrayal and types of roles assigned (Goodman, 1993; Purcell and Steward, 1990). Children's picture books also show greater male representation in titles, pictures, and central roles (Tepper and Cassidy, 1999). Studies reveal that science, social studies, and even math books depict girls and women in stereotypical sex roles. For instance, math problems involving girls often show them jumping rope, buying clothes, sewing, cooking, or calculating the grocery bill (Goodman, 1993). These socialization experiences influence what boys and girls learn about their gender roles. Though textbook publishers are improving accuracy in examples and coverage, many school districts cannot afford to buy the updated books (Cohen, 1992, p. A1).

Differences in behaviors begin early, when children as young as three-and-a-half start to influence their peers. Girls tend to be ignored by boys and even teachers and may stop trying to get attention. Girls form intimate "chumships," whereas boys relate through groups organized around activities, such as sports, similar to future job structures. Even speech patterns differ, with boys using speech for egoistic purposes and girls for social bonding (Hibbard and Buhrmester, 1998; Tavris, 1990, p. B5).

Girls learn "hidden" sexist lessons (Sadker and Sadker, 1994, p. 2). For instance, boys are called on more, asked to solve problems, disciplined more, and have more interaction with teachers. The accumulated messages may lead girls to experience other problems and disorders including eating problems, harassment, pregnancy and dropping out, and low self-esteem.

Societies' stereotypes of male and female behavior are learned fairly early in a child's life. Evidence of these stereotypes is apparent around the world. Statistics on enrollments and literacy rates for men and women exemplify the different societal expectations for the sexes (see Figure 4–1). Of 50 countries with significantly fewer girls than boys enrolled in school, most are located in the poorest regions of South Asia, Africa, and the Middle East, according to a

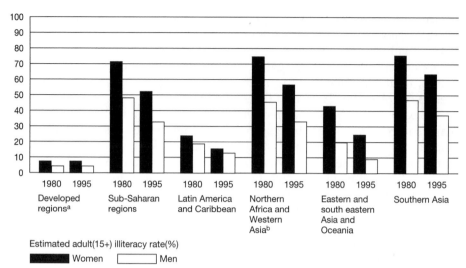

Estimated adult(15+) illiteracy rate(%)

■ Women ☐ Men

ᵃBased on limited data.

ᵇAlso including Djibouti, Mauritania, and Somalia.

FIGURE 4-1 Illiterate women and men age 15 and over, 1980 and 1995.

Source: United Nations Educational, Scientific and Cultural Organization, "Statistics on adult illiteracy; preliminary results of the 1994 estimates and projections" (STE-16). Based on estimated total illiterate population in each region. Reprinted in United Nations, *The World's Women 1995*, p. 90. © United Nations. All United Nations rights reserved.

study by Population Action International (1994). Only 23 percent of women in poor countries go to secondary school (United Nations Development Program, 1993). Without education, women cannot participate fully in the economic and political aspects of society, yet access to literacy and education remains a major problem for much of the world's population. The United Nation's Fourth World Conference on Women, held in Beijing in 1995, pointed out that by the year 2000 more than half of the world's population will be under the age of 20. Approximately half of these are women, who need to be educated if their countries are to reduce poverty (Geewax, 1995, p. A16).

Sex Differences in the Educational System

The sex-role differences in education in the United States are not new. The Puritans in the United States discouraged literacy for women, except to ensure salvation by reading the Bible. After the American Revolution, it became the responsibility of women to teach young children and pass on moral standards; thus, a limited amount of education became acceptable, perhaps even encouraged, in a male-dominated society. This attitude is illustrated in the following quotation from a school observer in the 1880s:

We noticed the boys all writing, but none of the girls; turning to our friend Tullis for an explanation, he said it was not safe for girls to learn to write, as it would culminate in love-letter writing, clandestine engagements and elopements. He said women were allowed to study arithmetic, though, for Miss Polly Caldwell studied as far as long division, and Mrs. Kyle, while a widow, got as far as reduction. He says Polly Caldwell was a weaver, and required the aid of figures to make her calculations for warping. (*History*, 1973)

Societal systems are dependent on schools to pass along crucial beliefs and values—among them, sex-role behaviors and expectations. In part, this occurs formally through courses and texts used in the curriculum or through the structure that assigns privileges and tasks by sex. But many of society's expectations are passed on through the informal or "hidden" curriculum (discussed in Chapter 8), including materials, activities, differential treatment, and counseling. Sex roles in schools mirror those in society. Our behavior and our expectations for each sex, from child-rearing activities to school expectations, are greatly affected by stereotypes (Rothenberg, 1995, p. 8). Stereotypes about male and female characteristics are fairly consistently held by members of our society: Girls are docile, gentle, cooperative, affectionate, nurturant; boys are aggressive, curious, competitive, ambitious.

Higher education presents a mixed picture for women; increasing numbers are enrolling, but not in all fields. Oberlin was the first U.S. college, in 1833, to open its doors officially to women, but their education was restricted to domestic subjects. With the development of women's colleges in the mid-nineteenth century came women reformers and women professionals. Since that time, the picture has been one of steady advancement for women in education, with both all-female and coeducational schools and with their entry into a wide range of professions. In recent years, many of even the staunchest male institutions have become coeducational. One area that continues to be controversial is women's athletics. Ongoing lawsuits in higher education point out the discrepancies—universities give less support to women's athletics than to men's, and Title IX requires equal treatment (Lederman, 1994, p. A51).

Over the past 20 years, the gap between the number of women and men going to college has disappeared for the 25- to 29-year-old age group (see Figure 4–2). It is predicted that by 2007, 9.2 million women but only 6.9 million men will be enrolled in colleges in the United States (Sommers, 2000). Women are enrolling in graduate education in increasing numbers and are strongly represented in education, health professions, and the social and behavioral sciences (see Table 4–1) (National Center for Education Statistics, 1999, p. 150).

Despite their increasing numbers, women do not always receive respect for intellectual achievements. For instance, African American intellectuals, especially women, are caught in a bind, living in a basically "anti-intellectual society." They often believe that their intellectual work is perceived as less valuable than that of activists (Hooks and West, 1991), though their contributions

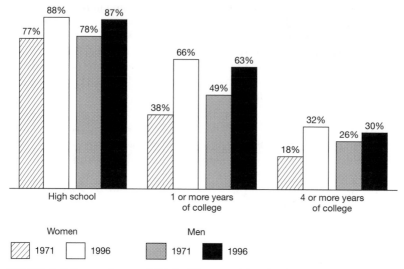

FIGURE 4–2 Percentage of 25- to 29-year-olds who have completed selected levels of education, by sex, March 1971 and 1996.

Source: U.S. Department of Commerce, Bureau of the Census, March Current Population Surveys.

lay the groundwork for activism. "Be smart, but not too smart—and always expect confrontation with harsh realities" is the advice of one woman.

There is some evidence that girls and women are excelling in school, and that it is the boys who are dropping out in greater numbers and attending college in fewer numbers. Many statistics on educational participation and achievement now favor girls (Sommers, 2000). However, these educational advances do not always translate into equal access to all fields, better job opportunities, and equal salaries after school.

Sex-Role Composition of Schools. Major sex composition differences remain in the structure of educational systems. For instance, in the United States in 1996, 74.4 percent of public school teachers were women; more than 86 percent of the elementary school teachers were women, whereas only 56 percent of high school teachers were women (National Center for Education Statistics, *Digest*, 1995, 1997).

The pattern of "the higher, the fewer" continues at the university level where 32.5 percent of the teaching faculty are women, primarily in lower ranks (*The Chronicle of Higher Education Almanac*, 1999–2000, p. 36). Why do these inequalities exist? Socialization affects attitudes; structural barriers limit access. And the educational system is slow to change. For instance, socialization and the hierarchical and power structures of organizations have influenced women not to seek administrative responsibilities; interpersonal barriers confront aspiring women when they face the dominant power structure; organizational

TABLE 4-1   Percentage Distribution of Bachelor's Degrees Earned by Women and Men, by Field

Major Field	1972 Female	1972 Male	1992 Female	1992 Male
Total	100	100	100	100
Biological/life sciences	3	5	4	4
Business	3	22	20	26
Communications	1	2	5	4
Computer science	0	1	1	3
Education	37	10	14	4
Engineering	0	10	2	13
English	11	5	6	4
Modern foreign languages	4	1	2	1
Health sciences	6	1	8	2
Mathematics	2	3	1	2
Physical sciences	1	4	1	2
Psychology	5	5	8	3
Social sciences	15	20	10	14
Other	13	13	19	18

Source: Digest of Education Statistics, 1994, tables 268–285. Reprinted in National Center for Education Statistics, "The Educational Progress of Women." Findings from *The Condition of Education 1995*, U.S. Department of Education, p. 13.

and institutional barriers occur during recruitment, selection, placement, evaluation, and other processes. Thus, at several levels women face obstacles to achieving higher positions in the structure.

Single-sex high schools and colleges have been dwindling since the 1960s, but research shows that they can provide support by separating academic from social concerns of adolescents, especially for girls. Some school districts are now considering single-sex classes in math and some sciences (Estrich, 1994, p. A11). Differences in learning styles and problems with teacher reactions to girls and boys could be eliminated with single-sex classes according to advocates (Fox-Genovese, 1995, p. C7). In academic achievement, achievement gains, educational aspirations, reduced sex-role stereotyping, and positive attitudes related to academics, single-sex schools have advantages. Whether there will be much expansion in single-sex schools, however, is questionable because of court cases in several cities (Brown and Russo, 1999).

In higher education, women's colleges are experiencing an increase in applications. Research indicates that women at single-sex colleges have higher self-esteem and self-control than women from coeducational colleges (Riordan, 1992), though debate about the value of single-sex college education continues; evidence indicates that faculty members at coed institutions take male contributions to classroom discussions more seriously than those of females, and they permit males to dominate (Fiske, 1992, pp. 52–53). Studies at a formerly women's college that became coed indicated that there were fewer overall interactions in all classes, which was attributed to a gender political environment (Canada and Pringle, 1995). When all-women Mills College in California decided to admit men, storms of protest arose. In this instance, the wishes of the students prevailed and the college remained all women. Without the social distractions of a coeducational institution and with norms of academic focus, encouragement to excel is stronger at single-sex institutions. Though no challenges have been through the courts, single-sex colleges may face "separate but equal" challenges in the future.

Experiences and Activities in Schools. Activities of persons in contact with children—parents, classroom teachers, administrators, and other school decision makers—also must be taken into account in understanding girls' experiences in schools. In elementary school, a child is most likely to have a female teacher. Although most classrooms are coeducational, many activities within the classroom are sex-linked. Evidence indicates that girls do not receive the same attention boys do; for instance, boys are encouraged to solve problems, whereas girls are given the answers. Thus, teacher actions reinforce sex stereotypes. Girls often are asked to water the plants and boys to clean the blackboards. Children line up for activities by sex. Even in discipline and in the amount of time teachers spend with children, there are sex differences; studies find that boys receive more and harsher discipline, but also more teacher time and praise. Teacher expectations enter into differential treatment of students by sex as well as by class and race (National Association for Women in Education, 1996).

Activities reflect stereotypical attitudes, as exemplified by studies of classroom and playground play behavior. As early as preschool, girls' play is more cooperative, whereas boys' play is more functional or "purposeful" (Neppl and Murray, 1997). In fact, boys in elementary school come to believe masculinity is avoiding whatever is done by girls (Jordon, 1995). As one observer of playground activity writes:

> Differences between the sexes are easily perceptible in the playground, always allowing for the presence of a few girls who are keen footballers and marbles players, and who are known (and accepted) as "tomboys," and a few timid little boys who stay under the protection of the older girls. Boys, in general, are more egotistical, enterprising, competitive, aggressive, and daring than the girls. They are comedians, exhibitionists. They do not mind making fools of themselves and provide most of the clowning that is such an important part of playground fun. They concentrate all their attention upon a game. (Opie, 1993, p. 7)

Many young women experience sexual harassment, usually from peers in school (see Box 4–1). In a recent study of students in grades 8 to 11, 85 percent of girls and 76 percent of boys experienced some form of sexual harassment,

---

••Box 4–1   *Hostile Hallways*

During your whole school life, how often, if at all, has anyone (this includes students, teachers, other school employees, or anyone else) done the following things to you when you did not want them to?

- Made sexual comments, jokes, gestures, or looks in your presence
- Showed, gave, or left you sexual pictures, photographs, illustrations, messages, or notes
- Wrote sexual messages/graffiti about you on bathroom walls, in locker rooms, and so on
- Spread sexual rumors about you
- Said you were gay or lesbian
- Spied on you as you dressed or showered at school
- Flashed or "mooned" you
- Touched, grabbed, or pinched you in a sexual way
- Pulled at your clothing in a sexual way
- Intentionally brushed against you in a sexual way
- Pulled your clothing off or down
- Blocked your way or cornered you in a sexual way
- Forced you to kiss him/her
- Forced you to do something sexual, other than kissing

Source: American Association of University Women, *Hostile Hallways: The AAUW Survey of Sexual Harassment in America's Schools*, 1993, p. 5.

---

with sexual jokes, gestures, and comments most common, followed by touching or grabbing in a sexual way. The harassment takes a greater toll on girls who report feeling less confident and more afraid in school (American Association of University Women, 1993).

Achievement and Motivation: The Case of Math and Science. "Girls face pervasive barriers to achievement throughout their precollegiate schooling and are 'systematically discouraged' from pursuing studies that would enhance their prospects for well-paying jobs" (American Association of University Women, 1991). This finding came from a study in 1992, "How Schools Shortchange Girls." Since the report made the headlines, some change has taken place in math and science courses. Girls are taking more math and science courses, though not at the highest levels where there are still gender gaps, especially in physics and computer science. The computer science gap is particularly problematic as it is becoming a "boys' club" (American Association of University Women, 1998; National Center for Education Statistics, 1997). Though girls achieve higher grades throughout their public school education, they were "systematically tracked toward traditional, sex-segregated jobs, and away from areas of study that lead to high-paying jobs in science, technology, and engineering" (Lawton, 1992, p. 17; National Research Council, 1989). This invisible "glass ceiling" started in elementary and high school. The Gender Equity in Education Package introduced to Congress sought to redress these gender differences (Hegger, 1993, p. A5).

In middle school, changes caused by the onset of adolescence enter the picture; girls' perceptions of who they are and how they should behave begin to affect their career choices. By the time girls are seniors, their plans and values for future participation in the workforce closely parallel the actual sex differences in occupations.

On standardized test measures of achievement, the male and female scores depend on the content of the tests; girls do better in reading, writing, and literature, boys in math and science. Composite SAT and ACT scores are higher for males, though the gap is not great (*The Chronicle of Higher Education Almanac*, 1999–2000). High school females received somewhat higher science grades than males, especially those who participate in sports (Hanson and Kraus, 1998), but males tended to take more optional math and science courses than females (National Center for Education Statistics, *Conditions*, 1997).

Why do boys outscore girls on math achievement tests in all countries except Taiwan (National Center for Education Statistics, 1995, p. 64), with the international average on the International Mathematics and Science Study being 518 for boys and 485 for girls? This question is of particular interest because of concerns about equal opportunity for women and the loss of valuable human resources that occurs when some fail to achieve at a high level in mathematics and science. Some claim there is sexist bias in the construction and content of achievement tests, and this creates problems for women competing for college admission and merit scholarships (e.g., Levine and Levine, 1996).

The percentage of women taking various science and math classes has been increasing steadily. For example, the percentage of girls taking high school physics increased from 9.4 percent in 1982 to 22 percent in 1994. The percentage taking calculus increased from 4.6 percent to more than 9 percent (National Center for Education Statistics, *Digest*, 1999, p. 152) (see Table 4–2). However, more males are enrolled in related computer science and science courses that use the math knowledge. Achievement is similar if male and female students take the same amount of math, but at the advanced level results are less clear and males seem to have an advantage. Those talented math students, both male and female, have favorable attitudes and take more science, the exception being physics, in which more boys are enrolled. However, many girls tend to lose interest after age 12 (Marklein, 1992, p. D6) and often take less science or drop it because they find it "dull" (Fennema and Leder, 1990).

Most researchers theorize that the differences in mathematical achievement result from socialization and experiences of boys and girls. These experiences start as early as primary school. White males have been encouraged to

TABLE 4–2 Percentage of High School Graduates Taking Selected Mathematics and Science Courses

Mathematics and Science Courses	1982		1994	
	Female	Male	Female	Male
Mathematics				
Geometry	49	48	72	68
Algebra II	36	38	62	55
Trigonometry	11	13	18	17
Calculus	4	5	9	9
Science				
Biology	81	77	95	92
Chemistry	31	32	59	53
Physics	9	18	22	27
Biology, chemistry, and physics	7	13	20	23

Source: U.S. Department of Education, National Center for Education Statistics, National Assessment of Educational Progress, *The 1994 High School Transcript Study Tabulations: Comparative Data on Credits Earned and Demographics for 1994, 1990, 1987, and 1982 High School Graduates*, 1996.

be independent thinkers and can develop creative ways of dealing with mathematics rather than following rigid norms of math formulas. Women believe the stereotypes, just as do many minority students, that they are not as smart in math or science as their male counterparts. Thus, they stop caring (Gose, 1995, p. A31; Bellisari, 1991). Many teachers expect boys to be better problem solvers and often ask them more high-level questions than girls, and high-achieving girls receive less attention than boys. A simple summary states that "males tend to attribute successes to internal causes and failure to external or unstable causes. Females tend to attribute success to external or unstable causes and failure to internal causes" (Fennema and Leder, 1990, p. 82).

Parental support and involvement also influence attitudes toward math and science and other curricular choices in the United States and other countries (Tocci and Engelhard, 1991, p. 280). Parents with higher-socioeconomic status are more likely to be "active managers" of their daughters' school course selections (Muller, 1998; Useem, 1991). These girls tend to have more advanced course work, which in turn contributes to social class reproduction (Useem, 1990). Cross-cultural studies of differences in parental support, teacher expectations, study habits, and values and beliefs that affect achievement indicate that girls in some countries excel in math. This is attributed to the country's gender stratification in education and occupational opportunities (Baker and Jones, 1993). Math lessons in a Japanese school encouraged children to think through the problem rather than give the answer. Comparative data show that female and minority students in the United States are not taught to think through a problem in other than a set formula or procedure.

If disproportionately smaller numbers of women pursue math, science, and technical careers, they will be left farther behind in a world that increasingly values and rewards these skills. In the United States, this problem has stimulated a number of federally funded projects to ascertain the causes. The problem of gender inequities in math and science is international, however. Where women have lower status, the gender achievement differential in math and science is also greater (Baker and Jones, 1991).

Attempts to narrow the gap between the mathematical performance of boys and girls has resulted in a plethora of innovative programs for teaching math and for attacking the problem from both attitudinal and organizational perspectives (McCormick, 1994; "What We Know," 1993; Clewell et al., 1992). For instance, according to a University of Michigan study, giving girls more "hands-on" lab work and reducing gender bias in texts can reduce the gender gap ("Science Study," 1995, p. E2). Positive female role models are another helpful way to increase young women's confidence in their abilities (Otter, 1994). As the socialization experience of students and school structural elements regarding math are altered in positive ways, we will continue to see positive changes and a narrowing of the gender gap in math and in the sciences.

Is there evidence that inborn characteristics are at the root of differences in educational experiences of girls and boys, that biological factors predestine some to success and some to failure by gender? Studies by sociobiologists look to possible biological factors to explain gender differences in girls' math and science ability, biological learning styles of each sex, and general intelligence of each sex. The problem with biological explanations is that they seldom give enough weight to the strong influence of cultural expectations and environmental constraints on students and, therefore, provide incomplete explanations when examined alone; evidence is still inadequate to draw conclusions about what role biology plays in sex differences in learning and achievement. Though researchers have looked for biological explanations for differences in math achievement, that does not explain Asian American women's relatively higher representation in science and engineering positions than the general workforce in the United States. Explanations are found in culture and home environment (Bellisari, 1989).

Combating Gender Differences

Evidence indicates that subtle and blatant differences in treatment of girls and boys occurs at all levels of the educational system. There is no one solution for dealing with these differences, but steps are being taken where boys or girls are disadvantaged by the system to lessen negative effects.

1. In teacher education, awareness of self-identity, stereotypes, and practices that commonly operate in the classroom can make teachers more sensitive to the formal and informal curriculum that perpetuates such practices (McCormick, 1994, p. 52). Simple changes in classroom practices are the easiest to tackle.

2. Dealing with concerns of women outside the classroom helps women learn in the classroom. Questions about relationships, career choices, violence, and futures are all concerns that impinge on the learning process. (Gilligan, Lyons, and Hanmer, 1990, p. 26)
3. The Title IX program mandated that school districts provide a nondiscriminatory educational environment for students; the law covers admissions quotas by sex, different course offerings by sex, and athletic programs. Regulations for schools include analysis of existing programs and equal treatment of all students in courses, financial aid, counseling, services, and employment. In fact, many changes in school programs have been attributed to Title IX.

Probably the biggest impact of Title IX has been on men's and women's sports. Facilities, physical education equipment, and course offerings must be equivalent for men and women. However, only 3 of the top 300 college programs were in compliance in 1998 (Weistart, 1998). Since 1992, more than 350 men's sports teams have been eliminated at colleges around the United States and opportunities for men have dropped 12 percent, whereas opportunities for women have increased by 16 percent (Gavora and Schuld, 1999).

Every institution in society has been affected by the changing roles of men and women. The changes are occurring rapidly, and we have not seen their end effect on education, other institutions, or equality of opportunity for women yet.

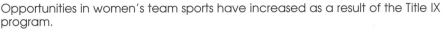

Opportunities in women's team sports have increased as a result of the Title IX program.

CLASS, RACE, AND ATTEMPTS TO RECTIFY INEQUALITIES IN EDUCATIONAL OPPORTUNITY

The question of how to achieve equality of educational opportunity is an issue considered by society's decision makers. The problems include disadvantage, poverty, and discrimination. Is it society's job to do something to correct the injustices suffered by racial minorities? One of the premises behind affirmative action is that it is.

Educational disadvantage stems from schooling, family, and community sources, which cannot be controlled by any individual student. There are demands for equal school facilities, experienced and trained teachers; equitable per pupil expenditures; an integrated racial composition; and for preferential treatment, such as affirmative action, to make up for past inequities (Coleman, 1990). These demands will increase as minority populations grow.

Trends in Public School Enrollments

Dramatic shifts in public school enrollments are under way. In most states the number of white students will shrink, whereas the number of African American and other minority students will increase. In 1996, minority children made up 37.5 percent of public school enrollment, with the largest minority, African Americans, at 16.7 percent, and Hispanics, at 11.9 percent (Table 4–3) (National Center for Education Statistics, *Conditions*, 1999, p. 126). The picture

TABLE 4–3   Percentage of Public School Enrollment by Ethnicity, 1976 to 1996

	1966	1976	1986	1996
Total Number	43,039[a]	43,714[b]	41,156[c]	43,775
		Percentage		
White	80.2	76.0	70.4	62.5[c]
Total Minority	19.8	24.0	29.6	37.5[c]
Black	14.3	15.5	16.1	16.7
Hispanic	4.6	6.4	9.9	11.9
Asian	0.4	1.2	2.8	4.4[c]
American Indian	0.5	0.8	0.9	1.0[c]

[a]Number in thousands
[b]Based on U.S. government projections that extended to 1997
[c]Based on extrapolation of U.S. data and population reference data by author (Ornslein, 1984; Bouvier & Davis, 1982).

Source: From *The Condition of Education 1989*, Vol. 1 (Washington, DC: U.S. Government Printing Office, 1989), pp. 110–111; *Digest of Education Statistics 1976* (Washington, DC: U.S. Government Printing Office, 1977), p. 40; and *Projections of Educational Statistics to 2000* (Washington, DC: U.S. Government Printing Office, 1989), p. 5; and *Conditions of Education Digest, 1999*, p. 152, Table 138.

looks quite different than the way it did in 1966 when 19 percent of the graduates were African American or Hispanic. In 1994, 86.1 percent of 25- to 29-year-olds had graduated from high school, with whites at 91 percent, African Americans at 84 percent, and Hispanic students at 60 percent (National Center for Education Statistics, 1995, p. 72). Ninety-eight percent of the high school graduates in the District of Columbia are minority graduates, and in California, Hawaii, Mississippi, and New Mexico, minority students became the majority in about 1995. Figure 4–3 shows the distribution of minority students by state.

The fastest growth is in the Asian and Pacific Islander population, rising 58 percent in less than ten years because of immigration and high birthrates among some groups. Hispanics will have the largest increase in graduates, whereas the number of African American and white students who graduate from high school will decline. One concern is that the growing groups do not graduate at the same rate as whites and are often not prepared for the workforce. The high school dropout rate for Native Americans was 27 percent; for Asians, 2 percent; for African Americans, 11 percent; for Hispanics, 18 percent; and for whites, 8 percent (Zuniga, 1991).

FIGURE 4–3 State enrollment by race and ethnic group, 1997. (The map shows the proportion of students enrolled in each state who are American Indian, Asian, African American, or Hispanic.)

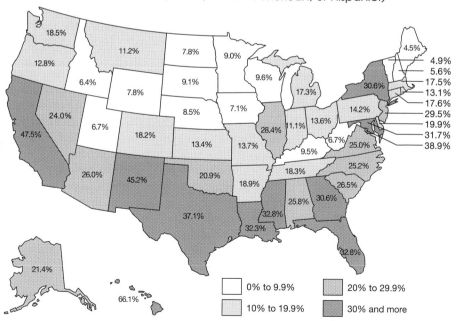

Source: The Cronicle of Higher Education, December 17, 1999, p. A53.

The Underclass and At-Risk Students

The term *underclass* was coined by Gunnar Myrdal, a Swedish observer of American society, and was brought into current usage by William Julius Wilson. The ghetto underclass is characterized by "low aspirations, poor education, family instability, illegitimacy, unemployment, crimes, drug addiction, alcoholism, frequent illness, and early death" (Wilson, 1987, p. 4). It has also come to refer primarily to minorities.

However, some scientists disagree with the concept and its implications of "blaming the victim" for the problem; thus, underclass has become a political policy issue. Herbert Gans describes it this way: "On the right and the left, the former arguing that underclass behavior is the product of the unwillingness of the black poor to adhere to the American work ethic, among other cultural deficiencies, and the latter claiming that the underclass is the consequence of changes in the industrial economy" (Winkler, 1990, p. A5). One study of Hispanic populations points out that, despite poverty and deprivation, Hispanics do not have many of the traits associated with underclass, such as poor health indicators and family breakdown (Moore and Pinderhughes, 1993).

Research on Equality of Educational Opportunity

Although literature related to equality abounds, two studies stand out because of the impact they have made on the ensuing debate, and their comprehensive data collection, analysis, and contribution to understanding inequality: the Coleman Report (Coleman et al., 1966) and Jencks's study of inequality (Jencks et al., 1972).

The Coleman Report. The best-known study of desegregation is the Coleman Report. The Department of Health, Education, and Welfare hired Coleman and his associates to do a study ten years after the *Brown* decision was handed down to determine the state of affairs in education. Coleman's findings turned up both some expected results and some quite unexpected ones. Indeed, the report proved highly controversial, partly because it challenged some strongly held but untested assumptions about schools and education.

The purpose of the study was to evaluate opportunities and performance of minority students compared with white students. Coleman's survey extended to about 5 percent of the schools in the United States and covered 645,000 students at five grade levels. The children were given tests of several types; information about the children's backgrounds and attitudes was collected; and school administrators filled out questionnaires about their schools. Coleman's findings revealed a number of interesting points.

1. Minority students (except for Asian Americans) scored lower on tests at each level of schooling than did white students, and this disparity increased from the first to twelfth grades. Coleman attributed the disadvantage of minority students to a

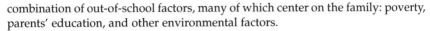

combination of out-of-school factors, many of which center on the family: poverty, parents' education, and other environmental factors.

2. The majority of children at the time of the report attended segregated schools. Teachers also tended to teach children of their own race.

3. The socioeconomic makeup of the school, the home background, and the background of other students in the school were factors that made the biggest difference in students' school achievement levels. This was a surprising finding and led to the recommendation that schools be integrated in order to have a racial-class mix of students.

4. Curriculum and facilities made little difference in student achievement levels—another surprising finding. In fact, school facilities turned out to differ very little across predominantly African American or white schools.

5. White children had somewhat greater access to physics, chemistry, language labs, textbooks, college curricula, and better-qualified and higher-paid teachers, but the differences were not very great.

The findings have been tested and retested by researchers, and although there are variations in the results, Coleman's general conclusions have been upheld. It was these findings that led to Coleman's recommendation that one way to improve the academic achievement of poor and minority children would be to integrate the schools, putting minority children with white children to produce an environment for achievement and to provide educational role models. The study provided the impetus for increased efforts to desegregate, especially through the use of busing.

Jencks's Study of Inequality. Another famous and often quoted study questions the use of schools to attain equal opportunity in society. In their report, Christopher Jencks and his colleagues reanalyzed the Coleman data plus many other data sets and argued that no evidence suggests that school reform can bring about significant social change outside schools. A summary of Jencks's findings follows:

> [T]he evidence suggests that equalizing educational opportunity would do very little to make adults more equal. If all elementary schools were equally effective, cognitive inequality among sixth-graders would decline less than 3 percent . . . cognitive inequality among twelfth-graders would hardly decline at all and disparities in their eventual attainment would decline less than 1 percent. Eliminating all economic and academic obstacles to college attendance might somewhat reduce disparities in educational attainment, but the change would not be large. (Aronson, 1978, p. 409)

Jencks points out that experience over the past 25 years suggests that even though the educational attainment gap between minorities and whites narrowed, economic inequality among adults continues to exist.

Jencks concluded that schools can do little to change people's status in society after graduation. Even school reform and compensatory education programs are not seen as effective in substantially changing the differences among adults. These conclusions both startled and angered educators and others; it is not pleasant to hear that schools make little difference. In the study, Jencks did not deny that schools are important for everyone—he did say that they cannot solve society's problems. He also concluded, as did Coleman, that the school achievement of children is dependent on one major factor—their families. Family background and attitudes toward education are primary determinants of school experience. Jencks argued that because school cannot achieve an egalitarian society and economic equality, we must redistribute income by changing the economic institution into a more socialistic system.

In further analysis of data, Jencks reports that family background accounts for about 48 percent of one's occupational status and 15 to 35 percent of income differences among individuals. The amount of education and family status are closely associated (Jencks et al., 1979).

Although the tests and retests of Coleman's and Jencks's conclusions come up with varied results, most uphold the importance of students' families and the backgrounds of peers. The importance of desegregation in equal opportunity is discussed next, and the significance of school "climate" is discussed in Chapter 8.

The Battle over Desegregation

Poverty and racism have been ugly realities in the history of the United States. Kidnappings, lynchings, mob violence, and abuse could not stop protests against unfair treatment of large segments of the population. These problems were reflected in the school system as in every other part of society, and the schools developed as segregated institutions in much of the country.

When discussing desegregation, people often use two terms interchangeably; however, their meanings are technically different. "*Desegregation* of schools refers to enrollment patterns wherein students of different racial groups attend the same schools, and students are not separated in racially isolated schools or classrooms. *Integration* refers to situations in which students of different racial groups not only attend schools together, but effective steps have been taken to . . . overcome the disadvantages of minority students and develop positive interracial relationships" (Ornstein and Levine, 1985, p. 398).

Court Cases on Desegregation

In 1954, the Supreme Court pronounced its landmark "separate is not equal" decision in the *Brown* v. *Board of Education* case, a ruling that has been seen as a blessing by some and a curse by others. Has it made any difference in the education or social status of minority groups in our society? Ten years after the *Brown* decision, the courts still had made no rulings on what desegregation meant. Therefore, in 1964, the Civil Rights Act ruled that delays in desegregation were no longer tolerable. In order to achieve equality of opportunity, desegregation was ordered, meaning that schools had to have 20 to 30 percent enrollment from each group. Some major desegregation efforts, especially in the South, produced change, but large cities remained and became even more segregated. A 1973 court case in Denver ruled there was intentional segregation, and the city must change this pattern. This ruling led to change in other large cities as well, with most using busing of children to attain the goals. Patterns of enforcement have varied; however, and the rulings in test cases— from the Supreme Court down to district courts—have been inconsistent. Since the 1954 "separate is not equal" Supreme Court ruling, and the order to change with all deliberate speed, courts at every level have been busy interpreting the ruling for their districts. The picture remains muddled.

More than three decades have passed since the U.S. Supreme Court rejected voluntary desegregation and required cities to initiate desegregation plans, but the national debate about desegregation continues. The pattern of segregation is like a patchwork quilt: Some areas have successfully desegregated, whereas others remain almost exclusively African American or white.

Efforts to desegregate can be divided into five periods: first, the 1954 Supreme Court decision; second, the 1968 ruling requiring southern rural schools to adopt desegregation plans; third, in 1973, when desegregation moved from the South to the North and West when Denver was required to rectify segregation; fourth, the current court cases that are rescinding mandatory busing in some cities; and fifth, the emphasis on improving quality of education in minority schools. Minority schools are those that have 90 percent or more minority students, and in 1980 one-third of African American students attended such schools. "Predominantly" minority schools are those in which 50 percent or more of the students are from minority groups (Orfield, 1983).

The Coleman Report documented the extent of segregation in the nation's public schools and the benefits to children where integration had occurred. With these data, pro-integration forces stepped up efforts to force integration, bringing numerous cases before the courts. But by the mid-1980s, there seemed to be a slow but steady reversal of years of desegregation efforts.

A key trend today is court cases that release school districts from court supervision of their desegregation efforts; several Supreme Court cases have approved dismantling of school desegregation plans, referred to as "unitary standards" (DeLacy, 1997). Examples include the following cases: *Board of Education of Oklahoma* v. *Dowell* (1991), *Freeman* v. *Pitts* (1992), *Missouri* v. *Jenkins* (1995), the Connecticut state case of *Sheff* v. *O'Neill* (1996), and *Wessmann* v. *Gittens* (1998). The results of the dismantling is that many students return to their segregated neighborhood schools. School segregation has been increasing steadily over the past 15 years, especially in non-Southern states (Weiler, 1998). This is because of a combination of dismantling plans, demographic changes caused by immigration (especially in urban areas), and the growth of suburbs. Hispanic students are more educationally isolated than African American students (Orfield et al., 1997). More focus is being centered on access to education and within-school tracking as these affect academic performance of minorities.

Extent of the Desegregation–Integration Problem. Social scientists have conducted more than 100 studies of busing and desegregation, with research focused on several primary questions:

1. Are desegregation plans accomplishing the goals of integrating schools, improving the quality of education for minority children, and improving relations between the races?
2. Are efforts to desegregate causing neighborhoods and schools to become more segregated because of "white flight" from the affected school districts?
3. What are the effects of integration on children's achievement and self-concept?
4. Can busing help accomplish the ultimate goal—equality of opportunity in society? Or are we piling our societal racial problems on a yellow school bus and shutting the door?

In some inner cities, education officials, resigned to the growing segregation of schools, have tried to ameliorate the problem by instigating new, innovative programs for their minority constituents. This has led some to dispute whether "better but segregated" is just a return to "separate but equal." Concerned over the controversy about the importance and value of desegregation, a number of scholars, including Gary A. Orfield, presented a summary statement of social science research over the past 20 years. The findings fall into four areas and show the following:

1. The desegregation of a school district can positively influence residential integration in the community.
2. Desegregation is associated with moderate academic gains for minority-group students and does no harm to white students.
3. Desegregation plans work best when they cover as many grades as possible, when they encompass as large a geographic area as possible, and when they stick to clearly defined goals over the long haul.
4. Effective desegregation is linked to other types of educational reform. (Orfield et al., 1992)

A more recent study by Orfield from The Harvard Project on School Desegregation found that there was a significant decline in segregation in the South from the mid-1960s to the 1970s, followed by a stable period until about 1988, and an increase in segregation from 1988 to the present (Orfield, 1997, 1994).

Effects of Efforts to Desegregate Schools

What happens when minorities and whites go to school together? Are students helped or hurt? Studies have considered the interpersonal relations, the self-esteem of students, the academic achievement and social roles of both African American and white students, and the effect of "white flight" on the communities involved. Volumes of information have been collected on each of these topics; a few examples follow.

Self-Esteem, Self-Concept, and Achievement. Self-esteem is important to achievement in school. African American children have been of concern to psychologists for many years because measurements of racial preference have shown that they lack a positive sense of racial identity and self-esteem. In a replication of studies conducted since the 1940s, questions about African American or white doll preference were asked. "Pick the nice, bad, pretty doll, and the one you'd most like to play with." Sixty-five percent of the African American children and 75 percent of the white children preferred the white doll (Talan, 1987, p. E11). This finding is especially significant for African American children in desegregated schools. The question raised is whether normally self-confident African American students are less confident in integrated school settings. Studies' findings show that African American students in integrated settings have lower self-confidence, self-esteem, and levels of aspiration than African Americans in less integrated schools, even though they do better, go to college more often, and are more successful in finding jobs and receiving higher incomes (Trent, 1997). And although schools may be desegregated, there is concern about within-school segregation from tracking policies (Weiler, 1998).

Student Goals, Aspirations, and Future Prospects

African American students have high aspirations. Positive and high expectations from teachers as well as parents can help aspirations become reality (Voelki, 1993). In fact, the high aspiration of African Americans may be responsible for the narrowing educational gap between them and whites, and those aspirations will continue to be useful to African Americans in making advancements (Portes and Wilson, 1976).

The effect of desegregation on aspirations and achievement has been an area of concern for researchers, especially because there has been a decline in African American college entry compared with whites. Plans to complete four-year college programs increased for both African American and white students, but actualization of plans decreased for African Americans (Hauser and Anderson, 1991, p. 272).

The norms that dominate a high school influence what students believe is possible. Thus, African American students in desegregated schools, especially males, have a higher likelihood of attending college and completing more years of schooling than do those from segregated schools. This is probably related to the aspiration and achievement levels at the schools and to available opportunities. African Americans who attend desegregated high schools also get better jobs than those from segregated high schools, and they have better chances for promotion (Trent, 1997; McPartland et al., 1985). Desegregation has been found to have a small positive effect on achievement in reading for African American students but no effect on their achievement in mathematics (Schofield, 1995; McPartland et al., 1985). In summary, desegregation seldom lowers the achievement of minorities and most often raises it. Also, there is virtually no evidence that desegregation lowers the achievement levels of whites.

The results of numerous studies indicate that achieving the goals of integration and positive race relations will not be easy, but lessons from successful programs provide models for reaching goals. Key in these programs are good human relations within classrooms, use of cooperative learning to involve all students and reduce tracking, efforts to involve students in extracurricular activities, fair enforcement of clear rules, and positive involvement of parents and other community members.

"White Flight." While citizens and policymakers were arguing over the effects of busing, social scientists began debating "white flight." Was busing or the threat of busing to achieve desegregation causing cities to become more segregated than before because whites were moving out of the cities to avoid school integration?

In 1975, James Coleman released some results of a new study. In it, he concluded that school desegregation contributed to "white flight" from big cities and was fostering resegregation of urban districts. Whites were leaving large and middle-sized cities with high proportions of African Americans. Coleman and his supporters now seemed to be suggesting less integration and more segregation to remedy "white flight."

Table 4–4 (p. 112) illustrates the change in percentage of minority students in major city schools between 1968 and 1998 (projected). Other studies since Coleman's have revealed important variables related to "white flight" that account for much of the decline of the white population in large urban areas:

1. Higher birthrate of minority families, resulting in more school-age children
2. Economic and class differences in upward mobility with whites moving to suburbs
3. New minority families moving into urban areas

4. Discrimination against minorities in suburban housing
5. Differences in "white instability" related to percentage of African American concentration (McDonald, 1997)

Court rulings have varied: In Denver, Boston, Memphis, and other cities courts ruled that "schools must be within 10 to 15 percent of the overall racial composition of the district," even if this requires busing. Other court rulings such as those in Dallas and Houston have allowed minority schools to remain segregated on the grounds that to integrate would be impractical. However, nonminority schools do have to desegregate (Levine and Levine, 1996, p. 266). Big-city school desegregation plans have been undergoing new analysis to study the effects of various plans (Carter, 1995).

A national study evaluating the impact of school desegregation programs on white public school enrollment trends found that, comparing districts that desegregated with those that did not, desegregation enrollment trends are the same. Prior to desegregation, enrollments declined, and the largest decline occurred during the year of actual desegregation and increased racial contact. Districts with more than one-third African American enrollment experienced twice as much enrollment loss (Wilson, 1985). Specific district-level characteristics associated with reduced white school enrollments include the proportion of African American pupils in the district, implementation of minor desegregation programs, and substantial proportions of Hispanic pupils (Ornstein, 1991, p. 66). Otherwise, there is little evidence that desegregation promotes resegregation (Smock and Wilson, 1991).

The overall results of efforts to desegregate seem to be positive if measured in terms of benefit to the most people. Because many schools remain predominantly minority, however, current efforts focus largely on instructional improvement in these schools (Levine and Levine, 1996, p. 268).

INTEGRATION ATTEMPTS

School districts have adopted numerous plans to work toward desegregation—redistricting, magnet schools, and busing and other student transfers, to name a few. In some cases, school districts have been desegregated, but separation exists within the schools. Segregated classes, minority groupings within classrooms, segregated athletics and extracurricular activities, differential discipline and suspension practices, and teacher assignments may all hamper efforts to integrate schools and classrooms (Metz, 1994).

Various steps have been taken to achieve educational equality within and between schools. The best known of these are the federally sponsored compensatory educational programs. The Elementary and Secondary Education Act was passed in 1965 with the expressed goal of improving the education of poor

TABLE 4-4 Minority Student Enrollment of the 25 Largest City School Systems, 1968–1998

City	1968 Student Enrollment	1968 Percent Minority	1978 Student Enrollment	1978 Percent Minority	1988 Student Enrollment	1988 Percent Minority	1998 Student[c] Enrollment	1998 Percent[d] Minority
New York City	1,063,787	54.2[c]	998,947	71.3	960,000	79.0	935,000	85
Los Angeles	653,549	42.6[c]	556,236	70.3	594,802	84.4	635,000	92
Chicago	582,274	61.5[c]	494,888	78.5	410,230	87.6	355,000	94
Philadelphia	282,617	61.0	244,723	69.0	191,141	76.5	160,000	81
Detroit	296,097	61.2	220,657	85.8	175,469	95.5	135,000	98
Houston	246,098	46.2	142,553	70.6	190,381	84.5	235,000	94
Dade County (Miami)	232,465	41.3	229,254	62.2	251,100	68.0	275,000	79
Baltimore	192,171	65.1	149,465	77.6	107,250	83.0	90,000	88
Dallas	159,924	38.4	133,289	66.2	131,582	81.8	145,000	91
Cleveland	156,054	57.9	103,627	67.6	73,350	76.0	60,000	85
Washington, DC	148,725	93.5	108,903	96.0	88,631	96.5	75,000	99
Milwaukee	130,445	23.9	95,502	49.4[a]	88,832	68.3	80,000	80
San Diego	128,914	21.7	115,007	38.3	117,057	58.6	125,000	70
Memphis	125,813	53.6	113,108	74.0	103,099	78.0	93,000	82
St. Louis	115,582	63.5	72,515	74.8	47,117[e]	80.7	40,000	88
Atlanta	111,227	61.7	76,625	90.5	61,718	93.4	55,000	96

112

New Orleans	110,783	67.1	88,714	85.8	85,113	92.7	75,000	96
Columbus	110,699	26.0	82,691	36.8	65,160	50.4	55,000	60
Indianapolis	108,587	33.7	73,569	48.2[a]	50,143[e]	50.6	40,000	55
Denver	96,577	33.4	68,830	55.6	58,626	64.8	50,000	72
Boston	94,174	27.1	71,303	60.4	54,765[e]	75.5	45,000	85
Fort Worth	86,528	32.7	68,224	52.6	68,410	64.4	75,000	74
Albuquerque	79,669	37.7	81,913	46.7[a]	84,783	51.0	85,000	55
San Antonio	79,353	72.9	63,214	87.1	61,246	93.1	70,000	96
Newark	75,960	81.8	65,575	90.7	49,728[e]	92.3	40,000	95
Totals	5,468,072	51.9[b]	4,519,334	71.3[b]	3,863,027	85.8[b]	4,028,000[c]	87.2[b]

[a]By 1980, these school systems (Milwaukee, Albuquerque, and Indianapolis) were more than 50% minority.

[b]Weighted percentage minority based on total population.

[c]Projections include a slight increase in student enrollments, most of it in California and Texas.

[d]Projections are conservative for minority enrollments, based on 50% or less of the growth rate between 1978 and 1988. The assumption is that most white flight has already occurred; however, immigration trends and family size of minorities will affect school enrollments.

[e]From 1968 to 1978 the 25 city school districts were the largest city districts nationwide. By 1988–89, Mobile (69,000), Nashville (63,000), Fresno (65,500), and Tucson (57,000) had replaced St. Louis, Newark, Indianapolis, and Boston in the top 25 list.

Source: Allan C. Ornstein, "Urban Demographics for the 1980s," *Education and Urban Society*, August 1984, pp. 477–496, Ornstein, 1990, preliminary data from a nationwide survey, unpublished; reprinted in Ornstein, Allan C., "The Relationship of the School Organization to Minority Students," *Peabody Journal of Education*, Vol. 66, No 4, Summer 1984, published 1991.

and minority children. Initially, $1 billion was appropriated, and the figure has continued to grow. Compensatory educational programs, funded primarily by federal government agencies, have included programs from preschool to higher education; the following describes several of these programs.

1. *Early childhood education.* Head Start and Follow-Through are the most common programs in this category. Whereas Head Start attempts to help disadvantaged children achieve "readiness" for the first grade, Follow-Through concentrates on sustaining readiness and supplementing in the early grades whatever gains are made by the children who have had a year's experience in Head Start. The children in those early childhood programs, which encourage child-initiated activities rather than teacher-directed activities, showed more short- and long-term academic and social development, and the children in these programs achieved benefits that the many unserved but eligible children did not (Schweinhart, 1997).

2. *Bilingual education.* An estimated three million public school students cannot do regular work in English. The Supreme Court ruled that states must assist limited-English-proficient students, but it did not indicate how; states have developed a variety of programs, from bilingual education to English as a Second Language training. In 1997, 11 state mandated bilingual education programs, and three forbad bilingual education (Garcia and Morgan, 1997). Emphasis and content of these programs vary, but they commonly focus on children whose native language is not English.

   Spanish-speaking children are the major target groups in these programs. Debate surrounding bilingual education centers in part on the best way to integrate non-English-speakers into American society (McGroarty, 1992, pp. 7–9). How people attain literacy in a second language is influenced by their culture and the social context in which the language training takes place. Effective programs will take this into consideration in developing methods of instruction (Ferdman, 1990, p. 201). One concern among those teaching English as a second language is how long federal funds should support children in bilingual programs; the current limit is five years, but many argue that more time is needed to integrate students into regular classes (Schmidt, 1992, p. 21). There is great demand for teachers who can teach bilingual classes, and many schools are having difficulty filling these positions; in California alone, 8,000 additional bilingual teachers are needed (National Center for Education Statistics, *Conditions*, 1997, Indicator 45; Office of Bilingual Education and Minority Languages Affairs, 1996).

3. *Guidance and counseling programs.* Various social, psychological, and vocational services have been provided for the disadvantaged. Social workers and community aides have been involved in helping to bridge the gap between the school and home.

4. *Higher education.* Special programs in higher education include the following: (a) identifying students with college potential early in the secondary schools and enriching their program; (b) accepting special provisions and lower academic requirements for college admission; (c) using admission criteria that allow open enrollment, whereby every high school graduate has the opportunity to attend a two-year or four-year college, thus favoring low academic achievers who might

not otherwise be granted admission; (d) transition programs to increase the probability of success for disadvantaged youth once admitted into college; and (e) special scholarships, loans, and jobs based solely on financial need and minority status (Ornstein and Levine, 1985, pp. 546–48).

Special programs also help schools revise curricula, pay for instructional materials, hire auxiliary personnel for tutoring, and provide adult education programs.

There are other, less tangible results of compensatory education. Upward Bound is a federal program to help disadvantaged students prepare to enter and succeed in college. Students enter the program in their first or second year of high school and can remain through the summer after high school graduation. The program provides instruction, tutoring, and counseling. Statistics have revealed mixed results on achievement, indicating that many students stay in the program only a short time, and the program has little impact on high school graduation rates. However, it may impact students' postsecondary plans and experiences (Myers and Schirm, 1999). Despite the inconclusive impact of the program, young minority and white students who have never before met children of other races live and study together, play together, and make new friendships. The overall atmosphere is cooperative. Many of these programs are held on college campuses where the students not only experience a campus atmosphere but also live in dormitories away from home. These students might not have seen college life as a possibility before this experience.

On the pessimistic side, some (e.g., Levine and Levine, 1996) believe that compensatory educational experiences do not provide significant results toward societal change and are insufficient to counteract the existing differences. Schools reflect and reinforce prejudices of the outside world, which cannot be equalized by special programs, improved teacher quality, or other patchwork remedies. According to some conflict theorists, increasing resources cannot equalize the inequality built into societies:

> The solution may be to change schooling for all children and to create an educational process that does not preconceive social roles or even clearly define what or how a child must learn. This process would require new kinds of tests to measure results and a different kind of teacher to produce them. Education of this type could allow a child's own stereotypes of himself and others to be destroyed and be replaced by personal relationships. The alternative strategy, then, creates equality among groups of children, by believing that all children are equally acceptable. (Carnoy, 1975, pp. 188–89)

The structure of schools, hierarchical role structure, student–teacher relations, and student role perception would need to be altered to bring about real change. Whether leaders of societies are willing to make radical changes is questionable.

EDUCATIONAL EXPERIENCE OF SELECTED MINORITIES IN THE UNITED STATES

We have discussed minorities in general terms, lumping all groups together, but focusing mainly on African Americans. There are, however, unique differences in the problems facing specific groups. For instance, children of migrant farm workers have little chance of receiving a consistent or continuous education, though mobile school programs have been set up to move from camp to camp with the migrants. Children whose native language is not English suffer from that limitation in the middle-class American school. Bilingual programs are provided in areas with a concentration of non-English-speaking groups—for instance, schools with heavy concentrations of Mexican American and Puerto Rican children. Influxes of Southeast Asian, Cuban, and Haitian refugees also have created a need for special language and culture programs.

Hispanic Students

Today close to half of America's population growth comes from immigration, primarily of Hispanics and Asians (Macionis, 2000). Hispanics are the fastest-growing ethnic group in the U.S. public schools, doubling over the past two decades from 6 percent in 1973 to 15 percent in 1997, and they are estimated to reach 20 percent by the year 2030. Segregation of Hispanic students rose dramatically between 1970 and 1997, with 75 percent attending predominantly minority schools (see Table 4–5). More than one-third were in schools with minority populations of more than 90 percent ("A New Divide . . .," 1999; "The Educational Progress," 1995, p. 3). With the increase in numbers has come an increase in segregation in states with the highest Hispanic population. Of the 50 schools with the highest concentration of Hispanic students, 85 percent are located in Texas, California, and Florida ("White House Initiative on Educational Excellence . . .," 1999, www.ed.gov/offices/OIIA/Hispanic/hssd/). The average age of Hispanics is much younger than that of whites because of high birthrates and youth immigration. Hispanic preschool-age children are less likely than white or African American preschoolers to be enrolled in school, but the difference evens out in kindergarten ("Hispanic Education Fact Sheet," 1999).

Although Spanish-speaking residents are often grouped under the label "Hispanic," there are differences among the groups, with Cubans and some other Latin Americans faring well in school compared with whites, Puerto Ricans, and Mexicans (Velez, 1994). Two factors stand out concerning Hispanics and schools. First is the issue of increasingly segregated schools, and second is bilingual education (Moore and Pinderhughes, 1993).

The gradually increasing segregation leads to several results: As the number of Hispanics in an area grows, their percentage in school grows; many

TABLE 4–5 Percentage of Hispanic Students in Predominantly Minority and 90 to 100 Percent Minority Schools, 1968–1992

Year	Predominantly Minority	90–100% Minority
1968	54.8	23.1
1970	55.8	23.0
1972	56.6	23.3
1974	57.9	23.9
1976	60.8	24.8
1978	63.1	25.9
1980	68.1	28.8
1986	70	33
1992		34

Source: Orfield, Gary, *Public School Desegregation in the United States, 1968–1980* (Washington, DC: Joint Center for Political Studies, 1983), p. 4. U.S. Department of Education data; and *The Condition of Education,* 1995.

are concentrated in urban areas that are losing white population. Language and cultural barriers may limit interaction with others and encourage concentrations. High school dropout rates are more than double that of white students, 25 percent of 16- to 24-year-olds who were not enrolled in school and had not completed high school, versus 8.6 percent of non-Hispanics. The noncompletion rate for Hispanics born outside the United States was 38.5 percent (National Center for Education Statistics, *Conditions,* 1999, p. 112).

Behaviors that increase the chances of dropping out include cutting classes, suspensions, early dating, being older than classmates, and being female and pregnant. School factors such as counseling, tracking, changing schools, and students' mobility between school districts are important factors to consider in prevention, along with recency of migration and country of origin. It is important to note that Mexican Americans born and raised in the United States often fare as well as their classmates from other backgrounds.

Bilingual Education. A concentration of Hispanics means that many children are surrounded by Spanish-speaking people in their schools as well as their homes. The controversial issue of bilingual education has been debated for a number of years, not only for Hispanics but for other minorities as well. Should state and federal governments provide special funds to teach minority children in their own languages? Will teaching in native languages help or disadvantage minority children? What will be the results for states and the nation?

Many argue that teaching children in their native languages hurts them in the competitive system and that English facility is crucial to get ahead (Levine and Levine, 1996, p. 324). Others argue that children are disadvantaged by being taught in a language they do not know, that they wish to retain their cultural language, and that they resent being considered "unacceptable" the way they are. The debate continues even in minority communities. In the 1993–94 school year, 23 percent of fourth graders were in schools offering bilingual education, and 52 percent were in schools offering English as a second language. The current thinking seems to favor two-way bilingual education that gives English-speaking children and other native speakers the chance to learn in both languages; this policy is being implemented in California (Garcia, 1993). A study of Mexican American middle-school students found that those who were proficient in both English and Spanish had better grades and higher numbers of credits at the end of ninth grade than those from limited English or English-only backgrounds (Rumberger and Larson, 1998). Most students that were studied wanted to learn English, and only a minority remained fluent in their parents' language after a generation (Portes and Hao, 1998).

Immigrants

Immigration is the "sincerest form of flattery," people selecting a country because it is desirable. It also means "open season on immigrants, from Europe to the United States" (Rumbaut, 1995, p. 307). Much recent immigration stems from the former Soviet bloc countries, Kurds in Northern Iraq, the former Yugoslavia, and from Central America and Cambodia. Immigration often starts because of wars or military occupations, and economic problems and opportunities; once families are established in a new location, other members join them, expanding the immigrant community in the new location.

Most immigrant parents encourage their children to work hard and get good grades in the schools in their new homeland as means of getting ahead; children may believe adjusting socially is more important, and these two ideas can be contradictory (Ogbu, 1991). Children's ethnic identities influence their self-esteem and assimilation into the culture, and hence their attitude toward schooling (Rumbaut, 1994).

In 1991, the United States legally admitted 1,827,167 immigrants, the highest number since World War II. By 1993, the number decreased to 904,300, but with the addition of illegal immigrants, the numbers probably remain close to the 1991 figures. The legal immigrants generally had a sponsor and a U.S. employer (or for refugees, the government). More than 75 percent had close family ties in the United States. Of the total, 145,843 were spouses of U.S. citizens (Rumbaut, 1996, pp. 1–2).

Immigration accounts for one-fifth of the population growth in the past decade in the United States (Stewart, 1992), mostly from Latin America (especially Mexico and Cuba) and Asia (especially Southeast Asia). In recent years, the proportion of immigrants from Latin America and the Caribbean has been close to 60 percent; from Asia, 27 percent; and from Europe and Canada, 18 percent (Aguirre and Turner, 2001, p. 227) (see Table 4–6). The 1990 immigration law not only increased by 40 percent those permitted to enter, but it also allowed more Europeans and Africans to enter. This means more and diverse students and faculty from abroad will be part of the U.S. educational systems. The law also requires that immigrants have contacts for employment or a skill to obtain employment, allowing them to become mobile in the society. Each group has a different history of why they immigrated and their experience in their new country (Sowell, 1994).

A study of the educational aspirations and attainment of eighth- and ninth-grade immigrant children, both native and foreign-born, resulted in the following findings: three-fourths of the sample from a wide variety of immigrant groups preferred speaking English, the exception being Mexicans living near the border. Some groups have high educational attainment and aspirations as shown by scores well above the norms on mathematics and other standardized tests—particularly Asians (Chinese, Japanese, Koreans, and Indians), followed by Vietnamese, Filipinos, Cubans, and Colombians. Below the national norms were Hmong, Mexican, and Cambodian immigrants, also reflecting socioeconomic status of the families. The Hmong, however, received very high grade point averages (GPA), compared to many other groups, and did more hours of homework. Immigrant groups as a whole outperform native-born American students in GPAs (Rumbaut, 1996, pp. 23–24).

Several issues become important in the new immigration wave. Each skilled immigrant who enters a new country is creating a "brain drain" in the country of origin. New immigrants have different needs, and schools are often forced to take into account different value systems and behavior patterns (Stewart, 1992, p. 23). Language barriers create challenges for school districts, and the issue of illegal immigrants raises questions about the educational rights of these groups.

TABLE 4–6 The Shifting Profile of Immigrants to the United States, 1951–1993

Area of Origin	1951–60	1961–70	1971–80	1981–90	1991–93	1997
Europe and Canada	67.7%	46.3%	21.6%	12.5%	13.1%	18.4%
Asia	6.1	12.9	35.5	37.5	30.0	26.5
Latin America and the Caribbean	24.6	39.2	40.3	47.1	49.9	61.5

Sources: Elizabeth Rolph, *Immigration Policies: Legacy from the 1980s and Issues for the 1990s* (Santa Monica, CA: The RAND Corporation, 1992); U.S. Department of Justice, 1991a; U.S. Bureau of the Census, 1995; U.S. Bureau of the Census, March 1997; Current Population Survey, Internet release date: October 5, 1999.

Asian American Students

The list of Asian American cultures and languages is extensive—Chinese, Filipino, Hawaiian, Korean, Japanese—making categorization difficult. Asian Americans make up more than 4 percent of the U.S. population, with 11,022,000 in 1999 (U.S. Census Bureau, 1999). By 2050 the estimated population of Asian Americans will be 32 to 34 million (U.S. Department of Commerce, 1996). More than 800,000 Southeast Asian refugees—Vietnamese, Cambodians, Laotians, Hmong—have come to the United States since 1975. They now number more than 1 million. California has 40 percent of this population. Because their values differ from those of Americans in some key areas that affect education, it is important for educators to be aware of these differences and work with them. For instance, "filial piety," unquestioning loyalty and obedience to parents and other authority figures, means that some parents do not attempt to see teachers; yet it is important to have parental involvement to help children. Several factors are directly related to parental involvement: level of literacy, educational level, and perceptions of what the school expects (Morrow, 1991, p. 20).

Many Asians come from large, tightly knit kin groups; the largest groups are Indochinese and Filipino; there are significant differences among Asian groups, and Vietnamese children generally are most successful (Blair and Qian, 1998; Rumbaut and Ima, 1987). Because close families and education are highly valued in many Asian cultures, especially those with a Confucian value system that emphasizes family closeness to achieve shared goals (Caplan, Choy, and Whitmore, 1993), students are cooperative and teachers are held in high esteem. The general attitude is that Asian students are good students, and schools with high percentages of Asian students are good.

Despite language barriers, Asian students as a group outscore other minorities, native-born white students, and international students on the International Assessment of Educational Progress and National Assessment of Educational Progress standardized examinations (Bracey, 1998; Levine and Levine, 1996, p. 312; National Education Goals Panel, 1993). Many Asian students take more courses in foreign languages, mathematics, and natural science than other students. Asian American students are also overrepresented in college-preparatory programs and in gifted-and-talented programs in high schools.

Explanations for the high educational achievement of Asian American students, and Chinese Americans in particular, are related to the group's traditional family values and values placed on education, especially parents with advanced educations themselves; favorable socioeconomic characteristics; and small-business owners who believe education is a channel of intergenerational mobility (Goyette and Xie, 1999; House, 1997; Sanchirico, 1991).

Recent studies, however, are showing that with successive generations in American society, the Asian American achievement differential is coming more in line with white student achievement, rather than exceeding it (e.g., Goyette and Xie, 1999). This may be caused in part by successive strains on the close-knit family and community, and by integration into the dominant peer-group value system.

Native American Students

The case of Native Americans is unique. When colonists first settled in the United States, Native Americans spoke more than 2,000 different languages, 300 of which are still spoken today. At first, missionaries provided education, but by the 1890s education was under government control (Chavers, 1991, pp. 28–29). The government and churches believed it was their duty to "civilize the Indian population," to eliminate their linguistic and cultural differences. They were relegated to poor land, and today many live in poverty as a result of low incomes, poor education, and unemployment or underemployment (Diamond, 1993).

In the early nineteenth century, Congress appropriated monies for a "civilization fund." Boarding schools were established to remove children from tribal and family influences and assimilate them into American culture. In 1928, the "Meriam Report" (Report of the Board of Indian Commissions, 1928, pp. iii, 41) questioned the government's "respect for rights of the Indian . . . as a human being living in a free country," criticizing the government policy of boarding schools, where 40 percent of Native American children were enrolled.

Gradually policies changed; schools became day schools, and bilingual Native American teachers were employed. In 1968, then-President Johnson urged putting control of Native American schools into Native American hands, and in 1972 the Indian Education Act was passed, allowing tribes to control and operate their schools. For the most part, this shift has taken place, and it seems unlikely that control will revert again to the Bureau of Indian Affairs. In one plan, the Choctaw Indians have been given complete control of educational programs on a Mississippi reservation, and they have built a new, modern school. The result of this local autonomy from the Bureau of Indian Affairs is that educational programs are geared toward the needs of the community; more students are attending and staying in school longer (Johnson, 1995).

In the early 1990s, more than 80 percent of the approximately 300,000 Native American students were in public schools, many in major cities. Others were in tribally contracted schools. Parental involvement is low in non-Native American-controlled schools, absenteeism is high, and the dropout rate for high school students is near 50 percent. Of the 25 percent of high school graduates who go on to attend college, 65 percent leave without degrees (Gipp and Fox, 1991, pp. 2–4). The picture is not all bleak, however. Some groups have increased high school graduation rates and college attendance, and tribal colleges are meeting the needs of many students (Johnson, 1995). Academic success in college is greatest for students who have family support, student support services, and precollege preparation programs such as Upward Bound; the highest failure rates for college students are related to financial problems and cultural differences (Jenkins, 1999; Kastl, 1997).

In order to improve the educational and other opportunities for Native Americans, some tribal leaders have established businesses on reservations, including gambling casinos. Some, though not all, have been successful in bringing needed dollars to tribal coffers (Richardson, 1993, p. A11).

The clash of cultures experienced by Native American children in the traditional school setting is described in Box 4–2. In order to meet the needs of Native American children, educators need to understand the cultures and be sensitive to the needs of these children, plan appropriate student-centered curricula, hold high expectations, and maintain good home–school relations.

Special Education Students

Which children can attend regular classrooms, and which should be separated for part or all of their education? This question of school and classroom organization and where students with disabilities fit into this environment has stimulated both commentaries and research. In order to be classified as disabled, a child must have a health condition or impairment that (1) limits the ability of the child to perform a major life activity (2) for an extended period of time. Conditions include learning disabilities; speech, hearing, orthopedic, and visual disabilities; mental retardation; serious emotional disturbance; and other forms of disability.

The era of the special education student began with the 1975 passage by Congress of PL 94-142, the Education for All Handicapped Children Act. It stated that all children with disabilities must be educated in the "least restrictive environment" possible. More recently, PL 99-457 (the Individuals with Disabilities Education Act) has been added, requiring school districts to educate all disabled children between the ages of 3 and 21. The interpretation of these laws and how to carry out their intentions have varied greatly, but they brought to the attention of educators and the public the importance of considering each child's special needs and then designing programs suited to them.

Under the federal acts, about 13 percent of all children from birth to 21 years (most between ages 6 and 17) qualified for services under either Chapter 1 or Part B programs. The percentage of students diagnosed as having learning disabilities rose from 22 to 51.1 percent of those with disabilities between 1977 and 1997, and an additional 41.4 percent of all students ages 6 through 21 had speech or language impairments, mental retardation, and serious emotional disturbances ("Seventeenth Annual Report to Congress, 1995) (see Figure 4–4).

Ninty-five percent of students with disabilities were served in regular school buildings and classrooms. About 30 percent are in regular classes all day, 38 percent are in resource rooms for special help at least part of the day, and

---

◆◆Box 4–2 *An Indian Father's Plea by Robert Lake (Medicine Grizzlybear)*

Dear Teacher,

I would like to introduce you to my son, Wind-Wolf. He is probably what you would consider a typical Indian kid. He was born and raised on the reservation. He has black hair, dark brown eyes, and an olive complexion. And, like so many Indian children his age, he is shy and quiet in the classroom. He is 5 years old, in kindergarten, and I can't understand why you have already labeled him a "slow learner."

He has already been through quite an education compared with his peers in Western society. He was bonded to his mother and to the Mother Earth in a traditional native childbirth ceremony. And he has been continuously cared for by his mother, father, sisters, cousins, aunts, uncles, grandparents, and extended tribal family since this ceremony.

The traditional Indian baby basket became his "turtle's shell" and served as the first seat for his classroom. It is the same kind of basket our people have used for thousands of years. It is specially designed to provide the child with the kind of knowledge and experience he will need to survive in his culture and environment.

Wind-Wolf was strapped in snugly with a deliberate restriction on his arms and legs. Although Western society may argue this hinders motor-skill development and abstract reasoning, we believe it forces the child to first develop his intuitive faculties, rational intellect, symbolic thinking, and five senses. Wind-Wolf was with his mother constantly, closely bonded physically, as she carried him on her back or held him while breast-feeding. She carried him everywhere she went, and every night he slept with both parents. Because of this, Wind-Wolf's educational setting was not only a "secure" environment, but it was also very colorful, complicated, sensitive, and diverse.

As he grew older, Wind-Wolf began to crawl out of the baby basket, develop his motor skills, and explore the world around him. When frightened or sleepy he could always return to the basket, as a turtle withdraws into its shell. Such an inward journey allows one to reflect in privacy on what he has learned and to carry the new knowledge deeply into the unconscious and the soul. Shapes, sizes, colors, texture, sound, smell, feeling, taste, and the learning process are therefore functionally integrated—the physical and spiritual, matter and energy, and conscious and unconscious, individual and social.

It takes a long time to absorb and reflect on these kinds of experiences, so maybe that is why you think my Indian child is a slow learner. His aunts and grandmothers taught him to count and know his numbers while they sorted materials for making abstract designs in native baskets. And he was taught to learn mathematics by counting the sticks we use in our traditional native hand game. So he may be slow in grasping the methods and tools you use in your classroom, ones quite familiar to his white peers, but I hope you will be patient with him. It takes time to adjust to a new cultural system and learn new things.

He is not culturally "disadvantaged," but he is culturally "different."

Source: Lake, Robert, "An Indian Father's Plea," *Teacher Magazine*, Vol. 2, September 1990, pp. 48–53. Reprinted with permission from *Teacher Magazine*.

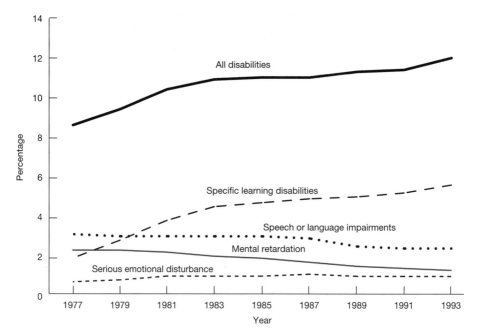

FIGURE 4–4 Number of children with disabilities served in federal programs as a percentage of total public K–12 enrollment, by type of disability.

Note: Includes students served under Chapter 1 of ECIA and Part B of IDEA. Prior to school year 1987–88, preschool students were included in the counts by disabling condition. Beginning in the 1987–88 school year, states are no longer required to report preschool students (0–5 years) with disabilities by disabling condition.

Source: U.S. Department of Education, Office of Special Education and Rehabilitative Services, *Annual Report to Congress on the Implementation of the Individuals with Disabilities Education Act,* various years. Reprinted in National Center for Education Statistics, *The Condition of Education,* 1995, p. 125.

7 percent are in separate classrooms or buildings. Services are provided for a variety of students. About twice as much money is spent to educate a disabled child as before PL 94-142, yet many are not receiving special education even now. Part of the problem is assessment: determining whether a child is learning disabled or has some other problem.

Most research results show that integration of as many special education students as possible has positive results; students have peer models from whom to learn social skills and competencies, and other students learn about disabilities. Integrating special education students into classrooms provides models and expectations that are powerful influences on children. However, low self-esteem is a concern when mainstreaming special education students. Some studies indicate that they have lower self-concepts in relation to academic achievement in regular classes than in separate classes (Ayres, Cooley, and Dunn, 1990). The effects of labeling students for special placement can influence peer-group relations, but the research has not clearly documented whether separate placement or mainstreaming has any detrimental effects. Of major concern is the number of minority students labeled retarded or learning disabled. It is estimated that 300 percent more Hispanics are represented in this group than the average. Clearly, careful and fair assessment is in order.

Gifted Students

Few think of gifted students as disadvantaged, but if their talents are not being developed, we may argue that they are in a disadvantaged position. Societies need to develop and use the talents of their most gifted members, but this presents dilemmas and controversies in democracies: To single out some students for special treatment or training is to give advantage to some and create an elite intelligentsia; yet if ability is considered regardless of other factors, such as family position, we are developing and using needed resources.

◆◆Box 4–3　*The Case of a "Dull" Genius*

Perhaps a good place to begin is with the case of a boy who was a slow developer, particularly with respect to language. He did not begin to talk until after his second birthday, and language difficulties persisted for him into adulthood. He did poorly in school; his temper tantrums proved highly disruptive to the classroom. Both his parents and his teachers thought him dull, and neither envisioned much of a future for him.

Finally, however, when he was 14, his parents happened upon a different kind of school pursuing a more holistic approach to education, and a less exclusively linguistically oriented one. The boy blossomed and his world changed. His name was Albert Einstein. His later writings suggest what may well have been the key problem: Even as an adult, Einstein continued—unlike most of us—to think in visual images rather than in words. Thus, he might understandably have found classrooms dealing only in words very hard to handle. (It may be worth noting, however, that the apparent language deficiency that handicapped him as a pupil may have empowered him as a creative genius. It has been said that Einstein's ability to depart from traditional physics may well have been associated with his independence from its concepts, as he dealt instead with visual images.)

Source: Raywid, Mary Anne, "Separate Classes for the Gifted? A Skeptical Look," *Educational Perspectives*, Vol. 26, No. 1, 1989, p. 44.

Controversy continues when schools consider which students to place in gifted programs. Congressional Act PL 95-561 defined "gifted" as including general intellectual ability, specific academic aptitude, creative or productive thinking, leadership, and visual and performing arts talents. But who is gifted is actually defined by each program that singles out children for special treatment, and herein lies the controversy (see Box 4–3). Low test scores and institutional discrimination may hide the talents of some students, especially minority students.

We know that gifted students benefit from homogeneous ability grouping. But in the process, some students are labeled "better" than others, and a self-fulfilling prophecy can result in which there is added stress and pressure to succeed and play a "significant" role in society.

Although there is lack of agreement on one strategy, many feel that individualized instruction combined with some joint classroom activities with other students may best serve both groups. Separating students from their peers does occur when students are tracked, sent to special programs or classes, or "pulled out" of classrooms for any purpose. Most useful to gifted and other students are programs that support a variety of learning styles (Raywid, 1989, p. 44) and use students in the teaching process.

IMPROVING SCHOOLS FOR MINORITY STUDENTS

The U.S. educational system is built on the premise that all students should be educated regardless of race, ethnic group, sex, ability, or other characteristics. This responsibility has been entrusted to the state and federal government, to take an active role in ensuring rights for minorities, including African Americans, Hispanics, immigrants from other countries, women, and other disadvantaged groups. Though there is an impatience to reform education, any new programs need to take all students into account; thus, reforms must come from old and new ideas, from the powerful and not so powerful in society, and from the various groups who will be affected (Coleman, 1990). Real change in the situation of minority students will not come about without individual and structural changes involving education, family, and other groups that act to empower minority students rather than disenfranchise them. This is a formidable task, considering the difficulty of changing power relations in society. Many programs only perpetuate the structure as it is and produce little change, in part because they deal with only part of the system. Some general conclusions and recommendations that stem from the research, especially that related to "at-risk" students, recommend that schools intervene early, make sure students spend time "on task," have high expectations of students and mainstream potential dropouts, provide support services such as day care for student parents, and reduce class sizes to fewer than 20 students (Lindjord,

1998). Many researchers and policymakers are experimenting with program ideas such as multicultural educational programs, school climates that reduce prejudice, and community service and career involvement programs to keep students in school.

Effective Schools. Effective schools create positive academic achievement environments, and they raise students' self-esteem, reduce student alienation and delinquency, encourage interracial friendships, and integrate teaching of racial equality into the school curriculum (Hammack, 1990). All students are highly involved in extracurricular activities, and teachers display behaviors that favor racial integration and prejudice reduction. In addition, many parents play an active role in these schools. Effective schools should benefit all students, including minority students, by attending to the following issues:

1. Clear-cut goals and objectives
2. Adequate funding and appropriate use of funds
3. Quality academic programs
4. Valid assessment programs and effective monitoring of progress
5. Parent, family, and community involvement
6. Teacher and staff development
7. High expectations for students
8. Comprehensive support services
9. Adequate school facilities
10. Productive school climate and culture
11. Multicultural instruction and sensitivity ("Effective Schools," 1998; Levine, 1995)

Choice Programs, Vouchers, and Charter Schools. Proposed plans for revitalizing education allow parents to choose the kind of school that meets their children's needs. In theory, this should provide competition and improve schools. However, there are many problems with the concept, as outlined in other chapters in this text.

Cooperative Learning. Cooperative learning involves groups of four to six heterogeneous members who work together toward achieving a goal. This idea stems from the work of Slavin and others at the Center for Social Organization of Schools at The Johns Hopkins University (Slavin, 1995, 1983). Findings show that cooperative learning positively affects student relationships and achievement.

Attitudes of Schools and Teachers. Among the many recent reports on how to improve schools are *What Works* and *Creating Effective Schools*. They document a number of findings from research that result in effective schools. The general conclusions support our discussion here concerning the need for improving the achievement and attitudes toward minority students. Teachers must communicate high expectations to all of their students; schools need strong educational leadership that emphasizes academic achievement; and parents need to be involved in the education of their children (Brookover, Erickson, and McEvoy, 1996; *What Works*, 1986).

Community Involvement. Community involvement addresses the need to approach school reform from many angles as suggested by the systems model. Schools alone cannot change the situation for minority students. Involvement of parents and businesses are two methods of changing the situation. For example, a New York City businessman promised sixth graders from his alma mater financial support to attend college if they finished high school. Instead of up to 75 percent dropping out, as was the norm, 83 percent finished high school and many have gone on to college. This one case started a national business–school liaison, the "I Have a Dream Foundation," to help 10,000 children pursue higher education (Sommerfeld, 1992, p. 1).

Although we may not agree with all of these recommendations, they point again to the importance of considering all levels of the system, from individual to the total educational system and its environment, in order to bring about change.

The process of stratification pervades educational systems both as a reflection of the stratification patterns in the society and its institutions, and as a mechanism to reinforce and perpetuate those patterns within society. From children's homes, neighborhoods, and peer groups to the political and economic systems, children are socialized to play their roles in society and to occupy a place in the societal system. Issues of equal opportunity have been raised, especially by those who feel that they are receiving unfair treatment and unequal chances for the rewards society can offer. Education is a target for these criticisms because of its perceived importance in providing opportunities for a better life. The open systems perspective reminds us that problems of equality go far beyond the effect of schools alone. Schools may be the nursery of integration, but equal access to housing, equal pay for equal work, employment opportunities, and many other areas must also be considered in the fight for equality of opportunity.

In summary, education is still a route to social mobility for many students, but for those locked into minority schools and neighborhoods and those who suffer from other disadvantages, achievement is more of a challenge.

◆ Summary

In this chapter we continued our discussion of the process of stratification in education and society. We focused on the problem of sex inequality in schools and attempts to rectify sexism, followed by problems facing minority groups in American education, including discussions of African Americans, Native Americans, Hispanics, and Asian Americans.

I. Gender and Equality of Educational Opportunity

Girls and boys have different school experiences, partly because of differences in expectations, encouragement, and treatment. The sex-role socialization process begins at birth, influencing what children feel is appropriate to their sex. Male and female achievement is affected by parental expectations; books, texts, and other materials; TV and media; toys; achievement motivation; sex-role models; teacher stereotypes and expectations; and peer-group pressures. The reasons for differences in math achievement are discussed, concluding that there is little evidence for biological explanations of differences. Efforts that combat the negative effects of sexism, such as Title IX programs, also are discussed.

II. Class, Race, and Attempts to Rectify Inequalities in Educational Opportunity

Do schools make a difference? Findings related to this question indicate a complex interaction between family and schools that affects equal opportunity. Because of inequalities in educational opportunities for minorities, the political and legal systems have intervened. Numerous court cases have ordered school districts to desegregate through busing children. Attempts to bus, the effects of busing and "white flight," self-concept, and achievement are discussed.

III. Integration Attempts

The attempt to rectify inequality through compensatory educational programs is described and evaluated.

IV. Educational Experience of Selected Minorities in the United States

Hispanic students are the fastest-growing and most segregated group in schools, and they also come from many different backgrounds. Whether to teach these students in English or their native language is a controversial subject. Which will give them greater opportunity in the future?

Asian American students do best of the minority groups, whereas Native Americans have perhaps the most difficult time. Other groups, such as special education students, are discussed briefly.

V. Improving Schools for Minority Students

Several programs that attempt to change the situation for minority students are discussed: changing patterns of interaction in schools, multicultural education programs, school climate, and community involvement are examples.

◆ Putting Sociology to Work

1. At your local library, randomly select a sample of children's books. Tabulate the following:

	Male	Female
Number of stories where main character is	_____	_____
Number of illustrations of	_____	_____
Number of times children are shown		
in active play	_____	_____
using initiative	_____	_____
displaying independence	_____	_____
solving problems	_____	_____
earning money	_____	_____
receiving recognition	_____	_____
being inventive	_____	_____
involved in sports	_____	_____
fearful or helpless	_____	_____
receiving help	_____	_____

2. Interview a group of eighth-grade girls, then boys, about their aspirations, future career plans, and high school curriculum plans. Compare these aspirations.

3. Talk with students who are being bused in order to desegregate schools. What are their experiences and feelings both about busing and about its effects on the school, academic work, their own attitudes, and friendships or peer-group relations?

4. What are the admissions policies with regard to race and sex for professional schools (medical, law, nursing, dental) in your area?

CHAPTER 5

The School as an Organization

It is Monday morning at 8:45. We are entering high school. Sounds of loud voices, banging lockers, and running feet greet us as the big, heavy doors slam behind us. A loud bell clangs through the chaos, and students begin disappearing behind closing doors along the corridor. And so another day begins. Each student knows his or her proper place in the system. If a late student enters, disrupting the routine, the school personnel will attempt to socialize this disruptive student into proper behavior and instill the value of punctuality.

There are many ways of looking at the school as an organization; in Chapter 6 we focus on the role structure of the school, and in Chapter 7 on its informal organization—classroom interactions, teaching and learning processes, and school climate. Here we look at the important structural components of the system and analyze aspects of the school as a bureaucracy.

Although each school has its own culture and subcultures, complete with legends, heroes, stories, rituals, and ceremonies, certain organizational facts are relevant to any discussion of schools. For instance, the size of a school is correlated with the type of organizational structure and degree of bureaucratization—the larger the school, the higher the degree of bureaucracy. The region of the country and a school's setting affect the degree of centralization—many rural schools tend to become more centralized because the area covered is more sparsely populated; community residents in urban school districts often push toward decentralization because of the diverse needs of different urban populations. The community's class and racial composition influence the school structure and climate, and private or religious schools are affected by other unique variables.

In considering the social structure of the school as an organization, our open system boundaries fall around the school and classroom (see Figure 5–1). Although the internal structure of the school system is our focus, we must keep in mind that the system is shaped and changed through interaction with the environment. Schools serve purposes for other organizations and institutions in society, and they cannot exist independently of other organizations. For instance, when we discuss school goals we are really discussing what is expected of schools by their environments and how that is reflected in school goals. We separate out the school as an organization for analytical purposes only, to understand the whole educational system.

SOCIAL SYSTEM OF THE SCHOOL

According to the functionalist approach, the school system is composed of many distinct subsystems or parts, each with goals; together these parts make up a functioning whole (see Figure 5–2). If one of these parts experiences problems or breakdown or does not carry out its functions, other interdependent parts are affected. Each part is dependent on the others for smooth operation, for the materials or resources it needs to function, and even for its existence. As you read, picture a school with which you are familiar.

1. As we enter the school we are directed to the office. Here a member of the school staff, usually the secretary, greets us and ascertains our business. The office and its staff act as buffers to protect the rest of the school from interruptions in routine.

FIGURE 5–1 Open system model of educational organizations.

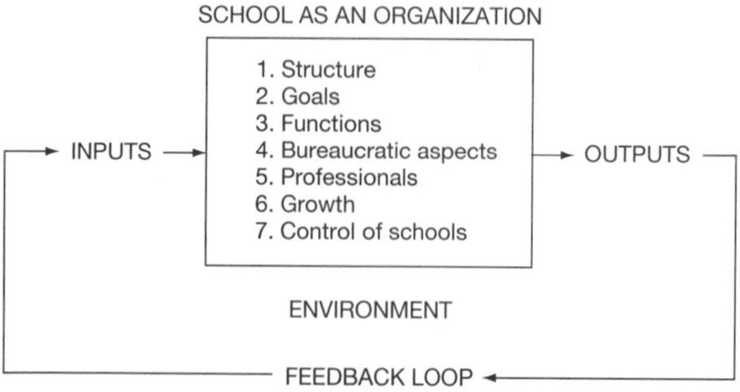

SCHOOL AS AN ORGANIZATION

INPUTS →
1. Structure
2. Goals
3. Functions
4. Bureaucratic aspects
5. Professionals
6. Growth
7. Control of schools
→ OUTPUTS

ENVIRONMENT

FEEDBACK LOOP ◄

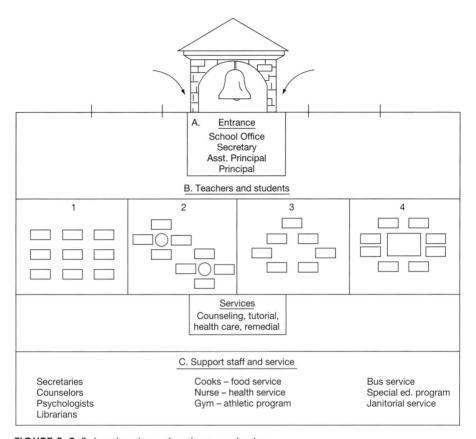

FIGURE 5–2 School system structure and roles.

2. Classrooms take up most of the physical structure of the school; within the class-room, teacher and students are the main occupants. However, the order of the classroom—including seating arrangement, work groups, location, style of leadership, class size, and the types of students—affects the relationships between position-holders and the consequent roles they play. These in turn affect the activities taking place within the classroom. Each classroom has a distinct climate and social structure.

3. Support services are necessary for classrooms to function; standard services include food, janitorial, and emergency health services. In addition, most schools have facilities for counseling, special services such as psychological testing or tutoring, bus service, and library service. This total school system exists in a larger societal context, including the local community with its social class and minority-group compositions and interest groups; the regional setting; the state government with its board of education, legislative bodies, rules, and regulations; and the federal government with its federal regulations and funding. A school system—people, buildings, classrooms, textbooks, and equipment—becomes what it is through interaction with the environment.

GOALS OF THE SCHOOL SYSTEM

Formal goals serve several purposes for social systems. They provide guidelines for activities of the system and focus the activities of members; they imply social acceptance of the stated purposes and of means to achieve them; and they legitimize the activities of the system. There is not always consensus, however, on what goals should receive highest priority or how they should be achieved. Witness the controversies over school curricula: Some adults are concerned that schools are not putting enough emphasis on basic skills and that too many "frills" (art and music, for example) are included in the program. Others argue that children need exposure to a broad curriculum. Schools also are under pressure from many community members to take on ever greater roles, especially in social service areas such as after school child-care programs and intervention in personal and family problems.

Thus, goals are constantly being "negotiated" and reconsidered depending on the interests of the powerful and the needs of the system. We now consider briefly some goal expectations of various societal sectors that influence official school goals.

Societal and Community Goals

Each society has certain goals for its educational system that, ideally, are put into practice in the schools and classrooms. In homogeneous societies there is often consensus on key goals, and national educational programs determine uniform curriculum and materials; but heterogeneous societies have constituencies with competing goals. Functional theorists hold that these goals give direction to the school, helping it to function smoothly and to support the societal system. Conflict theorists argue that these are goals of the dominant power groups in society, that they represent only one segment of society, and that they serve to perpetuate the stratification system. There are competing and contradictory goals held by other groups in society. School systems are often at the center of political struggles for control of resources and ideas (Torres, 1994).

Over time, goals change. For instance, the early sociologist Émile Durkheim spoke of the social organization of the school classroom that fosters the moral habits that keep societies together (Durkheim, 1961). Today educators debate goals for school curriculum, structure, outcomes, and even what values and morals should be taught, if any (Jackson, Boostrom, and Hansen, 1993).

The diversity of goals and expectations in the United States is exemplified by the fact that there is little consensus among those who have vested interests in schools—students, social scientists, educators, parents, and politicians, to name a few. This diversity of goals presents a dilemma for school districts beholden to their constituencies.

Each new national administration presents its goals for education. During the Bush administration, the plan was called *America 2000: An Education Strategy*

One goal for schools is that they function smoothly.

(*America 2000*, 1991). The Clinton administration's plan is called *Goals 2000: Educate America Act* (*Goals 2000*, 1994). It called for systematic national reform (see Box E–2 for goals). The next administration will put forth another statement of goals, supporting more or less government aid and intervention. During the 2000 presidential campaign in the United States, the major candidates also put forth platforms on education indicating their respective philosophies of the government's role in education ("Comparing Two Plans for Education," 2000, p. A18).

Other plans for reform also receive national attention. In K–12 education, Theodore Sizer has influenced educational reformers with his call for teachers to teach fewer subjects in greater depth, for students to be active learners, and to give diplomas only after mastery of certain subjects (Sizer, 1985). Other reforms such as the Paideia classroom (Roberts and Billings, 1999) and programs for at-risk students such as Accelerated Schools, Coalition of Essential Schools, Community for Learning, and School Development (Wang, Haertel, and Walberg, 1998) are being carried out in schools across the United States. John Goodlad, another visionary, has stimulated reform at teachers' colleges as well with his propositions for improving education (Bernhardt and Ballantine, 1995; Goodlad, 1984).

The expectations that individual communities have of their schools are likely to be far more specific than the general goals of society. For instance, schools in old, small towns in rural areas, such as that described in the classic work, *Elmtown's Youth* (Hollingshead, 1975), are likely to stress hard work, moral orientation, and other major American values (Williams, 1970). The dominant community members (business leaders, politicians) control school board elections and screen out teachers who might try to change things. Urban schools, because of the heterogeneous population served, have less consensus on academic goals and spend more energy on the "goals" of discipline and control. Suburban schools are likely to focus on success and achievement goals. Emblems, mottoes, and student handbooks stating very general goals are redefined and operationalized constantly to meet community needs and expectations. Local school goals are influenced by political pressures from community groups, especially where decision making rests in the hands of the local school (Hannaway, 1993, p. 147). It is precisely because of the constant pressures for change that goal statements are kept on a broad and widely acceptable level. This avoids clashes between schools and government, community, family, and other groups. Vague general goal statements, however, also mean that schools are vulnerable to influence and pressure from many conflicting interest groups.

School Goals

A broad and generally accepted model for most schools' formal goal statements was developed in 1918 by the National Education Association's Commission on the Reorganization of Secondary Education. It recommended that secondary education should "Develop in each individual the knowledge, interests, ideals, habits and powers whereby he will find his place and use that place to shape both himself and society toward ever nobler ends." Although it is dated, this statement reflects some basic American values, which ideally should be reflected in local schools: good citizenship, or fitting into society; and individuality, or making one's own way by using acceptable means. In reality, these goals are not working for some groups in American society; equal opportunity is far from reality, as we discussed in Chapters 3 and 4.

The stated goals are often different from the operational procedures, which outline what is to happen and what programs are to be carried out in each school. These procedures focus on curricular content, classroom style, and organizational structure to accomplish the stated goals. It is in the school that stated goals must be translated into action; in this process, conflicts over purpose and interpretation can arise.

Subsystems within the community and school may have informal unstated goals that differ from, and perhaps even contradict, the stated formal school goals. For instance, teachers may seek to buffer themselves from the community to protect their professional autonomy, whereas the school may profess an open-door policy toward parents and community members and at the same time put up protective barriers to maintain the school's operational goals and control over the academic program.

Two models dominate the organizational control of schools: highly decentralized schools in which teachers have workplace autonomy, and top-down bureaucracies in which teachers have little autonomy. Some assume that large, bureaucratic districts will have more top-down decision making and goal setting, but data indicates that small private schools often have great central control as well. The degree of control over goals, stated or unstated, and the autonomy of teachers and schools depends on what activities are considered and on differences in the degree of control exerted by boards of education, principals, and teachers in different types of schools (Ingersoll, 1994).

Individual Goals

Members of the organization holding different roles are also likely to have different goals. For instance, administrators and teachers desire high-quality education, but they also have personal motivations such as the need for money, prestige, and knowledge. For students, school is obligatory; they are required to attend. Their goals will vary depending on individual motivations, ranging from dropping out at 16 to attending college. Students can be encouraged to take academic courses that seem accessible (not too difficult) when they see rewards in doing so (Kilgore, 1993, p. 81). Parents' goals are sometimes in conflict with school policies, as we shall see.

SCHOOL FUNCTIONS: THE PURPOSES OF THE SCHOOL

The goals just discussed reflect many of the functions or purposes that education serves in society and that help prepare children for society. Several manifest (obvious and stated) functions apply to all school systems in industrialized societies, and they are often made explicit in goal statements. But competing interests illustrate that there are differences in views concerning functions of schools.

Diverse Functions

Because schools include many diverse functions reflecting competing interest groups in communities, it is useful to look at these functions of schooling from differing perspectives within the system—those of society, community, family, and individual student.

For society, important school functions are to socialize the young to perform needed adult roles; keep the young occupied; delay entry into the job market; help perpetuate society; socialize the young into particular societal values, traditions, and beliefs; develop skills needed to live in society, such as reading, writing, and responsibility; and select and allocate the young to needed roles, from professionals to laborers.

For the community and family, the functions of schools that are believed to be important are to formalize socialization experiences, especially in formal learning; facilitate peer interaction; structure socialization experience; help meet family goals for successful children; give children more options in the competitive marketplace; and produce young people who will fit into the community. Individual groups or families in a community may differ on goals because of social class, religious affiliation, or minority status.

For individual students, school provides an opportunity to get together with peers and engage in sports and other activities. Student attitudes toward and cooperation with adults help socialize them into having acceptable attitudes and behaviors, and they provide skills and knowledge for them to fit into society's competitive bureaucracies.

Although these functions overlap, it is also apparent that conflicts may arise between the different groups over the importance of various functions and methods of carrying out functions in the school setting.

Unanticipated Consequences of Functions

Each of the functions noted may have both positive and negative outcomes; the intended purpose is not always the only result or even the main result of the process of education. For instance, schools bring age peers together in the classroom and for other school-related activities. This bringing together enables friendship groups or cliques to develop and the youth subculture to flourish; these groups in turn may profoundly influence the school, as we shall see in Chapter 7. Delaying young people's entry into the job market may serve the purpose of keeping more adults employed while the students receive more education, but it may also cause strain when overeducated, unemployed young people do reach the job market.

Conflicting Goals and Functions

Controversies occur between community members and the school over issues such as curriculum and school structure. Many families want their children to learn but not to be exposed to ideas that contradict the families' values and teaching. For example, school personnel may consider sex education important for teenagers; some families object to the school's taking over this educational task. The court cases brought by religious groups such as the Amish and fundamentalist Christians are other examples of community-school conflicts.

What can be done with early adolescents? This is the question underlying debate about the virtues of middle school structures versus junior high or other organizations. The middle school model—typically grades 6, 7, and 8 or 7 and 8—is winning out and growing in popularity. "Trends over the past two decades indicate a shift from junior high schools (grades 7–9) to middle schools (grades 5–8 and 6–8)" with more than 55 percent of schools using the 6–7–8 pattern (National Middle School Association, 1995). This period serves as a transition from the nurturing elementary school years to the all-important high school years. It is during the early adolescent period that some students exhibit behaviors that begin a cycle of academic failure and dropping out of school (Ames and Miller, 1994).

Promising programs for middle schools share several features: individualized instruction, evaluation techniques to determine progress, flexible temporary student groupings to avoid labeling of students, attention to different styles of learning, family involvement, student responsibility for learning, extra staff and resources, and staff development (Epstein and Salinas, 1991). "They are organized in ways that correspond as much as possible to the distinct developmental needs of youngsters between the ages of 10 and 15" (George et al., 1992, p. 38).

The Carnegie Task Force on Education of Young Adolescents produced a report, *Turning Points: Preparing American Youth for the 21st Century.* Its recommendations address the mismatch between the intellectual and emotional needs of 10- to 15-year-olds and the organization and curriculum of middle grades; for instance, they suggest building on the preoccupation with social relations by forming small work groups and having an adult available to talk with individual students (Carnegie Task Force, 1989). The director of the middle school programs at The Johns Hopkins University Center for Research on Elementary and Middle Schools suggests a transition team to give guidance and control in moving from elementary to high school (MacIver and Epstein, 1990).

Individual students face conflicts also. Formal schooling may broaden opportunities and career options, but it may also narrow freedom to choose what to learn and how to act. Students may gain security and a sense of belonging from peer groups or "youth subcultures" with their own special values, but at the same time these groups' values may contradict school academic programs and family goals such as achievement, success, and conformity.

School goals and functions are carried out within a formal structure. Our next step in understanding the organization is to look at the structural elements making up the school system.

> **A**pplying Sociology to Education: What conflicts over goals and functions have dominated school board meetings in your local schools? ◈

THE SCHOOL AS AN ORGANIZATION

Sally Joseph is a fifth-grade teacher, popular among students and parents because of the results she achieves in reading and math and her ability to relate to children in her classes. Ms. Joseph has relative autonomy in leading her classroom. How she organizes and presents her materials is primarily her decision, within the parameters of her physical space and the broad goals outlined by the school district. Yet she functions within a larger organizational system that presents her with both opportunities and constraints. Traditionally, sociologists have viewed the situation within which Ms. Joseph works as a bureaucracy, but they have pointed out the limitations of this model for educational organizations; what works in formal bureaucracies such as business organizations may be dysfunctional in schools. Another model views educational systems as "loosely coupled" organizations. We shall look at schools as bureaucracies and problems related to this model.

The School as a Bureaucracy

Bureaucracy! How often do we throw up our hands in disgust at the red tape, forms, impersonal attitudes, and coldness of bureaucracies? How infuriating is it to be treated as a number? Behind the stereotypical face of bureaucracy are millions of individuals with histories and feelings and experiences like ours. What is it that makes us bristle at the idea of bureaucracy? Bureaucracy is a rational, efficient way of completing tasks and rewarding individuals based on their contributions. However, it can also represent an impersonal, inefficient, cumbersome organization unresponsive to human needs, as perhaps you have experienced when you waited in line to accomplish some task, such as registering, paying fees, or renewing a drivers license.

By dividing organizations into formal and informal parts (discussed in Chapter 8), we can better understand the working bureaucracy and the way it relates to schools. Although we may complain, bureaucracy serves a vital function in our society. A system based on nepotism and favoritism rather than selection and promotion based on merit, for example, would be certain to raise cries of unfairness and discrimination, and it would be dysfunctional for most societies.

A note of caution is necessary in discussing schools as bureaucracies, because schools are unique organizations. As Christopher Hurn indicates, schools are distinctive because they are expected to transmit values, ideals, and shared knowledge; foster cognitive and emotional growth; and sort and select students into different categories—college material, promising, bright, and so forth—with consequences for future adult status. Organizationally, schools are divided into classrooms, the day into periods, and students into groups by grades or performance on examinations (Hurn, 1992). Other bureaucracies have different purposes and structures.

Characteristics of Bureaucracy

The bureaucratic form of organization became prominent in Western Europe and the United States during the Industrial Revolution, primarily because it was believed to be the most efficient and rational form for organizations with goals of high productivity and efficiency.

Max Weber, whose ideas were discussed briefly in Chapter 1, described the elements that make up a bureaucratic organization (Weber, 1947). His typology of characteristics is what is called an "ideal type"; no real organization is going to match these characteristics completely, but it gives a set of characteristics against which to compare real organizations. The italicized points in the following five statements are Weber's characteristics; these are followed by an explanation of their relation to schools, as outlined by David Goslin (1965, p. 133).

1. An increasingly fine *division of labor*, at both the administrative and teaching levels, together with a concern for allocating personnel to those positions for which they are best suited and a formalization of recruitment and promotion policies
2. The development of an *administrative hierarchy* incorporating a specified chain of command and designated channels of communications
3. The gradual accumulation of *specific rules of procedure* that cover everything from counseling and guidance to schoolwide or systemwide testing programs and requirements concerning topics to be covered in many subjects such as history, civics, and social studies
4. A deemphasis of personal relationship between students and teachers and between teachers and administrators, and a consequent reorientation toward more *formalized and effectively neutral role relationships*
5. An emphasis on the *rationality* of the total organization and the processes going on within the organization. In general, the movement, particularly at the secondary school level, has been in the direction of the rational bureaucratic organization that is typified by most government agencies and many business and industrial firms.
6. In addition to these characteristics discussed by Goslin is Weber's point that the *positions individuals hold in the organization belong to the organization.* Thus, when an administrator, teacher, or student leaves the system, new individuals will move in to hold those positions.

Let us look at each of Weber's characteristics more closely.

Division of Labor, Hiring and Firing, Promotion Policies, and Authority System

Division of labor. Each of us has specific tasks on the job and at home. We become specialists. With busy schedules, efficiency is high if we each know the tasks for which we are responsible and become adept at performing them. One problem that can result from a high degree of specialization is boredom—consider the assembly-line worker who faces eight hours daily at a single monotonous task. For a teacher, however, each student and class is different and challenging. There is constant updating of material and techniques and learning of new knowledge. This relieves boredom, but the intensity of the work can also cause burnout, a problem discussed in Chapter 6.

Hiring and firing based on competence and skill. The following is taken from a teacher job description of a large school district:

Duties of teachers. Teachers shall take charge of the division of classes assigned to them by the principal. They shall be held responsible for the instruction, progress and discipline of their classes and shall devote themselves exclusively to their duties during school hours. Teachers shall render such assistance in the educational program in and about the buildings as the principal may direct, including parent-interviews, pupil-counseling, corridor, lunchroom, and playground supervision, and attendance at professional staff meetings. (Teacher job description)

With extensive certification regulations and testing, personnel policies, hiring committees and procedures, and equal opportunity regulations, school personnel must be clearly qualified for the positions to be filled. Training institutions become important for preparing individuals with the skills and attitudes necessary for the job. Colleges of education are usually accredited by state and regional organizations. They are required to teach the needed job skills and must be run in accordance with federal and state regulations governing education. The colleges also serve as screening points; those who can fit into the system and abide by rules are likely to be passed on to school systems with high recommendations.

Promotion and salary based on merit. Salary schedules and criteria for promotion are usually formulated by the superintendent's office and approved by the school board. These two are closely linked to the individual's level of education and number of years of service.

Hierarchical System of Authority. You need spend little time in the halls of learning to know who is the boss and who is being bossed. The hierarchy of authority in any bureaucracy can be diagrammed, and most schools fit into the model shown in Figure 5–3. The hierarchy has implications for communication channels in schools. Depending on the position in the hierarchy, a person will receive and give out varying numbers and types of messages. Consider your college classrooms: There is a variety of teaching styles, class size, and information flow. One typical pattern is a downward flow of communication from instructor to student. Some educators have suggested that modifying the one-way flow and encouraging more interaction would lessen the alienation created in a large bureaucracy. More teachers would become "facilitators" in the learning process instead of "directors" or one-way communicators.

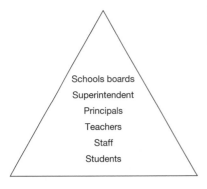

FIGURE 5–3
Hierarchical system of authority in schools.

Part of the individual's responsibilities in the hierarchy involve reciprocal relationships; that is, relating to others in the organization. This is illustrated in the use of names: Teachers call students by first names, but the reverse is seldom true. The hierarchical differences are acknowledged in the formal title. The formal organization hierarchy chart alone cannot provide an accurate picture of where authority and power lie and how they are used, but it can give a picture of structure and formal relations.

Rules, Regulations, and Procedures. School begins at 8:40 A.M. Late students must report to the office for a tardy slip. At 8:50 A.M. students move to class period 1. . . . This is the routine set up by rules, but in addition there are rules covering most forms of behavior in the school, including dress, restroom behavior, cafeteria time, recess, after-school activities, bus behavior, and on and on.

Each individual is socialized into the system's rules and regulations. Often these rules are formalized in an orientation program for new students or written in a student or teacher handbook. Most of the expectations, however, are passed on informally through observation, discussion, and ridicule, or by more severe sanctions if rules are violated. Part of our anxiety about entering new situations is the fear of violating the rules, making faux pas, and being singled out for ridicule. Most of us wish to avoid such embarrassment, so we do our utmost to conform. Bel Kaufman, in her classic amusing but sobering account of the bureaucracy, provides us with vivid examples of rules and regulations. In Box 5-1 she outlines the tasks to be accomplished by the teacher during the homeroom period.

Formalized and affectively neutral role relationships. Those individuals holding a certain position in the bureaucratic organization are treated alike in a formal "neutral" manner; at least, that is the way it is supposed to be to avoid favoritism. The following example will sound familiar. The school is giving standardized examinations. All the children will sit in rows in the auditorium, where they are handed a test book and told to "Begin," "Stop," "Now turn the page," "Close your test booklet," and "Pass it to the right."

Exceptions to the rule may cause problems for bureaucracies. Efficiency is based on an assumption of sameness, and each exception takes time and energy from the organizational routine. If an individual is treated "differently," there may be charges of preferential treatment, prejudice, or discrimination. Formalized, impersonal treatment pervades many aspects of our school systems, but where human relations are involved, formal relations are constantly being challenged, as we discuss in Chapter 7. Human beings do not fit into simple boxes.

Rationality of the Total Organization. The tendency in organizational administrations is to seek more efficient means of carrying out functions. Schools are no exception in the attempt to achieve greater efficiency; as the size

---

◆◆**Box 5–1** *Program for Today's Homeroom Period (Check Off*
Each Item Before Leaving Building Today)

- Make out Delaney cards and seating plan
- Take attendance
- Fill out attendance sheets
- Send out absentee cards
- Make out transcripts for transfers
- Make out three sets of students' program cards (yellow) from master program card (blue), alphabetize and send to 201
- Make out five copies of teacher's program card (white) and send to 211
- Sign transportation cards
- Requisition supplies
- Assign lockers and send names and numbers to 201
- Fill out age-level reports
- Announce and post assembly schedule and assign rows in auditorium
- Announce and post fire, shelter, and dispersal drills regulations
- Check last term's book and dental blacklists
- Check library blacklist
- Fill out condition of room report
- Elect class officers
- Urge joining C.O. and begin collecting money
- Appoint room decorations monitor and begin decorating room
- Salute flag (only for non-assembly or Y2 sections)
- Point out the nature and function of homeroom: literally, a room that is a home, where students will find a friendly atmosphere and guidance

Teachers with extra time are to report to the office to assist with activities which demand attention.

Source: Reprinted with the permission of Simon & Schuster from *Up the Down Staircase* by Bel Kaufman. Copyright © 1964, 1988 by Bel Kaufman.

---

of schools has grown, so have formalization, specialization, and centralization. There are attempts, however, in many districts to decentralize.

Positions Belong to the Organization. The retirement dinner was crowded with well-wishers; she has been a popular teacher, well liked by colleagues and students. She will leave, but the position will be refilled. Next fall a new, younger teacher will come, bringing a new personality and different talents to the job.

One thing is clear: The job description belongs to the organization and carries with it the rights and responsibilities of the position. Each individual hired to fill a role will do so in a unique way, interjecting his or her own personality and experience into the job. We know that Mrs. Jones has a reputation for being a strong disciplinarian, Mr. Smith for being good at teaching math concepts, and so forth. Yet each holds a position with the same job description.

The holder of the position has authority or legitimacy over others only in areas related to the job. Authority is one type of power that gives the role-holder the right to make decisions and exert influence and control in specified areas. In school systems, legitimacy is granted on the basis of expertise and position in the hierarchy. Should a teacher overstep the power vested in the position, the teacher's legitimacy could be challenged. For instance, your teacher or professor cannot require you to get a good night's rest, eat a good breakfast, or even spend a certain number of hours outside school working on school-related activities.

When a teacher retires, resigns, or is fired, the replacement assumes the same responsibilities, and allegiance is given to the new position-holder. Personal reasons for allegiance may vary—respect for authority or for the person's expertise, or knowledge that the person holds power in the form of job security, money, or responsibility for giving grades. But the position remains the same.

Professionals are generally highly trained and have more autonomy and freedom in the way they execute their roles than do those lower in the hierarchy. How much freedom they have depends on their reciprocal roles and the setting in which they are working, as discussed in Chapter 6.

Part of learning our roles in an organization involves understanding the reciprocal roles. Symbolic interaction theory explains the process that is constantly taking place in our adjustment to situations as "taking the role of the other." This helps us learn our own roles and their limitations and anticipate the mind-set of the reciprocal role-holders so that we can understand and meet their expectations. This process is discussed further in Chapter 7.

Development of Schools as Bureaucracies

In the nineteenth century, schools were scattered throughout the country; their size depended on location, but most were small compared with today's inner-city and consolidated rural schools.

> By 1865 systems of common schooling had been established throughout the northern, midwestern and western states. . . . The common schools of the period varied in terms of size, organization and curricula depending on their location. In rural areas, where the majority of Americans lived, one would most likely find the one- or two-room schoolhouse in which a pupil's progress was marked not by annual movement from one grade to the next but by his completion of one text and beginning of the next in the series. Only in larger towns and cities had grading been introduced. (Binder, 1974, pp. 94–95)

The movement to mass secondary schooling forced a change in early high schools to more modern models. The main changes included the bureaucratization of public education and the move from the innovative structures of individual schools to strong, centralized structures and administrations in which teachers had little power.

Since the turn of the twentieth century, schools have become larger and increasingly more bureaucratic, exhibiting many characteristics similar to those presented in Weber's "ideal type" bureaucracy. A result of the changing size of school populations and movement to urban centers was the centralization and bureaucratization of schools. These moves toward consolidation of school districts resulted in part from modernizing state bureaucracies that pushed for change and increasing numbers of students. The enrollments in public and private elementary and secondary schools from 1970 to 2008 are presented in Figure 5–4.

The growth of "corporate schooling," according to Meyer and Rowan (1978), relates to the worldwide trend of national development; educational bureaucracies serve the societies, not individuals or families, and as such they help those in control "sort, select, and allocate" individuals from the many groups in society. Standardization of the system facilitates this process and has led to larger and larger bureaucracies with increasing numbers of administrators. Today there is more than one administrator for every ten teachers, and in some districts less than half of the employees are teachers. The main role of

FIGURE 5–4 Elementary and secondary school enrollment, by control and grade level of school, fall 1970–2008.

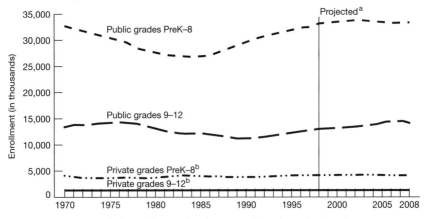

[a]Enrollment includes students in kindergarten through grade 12 and some nursery school students.

[b]Beginning in fall 1980, data include estimates for the expanded universe of private schools.

Source: U.S. Department of Education, National Center for Education Statistics, *Digest of Education Statistics 1998* (based on Common Care of Data) and *Projections of Education Statistics to 2008*, 1998.

many administrators is to respond to higher administrative levels in the state or federal governments (National Center for Education Statistics, 1999).

In recent years a number of researchers have pointed out both academic and personal value in small schools, both urban and rural; they tend to have higher academic achievement, be more personal, have higher student and teacher satisfaction and morale, lower dropout rates and behavior problems, and students are more involved in extracurricular activities. They have particular benefits for disadvantaged students (Raywid, 1999; Cotton, 1998). A small but consistent relationship exists between size and disorder as well; small schools are safer, have greater communication and performance feedback, and have more individuals involved in decision making (Raywid, 1999; Gottfredson, 1986). Because of the apparent advantages of small schools, some educators are creating mini-schools or schools-within-schools in larger school buildings (Lashway, 1999). In fact, some researchers argue that small school size is essential if meaningful school reform is to take place.

Problems in Educational Bureaucracies

Any time we attempt to put people into neat categories to maximize efficiency in an organization, there will be some who do not fit into the categories. A further problem is that its very structure as a bureaucracy may cause a school to experience difficulties. Consider the following types of problems:

1. Huge enrollments make test scores, rather than in-depth knowledge of a student's family, background, problems, motivations, and other personal characteristics, the major criteria for screening and placement of students, and thus the determinants of their future.
2. Because relationships are expected to be impersonal, students, particularly the disadvantaged, cannot receive the counseling and support, or the exposure to "acceptable" role models that they need to develop a positive self-image.
3. Official rules tend to overcontrol the behavior of school personnel and are difficult to circumvent when problems arise.
4. Teachers and students often feel powerless to change school conditions and so become apathetic about solving problems.
5. Teachers, and particularly administrators, can develop bureaucratic personalities, becoming insecure, overly protective of their jobs, narrowly specialized, less and less concerned with teaching, and inflexible in their daily behavior.

For students who conform to bureaucratic expectations, life in school is most probably rewarding. For many students, however, school bureaucracy presents a bewildering and alienating maze through which they must struggle.

Our negative feelings toward bureaucracy come into play as the system gets larger and we are caught up in the rules and regulations and we are treated as numbers that are being processed. The following extract from Roger's classic description of the New York City school bureaucracy, *110 Livingston Street*, describes the morass in the impersonal system:

> The New York City school system is typical of what social scientists call a "sick bureaucracy"—a term for organizations whose traditions, structure, and operations subvert their stated missions and prevent any flexible accommodation to changing client demands. It has all those characteristics that every large bureaucratic organization has; but they have been instituted and followed to such a degree that they no longer serve their original purpose. Such characteristics as (1) overcentralization, the development of many levels in the chain of command, and an upward orientation of anxious subordinates; (2) vertical and horizontal fragmentation, isolating units from one another and limiting communication and coordination of functions; (3) the consequent development of chauvinism within particular units, reflected in actions to protect and expand their power; (4) the exercise of strong, informal pressure from peers within units to conform to their codes, geared toward political protection and expansion and ignoring the organization's wider goals; (5) compulsive rule following and rule enforcing; (6) the rebellion of lower-level supervisors against headquarters directives; alternating at times with overconformity, as they develop concerns about ratings and promotions; (7) increasing insulation from clients, as internal politics and personal career interests override interests in serving various publics; and (8) the tendency to make decisions in committees, making it difficult to pinpoint responsibility and authority, are the institution's main pathologies. (Roger, 1969, p. 267)

The larger the system and the more entrenched the bureaucracy, the more there is resistance to change, as illustrated in the description of New York City's school system. A teacher facing 30 or more students each period, six periods a day, is unlikely to recognize an individual student's problem and take time and energy to deal with it. And that individual student may retreat further and further into the faceless mass at the high school, where 5,000 bodies are processed through the system. Various solutions to the impersonal bureaucracy have been proposed: decentralization of decision making; curricular changes; personalizing instruction; and having students more involved in community settings.

Schools as "Loosely Coupled" Organizations

Organizations in which activities and decisions made at one level are not necessarily reflected at other levels have been called "loosely coupled" organizations. This description characterizes many school districts. Part of this problem comes from the autonomy and physical separation of levels of hierarchy in educational systems. Teachers, such as Sally Joseph in the earlier example, are spatially isolated and professionally autonomous in classrooms (Gamoran and Dreeban, 1989); many teachers who desire autonomy support this situation. Actions of administrators also may facilitate teacher autonomy by granting them control over the organization of the classroom. Viewing schools as "loosely coupled" may be closer to the reality faced by teachers than trying to understand their behavior and feelings of control over decision making through more traditional theories that focus on bureaucracy, control mechanisms of schools, or environmental pressures.

Intervention in classroom teaching is often virtually impossible; therefore, decisions made at administrative levels have little impact on classrooms, and what goes on in classrooms is removed from the school's formal hierarchy, according to this model. Many administrators spend little time on instructional matters. The dilemma for schools and their administrators is central coordination of educational activities in a situation where teachers are largely autonomous.

Schools are more tightly controlled in some districts, however. Where administrations control the availability and use of resources, such as funds for materials, units of the educational system may be more dependent on each other. How tightly or loosely coupled the system is also varies by grade and subject matter (Gamoran and Dreeban, 1989), and by pressure from communities for accountability of school systems and teachers.

One example of a loosely coupled educational system can be seen in large metropolitan districts with multiple layers of administration (see the New York City model, Figure 6–2). In contrast, private schools in the United States, such as preparatory and Catholic schools, are more tightly coupled with administrations that are less complex; the result of the latter in most cases is more curricular coherence (Scott and Meyer, 1984). Teachers have more sense of control over classroom practice within the curriculum guidelines in Catholic schools, which leads to higher levels of satisfaction (Lee, Dedrick, and Smith, 1991).

*A*pplying Sociology to Education: In what ways is a bureaucratic organizational model useful to schools? In what ways can it be dysfunctional? ◆

CENTRALIZED VERSUS DECENTRALIZED DECISION MAKING: THE FIGHT OVER CONTROL OF SCHOOLS

In every system there are centers of power where decision making takes place. In the social system of the school, the locus of power has been in contention over the years. Key questions concern whether power should be concentrated in one central place or be distributed among parts of a system, who should make decisions for whom, and at what level. Some decision making takes place at each level of the system, from the superintendent to the teacher in the classroom, to individuals in the school (Barr and Dreeben, 1983). Most models break down decision making into two types: centralized and decentralized (Ingersoll, 1994, p. 150).

Centralization of Decision Making

The degree to which decision making is centralized varies with the size of the system, the degree of homogeneity of the people involved in the system, and their goals for the system. Different degrees of centralization can be found at the national, state, or local level. Certainly, control of the purse strings is one key determinant of the locus of power (Meyer, Scott, and Strang, 1986). For instance, the federal government has garnered increased control in education in recent years by determining areas of national concern and allocating funds for education in those areas.

When federal funds are provided for new programs, new administrators are hired to take on program responsibilities. This increases local educational bureaucracy and administrative expenditures, but without integration of the administrative unit. This phenomenon of increased administrative size without integration has been called "fragmented centralization." Funds were allocated for accelerated science and math programs in the "Sputnik Era" of the 1950s, when the U.S. government was concerned that the former Soviet Union was gaining a technological lead in the space program. More recently, laws have been passed requiring that all disabled children have access to education (Americans with Disabilities Act, 1990). Centralized power and decision making in education, however, are not necessarily representative of the interests and concerns of the local community.

Powerful countries and organizations influence policies and programs of less developed countries. For instance, the World Bank makes monetary policy, but it also "helps guide and create knowledge," which leads to the production of knowledge. For instance, foreign assistance has an impact on African educational systems; education is essential for development, and many African educational systems are in disarray. Therefore, dependence on funds from foreign sources is necessary. The price is often lack of local imagination and initiative in how to best educate a country's citizens. "Instead, as it becomes a set of largely externally defined rules specifying acceptable courses of action, research disorients and imprisons" (Samoff, 1993, p. 221).

State initiatives in educational reform are now moving to the foreground, spurred on by federal and private foundation commission reports lamenting the condition of education. State boards and commissions of education are recommending new policies at an unprecedented rate: tougher graduation standards, proficiency exams, textbook and curricular revisions, longer school days, year-round school, and many other reforms.

Many of these new state initiatives are aimed at the very core of the instructional process—what is taught, how, and by whom—reducing the autonomy and decision making of local boards, administrators, and teachers. Consider the recent discussions over the teaching of evolution in Kansas when the Kansas school board voted to remove most references to evolution from state education standards ("Poll: Origin Theories," 2000). State representatives argue, however, that until the local units and professional organizations take leadership, someone else must. Elected or appointed boards of education at the local and state level have the ultimate decision-making power—on paper. In reality, as school districts have become larger and more centralized—and as the issues have become complex, requiring trained experts—school boards have tended to leave issues of educational policy to the school administrators, giving them rubber-stamp approval. They have retained for themselves the role of mediators between the schools and the community. In this way, professional educators have gained more autonomy over policy issues.

Another contender in the "control of education" contest is private organizations such as foundations and industries, which are becoming increasingly involved in educational practice and policy. School boards are contracting out for more services, negotiating with the company that can provide the most for the least, including technology as discussed in Chapter 2. For example, Fairfax County, Virginia, and Houston, Texas, have "last-resort" or "second chance" programs in which they send high risk or expelled students to privately operated schools where the students get more teacher attention (Hardy, 1999). This occurs most often in noninstructional areas, such as food and janitorial services, but also is moving into instructional services. In Hartford, Connecticut, "desparate for a remedy for high dropout rates, low test scores and deteriorating buildings, [the board of education voted to make it] the nation's first city to put a private company fully in charge of its public school system" ("Hartford First," 1994). The experiment, however, met with considerable opposition and after several years failed (Uline, 1998). Another example is that of private-company reading programs that promise to raise reading levels of children. In some areas, businesses are providing financial support for teacher training and special programs for children. Privatization could leave the school board more time to deal with educational issues, but it also gives other organizations influence in school decision making and signifies another level of educational control.

Many suburban schools have a core of motivated students and parents who are involved with and influence the decisions of school boards and school officials (Wexler et al., 1992). Involvement is possible when classes are small, expectations are high, and discipline is fair but firm, and where classrooms are structured for cooperative learning to meet more student needs than rigidly structured classes (Eccles, 1994, p. 10). In urban schools it is harder to get parents involved. Large school districts such as New York City have had major disputes over control of local schools, with concerned local citizens wanting to be involved in decision making concerning staff hiring and firing, building maintenance, construction plans, and curriculum.

Decentralization

Decentralization is an ambiguous word. Some view decentralization simply as an administrative device—as a shift in administration from the national to the state or city governments, or from central city administrative offices to the local schools. Others insist that decentralization plans should embody a design for meaningful shifts in power from central agencies to local communities, not merely administrative adjustments, and that plans should go beyond education to other crucial areas such as health. Advocates of local control maintain that only such plans can temper the central bureaucratic monopoly on power and decision making. Studies of schools that have restructured reveal that students improve in their academics and in achievement; this is especially true in smaller high schools. Communal reforms go beyond decision making to meeting local needs, being flexible, promoting interdisciplinary work, being responsive to student talents and abilities, and providing mixed-ability classes and cooperative learning. Local schools can target a few key efforts and make a difference (Lee and Smith, 1995).

Decentralization has different meanings for different people. Often referred to as site-based management, and popular in discussions of educational reform, the idea involves shifting the initiative in public education from school boards, superintendents, and central administrative offices to individual schools. The idea is to give local schools more responsibility for school operations (Bauer, 1998; Hannaway, 1993). In Chicago, for instance, parents made a grassroots push for site-based management that resulted in the School Reform Act.

In a study of major urban and suburban school systems (Hill and Bonan, 1991), researchers drew five conclusions about site-based management:

1. Though site-based management focuses on individual schools, it is in fact a reform of the entire school system.
2. Site-based management will lead to real changes at the school level only if it is a school system's basic reform strategy, not just one among several.
3. Site-managed schools are likely to evolve over time and develop distinctive characters, goals, and operating styles.
4. A system of distinctive site-managed schools requires rethinking accountability.
5. The ultimate accountability mechanism for a system of distinctive site-managed schools is parental choice.

Systems moving toward site-based management need to have the support of school boards, teachers' unions, business and community leaders, and parents. "This involves a growing trend to grant increased decision-making power to the users of the education system (parents and students) and to its agents (teachers and headmasters)" ("Information and Decision Making," 1994, p. 1). Philadelphia, with help from several agencies, funded a school initiative to give local school sites greater autonomy to coordinate curriculum and instruction across disciplines and grades. Teachers working together was the key to revamping schools' organizational structures and to ongoing success of decentralized decision making. The conclusions from this largely successful experiment indicate that restructuring initiatives should be teacher-driven at local sites with external change agents and funding of necessary components in the initial phases (Useem, 1994). Giving teachers decision-making power makes a difference in teachers' perceptions of their daily lives and quality of their teaching. Other countries such as Russia are also experimenting with decentralization of educational systems and giving teachers more autonomy (Poppleton, Gershunsky, and Pullin, 1994, p. 323).

Although the power struggles continue, some parents are expressing their concern about the direction of the schools by withdrawing their children altogether and placing them in private schools. Some proposals for alternative structures of education have been realized in New York and elsewhere in the form of alternative and free schools. Charter schools (discussed in Chapters 3 and 11) have been springing up like mushrooms, but with their rapid growth have come many questions, court cases, and some failures. Parent and student input into decision making is built into these school structures. Critics such as Ivan Illich (1971, p. 154; National Center for Education Statistics, 1995, p. 160) have recommended total restructuring or "deschooling" of education, as we know it today, in order to change the locus of power. (These alternatives are discussed in Chapter 13, which is concerned with educational alternatives and movements.)

One thing is clear: The issues that fuel locus-of-control fires are still hot. The issue of school control concerns more than just the control of education; for minority groups, it reflects issues of control over life chances.

*A*pplying Sociology to Education: Considering local needs, national needs, teacher and student morale, and other relevant factors, where is centralization versus decentralization the best organizational model for schools? ◆

PROFESSIONALS IN THE EDUCATIONAL SYSTEM

Professionals are characterized by several factors: specialized competencies involving an intellectual component, strong commitment to a career based on a special competence, monopoly over service offered because of special competence, influence and responsibility in the use of that special competence, and a service orientation to clients. Certain occupations, such as law and medicine, fall clearly into the category of professions.

Because of professionals' commitment to fellow professionals in their area of expertise, and to their professional organizations, conflict can arise between the principles governing bureaucracies and those governing professionals. Thus, professionals often have a hard time adjusting to bureaucratic structures.

The school system presents a unique situation. Teachers—who make up the majority of staff members—are "marginal professionals," or what has been referred to as "semiprofessionals." They share this not-quite-professional status with nurses, social workers, and librarians, among others. These semiprofessions have some common characteristics: They involve nurturing, helping, and supporting. They also include a preponderance of females. For instance, in 1961, 69 percent of public elementary and secondary schoolteachers in the United States were female; in 1971, 66 percent; in 1981 and 1983, 67 percent; in 1991, 72 percent; and in 1996, 74.4 percent (*Digest*, 1999). Although more males are entering teaching each year, many are skimmed off for administration and move into positions of power. Even at secondary school levels, teaching has been characterized as a "feminine role," though there is more of a balance between male and female teachers.

Strong arguments have been made that only predominantly male occupations receive professional status and that predominantly female occupations have failed to reach this level because of a male political and economic elite that keeps job status and pay of teachers and other semiprofessionals down and leaves them little autonomy within the bureaucratic system.

Teachers have made claims for professional status in order to gain higher prestige and pay, but they have not yet developed the "teacher subculture" (unity as a group) to claim full professional status (Ingersoll, 2000). This difficulty stems from several factors related to the nature of teaching. First, teaching was not considered to be "regular" employment in this country until the mid-nineteenth century; it acquired serious occupational status with the advent of free, public education, and the founding, in 1857, of the professional organization, the National Teachers Association (now the National Education Association). Teachers are still employed by bureaucracies, however, under the direction of principals, superintendents, and boards of education; this they have generally not contested. Direction, then, comes from the bureaucracy rather than the professional organizations.

Another factor making professional status unclear is the question of membership. Professions have clear qualifications and boundaries for membership, whereas membership in the teaching occupation is much less clearly defined.

Professions have high prestige in occupational rankings. Teaching is not at the top, however. In data comparing 60 countries with the United States on occupational prestige rankings, high school teachers ranked 64 and 63.1 out of 90, respectively (Tremain, 1977). Secondary school teachers in the United States have an occupation prestige score of 66, the same as registerd nurses, the second of the two highest-ranked "female" occupations; and elementary school teachers have a score of 64 (*General Social Survey*, 1998). This indicates that occupational rankings in general have changed little since the 1920s, when data began to be collected. Nevertheless, teaching is still one of the higher-prestige occupations readily available to women.

Whereas most professions operate on a "fee-for-service" basis, teachers receive a salary in exchange for teaching students, and they are expected to prepare students for life after school. A further distinction is that professionals have expert training and a command of knowledge not generally possessed by lay persons, and they are scrutinized by colleagues, whereas teachers do not possess unique knowledge (though their skills are specialized) and are scrutinized and regulated by the bureaucracy and lay public. To put it bluntly, the knowledge and skills of professionals are seen as vital, but "no one ever died of a split infinitive" (Hannaway, 1993).

In bureaucratic settings, teachers must contend with close supervision, emphasis on rules, and centralization of decision making. These factors of standardization and centralization are alienating to those who want to be considered and treated as professionals. The desire for professional status and the frustration of trying to gain recognition, prestige, autonomy, and higher salaries in the bureaucratic setting has led to reform movements, militancy, and unionization of teachers, which are discussed in Chapter 6.

◆ Summary

In this chapter we have discussed the school as an organization, focusing on formal aspects of the internal functioning of schools. In our systems model, the organization represents the actual school or system being considered. For analytical purposes, the focus here is on the internal organization more than on the interaction of the organization with its environment. However, when discussing goals and centralized versus decentralized decision making, the influence of the environment cannot be ignored. The following outline summarizes major topics covered.

I. Social System of the School

The relation of the organization to the systems model is discussed, summarizing structural components of the system such as classrooms and positions of participants within the school.

II. Goals of the School System

School goals serve multiple purposes in helping define the system's activities. Goals are not the product of isolated educational systems but reflect the concerns of the larger society, the community, participants in the school, and individuals.

III. School Functions: The Purposes of the School

Societies have several manifest functions for schools that relate to perpetuation of society. Communities refine these functions to represent their particular needs. Because there are sometimes diverse needs within a community or society, agreement on goals may be difficult to reach and conflict may erupt. Goals also serve certain latent functions—functions that are not stated.

IV. The School as an Organization

Two models of school organization are discussed: bureaucracy and loosely coupled. Characteristics of bureaucracy as outlined by Max Weber are discussed:

1. Division of labor, recruitment, and promotion policies
2. Hierarchical system of authority
3. Rules, regulations, and procedures
4. Holders of similar positions being treated the same
5. Rationality of the organization

Problems in using a bureaucratic model in education settings are outlined, and the relationship between growth and bureaucracy is discussed. Loosely coupled organizations reflect activities and decisions that are made at one level, but not necessarily carried out at other levels. Because teachers have autonomy, this model may come close to fitting many schools.

V. Centralized versus Decentralized Decision Making: The Fight over Control of Schools

With the growth of schools has come more centralized decision making. However, challenges from local residents of huge bureaucratic systems have forced school officials to heed demands for greater local representation. One movement for decentralization is site-based management. Another is "choice," discussed in Chapters 3 and 11.

VI. Professionals in the Educational System

Professionals present unique challenges for organizations. The semiprofessional status of teaching, female–male composition of the occupation, and conflicts between teachers and the bureaucratic organization are discussed.

◆ *Putting Sociology to Work*

1. Visit a high school—the one you attended, if possible. In your field notes, indicate examples of Weber's characteristics of bureaucracies and decision-making patterns in the school and classroom.
2. Imagine you are from another culture; describe the school you visit as if you had no familiarity with it. Note the norms (rules, behavior patterns, communication patterns, and so forth) and functioning of the organization.
3. What are your most memorable school experiences? How do they relate to the material in this chapter? (For example, what were your positions in the structure?)
4. Compare your goals for high school when you were a student with your goals for high schools now. What were your goals for college while in high school? Have they changed?

CHAPTER 6

Formal School Statuses and Roles

"The Way It Spozed to Be"

For each of us there is a degree of discontinuity in the status we hold. We have a high status in one social setting—parent, oldest sibling, supervisor over other workers, president of a club—and low status in other social settings—patient, student, low-guy-on-the-totem-pole at the neighborhood gym.

THE MEANING OF ROLES

Try to recall your experience as a student in elementary and high school. Not only did your status and role change as you progressed through the system, but in some classroom situations your status was higher than in others. Perhaps you won the English composition competition but were unskilled in math; you may have been the fastest runner on the playground but could not spell "whether."

Status and Roles in the System

This section on status and role structure in the organization is a continuation of our discussion of the internal organizational structure of the educational system (Figure 6–1). Every organization is made up of an interrelated set of statuses

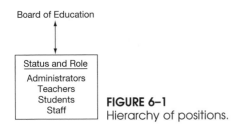

FIGURE 6–1
Hierarchy of positions.

or positions that members of the system occupy. They are needed to perform duties and meet the goals of the system. Implicit in each position is a set of responsibilities or parts to be played that the individual holding the position is expected to perform; these activities make up the role. Sometimes the specific requirements of the position are written out; these represent the ideal for that position. Sometimes positions are only roughly defined, allowing considerable room to determine one's own role behavior. Often, there is a great deal of flexibility in role performance, especially as one moves up in the hierarchy and gains seniority. All individuals bring their own experiences and personalities into the position. Principal A is not identical to principal B, although the job descriptions may be the same.

Role expectations held by those outside the role affect the selection of persons for particular positions. Choices may reflect prevailing stereotypes or norms, such as those that encourage selecting women for elementary-level teaching positions or males for administrative positions.

The School Organization and Roles

The organizational settings in which we play our roles define and limit the ways we behave. For example, David Rogers (1969, p. 272) describes the types of pressures toward centralization in the New York City system: "to guarantee uniform standards across the city, to preserve professional autonomy from outside political interference at the local level, to prevent ethnic separation, and to maintain headquarters control over field officials." As a result of such organizational trends, decision making and autonomy in carrying out one's role are affected. "Most decisions on such matters as curriculum, staffing, budgeting, supplies, construction, and maintenance are made by professionals at central headquarters, several layers removed from the schools themselves" (p. 271).

Centralization is but one organizational factor that affects role performance. Among the other factors are rules, especially rigid ones that work against what teachers, parents, and students believe is important. Teachers in autonomous classrooms, however, have a great deal of flexibility in how to implement programs and the curriculum.

Role Expectations and Conflict

Schools function smoothly when people agree on role expectations; however, when they disagree, conflicts arise. A key problem here is that the goals of education are often ambiguous, even contradictory, and not universally shared; this causes confusion in role expectations.

In Chapter 5 we discussed conflicting goals held by various members of the educational system. Role expectations also vary depending on one's position in the organization. Role conflict occurs for individuals when their own role expectations are in conflict with expectations of others or cannot be met—for instance, when students must study for exams and carry out family responsibilities; or when one's expectations are in conflict with those of other members of the system—for instance, when teachers differ with parents over course content or discipline techniques. This may happen when definitions of the position and the function the position plays toward meeting system goals differ among members of the organization.

Perspectives on Roles

How roles should be viewed is debatable. From the functionalist perspective, role expectations as defined by the organization should benefit all by helping to maintain the system. If individuals carry out their roles, the organization functions smoothly. Teachers fill the expectations of their job contract and position description. However, this is not always simple. From the conflict perspective, roles held by some should put them in advantageous positions for obtaining the scarce resources of society, such as prestige and salary. The more authority there is in a role, the greater the possibility of conflict between that role and roles of those with less authority. For instance, persons in the teacher role have the authority to dominate those in the student role. Conflict theorists might argue that this domination is achieved in subtle ways through the socialization process, which forces students into a subordinate role. Each theoretical approach is useful for analysis and explanation of some situations. In this chapter we focus on the ideal-typical role types of employees in the school; while recognizing that there is great variation in role expectation and performance, depending on the position held in the system and the theoretical approach one uses.

*A*pplying Sociology to Education: Describe some reciprocal roles you hold in the educational system. ◆

ROLES IN SCHOOLS

Roles locate us in relation to others who hold reciprocal positions, for no role exists in a vacuum. Following the role hierarchy, we can now look at the role responsibilities of each of these position-holders and evaluate their relationship to one another.

School Boards: Liaison Between School and Community

It was an exciting meeting! Half the town turned out to express views and hear discussion on the issue of a sex education course in the local middle school. The seventh graders were being shown anatomy videos and contraceptives, and a large group of parents disapproved, arguing that these matters should be dealt with in the home. Other parents took the position that teenagers need all the information they can get, especially with the rising rate of teenage pregnancy. Because the topic is not dealt with in many homes, they felt schools should cover it. Such a situation is typical of the conflicting pressures facing school boards around the country.

Role of the Local School Board. Theoretically, local school boards have a tremendous amount of power awarded to them by the state. This power stems from the tradition in our country of democratic lay control over schools. This group of individuals may be known as a board of regents, a board of education, a board of trustees, a board of directors, or a school board. Whatever the label, nearly every school at every level, public or private, has its board.

The National School Boards Association compiled the following list of formal duties representing the legal role of school boards:

1. Hiring superintendent, principals, and teachers
2. Determining teachers' salaries and contracts
3. Providing transportation for students
4. Determining the size of the school budgets
5. Deciding the length of the school term
6. Building new schools and facilities
7. Changing school attendance boundaries
8. Selecting textbooks and subjects to be taught
9. Maintaining school discipline

In reality, once the board has selected the superintendent, it generally exerts little control over the administration or teaching but concerns itself with school policy matters.

State boards of education, often appointed by state governors and subject to the approval of legislators, oversee state standards and district policies, especially where state monies are concerned. In recent cases of bankruptcy of large school districts, state boards of education have played major roles devising new financing plans. Although decisions over curriculum are primarily a local matter, states may wield considerable influence in decisions on expenditures and methods for financing schools.

Elected Versus Appointed School Boards. In the United States, each state's laws determine how board members are selected and delegates certain powers to local school boards. Virginia had been the only state that required appointed school boards; 19 states now allow elected or appointed school boards depending on the local preference, and the rest require elected boards (Underwood, 1992). Neo-Marxists Samuel Bowles and Herbert Gintis argue that schools serve the interests of those who dominate the economy in a capitalist system (Bowles and Gintis, 1976). Appointed school board members are more likely than elected members to represent bourgeois interests of those in power, and the potential for conflict with other community interest groups is great.

The New York City Board of Education was a case in point: The appointed board was not very responsive to external political pressures from community groups. Today, in New York City, largely thanks to community pressure groups that demanded control of schools, there are local community boards *elected* by their districts under a system of decentralization. In Massachusetts the governor signed into law a bill that allows Boston's mayor to appoint a seven-member panel (Freeman, Underwood, and Fortune, 1991).

Composition and Expectations of School Boards. Boards are composed predominantly of married, white, professional males with graduate degrees; 41 to 50 years of age; and with children in school. Females make up 33.8 percent of board members nationally; African Americans, 4.6 percent; and Hispanics, 1.4 percent.

Many conflict theorists argue that this means that minority views are not represented or influential in decision making. Not all agree. Members of the community likely to serve on the volunteer school boards generally have a genuine interest in the educational system and represent a cross-section of community interests, yet they usually have little orientation or training for their job.

Community members have certain expectations of school board members. Although these may differ depending on the individual's position in the community structure, six role expectations stand out: promote public interest in education; defend community values; hear complaints and grievances; supervise school personnel; conserve resources; and promote individual rights and interests within the school.

When the priorities of school board members and the public are compared, the discrepancies represent the boards' concerns with managerial problems and different community and parent concerns. In fact, the gap between views of the public and board members is wide on a number of issues; asked whether the schools are doing a good job, 71 percent of urban board members said yes, and only 37 percent of urban adults agreed. Although 82 percent of urban board members said their districts were effective at keeping violence and drugs out of schools, only 33 percent of urban adults agreed (National School Board Foundation, 1999). Boards also influence how school funds are spent. Note the thoughts of a school board member recounted in Box 6–1.

Factors Affecting Board Decisions. The most troublesome issues facing board members are state mandates and money issues; for example, funds may be needed to renovate facilities. Boards may become mired in controversial issues that prevent them from dealing with long-term planning and policy issues.

Boards are limited in their effectiveness and influence in part because they are caught in the middle between the demands of electors or appointers and the needs of the school. As revealed in the example concerning sex education at the beginning of the section, some issues faced by school boards are specific, perhaps isolated, concerns, causing brief episodes of conflict. Most of the board's decision making, however, is routine, and interactions are primarily with the PTA, administration, and teachers. School boards cannot be expected to command the knowledge of the professional educators—superintendents, principals, and teachers—and this fact alone limits their decision-making capabilities and control. In fact, boards often rely on the knowledge and expertise of professional educators when making decisions. Some educational analysts feel boards have too much power, considering the limitations on their roles, and propose a more limited role for local school boards; one suggestion is for states to take on more responsibility for local decisions (Education Commission of the States, Draft Report, 1999).

School boards have reciprocal relationships with other role-holders in the system. The most direct link is through the superintendent they hire. This relationship has been compared to a marriage, and for the most part the partnership is a happy one, with board members supportive of superintendents. However, breaks do occur, primarily because of loss of confidence and faith, or evidence of mismanagement of finances.

This interdependence between roles also affects decision making. Boards receive carefully selected information on issues from teachers and administrators; some issues may be filtered out and never reach the board. Effective superintendents have developed good communication and trust, and they possess knowledge that no board member can fully master; by controlling information, superintendents have great influence over board decisions.

Applying Sociology to Education: How is the school board selected in your community, and what segments of the community are represented? ◆

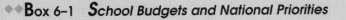

◆◆Box 6–1   *School Budgets and National Priorities*

[I have] the budget report for next year. The bottom line: approximately a million in the red. Just about the cost of one of those Patriot missiles, I reflect. Calculating quickly, I realize that every time one of them exploded, we blew away, in effect, another 43 school teaching positions or another 1,500 classroom computers or another 25 or 30 college educations.

Somehow I find myself wondering what I'd say if I had Secretary of Defense Dick Cheney's ear for a few minutes to present a school board member's ideal budget. Here's the list I come up with—just for our 8,300-student, K–12 district:

◆ Merge interactive video learning technologies with computer labs in our 16 schools: $120,000.

◆ Install fully equipped science labs in all 16 high schools: $70,000.

◆ Hire 40 counselors to track, monitor, and advise every child, K–12: $1.25 million.

◆ Set up a central computer program for tracking every child, K–12, so kids can't fall through the cracks: $200,000.

◆ Build a new school to eliminate overcrowding: $5 million.

◆ Offer every hungry kid a hot breakfast and lunch: $100,000.

◆ Provide after-school tutoring: $45,000.

◆ Reduce class sizes by hiring 50 new teachers: $1.5 million.

◆ Give every teacher a $1,000 tuition grant for professional development: $530,000.

◆ Grant sabbaticals to prevent burnout and ensure teacher renewal: $1.9 million.

◆ Expand travel budgets so half of our teachers can attend two professional conferences: $530,000.

"Mr. Secretary," I would say, "this comes to a grand total of $11.2 million. If I have my figures right, sir, this is approximately 1/47th the cost of just one Stealth bomber."

But reality, of course, comes crashing back.

Source: Nolen, Donald M., "Smart Bombs or Smart People?" *The American School Board Journal,* September 1991, p. 52.

Superintendent: Manager of the School System

The office was large. A long table covered with computer printouts and charts took up one side of the room, and a rather large desk faced by two easy chairs stood on the other side. Books on administration matters, teaching, and curriculum were shelved around the walls. As I entered, the superintendent jumped up, looking relieved to take his eyes off the figures for a few minutes and discuss his role. The responsibilities of a superintendent of a small school district include a large number of routine roles: issuing budget reports; engaging in staff negotiations; answering mail and phone calls; meeting with principals, staff, and others; carrying out routine "blessings" on projects; giving symbolic gestures of support and approval; preparing reports for the board, the state, and the federal government; keeping up with new regulations; responding to questions; making staff recommendations. These tasks take up the bulk of time. If time remains, matters such as long-term planning and curriculum evaluation can be considered.

Crises interrupt the normal flow of work, making it difficult to plan a firm schedule. An unexpected shortage of heating fuel, for example, can make it suddenly necessary to arrange for double sessions. Successful superintendents juggle their various constituencies—community groups, the school board, principals, teachers, and staff—with skill. In large districts the responsibilities of the role may be divided between several assistant superintendents, each of whom specializes in an aspect of the role such as curriculum, public relations, and staffing.

Superintendents are usually white males, mostly in midcareer. Of the nation's superintendents, 88 percent are men, though two-thirds of public school teachers are women (Vail, 1999). Why is this the case? Some explanations have been put forth, though few studies have been done; the superintendency is a "hot seat" offering little security; if women appear to be too authoritarian in their decision making, they risk censure; yet that is what the position requires, according to some experts (Vail, 1999).

Large urban school districts are finding it increasingly difficult to attract superintendent candidates. Why? Some reasons include problems with hostile boards, shabby treatment, negative publicity, graft and corruption, conflicting expectations, and rigid requirements for the job.

The Advent of Administration. Until the late nineteenth century, boards were responsible for running the schools. With smaller districts and fewer compulsory years of schooling, this was possible. As school systems became increasingly large and complex, a force of trained, full-time professionals took over the day-to-day running of the schools; school boards relied on these hired agents, delegating significant power to them.

The number and specialization of administrators depends largely on the size and complexity of the system. Small districts may have one superintendent who is a generalist, as in the preceding example; large districts need specialized managerial expertise in such areas as business, legal matters, personnel, public relations, and data-processing operations.

Today administrative structures vary directly with the size of the system. The hierarchical design of the huge New York City system is shown in Figure 6–2 (NYC Board of Education, 2000). It is difficult to give a single description of the responsibilities of an administrator in such a complex system.

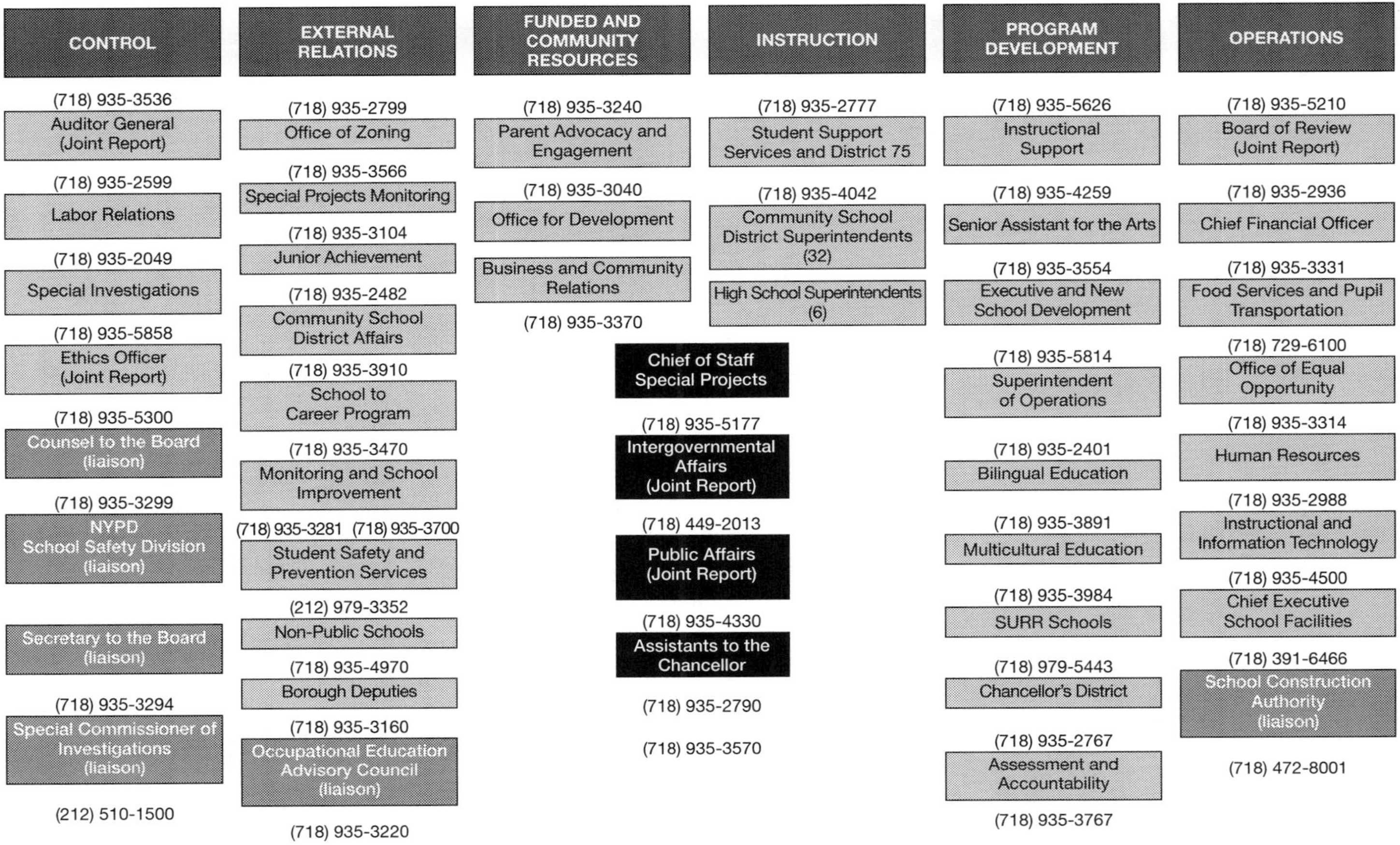

CONTROL

- (718) 935-3536 — Auditor General (Joint Report)
- (718) 935-2599 — Labor Relations
- (718) 935-2049 — Special Investigations
- (718) 935-5858 — Ethics Officer (Joint Report)
- (718) 935-5300 — Counsel to the Board (liaison)
- (718) 935-3299 — NYPD School Safety Division (liaison)
- Secretary to the Board (liaison)
- (718) 935-3294 — Borough Deputies
- Special Commissioner of Investigations (liaison)
- (212) 510-1500

EXTERNAL RELATIONS

- (718) 935-2799 — Office of Zoning
- (718) 935-3566 — Special Projects Monitoring
- (718) 935-3104 — Junior Achievement
- (718) 935-2482 — Community School District Affairs
- (718) 935-3910 — School to Career Program
- (718) 935-3470 — Monitoring and School Improvement
- (718) 935-3281 (718) 935-3700 — Student Safety and Prevention Services
- (212) 979-3352 — Non-Public Schools
- (718) 935-4970
- (718) 935-3160 — Occupational Education Advisory Council (liaison)
- (718) 935-3220

FUNDED AND COMMUNITY RESOURCES

- (718) 935-3240 — Parent Advocacy and Engagement
- (718) 935-3040 — Office for Development
- Business and Community Relations
- (718) 935-3370

INSTRUCTION

- (718) 935-2777 — Student Support Services and District 75
- (718) 935-4042 — Community School District Superintendents (32)
- High School Superintendents (6)

Chief of Staff Special Projects

- (718) 935-5177 — Intergovernmental Affairs (Joint Report)
- (718) 449-2013 — Public Affairs (Joint Report)
- (718) 935-4330 — Assistants to the Chancellor
- (718) 935-2790
- (718) 935-3570

PROGRAM DEVELOPMENT

- (718) 935-5626 — Instructional Support
- (718) 935-4259 — Senior Assistant for the Arts
- (718) 935-3554 — Executive and New School Development
- (718) 935-5814 — Superintendent of Operations
- (718) 935-2401 — Bilingual Education
- (718) 935-3891 — Multicultural Education
- (718) 935-3984 — SURR Schools
- (718) 979-5443 — Chancellor's District
- (718) 935-2767 — Assessment and Accountability
- (718) 935-3767

OPERATIONS

- (718) 935-5210 — Board of Review (Joint Report)
- (718) 935-2936 — Chief Financial Officer
- (718) 935-3331 — Food Services and Pupil Transportation
- (718) 729-6100 — Office of Equal Opportunity
- (718) 935-3314 — Human Resources
- (718) 935-2988 — Instructional and Information Technology
- (718) 935-4500 — Chief Executive School Facilities
- (718) 391-6466 — School Construction Authority (liaison)
- (718) 472-8001

FIGURE 6-2 New York City board of education, 2000.

165

Power of the Superintendent. The actual power of the superintendent to make decisions for the system is related to such diverse factors as the type of community in which the position is held; the school board; baby booms, which cause expanding student populations; teacher strikes; demands by teachers, students, and community for more power and autonomy in decision making; federal guidelines and control; and court orders.

In attempts to exercise power, the superintendent may be faced with conflicting demands from the school board, teachers, and other constituencies. For example, pressures may be brought to bear on superintendents to cut costs radically at the same time that the teachers are demanding higher salaries.

Often the outcome of power conflicts depends on the superintendent's style. Being politically suave in dealing with the board and the public and using expertise to its greatest advantage puts the superintendent in a powerful position. As Willard Waller suggested early in the history of sociology of education in the United States:

> [W]e must conclude that it is a difference in [superintendents'] personal techniques which accounts for this [ability to deal with the school board] . . . that ability to dominate a school board pleasantly is a greater factor in determining personal advancement in this walk of life than the ability to administer a school system of students and teachers. (Waller, [1932] 1961, p. 94)

Regardless of the distribution and degree of power, the role of superintendent has become a firmly established and essential part of most districts.

The Principal: School Boss-in-the-Middle

Principals are managers and coordinators. Their roles include supporting teachers, disciplining students, counseling students and teachers, managing the budget, scheduling classes, and handling the myriad problems that arise each day in the school.

Role of the Principal. A careful look at the roles of the principal shows that most, by definition, involve interaction with other individuals—teachers, superintendents, parents, and students. Principals have more direct contact with the public than do superintendents. They hold a position in the middle, and the interests presented them are often conflicting. They are the bosses of their schools, and as such they must make recommendations on the hiring and firing of teachers and give moral support to their teachers. Handling such potentially conflicting responsibilities is not easy. Many variables affect the role and expectations of a principal—size of the school and district, a rural or big-city location, and the social class background of the children attending the school.

Principals must deal with professionals and technical experts in education, parents and community members, superintendents, and students.

Research on effective schools stresses the importance of the principal (or designated leader) as instructional leader in creating the school culture to support strong academics and achievement (Brookover, 1996). If the principal receives support from the teaching staff, planned change is more likely to occur (Deal and Peterson, 1993).

Principals can exert control over the teaching staff by rewarding cooperative teachers and causing less desirable situations for less cooperative ones through such mechanisms as classroom placements, assignments of unruly students, and undesirable scheduling. The principal's expectations of teachers strongly influence their morale, performance, and self-concept; teachers indicate that they are more satisfied with principals who make clear what is expected and reward good work. Nevertheless, teachers claim professional status and the need for autonomy. They expect the principal to stand up for them in situations where their authority is challenged, and they sometimes use their collective power to make this clear to the principal (Becker, 1973), as in cases where grievances are filed or strikes occur.

When we hear little from the principals' offices, things are probably going smoothly. They are busy managing their schools; facilitating the processes taking place; dealing with daily, routine, teacher needs, and student concerns; and maintaining good relationships with groups outside the school. Principals report that their priorities are shaped by results on measures of school effectiveness such as standardized tests, efforts to ensure school safety, developing good teachers, maintaining effective community relations, and creating a sense of shared purpose within the school (Genzen, 2000; Lyons, 1999; Smith, 1999).

School administrators spend part of each day dealing with the unexpected; this includes disasters such as bus accidents, suicides or murders, bomb threats or weapons in the school; and natural disasters such as tornadoes. Here is a description of a typical day from a small-town elementary school principal:

> My day starts before the school opens. I check to make sure the building is in order and teachers in place. When possible, I like to be in the halls to greet students as they come in; seeing them gives me a lift.
>
> Many of my interactions with teachers take place in the halls where we exchange a few words about an issue or problems. Most problems for teachers can be solved in this way. Of course, we have team leaders' meetings too.
>
> Only severe discipline problems come to me. Most are handled in the classroom. But if students are damaging property or endangering other children or fighting, then I see them.
>
> There are always the routine things to do—reports, curriculum matters, budgeting, and so forth. But when a parent comes in, I drop everything, if possible, to see that parent.
>
> I think some people feel we sit behind a desk and shuffle papers, but that's only the tip of the iceberg. I have a daily plan, but more often than not things come up which need immediate intervention. (Interview with elementary school principal by the author)

The principals of middle schools or junior high schools face a different type of situation than elementary school principals. Students in the junior high age group have been described as a "jumble of hormones." They are trying to "get it all together," and each child copes in a different way. Discipline may become more of an issue at this level, and children may be less manageable within the classroom, thus involving the principal and assistant principal more often.

High school principals have the additional role of preparing students for the transition to college and the work world. High school principals and school districts are being held accountable for the students they pass from grade to grade and graduate. Several legal suits have been brought against school systems on the grounds that they graduate students who cannot read or write at a twelfth-grade or even tenth-grade level. Competency testing of students and testing of new teachers is also being carried out in some states and school districts. These issues are discussed further in Chapter 13. Being both effective managers and instructional leaders is difficult, and some suggest that these tasks should not fall to the same person.

Many persons in the school system play roles complementary to that of the principal, including teachers, supervisors, and the like. Principals cannot perform their own roles without giving some consideration to how their performance might affect or infringe on the roles of others. In essence, then, these others play an important part in the definition and delineation of the principal's roles.

In some schools, issues of safety are paramount. In 1998, 44 percent of students indicated that they always feel safe in school compared to 37 percent in 1999 (Horatio Alger Association, 1999). Students who do not feel safe at school indicate that it is usually because of threats from bullies and weapons (McEvoy, 1992). Others, including large percentages of African American and Hispanic students, report fear of being attacked at school or when going to and from school, usually by street gangs (U.S. Department of Justice, 1998). *When Disaster Strikes* recommends having a plan in place to deal with safety issues and tragedies. Using knowledge from the social sciences to deal with problems, knowing what to expect in the way of reactions and grief, and having the mechanisms in place are important steps a principal can take to prevent damage (McEvoy, 1992).

Surprisingly, there have been few studies of the principal, but those that have been done provide us with information on the characteristics of principals. Table 6–1 presents the results of one study.

Though women dominate the field of education as teachers, female administrators are few in number; in 1994, women held 36 percent (79,618) of principal positions in public schools. Women, however, held a majority (54 percent) of principal positions in private schools (13,410) (National Center for Education Statistics, *Digest*, 1999). Women bring different leadership, communication, and decision-making styles and skills to school leadership (Gross and

TABLE 6–1 Principals in Public Schools

Selected Characteristics	Total[a]	Percent of Principals, by Highest Degree Earned[b]				Average Years of Experience		
		Bachelor's	Master's	Education Specialist	Doctor's and First Professional	As a Principal	Other School Position	As a Teacher
Sex								
Men	58,585	1.9	55.7	34.3	8.2	11.2	3.6	9.0
Women	19,118	3.9	46.6	37.8	11.3	6.1	4.0	12.3
Race/Ethnicity								
White[c]	69,048	2.5	53.7	35.0	8.6	10.1	3.6	9.6
Black[c]	6,696	(e)	51.4	36.9	11.5	8.8	4.8	11.8
Hispanic[d]	2,483	(e)	54.2	30.2	(e)	6.6	5.4	9.8
Asian or Pacific Islander	434	(e)	52.8	33.4	(e)	7.7	4.5	10.8
American Indian or Alaskan native[c]	821	(e)	51.2	(e)	(e)	9.9	4.6	9.1
Age								
Under 40	14,430	3.6	54.7	33.7	(e)	4.3	2.5	7.8
40 to 44	17,755	2.0	49.0	39.7	9.2	6.8	3.7	9.2
45 to 49	16,408	0.0	52.8	35.8	9.6	10.0	4.0	10.3
50 to 54	14,936	2.2	56.6	33.2	7.9	13.2	4.3	10.6
55 or over	13,891	2.7	55.9	31.7	9.6	16.5	4.1	11.4
Total	**77,890**	**2.4**	**53.4**	**35.1**	**8.9**	**10.0**	**3.8**	**9.8**

Note. Details may not add to 100 percent because of rounding and survey item nonresponse.
[a]Total differs from data appearing in other tables because of varying survey processing procedures and time period coverages.
[b]Percentages for those with less than a bachelor's degree are not shown.
[c]Includes persons of Hispanic origin.
[d]Persons of Hispanic origin may be of any race.
[e]Too few sample cases (fewer than 30) for a reliable estimate.

Source: National Center for Education Statistics; reprinted in *Education Week,* February 5, 1992. p 7.

Trask, 1991). They spend more time on instructional leadership activities such as "interacting with teachers as a resource provider, instructional resource, communicator, and visible presence" (Andrews and Basom, 1990, p. 38). The instructional leadership style is compatible with the characteristics of effective leadership behavior in schools:

◆ Emphasize achievement and convey to teachers their commitment to fostering academic success

◆ Set instructional strategies and accept responsibility for facilitating their accomplishment

◆ Provide an orderly atmosphere and ensure that the school's climate is conducive to learning

◆ Frequently evaluate student progress in light of performance expectations

◆ Coordinate instructional programs consistent with the overall goals of the program and the school

◆ Support teachers with regard to staff development (Shakeshaft, 1986)

The Principal's Power and Effect on Change in the School. Principals and other administrators have power to influence school effectiveness through their leadership and interactions. In successful schools, principals meet with teachers regularly, ask for suggestions regarding curriculum, and give teachers information concerning effectiveness (Brookover, Erickson, and McEvoy, 1996). Those concerned with effective schools argue that principals should spend the majority of their time improving instruction, but this seldom happens because of the many responsibilities of principals.

Teachers' primary responsibility is in the classroom; they feel less successful in their efforts at schoolwide decision making, which intensifies teachers' autonomous "culture of teaching" and acts as an obstacle to change and innovation proposed by principals (Hargreaves, 1984).

Although the principal has the power to run the school, he or she is also constrained by the environment: the superintendent and board, teachers' unions, student demands, and state and local regulations. Principals are involved in decision making in many areas but share the responsibility with those holding reciprocal roles.

*A*pplying Sociology to Education: What are some conflicting roles held by principals? ◆

Teachers: The Front Line

Looking back at our school days, the persons we remember most fondly or with the greatest dislike are teachers. Occasionally a principal makes an imprint in our memory, or a counselor influences our decisions. But the teacher is the one with whom we have the most contact, and his or her classroom is where we lay ourselves open for scrutiny, praise, and criticism. Often not even our parents spend as much time with us and understand our capabilities as well as our teachers do.

Why Teachers Teach. Why do teachers choose to become teachers? Most teachers indicated one or more of the following reasons: the desire to work with young people and impart knowledge; love of children; desire to do something valuable for society and make a difference; the challenges and responsibilities of teaching; interest and excitement about teaching and subject-matter field; security and financial rewards; and fulfilling a dream (Phillips and Hatch, 1999).

Characteristics of Teachers. Approximately 2,164,000 Americans are employed as professional educators in American primary and secondary schools. Some characteristics of teachers are outlined in Table 6–2 (National Education Association, 1997). Of elementary and secondary teachers, 90.7 percent are white, 7.3 percent African American, with 9 percent total minority teachers, a drop from 13.7 percent in 1991 (National Education Association, 1997). The average teacher in 1997 earned $36,498 per year, with beginning teachers earning $24,641 (National Center for Education Statistics, 1997). Median salaries have increased, in part because of more teaching experience, from an average of 12 years in 1981 to 15 years in 1996 (National Education Association, 1997). An individual writing "teacher" in the occupation blank on a form would generally fall into the category "middle class." Teaching is believed by many to be an easy route to upward mobility from lower classes; not only is the cost of training for this profession lower than for many others, but the occupation is a familiar one. We all "understand" teachers.

In the 1960s there was a shortage of teachers brought about by the rapid increase in the number of school-age children from the baby boom. As the 1970s came to an end, however, more than 600,000 teachers were labeled "surplus" and most could not find jobs. The predicted job market low passed in 1983, and the situation for teachers has improved. By 2007, the number of classroom teachers is expected to increase to 3.17 million, an increase from 3.04 million in 1997 and 2.51 in 1984 (National Center for Education Statistics, 1999). The average number of students in public school elementary classrooms has decreased from 29 in 1961 to 24 in 1996, in part because more teachers teach smaller classes of special education, compensatory education, and bilingual education.

Not all agree that the job shortage will ease, pointing out the reservoir of unemployed teachers certified during the slump; the increase in applicants to teachers' colleges; and the rising salaries of starting teachers, which will attract some professionals from other fields. Supply and demand forces, it is argued, will balance the equation. One of the most difficult tasks for school

TABLE 6-2 Public Elementary and Secondary School Teachers—Selected Characteristics, 1990–1991[a]

Characteristic	Unit	Age				Sex		Race/Ethnicity			Level of Control	
		Under 30	30–39	40–49	Over 50	Male	Female	White[b]	Black[b]	His-panic	Elemen-tary	Sec-ondary
Total Teachers[c]	1,000	312	732	1,003	514	720	1,842	2,216	212	87	1,298	1,264
Highest degree held:												
Bachelor's	Percent	84.1	56.4	43.8	41.6	44.7	54.7	51.5	50.8	61.0	56.7	46.9
Master's	Percent	14.4	39.1	48.8	49.9	47.0	40.1	42.7	42.1	32.9	38.7	45.5
Education specialist	Percent	1.2	3.4	5.9	5.9	5.3	4.3	4.5	5.0	4.3	4.1	5.2
Doctorate	Percent	—*	0.4	1.0	1.4	1.3	0.6	0.7	1.3	0.9	0.4	1.2
Full-time teaching experience:												
Less than 3 years	Percent	40.0	8.4	3.0	1.3	7.1	9.3	8.7	5.9	13.0	9.4	8.0
3–9 years	Percent	59.8	37.1	14.5	6.1	18.9	27.1	25.0	19.0	31.8	26.2	23.3
10–20 years	Percent	0.2	54.4	49.8	24.8	37.6	41.0	40.0	41.7	41.4	40.3	39.8
20 years or more	Percent	NA	0.13	2.7	67.8	36.5	22.5	26.4	33.6	13.8	24.1	28.9
Full-time teachers	1,000	283	650	925	481	666	1,273	2,015	199	81	1,170	1,169
Earned income (dollars)		24,892	30,126	36,095	38,642	37,895	31,897	33,631	33,666	32,960	31,972	35,241
Salary (dollars)		22,754	27,934	33,702	36,361	33,383	30,501	31,313	31,707	30,774	30,611	32,034

Supplemental contract during school year:												
Teachers receiving	1,000	121	231	313	122	353	434	701	49	25	238	549
Salary (dollars)		1,675	2,045	1,914	2,088	2,663	1,357	1,977	1,664	1,709	1,172	2,276
Supplemental contract during summer:												
Teachers receiving	1,000	56	118	169	65	164	244	334	46	19	167	241
Salary (dollars)		1,608	1,952	2,003	2,284	2,309	1,763	1,919	2,272	2,360	1,803	2,104
Teachers with nonschool employment:												
Teaching/tutoring	1,000	13	30	47	20	39	70	95	8	5	41	69
Education related	1,000	9	18	28	12	31	36	59	5	2	23	44
Not education related	1,000	32	63	91	42	130	99	203	16	5	52	147

[a]For school year. Based on survey and subject to sampling error; for details, see source.
[b]Non-Hispanic.
[c]Includes teachers with no degrees and associates degrees, not shown separately.
*—represents or rounds to zero.
NA = Not applicable.

Source: National Center for Education Statistics, Digest of Education Statistics, 1993.

Formal rules and regulations guide the behavior of students and teachers.

administrators is to predict the population fluctuations in their districts and prepare for them by having an appropriate number of classrooms and teachers.

At one time, teaching was one of the few career paths accessible to highly qualified women and minorities. In 1972, 37 percent of women college graduates were headed for teaching; by 1995, that number was only 14 percent (National Center for Education Statistics, 1995). Nine percent of all college graduates majored in education; yet the number of women in that 9 percent is still high, 75.8 percent. Asked if they would select teaching as a profession again, 32 percent said definitely and 31 percent said probably, 20 percent said probably or certainly not (National Education Association, 1997).

It is no secret that there is a heavy preponderance of women in teaching's lower levels—both grade level and professional rank. This fact has not been overlooked by researchers or feminists. In elementary schools, 85 percent of teachers are female and 15 percent are male. In high schools, 46 percent of teachers are male and 54 percent female. Between 80 and 90 percent of primary school teachers have been female since the early 1900s. The figure for secondary school female teachers has fluctuated from 47 to 65 percent in the same period. Overall, about 74.4 percent of all public school teachers were female in 1996 (National Center for Education Statistics, *Digest*, 1999, p. 80). Males predominate as school administrators and superintendents.

Women who do move into administration do so slowly, spending many more years in the classroom than men. There appear to be two overlapping reasons for this imbalance: convenience and discrimination. For women, teaching has been more available and acceptable than other professions; the accessibility of education is greater than in many other fields; time and cost of getting a degree are less in education than in some other fields; the hours, vacations, and schedule are compatible with home and children; the job can be pursued in many locations; and for many, the "nurturing" experience coincides with life experiences (Tannen, 1991). Discrimination is a factor in the imbalance because many other career paths are closed to women at the training or entrance level. Men have a greater variety of career opportunities available; many male teachers make the teaching career decision after realizing that other goals are unattainable. Yet as more jobs become available, fewer highly qualified women and minorities choose education.

Of public school teachers, more than 90 percent return to teach the following year. Of those who do not, the most common reason is retirement, followed by pursuit of another career, pregnancy and child-rearing, and other family or personal issues. Fewer leave because of dissatisfaction (National Center for Education Statistics, "Schools and Staffing Survey," 1993–94).

Teachers' career cycles typically follow three stages: survival in the new setting and discovery of new challenges; stabilization through the middle years; and *disengagement* from their strong investment in teaching as their careers come to an end. Teachers' commitment differs depending on the career stage, with midcareer teachers having lower commitment to their jobs (Rosenholtz and Simpson 1990).

Today, the median age of teachers is 44, up from 37 in 1981 (National Education Association, 1997). There are certainly advantages to having a high concentration of older teachers. They have much teaching experience and consider themselves professionals. Collectively, they belong to more professional organizations and have more ties in the community than younger teachers. But there are disadvantages, too: Some tenured teachers are not competent, but they must be kept on; older teachers are more expensive to the system; their presence prevents younger teachers from filling a percentage of the teacher slots. Young teachers bring new teaching ideas and new developments in the discipline to their first jobs, helping to keep older colleagues in touch with their fields. Thus, a two-way socialization takes place between older and younger teachers.

Are we asking too much of our teachers? Consider the following hypothetical advertisement characterizing the role expectations for teachers:

Wanted

College graduate with academic major (master's degree preferred). Excellent communication/leadership skills required. Challenging opportunity to serve 150 clients daily on a tight schedule, developing up to five different products each day to meet individual needs, while adhering to multiple product specifications. Adaptability helpful, as suppliers cannot always deliver goods on time, incumbent must arrange for own support services, and customers rarely know what they want. Ideal candidate will enjoy working in isolation from colleagues. This diversified position allows employees to exercise typing, clerical, law enforcement, and social work skills between assignments and after hours. Typical workweek: 50 hours. Special nature of the work precludes amenities such as telephones or computers, but work has many intrinsic awards. Starting salary $24,661, rising to $36,495 after only 15 years. ("What Matters Most," 1996, p. 54)

Role Expectations for Teachers. Teachers are primary socializers of children; that is, they play an important role in teaching the child how to be a member of society. The primary reciprocal role for the teacher is that with the student (Brophy and Good, 1974). It is an involuntary relationship for both. The teacher holds power and has several means of exerting it: adult authority, grades, punishments such as detention or humiliation—and also affective behavior, praise, reinforcement, and personal contact. The question of how to socialize young people most effectively in the schools is, according to some, the most pressing issue schools face. Though parents and principals may be in the background making curricular and instructional decisions (Apple, 1988), "the final responsibility for delivery of an effective school learning climate rests with teachers" (Brookover et al., 1996, p. 101).

Teachers are expected to teach children the three Rs, manage and facilitate classrooms, provide an atmosphere conducive to maximum learning, and in general be gatekeepers who control the flow of activity and students. As socializers, teachers are in very visible roles and are expected to set good moral examples for students. Yet what is defined as "good" is often controversial. For example, some court cases challenge teachers' negative influence on their students because of their dress, appearance, alcohol or drug charges outside of school, sexual orientation, or unseemly behavior with students.

Whether or not they have tenure, teachers can be fired only with good and just cause. Such causes, though difficult to prove, generally include incompetence (knowledge of subject matter, teaching methods); immorality (lying, falsification of records, misappropriation of funds, and cheating); drug abuse; critical and derogatory statements about the employer; and profane language.

Teacher Preparation. The reality of facing that first class full of children challenges every beginning teacher—that is, one-third of the teaching force each year (National Center for Education Statistics, 1996, 1992). About one-third of first year teachers transfers from other schools and 57 percent come directly from college (National Center for Education Statistics, *Condition*, 1996). More than 50 percent of public school teachers have returned to colleges for master's, specialist, or doctoral degrees, and most teachers are certified in their main field of teaching (National Center for Education Statistics, 1995). The majority of public school teachers (71 percent) believed they were well prepared to maintain order and discipline in their classrooms, but fewer (41 percent) believed they were prepared to implement new teaching methods or mandates from the state or district (36 percent). The smallest number of teachers believed they were prepared to integrate educational technology into teaching methods (21 percent). With the new initiatives, technologies, and changing student populations, the demand on teachers to go beyond their preparation are great (National Center for Education Statistics, *Condition*, 1999, p. 48).

Revamping teacher education programs is being considered by many teaching colleges. Reformers such as John Goodlad (1998, 1984) and reports, including *A Nation Prepared: Teachers for the 21st Century* (1986), provide models for changing teacher education. Some recommendations include having teachers major in a subject area, giving teachers more say over what happens in schools, establishing a national board of standards, and increasing the number of minority teachers. In fact, a National Board for Professional Teaching Standards has been established and is working to implement recommendations.

Dissatisfaction with schools has forced educators to examine the total system, including teacher education. Evaluating curricula and redesigning content to address current concerns includes everything from classroom management practices to multicultural and global education, to special training for teaching in the middle grades, to improving the quality of math and science education, to working with differences in male and female learning styles (Banks, 1999).

Interest in careers in teaching dropped steadily from the 1970s to the early 1990s, but it is now rising slightly as the number of both students and teachers is expected to rise 4 percent between 1997 and 2009 (National Center for Education Statistics, *Projections*, 1999). Schools may see a teacher shortage, however, as larger cohorts of students enter the system. School districts are resorting to several techniques to meet the need; one is to retool current teachers who are in fields with less demand by training them in other areas. Another is "alternative credentialing," to attract qualified individuals working in other areas into teaching ("Alternatives, yes," 1989). In most cases, pedagogical training is provided when a person begins teaching. The Holmes Group, a group of education deans from colleges of education throughout the United States, recommended that a fifth year of graduate education be provided to certify new teachers (Levine and Levine, 1996, p. 405). The public favors hiring these individuals for their subject-area expertise, especially if they have shown talent for teaching (Elam, Rose, and Gallup, 1995).

To improve teachers' effectiveness, especially in content areas, some educators propose a universal master's degree. However, critics point out that this additional time and cost might discourage minority students from studying for teaching degrees. Other efforts focus on providing settings in which prospective teachers can receive classroom training in professional development schools, schools that work in conjunction with colleges of education to provide training for new teachers (Holmes Group, 1995).

Testing and Licensing. In an effort to raise standards, most states now require national or state tests for licensure of teacher candidates; the vast majority require teachers to pass minimum competency/basic skills tests. In 1998, the only states that did not require at a minimum an entrance exam for teacher education programs were Alaska, Idaho, Iowa, Utah, Vermont, and Wyoming (National Center for Education Statistics, *Digest*, 1999, Table 156). The National Teacher Examination is widely used by school districts, but a number of competing testing companies offer alternatives, and some states have developed their own tests. The two national teachers' unions, the National Education Association and the American Federation of Teachers, support teacher testing, though their views of what is tested and the basic purpose for the tests vary.

Controversy over testing and licensing of teachers continues, with some arguing that skills tests may not be valid, are not the only measure of competent teachers, and may discriminate against minority teachers. Others support the testing, arguing that it is harmful to children to have teachers in the classroom who lack basic skills. Court cases challenging the fairness of state testing have been brought forth in several states.

National Reports and Teaching Recommendations. The concern with rising dropout rates, poor performance of American students on international exams, and other problems have set off the alarm bells in the Department of Education and in private foundations and organizations devoted to the betterment of education. In the 1980s a spate of reports were produced, dealing with the "crisis in education" and making some radical suggestions for change.

Several reports argued that before the United States could upgrade educational programs and curricula, it would have to make teaching a more attractive profession. As older, experienced teachers retire and gifted young ones leave for other professions, the qualifications of the teaching force dwindle. During teacher shortages, the United States will have to "scrape the bottom of the barrel" unless it raises standards and salaries.

The catch-22 is that as educational administrations have to dictate policy to control the quality of education, fewer professional teachers will be attracted to education. Good teachers want autonomy and need competitive pay and working conditions; yet 10 to 50 percent of teachers' time is spent on noninstructional duties: keeping records; monitoring playgrounds, lunchrooms, and hallways; making copies—many of which take away from important instructional duties.

One of the many reports on educational reform comes from the National Commission on Teaching and America's Future, 1996, funded by the Rockefeller Foundation and Carnegie Corporation of New York, which proposed the following goal: "By the year 2006, America will provide all students in the country with what should be their educational birthright: access to competent, caring, and qualified teachers." To help accomplish this ambitious goal, the Commission created a reform agenda, *What Matters Most: Teaching for America's Future* (National Commission, 1996), outlining how to prepare, recruit, select, induct, and support teachers, and how schools support, assess, and reward teachers' work.

Another Commission report, The National Commission on Excellence in Teacher Education, focused on two general recommendations: that all teachers be required to take a competency exam, and that teacher-preparation programs be improved and extended to five years—in particular that teachers be required to obtain a degree in a particular content area and then take teacher training. Although these recommendations appeal to many, there is fear that a five-year program would discourage some potential teachers.

The main message is that teachers need more pay, more respect, more professional treatment, and more opportunity for advancement if we are to attract and keep high-quality individuals in the field. Progress is being made on some of these recommendations, such as higher salaries, but faculty still report having little infuence over school policies and only moderate control over classroom decisions.

Merit, incentive, or performance-based pay has been proposed as a way to reward teacher excellence, and some administrators are implementing such plans. A majority of the public favors merit-based reward systems, and many states in the United States have projects on merit pay. However, some argue that these plans lower teacher morale, create dissension, make the situation competitive, and are impossible to administer.

Bad conditions in schools need to be rectified before real change can occur. Private and parochial schools, which have less money for salaries, structure the system so that teachers have more freedom and fewer bureaucratic rules, allowing professionals to flourish and share a mission in a team atmosphere. Public schools, because of the hierarchy and bureaucracy, must be routinized, standardized, and regulated. Some suggest that parents and children could provide controls through choice of schools and the use of vouchers (Chubb and Moe, 1986).

Teacher Stress and Burnout. Schools can lose teachers in three ways: teachers leave teaching, they transfer to another school, or they are fired. Many transfer from one school to another, better situation (Boe et al., 1998). Because of hiring practices, many classrooms are staffed with unqualified teachers, mainly those teaching out of their field of expertise (Ingersoll, 1997).

Problems in schools also affect teacher stress and burnout, especially in urban areas. Teachers often feel that their work is meaningless and that they are powerless to effect changes in their situations. A number of factors contribute to the problem: Some are characteristics of teachers, others are found in societal pressures. For instance burnout begins between seven and ten years of teaching; the level of burnout rises with age and years of experience in teaching (Byrne, 1998), peaks at age 41 through 45, and then declines. Teachers with higher levels of education, and, therefore, higher career expectations, experienced more frustration (Friedman, 1991). The main factors contributing to burnout are unappreciative and uncaring administrators and students.

The following is a list of characteristics identified in a study of teacher burnout. Specifically, the report indicated that burnout was more common among teachers who

1. Were under 30 years of age
2. Were white and from middle-class backgrounds
3. Were inexperienced, having taught for fewer than five years
4. Were racially isolated, teaching in schools where most of the student body is of a race other than their own
5. Felt that members of their own race have been targets of discrimination at their school
6. Preferred not to be assigned to the school at which they teach
7. Believed that fate or luck controls their destinies and, hence, their future is out of their hands
8. Disagreed with their principals on the appropriate role for a campus administrator

The research revealed that the best single predictor of the likelihood that a teacher would plan to quit teaching was a sense of burnout. Teachers who wanted to quit also fit the characteristics of the teachers who were burned out. (Dworkin, 1985, p. 9)

Teachers in some urban school settings feel physically and emotionally victimized, situations that increase stress and burnout. Sixty percent of urban school districts responding to a study reported student assaults on teachers, 28 percent of all districts reported student–teacher violence, and three-quarters of teachers know of verbal abuse against teachers (National School Boards Association, 1993; McEvoy, 1990).

School culture and structural variables that cause teachers to burn out and quit are equally important (LeCompte and Dworkin, 1992). Highly organized schools may not provide the flexibility teachers need to be spontaneous and initiate new ideas. Teachers need to feel that they have some control over the environment and that they have some say in school policies. Effective teachers have a sense of control over their classrooms; they minimize lost class time and reduce interruptions by being good managers and enforcing necessary rules.

Are there solutions? Studies suggest two tentative ideas: First, teachers need to feel a sense of control over their domain, that they can be creative and spontaneous; second, supportive principals are a key factor in reducing stress and burnout (Dworkin and Townsend, 1993; Dworkin et al., 1990).

In sum, when a group is faced with threats from its environment—low prestige and low salaries; poor working conditions; lack of autonomy and professionalism; physical threats; hurt pride because of difficulty dealing with some students; and criticisms from angry minorities, parents, and administrators—there are bound to be reactions: stress, burnout, dropping out, and joining teachers' unions to fight for better conditions and more autonomy.

Recommendations to Improve the Role of Teacher. "I like the kids; I like the job; I like the satisfaction I get from the work. But I feel I'm not doing something which is really valued by society. Look at our pay scale and the lack of autonomy we as professionals have. So I don't know what the future holds for me or for the profession" (Dworkin and Haney, 1988). Task forces and commission reports have made suggestions for sweeping changes, some of which we have discussed. How do teachers feel about their circumstances? Despite the problems, teachers seem to be happier about their profession today than they were a decade ago, and almost 60 percent say they probably or certainly would be willing to teach again (National Center for Education Statistics, *Digest*, 1997). This may be due in part to greater recognition and appreciation of the essential role teachers play in society.

In 1979 Houston, Texas, began giving incentive pay to teachers in several categories: for teaching in high-priority schools; for teaching subjects in which there was a staff shortage; for good attendance; for professional training; for student gains on standardized tests; and for teaching at an experimental school. According to officials, the results were positive. However, the idea of merit pay, paying teachers for performance, has been controversial and not gained much support; establishing fair criteria for rewarding teachers has proven difficult, and allowing administrators to control the evaluation system is opposed by teachers' unions. Certainly there are areas of agreement between teachers and administrators on how to improve the teaching profession, and some changes are taking place.

Teachers work with students daily and have certain expectations of the student role. The student role and the reciprocal role relationship between students and teachers is our next topic.

*A*pplying *Sociology to Education:* Describe an effective teacher you know. What makes this teacher effective? ◆

Support Roles in the School: Behind the Scenes

School Staff: Guardians of the Gateway. Most schools have a supporting staff of both professional specialists and service workers. On entering the school, our first contact is usually with an office worker behind a counter who serves the important functions of "buffering" and "filtering" in dealing with the community. The irate parent comes in demanding to see the principal immediately; the text salesperson would like to speak to someone "in charge."

The office worker must determine the appropriate place for the complaint or request, screen out unnecessary interruptions of school personnel, and match the visitor with the appropriate person.

Office workers also control such key information as the contents of files. For example, if the vice principal needs information on the arrangement made with the food distributor for deliveries, he or she relies on the office worker to locate the material. Teachers and students also depend on office workers for many services and information. In this respect the person holding the role may wield a great deal of influence.

Other important support roles include librarians, special education teachers, paraprofessionals, food service workers, bus drivers, and nurses. One important role is often overlooked: Janitors are in a unique position. Although they hold little formal power in the hierarchy, they may be extremely influential members of the community in which a school is located. They have an insider's view about the running of the school, a vantage point almost no others, often not even the principals, have. Although many janitors are neutral entities, some have used the position in a political way, as exemplified in the following excerpt from Waller (1965, p. 80):

> [T]he janitor is always a member of the local community, whereas teachers belong rather to the outside world. . . . The janitor is important, too, as a talebearer. Often he regards himself as an official lookout for the community; it is his role to see what he can and to report what he observes to his friends and connections by way of gossip.

Another crucial role in schools is carried out by paraprofessionals—individuals with less than a four-year college degree. Although they do not have total control of a classroom, they do carry out numerous tasks in classrooms and schools. The largest number work with special education programs, including remedial and bilingual classes (Blalock, 1991).

The role of school nurses has changed dramatically, from giving bandages and immunizations to handling medications for chronically ill and hyperactive students, to dealing with abuse, and working with other social problems that affect health services. Sometimes this involves coordinating social services to get children the help they need One controversial aspect of this role in some schools is sex education, pregnancy testing, and dispensing condoms.

Counselors: The Selection and Allocation Function. As high schools have become larger and more diverse in programs and courses offered, their personnel have become more specialized. Counselors are hired by many school systems, mostly to deal with students at the high school level. They usually have degrees in school counseling and often have had teaching experience. From the American School Counselor Association (ASCA) (1999) web site comes a policy statement that includes a clear definition of the formal role of the counselor:

The professional school counselor is a certified/licensed educator who addresses the needs of students comprehensively through the implementation of a developmental school counseling program. . . . School counselors work with all students, including those who are considered "at-risk" and those with special needs . . . they provide assistance to students through four primary interventions: counseling (individual and group); large group guidance; consultation; and coordination.

Counselors have a great deal of power in determining what happens to each student—a "gatekeeping" role. They often determine the road students will follow when they leave secondary school (Brookover et al., 1996, p. 100). With all the student records at hand, they can guide students into courses and programs to meet students' and society's needs. The counselor can make lifetime decisions for young people. Counselors use not only the objective criteria of grades and test scores but also their impressions of the students, often formed during brief encounters taking place over several years. Labels attached to students from teachers and peers can influence the counselor's impressions. Factors such as the student's class background, dress, and manner of speaking influence the counselor's opinions of what the student can do and recommendations for future plans. A dilemma is present for the counselor who is expected to keep "societal" goals in mind, get to know students well enough to plan their futures, and work with students and parents to achieve what are sometimes unrealistic goals.

Special Support Roles. Because of growing concern in the nation in the 1970s over the apparent decline of basic skills, Title I (Elementary and Secondary Education Act) was passed to provide supplementary monies to districts for additional personnel and special programs. Schools can hire specialists in reading, mathematics, and sometimes preschool education to work with children who score below third-grade level on standardized tests. In addition, needy children in Title I programs are offered some auxiliary services such as food, medicine, dental services, and clothing. Special education staff can make a significant difference for marginal students, especially those who have attention deficit, are learning disabled, emotionally impaired, or mentally impaired, if they have high expectations and provide support rather than give up on these students (Brookover et al., 1996, p. 105).

The national report *A Nation at Risk* recommended use of "the voluntary efforts of individuals, businesses, and civic groups to cooperate in strengthening educational programs" (National Commission on Education, 1983). Operation Rescue, administered by the Washington, DC, Urban League and the public schools uses residents, businesses, organizations, and churches to tutor first- through third-grade students who are having trouble with basic skills. "Rather than 10,000 students failing, over 7,000 students graduated to the next grade level, due in part to the one-on-one or small group tutorial assistance they had received through Operation Rescue" (Epperson, 1991). The program incorporates recommendations of the report *Schools That Work* (U.S. Department of Education, 1989).

Reports of schools with volunteer programs abound. With shortages of funds and personnel, extra hands to do special tasks can be invaluable. Retired teachers and other professionals, community citizens with skills, parents, business members, substitute teachers, even upper-level students or college students volunteer to tutor; aid teachers or substitute in classes; give lessons on specific topics; help in the office, library, or other areas; chaperone; and run after-school programs in sports or other special-interest activities. Some programs use community resources to place students for internships, and in other communities businesses provide personnel and resources to the schools for special programs.

Alumni are the biggest school boosters and the strongest school critics. They provide financial support, especially at the college level, and are often community members in their high school hometowns, attending sporting events and volunteering help in various capacities.

However, alumni can be a hindrance in efforts to change. A prestigious preparatory school set quotas for accepting a percentage of minority students each year; it then considered becoming coeducational. Protests and loss of alumni support—including financial help—followed these moves.

How individuals carry out roles varies greatly. In the next chapter we consider student status and role.

*A*pplying Sociology to Education: Draw a diagram of a school and describe different roles within the school. ◆

◆ Summary

No system can work without individuals who fill the necessary roles, which in turn make the system alive. Although the major obligations for most positions are usually clearly defined, individuals bring unique sets of characteristics, training, abilities, and background experiences with them when playing their roles. Hence, no one description can capture the richness and variety that enter into the system of roles.

I. The Meaning of Roles

Roles refer to the parts individuals play in the social system. In school organizations, roles include administrators, teachers, students, and support staff. Conflicts may arise from incompatible demands on those holding particular roles. Reciprocal roles in the educational system illustrate the interdependence of parts; for instance, without students other roles in the educational system would be nonexistent. Those taking on a role are usually socialized rather rapidly into that role; few can tolerate the uncertainty of an ill-defined role, and few want to face the ridicule or punishment likely to follow defiance of role expectations. Hence, the school system has a built-in guarantee into which most neophytes will fit nicely and without disruption. This is one reason why change in the system is often slow.

II. Roles in Schools

School boards consist of lay community members who have varying degrees of control over school personnel, budget, and policy; these may be points of tension.

Superintendents are the overall managers of schools. They provide the liaison between the schools, the board, and the community.

Principals are bosses of individual schools, but their authority lies between that of the superintendent and the teachers. This often requires them to play a balancing act to keep both satisfied.

Teachers are on the front line, running the classrooms. The conflict between their desire for autonomy and pressures from the environment can lead to tensions. Recently, there have been controversies over teacher accountability, testing of teachers, and teacher training. Several national U.S. commission reports have addressed the problem of how to improve teaching.

A number of other support roles exist in schools, each playing an important role in the overall functioning of the school.

◆ *Putting Sociology to Work*

1. Imagine yourself in the various roles of a specific school system. Compare your role behavior in each role.
2. Try to recall the highlights of your education at different levels in your role as a student. What were different role expectations at different levels?
3. Observe the people in a school. Note the differing roles and the reciprocal relationships.
4. View the documentary film *High School* and try to identify some of the formal school roles you see individuals performing. Describe the reciprocal role relationships.
5. Examine several of the "Problems in Teaching Series" (Science Research Associates) films of teaching anecdotes and identify the roles the teacher, students, and administrators are taking or might take in performing their formal roles.

CHAPTER 7

Students

The Core of the School

I chatted with a group of fourth-grade boys about their school experiences. There was no question about their knowing what was expected of them by the adult world and why they go to school. They all chimed in that they must learn to read and write to survive in today's world, that they couldn't get a job if their skills weren't developed. What does it mean to be a good or bad kid in school? Again, they did not need to stop and think. A good kid is one who turns in assignments on time, listens and pays attention in class, and doesn't mess around. Bad kids are disruptive, sometimes mean and aggressive, and don't really care about learning. Is it hard to be a good kid in school? When the teachers are picky or in a bad mood, it is; but most of the time it's not, if you want to be good. I had a feeling of déjà vu; things hadn't changed much since I was in school. The continuity in expectations is remarkable.

STUDENT CHARACTERISTICS

Students come in many sizes, shapes, intellectual capacities, and motivation levels. They can be active learners, passive attendees, or disruptive trouble-makers. Estimates indicate that most children in the world between the ages of six and nine attend school all or part of the time, but after about third grade the picture is spotty. Attendance is near 100 percent in industrialized nations, but it is much lower in less developed countries, as we shall see in Chapter 11 (see Box 7–1).

In 1983, the report *A Nation at Risk* recommended that all students seeking a diploma be required to complete the "new basics." This included four units of English; three units each of science, social studies, and mathematics; and one-half unit of computer science. From 1982 to 1994, the percentage of public school students completing this curriculum jumped from 13 to 32 percent. High school students are taking more courses (seven per year) than they did in 1982–83, but they are spending less time on work for these classes. The largest increase in courses taken was in math and science, but social studies and English also increased. The number of students taking foreign language was 39 percent in 1994. This trend toward more academic courses being offered and taken may reflect the recommendations of early commission reports arguing that we needed to upgrade our programs. These changes are affecting students of all types and abilities at all levels of the educational system. The following is a description of some of those students and their needs.

Minority students made up 10 percent of the enrollments in metropolitan-area public schools outside of central cities, up from 6 percent in 1970. In 1996, one of every four students in central-city public schools was Hispanic (National Center for Education Statistics, 1999). In 2000, minority students were a majority in ten states. These students need minority role models and bridges between the middle-class culture of the school and minority subcultures. The number of minority teachers, however, declined from 12.5 percent in 1980 to 9 percent in 1996 (National Center for Education Statistics, *Digest*, 1999, p. 80). Estimates indicate that minority students could be as high as 39 percent by 2020, but minority teachers would still constitute only a small percentage of the teaching force.

The low percentage of minority teachers is understandable considering the teaching conditions in unappealing classrooms and schools, relatively low salaries, and what some claim are culturally biased teacher exams (Stephens, 1999). Techniques for increasing the number of minority teachers must approach the problem at many levels, from individual incentives to teacher-college programs, to state and national policies. Equitable placement procedures, incentives, competitive salaries, mentoring programs, subject-area recruitment, and multicultural training are all recommendations (Stephens, 1999). In Georgia, the state has instituted a plan to train noncertified school district employees, mostly paraprofessionals, by giving them tuition and support so that they can become certified teachers (Dandy, 1998). Increasing the number of minority teachers would provide more role models for the many students coming through the academic pipeline.

◆◆**Box 7-1** *School Enrollments, 1998–99*

Total enrollment in the nation's public and private elementary and secondary schools, K–12, in 1998–99 was estimated at 58.6 million, according to the U.S. Education Department's National Center for Education Statistics (1999). Of that total, 52 million students were attending public schools, compared with 39.2 million in 1984. Private school enrollment was estimated at 6.6 million. Public school enrollment has increased some 12.8 million since 1984, whereas private school enrollment has remained relatively steady.

"In 1993, over 63 million people in the United States, almost one in four, were enrolled in elementary or secondary schools, colleges and universities. This included about 37 million students in kindergarten through grade 8, 13 million in grades 9 through 12, 6 million in two-year colleges, and 9 million in four-year colleges and universities" (National Center for Education Statistics, 1995, p. 104).

"Enrollment in public schools in kindergarten through grade 8 declined through the 1970s, reaching a low point in 1984, and has been rising since then. Enrollment in public schools in grades 9–12 declined from 1976 through 1990, with some minor fluctuations in the mid-1980s. It then increased between 1990 and 1994 and is projected to continue increasing" (National Center for Education Statistics, 1995, p. 106).

Expectations for the Student Role

In most public school systems, formal role expectations for students are standardized by grade. Elaborate plans outline where a student's academic position should be. Formal student roles—club officer, athletic team member; or (at the lower grades) trash emptier, board eraser, or traffic guard—are found in most schools, but these roles do not capture the flavor and variety of the classroom and student roles.

Student culture, that complex of "strange customs," constitutes a "participation mystique, complex rituals of personal relationships, a set of folkways, mores, and irrational sanctions, a moral code based upon them" (Waller, [1932] 1961, p. 103). This description is part of the informal student role and reflects the uniqueness of student culture.

In describing the expectations for student roles in schools we must consider both the formal and informal aspects of student culture. We were all a part of it once, but memories fade and times change, keeping the student culture apart from the world of adults. Students are at the bottom of the role hierarchy with a power structure looming over their heads; although they are a numerical majority in the system, they are a distinct minority in decision making. Often students are spoken of as an almost alien group—the group to be "subdued," disciplined, or conquered by the school staff.

The student subculture determines for many young people the acceptable behaviors for peer survival, behaviors that are often at odds with adult expectations. Peer groups come in different types: Some support the importance of school learning and achievement, some are more interested in social activities, and a proportion of peer groups engage in delinquent activities. Those students whose friends care about learning have better educational outcomes than those whose friends have little interest in learning (Chen, 1997).

If a student's *friendship patterns* are "high-quality," meaning with students who value their education, students are more likely to adjust and even take on leadership roles. However, those students whose friends have been defined as having behavioral problems have a more difficult time adjusting, especially in junior high school (Berndt, Hawkins, and Jiao, 1999). Who children select as friends is not only personal choice, but also a cultural process, and may reflect their self-concept and feeling about their place in the society or in school practices such as tracking; in other words, friendship patterns can be seen as part of the process of class reproduction (Corsaro, 1994).

The following two studies of "jocks" and "burnouts" and of athletes and nonathletes provide examples of student subcultures. Class reproduction can occur through adolescent peer groups. "Jocks," college-bound, middle-class students, have an investment in the school system, whereas "burnouts," working-class students who often feel hostile or alienated in the school environment, are stigmatized in schools. Working-class students engage in behaviors that will prevent them from succeeding in high school (Eckert, 1989; Willis, 1979). Scholar–athletes and pure scholars have higher self-esteem, extracurricular involvement, and leadership ability than do pure athletes or students who are neither scholars nor athletes; one example is that women who participate in sports (excluding cheerleading) have higher achievement in science (Hanson and Kraus, 1998; Snyder and Spreitzer, 1992).

Another variable that affects the student role is gender. Even such subtleties as language usage can have an impact on the student experience. If teachers are aware of the different uses of language, they may be able to use this knowledge effectively in teaching girls and boys. According to a study of student language usage, girls tell secrets to their best friends, whereas boys participate in activities in larger groups and develop hierarchies of status. Boys are more comfortable putting themselves forward and are more willing to argue, whereas girls resist "hostile" discussions. Because of such differences, some argue that single-sex education may lead to more positive social and academic outcomes for female students (Riordan, 1990). Gender and achievement are discussed in Chapter 4.

Learning the Student Role

Each year a new crop of students must be socialized into their roles and the expectations of kindergarten and the elementary school classroom. Students preparing to enter a new classroom or school are concerned about making mistakes in front of their peers or getting in trouble because they have not yet learned their role expectations. Most children want to be accepted. Much of the student's

Learning the rules, roles, and routines is part of becoming a "good" student.

role learning ties in with the social control function of education—learning how to adjust, take orders, and obey. To become a "good" student means to follow the school's routine and rules. These early experiences have an impact on the later adjustment of students and their attitudes toward schooling.

School deals with the intellectual abilities of the child; in contrast, the family deals with the whole child. Preschool programs and kindergarten introduce the child to the institution of education and have been described as "academic boot camp." In a classic article describing the kindergarten routine, Gracey recounts a day in the life of both the children and the teacher, pointing out the socialization of children into the formal world (Gracey, 1967). Students are the most transient members of the educational system in that they move through and eventually leave the system; the school system is geared toward facilitating the successful movement of students through the system. Movement requires progress, which in turn requires control and cooperation. Because students are not in school by choice, most schools find it necessary to keep them in line by using incentives such as positive reinforcement and interesting subjects, or punishment such as extra work, detentions, and suspensions, and by giving grades as incentives for students to accomplish the school's goals.

Each year's crop of students becomes a "class" and is processed through the system as a group, or cohort. Picture a giant sieve with layers. Students are put in the top and pass through the layers, which have succeedingly smaller holes. Those who fail to pass through a level are retained or drop out of the sorting and selecting process. At the bottom of the sieve comes graduation.

If students with common experiences and values are placed according to ability levels, their labels—brains, jocks, losers—may affect their role patterns. The fact that students are placed in different tracks also points to a major cause of variation in students' educational experiences. The courses students pursue are generally influenced by and selected on the basis of their future plans for either further schooling or work. In several European countries—Germany and England, for example—tracking or "streaming" becomes increasingly rigid as students move through the system. Exams at several school levels in Germany, at age 16 in England, and for university entrance in Japan and many other countries have a major impact on determining a student's future educational opportunities. SATs or other exams are required by many U.S. colleges and universities.

Conflicting Expectations for the Student Role

The school is expected to socialize children to be successful members of society; this implies academic and social skill development for students in the school. The school expects "successful" students to carry out two components of achievement at the elementary level, according to Talcott Parsons. The first is "cognitive" learning of information—skills, frames of reference, and factual information about the world. The second is a "moral" component, including responsible citizenship, respect, consideration, cooperation, work habits, leadership, and initiative (Parsons, 1959). To the extent that student peer groups rebel against these goals, division and conflict are created. High school students may have another agenda, centered on peer-group involvement and acceptance. Willard Waller points out this conflict between adult and student values very aptly. His analysis describes a basic function of schools, cultural transmission:

> Certain cultural conflicts are at the center of the life of the school. . . . A conflict arises between teachers and students because teachers represent the culture of the wider group and students are impregnated with the culture of the local community. . . . A second and more universal conflict between students and teachers arises from the fact that teachers are adults and students are not, so that teachers are the bearers of the culture of the society of adults, and try to impose that culture upon students, whereas students represent the indigenous culture of the group of children. (Waller, 1965, p. 104)

Student Coping Mechanisms

Students use different coping mechanisms to get through the levels of the system. Varying roles are adopted—the leader, the clown, the bully. Playing these roles requires adapting to the demands of differing situations.

> Thus the leader may remain a leader, but he must adapt his leadership to the (usually) superior force of the teacher, which he may do through alliance, opposition, rivalry, or other means. The clown is still a clown, but his buffoonery must be disguised, it may become covert, or it may adopt a mien of innocence and pose as blundering stupidity. (Waller, 1965, pp. 332–33)

Waller points out that a clever teacher recognizes student roles, manipulates them, and uses them effectively. Teachers speak differently to students for whom they have high expectations and low expectations. Students can pick up cues about how teachers feel about them (Charles, 1999; Babad, Bernieri, and Rosenthal, 1991; Waller, 1965).

Teachers also have different stereotypes of male and female students, resulting in different experiences for boys and girls in school. For instance, many teachers believe that males have higher math capacity and, therefore, have higher expectations for males in math performance (Li, 1999). Students who are alienated from the system may also attempt to sabotage the teaching effort by maintaining an emotional detachment from what is happening in the classroom, devaluing what is taking place, cheating, daydreaming, or acting bored (Jackson, 1968).

Another student coping mechanism is apathy—protecting themselves against total failure in a competition they feel they cannot win. If their sense of self-worth is threatened, it may reduce their desire to try to achieve. Until these students see the possibility of success from effort rather than feeling a sense of futility, they are unlikely to put forth that effort. Those students with positive attitudes are likely to be high achievers. Those who are defensive or have low self-esteem or other problems often need help to succeed. Although schools cannot solve society's problems, they can attempt to recognize students in trouble and collaborate with other human service agencies to meet student needs.

Why should we care about alienated, bored, apathetic students? The loss in human potential is tremendous. "Our society is aging and the number of children and youth in relation to other age groups in the population is declining. If current trends continue, a disproportionate number of our young will grow up poor, undereducated, and untrained at the very time that our society will need all of our young to be healthy, educated, and productive" (Children's Defense Fund, 1996).

SCHOOL FAILURES AND DROPOUTS

Alienation is a sense of powerlessness, normlessness, meaninglessness, isolation, or self-estrangement. In schools, its roots are found in the formal, impersonal, bureaucratic, educational system. Complete overhaul of the school structure would be necessary to prevent the feelings that drive some students to drop out of the system.

Dropouts (called "status" dropouts) are persons who are 16- to 24-years-old who are not enrolled in school and who have not completed a high school program, regardless of when they left school. People who have received GED (General Education Degree) credentials are counted as high school completers. (U.S. Department of Commerce, 1998)

Who Drops Out?

Sheri is a high school dropout and an unwed mother, a double stigma. Her intentions were to finish high school while her baby attended day care; then she could get a good job to support the baby. But when winter came and the baby got sick, she could not get to school regularly and dropped out. Juan's family moved to a large city from his native Puerto Rico when he was in elementary school. He worked part-time while attending high school because his family needed the money. With the language barrier, need for immediate cash, and little support from home, he dropped out to work longer hours at his menial job. Sheri and Juan are just two examples of the many youths who leave high school.

Eleven percent of all students between the ages of 16 and 24 drop out of high school (National Center for Education Statistics, *Digest*, 1999, p. 124, Table 104). Where ethnic diversity is greatest, retention rates are lowest. African Americans and Latino students feel more alienated, with a higher sense of powerlessness and isolation than white students; these feelings are especially influential in dropout decisions for males. Note the dropout rates for different groups in Table 7–1.

Almost one-half of all Hispanic students dropped out before completing high school in the 1980s, many to help their families, but most ended up in deeper poverty. Almost 40 percent of Hispanic dropouts over age 25 had not finished high school in 1997, compared with 7.7 percent non-Hispanic (National Center for Educational Statistics, *Conditions*, 1999, p. 138). The percentage of Hispanics from 16 to 24 years old who had not completed high school by 1997 was 25.3 percent. Those Hispanics ages 25 to 34 who had not finished high school dropped slightly between 1989 and 1997, from 39.1 to 38.5 percent (National Center for Education Statistics, 1999, p. 138).

Students from Mexican American non-English-speaking homes in the United States have additional possibilities of being alienated; bilingual students tend to cope better than non-English-speakers because they are able to acquire the institutional support for school success and social mobility (Stanton-Salazar and Dornbusch, 1995, p. 116).

Dropouts are disproportionately male, older than average (two or more years behind grade level), burdened with low grades and behavior problems, minorities, from low-income families with low educational attainment, and given little educational encouragement. It is these individuals who make up the reserve labor force in capitalistic systems. About 14 percent of the male

TABLE 7–1 Event Dropout Rates[a] for Those in Grades 10–12, Ages 15–24, by Sex, Race–Ethnicity, and Family Income, October 1972–97

October	Total	Sex		Race–Ethnicity[b]			Family Income[c]		
		Male	Female	White	Black	Hispanic	Low	Middle	High
1972	6.1	5.9	6.3	5.3	9.5	11.2	14.1	6.7	2.5
1974	6.7	7.4	6.0	5.8	11.6	9.9	—	—	—
1976	5.9	6.6	5.2	5.6	7.4	7.3	15.4	6.8	2.1
1978	6.7	7.5	5.9	5.8	10.2	12.3	17.4	7.3	3.0
1980	6.1	6.7	5.5	5.2	8.2	11.7	15.8	6.4	2.5
1982	5.5	5.8	5.1	4.7	7.8	9.2	15.2	5.6	1.8
1984	5.1	5.4	4.8	4.4	5.7	11.1	13.9	5.1	1.8
1986	4.7	4.7	4.7	3.7	5.4	11.9	10.9	5.1	1.6
1988	4.8	5.1	4.4	4.2	5.9	10.4	13.7	4.7	1.3
1990	4.0	4.0	3.9	3.3	5.0	7.9	9.5	4.3	1.1
1991	4.0	3.8	4.2	3.2	6.0	7.3	10.6	4.0	1.0
1992	4.4	3.9	4.9	3.7	5.0	8.2	10.9	4.4	1.3
1993	4.5	4.6	4.3	3.9	5.8	6.7	12.3	4.3	1.3
1994[d]	5.3	5.2	5.4	4.2	6.6	10.0	13.0	5.2	2.1
1995[d]	5.7	6.2	5.3	4.5	6.4	12.4	13.3	5.7	2.0
1996[d]	5.0	5.0	5.1	4.1	6.7	9.0	11.1	5.1	2.1
1997[d]	4.6	5.0	4.1	3.6	5.0	9.5	12.3	4.1	1.8

—Not available
[a]The event dropout rate is the percentage of those in grades 10–12, ages 15–24, who were enrolled the previous October, but who were not enrolled and had not graduated in October of the current year.
[b]Included in the total but not shown separately are dropouts from other racial–ethnic groups.
[c]Low income is the bottom 20 percent of all family incomes; high income is the top 20 percent of all family incomes; and middle income is the 60 percent in between.
[d]In 1994, the survey instrument for the Current Population Survey (CPS) was changed and weights were adjusted.

Note: Beginning in 1992, the Current Population Survey (CPS) changed the questions used to obtain the educational attainment of respondents. *Source:* U.S. Department of Education, National Center for Education Statistics, *Dropout Rates in the United States, 1997,* 1999 (based on the October Current Population Surveys).

dropouts and almost 20 percent of the female dropouts between the ages of 16 and 24 were unemployed in 1998 (*Statistical Abstracts of the United States, 1999,* U.S. Census Bureau, 1999, p. 191).

The dropout problem is growing worse in many major U.S. cities, where the average rate is more than 40 percent; in New York City the rate is about 50 percent. In the nation as a whole, however, the rate has leveled off and is declining slightly (see Table 7–2).

Why Students Drop Out

"Many youngsters arrive in school homeless, sick, hungry, and destitute—plagued by problems that often make staying and succeeding in school virtually impossible" (DeRidder, 1990, p. 153). Problems faced by students range from school conditions to family breakups to neighborhood dangers from gangs and drugs (see Table 7–2).

Some schools are so poor and crowded that they cannot begin to offer in-school support, much less coordinate with other agencies to meet student needs. Kozol describes differences in two Chicago-area schools—one wealthy, one poor. The wealthy school has an average class size of 24 children, and there are 15 students in classes for slow learners. The poor school has remedial classes with 39 students, and classes for the "gifted" of 36 students. Each student at the wealthy school has an adviser assigned; at the poor school, one guidance counselor advises 420 children (Kozol, 1991, p. 66). It is difficult to cope with the requirements of the compulsory, rigid, formal, educational system, which has no room for misfits who frequently drop out when they reach legal age (National Dropout Prevention Network Web site).

Problems such as teenage pregnancy and peer group pressure from gangs are two examples of factors affecting dropout rates. Teenage pregnancy often prevents young mothers from finishing school. This problem is most prevalent in the inner city. Early intervention to provide sex education, parenting training, child care, and easy access to education are necessary. Many programs are being targeted to inner-city schools ("Teen Pregnancy," 1998; Scott-Jones, 1991, p. 461). Gang violence is a threat to neighborhoods and schools. Armed, angry, and impulsive, these hostile youths have little regard for others. Social ills are directly related to youths joining gangs (McEvoy, 1990, p. 1).

Gangs and Schools

Youth gangs are found in every area of the United States and many other countries. Why do youth join gangs? Joining a gang, some argue, is a class and ethnic group issue. Most gangs are made up of disaffected youth living in poor neighborhoods, having difficulty in school, and sometimes from ethnic groups that are not integrated into the mainstream society. Youths join gangs for protection and

TABLE 7–2   Reasons for Dropping Out

Reasons for Dropping Out	Total	Sex		Race–Ethnicity		
		Male	Female	Hispanic	Black, Non-Hispanic	White, Non-Hispanic
School-related						
Did not like school	51.2	57.8	44.2	42.3	44.9	57.5
Could not get along with teachers	35.0	51.6	17.2	26.8	30.2	39.2
Could not get along with students	20.1	18.3	21.9	18.2	31.9	17.4
Was suspended too often	16.1	19.2	12.7	14.5	26.3	13.1
Did not feel safe at school	12.1	11.5	12.8	12.8	19.7	9.5
Was expelled	13.4	17.6	8.9	12.5	24.4	8.7
Felt I didn't belong	23.2	31.5	14.4	19.3	7.5	31.3
Could not keep up with schoolwork	31.3	37.6	24.7	19.5	30.1	35.8
Was failing school	39.9	46.2	33.1	39.3	30.1	44.8
Changed school and did not like new school	13.2	10.8	15.8	10.3	21.3	9.8
Job-related						
Could not work and go to school at same time	14.1	20.0	7.8	14.3	9.0	15.9
Had to get a job	15.3	14.7	16.0	17.5	11.8	14.3
Found a job	15.3	18.6	11.8	20.8	6.3	17.6
Family-related						
Had to support family	9.2	4.8	14.0	13.1	8.1	9.0
Wanted to have family	6.2	4.2	8.4	8.9	6.7	5.4
Was pregnant[a]	31.0	—	31.0	20.7	40.6	32.1
Became parent	13.6	5.1	22.6	10.3	18.9	12.9
Got married	13.1	3.4	23.6	21.6	1.4	15.3
Had to care for family member	8.3	4.6	12.2	7.0	19.2	4.5
Other						
Wanted to travel	2.1	2.5	1.7	([b])	2.9	1.9
Friends dropped out	14.1	16.8	11.3	10.0	25.4	10.9

—Not applicable.
[a]Females only.
[b]Too few cases for a reliable estimate.

Source: U.S. Department of Education, National Center for Education Statistics, National Education Longitudinal Study of 1988 First Follow-up Survey, 1990.

to show strong loyalty to their neighborhood and "protect their turf." Gang involvement is also related to risk-taking behaviors, and the rate of delinquent acts is high for gang members (Thornberry and Burch, 1997; Crowley et al, 1997). Add ethnic differences, difficulties assimilating, and limited opportunities, and one has a recipe for gang membership (Rodriguez, 1993). Immigrants join gangs to defend and maintain their ethnic identity and create a sense of belonging.

The National Youth Gang Survey (NYGS), sponsored by the U.S. Department of Justice (1999), has been conducted since 1995 and provides a representation of gang members and their activities. The survey is given to police and sheriff departments of all sizes. From these surveys, NYGS estimates that there were 28,700 active gangs and 780,000 gang members in the United States in 1998, a slight decline from the previous year. Most members (92 percent) are male; only 1.5 percent of gangs are female dominated. The majority of gang members are between ages 18 and 24 (46 percent), with 11 percent less than 15 years old, 29 percent between 15 and 17, and 14 percent older than 24 years old. Hispanic members make up 46 percent of all gang members; African Americans, 34 percent; Caucasians, 12 percent; and Asians, 6 percent of gang members. About one-third of the gangs have a mix of ethnic groups. Though gangs are most prevalent in urban areas, they also are found in suburbs, small cities, and rural counties; the only increase in membership in 1998 was seen in rural areas.

What do gang members do? Many gangs are involved in serious and violent crimes. Twenty-eight percent of the gangs were organized specifically for trafficking in drugs; other gangs committed assaults and robberies, sometimes along with drug activities. Fighting, stealing, alcohol dealing, and drug dealing leads to power and respect from other gang members. An estimated 50 percent of assaults involved carrying a gun.

How do gangs affect schools? In fact, the number of gang members in schools is usually fairly small, but the gang presence can be quite disruptive, bringing into schools fear, violence, drugs, and recruitment for gangs (Burnett and Walz, 1994).

Some ethnic groups are labeled by teachers and peers in school and are expected to fail and to be gang members; Latino youth often experience this stereotype (Katz, 1997). By stereotyping certain students, they may be labeled unfairly. The school atmosphere can contribute to a sense of failure, restrictions on language, lack of respect for different cultures, and lack of a sense of belonging (Burnett and Walz, 1994).

What can schools do about gang influence? First, they can legally protect the learning environment for students from intimidation, fear, or threat of violence. Dress codes that forbid student gang apparel, however, are not legal unless it can be shown that the apparel interferes with learning and with freedom of expression (Gluckman, 1996). School atmosphere plays a significant role.

Communities can help youth by providing alternatives to gangs. For instance, youth clubs, sports activities, midnight basketball, boxing, rap sessions, and other activities draw youth away from gangs. The best remedy is to integrate all young people into the school so that they feel a vested interest in participating and know their efforts will lead to success in the job market.

School Crime and Violence

School-based crime and violence are ranked as the number one problems in public polls of attitudes toward schools (Elam and Gallup, 1999). Shootings in schools make the headlines, but many students face daily bullying, sexual harassment, and beatings. In fact, some children are afraid to go to school or carry weapons to school for protection, issues discussed in Chapter 2 and elsewhere in the text. Parents, educators, and community members are concerned for the safety of students and the integrity of the learning process. Studies show, however, that most schools are safe, that 80 to 90 percent of school employees rate their schools as safe (Verdugo and Schneider, 1999). Why, then, is there a perception of unsafe schools? Newspaper headlines report dramatic happenings on school grounds, incidents that seem random yet are real. Educators in most schools affected are shocked by these incidents; it is the very randomness of the acts and lack of ability to predict them that frightens people. Though violent acts are unlikely in 90 percent of schools, the other 10 percent are problematic. The public seldom hears about problems in some inner-city schools where crime and violence are daily events and the schools are armed fortresses with metal detectors and police guards.

Consider the case of a group of Chicana adolescents. Conditions in their school are poor with overcrowded classrooms, underfunded programs, high dropout rates, many students in poverty, teacher burnout and discouragement, social promotions, and no programs to remediate these students, resulting in few graduates prepared for college, and sexism and racism. Young women in the school make choices based on the reality of their situations, and those choices often involve early pregnancy, gang affiliation, and dropping out of school (Dietrich, 1998).

Students like these girls who are engaged in antisocial behavior are likely headed for academic failure. Yet programs that do exist to deal with the problems focus on either the antisocial behavior or academic success and do not link the two; programs also focus narrowly on changing attitudes or behaviors, but not the context or climate within which behaviors occur. By identifying climates that allow for academic failure and antisocial behavior, schools may be able to attack the problems more effectively (McEvoy and Welker, 2000; Noguera, 1995).

The Safe Schools Movement formed to combat school violence. Movements arise when there is collective action around a common purpose. Violence reduction is a goal of almost all schools in the United States and of the Safe Schools Movement. However, developing effective school-based programs that are integrated into the school systems and can change the climate of the schools is challenging. Problems include "conflicts over violence reduction programs and services, lack of appropriate program evaluation, limited programs that attempt to change attributes of the individual rather than the environment in which violence emerges, and lack of a theoretical rationale to guide the development of school-based violence prevention and intervention efforts" (McEvoy, 1999).

Retention and Suspension: School Reactions to Problem Students

Schools need to rethink how they deal with "at-risk" and troublesome students based on sociological study results. Grade retention is one factor that contributes to the decision to drop out of school. Retention does not appear to improve school performance of poor students, but it does tell students that they are not considered capable, which increases the chances of their leaving because of frustration and disengagement (Roderick, 1995, 1994).

Students who are retained have low self-esteem and seldom make up the academic deficiencies that held them back in the first place (McCollum et al., 1999). Retained students lose achievement and have higher dropout rates. Estimates are that 2.6 million students are retained at a cost of $10 billion. These students are often young males with low socioeconomic status, poor self-esteem, and low motivation, a description that matches that of the typical dropout (Nason, 1991).

Schools seeking funding for special programs as alternatives to retention have had difficulty finding funds, leaving few alternatives to retention (Natriello, 1998). Thus, budgetary constraints are leading to retention, which is leading to a higher rate of dropping out, ultimately costing schools and society in both loss of human power and social services.

Unfortunately, too many schools use strategies such as suspensions that reduce expectations and stigmatize students. The students who are suspended are often at-risk students to begin with. Suspending students may eliminate the immediate problem but cause many long-term problems, including increased dropout rates because suspended students get behind in class work. "Tragically, although removing troubled and troubling students may provide systematic relief for schools, such strategies ignore the root causes of aggressive behavior and banish those children who are most in need of the benefit of a strong academic foundation, a caring school environment, and positive peer relations" (Hudley et al., 1998).

To prevent students from dropping out, programs that focus on the most vulnerable populations, try to reduce causes of apathy and alienation, raise self-esteem and success of students, and begin early in students' careers are important. Most experts advise identifying at-risk students early and intervening quickly. Many intervention programs have been proposed and some have been tested at the elementary and middle school grades. Accelerated academics, alternative schools, and Saturday and after-school programs are some of the academic approaches used. Laws to deny drivers' licenses to students in academic difficulty or to those who drop out of school before age 18 are being passed in a number of states. Getting parents involved in programs to keep students in school and holding parents accountable for students who do not attend school are other strategies. Finally, for those students who do drop out, an increasing number of programs for completing high school are available.

About half of the students who drop out eventually complete high school; some return to high school, others complete the GED (General Educational Development) exam. Their completion of high school is associated with several variables: Those students who demonstrated academic ability even if they did not perform well were most likely to complete high school. Seventy-five percent of those students from higher SES families completed high school. About one-quarter of dropouts enroll in postsecondary education (National Center for Educational Statistics, June 1998).

Adolescent Employment and Dropping Out of School

Adolescent employment creates conflicting expectations for students; adolescents supply labor as workers in fast-food restaurants, as newspaper carriers, and in many other positions in evenings and on weekends. Work experience is valuable training for adult roles, especially in responsibility, punctuality, working for a boss, following orders, handling money, and practicing whatever skills may be acquired. However, work takes time from studies, extracurricular activities, peer associations, and "growing up."

Two major questions have been asked about the effect of high school students' employment: What is the effect on school achievement of the number of hours worked, and are working students more likely to drop out of high school? More than half of tenth graders, and almost all eleventh and twelfth graders work sometime during the school year (Schoenhals, Tienda, and Schneider, 1998). The number of hours worked and the type of employment significantly impact students' decisions to drop out of school. Students working in traditional student occupations such as baby-sitting, lawn work, odd jobs, and farming chores experience a different work environment than students working in retail or the private sector economy. Traditional work settings are less mundane and may entail meaningful interactions with adults, another source of socialization. However, long hours working in service sector occupations can be detrimental for both male and female students.

Unfortunately, this means that the majority of high school student jobs can have a detrimental affect on staying in high school. "Policy makers have long contended that one way to socialize teenagers to become young adults is to encourage them to work. However, these findings indicate that there is a negative unintended consequence of adolescent employment: a higher likelihood of dropping out" (McNeal, 1997, p. 217).

If adolescents work limited hours at times that do not interfere substantially with other activities, there are benefits from the experience. Many cite the ability to buy clothes, cars, electronic goods, music CDs, and other desired goods as a motivation for working. Almost one in three high school students worked in 1990, but African American students were less than half as likely as white students to work (see Figure 7–1).

Dropping out of high school is related to the number of hours a student works during high school and to the motivation for work; some students work more hours than allowed by law. Other students work because they have school-related problems, need money, or have family problems. Though some students must work to help their families, fewer than one in ten donate part or all of their earnings to help support their families.

The Future for Dropouts

Many dropouts face a grim future. Only 47 percent of recent high school dropouts were employed in 1997 (see Figure 7–2). They are more likely to be on welfare and to have dependent children; a disproportionate number of dropouts end up in the nation's jails and prisons and are four times as likely to engage in unlawful behavior; dropouts have difficulty competing in the labor market; they lack skills for today's jobs, have less knowledge for daily living, and have low self-esteem. But most important is the human cost to society of individuals who cannot compete in the world. Unfortunately, some proposals to raise standards in schools and require graduation examinations could also increase the dropout rates of marginal students, although a proportion of dropouts end up completing their high school degrees through GED exams.

One program developed by sociologists, which combines knowledge from the numerous studies on dropouts, is called Project RAISE. It involves at-risk middle school students in one-on-one mentoring using community adults. During the first two years of the program's operation, students improved in attendance and in report card grades in English; but this program alone is not enough to remove the years that led up to the risk of dropping out (McPartland and Nettles, 1991, p. 568). Another program for older students is the federal government's "ability to benefit" program that allows students without a high school degree or equivalent to pass a test administered by a college and qualify for federal aid to attend that college. Though these students are considered high-risk for dropping out, many find this opportunity to restart just what they need (Burd, 1996). Increased resources, more flexible time requirements, altered

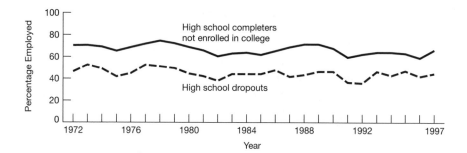

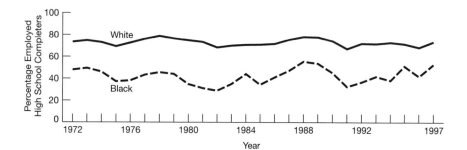

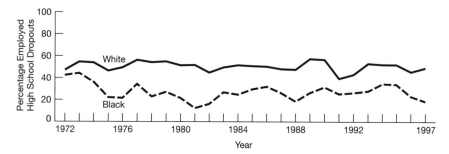

Note: Recent high school completers are individuals ages 16–24 who completed high school during the survey year. Recent high school dropouts are individuals ages 16–24 who had not completed high school, were not enrolled during the survey month, and were in school 12 months earlier. In 1994, the survey instrument for the CPS was changed and weights were adjusted. In 1992, there were too few sample observations for a reliable estimate of black recent school dropouts.

FIGURE 7-1 Employment rates for recent high school completers not enrolled in college and for recent school dropouts, October 1972–97.

Source: U.S. Department of Commerce, Bureau of the Census, October Current Population Surveys.

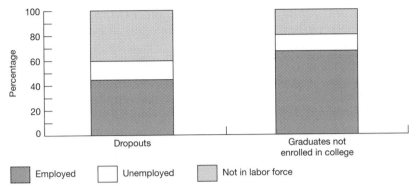

FIGURE 7-2 Labor force status of 1996–97 high school dropouts and graduates not enrolled in college, October 1997.

Source: U.S. Department of Labor, Bureau of Labor Statistics, "Employment Status of School Age Youth, High School Graduates and Dropouts, 1997."

suspension policies, and special counseling services are but a few suggestions (McEvoy, 1988, p. 7).

Schools contribute to the dropout process—or, as some have referred to it, the "pushout" process—by giving signals that the schools cannot deal with certain students. Detentions, suspensions, expulsions, and no school support system are recipes for creating dropouts (Herbert, 1989, p. 84).

Criticisms of the Student Role

Students are generally well aware of where they stand academically. They have been labeled by teachers and other students from their earliest days in school. In one second-grade classroom the teacher divided the children into reading groups—the Rocket ships, Jet airplanes, and Piper cubs. There was no doubt in those children's minds as to where they stood! Even the types of subjects taken by older students encourage role definitions; there are "dumbbell" courses and "elite" ones. These placements and labels can have a permanent, sometimes detrimental, effect on a student's self-perception.

Attitudes toward student learning differ across cultures. The Japanese have few student "failures," in part because they do not define students as failures. If a student is not succeeding, parents and teachers expect him or her to work harder to accomplish what is expected. Instead of assuming that some students cannot do the work, the assumption is that all (except those with a disability) can pass if they put in enough time and effort. This corresponds with the findings on effective schools in the United States, which hold that high academic expectations for students and teachers result in high achievement.

According to anthropologist Jules Henry and other critics of schools, students are put in a position that compromises their integrity; they must "give the teacher what she wants." Henry elaborates the reason for this in his book *Culture Against Man:*

> American classrooms, like educational institutions anywhere, express the values, preoccupations, and fears found in the culture as a whole. School has no choice; it must train the children to fit the culture as it is. School can give training in skills; it cannot teach creativity. . . . Schools deal with masses of children, and can manage therefore only by reducing them all to a common definition. (Henry, 1963, pp. 287, 320–21)

Thus, students are not encouraged to be creative, but only to toe the line, according to Henry.

Many educators have raised criticisms about the student role that concern the core of society itself. Bowles and Gintis (1976) argued that the roles of students in schools prepare them for the unequal stratification system in society at large. Students divided into tracks conform to different behavioral norms. "Vocational and general tracks emphasize rule-following and close supervision, while the college track tends toward a more open atmosphere emphasizing the internalization of norms." These differences in social relationships reflect students' social backgrounds and likely future economic positions.

> Thus blacks and other minorities are concentrated in schools whose repressive arbitrary, generally chaotic internal order, coercive authority structures, and minimal possibilities for advancement mirror the characteristics of inferior situations. Similarly, predominantly working-class schools tend to emphasize behavioral control and rule-following, while schools in well-to-do suburbs employ relatively open systems that favor greater student participation, less direct supervision, more student electives, and, in general, a value system stressing internalizing standards of control. (Bowles and Gintis, 1976)

According to this perspective, docility, lack of creativity, and conformity are the goals being met by schools in preparing students for the work world.

The student role has not changed significantly in most school settings, even with educational movements advocating more rights, power, equal opportunity, and freedom for students. Students are the clients of education, yet they have almost no control over the service rendered. Do students have the right to determine what they learn and how they should learn it? Radical educators such as Illich (1971) and Kozol (1991) argue that this is a basic right that is being denied to students for reasons other than sound pedagogy.

*A*pplying Sociology to Education: Describe your role as student at various levels of the educational system. How has it changed? ◆

STUDENTS AND THE INFORMAL SYSTEM

To carry out a role, individuals must believe that they can be successful. Therefore, students must believe that they can be high achievers in order to try to be so. Our evaluation of our ability can be altered depending on what we believe to be the costs, rewards, and motivations involved. The following sections reveal the subtle influences on students' academic achievement and school experiences.

Student's Self Concept

Wilbur Brookover and colleagues (1996) show that self-concept of academic ability is significantly correlated with academic performance. Labeling and conditioning influence the way we see our abilities in any area. If many students in a school have low achievement expectations, this influences the school's achievement level. Manipulating school variables may improve students' chances of academic success. School value climate, background experiences, peer-group relationships, and other factors in students' careers influence academic self-concept, and vice versa. Thus, the recommendation in the effective schools literature is to raise students' self-concept and academic expectations.

School Value Climate and Student Achievement

Schools reward incompetence. So argues Jackson (1968), pointing out that the average student spends 20 hours a week on courses, does little to no homework, and plays dumb. The reward for success in school is more hard work, so why try? Here we examine how school affects student achievement.

Brookover and his colleagues (1973) set about to test Coleman's and Jencks's findings that the home environment supersedes school influence in students' school achievement. In ongoing research on school climate and performance, they administered questionnaires to students and teachers. Results showed that academic value climate of school for elementary students is affected by four types of perceptions:

1. Student perceptions of the present "evaluations/expectations" of "others" (parents, teachers, friends) in their school and social system
2. Student perceptions of the future "evaluations/expectations" of "others" in their school and social system
3. Student perceptions about the level of feelings of futility permeating the social system of the school
4. Student perceptions of those academic norms stressing academic achievement that exist in their school and social system (Brookover and Erickson, 1975)

The most important variable by far was the students' reported sense of futility—their feelings of hopelessness and their sense that teachers do not care about their academic achievement. The role of teachers' and classmates' attitudes in establishing these feelings is obviously an important part of the school climate.

In a more recent study, Brookover and colleagues (1996) considered the effects of school social structure and social climate on student achievement. *Student achievement* was measured by reading and writing competencies, academic self-concept, and self-reliance. The *school social structure* was measured by teacher satisfaction with the school structure, parental involvement, differentiation in student programs, principals' reports of time devoted to instruction, and student mobility in school. The *school climate* was measured by student perceptions, teacher perceptions, and principal perceptions. More than 85 percent of the variance in student attainment was explained by the combination of these variables. In a summary of findings, which compared improving and declining schools, Brookover and colleagues found the following: The staff of improving schools place more emphasis on accomplishing basic reading and mathematics objectives; they believe all students can master basic objectives and they hold high expectations; they assume responsibility for learning and accept being held accountable. Principals in improving schools are instructional leaders and disciplinarians. In short, Brookover argues that schools can and do make a difference.

To illustrate this point and to put the concept of "school climate" into practice, Brookover and colleagues designed a pragmatic program in the Chicago public school system using the variables mentioned to alter school climate. As a result, school achievement levels increased significantly.

The findings of an English study confirm those of other studies on the question "What difference do schools make?" The researchers studied 12 inner-city London secondary schools, which varied greatly on factors such as student behavior and academic ability. School variations remained fairly constant over time, even when controlling for students' family background and personal characteristics. Examination results, behavior, and degree of delinquency were closely related in successful schools, but not related to school size, physical aspects of the building, or administrative structure.

Outcomes were related to school characteristics as social institutions—"academic emphasis, teacher action in lessons, the availability of incentives and rewards, good conditions for pupils, and the extent to which children were able to take responsibility." These factors could all be influenced by staff. The abilities of the children also affected outcomes. The combined factors created "a particular ethos, or set of values, attitudes, and behaviors which [will] become characteristic of the school as a whole. This is the school value climate. Behaviors and attitudes are shaped by school experience, and these in turn shape outcomes of schools" (Rutter et al., 1979, pp. 177–79).

Many recent commission reports encourage teachers to set high academic standards, assign well-constructed homework, and provide grades and meaningful comments. In fact, there is a relationship between the high standards and homework; research indicates that achievement and test scores improve with increased study time spent outside the classroom. High achievement performance standards set by teachers, parents, and peers also generate greater effort on homework. Higher standards are set by teachers and peers for high-ability students who can handle a challenge. Parents are more likely to set higher standards for lower-ability students less able to deal with the challenge. This difference may result from teachers' expectations of high-ability students and parents' response to their student's poor performance (Coon et al., 1993; Natriello and McDill, 1986; Pashal et al., 1984).

The bottom line is that student self-concept, home environment, teacher expectations, school climate, and many other factors all interact to affect a student's achievement. Whatever the academic norms of a school, students tend to conform. Where academic achievement is rewarded by faculty and peers, students tend to achieve better (McDill et al., 1967). School climate explains much of the difference in levels of school achievement, differences sometimes attributed solely to race, SES, and home effects (Brookover and Erickson, 1975).

Teacher and Student Expectations

Within schools, groups of student peers can be identified by their cohesiveness; along with that cohesiveness goes a set of expectations, values, and aspirations. Willis (1977) describes how boys in an all-male comprehensive secondary school in England were divided into the "lads," who "worked the system" to gain control over their time; and the "ear 'oles" (earholes), who complied with authority and the expectations of the school. Lads were learning to belong to the working class by rejecting the mental work of the school; they were reinforcing and reproducing their status. The culture lads reproduced for themselves was actually their realistic assessment of chances within the school and social class context, according to Willis. School reformers argue that a sense of futility among students can be altered by setting high expectations: "No students are expected to fall below the level of learning needed to be successful at the next level of education" (*Effective School Practices*, 1990).

> **A**pplying Sociology to Education: How would you change the value climate of your community's schools to improve students' learning and achievement? ◆

Peer Groups and Student Culture

When we enter a school or observe playground activity, we see the school's unique culture manifest itself. The norms that control behavior of peer-group members are strong. One need only observe the conformity in dress, gestures, language, and slang to discover what is acceptable in a particular school. Fads and crazes are key aspects of student culture, holding the group together.

Playground activities and games help set the students' world apart from the adult culture. Even in playground games, children are learning to relate to their peers by following rules, taking turns, and verbally and nonverbally expressing themselves. These behaviors will carry over into their formal encounters with the adult world and are an important socializing agent in the child's life.

The student subculture has strong influence in determining what happens in school. Because students are grouped together by age and subjected to a series of age-related requirements, they develop a separate subculture with norms, expectations, and methods or "strategies" for coping with these demands. This subculture of peers evolves as a result of the long period of school training, necessary for industrial societies, that delays the entry of young people into the adult world. Peer groups serve a number of purposes for their members: Young people of similiar age and status in the social and educational system can express themselves freely; experiment with social interactions and friendships while learning to get along with others; learn sex roles; and serve as reinforcers for norms, rules, and morality. Age-mates are important in this process because they are thrown together in school activities.

In *The Adolescent Society*, Coleman (1961) writes that the strength of this subculture lies in its power over its members. He found that for an adolescent, the disapproval of one's peers is almost as hard to accept as that of one's parents, and that one pays a price for nonconformity. For most adolescents, their peers are a reference group that influences their dress, mannerisms, speech patterns, preferences—their whole way of life. Smoking, early sexual involvement, drinking alcohol, and using drugs, for instance, are closely correlated with best friends' and close peers' behavior (Wang et al., 1995; Bauman and Ennett, 1994; Webb et al., 1993).

High school subcultures often place high value on athletics for males and on leadership activities for females, but little value—for either sex—on being very bright or academically oriented. For girls, good grades are often believed to detract from popularity. Some students even try not to appear smart for fear of losing peer-group approval. The students with the highest status in high schools tend to be from the dominant socioeconomic status group in the school, oriented toward school activities, and not primarily concerned with gaining adult approval. Students who are academically outstanding gain little peer acceptance or reward and are sometimes ridiculed. Coleman (1960) suggests that schools could shift the focus so that the norms of the teen communities reinforce educational goals rather than inhibit them. However, in those high schools where students have high educational and occupational expectations, competition for grades can be intense. High achievement in these schools is rewarded, and some students may even resort to cheating rather than risk doing poorly.

Student peer groups often form around neighborhood friendships, which may have existed since grade school. Their activities may have little to do with the academic aspects of school, though they can influence academic achievement and other organizational aspects, such as extracurricular activities (Garner and Raudenbush, 1991, p. 251).

Student peer-group actions are constructed within the framework or environment of the school. Philip Cusick outlines key parts of this *sociocultural environment*, which had the *intended effects* of denying freedom of activity and lumping students in an undifferentiated mass, and the *unintended effects* shown in Figure 7–3 (Cusick, 1973, pp. 216–17). As Cusick discovered in the high school he studied: "The tendency of the students . . . to maintain tight, in-school groups was a natural, but unrecognized, consequence of the school's basic organizational structure. As long as the supporting structure exists, the students will probably continue to form groups" (pp. 208–209).

Within this potentially alienating culture of high school, it is important to have friends with whom to walk, sit at lunch, and attend activities. There is usually a core of elite "jocks" and good-looking female students, and some schools may have high-status music and drama groups. There are, unfortunately, social isolates who have no friends and, therefore, no "protection" in the system (Cusick, 1973, p. 173). Generally, their number is small. In his study of high schools, Hargreaves (1967) describes two main student groups or subcultures:

FIGURE 7–3 Relationship between student behavior and the school organization.

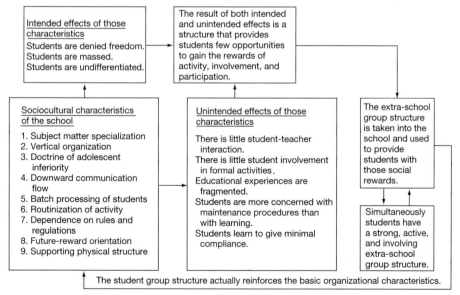

Source: Cusick, Philip A., *Inside High School. The Student's World* (New York: Holt, Rinehart and Winston, 1973).

those with positive orientations and those with negative orientations. Students with positive orientations toward the values of schools end up in the higher groups, which reinforce their orientations; negative students end up in the lower groups. For members of the negative subcultures, peer culture becomes the primary identification, whereas positive students are influenced by school values as well as by peers.

School organization sometimes contributes to the polarization of students through ability grouping, or "streaming," as do social class differences in students. Willis gives evidence that those from working-class or lower-class backgrounds may see little hope for an improved future and concentrate in negative-orientation groups:

> [A]nti-school culture provides powerful informal criteria and binding experiential processes which lead working-class lads to make the "voluntary" choice to enter the factory, and to help reproduce both the existing class structure of employment, and the "culture of the shop floor" as a segment of the overarching working-class culture. (Willis, 1977, pp. 53–54)

There is evidence that the influence of peer groups is growing in many countries as the influence of family on adolescents decreases. Studies indicate that parenting practices do influence the child's peer associations (Brown et al., 1993). The amount of time parents spend with adolescents does affect their tendency toward delinquency and inhibits formation of delinquent friends (Warr, 1993). Although the family in America used to have the dominant influence on adolescent values and behavior, the home as a socializing agent is now in competition with peer groups for the child's attention (Goodlad, 1990, 1984).

Student Coping Strategies

Student "coping" strategies, or ways of adapting to the power structure of school culture, are major aspects of the informal system. Students develop strategies related to their own needs, based on their own experiences with schooling, self-concept, peer-group relations, ability grouping, and other factors. School requires strategies very different from those learned at home in early socialization, although early learning is crucial to the student's success in school. The child is gradually eased into the competitive, judgmental, disciplined world of school. The social distance between students and teachers is established early because teachers have authority as a result of their position in the educational system. Thus, students begin to learn strategies to cope with the world of the school and classroom from an early age.

Much of the research in this area is an offshoot of the interactionist theoretical approach, which contends in part that we construct our realities within an environmental context and behave in accordance with those constructions. From this perspective, the development of strategies can be seen as a kind of negotiation requiring students to understand the teachers' roles and needs while attempting to maximize their own interests. Students' attitudes vary from almost complete compliance with the teachers' goals to total lack of commitment. Teachers have power, but getting students to do what is desired takes strategies other than the direct use of power (Woods, 1980). "Negotiations" between individual students, students and teachers, and the class as a group are constantly changing, although some interactions are fairly routine.

Different strategies are appropriate at different times in the maturational development of students. Learning how to work and solve problems may be key at one time, whereas mastering skills in taking examinations is the focus at another stage in the student's career (Woods, 1980). Turning points in children's careers can change them from "drifters" to "experts," or from excited students to bored ones. Peers play a major role in students' self-concepts as the peers define the role of each student in the class and school. Unpopular teens may be labeled "nerds," a label that is overcome by some teens through activities and friendship groups leading to greater self-confidence (Kinney, 1993).

Martyn Hammersley and Glenn Turner (1980) have developed an interactional model that takes into account student and teacher strategies. It begins with an analysis of the intentions, motives, and perspectives for student actions. The student considers possible actions, their costs and payoffs, and makes a decision based on the perceived and actual consequences of various behaviors. The teacher sets guidelines, expectations, or "frames" that operate in the classroom situation or that relate to specific segments, lessons, or problems. Students may conform to teacher "frames" or set up alternative options or "frames" that deviate from the teacher's. Whether students conform or deviate depends in part on student peer-group behaviors and on their involvement in the lesson content.

The sociocultural structure of the school is also important in determining student experiences and strategies. Recognizing this, Robert Merton developed a typology of students' reactions to school goals and means (the school's methods of attaining goals). Individual student reactions to school goals and means range from acceptance to rejection, as indicated by Merton's (1957) four types:

1. *Conformity*: acceptance of goals and means
2. *Retreatism*: rejection of goals and means
3. *Ambivalence*: indifference
4. *Rejection with replacement*: something else in mind

Peter Woods (1980) tested the goals–means typology on English public boarding school boys and revised the model to make it represent more of the variations in individual pupils' responses. He adds to the goals–means typology several categories:

1. *Colonization*. Colonization combines indifference to goals with ambivalence about means. The students accept school as a place where they must spend their time and try to maximize available gratifications, permitted and not, official and unofficial. Parts of the school system are acceptable to them, but illegal means may be used to cope, such as copying work or cheating on tests.

2. *Indulgence*. There is a strongly positive response to goals and means.

3. *Conformity*. This is broken down into several categories.

    a. *Compliance*. Students "feel some affinity for and identification with the goals and means."

    b. *Ingratiation*. Students "aim to maximize their benefits by earning the favor of those with power, and are usually undisturbed by unpopularity among their peers."

    c. *Opportunism*. Students show "less consistent application to work and frequent but momentary leanings toward other modes," trying them out before settling on one. This can result in fluctuations of behavior.

4. *Intransigence*. Students adopting this strategy are indifferent to the school's goals and reject its means to achieve goals through rules, rituals, and regulations. They may disrupt lessons and even physically assault staff or destroy property. Appearance may distinguish this type of student—hair, dress, shoes, or boots. These students are generally difficult for the school to handle.

5. *Rebellion*. Students reject the school's goals and means, but they substitute others. This is common later in school careers. The replacement of goals makes this group less of a threat than the intransigents.

In this model, developed by Merton and modified by Woods, student strategies in relation to school goals and means of achieving goals are laid out for students in elementary and high school. At the college level, strategies differ because of the different demands and nature of the situation. College students' coping mechanisms are oriented to the work they must complete in each class. Snyder (1971) documents many of the gaps between the hidden and formal curricula in higher education; that is, the implicit demands versus the visible ones, which can be recognized more easily.

Some college students quickly discover that those who master the hidden curriculum, who learn to "play the system," have learned important coping strategies. For example, C. M. L. Miller and M. Parlett (1976) write about "cue-consciousness," the degree to which students pick up cues from professors on such things as exam topics and favored subject areas. They describe three types of students:

1. *Cue-conscious*. Students who rely on hard work and luck to do well. They are less well prepared for exams because they try to learn more topics. They pick up a limited number of cues.

2. *Cue-seekers*. Students who learn selectively. They often actively seek information from faculty and try to make a good impression while seeking cues as to which topics are important.

3. *Cue-deaf.* Students who pick up virtually no cues about what is important and try to study all of the material rather than being selective.

The researchers found a correlation between the most cue-conscious students and high exam scores.

In recent years some researchers have studied students' learning styles. Each person has dominant modes of learning; if teachers are aware of the range of individual variations and class profiles in learning styles, they can plan lessons to match dominant modes or the variety of learning styles. Students who know their style can adapt study patterns. We learn from auditory stimuli, visual stimuli, and tactile stimuli; in cooperative groups, in competitive situations, or in isolation. Several scales to evaluate learning styles have been developed (see Box 7–2).

Student strategies result in a variety of individual roles and a variety of labels: conformists, drifters, planners, retreatists, intransigents, rebels, teacher's pet, nobodies, troublemakers, jocks, dumb kids, brains, eggheads, popular, sleepers, or hand-wavers (Jackson, 1968). Any label can change. Once labeled, however, a child may come to behave more and more in the manner associated with the label, carrying out the self-fulfilling prophecy.

When evaluating student strategies, it is important to consider the entire system within which the student is operating, including the power dynamics, strategies of other students and teachers, and the sociocultural structure or goals and means of the school. We now consider the environment of students.

*A*pplying Sociology to Education: What strategies do you as a student use to cope with your course(s)? ◈

STUDENTS AND THEIR ENVIRONMENTS

Effects of Home Environment on Educational Achievement

A school social worker who had in her district an elementary school that served a poverty-stricken area told of children whose parents could not care for them because of their working hours, illness, or other social problems, and of young children who took care of younger siblings. She told of children who had cola and potato chips for breakfast; of children who came to school in winter with holes in their shoes and wet feet; and of children who had unexplained bruises and even rat bites. Children facing such environmental hardships do not have the support system necessary to do well in school. We all have solutions to the problem—so why doesn't someone do something?

◆◆Box 7-2   *Learning Styles Inventory*

The following are sample statements from the Grasha-Reichman learning styles inventory (Grasha, 1975). (Students respond on a scale from "agree" to "disagree.")

1. Most of what I know, I learned on my own.
2. I find the ideas of other students relatively useful for helping me to understand the course material.
3. I try to participate as much as I can in all aspects of a course.
4. I study what is important to me and not necessarily what the instructor says is important.
5. I think an important part of classes is to learn to get along with other people.
6. I accept the structure a teacher sets for a course.
7. I do not have trouble paying attention in classes.
8. I think students can learn more by sharing their ideas than by keeping their ideas to themselves.
9. I like to study for tests with other students.
10. I feel that I must compete with the other students to get a grade.

The researchers analyze the responses of each student and of the class; with this information, both students and teacher have a better understanding of which style of learning is most effective.

Children's positions in school and society are determined in large part by their family background. Studies by Coleman (1966) and Jencks (1972), discussed below, found that one-half to two-thirds of student achievement variance is directly related to home variables such as socioeconomic level (Greenwood and Hickman, 1991, p. 287). Family "processes" are a better predictor of positive achievement and grades than all other variables (Dornbusch and Ritter, 1992).

An underlying question here is how schools can meet every child's needs. We know that schools use social constructs, with organization and language that are more familiar to middle- and upper-class children. These children are more likely to have home experiences supporting the values, attitudes, and training in cognitive skills that will help them adapt to school demands. During the early formative years, children learn languages, values, and an orientation toward the world. The early home learning environment of children is crucial; Bloom estimates that 80 percent of our potential intelligence is developed by age eight. Stimulating environments can help recover lost potential, but the process becomes more difficult (Bloom, 1981).

Let us follow two 5-year-old children of equal ability into school. Joey comes from a working-class family, Billy from a middle-class family. Why is it likely from the outset that Joey will achieve at a lower level than Billy? We must be ever cautious of generalizing from two cases, and we must be aware that there are many variations in patterns of child-rearing; yet research in the United States and Britain has identified some common class-related child-rearing patterns, and these give Joey and Billy different tools with which to approach the school experience.

Joey and Billy's differences fall into several categories: cultural capital they bring to school, learning right and wrong, attitudes and values, language ability and cognitive skills, family structure, and parent–child interaction. When Joey misbehaves, his parents are quick to discipline him. The most common punishments are threats about consequences of his actions or withdrawal of privileges or belting him with a strap. Billy is also disciplined, but the method is very different. His parents use reasoning, guilt, and shame to instill values. Joey's socialization may be useful training for living in a sometimes dangerous environment, but it does not help him meet certain demands of the classroom situation, such as creative or independent thinking.

Joey and Billy are likely to develop different language patterns. Both speak English, but middle-class children learn formal or elaborated language in addition to "public" language used in everyday conversing by both children. The more restricted "public" language limits the child's ability to conceptualize new ideas and concepts. Formal language allows Billy to deal with more complex ideas and feelings (Bernstein, 1981).

Although most parents place a high value on the education and achievement of their children, their methods of encouraging education are different. Working-class parents expect their children to "behave" in school, stressing conformity and obedience to authority, behaviors necessary for working-class jobs. Socialization of middle-class children stresses independence and self-direction, important in decision making and carrying out white-collar jobs.

Family Background and Parental Involvement

Children succeed in large part because of their family background and what parents do to support their children in their education. Parenting styles and parental expectations play crucial roles in setting the child's educational agenda. Guidelines about after-school and weekend activities, television watching, homework, and other school-related decisions give the child structure and help the child set goals (Dornbusch and Ritter, 1992; Lee, Dedrick, and Smith, 1991). One of the most important ingredients in a child's success in school is the degree of parental involvement in the educational process of the child. Questions concern what parental activities help or harm a child's school achievement. Involvement of parents is shaped by their social and financial resources, their opportunities to be involved, and their own orientation toward education (see Figure 7–4).

Some home environment factors that influence student achievement include social class of family, early home environment, parenting style, "type" of mother–child interaction, effect of the mother working, parent involvement in school decisions and activities, family and student aspirations, and number of children in the family (Rubin and Borgers, 1991). The more children in the family, the less time parents interact with each child. Let us consider several of these factors.

Social Class Background

Parents' involvement in the educational process differs by social class. A great deal of research has focused on the "cultural capital" that children bring to school from their family life (Kalmijn and Kraaykamp, 1996). Some types of cultural capital facilitate school learning, some do not (Bourdieu, 1977). In fact,

FIGURE 7–4 Factors affecting parental influence on children's achievement and behavior.

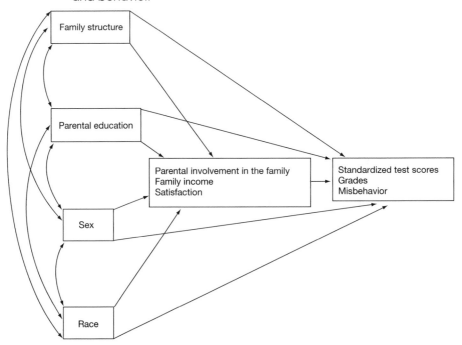

Source: From *Parents, Their Children, and Schools* by Barbara Schneider, Copyright © 1993 by Westview Press, A Member of the Perseus Books Group. Reprinted by permission of Westview Press, a member of Perseus Books, L.L.C.

social class position can become a form of "cultural capital" leading to different schooling experiences. The cultural capital of middle- and upper-class children—for instance, those with educated mothers (Rosenweig, 1994)—provides useful resources for educational experiences, whereas that of the lower classes provides resources not valued by dominant social institutions such as education (Lareau, 1985).

Higher-class parents are active in managing their children's education at home and at school, whereas lower-class parents do what the schools ask but little more. Both sets of parents hold similar educational values, and parents are treated the same by the school. Higher-class parents, however, have more "cultural capital," and if they use it, their children benefit. Parents of working-class children are less comfortable dealing with schools and teachers than those of higher-class students, who feel more comfortable communicating with teachers and are more involved with school activities (Lareau, 1989).

Middle-class families tend to have more educational materials in the home—books, newspapers, magazines. These students read a lot at home and score higher than lower-class students on reading achievement tests. Their parents read, visit the library, and participate in school activities (Anderson et al., 1985). They also visit more museums and attend concerts, and provide extra educational opportunities during school breaks (Entwisle and Alexander, 1995); all of these are activities that reinforce values of education and supplement learning.

Though children from different social class backgrounds attend colleges, their cultural capital is closely related to the type of college they attend. Students' choice of college is related to their family background, friends, and outlook on their life chances (McDonough, 1997). In addition, the long-term differences indicate that low-SES students' income levels, educational attainment, educational aspirations, and graduate school attendance were lower than those of high-SES students (Walpole, 1997).

Parenting Styles

Parenting styles also affect student achievement. Authoritarian, overprotective, and permissive parenting styles (very rigid or very lax) in American society are negatively associated with student achievement, and higher percentages of students from these backgrounds drop out of school (Taris and Bok, 1996). An authoritative style (guidance with reasoning) balances clear, high parental demands with emotional responsiveness and recognition of the child's autonomy. This latter approach is positively related to achievement (Darling, 1999). It involves a high degree of monitoring on the part of the parents, high support and involvement, and a high degree of psychological autonomy for the child (Lam, 1997). In some societies, rigidly structured and cohesive families are associated with high achievement (Georgiou, 1995; Fontaine, 1994).

Family Aspirations

Family and student aspirations for the future are another aspect of the influence of class, racial, or ethnic background. Parents who set high standards and have high aspirations for their children are more likely to have high-achieving children. James Coleman and colleagues found that African American and white seniors had comparable aspirations; the difference was in taking the necessary steps to carry out their goals. African American students believed that they had less control over their environment and left their fate to luck and chance (Coleman et al., 1966), though many lower-class African American mothers find multiple strategies to encourage their children's school achievement (Rosier, 1993). From Coleman's research in Equality of Educational Opportunity (the Coleman Report), the most extensive study done in the field of education, comes evidence that the effects of the home environment far outweigh the effects of the school program on achievement. Educational and social class background is the most important factor in determining differences among students. The next most important factor is the school composition—the backgrounds of other children in the same school.

Another extensive study, by Christopher Jencks and others (1972), reached the same general conclusion: Family characteristics are the main variable in a student's school environment. In fact, Jencks's findings indicate that family background accounts for more than one-half of the variation in educational attainment. Regardless of the measure used—occupation, income, parent education—family socioeconomic status is a powerful predictor of school performance.

Single-Parent Homes

Children from one-parent households have lower grades, lower test scores, and higher dropout rates on average than those from two-parent households; these results also are influenced by the race or ethnicity of the family, the educational level of the parent(s), and low level of involvement by the absence of a parent. Warning signs that children are likely to have problems in school appear as early as ages three to five in many welfare children who receive little cognitive stimulation and emotional support. Unless there is significant parental support and supervision, these factors are correlated with children being tardy or absent from school, not doing homework, not having contact with their parents, and engaging in frequent dating and early sex (Moore et al., 1996; Pallas, 1989; Mulkey, Crain, and Harrington, 1992).

Children who live with single parents receive less parental encouragement and attention with respect to educational activities than children who live with both biological parents. These children report lower educational expectations, less monitoring of school work, and overall less supervision than children from intact families (Astone and McLanahan, 1991, pp. 318-19).

The Role of Mothers

Poor mothers are less likely to be involved in their children's schooling because of discomfort with teachers and lack of social support (Thurston and Navarrete, 1996). Children who are left to make their own educational plans and decisions, where parents have little involvement, are more likely to be dropouts (Rumberger, 1990). These findings are confirmed by a study in the Netherlands, which reported that the negative effects of the single-parent family have increased since the 1980s (Dronkers, 1992). Single parents, however, who do become involved in their children's education can compensate for these problems (Lee et al., 1991; Pallas, 1989). Recent findings indicate that mothers who work part-time tend to be very involved with their children's education, and their children perform at a higher rate. Full-time work affects after-school supervised time for the child; it is here that differences exist (Muller, 1991).

Other evidence shows the impact of involvement of mothers in the schooling process. For instance, mothers with an eighth-grade education discuss similar strategies to other parents for encouraging their children's school achievement, but their use and implementation of these strategies differed by their socioeconomic level. College-educated mothers "managed" their children's high school schedule by selecting college preparatory courses. High-socioeconomic-background children do better in the school system partly because their parents have better management skills (Baker and Stevenson, 1986). In fact, some middle-class parents may try to "control" schools and take action if a child is having problems, whereas lower-class parents feel helpless and alienated in their interactions with schools.

A question of concern to many families is the effect of working mothers on the achievement of children. Study results are mixed, and many variables are involved such as the number of hours worked and intensity of the work, care of children, and the socioeconomic level of the family (Williams, 1993). Summarizing the major findings, we can say that working women provide positive role models and their children often score higher on achievement tests (Radin, 1990). More specifically, African American, single, working mothers have a positive effect on the achievement of African American elementary school children. Working mothers from African American two-parent families have little affect on children's achievement. Findings show little relationship between a mother's occupation and her daughter's occupational aspirations, perhaps because many mothers' occupations were routine jobs. When the mother was in a female-gendered occupation, however, the daughter was more likely to aspire to a female-gendered occupation (Mickelson and Velasco, 1998).

The Number of Siblings

The number of children in the family is another variable that affects school experience, especially the years of schooling that a child completes. Parents with smaller families offer children greater intellectual and educational advantages. We know that boys who come from families with a small number of siblings have more mobility; that is, they more often complete more years of schooling than did their fathers. The more siblings in a family, the more diluted the parents' attention and material resources (Blake, 1991), and the lower the achievement (Hanushek, 1992).

Children from families with a small number of siblings "gain many advantages of a personal nature, including markedly higher verbal ability, motivation to perform in school, a preference for 'intellectual' extracurricular activities, a family setting that is typically conducive to study and academic pursuits, and encouragement to go to college." Those from families with a large number of siblings, "on average, have lower verbal IQs, perform less well in school, engage less in intellectual extracurricular activities and more in sports and community activities, are less likely to be encouraged to go to college, and, as a consequence, are more dependent on being shored up by familial status if they are to graduate from high school" (Blake, 1986, p. 416).

Schools play a role in making it possible to involve parents (Spencer, 1994, p. 5f). Not all schools are welcoming; teachers are overworked and parents add one more layer to the workload (Dornbusch and Ritter, 1992). Some parents expect too much from teachers or are downright abusive (Ostrander, 1991, p. 37). However, there are constructive ways to involve parents both in the education of their own children and in the school program (Epstein and Dauber, 1991, p. 289).

Applying Sociology to Education: What can families do to enhance the academic achievement of their children? ◆

Students make up the largest group of school participants, and, therefore, have the major role in influencing the achievement level and climate of the school. The importance of understanding their roles is to know what they bring to the school in terms of environmental influences and what they take out of the school in terms of preparation for participation in society.

◆ Summary

The largest group making up the school system are students. School exist to socialize students into productive roles in the larger society. This chapter deals with a variety of aspects of the student role.

I. Characteristics of Students

Minority student enrollments are increasing in primary and secondary education in the United States. Students are caught between school, peer, and the family expectations, affecting student achievement. Student subcultures and friendship patterns can influence a student's self-concept and achievement in school, as can social class and gender. Students learn their roles early in school—in nursery school or kindergarten—and carry out these roles throughout their school careers. Each new group is processed as a cohort or class. Some students face conflicting expectations between teachers and administrators representing adult authority, and peers. Students cope with expectations by adopting different roles in classrooms; they may be apathetic, alienated, or go along with the school program. For those that have problems with the system, failure is possible.

II. School Failures and Dropouts

Some students fail. These are the students who are most at-risk to drop out of school. Home problems, pregnancy, second-language issues, gang affiliation, immigrant status, poverty, feeling alienated from the school system can all lead to dropping out. Youth join gangs for protection and belonging; many gangs are involved in illegal activities, and their influence can spill over into schools. Though their numbers may be small, their impact on schools can be great, creating fear, violence, intimidation, drug use, and gang recruitment. In order to control the influence of gangs, schools try to influence the learning environment so that it is more accepting of at-risk students, but at the same time protect schools for the other students. The Safe Schools Movement develops programs to reduce violence and the threat of violence in schools. Some students are retained or suspended from schools; often those students are more at risk for dropping out. Several suggestions for reducing these problems are given. Employment can be helpful or harmful to student achievement, depending on the type of work and the number of hours worked. Dropouts face a difficult future; therefore, trying to keep students in school is an important goal. Conflict theorists argue that school prepares students for their social class status in society.

III. Students and the Informal System

Self-concept impacts a student's achievement. Low expectations in a school or classroom result in low achievement. The value climate of the school influences expectations; schools do make a difference in student achievement, and characteristics of effective schools are discussed, such as teachers setting high standards. Teacher expectations of students and peer-group influences compete to affect student achievement. High school athletic groups is one example. Ability grouping can influence student peer grouping, not always with positive results. Coping strategies, discussed by interaction theorists, refer to ways students interpret and respond to school expectations. One model for looking at student strategies considers students' goals and means as related to their achievement.

IV. Students and Their Environments

Environments refer to influences outside the school that affect the student's role in the school. For instance, home environment has a major impact. Whether the student receives support from home, role models, and other requirements to do well in school will impact on achievement. When parents are involved with their children's schooling, children's achievement is higher. Involvement of parents differs by social class and parenting styles. Family aspirations for the future also influence student achievement. More highly educated mothers, for instance, take a more active role in managing their children's education. Whether a mother's working affects the child's achievement varies. Number of siblings also can affect achievement, with smaller families giving more attention to each child.

Many factors, then, affect the student's achievement in school.

◆ *Putting Sociology to Work*

1. Discuss how teacher expectations have affected your education or your children's education.

2. What peer groups or cliques were evident in your high school? How did these affect the attitudes toward school and achievement levels of the students involved?

3. How can a child's self-concept affect his or her learning? Give a specific case example.

4. Interview parents from several different backgrounds—class, minority status, gender. Ask about their involvement in their children's schooling and what their philosophy of being involved is.

5. What are the most important influences in the lives of students you know—your children, siblings, others you know—their families, peers, or other influences?

CHAPTER 8

The Informal System and the "Hidden Curriculum"

What Really Happens in School?

Ginger held back tears as her father left her at the first-grade classroom door. Would she know any classmates or make friends? Like the teacher? Understand the rules? Be successful? These questions go through the minds of students as they face new challenges that may mean success or failure. Remember your first day in a new school year or new school? These memories are vivid and lasting because we invest a tremendous amount of time and energy in adjusting to schooling. During our time as students, we spend more than 1,000 hours each year in school (Jackson, 1968). Probably our clearest memories of school are the high and low points, not the daily routine. Ask your friends what they remember about early school experiences and you will hear about winning the spelling bee; standing in front of the class to recite a poem; getting detention for nothing; searching for the hamster that got loose in the school and missing math period; falling on the playground and getting stitches; starring in the school play and forgetting the lines. These highs and lows help make up our attitude toward schools and how we shape our school experience. They are part of the *informal system*. In this chapter we look at several aspects of the informal system of schools, those unplanned experiences that happen apart from or as a result of the formal, planned curriculum of schools.

We tend to define ourselves in relation to those around us in school—our peers and teachers. We are tested, rewarded, accused, cajoled, punished, favored, ridiculed, praised, or mocked. And possibly, we fail. John Holt (1968) discusses this topic and in doing so points out some of the variables that shape children's school experiences:

> They are afraid, above all else, of failing, of disappointing or displeasing the many anxious adults around them, whose limitless hopes and expectations for them hang over their heads like a cloud. They are bored because the things they are told to do in school are so trivial, so dull, and make such limited and narrow demands on the wide spectrum of their intelligence, capabilities, and talents. They are confused because most of the torrent of words that pours over them in school makes little or no sense. It often flatly contradicts other things they have been told, and hardly ever has any relation to what they really know—to the rough model of reality that they carry around in their minds. (pp. xiii, xiv)

Our beliefs about school are affected by the teacher, by the atmosphere of the classroom, by events taking place outside the school, and by our own perceptions and interpretations. Yet most of us have not given much thought to our beliefs about school. Social scientists and educators have not paid much attention to this topic until recently. Judging by the scarcity of studies, students' beliefs about school would seem to be of little concern; after all, kids must go to school, so why question how they feel about it? What good would it do anyway? Schools have functions to perform and they cannot always be to the liking of students, who probably do not know anyway what is important to learn.

The informal system covers topics ranging from coping strategies of individual students and teachers at the microlevel of analysis to the structure and culture of schools at the macrolevel. Because the informal system permeates every aspect of education, we can only give examples of what this system is and how it works.

THE OPEN SYSTEMS APPROACH AND THE INFORMAL SYSTEM

The internal system of the school has both a formal part, consisting of roles and structure, and an informal aspect. Consider the model shown in Figure 8–1, and note the interaction between the internal system and the environment, which is discussed further in Chapter 9. Our topics in this chapter cover several aspects of the informal system: the hidden curriculum and reproduction theories, pedagogical "codes," educational climate and effective schools, peer cultures and peer-group influences, the school as an informal agent of socialization, power dynamics in the school, and student and teacher coping mechanisms.

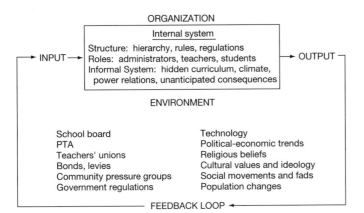

FIGURE 8–1 The open system of schools.

The Hidden Curriculum

Under the organized, structured curriculum lies another, the three Rs: rules, routines, and regulations of the "hidden curriculum," as demonstrated in the syllabus outlined in Table 8–1. Most of us have had similar questions as we entered each new class and evaluated each new teacher. The name *hidden curriculum* was coined by Benson Snyder (1971), and the concept has been used for many years by educators, sociologists, and psychologists in describing the informal system of schools. Snyder refers to the "implicit demands (as opposed to the explicit obligations of the 'visible curriculum') that are found in every learning institution and which students have to find out and respond to in order to survive within it" (p. 6).

Many alternative adjectives exist for the "hidden" curriculum: unwritten, unstudied, tacit, latent, unnoticed, and paracurriculum. In David Hargreaves's

TABLE 8–1 Syllabus for Course 101

Actual or Visible Curriculum	*Hidden Curriculum*
Instructor: Name	*Instructor:* What should I call the instructor?
Texts: Names	*Texts:* Do we really have to have them and read them?
Course topics: Listed	*Course topics:* What is the instructor really going to teach? What is he or she really interested in?
Requirements:	*Requirements:*
Readings	What do I really have to do to get by?
Projects	Will it help if I speak up in class?
Exams	Will it help if I go see the instructor?
Bibliography	*Bibliography:* Am I really supposed to use this?

(1977) analysis of the research done on the "paracurriculum," he finds two major categories: (1) the social-psychological aspects of the paracurriculum from functionalist-conservative or radical-conflict points of view; and (2) the sociological aspects from a functionalist-conservative account or the more radical-conflict position. We will refer to these perspectives in our discussion of the informal system.

From the systems perspective, the hidden curriculum is one part of the total system, and we can understand it only by understanding the context or school setting. We now review some of the elements that make up the informal system.

Reproduction Theory and the Informal System

To conflict theorists, the social control function of the hidden curriculum reproduces the social class of students (Bowles and Gintis, 1976); for instance, working-class students learn to cope with boredom in schools, which enables them to endure a life of boredom on the job. They learn through the hidden curriculum that they are "written off" in the educational system.

The hidden curriculum contains a social and economic agenda that is responsible for separating social classes, giving elites more freedom and opportunity, and training nonelites to accept their lot as obedient, punctual workers. Most students learn to accept their political-economic system as best, whatever their position within it.

Anyon (1980) documents the differences in school experiences and expectations by describing several types of elementary schools in contrasting communities, from working-class to professional and executive elite schools. Although many outward similarities exist, the hidden curriculum in each school addresses the "needs" of the social class represented by the majority of students in the school.

1. The working-class school stressed following the steps of a procedure, mechanically, by rote, with little decision making, choice, or explanation why it was done a particular way. Grading is based on following procedures.

2. The middle-class school stressed getting the right answer. There is some figuring, choice, and decision making; for instance, asking the children how they got an answer.

3. The affluent professional school stressed creative activity carried out independently, with students asked to express and apply ideas and concepts, and think about the ideas.

4. The executive elite school stressed developing analytical intellectual powers, reasoning through problems, conceptualizing rules by which elements may fit together in systems and applying these to solving problems. Included here is successful presentation of self.

Anyon points out that these aspects of the hidden curriculum are preparing the students for their future productive roles in society. The working class is being prepared for future wage labor that is mechanical and routine, the middle class for bureaucratic relations to capital, the professionals for instrumental and expressive roles that involve substantial negotiation, and the elite for analyzing and manipulating the system. In conclusion, the hidden curriculum prepares students for their future roles in society.

MacLeod (1995) describes the life of two groups of young men in a poor housing project in Chicago. In his ethnographic study, he observes, "hangs out with," and interviews members of the group; his focus is on their relationship to their schooling, the barriers to success in school and life, and how they reproduce their life chances by their actions. In another ethnographic study, Lubeck (1984, p. 230) reports on early childhood education, documenting the importance of the use of time and space to transmit adult values. The differences between the Head Start and other child-care settings she studied illustrate the importance of values for reproducing class. In Head Start settings serving low-income children, time and space tended to be more rigidly structured for the children than in other centers where children had some control. The meaning for the students is in the long-term results of reproducing their class status.

Students at all levels of education develop coping mechanisms or strategies for survival within the structure of contradictions—delays while much of the day is spent waiting to hurry up, or denials when students are told the many things they cannot do. Students try to find the approved responses among the mixed messages; successful students become adept at beating the system (Holt, 1968).

*A*pplying Sociology to Education: Describe "the hidden curriculum" in your educational setting and in the courses you are taking.

THE EDUCATIONAL "CLIMATE" AND SCHOOL EFFECTIVENESS

Let us enter the school again as we did when we discussed the formal school system. However, this time we are looking for the informal aspects of the system. We can observe only a handful of situations, but these few will provide examples of the informal system within schools.

"Climate refers to a general social condition that characterizes a group, organization, or community, such as the general opinion in a community" (Brookover, Erickson, and McEvoy, 1996, p. 26), as it affects what happens in

Much student learning takes place outside the classroom in interaction with peers.

schools and classrooms and as it contributes to effective schools. Put less formally, climate and culture are the unofficial happenings and the atmosphere that pervade each educational setting—warm and accepting, strict and intolerant, large and impersonal. The concept of organizational climate has interested researchers since the 1960s; early research indicated that attention to the school climate could influence student academic achievement. Therefore, understanding conditions or environment needed to maximize student learning became a focus of researchers in both the United States and other countries (Johnson et al., 1999). Some elements of the informal system are fairly easily observed: the school's architecture, open versus closed classrooms, ability grouping, age grading, and team teaching. Many of these are discussed elsewhere in the text. Others are not so easily observed. Here we are particularly interested in the educational "climate" or "culture" as it affects the experience of school participants. Factors both inside and outside the school influence the value climate, our first topic.

The Value Climate

What affects students' motivations, aspirations, and achievement? Why are some schools more productive than others? Do peers have more influence over students than teachers and parents? It is difficult to unravel this interlocking group of questions, for the variables are closely interrelated and no single one can provide an answer. Each major research project concerned with the value climate has included slightly different research questions, variables, methods, and settings, resulting in conclusions that are often diverse and even contradictory. Although this is a field in the process of development and change, the studies cited here show the relationship of value climate to home environment, self-concept, achievement, and teacher expectations, and illustrate some of the major interests and findings in the field.

Schools teach more than reading, writing and 'rithmetic. Both the formal and informal organization include lessons in values and morals. Philip Jackson and colleagues (1993) studied practices in schools that pass on moral values to students. For instance, teaching of morals as a part of the formal curriculum of public schools was almost absent. Though lessons in morals came up within the curriculum content of other subjects, seldom was the purpose of a lesson to instill moral content. Moral education came in other forms, such as the rituals and ceremonies in schools—speakers on drug abuse, pep rallies, graduations, the Pledge of Allegiance, or holiday celebrations such as Martin Luther King day. Visual displays of signs, pictures, and posters contained moral messages such as "Take pride in what you do" and "Peace on Earth," promoting a kind of "bumper sticker morality." At times teachers would interject moral lessons into the day; commenting on a theft, act of cruelty, or poor sportsmanship are examples.

Some moral messages were not taught, but absorbed as part of the educational environment. For instance, each classroom and school has its do's and don'ts—rules, regulations, customs, and traditions. Verbal and nonverbal cues let students know when their behavior is unacceptable. It is through these messages that students learn the informal lessons of school.

The School Climate and Effective Schools

Many aspects of schools are familiar: corridors, classrooms behind closed doors, a big clock, signs directing us to the school office. But there is something unique about each school's environment or atmosphere, something intangible. This forms the school *climate*.

School Culture. Each school has a culture of its own, like a miniature society. This is part of school climate. It consists of the values, attitudes, beliefs, norms, and customs of those making up the system. Each school's culture includes its rituals and ceremonies (Waller, [1932] 1961). A key purpose or function of this culture is to bring about a group feeling of loyalty. Pep rallies, cheering at athletic events, assemblies, singing, devotions, fire drills, honors and awards ceremonies, opening exercises, commencement, and even passing to classes constitute ceremonies common to most schools, but these are unique in each school. Many ceremonies take place around athletics;

athletes are often leading figures among the students and may even be given special privileges and status in the school. Similar ceremonies are found at the college level in fraternities and sororities; they distinguish participants from the more "serious" world of academics and professors, and provide a buffer between the two.

Students are assigned to a public school by chance of residence. The school culture reflects the immediate community in which the school is located and its students' characteristics. Norms in both the school setting and the larger culture encourage distance between teachers and students. A new teacher who tries to be too friendly to students may receive sanctions from teachers, ranging from teasing to ostracism. In most school situations, teachers maintain distance as a sign of authority, and perhaps also to discourage close relations, which might lead to indiscretions between students and teachers.

Teachers represent the culture of the adult society and the dominant group; students have a more limited cultural boundary centered on age-peer group, school, and local community. The worldview held by the two groups is a separating influence. Teachers are considered "different" by students; mystique surrounds them. Recall your impressions of various teachers, the rumors that circulated about them, and nicknames they were given. Students make their own culture, which is passed on to each new generation entering the school; it involves language, dress, humor, music, games, and hazing.

School Learning Climate. We can all document problems found in schools, but how do we define effective schools? Learning climate refers to "the normative attitudinal and behavioral patterns in a school which impact on the level of academic achievement of the student body as a whole"—teacher expectations, academic norms, students' sense of futility, role definitions, grouping patterns, and instructional practices (Brookover et al., 1996, p. 28). The concept of effective schools addresses both formal structural variables and informal climate variables, recognizing the interrelationship between the two.

Pervading all of these characteristics is the idea that a positive school climate emphasizes and rewards academic achievement, the importance of scholastic success, and the maintenance of order and fair discipline. Complementing these should be positive home–school relations: a supportive home environment for students, involvement of parents with the school, and support of students doing homework (Epstein, 1995).

These relationships within the school and classroom context make up the system of education that must be manipulated at the local, state, and national levels to improve schools and make them more effective (Levine and Ornstein, 1993).

A*pplying Sociology to Education:* Based on what you have learned about effective schools, what needs to be changed to make your community schools more effective? ◆

Classroom Learning Climate

The class has often been described and viewed as a self-contained system, sealed off from society. Psychologists and sociologists have concentrated on the "one teacher–many students" model, rather than viewing the classroom in a broader context advocated by the open system model. The classroom also has been equated with a crowd situation (Jackson, 1968, p. 10): many people in close proximity and a central figure trying to maintain control, often through the use of discipline. Whatever the model, the dynamics of classroom behavior cannot be understood unless the importance of the environment is recognized. Did Johnny have breakfast this morning; did Linda have an argument with her best friend; are Stephen's parents separating; does the teacher have personal or professional problems?

The learning climate is made up of routines imposed on students in classrooms in order to maintain control and discipline. In fact, the instructional patterns are remarkably similar. Students often play passive learning roles and are not actively involved in thinking or in hands-on activity. Teachers can take into account different types of intelligences and learning styles, however, in teaching to student needs (Lazear, 1992). Teachers call the shots and determine the activities. If they believe they can make a difference, they usually do (Weber and Omotani, 1994).

Classrooms, because of their structure and organization, assume certain behaviors and attitudes on the part of students—delayed gratification, for example, and support of group cohesion and purpose over individual desires. These attitudes are not taught easily in school but are necessary components of the teaching situation. Children must begin to acquire the behaviors and attitudes necessary for classroom learning before coming to school. The school experience can be meaningless for "unprepared" children. Problems in families, lack of discipline in some homes, and the influence of television have not aided the adjustment to traditional classrooms. Preparation for school can no longer be assumed by teachers. What can be done to prepare students? Suggestions range from solving societal-economic problems in order to increase family stability, to "deschooling society," as described in Chapter 13.

Students understand their classroom experiences in many different ways, most of which are influenced by relations among students. Especially for early adolescents, social and personal development needs suggest that cooperative learning activities are important and effective (Gilmore and Murphy, 1991).

Classroom climate can produce antischool feelings, especially in competitive, restrictive classrooms, or it can produce students who are motivated toward self-improvement, academic success, and enjoyment of learning. Where student motivation is low, increasing teacher concern and involvement may reduce classroom problems. An unfortunate downward trend in positive, encouraging teacher behaviors occurs, however, as students progress through levels of school. By the high school years, "the frequency of teacher praise, encouragement, connection with guidance, and positive interaction with students had dropped by nearly 50 percent from the number of observed occurrences at the early elementary level" (Benham, Giesen, and Oakes, 1980, p. 339).

Classroom Codes: Interaction in the Classroom. A major process in the school system is interaction. Messages concerning expectations, power relations, and attitudes toward others and the learning process are passed on through verbal and nonverbal cues. The type and extent of classroom interaction is related to teacher styles, which can be grouped into three types:

◆ *Authoritarian*: Formal power is vested and used by the teacher.
◆ *Democratic*: Students are involved in the decision making that affects classroom activities.
◆ *Laissez-faire*: There is general freedom in the classroom.

The daily student–teacher interactions and interpersonal relations determine the atmosphere of the classroom. In the average classroom a routine develops, though a day in a classroom is seldom really routine. Consider the fact that between 300 and 600 interactions take place in one hour of class time. Consider also that for every spoken message there are several unspoken messages given through tone, gesture, and facial expressions. The silent language can tell us more about the atmosphere of the classroom than any spoken words.

Basil Bernstein, an English sociologist who has written extensively on processes in schools, is concerned with the formal and informal processes that take place in classrooms, the rules that govern interaction, power relationships between teachers and students, and how these relate to the social class of students. He argues that these classroom dynamics lead to the social reproduction of class (Bernstein, 1996). Classrooms, he contends, have interaction "codes"— rules, practices, and agencies regulating communication that determine the distribution of power. *Code* refers to a "regulative principle which underlies various message systems, especially curriculum and pedagogy." *Pedagogy* refers to the transmission of knowledge, usually through structured curricula. Among the codes are hierarchy—the interaction between the transmitter (teacher) and acquirer (student); the sequencing and pacing, or progression and rate, at which information is transmitted; and the criteria, or whether the student accepts as legitimate or illegitimate what is being transmitted in the educational process. All of these factors affect the student's learning. Control, then, relates to the power structures and social division of labor. Those who control *what* knowledge is transmitted in the curriculum also have control over *how* knowledge is transmitted—the materials, organization, pacing, and timing of knowledge transmitted and received (Bernstein, 1990). "That schools require an elaborated code for success means that working class children are disadvantaged by the dominant code of schooling, not deficient . . . difference becomes deficit in the context of macro-power relations" (Sadovnik, 2001).

In a test of Bernstein's concept of "pedagogical codes," Kalekin-Fishman (1991) studied the way messages are transmitted between teachers and students in kindergartens in Germany and Israel. The "noise" patterns in classrooms reflected the goals and structure of classrooms. For instance, a teacher's authoritarian directives resulted in more controlled noise patterns, with children speaking when permitted. This pattern was more effective in some settings, such as working-class areas, in bringing about desired results. Teachers as "facilitators" produced more "white noise" or undifferentiated sound in the classroom, because students were freer to talk with fewer direct teacher commands. The different pedagogical codes do affect the learning environment and the reproduction of social class.

Student Friendship and Interaction Patterns in the Classroom

Who students "hang out" with is an important part of the informal experience in schools. These friendship patterns affect each student's peer-group affiliation and in turn aspirations for educational attainment. Student friendship patterns and interactions vary depending on whether the classroom is structured in an open or a traditional manner. Open, flexible, and democratic classrooms stress the affective or emotional growth of students (Grubaugh and Houston 1990), whereas traditional classrooms are teacher centered and often stress learning the basics. According to a study of friendship patterns (Hallinan, 1976), affective classrooms include increased interaction and shared activities, more uniform distribution of popularity among students, and an increased opportunity for students to be good at some task. Open classrooms encourage more and longer-lasting friendships. Hallinan considered the context in which students meet friends in traditional and open classes. Students in open classes had fewer best friends (Hallinan, 1979), but more general friendships. In traditional classrooms, children have potential friends who are seated near them because of imposed seating assignments.

Friendship patterns begin in preschool; children develop friendships in the course of their play, and these patterns continue through childhood (Evaldsson and Corsaro, 1998; Corsaro, 1994). Having friends is related to popularity of young children and facilitates socioemotional growth and behavior (Walden, Lemerise, and Smith, 1999). For adolescents, having a best friend is important as a source of mutual intimacy and provides acceptance, understanding, a place for self-disclosure, and mutual advice. Loyalty and commitment become increasingly important aspects of friendships as adolescents become older.

Peer social status and friendships do not necessarily go hand in hand. Some rejected, neglected children have friends, and some popular children do not. The point is that all children need social peers and close friends to feel that they belong; to the extent that teachers can facilitate these relationships, children's achievement may improve (Vandell and Hembree, 1994).

There are clear differences between female and male popularity and friendship patterns: Females are closely knit and egalitarian, sharing intimacies and problems; males are loosely knit, with clear status hierarchies based on shared activities such as sports (Corsaro and Eder, 1990). Popularity of boys and girls in elementary school relates to gender socialization. Boys achieve high status because of athletic ability, coolness, toughness, social skills, and success in cross-gender relations. Girls are popular because of their parents' socioeconomic status, their appearance, social skills, and academic success (Adler, Kless, and Adler, 1992).

Eder (1985, Eder et al., 1995) describes a hierarchy of cliques that are evident among girls in junior high school. Popular girls avoid interactions with lower-status girls, but this engenders dislike toward the popular girls, hence a cycle of popularity. Many girls want to appear friendly and interact with people they dislike to avoid a "snobbish" or "stuck-up" label. Adolescent boys are often insensitive and aggressive, patterns they adopt as part of the stress on competitiveness for success (Eder et al., 1995). For the most part different experiences of girls and boys in elementary school classrooms result from gender-role expectations; there are subtle differences in teaching boys more self-reliance and independence and girls more conformity and responsibility (Brophy, 1985).

The organizational structure of the school can also affect interactions. For instance, tracking or ability grouping constricts the number and variety of students with whom one comes in contact, influencing student contacts such as racial interactions in schools where groupings break down along racial lines. Interracial friendships are important as a training ground for future work environments and as an influence on college aspirations and attendance. The closer the peers, the greater the influence, especially in the same track and gender (Hallinan and Williams, 1990). Teachers often manipulate the classroom situation in order to have better control over interaction patterns of individuals or groups of students. Moving seats, rearranging desks, and regrouping students all influence interaction patterns and climate.

Special events or organizational changes can alter the classroom routine and also affect classroom participation: when a substitute teacher comes; when a child moves from one reading group to the next level group; when the principal visits the classroom; when testing days are held; and when the school has a special assembly or holiday program.

Seating Arrangements and Physical Conditions in Classrooms and Schools.
A persistent question in the field of school facilities planning is the relationship
between the building environment and the performance and behavior of users,
particularly students (Earthman and Lemasters, 1996). Evidence points to the
influence of classroom structure and school conditions in the achievement of
students.

Most classrooms are set up so that the teacher is the center of activity; students face the teacher and are placed so that maximum attention can be focused
toward the central point. In this way, students' attention can be better controlled by teachers. If a student is inattentive, or a group of students is disruptive, seat reassignment may solve the problem.

The location of a student's seat affects both that student's behavior and the
teacher's attitude toward the student. Students focus better on individual tasks
when they are in rows; one study showed that time on task went from 75 percent
in rows to 56 percent in groups, back to 79 percent when reorganized into rows.
For some tasks, sofas and effective room decor, such as popular posters, create
an optimal learning environment. The message is that the seating arrangement
is most effective when it matches the task; group seating is most appropriate for
cooperative learning tasks (Hastings, 1995; Arnold, 1993).

Studies from elementary schools to college classrooms show that students
sitting in the front or center of the classroom participate more and achieve
better. These students are also regarded more highly by teachers and peers.
Teachers tend to be more permissive in their verbal interactions and use fewer
formal directives with pupils who are near the front. In college classrooms, students in these positions tend to be brighter and more interested, to get better
grades, and to like the instructor better, perhaps because they can see and hear
better, are more involved, and can watch and participate more. Yet for some
students seating choice is related to the need for privacy (Pedersen, 1994; Stires,
1980); they may select seats out of the main focus area.

Attention has also been paid to the physical conditions that produce the
best working conditions, including open-space programs, school building age,
thermal factors, visual factors, color and interior painting, hearing factors,
windowless facilities, underground facilities, site size, and building maintenance (Earthman and Lemasters, 1996). Estimates indicate that 25 percent of
learning is dependent on the physical environment (Hayward, 1994).
Researchers found that the most important factors affecting student performance and achievement were the thermal environment, lighting, adequate space,
and equipment and furnishings, especially in science education. The ideal temperature for optimum learning in the classroom is about 20°C, with variability
depending on such factors as activity, clothing, and amount of stress. Little
research has been done on lighting, though windowless schools are not considered advisable. Even the "electrical atmosphere," or ionization of the
climate, has been suggested as a factor that affects learning and performance,
with negative ionization thought to be beneficial (Kevan and Howes, 1980).

Other factors, such as types of seats, wall color, shape of room, music and noise level in and outside the classroom, all have some affect on learning, though evidence in this field is scanty. Figure 8–2 shows physical conditions that may affect learning. Note the relationships suggested between psychocultural, biological, and physical factors.

Concerns about classroom and school health hazards abound. The U.S. General Accounting Office (GAO) prepared a study of state-by-state conditions of school facilities, which examined the condition of buildings, environmental conditions, and other variables related to safety (General Accounting Office, 1996). Estimates are that one in eight schools is old, dilapidated, and in poor condition for learning; and 25 percent lack adequate space, maintenance, and safety. But funds to repair buildings are lacking. Building contaminants such as carbon dioxide, carbon monoxide, water vapor, nitrogen dioxide, asbestos, formaldehyde, bioaerosols, bioeffluents, lead, and radon exist in almost every school building (Greim, 1991, p. 29).

FIGURE 8–2 Schematic representation of factors to be considered when determining human thermal environment.

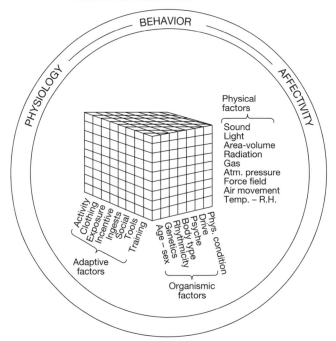

Source: Rohles, F.H., "Environmental Ergonomics in Agricultural Systems," *Applied Ergonomics*, Vol. 16, No. 3, 1985, pp. 163–66 (chart p. 163). Reprinted with kind permission from Elsevier Science Ltd., The Boulevard, Langford Lane, Kidlington OX5 1GB, UK.

A look at one of the largest school systems in the United States, New York City public schools, illustrates the problems of aging facilities. The system is trying to provide for a large increase in student enrollment while improving conditions of old buildings. Unfortunately, the results are not positive. In the 1990s, already crowded school buildings grew more crowded; class sizes increased; the conditions of buildings deteriorated; and academic achievement remained poor, with average reading and math scores at least one grade level below average. The average class sizes in 1996 were 32 or more in high schools, 26 in grades four through nine, and 29 for kindergarten through grade three. And the situation is getting worse (Rein, 1997).

Size of School and Classroom. One assumes that "smaller is better" in the classroom; that smaller classes mean fewer control problems, less work for teachers, and more interaction and communication between teachers and students. There is evidence at the elementary level (K–3) that reduced class size does enhance achievement. In fact, the federal government spent $1.2 billion in 1999–2000 on the administration's "Class Size Reduction Initiative" and several states including California and Tennessee have introduced programs to lower class size at the elementary level (Sulllivan, 1998). Tennessee's Project STAR (Student/Teacher Achievement Ratio) began in the 1991–92 school year, and reduced class sizes in grades one to three to a ratio of one teacher for fifteen students. The Lasting Benefits Study (Nye et al., 1994), an evaluation of the project, revealed that reduced class size increased achievement and improved instruction (Achilles, Harman, and Egelson, 1995), and those effects lasted at least through fifth grade. Minority and inner-city students gained the most (Black, 1999).

Another question to ask is "what happens in small classes and small groups within classes?" Schools with smaller class sizes and fewer students per teacher have more positive classroom climates, a factor associated with higher achievement. Classrooms in which children teach each other specific material in small groups also have high achievement levels. However, teachers do not always take advantage of the smaller class size to create climates more conducive to learning (Galton, 1998); teacher training is important to maximize learning potential in small classes.

As early as 1974, smaller school size was recommended by the Panel on Youth (Coleman et al., 1974, pp. 154–56), chaired by James Coleman, because of the impact on social interactions. Since that time, other studies have pointed to the benefits of small schools, including greater interest in school activities, higher achievement levels, and more social equality (Griffith, 1995; Lee, 1995). Students can play a more active role in school life, and interact more informally with teachers and administrators in smaller schools. In contrast, the climate in large schools leads students to be more passive with adults, to be followers, to depend on others to manage their affairs, and to have fewer leadership opportunities. Percentage of participation decreases with increased size of the school.

Certain types of activities, such as hobby clubs, can increase in size to include any number, but other activities—athletic teams, music, and drama—are inelastic; students attending larger schools are at a disadvantage because a smaller percentage of the school population can participate.

Architecture of Schools. Architectural designs reflect the purpose that a building is to serve; in turn, the design influences activities within a building, and how these will interact with surrounding activities and buildings. School architectural style and sites make schools stand out among buildings, indicating their distinct function. Whether school buildings are squeezed between other buildings or located on sprawling campuses, their fenced-in area or other physical separation distinguishes them from the community at large. Some educators object to this physical isolation from the surrounding community. Separation isolates schools from valuable interactions with the wider community. Yet it serves the function of concentrating students in one place for one specific activity ("An Architectural Revolution," 1990, p. 9).

Based on the book *Savage Inequalities* (Kozol, 1992), the video "Children in America's Schools" provides the visual companion, showing the condition of many schools—overcrowded; underheated; condemned buildings with paint chips, asbestos, and pipes falling down; leaks in roofs and walls; and torn-up, dated textbooks. It raises questions about the learning that can take place when the surroundings are poor and even dangerous.

The school is composed of many dynamic parts that fit together, from buildings that make possible certain interaction patterns to the atmospheres or climates that influence the learning process. All these are part of the complex informal system of education. We now turn to another major aspect of the informal system: power relationships.

*A*pplying Sociology to Education: Describe what you would call an ideal school in terms of architecture, size, and physical conditions. ◆

POWER DYNAMICS AND ROLES IN THE INFORMAL SYSTEM

In the classroom there is a delicate balance between formal expectations and informal processes. Many rules prescribing formal behavior in schools are informally transmitted. Some argue that this informality serves the school and classroom well; the classroom is less bureaucratic than many formal organizations (Dreeben, 1973), providing a transition from home to workplace. When students are not hampered by formal rules, they are more likely to unconsciously assimilate rules. Through this informal process students learn to deal with the formal and informal expectations of organizations. Broadly defined, *power* refers both to actual practice that promotes teacher and adult interests, and to informal threats that need not always be exercised in order to control or secure desired outcomes.

Theoretical Explanations of Power Dynamics in the Classroom

The theoretical approaches that have been discussed in other chapters are also important in discussions of power dynamics. Functional theorists emphasize the consensus resulting from the socialization function of the classroom as it prepares students for societal roles (Parsons, 1959). Another primary function is that of selection and allocation, which begins in elementary classrooms and continues throughout schooling. Not only achievement but also obedience and cooperation are important aspects of schooling. Children learn quickly what is expected of them, and their cooperation makes the school system work. Those most successful in meeting achievement and behavioral expectations do best in the school system. Students are "selected" according to how successfully they have been socialized into the system and how well they cooperate with those in power.

Conflict theorists have other interpretations of classroom dynamics. They see a power struggle between school staff, representing the dominant group and values of the adult world, and students who must be controlled, coerced, and co-opted using a variety of strategies. The theme of conflict in the classroom is dominant in Waller's book, written in 1932 (1961). He describes the difference between adult and student cultures, mechanisms to maintain the social distance between the two, and the "battles" in classrooms over requirements.

Capitalism, which demands that schools prepare a loyal, docile, disciplined workforce for society, is seen as a societal force behind the "coercion" in classrooms:

> Schools foster types of personal development compatible with the relationships of dominance and subordinancy in the economic sphere . . . through a close correspondence between the social relationships which govern personal interaction in the workplace and the social relationships of the educational system. (Bowles and Gintis, 1976, pp. 11–12)

From this perspective, conflict is seen as built into the dynamic system. Power influences how "cultural capital" is transmitted and reproduced. Teachers control the use of space and time, initiate interactions, and define the rules. Thus, the routines and rituals of schools represent the dominant value system that the schools are passing on to young people. Those who are successfully selected, classified, and evaluated in school are likely to be successful in society as adults (Bernstein, 1990; Bourdieu, 1977). Part of the reason for the convergence of minority and dominant groups in higher levels of educational achievement is the conscious passing on of cultural capital from parents to their children; this may prove to be an effective means of upward mobility for less privileged minority groups (Kalmijn and Kraaykamp, 1996). Parents of minority students "play their hands" in a variety of ways, depending on the interplay between the individual parents and the particular school that is dealing with their child (Lareau and Horvat, 1999; Fordham, 1996).

Schools alone do not determine their own internal power structure or their unequal outcomes. Rather, we must view schools within the larger societal context of social class, ideological, and material forces (Apple, 1980). Some of the recent "reforms" of education coming from government sources and justified by conservative ideologies and policies are exacerbating inequalities (Apple, 1997, 1996), yet educational theorists have spent little time analyzing the impact of power systems outside schools.

From the interactionist perspective, each member of the class has a distinctive perception of the world of the classroom. Each individual's plan of action is dependent on how she or he views the world and responds to it. Many factors affect perceptions. Consider Howard Becker's classic study of Chicago teachers (Becker, 1952). Their perceptions of students were related to cultural differences and class origins among pupils, which in turn related to the degree of trouble teachers had with students.

Students are often labeled early in their school careers and put into rigid, inflexible tracks. For instance, one teacher grouped students into "tigers, cardinals, and clowns"; labels given were internalized by pupils and acted as a self-fulfilling prophecy. Tigers received the most positive interaction, whereas those in lower groups were given less attention. The groups were correlated by researchers with students' social class, tigers being from higher classes than the other groups (Gouldner, 1978). These different expectations based on class influenced the selection and allocation process, with students from lower-class backgrounds at a disadvantage. Another indication of the effect of labeling on student behavior is seen in a study of individual student's perceptions of their teachers' disapproval; perceptions of teacher disapproval are related to more delinquency (Adams and Evans, 1996).

Student perceptions of their own chances for success influenced their decisions about what role to play in school. For example, some studies show that the "climate" in all-women's classes is more conducive to women's participation if separation does not lead to different opportunities and values (Stromquist, 1995, p. 423). Issues surrounding women's education continue to generate controversy and research, as discussed in Chapter 4.

Teacher Strategies and the Informal System

"'Classroom management' refers to the entire range of teacher-directed planning, managing, and monitoring of student learning activities and behavior. The school climate incorporates not only collective classroom management by the staff, but also schoolwide rules and norms for defining and enforcing proper student behavior" (Brookover et al., 1996, p. 184) (see Box 8–1). Different teacher strategies are necessary in each new circumstance. The philosophy of the teacher and school, the organization of school and classroom, available resources, number of students and their interest level—all affect the goals and strategies of teachers.

Martyn Hammersley and Peter Woods outline several alternative techniques or strategies that may be used by teachers to deal with classes:

1. Formal organization implies that the teacher is the center of activity; typical strategies are to have students recite material, or do question-and-answer and written work. Informal organization implies groups of students working together and more interaction between class members.
2. The teacher may supervise student action and intervene when deviation occurs. Alternatively, the teacher may act more as participant.
3. The teacher may make use of orders and demands backed by coercion and the authority of the position. Alternatively, the teacher may make personal appeals to the rights and obligations of any person, backed by legitimate resources.
4. Class or school tests may be used for comparison of student performance. Alternatively, there may be no formal assessment. Many commonly used informal strategies of grouping are based on age, ability, or "troublemakers" versus random grouping based on student choice, friendship groups, or no formal grouping. (Hammersley and Woods, 1977, p. 37)

Techniques employed by teachers influence the climate of the classroom and type of learning taking place, though on many dimensions there is no clear evidence which technique is more effective.

Students often challenge teacher authority, and teachers often end up going further in adjusting to students than students to teachers. Students in lower tracks, according to Mary Haywood Metz, most often use physical and verbal disorder strategies in challenging, whereas those in higher tracks test the teacher's mastery of the subject. Students challenge teachers on the ground where they feel most competent (Metz, 1978, pp. 91–92). New teachers, even when armed with the best training and teaching techniques, must experience the realities of the classroom to develop their own strategies to meet goals for their classes.

Consider the task of getting and keeping student attention. Teachers have plans in mind for the activities and lessons of the day, but they must convince students of the importance of the lessons and motivate them to comply—and even to participate. Time on and off task is related to classroom management; "teachers in typical classrooms lose approximately 50 percent of their teaching time because students are off task or otherwise disrupting learning" (Charles, 1999, p. 107). Studies of effective schools find that teachers can save wasted time by having well-planned and paced lessons, making quick transitions between topics, using students to do some simple tasks and

---

◆◆**Box 8–1** *Research on Effective Schools*

"Teachers

- ◆ . . . at the beginning of the year or course . . . review key concepts and skills thoroughly but quickly;
- ◆ use different materials and examples for reteaching than those used for initial instruction . . . more than a rehash;
- ◆ reteach priority lesson content until students show they've learned it;
- ◆ provide regular focused reviews of key concepts throughout the year;
- ◆ select computer-assisted instructional activities that include review and reinforcing."

Source: From Brookover, Wilbur, et al., *Creating Effective Schools: An In-Service Program.* Holmes Beach, FL: Learning Publications, Inc., 1996, p. 140; and Cotton, K. *Effective Schooling Practices: A Research Synthesis 1995 Update,* Northwest Regional Educational Laboratory, 1995.

---

paperwork, establishing daily routines, and using other time-saving techniques (Brookover et al., 1996, pp. 185, 198).

The teacher must defend the lesson from disintegration and internal defection. The student is being asked to pay attention to the "official environment"—that is, what is going on in the class directed by the teacher—rather than to a friend, comic book, or other distraction. In the typical situation, teachers are at the front of the classroom with students facing them. They watch for inattention and may use strategies such as questioning to get attention. Students may attempt to disguise illicit activities. Teachers can exert power in the form of control over valued things—recess, physical education, games.

Most people perceive deviant students as detrimental to the classroom situation. Some teachers, however, find that using disruptive students as a "resource" may turn them into an asset. Deviants are products of the social organization of the classroom; by considering three factors in their place in the total social context, teachers may discover how to manipulate the classroom structure to their benefit: (1) how ranks of deviants are established; (2) how deviant status is maintained; and (3) how deviants contribute to maintaining order or gain from their disruptions (Stevenson, 1991).

Students today have a need to be entertained; they expect instant gratification. Attention spans are shorter. They need more attention, are harder to please, have higher expectations of teachers, are less willing to put forth effort to learn, and are motivated by external rather than internal rewards.

*A**pplying Sociology to Education:* What coping strategies do(es) your professor(s) use in class?

Decision Making in the Classroom. We have discussed teachers' roles in the educational system in Chapter 6 and the effect of teacher decisions and actions on students' achievement in Chapter 4. Implicit in these discussions is the teacher's role as primary decision maker in the classroom. What really happens in the classroom and what influences the decision-making process is complex. Much of the research on this topic comes from "interaction" theorists and the "new sociology of education" and focuses on the dynamics of class-room interaction and how individuals perceive the situation. It is not easy to observe these dynamics, but, despite methodological difficulties, the "how and why" of decision making is now a topic of concern.

Most of a teacher's decision-making behavior is almost instinctive, based on experience. But teachers do have decision-making strategies, conscious or unconscious. They may be "situationally specific decisions, or negotiative strategies," used to deal with special circumstances that arise. Teachers' strate-gies, especially those of the new teacher, are often based on a textbook ideal world. Students deviate from ideals, however, forcing teachers to deviate from their ideal models to more realistic strategies for the situation.

Using a role conflict model, which focuses on incongruities in the teacher's role, we can see how decision making is influenced not only by the views and expectations of students, parents, other teachers, and administra-tion, but also by teachers' own definitions of the task to be performed. Teachers must consider what they can and cannot, will and will not do. They may exploit rules, use their expertise, and bargain to gain power. Decision making is a complex process influenced by many interacting elements. Teacher dissatisfac-tion and burnout are increased when teachers are given little control in deter-mining the classroom environment (Lee, Dedrick, and Smith, 1991).

The importance of recognizing the informal system of schools—the hidden curriculum, the educational climate, power dynamics, and other topics—is in understanding aspects of the educational system that lie beneath the surface. This chapter has provided a few examples of this large part of edu-cation. Also crucial to dynamics of schools is the environment, our next topic.

Summary

To understand the processes taking place within the school and classroom, one must be aware of the informal system, an important area of social research. In this brief discussion, we have attempted to acknowledge its importance for complete understanding of the system and its integral part in a systems approach.

I. The Open Systems Approach and the Informal System

The hidden curriculum of the informal system includes the curriculum students learn that is not part of the formal curriculum—implicit demands, values, latent functions. Some conflict theorists argue that schools reproduce students' social class, largely through the hidden curriculum. Students experience schools differently depending on their class backgrounds.

II. The Educational "Climate" and School Effectiveness

The climate or atmosphere of schools and classrooms includes the school's architecture, type of classroom, ability and age grouping, and other aspects of the school. Value climate influences motivations, aspirations, and achievement of students. Factors such as home environment, self-concept, and school values influence the effectiveness of schools. The school culture is distinctive in each school. Interaction patterns in classrooms are also part of the climate. Factors, such as gender, that affect interaction are discussed.

III. Power Dynamics and Roles in the Informal System

Power dynamics are present in any hierarchical system. In schools a look at the teacher–student relationship acquaints us with some of the issues. Both students and teachers develop coping strategies to deal with the dynamics. Power in schools can be actively used or can be seen as latent potential to keep students in line. Functional theorists argue that students learn societal roles by cooperation with adult-enforced rules, whereas conflict theorists feel that there is constant potential for conflict because of power dynamics.

Teachers attempt to maintain a delicate balance between overt use of power and gaining student cooperation. Teachers must make decisions about strategies to use in the classroom; numerous factors affecting these decisions are discussed. The strategies used range from power to subtle cues to changing the physical or social arrangement of the class.

In order to understand how educational systems work, an understanding of the informal system is essential.

◆ *Putting Sociology To Work*

1. Interview a sample of students concerning their outstanding memories of school experiences.

2. Describe the student peer subculture in your high school and college. Were there social isolates, and can you recall their characteristics? Compare your high school with a high school today through observation or interviews.

3. What were some roles students played in your high school? Talk to some students about roles they play today.

4. What are some strategies used by teachers you observe in high schools to get students to cooperate?

CHAPTER 9

The Educational System and the Environment

A Symbiotic Relationship

Our environment surrounds us. It encompasses us. No one and nothing exists in a vacuum, for we cannot exist outside our environment. That environment differs for each of us just as it differs for each educational system. What makes our environment unique depends on our background experiences, the family into which we were born, and the individuals and institutions with which we come into contact.

As college students, we pay tuition, take classes, study, receive grades, and eventually graduate. The roles we carry out as students are dictated by our educational environment. Also in our environment are other factors: family, church, job, children, friends. Events related to one set of behaviors or roles will affect the other roles we play because they are all interrelated. Let us suppose that we have an important exam coming up. We may experience role conflict because of time pressure. Perhaps our family or friends will be neglected; perhaps we will decide not to spend much time studying for the exam. Every element of our environment is affected by demands from other elements.

In this chapter we consider the meaning of environments and examples of institutional environments of schools: family, religion, politics and the legal system, economics, and communities. As part of the larger societal system, school systems are surrounded by pressures from ideological groups, political systems, economic conditions, and other trends in society. Each sphere of society is interrelated; schools cannot ignore the political, economic, and cultural-ideological spheres that make up their environments (Apple and Weis, 1986).

THE ENVIRONMENT AND THE EDUCATIONAL SYSTEM

Educational systems have environments that give them purpose and meaning and define their functions, limitations, and conflicts. Schools are particularly vulnerable to environmental influences where issues relate to their function of socializing the young. Children are often perceived as sponges, waiting to absorb the knowledge presented to them, and many parts of the environment—government, community pressure groups, religious and other special-interest groups—demand input into what children are taught and how they are taught.

Population changes, technological advances, fads, and social movements are some of the environmental factors that influence the functions of education. For example, in the 1960s, there was much experimentation with avant-garde programs in the United States, producing ideas that influenced the public schools. In the 1970s, there was great concern with establishing more discipline in schools; "back-to-basics" became the theme. The 1980s and 1990s brought accountability and proficiency testing of teachers and students. Such movements constitute environmental pressures on the schools.

In our discussion of the internal workings of the system, we considered the connection between the many individual positions people hold in educational systems and the structural units of the school organization. But no organization, unit, or individual can exist without being dependent on and influenced by the environment. Figure 9–1 emphasizes the relationship between the organization and its environment.

FIGURE 9–1 Environment of school systems.

ENVIRONMENT

School board	Technology
PTA	Political-economic trends
Teachers' unions	Religious beliefs
Bonds, levies	Cultural values and ideology
Community pressure groups	Social movements and fads
Government regulations	Population changes

FEEDBACK LOOP ◄

All individuals and organizations depend on their environments in order to survive and to meet needs; in turn, they affect the environment in which they live by leaving personal or institutional imprints on individuals and institutions.

The interdependence of organization and environment can be seen clearly in many systems. Consider the complexity of a system such as New York City and the chaos that occurs when one part of that system malfunctions (Rogers, 1969, p. 211). If the power goes out, or the sanitation engineers, subway workers, telephone operators, or schoolteachers go on strike, the city's interdependent structure breaks down and all parts of the system are strained to the breaking point. New York City's school system is likewise complex; it employed 75,209 teachers in 1998–99, with an additional 23,704 paraprofessionals, several thousand administrators and technicians, and served 1.1 million students. The school budget is more than $9 billion, and the system has almost 1,600 facilities. It is spread over the five boroughs of the city and services many different populations and communities (New York City Board of Education, 1999). The interdependence of parts of this tremendous school system forces it into a delicate balancing act between competing community interests.

Types of Environments

Some parts of our environment are more important to our survival than others; these are immediate environments. Less important to survival are secondary environments. Our families are key to our emotional, physical, and financial well-being, whereas a Friday night party is not a matter of survival for most of us. For an organization, the relevant parts of the environment fall into a number of categories: government, including local, state, and national legislatures and agencies; the judicial system; financial support units; the "physical" community surrounding each school, including the demographic composition (age, sex, religion, race, and social class); interest groups in the community; the technological environment, including teaching innovations and new scientific research; consumers of educational system products, such as those who hire graduates or incorporate new knowledge from educational systems; and religious institutions.

The distinction between immediate or primary environments and less crucial secondary environments is not always clear. Importance can change over time, but the fact remains that there are differing degrees of importance in environmental factors. Recognizing this allows us to single out those environmental factors that most affect decision making in a school system at any one time. The school is affected less as environmental units become farther removed, just as ripples in a pond become weaker as they move out from the center.

Organizations are not encapsulated but depend on the environment for resources, materials, people power, and, ultimately, existence. The importance, or salience, of environmental units for educational systems can be illustrated as a continuum (see Figure 9–2). The salience of environmental units will vary depending on the individual school situation being considered.

Another point needs to be explained. We generally consider the individuals who fill positions in the schools—the administrators, teachers, students, and support staff—to be parts of the internal organization. These groups fill the positions in the internal structure of the school and carry out the processes of the school. They provide the bases for the informal relationships in the school. However, there is no question that each of the position-holders in the school brings a unique background and personality into the school, which could be considered an "environmental influence." (Some sociologists consider students as clients of the school system, and, as such, they became a part of its environment.) Further, some school personnel, such as principals, school counselors, and social workers, carry out roles to provide a bridge between the school and the home or community environment. These "boundary-spanning" roles facilitate the movement of ideas and products in and out of the school system and are essential in maintaining relations and contact with the environment.

To summarize, the importance of environmental units must be viewed as varying in degree; some are crucial to the well-being, even survival, of the organization at a particular time. Effects of problems in one sector of the system's environment or in relations with the environment will have ramifications for other sectors, depending on that part's salience to the survival of the system.

In this chapter we focus on the institutional environment of the school. There are many elements in any school's environment, however, from the individuals who make it up to the ancillary organizations that surround it, put pressures on it, and provide services to it.

FIGURE 9–2 Environmental salience.

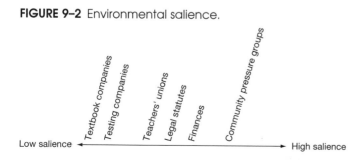

*A*pplying *Sociology* *to* *Education:* List some influences from various types of environments on your local schools. ◆

THE SCHOOL SYSTEMS' ENVIRONMENTS: INTERDEPENDENCE BETWEEN INSTITUTIONS

School officials deal with issues from their external environments daily:

◆ Parents and community members disenchanted with schools are demanding that schools and teachers become accountable for the education they are providing. This is resulting in many school districts' and even states' requiring standardized tests to measure achievement levels.

◆ Are parents violating any unwritten rules if they send their children to nonaccredited religious schools? Should both "scientific creationism" and evolutionary theory be taught in schools?

◆ Courts in numerous districts are dealing with questions regarding the separation of church and state: Can public school districts provide such services as transportation, remedial classes, and counseling to religiously affiliated schools?

◆ Financing schools leads to controversies when some districts have more property tax money for education than others.

◆ Hot debate rages in communities between special-interest groups representing differing points of view on minority studies, selection of textbooks, role of the schools in sex education, and numerous other issues.

In this section we look into some of the environmental pressures and resulting issues affecting schools:

1. Home influences and pressures
2. Separation of church and state in education
3. School financing
4. Governmental regulations and court rulings
5. Influence of the community and special-interest groups on schools

Home and Family Influences on School

When children walk into the school building they bring with them ambition, motivation, pressures, expectations, physical and mental strengths or weaknesses, and sometimes abuse, insecurities, stress, and other problems. Therefore, knowledge of the social and family context that students bring into school is essential for teachers in dealing with students (Henry, 1996). In Chapter 7 we discussed the influence of the family on achievement of students. Here we reemphasize that link between the family institution and education (Epstein, 1995).

Many families balance work and parenting. They must find reliable child care for preschool children. Six million children in the United States are in formal day-care settings daily. Congress passed the National Child Protection Act of 1993 to help safeguard young children in child care from abuse when they are outside the home (Clinton, 1993). Once a child enters formal schooling, the "curriculum of the home"—the development of attitudes and habits supporting learning and the high value placed on personal development—influences the child's learning and academic achievement in school. This "curriculum" includes family size, reading materials and reading at home, time spent watching TV, attention to homework and absences from school, parental involvement in school decisions, and family resources (Barton and Coley, 1992; Redding, 1992).

The key finding is that the higher the parents' involvement in their children's schooling, the higher the overall academic performance (Keith and Lichtman, 1994; "Parent Involvement in Education," 1994; Reynolds, 1993). Parents affect children's educational achievement and aspirations in several major ways. Boys and girls are strongly influenced by the "defining" behavior of parents through which expectations for appropriate behavior are established (Cohen, 1987). Also important, especially for girls, is "modeling," or emulation, of parents. Family influence is strong across social class, but mothers with higher educational status are more involved in school activities, have more contact with teachers, and choose college-preparatory courses for their children. Children of parents who are involved in schools have higher school performance levels (Stevenson and Baker, 1987; Baker and Stevenson, 1986). This includes children from minority families whose parents are involved in their children's education (Keith and Lichtman, 1994). Children from homes and neighborhoods considered "socially deprived," however, experience negative effects on their educational attainment (Garner and Raudenbush, 1991).

In ongoing research at the Center for Research on Elementary and Middle Schools, Epstein found that teachers who involve parents in home activities, especially reading, with their children have positive learning results for children (Epstein, 1988, 1987). Single parents tended to feel pressure to help with home learning; married parents assisted more at school (Epstein, 1984). Her research shows the positive impact of the home environment and involving parents in the education of their children (Epstein, 1987).

When we combine the influence of parents, peers, and teachers, we have strong effects on students' attitudes toward school, homework, achievement, and other aspects of schooling in the United States (Natriello and McDill, 1986).

Parents' investment in their children and support for higher education is related to their views of status attainment. Some parents perceive children as an investment, following the "human capital theory." Others view payment for education as "resource-dilution," often related to how many children are in the family compared with available resources. For instance, parents are more willing to pay for higher education for their children if their parents paid for their education, and they believe this to be a responsibility; they are also more willing to pay if the number of children in the family does not drain their resources (Steelman and Powell, 1991).

*A*pplying Sociology to Education: How can a positive or negative home environment affect a child's achievement in school? ◆

The Institution of Religion: Separation of Church and State

In many societies, religion and state are synonymous, and the educational system reflects the beliefs and values of both. Religious minorities may have their own schools, or they may tolerate the dominant religious themes. In England, for instance, holidays of non-Christian students living in England are often discussed to promote intercultural understanding.

In the United States, a unique experiment was attempted. Since the time of our nation's founding, the principle of separation of church and state has been espoused. It is expressed in the First Amendment, which states: "Congress shall make no law respecting an establishment of religion, or prohibiting the free exercise thereof." The framers of the U.S. Constitution built in guarantees to avoid the religious conflicts that had arisen in many other countries. The government's responsibility was to protect the rights and freedoms of all and favor none. Yet keeping church and state distinct has not always been easy. The roots of the problem lie in our pluralistic society, where freedom of worship is an integral part of the value system and political ideology. (See Box 9–1.)

We have seen in our open systems model the interdependence of each institution with all others. When individuals segment religion from the rest of daily life spent in institutions of family, economics, politics, and education, conflict is not likely to arise. But where religion is integrated into all aspects of a person's life, including education, demands for representation of this part of life take the form of pressures on the school from the religious environment.

Religious pressures on schools have led to court cases, initiated by both religious groups and those favoring secular education. Two types of cases have dominated the courts. First are those that claim that the school is infringing on individual beliefs; saying prayers in class or at ceremonies or teaching the theory of evolution are examples. Other cases occur when school officials or policies prevent individuals from participating in religious activities during school and in school, such as religious use of school facilities.

As early as 1948, religious released-time classes in public school buildings were ruled unconstitutional. In 1962, an extremely controversial ruling was passed by the Supreme Court against required recitation of prayers in public school (*Engle* v. *Vitale*, 370 US 421). Several states passed laws allowing for vol-

◆◆Box 9-1 *Church and State in American Education*

Should prayer be allowed in schools? Under what circumstances? Should students be allowed to lead prayers at events such as graduation? Should religious schools receive federal funds for special education? Should state schools pay for student religious publications?

In 1971 the U.S. Supreme Court established guidelines for what constitutes a violation of separation of church and state (Cook, 1995, p. 17). The Lemon test (from a court case *Lemon* v. *Kurtzman*, 1971) "established a prohibitive test of constitutionality. The challenged government action must (1) have a secular purpose; (2) have a principal or primary effect that neither advances nor inhibits religion; and (3) not foster an excessive government entanglement with religion" (Cord, 1992). Despite the guidelines, in recent years the Supreme Court has given little clear guidance to school districts as an increasing number of cases reach the courts. They have sought to avoid the appearance of persecuting religious groups and also to avoid advancing or endorsing religion. In the 1992 case, *Lee* v. *Weisman*, the court ruled that giving a nonsectarian invocation of God at a public school graduation ceremony violated the constitution.

Consider the case of a community, Kiryas Joel, of Hasidic Jews outside New York City. Yiddish is the main language, and dress and other cultural patterns are distinctive to the group. Children go to Jewish parochial schools funded by the Hasidic community.

Children with disabilities from the community went to school in an adjacent school district to receive special services, but parents withdrew them because of the "panic, fear, and trauma which (the children) suffered in leaving their own community . . ." (Drinan, 1994, p. 9). A new school district was set up in Kiryas Joel for the 220 children, attended only by children with special needs, taught in English, and with no religious symbols. A legal battle concerning students with special needs raised the question: Are the schools intended to help religion? The school was challenged and New York's highest court found the district violated the First Amendment of the Constitution, and in 1994 the U.S. Supreme Court upheld this decision (Rabkin, 1994).

Recently, the U.S. Supreme Court ruled on the funding of religious-oriented student publications in a case from the University of Virginia, declaring that the university must pay the printing cost for a religious-oriented student publication from the Student Activities Fund, arguing that the university violated free speech rights (Hernandez, 1995).

The separation of church and state is a controversial political issue and is unlikely to be resolved in a clear and straightforward manner any time soon.

untary prayers; Illinois, Connecticut, Arkansas, Massachusetts, and others passed laws allowing for a "period of silence," "in silent contemplation of the anticipated activities of the day." This has been ruled constitutional because it does not "advance religion." Reciting the Lord's Prayer and forcing students to recite the Pledge of Allegiance have been ruled unconstitutional.

In 1963, the decision in *Abington Township, Pennsylvania* v. *Schempp* was passed down, putting a different emphasis on religious education: "One's education is not complete without a study of comparative religion and its relationship to the advancement of civilization. . . ." The argument was that we cannot ignore religions as a field of academic study because they encompass a large part of many people's lives. Organizations exist to help provide schools with interpretations of the meaning of the law and materials for classroom use. Therefore, schools can teach about religion, comparative religion, history of religion, or the Bible as literature, but not a subject that promotes religion.

A related controversy has to do with providing parochial schools with instructional materials and services from public monies. In a 1975 Supreme Court case (*Meek* v. *Pittenger*), the conflict between strict and loose constitutional constructionists came to a head. The court ruled that "a state government may lend secular textbooks to pupils attending parochial and other religiously oriented schools." Government may also provide nonpublic schools with the following: buses; lunches; fire protection; water; police; sewers; tax exemptions; standardized tests and scoring; in-school diagnosis of speech, hearing, and psychological disorders; therapy, guidance, and remedial services off the school premises; payment for field trips; and loans to students of instructional materials and equipment. It was ruled unconstitutional, however, to make direct loans of instructional materials and direct provision of auxiliary services such as counseling, testing, therapy, and remedial aid, because such services result in the direct and substantial advancement of religious activities.

In *Aguilar* v. *Felton*, the public schools were legally required to administer federal aid, but questions about how to do so remain. Some court support has come for not providing aid for equipment such as computers and photocopiers, which could be used for religious purposes (Crawford, 1986, p. 15). Clearly, there is a fine line between the acceptable and nonacceptable, and more test cases are being brought to the courts.

Several state and federal court rulings in 1999 and 2000 on voucher systems and charter schools have created confusion over funding of private schools. Court rulings in Ohio, Maine, Vermont, Pennsylvania, and Florida have sent a message to voucher plans across the United States. The general concern is that vouchers are providing subsidies to students who attend religious schools, violating the church-school separation principles of the Constitution. The courts seem to be encouraging states to focus on improving the public schools rather than looking for solutions in funding private schools (www.nbsa.org).

Another issue in the church-state controversy is the clash between state standards and those of private schools. A case in point occurred in Darke County, Ohio, in 1976, when the Tabernacle Christian School, serving the Dunkard religious group, was told that it failed to comply with the state board of education requirements and that parents would be charged with failure to send children to school. This was seen by supporters and sympathizers of the school as an attempt to crush evangelical Christian schools. Other cases involve conflicts between religious groups such as the Amish and the states in which they live, centering on attendance laws. The church groups would prefer to have control over both the type and the amount of schooling children receive. Accommodations between the state and religious groups have been reached in most areas.

One of the most controversial cases involving separation of church and state was heard before the Little Rock, Arkansas, state courts in 1981 and 1982. Referred to popularly as Scopes II, *McLean* v. *Arkansas Board of Education* was similar to the 1925 trial of John Scopes for teaching evolutionary theory in the classroom. The 1981–82 case dealt with requiring equal time in the classroom for "scientific creationist" and "evolutionist" theories. This and similar cases have centered on the battle between "absolute truth" believed by creationists and "relative truth" of those who have been labeled by fundamentalist Christians as "secular humanists." Those in favor argued that evolution is not a proven theory and that other theories should receive equal time; those opposed maintained that the creationist view is taken from the Bible and would bring religion into the classroom.

After lengthy expert testimony, the court ruled that allowing the creationist view to be taught would be a violation of church and state separation. The case was particularly important because it set a precedent for cases being considered in 18 other states. One of these was brought before the Supreme Court in June 1987; the argument was that "creation science" had as much right to be taught in the classroom as evolution. Proponents argued that creation is a respectable scientific theory, that life forms did not evolve but appeared suddenly, and that this thesis should be given equal time. But by a 7 to 2 vote, the Court again held that this was a subterfuge to bring the Bible back to class and violate First Amendment rights ("Louisiana Creationism Law," 1987, p. 23).

Recently, the issue arose again in Kansas where the State Board of Education passed the "Kansas Curricular Standards for Science Education" which did not include the theory of evolution in the required science curriculum, leaving the choice of teaching evolution up to the local school boards ("Evolution/Creation Science Controversy Continues," 1999). Polls on public opinion concerning the issue indicate that 83 percent of Americans want the theory of evolution taught in science classes, and 70 percent do not see a contradiction between evolution taught in science classes and creationism as a religious concept. Less than 30 percent want creationism taught in science classes (People for the American Way, 2000).

Other recent court cases return to the issue of prayer in schools and to the complex issue of extracurricular religious clubs. In a 1981 ruling (*Widmar* v. *Vincent*), the Supreme Court granted public university students the right to form religious clubs on campus; in a June 1990 ruling (*Westside Community Schools* v. *Mergens*), it extended the ruling to apply to secondary schools under some circumstances (Sendor, 1990, p. 15). The Equal Access Act states that if a school allows any noncurriculum-related clubs to meet—recreational, political, philosophical—it must also allow religious groups to meet. The U.S. Congress has also entered into the issue of church and state, considering whether the Ten Commandments can be displayed in schools.

Another case (*Weisman* v. *Lee*) relates to the constitutionality of including prayer at graduation or promotion ceremonies. One side argues that invoking God's name should be upheld as constitutional; others argue that this violates the rights of separation by favoring some religions over others and by making nonadherents feel that they are "outsiders and the public school system does not belong to them" (Walsh, 1991, p. 1). Another current issue before the Supreme Court involves prayers at football games; in a Texas case, the issues of separation of church and state versus students free-speech rights are at issue. According to a national poll, two-thirds of Americans think students should be permitted to lead such prayers(Carelli, 2000).

*A*pplying *Sociology to Education:* Present arguments for and against religious presence, such as clubs and prayer, in public schools. ◆

The Economics of Education: Financing Schools

Most societies view education as an investment in the future. Training youth functions to socialize them into productive roles in society, prepares them to contribute to society, and "selects" them for future roles. In many countries, central governments provide local districts with funds to carry out equitable public education. These policies are based on goals of efficiency, equity, and liberty. However, wealthy members of society may buy their children elite educations, thus ensuring them high positions that reproduce the stratification system.

Schools serve the ever-growing expansion and technological sophistication of the economic sector. This is reflected in the rapid growth of schools to train populations for jobs. Growth of schooling in the United States has been dramatic. From 1890 to the 1960s, secondary education expanded from an enrollment of 7 percent of the high school-age people to more than 90 percent. Figures in 1997 reveal that almost 97 percent of 14- to 17-year-olds are enrolled in school, and the number drops to 61.5 percent for those aged 18 and 19 (National Center for Education Statistics, *Digest*, 1999, p. 15, Table 6).

The growth of schools is seen by functionalists as meeting the economic needs for an educated labor force. The two go hand in hand to support the economy of nations. The growth and improvement of schools enhances worker skills and character traits, which in turn improves economic growth and social progress. More schooling for individuals opens more economic possibilities for individuals and nations.

A counterargument to the functionalists, the social progress model, states that educational improvements alone do not cause social development. Schools serve as sifting and sorting institutions. Conflict theorists believe schools train individuals to meet the economic, occupational demands of society. Training stratifies by credentialing individuals for the labor force, just as testing sorts individuals, but it does not necessarily imply social progress.

The financial environment of schools in the United States is uncertain. Actual dollars for education keep rising; but school costs are rising faster than inflation, and school levies to help meet rising costs often fail. In 1997–98 constant dollars, the average cost of educating public school students in average daily attendance has risen from $453 per student in 1919–20 to $6,624 in 1997–98 (National Center for Education Statistics, 1999, p. 186).

School financing occurs at three levels: local, state, and federal. State funding has, on balance, provided the most funds for public education; however, this balance is shifting. The state share of funding grew steadily to about 50 percent in the 1980s. It declined as local funding rose from 43.9 percent in 1986–87 to 45.9 percent in 1995–96. In some states, the balance is quite different. For instance, in New Hampshire, 87 percent of the funding comes from local sources, with Vermont and Illinois at 64 percent each. The federal share is 6.6 percent (National Center for Education Statistics, *Digest*, 1999, p. 170, Table 158).

Inner-city schools with higher expenditures are particularly hard hit in attempting to fund schools: teachers' unions in cities are strong and often successfully demand more pay; school buildings need repairs; special programs, such as compensatory education, are greater in inner cities; turnover of students is higher. Unfortunately, as the tax rates go up to support the schools, some residents move to the suburbs, further reducing the city's tax base. Therefore, federal and state funding is higher in poor areas such as inner-city districts that do not have a strong tax base. In school districts with a high percentage of children in poverty, the federal government pays almost 13 percent of schools' revenues, the state pays 60 percent, and local revenues amount to 27 percent. Even with government subsidies, comparing poor districts with wealthy districts, the funding picture looks quite different: Federal funding in wealthy districts is as low as 3 percent, state funding 41 percent, and local funding 56 percent (National Center for Education Statistics, 1995, p. 390).

Local Funding. Property taxes have been the main collection method for local funding, but the disparities between districts are great. Inner cities have lower tax bases from property taxes and continue to lose their tax base, with wealthy individuals moving to suburbs and industries relocating; therefore, suburbs have greater tax bases to provide better schools. Should property taxes not provide adequate funds, bond levies can be put up for vote; but the record

Schools are often dependent on local funding sources such as tax levies.

of success does not bode well for schools depending on this source. Per pupil expenditures in central cities are generally less, though needs are usually greater to provide for students in poverty, to maintain and upgrade old school buildings, and to collect property taxes.

Across America, large districts and small towns alike face shortages of funds. In the early 1960s, local tax levies provided 6 percent of the school budget. By 1974, that figure was 26 percent and growing. Today, 56 percent of total school revenue in the wealthiest districts comes from local funding sources. Taxpayers are rebelling against this heavier burden. In the 1990s, school finance reform was a top priority; state support is providing an increasing proportion of the budget, wheras local and federal taxes provide less. The local tax base is affected by crises such as the closings of military bases and the bankruptcies of industries and savings and loan institutions. Thus, some local districts are resorting to four-day workweeks, selling children's art, and holding lotteries to raise needed funds.

State Funding. In recent years, state funding of education has increased to almost 60 percent of the total funding in poor districts; the money comes primarily from sales taxes, personal income taxes, and special funding like state lotteries. More than 40 states have statewide sales taxes, which make up more than 30 percent of state revenues. Personal income tax makes up the remainder. These tax rates vary by state. An increasing number of states are using lotteries to raise funds for education.

The issue of school funding was first initiated almost 25 years ago and is still an issue in the courts, with a majority of states involved in litigation. Leading court rulings are

1. Redefining the constitutionally required level of education a state must provide
2. Using new criteria for measuring constitutional compliance
3. Focusing on adequacy in addition to equity
4. Relying on the plain meaning of education clauses of state constitutions (Verstegen, 1994, p. 244)

The concern in distribution of funds is how to be fair to all groups and areas of a state. State monies come to local districts through four main methods:

1. *Flat grants* provide the same amount to all districts for all students regardless of special needs; some states modify this to provide more for poor districts.
2. *Foundation plans*, the most common approach since the *Serrano* case [discussed later], provide for a minimum annual expenditure per student.
3. In *power-equalizing plans*, "the state pays a percentage of the local school expenditures in inverse ratio to the wealth of the district."
4. *Weighted-student plans* allow students to be rated according to their special needs: bilingual, disabled, vocational education. (Ornstein and Levine, 1985, pp. 258–59)

Several of these plans attempt to take into consideration the differential in local ability to support schools and special needs of some districts, thus attempting to provide more equality among schools.

A continuing debate, which has reached the courts in a number of states, concerns the use of property taxes to help finance schools. The argument of groups opposed to this is that wealthier districts have more money to pour into schools and can afford a better-quality education for their children. Thus, states are seeking ways to reduce the disparities in funding between local districts.

Two well-known court cases addressed the issue of local school funding through property taxes. In 1971, in the case of *Serrano* v. *Priest*, the California Supreme Court ruled that "this funding scheme invidiously discriminates against the poor because it makes the quality of a child's education a function of the wealth of his parents and neighbors." This landmark ruling affected school funding in many other states. In a 1973 Texas case, *San Antonio* v. *Rodriquez*, it was argued that education is a fundamental right and all schools should have the same financial base. This case reached the U.S. Supreme Court, which held that "education is not a fundamental interest or right," and rejected the case against property tax support. The use of property taxes for schools was left undisturbed, though states were urged to devise new taxing and spending plans.

Other cases have resulted in a redistribution of monies for education among local, state, and federal funds. Since the *Serrano* v. *Priest* (1971) and

Rodriquez v. *San Antonio* (1973) landmark cases, court rulings on funding plans have been mixed (Fulton and Long, 1993). Currently, more than 34 states have cases pending on rural versus metropolitan funding of schools (Dayton, 1998).

Federal Funding. Federal funding for education is influenced by the economic state of the nation. When recession plagued the United States in the early 1980s, available monies from government revenues dropped. A nation's priorities also influence where money is channeled.

During the Reagan and Bush administrations, the philosophy was to leave education and decision making to state and local governments. Thus, federal programs for disadvantaged students, except for Head Start, were reduced. Twenty-seven federal programs were put together into single grants to states, resulting in some programs being lost at the state level, especially if they were unpopular among more powerful groups in the state; this caused many to argue that the federal government should continue to support programs to enhance equal opportunity. Urban schools are likely to suffer most from loss of programs and money. The end result is that the United States spends less money per student on education than several other industrial nations (see Figure 9–3).

Several ideas have been proposed to improve funding of education: Tuition tax credits, vouchers and charter schools, private-sector support and companies running schools, and lotteries are among the most common methods

FIGURE 9–3 Public expenditures for education as a percentage of the gross domestic product: Selected countries, 1994.

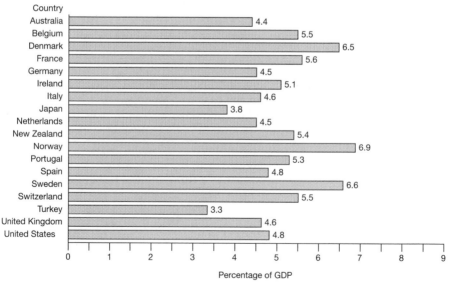

Source: Organization for Economic Cooperation and Development, unpublished data.

suggested. As mentioned, vouchers have generated controversy in various circles. The basic idea is that children and their families would receive a voucher to pay for a school of their choice, or for schools that would meet special needs of students. Some critics of this idea argue that it could lead to segregated schools, challenge teachers' unions, allow special-interest groups to dominate education, and destroy the concept of mass education.

Because of financial pressures, schools are put in the situation of having to market themselves to the environment, sell their program advantages, justify their staffing, and prove their success. The programs that are considered by the community to be "frills" are scrutinized most carefully. Thus, extracurricular activities—sports, music and art programs, counseling services, yearbooks, newspapers, debate teams, plays, and concerts—are often the first to be eliminated in a budget crunch. The financial environment of the school has a great impact on the type of school programming and planning that takes place.

Applying Sociology to Education: What are some implications of the balance of funding sources for public schools? ◈

The political climate and philosophy directly affects funding for education. Our next environmental institution is the political sector.

The Political and Legal Institution

Governments have direct involvement in education, whether through influencing content and values taught, funding for special programs, or setting policy. Educational systems in many countries are controlled by the central government, usually through a ministry of education. Other governments often have legal and financial control and influence over schools. Some of the political issues facing schools are worldwide, others are unique to particular systems. Consider the following issues that face local to national educational systems.

1. Should children be provided with broad, comprehensive education or tracked, with some taking vocational education and others academic courses?
2. Should schools be administered from a central "ministry of education" or a local authority?
3. Should parents be allowed to educate their children in schools of their choice (even if unaccredited, such as some church schools) or at home, or should children be required to go to accredited schools?
4. Should vouchers be given to parents to choose their children's school?
5. Should groups of parents with particular ideological concerns be allowed to ban textbooks from schools because they are offensive to the group?
6. Should controversial community or societal issues such as AIDS and sex education be taught in the classroom?

In many ways, education and politics cannot be separated:

◆ School programs are influenced by economic needs; some countries with planned economies designate how many people can be trained for each type of position.
◆ Parents and communities put pressure on schools to prepare children for success.
◆ Different interest groups conflict over what knowledge should be passed on to children through curriculum content and textbooks. (Apple and Weis, 1986, p. 8)

Schools have always been the testing ground for societal changes. In the United States, this means responsibility for public education and "promoting the general welfare." Early in U.S. history, the federal government was involved in setting aside land for education and raising funds as ordained in the Northwest Ordinance of 1785 and the Morrill Act of 1862 and in passing laws to ensure education for specific groups of students such as Native Americans. In recent years, laws have been passed to guarantee education for disabled students.

Courts at each level of the system hear education cases on interpretations of the law, ranging from desegregation to education for the disabled to voucher systems and charter schools. Community residents or interest groups initiate cases that are brought before the courts; we have considered several examples throughout the book: textbooks, creationism, busing and integration, special education, and many other issues.

One example of the enormous impact legislation can have on schools is in a federal government ruling that some predicted would have as profound an effect on education as the 1954 *Brown* v. *Board of Education* case, or the 1964 Civil Rights Act. Public Law 94-142, the Education for All Handicapped Children Act, enacted in 1975, requires schools to "mainstream" disabled children from ages 3 to 21. The Individuals with Disabilities Education Act (IDEA) changed the lives of many children. Before the passage of PL 94-142, one million disabled children could be excluded from the public school system, and hundreds of thousands more were denied appropriate services. Now many are graduating from high school, going to college, and entering the workforce. Arguments for integrating these children include the following (IDEA, 1997).

1. The disabled can achieve higher levels academically and socially if not isolated.
2. Regular school settings help them cope with the world in which they must live as adults.
3. Exposure to the disabled helps other children understand differences between children.

On the fifth anniversary of the Americans with Disabilities Act (ADA), a comprehensive civil rights law for people with disabilities, the Justice Department issued an evaluation of the effectiveness of the law. From mainstreaming students and ensuring participation in activities to offering fair testing opportunities, the situation for disabled students has improved greatly over the past few years ("Enforcing the ADA," 1995).

Opponents of the law argue that many disabled children will suffer from the taunting of classmates and from untrained teachers trying to make the program work. They recommend caution in placements, special training for teachers, and limited numbers of disabled children in classrooms.

Governmental bodies and agencies at various levels in the school's environment have responsibility for passing and enforcing legislation related to the functioning of schools, and, therefore, they have an impact on the school's internal operation. The whole educational system is affected. The structure must be altered to include appropriate materials, physical facilities, and support personnel; roles must be redefined to include new expectations; school goals must be restated to avoid conflicting statements. Laws requiring change in schools, classrooms, curricula, and individual role responsibilities mean a restructuring of the system and have repercussions for structure and positions at each level.

Applying Sociology to Education: What role does the political system play in your community's schools? ◆

Communities and Their Schools

At some time, most of us will take sides on an issue that is confronting the school system. It may involve the proper role of schools, the educational content of curricula, or the hiring or firing of personnel. Because of the school's vulnerability to environmental demands, administrators must consider the varying demands made on them. The school administration is in a double bind. It is under pressure to consider all opinions on an issue, yet not all views can be accepted.

Groups of parents complain that the school should not be teaching about sex. Businesses put pressure on the school to train students in industry-oriented computers and technology. Some immigrant groups want the school to teach students in their native languages. Peer groups compete with schools for the attention and loyalty of students. All of these examples show the vulnerability of the school system to environmental pressures from a variety of community sources. The composition of the community in which schools are located determines the "raw material" entering the local school.

School Partnerships. Businesses have become increasingly involved in schools, especially in some large cities where high school students are given internships, graduates are promised jobs, and those going to college are given tuition. Business leaders consider this support to be in their interests to provide a trained labor force and more livable cities. The link between corporations and students from inner-city schools who go on to attend college encourages some students to continue with their high school educations. Corporations also express frustration, however, at not always knowing the outcomes of their cash and in-kind contributions to schools. Measuring effectiveness is difficult, and many corporate leaders are questioning whether their efforts are having any impact.

Corporate America, realizing that its future workforce is at stake, is paying more attention to schools. This attention takes several forms, from outright cash donations to operating schools on corporate premises. Foundations are particularly active in awarding grants to school districts for projects; some are diverting funds that formerly went to universities in attempts to shore up elementary and secondary schools. Local small businesses give donations for special programs, libraries, and sports programs.

Some school personnel question the role of business in public education, fearing undue influence from the corporate sector, which has money to direct curriculum and policies; others feel that corporate partnerships provide hope for infusing more funds into poor school districts and for trying creative ideas to improve achievement levels.

Peer groups become increasingly important for children as they progress through the teen years; each child is likely to be influenced by several different groups—some are formally organized by the school, as in team sports; some are community activities through religious groups or scouts; and some are informal, such as neighborhood and peer groups.

Special-interest groups make constant demands on the school:

◆ More money should be funneled into athletic programs.
◆ Sex education is not the role of the schools, but should be taught at home.
◆ Teaching diverse cultural heritages should be a high priority for schools.
◆ Students should learn discipline and respect in the school in order to become solid citizens.
◆ Minority students should have special cultural programs.

Minority programming is one example of an issue put forth by special-interest groups. Classrooms are becoming more diverse in class, multicultural, and multiethnic composition. Understanding the interests and needs of the community improves the educational process (Drake, 1993).

Over the years, minority groups have requested that a number of programs be added to the school curriculum; African Americans studies, Hispanic studies, women's studies, and others have been initiated. More recently, grant money from such philanthropic organizations as the Ford and Rockefeller Foundations funded projects in ethnic studies. Many educators agree that the standard curriculum—originally designed to socialize children to be like the dominant group in society, and to assimilate groups to be "Americans"—needs revision. Trends today are in the direction of intercultural programs supporting the diversity of groups within the system. This could eventually put each group into perspective in the national picture and stress respect for cultural diversity and pluralism.

The stronger the power base of the interest group pushing an issue in a community, the more consideration the issue is likely to receive. Some small groups have had disproportionate influence because they were willing to speak out. Consider the examples of censorship of books in Chapter 2. The school's institutional environment shapes the internal processes of schools around the world, making each a unique organization within the educational setting.

The many influences from the educational system's environment cause some similarities between schools, but they also make each school unique because of different pressures from that school's environment. In order to understand the policies and activities within the school, it is necessary to understand environmental pressures on schools.

◆ Summary

I. The Environment and the Educational System

Schools respond to the many and varied demands of their environments in order to survive. Because they depend on the environment for resources, demands from the environment cannot be ignored. In this chapter we have focused on the institutional environment of schools: family and home, religious groups, financing and the economy, political and legal systems, and the community.

Conflicts of interest are an inherent part of the schools' environment, with opposing groups demanding that their views dominate. In order to receive the resources necessary for survival, schools must expend more energy dealing with the demands of the more salient parts of the environment.

II. The School Systems' Environments: Interdependence Between Institutions

Key institutions that make up the environment include the home, religious organizations, financial environment, government and legal systems, and the community and special-interest groups.

1. Children bring their attitudes toward school, among other attributes, from home. Parents have varying degrees of involvement in schools; the more active the parents, the more positive the results for their children's school experience.
2. In some societies, religion and the state, including education, are one and the same. In the United States, the separation of church and state has caused conflict on several issues, most notably what constitutes teaching religion in schools and what to teach in the classroom. The "creation story" issue is a prime example.
3. Funding of education comes from three primary sources: federal, state, and local levels. The percentage supplied by each of these has shifted over the years. Court

cases have challenged some local plans for financing schools as being unfair to poor districts, and in recent years there has been an increase in state funding. Funding comes from several sources: personal income tax, sales tax, property tax, levies, and—in some states—lotteries. Methods of distribution of funds also vary by state, with "foundation plans" being most common. Federal funding supports special programs for minorities, the disabled, and other targeted projects. Proposals for change, including tax credits and vouchers, continue to be discussed.

4. The government role in education involves passing laws and setting policies. Although local control in the United States is paramount, the federal government has great leverage by restricting funding of education to those who fail to adhere to federal educational guidelines. Where there are questions related to laws and policies, the courts are asked to make judgments; for instance, laws setting policy for education for the disabled have dramatically affected this group, and cases brought before the courts continue to test the law.

5. Communities provide the "raw material" entering the schools, as well as influencing the type of education offered in a particular community. Composition of the community determines the need for special programs such as bilingual education. Special interests in the community also put pressure on schools to accommodate their interests.

6. The school environment has a dramatic effect on the internal functioning of schools. We cannot completely understand schools without considering this crucial element affecting the educational system.

◆ Putting Sociology To Work

1. Describe the parts of your environment that affect your role as a student. Do any of these cause role conflict?

2. What are some movements or population trends affecting your school district? Ask teachers and principals what they perceive to be pressures on the schools related to current trends. Compare current influences with those of the 1960s (see also Chapter 10).

3. What are your local schools' immediate and secondary environments? Diagram them.

4. Discuss several examples of school system change brought about by environmental feedback.

The System
of Higher Education

"The path from school to college is poorly marked" (Boyer, 1987, pp. 13–14). Some of us have models—older siblings, parents, or a counselor—to point the way through college-preparatory curricula, college testing, the application and selection process, and admission. Others have little guidance, and often these are the very students who have less chance of going to college and succeeding in higher education. Elementary and secondary schooling are compulsory, but we choose whether to attend an institution of higher education. The atmosphere, the professional manner of the faculty, and the organization of the system are all unique features of higher education as compared with primary and secondary school.

In this chapter we deal with the system of higher education—its development and meaning; access to the system; the structure, process, and role relationships within the system; environmental pressures toward change; and outcomes and reforms in higher education. The open systems model helps us draw together the many aspects of higher education and see them in relation to the total system (see Figure 10–1). This model shows the parts of some systems of higher education today. However, it would look unfamiliar to many who have been involved in higher education throughout history.

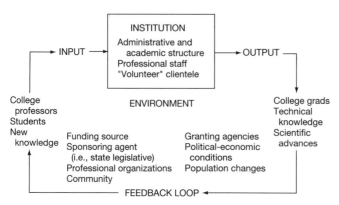

FIGURE 10–1 Systems model of higher education.

HISTORY AND DEVELOPMENT OF HIGHER EDUCATION

Walking through the colleges at Oxford and Cambridge universities in England, one is reminded that many traditions in higher education were established in the twelfth and thirteenth centuries in those very settings, with their courtyards, spires, formal gardens, long halls with stained-glass windows, and statues of notable early scholars. In the ancient library at Oxford University, medieval scholars sat and studied just as students in jeans with backpacks do today. The tradition of transmitting knowledge began with the early universities: Paris in France, Bologna and Venice in Italy, Salamanca in Spain, and Oxford and Cambridge in England (Perkins, 1973, p. 3). These universities established a delicate balance between independence and autonomy over their decision making and interaction with the church and state, a balance that set precedents for church-state-institution relations through the centuries and up to the present time.

Historical Functions of Higher Education

In the nineteenth century, a new mission or function was added to the traditional one of transmitting knowledge. Research became an end in itself (Perkins, 1973, pp. 6–7). This new mission created tension between teaching and research, causing strains on the teacher–student relationship and between faculty members with different orientations and interests. This tension is familiar to us today as professors divide their time between students and research. In many countries, research wins out because more monetary and prestige rewards are attached to these activities than to teaching (Ballantine, 1989).

Two further missions or purposes have developed during the present century: providing services to the community and creating an ideal democratic community within the institution (Perkins, 1973, pp. 10–13). Both have led to dilemmas for the university, as we shall see.

Over time, changes have occurred in the governance, the administrative structures, the curriculum, and the composition of the student body in higher education. New disciplines developed rapidly, requiring adaptation of existing structures. Pressure for more representative multicultural curriculum and higher educational opportunities for more segments of populations around the world became key issues over the years.

Trends in Development of Higher Education

Higher education developed somewhat differently in the United States compared with European countries such as England and Spain. In the colonial period, several small colleges were established in the United States, most sponsored by religious groups but run by lay persons, a pattern that was also typical in Scandinavian countries. In the period that followed, many other colleges sprang up—and many failed. The colleges were meant to serve men from "respectable families" and a few lucky young men selected from poor families. Generally, they were established by upper-middle-class men and perpetuated the existing distinctions between social classes in the United States. In 1776, only about one man in 200 had a college education, but many other young men learned from tutors or were self-taught (Jencks and Riesman, 1968, pp. 90–91). Women were excluded from higher education at this period; however, a few women met in small private groups to receive training from broad-minded male professors at nearby universities.

It was not until after the Civil War, with the passage of the Morrill Act, that many states established public land-grant colleges and universities with the purpose of providing liberal and practical education for a wide range of students. Public teacher-training colleges, or "normal schools," also sprang up to meet the growing need for teachers. The first American colleges to provide graduate education and, thus, become universities were Harvard University, chartered in 1869, and Johns Hopkins, in 1876.

By 1900, there were several hundred small, private, undergraduate colleges, most with a "classical" curriculum of Greek, Latin, mathematics, morals, and religion. In addition, more specialized colleges, forerunners of today's professional schools, were emerging—for example, the Massachusetts Institute of Technology (MIT) and the California Institute of Technology, both specializing in engineering.

England today has a relatively small number of higher education institutions that fall into the categories of universities, polytechnics, and colleges; about 15 percent of individuals between ages 25 and 34 have completed higher education. In contrast, the United States has more than 4,000 higher-education institutions, including two-year colleges (*The Chronicle of Higher Education Almanac*, 1999, p. 24), and enrolls almost 63.5 percent of male and 70.3 percent of female high school students the fall following graduation (National Center for Educational Statistics, *Digest*, 1999, p. 209), the highest percentage in the world. Canada, New Zealand, and Australia come next in percentage attending institutions of higher education. Various historical factors have led to the more restrictive model in England and the mass education model in the United States, among them the great diversity of student population in the United States. England is expanding its model, however, to provide education equivalent to the two-year college, as we shall see (Trow, 1987).

The advent of two-year colleges, sometimes called community or junior colleges, is a twentieth-century phenomenon. They provide terminal degrees or act as feeders for four-year colleges and universities, or both. "In comparison with four-year colleges and universities, community colleges are more likely to enroll academically less-well prepared students, minority students, part-time students, economically less-well off students, commuter students, older students, and first generation college students" (Oromaner, 1995, p. 1). This original American institution serves multiple purposes: a focus on students, remedial education where needed, vocational courses, community service, and nontraditional and minority student accessibility (Grubb, 1991; Vaughan, 1991). "Approximately half of all post-secondary students are beginning their college education at two-year colleges, and approximately 40 percent of the nation's students are currently enrolled at two-year institutions" (Olson, 1996; National Center for Education Statistics, 1995, p. 42). More than half of the minority students are enrolled at community colleges. Of those in higher education who attend community colleges, about one-fifth graduate from four-year colleges, a figure that has been constant over the past decade (Cohen, 1997; National Center for Education Statistics, 1995, p. 42). The likelihood of graduating in six years from a four-year college was the same (69 percent) for transfer students as for those who started at four-year institutions, according to one study (Lee, Mackie-Lewis, and Marks, 1993).

Four decades ago, Burton Clark observed that junior colleges in California in the 1950s served two functions: to provide terminal two-year degrees and to give a small group of students the preparation to transfer to four-year institutions. Clark points out that when it became clear that many students wished to transfer, they were dissuaded by the junior college and told of their academic weaknesses and the virtues of the career-oriented, two-year terminal programs. Clark calls this the "cooling-out function" (Clark, 1960).

This idea of the "cooling-out function" has been the stimulus for much debate about the role of two-year colleges. Critics fall into several categories: Elitists argue community colleges are inferior and do not measure up to academic standards of four-year institutions; mainstream critics are supportive in principle but believe community colleges could do a better job of serving less advantaged students and promoting transfers to four-year colleges; and structural critics see a stratified system of higher education producing inequalities, and two-year colleges playing a role in that system (Pincus, 1994) (see Figure 10–2). The latter argue that community colleges serve as a sieve to eliminate poor and minority students or prevent them from moving up the educational ladder; marginal students, who are often minority students, are filtered out from the higher-education system. For instance, Hispanic stu-

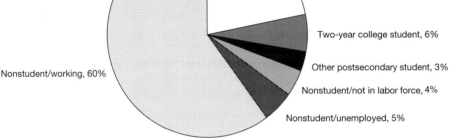
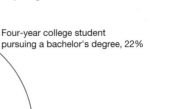

Four-year college student pursuing a bachelor's degree, 22%

Two-year college student, 6%

Other postsecondary student, 3%

Nonstudent/not in labor force, 4%

Nonstudent/unemployed, 5%

Nonstudent/working, 60%

FIGURE 10–2 Activities of two-year college students by years of college completed in October 1991.

Source: U.S. Department of Commerce, Bureau of the Census, Current Population Survey, October 1991. Reprinted in *The Condition of Education,* 1995, p. 45.

dents are disproportionately tracked into two-year colleges (Velez and Javalgi, 1994). Many minority students have inadequate college preparation programs at inner-city high schools, and nearly 90 percent of these students spend time in developmental educational programs at community colleges. Access to four-year degrees is limited (Littleton, 1998).

Another debate surrounding community colleges focuses on the shift in their purpose toward service to the corporate culture, with custom-contracted training programs to meet business needs. Because this is more of a community and vocational purpose, the traditional liberal arts and transfer functions of community colleges are weakened (Lee and Pincus, 1989). Until 1970, two-thirds of community college students transferred to four-year schools; by 1980, 70 percent of community college students were in two-year vocational programs. In a recent review of the situation, several reasons for this dramatic shift were suggested, from the high responsiveness to economic, social, and political environments of the community college to students' choices of programs (Dougherty, 2000; Dougherty and Bakia, 2000).

Research shows that the community colleges themselves may have pursued the more vocational and semiprofessional course because it was an available niche in the higher-education marketplace (Brint and Karabel, 1989). However, contracting with businesses to provide training, courses, and workshops for business employees points to the fear that community colleges may find the financial benefits more appealing than their educational autonomy and serving the educational needs of their unique student constituencies.

Educators are concerned also about the drop in the numbers of transfers, though articulation programs with universities make transferring easy (Eaton, 1990). Some argue for the importance of the transfer function because it confirms the academic purposes of community colleges; many students do aspire to a four-year degree but are discouraged in the process; and claims to be egalitarian depend on the transfer function, which purports to give all students an opportunity for a four-year higher education (Grubb, 1991, p. 194). Of those who do transfer, their likelihood of graduating and going on to graduate school differs little from those who started in four-year schools (Lee, Mackie-Lewis, and Marks, 1993).

What effect do community college degrees have on occupational placement and success? The type of college we enter shapes our occupational status. Community college male entrants achieve lower occupational status than those who begin at four-year colleges. For women, occupational return for each additional year of education is lower for community college entrants than for four-year entrants. On average, community college entrants achieve a lower occupational status than four-year college entrants. Of those who had completed two years of community college in 1990, 60 percent were working and almost 5 percent were unemployed one year later.

According to recent studies, students who enter community colleges have limited occupational and economic status advantages over students who take a job after high school. Considering the loss of work experience, the economic payoff is modest (Monk-Turner, 1992b). Completing the associate of arts degree may actually hinder a student's chances of getting additional years of education (Monk-Turner, 1992a). Community college, then, can perpetuate stratification in higher education (Lee and Frank, 1990, p. 191).

Vocational education offered at community colleges leads to certain types and levels of jobs, such as building trades or electronic or business skills; it benefits employers who need skilled workers and may give workers an opportunity to rise above low-paid, dead-end jobs (Pincus, 1985), but it may also lock workers into lower-level positions, as feared by conflict theorists.

It is clear that two-year colleges serve a distinct role and, despite the controversy, are expanding their presence around the world. For example, Britain has added "sixth-form" colleges to many comprehensive schools; these are similar in structure and function to two-year colleges. Japan also offers selected courses of study at two-year colleges.

> *A*pplying Sociology to Education: What role do you think community colleges can or should play for students and communities? ◆

THEORETICAL APPROACHES TO HIGHER EDUCATION

Higher education has expanded rapidly around the world in the past half-century. Major theoretical questions are why and what are the results? Another major theoretical debate has centered on access to higher education—whether

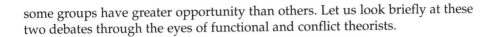

some groups have greater opportunity than others. Let us look briefly at these two debates through the eyes of functional and conflict theorists.

The Expansion of Higher Education

Functionalist or consensus theorists think that universities can go a long way toward solving societal problems through development and use of new knowledge; conflict theorists argue that universities often perpetuate the status quo and that more basic societal change is needed if we are to alter the current state of inequality.

Functional Approach. According to a functionalist perspective, higher education has developed rapidly in the United States and other countries for several reasons. First, higher education is desirable to help improve individual opportunities. Second, higher education increases the possibility of equal opportunities by teaching the skills required in a complex technological world, and thereby improving an individual's ability to compete and fit into the system in a productive way. Third, society needs higher education to help prepare individuals to fill essential roles; this argument has been put forward to expand higher education in developing regions.

Conflict Approach. Conflict theorists view the growth in higher education as directly related to changes in the needs of the capitalistic system. They believe that higher education, like primary and secondary education, is structured to serve the needs and perpetuate the advantaged position of the elite. Just as the secondary schools channel students into vocational or academic tracks, so too the higher-education system can be viewed as a series of tracks. The illusion of upward mobility is present, but its reality has been questioned. There is a major difference in the occupational status of the student graduating from a two-year college or technical school compared with that of the elite university-trained student. Samuel Bowles and Herbert Gintis interpret most of the system of higher education as channeling students to lower-level, white-collar occupations that permit little autonomy or discretion. Students have more choice and long-range work without supervision in institutions preparing students for elite status (Bowles and Gintis, 1976, Ch. 8). These authors are doubtful that even an elite education encourages students to raise questions about the system and its legitimacy. Research funding is also guided by the interests of the elite and perpetuates the status quo.

To understand the politics of "gatekeeping" (Karen, 1990), or who has access to elite colleges, one must study all parts of the educational system, including those who make decisions about access, which includes both college admissions officers and high school counselors (Rosenbaum, 1996), the criteria they use, and what type of university they are trying to create. The admissions process probably reflects the university's position in the larger society and how selective it can be. Therefore, the struggles for access in the society are reflected in the admissions process (Collier and Mayer, 1986).

Access to Higher Education

The issue around the globe is who gets into what university, and why. True or not, the belief in most countries is that education is the road to advancement and success. In many societies, the elite do dominate the halls of ivy, and as the opportunity structures change with modernization, others in society are demanding a share of the profits.

Old universities around the world are pressured to reconsider their restrictive entrance requirements, and new universities are opening their doors to new groups of students. For example, in Malaysia, the national university now serves primarily Malays, the indigenous group that until recent years was underrepresented in higher education compared with Indian and Chinese groups in the population.

In the United States, the situation is different. Admission to elite universities is similar to that in England and Japan, but it is not based primarily on a university exam. Ninety percent of the public institutions in the United States have "open-door policies," meaning that any high school graduate with required prerequisites will be admitted. Private schools are divided between open-door (47 percent) and selective (48 percent) admissions. Since 1980, public four-year institutions have become more selective, meaning that expectations for high school coursework and achievement test scores have increased. At one prestigious institution, Harvard College, admission decisions are tied to both the elite status of some students and affirmative action considerations for others (Karen, 1991). With this gradual closing of the doors has come protest over access to systems and elitism in higher education.

Stratification and Equal Opportunity in Higher Education

In the United States, several factors are considered by college admissions officers—high school grades, activities, recommendations, and test scores. Controversy centers on test scores in particular. Those in favor of using standardized test scores in the admissions process argue that scores help screen out students who "can't make it." Critics of the achievement tests argue that the tests do not give an accurate representation of what students have learned, that students who can afford it can be coached to raise their scores, that the tests do not measure what they say they do, and that they are unfair to minority stu-

TABLE 10–1 Average Scores on the SAT by Sex and Racial and Ethnic Group, 1998

	Verbal Section		Mathematical Section	
	Score	1-Year Change	Score	1-Year Change
Men	509	+2	531	+1
Women	502	−1	496	+2
American Indian	480	+5	483	+8
Asian	498	+2	562	+2
African American	434	0	426	+3
Mexican American	453	+2	460	+2
Puerto Rican	452	−2	447	0
Other Hispanic	461	−5	466	−2
White	526	0	528	+2
Other	511	−1	514	0
All	505	0	512	+1

Note: Each section of the SAT is scored on a scale from 200 to 800.

Source: The Chronicle of Higher Education Almanac, August 27, 1999.

dents. The scores of minority students have improved somewhat; on the SAT, scores of most groups rose slightly, as shown in Table 10–1.

In many countries in Europe, Latin America, Africa, Asia, and other parts of the world, one exam for university entrance determines one's future. Pass or fail—simple as that! This has created a category of young people in Japan called "ronin," students who failed the exam for the university of their choice and spend an extra year or more studying to retake the entrance exam. Some students in Japan, however, simply give up the competitive battle for top university placement and go to less prestigious institutions or to work; more often these are children of blue-collar workers, thus perpetuating the existing class system.

Gaining admission to Oxford University in England typifies the process of entrance to elite universities of the world; the university's entrance exam is most important. Next come the British A-level exams, which each high school graduate contemplating college takes. Socioeconomic variables (especially the type of school from which the student graduated) are highly significant in determining university admission. Pressure to open university admission to more students, stimulated by rapid social, economic, and political change in many countries, is forcing governments to consider new models such as the multiversity, to open more positions, and to consider allowing more private universities (Hayhoe, 1995). Partly as a result of the controversy over access, more institutions are adopting open admissions policies, our next topic.

Elite versus Public Colleges

Students from lower socioeconomic backgrounds are most likely to go to colleges with lower selectivity, such as two-year and open-enrollment institutions, regardless of their ability, achievement, and expectations. Although high school students in the United States know that some school will accept them, fewer middle-class students are enrolling, especially in selective schools. Elite boarding school students have the highest probability of attending highly selective colleges and universities (61 percent from elite schools versus 39 percent for a general sample of college-bound students) (Karen, 1990, p. 238). Admissions officers are working toward diversifying the student populations at their campuses, usually voluntarily, though they have complete autonomy in who they choose because of their independence from regulations (Farnum, 1997). However, these efforts have caused controversy and raised affirmative action questions.

Admissions and the Courts

Admission of minority students has not always been a voluntary decision by the institution. The government has put pressure on institutions by offering funding for special programs, passing affirmative action legislation, and denying research funds to universities that do not comply with government-set standards in minority admissions and staff hiring.

Increasingly the courts have become involved in major decisions affecting the direction of education at all levels; this sector of the educational systems'

Systems of higher education range from open admissions to highly selective.

environment has taken on increased importance. In higher education, court decisions and their implications have ranged from admissions and affirmative action to financing school sports and questions of students' rights. Two early cases related to equal opportunity demonstrate the role of the courts in the environment of higher education.

What is considered preferential treatment of minorities by some has not gone unchallenged. In 1970–71, a case was brought by DeFunis, who was denied admission to the University of Washington law school; he claimed that minority students with lower scores were given preference. The case reached the Supreme Court, which ruled in his favor but left unclear the issue of minority admissions and quota systems.

Admissions officers hoped that the 1978 *Bakke* case would resolve the unanswered questions about minority preferential treatment in minority quotas resulting from the DeFunis case. In this case, the medical school at the University of California at Davis set up quotas. Bakke came close to admission, but special applicants with lower scores were admitted. Bakke filed suit, arguing reverse discrimination. The Court supported the idea that institutions may attempt to achieve racial balance through admissions and affirmative action programs. But the idea of protecting individual rights was not to be ignored in admissions; thus, types of race-conscious plans other than quota systems should be adopted. This eagerly awaited decision left almost as many questions unanswered as answered. Postmortems ranged from disappointment that the Court was stepping backward in the push for minority progress, to realization that more cases must be heard to test the ramifications.

Then in March 1996, the U.S. Fifth Circuit Court of Appeals struck down the admissions policy of University of Texas School of Law. In *Hopwood* v. *State of Texas* the court barred their policy favoring Mexican American and African American applicants. The result has been a dramatic decline in the number of minority admissions to the school (Diaz, 1997). The ruling has left some states such as Louisiana and Mississippi with conflicting affirmative action directives (Healy, 1998).

Another recent issue facing higher-education admissions that has come under attack is race-based scholarships. A number of institutions have set aside scholarships for minority students to help with recruitment and retention, though these scholarships represent only 5 percent of all scholarships. Because of recent rulings against the practice, many colleges are dropping minority scholarships. A case in point is the University of Maryland. The Supreme Court has ruled that their scholarship program for African Americans only is unconstitutional ("Supreme Court," 1995, p. 22). Now some colleges are attempting to comply with the rulings by offering "first-generation student scholarships" that would include some disadvantaged white students as well as minority students (Gose, 1995). Critics argue and evidence indicates that minority enrollments will drop. We have not heard the end of this difficult issue.

Applying Sociology to Education: How can institutions of higher education provide equal opportunity and be fair to all groups of students? ◆

CHARACTERISTICS OF HIGHER EDUCATION IN THE UNITED STATES

Higher education is a catchall term for programs offering some academic degree after high school. In general, however, we will not be referring to vocational or occupational training programs in this section.

In selecting our college, we can pick from two-year, four-year, or university systems, public or private. Once we have made our selection, we move into the system where we will remain until either (1) we are graduated after two or four years, (2) we drop out, or (3) we transfer.

There are more than 4,000 institutions of higher education in the United States ("Number of Colleges," 1999, p. 24). First, sponsorship is an important division, with two main categories—public and private. Within the public category, institutions of higher education exist at the local, state, and even federal level. Most often public institutions are state-sponsored. Locally sponsored institutions tend to be two-year colleges and technical training institutions. More than half of the private institutions are religiously affiliated, usually with Protestant and Roman Catholic parent organizations.

Second, student composition tells us something about the institutions: percentage of males, females, minorities, foreign-speaking students; age and background of students (see Table 10-2).

Third, types of programs distinguish one institution from another: two-year, four-year, master's or graduate level, Ph.D.-granting, and professional schools such as law or medicine. Many of the institutions develop certain spe-

TABLE 10–2   Attitudes and Characteristics of Freshmen, Fall 1998

Racial and Ethnic Background	Total	Men	Women
American Indian	2.1	2.0	2.2
Asian American	4.0	4.1	3.8
African American	9.4	8.2	10.4
White	82.5	83.2	81.9
Mexican American	2.1	2.2	2.0
Puerto Rican American	1.0	1.0	1.0
Other Latino	1.4	1.5	1.4
Other	2.3	2.4	2.3

Source: Higher Education Research Institute at UCLA.

cialty areas or professional schools for which they become well known. Some institutions, especially public, state-sponsored systems, have moved toward multicampus facilities. The University of California is a case in point, with its nine university campuses, 19 four-year state universities, and more than 100 two-year programs, which can either be terminal or feed into the other parts of the system.

Within each classification, there may be further variations. For instance, there are many types of professional schools, including

Architecture	Journalism	Optometry
Business	Law	Pharmacy
Dentistry	Library science	Public health
Education	Medicine	Social work
Engineering	Music	Theology
Forestry	Nursing	Veterinary medicine

These schools vary as to size, financial resources, graduate or undergraduate training, affirmative action and sex distribution, and according to specific attributes of the universities with which they are affiliated. The variations between systems of higher education are great. What they have in common is their service to students who have completed 12 years of schooling and who are voluntarily furthering their education.

Higher education experienced a period of phenomenal growth and has now leveled off. We look at these trends and their implications next.

Growth of Higher Education

The growth of American higher education since the late nineteenth century (and especially in the 1960s) has been phenomenal as compared with any previous time. Despite the rapid increase in the size of institutions of higher education, the dropout rate has remained the same throughout the period. Recent data show enrollments of 15.5 million students (full and part time) in fall 1997. Much growth was at the two-year colleges (*The Chronicle of Higher Education Almanac*, 1999, p. 24). This number is expected to rise to more than 16 million in 2002 (Evangelauf, 1992). The minority population in these figures is also rising, wheras the white population is dropping slightly.

The School-to-Work Transition and the Credential Crisis

Does everyone have the right to go to college? Do those who don't go to college have a right to work? Who should decide who has the right? And, ultimately, must some people trying to enter the job market fail?

The United States does less to help its high school and college graduates prepare for and find jobs than other industrial countries. Those graduating from high school have seen little connection between school and work, yet they must adjust to the demands of the job market. College graduates fare better because they have trained in specific fields (Reich, 1994, p. A16). Employers need workers with specific skills that new employees often lack. This means employers must go to the effort and expense of training new workers, using supervisors' time to explain and oversee tasks. In addition, employers make extra efforts to keep their skilled employees (Rosenbaum and Binder, 1997).

An issue that affects college graduates is the "credential crisis," which has arisen because graduates can no longer be guaranteed a job after college. Large numbers of college graduates remain unemployed or are returning to graduate school to improve their chances of employment (Wilson, 1990). Various new types of credentials are being proposed and requirements for jobs are being raised, not as a result of new educational knowledge, but because of the increased number of people seeking higher-level jobs in the system. Thus, many people are overeducated for the jobs they receive, a phenomenon referred to as the "job gap." Jobs once held by poorly educated people are now held by more highly educated individuals until they can find appropriate jobs for their training (Halaby, 1994).

The inflation of credentials is closely related to the economic and stratification system; students want higher credentials to get better jobs to have higher status. However, the image of college and university as "a sure route to the better life" has lost ground. The narrowing gap between high school and college credentials is directly related to the economic status of countries and the failure of the economy to provide more and higher-paying jobs for the larger number of college graduates (Moore and Trenwith, 1997). In fact, many college graduates accept positions unrelated to their college majors. The functionalist interpretation of expanding educational opportunities to meet societal needs is challenged by the current economic picture. Tensions produced by the presence of large numbers of dissatisfied graduates could, according to conflict theorists, force a restructuring of the economic system, and in turn of the educational system.

Applying Sociology to Education: Should everyone have access to higher education, or are we overeducating the population? Who should make these decisions? ◆

FUNCTIONS OF THE HIGHER EDUCATION SYSTEM

Higher education serves certain functions or purposes in society. What these purposes are or should be is a matter of debate and may cause conflict between parents, educators, students, government officials, and other groups in society. In the following discussion we consider the university as a community, the functions of the university, and conflicts over functions.

The University as a Community

One way to consider the functions of the university is through the concept of community: what members have in common, the division of labor, and the interdependence among members (Sanders, 1973, p. 57). Universities are communities with an overall academic program, centralized physical settings, a form of governance, and a range of services. One can eat, sleep, and work there. Perhaps the best way to describe the modern university is as one institution fulfilling numerous functions.

The full university, with its expanse of programs, research facilities, graduate and professional schools, and support services, has set the standards for all academic systems of higher education. Yet it is caught between contradictory goals, especially in the area of organizational structure and autonomy. Bonds such as shared beliefs, attitudes, and values, which traditionally held the university together, have been disintegrating as more formal structures, rules, and procedures have replaced them (Perkins, 1973, p. 258). Questions have been raised about some basic values of the university community—the nature of the academic programs; whether to teach factual knowledge, or also values and beliefs, and even practical skills; the meaning of freedom of inquiry for scholars; and what should be included in the activities of a university.

The Function of Research

The expansion of knowledge is a generally accepted purpose of higher education, especially in universities with strong research components. The direction and extent of research programs has been determined largely by the financial support provided by business, industry, and government. This influence on the direction of research efforts has led some researchers to ask, "knowledge for whom?" Some research, especially in pure rather than applied science, is being eliminated because it is not a priority in this time of financial cutbacks. This could lead to future gaps in our knowledge, some argue. The cutting back of state and government funding from the university's environment will significantly affect research institutions dependent on such funding to support research scholars, students, and other departments ("The American Research University," 1993).

The Function of Teaching

Concerns regarding the balance of teaching and research roles of professors dominate institutions of higher education, especially those with graduate programs. Stanford University, followed by Cornell and others, took the lead in the early 1990s when they announced that evaluation of teaching would be a significant part of the promotion process. A number of disciplines are producing teaching materials and promoting professional development in teaching. Professional schools are also putting more emphasis on the art of teaching.

The Function of Service

Another function or purpose of the university is that of public service in the wider community. The faculty are expected to disseminate knowledge developed in research programs through such channels as publications, the media, and teaching and lecturing. This diffusion of ideas has wide repercussions, even to the point of stimulating social change in countries around the world. The degree to which scholars should become involved in attempts to sway opinions through social awareness or act to bring about changes is a matter of debate. Students in many colleges are involved in community service work, sometimes as a required part of their education.

The Function of the "National Security State"

Higher education, sometimes assumed to operate autonomously, is, in fact, central to the training of individuals for high-level technical human resource requirements; this is seen by some as necessary to national security and for a developing economy. Some argue that the university power structure is headed by boards of trustees who serve corporate interests, and that their interests impact on the organization of universities (Rhoades and Slaughter, 1991). Liaisons between universities and the corporate world, created by students employed in these organizations and research funded by private interests, provide evidence for the links.

University professors create ideas in laboratories; some of these ideas become commercial products. Structures for transferring the technology from labs to commercial use are most often controlled by university administrations, who use the idea of "the public good" to control the transfer; university faculty, however, hold that scientific norms should guide the transfer of technology. How the information is transferred affects who receives credit, patents, and financial benefits (Rhoades and Slaughter, 1991, p. 75).

Conflicts over the University's Function

It is a crisp autumn Saturday afternoon. The stands are packed for the big game, the traditional rivalry that will determine who goes to the bowl. College athletics is big business worth millions of dollars, and the issues surrounding athletics have become major targets in the conflicts over the functions of a university. Sports is a big moneymaker and attracts new students. Critics argue that athletics is not part of the major function of universities—the acquisition and transmission of knowledge, service, or other traditional functions. This case illustrates the conflict over the academic function of universities versus a big-business orientation.

The Academic Function of Universities versus Big Business

Issues that have been raised in recent years illustrate the conflicts. The "athlete as a hunk of meat" is one of these issues. Scouts and recruiters see star high school players and sign contracts. It is illegal to offer rewards or bribes such as cars or fancy living, but it has been known to happen. What is more common is that pressure to succeed in athletics is so great that there is temptation to skirt the rules. Reports of grade fixing at several institutions have caused scandals and led to sanctions against individuals and institutions. Young men and women with weak academic backgrounds are recruited to compete, but they sometimes fail to make progress toward a degree. Minority students are affected particularly hard. In recent years, however, student athletes have been entering as first year students with higher credentials than in the past, and their graduation rate after six years is 58 percent compared to 56 percent of all students at Division I institutions.

Statistics collected by the National Collegiate Athletic Association (NCAA) show that African American athletes attending Division I colleges are five times more likely to enter college with weaker credentials than other students, and are less likely to graduate (41 percent) when compared to all scholarship athletes (58 percent). However, a higher percentage of African American scholarship athletes graduate in six years than all other African American students (see Table 10–3); in some institutions, academic tutoring programs geared toward athletes assist them (1999 NCAA Graduation Rates Summary, 1999; Blum, 1995, p. 34). A recent concern is the drop from a 45 percent graduation rate in six years in 1991 data to a 41 percent rate in 1998 (Haworth, 1998, pp. A41–42).

Using participant observation, two sociologists spent several years studying athletes at a Division I college, observing the conflicting roles of players. Most players come to college expecting to play ball, have a social life, earn a degree, and perhaps to go on to the NBA or other professional leagues. Many quickly become disillusioned, however, and some feel exploited by the fans and even the coaches, who are interested in them only as long as they can perform well. The problem is that the athletes come poorly prepared for academics, and training is all-consuming. They are often housed separately, isolated from campus, and made to feel like outcasts. Some of the middle-class athletes graduate, but few recruited from the lower classes do so (Adler and Adler, 1991).

Another problem is the lack of support athletes get once they enter college. In some institutions they are used as long as they can play for the team; then they are dropped, leaving them little future. Several proposals have been made to curb the "meat market" phenomenon. In order to be considered a "qualifier," that is to play during first year, athletes must have graduated from high school, completed a core curriculum of 13 academic courses, and have a

TABLE 10–3 1998 NCAA Graduation Rates Summary

1. Division I Student-Athletes

Year Entered	Student-Athlete Graduation Rate (%)	Div. I Student Body Graduation Rate (%)
1992	58	56
1991	57	56
1990	58	56
1989	58	57
1988	58	57
1987	57	56
1986	57	55
1985	52	54
1984	52	53

2. Division I Male Student-Athletes

Year Entered	Student-Athlete Graduation Rate (%)	Div. I Male Student Body Graduation Rate (%)
1992	52	54
1991	51	53
1990	53	54
1989	53	55
1988	53	55
1987	53	54
1986	52	54
1985	48	52
1984	47	51

3. Division I African American Male Student-Athletes

Year Entered	Student-Athlete Graduation Rate (%)	Div. I. African American Male Student Body Graduation Rate (%)
1992	40	31
1991	41	34
1990	43	33
1989	43	35
1988	42	34
1987	43	33
1986	41	30
1985	34	30
1984	33	28

4. Division I White Male Student-Athletes

Year Entered	Student-Athlete Graduation Rate (%)	Div. I White Male Student Body Graduation Rate (%)
1992	58	57
1991	56	56
1990	57	57
1989	59	57
1988	58	57
1987	58	57
1986	57	56
1985	55	55
1984	55	54

Source: NCAA Graduation Rates Summary, National Collegiate Athletic Association. http://www.ncaa.org/grad-rates/

combination of grade point and SAT or ACT score specified in the NCAA academic eligibility standards. The combinations range from a 2.5 GPA or above and 17 on the ACT or 820 on the SAT to 2.0 GPA and 1,010 on the SAT or 21 on the ACT ("NCAA Guide," 1999, 1995). Foes of this requirement argue that it places a heavy emphasis on racially biased tests.

One proposal is to let athletes play five years, giving them more time to complete their college work. Programs for special tutorials, restrictions on "the season" and practice time, and counseling services are being put in place in many schools and could help poorly achieving students. Tutoring and mentoring programs at many universities are meant to supplement the athletes' programs; some help, some don't. Some of those athletes who flunk out or drop out end up sweeping floors or doing other menial labor. The academic "teaching" function is brought into question when emphasis is on "big business," but recent attention is focusing efforts, such as those mentioned previously, on bringing this function into balance. There is one bright spot—students who have participated in varsity sports are more likely to do better in the job market than those who did not, according to some findings (Lederman, 1990, p. A47).

What Type of Curriculum?

Conflicts persist over curricular issues. On the one hand are those who would have the university retain its traditional focus on a liberal education in the arts and sciences, which transmits to students knowledge for its own sake and produces a well-rounded person. On the other hand are those who advocate a practical, career-focused training that stresses the social utility of the knowledge transmitted. These conflicts are particularly relevant today, when universities and colleges face periods of dropping enrollments, and when economic conditions put pressures on students to get a degree they can "use"—one that will be functional and lead directly to employment. Only a few elite schools may be able to resist the pressures to diversify the curriculum and introduce more applied or practical programs as opposed to "pure" arts and sciences. For most institutions, ability to adapt to changing or conflicting environmental demands may determine survival.

Societal conflicts are reflected in debates over curriculum content and pressure to be "politically correct." Racism, discrimination, prejudice, intolerance, differential treatment, sexual harassment, and homophobia are all hot topics on university campuses. After the 1960s, there was a transformation from activism to "MEism," but we are seeing a recurrence of activism in the 1990s (Altbach, 1990, pp. 33–48). Extremes range from those who would throw out the "old" curriculum and replace it with entirely new materials sensitive to abuses of the past, to "hate speech" and racial or sexual incidents on campuses. The debate is between competing responsibilities to protect freedom of speech and to protect students, faculty, and staff who are victims of hate crimes (Munitz, 1991, p. 4). The Supreme Court has ruled in one decision that "hate speech" is free speech, but other court rulings challenge use of such words as the "N" word by teachers and students except in literature (Zirkel, 1999).

Most colleges are "internationalizing" their curricula to include Third World and environmental concerns; the numbers of students majoring in these fields are also increasing (Dodge, 1990, p. A31). Requirements to engage in community service show a curricular trend toward service learning and citizenship development.

Conflicts over purposes can also be seen in the changing roles of various members of the university community. For instance, in the 1950s administrators were expected to watch over their students like parents; hence the term *in loco parentis*. Dormitory hours were rigid, lights-out regulations were enforced, separation of the sexes in living quarters was expected, and the atmosphere was one that not only perpetuated an adolescent dependence but also carried the home structure to the school. Following student discontent and attacks on the university administration in the 1960s, most administrators gradually reduced or eliminated this role. Faculty roles are changing with new technologies, as described in Box 10–1.

> **A**pplying Sociology to Education: Should universities meet the needs of the community, remain independent of community needs, or find another option? ◆

HIGHER EDUCATION AS AN ORGANIZATION

Higher Education Structure and the Bureaucratic Model: Does It Work?

Universities face particular contradictions when trying to run on a bureaucratic or business model, yet that is what most are doing. The hierarchical charts of universities may resemble business organizations, but most of the similarities stop there.

1. There are two distinct structures in the university: the flat academic structure and the hierarchical administrative structure.
2. Many of the employees are knowledge specialists, professionals who by tradition expect autonomy and academic freedom; they may have only temporary loyalty to the institution but permanent allegiance to their disciplines.
3. Colleges are to a large extent detached from the community and larger society in pursuing their primary activities—transmitting knowledge and conducting research.
4. Teaching and research require individual faculty autonomy over the end product.

> ◆◆**Box 10–1** *The Future of Higher Education: Case of the Virtual University*
>
> Imagine a university that comes to all citizens who have a desire to learn and wish to take courses, from high school age to senior citizens. The setting can be the home, a library, or any place with Internet access.
>
> No need to imagine! In Kentucky and several other states, this scenario is reality. Faced with the changing state, national, and global economy that made former occupations in coal mining and tobacco growing obsolete, Kentucky's virtual university is being used as one solution to the problem of unemployment and poverty.
>
> How does the process work? The virtual university staff of 20, sitting in an office with cubicles and computers, arranges for services to be delivered on-line to students around the state and beyond. Public and private universities in Kentucky offer up to three-quarters of required degree credits on-line. Other services include contracts with professional designers of courses, on-line library resources, student counseling services, and bookstore services.
>
> The role of faculty changes from lecturing to mentoring—from discussing issues and problems with students to utilizing services such as on-line writing assistance, and of course grading student work. Concerns about lack of face-to-face interaction are being addressed by seeing the professor or class members on the computer screen.
>
> In the virtual university, students as consumers have control over the process of learning, are able to register and carry out all tasks on-line, move at an individually comfortable pace, watch and interact with professional on-line courses that include projects and assignments, read the text from on-line bookstores, and interact with the professor on-line. According to Susman, president of Kentucky Commonwealth Virtual University, virtual universities involve an "orbital shift." No longer do students need to be on site, running around between offices to register or to obtain professor permissions and parking passes. No longer are they concerned with getting to class on time—the Internet has 24-hour access.
>
> Looking for recreation as a part of the college experience? Join the virtual football team. Michigan Virtual University has challenged Kentucky's team to a match. Other opportunities for games such as chess, book clubs, and chatrooms in courses are being created as you read this; the possibilities are endless.
>
> The bottom line is that the university experience for some students is likely to be a very different one in the future with technology leading the way.
>
> *Source:* Taken in part from a lecture by Mary Beth Susman, president, Kentucky Commonwealth Virtual University, August 11, 2000, Bethesda, MD, at the meeting of the Society for Applied Sociology.

5. Policy decision making is spread throughout the organization, and students sometimes have a substantial voice in issues.

Let us consider the problems of hierarchy and decision making in greater detail.

The Dual Hierarchy. Academic institutions have two hierarchies. The *academic structure* of the university, with its many departments and programs, has one form of hierarchy, usually based on rank and tenure. Although faculty members hold differing ranks, their formal status within the university is the same. However, informal influence, power, responsibilities, and salary may differ. The *administrative structure* approximates more closely the business model and Weber's bureaucratic division of labor. At the top of the hierarchy are the president and other top administrators, including deans. Other administrative personnel carry out diverse functions, providing health services, bookstores, food services, building and grounds maintenance, financial services, and counseling.

The structural looseness of the university, with its focus on academic freedom, allows for little centralized decision making. The professional faculty expect to make decisions in their areas of expertise and resent others' usurping this power or making rules that infringe on this "right"; this is especially true in the area of hiring, promotion, retention of faculty, and curriculum matters. Once faculty members are granted tenure by their peers, their independence from administrative decisions is increased. Finally, there is inherent conflict between providing a good education and running an administratively economical and efficient operation—as is called for in business or a bureaucratic model.

These problems and inconsistencies have been accentuated by the rapid increase in size and corresponding administrative complexity of the "multiversity." With added departments, programs, and research components, the administrative structures increase in complexity along with the academic structure.

The University Hierarchical Structure and Decision Making. Despite the incongruities, it is useful to use characteristics of the bureaucratic model to describe the university, because this model is closer than any other to the realities of the situation. There are seven levels within the higher-education hierarchical structure.

1. *Department.* The department is an administrative unit with a head or chair who may be appointed or elected, or the position may rotate among department members. The chair is accountable to both department members and higher-level administrators. The position has inherent role conflict, because a chair must both support faculty and sit in judgment of them for salary increases and, sometimes, promotions. Departments are hierarchically structured, the usual ranks being instructor assistant professor, associate professor, and professor. Power and decision making for the unit are usually distributed among members, who use democratic procedures to make major unit decisions.

2. *College.* Several related disciplines are grouped as a college with a dean as administrative head. Professional schools in universities have similar status. At this level of the administrative hierarchy, decisions are made about finances, salaries, scheduling, new programs, and so forth, which affect all unit parts.

3. *Administration.* The president or chancellor, vice president, deans, and assistants may or may not be faculty members. They have responsibility for various aspects of the university, including academic matters, student services, and financial matters.

4. *Faculty representative bodies.* Faculty councils or senates composed of representatives from the various colleges and schools have decision-making power over academic issues.

5. *Board of trustees.* These lay persons from the community have ultimate legal responsibility. Members are usually selected through election, by other board members, or through appointment by state governors. Most boards will give their formal approval to recommendations of the institution's president and faculty senate. In recent years, central committees have been formed as coordinating structures for some multicampus universities. These "superboards" have ultimate control just as boards of trustees, but they remove decision making even further from the faculty and individual campus (Clark, 1976).

6. *Regional accrediting associations.* There are six voluntary associations around the country that evaluate institutions' achievements in comparison with their goals, using professionals from within the regions: North Central, North West, New England, Middle States, South, and West. The attempt is not to equalize or standardize institutions, but to help institutions achieve the standards they set for themselves.

7. *National organization.* Many countries have national coordination of public institutions. Although there is no formal national control of decision making in the United States, the federal government does wield its influence in many ways. To some extent a national educational policy has been developed in response to international pressures and competition and national needs in areas of economics, politics, and the military. Federal funding has had a major influence on what research an institution pursues, and it may constitute the financial support of entire programs in the university. If an institution is judged to be negligent in its affirmative action policies, funding will be withdrawn. Many institutions would suffer severe crises if they lost federal support.

Control and Decision Making. Major decisions are made or approved by the institution's president and board of trustees. The multiplicity of diverse programs is coordinated through the administrative hierarchy. Although the number of coordinating structures has been increasing, demands also are increasing for decentralized decision making, with power held by individual units. However, these units want money from outside agencies that require scrutiny of the units (Friedman, 1995, p. 746).

Lower-level participants in the university wield power that is not always recognized officially but that is influential in decision making. For instance, office workers have access to and control over people, information, and technology. Many office workers are irreplaceable because of the knowledge they hold. However, their compensation is seldom commensurate with their subtle power (Reyes and McCarty, 1990).

Students have varying degrees of power in the decision-making structure. They are with the organization for a short time; they bring new perspectives;

they pass through and leave their mark. Because of their short stay in the institution, students are not usually primary decision makers, but they may provide much-needed impetus for evaluation and change of the status quo.

> **A**pplying Sociology to Education: Can you identify areas of conflict between the university hierarchical structure and the business model?

ROLES IN HIGHER EDUCATION

Each of us has a role in the system of higher education. This is only one of our many roles, and herein lies one of the problems for higher education, as for any organization—it must compete for the loyalty of members who have multiple role obligations. A student may have family, work, and other role obligations. Faculty members have multiple loyalties, which lead to problems for the organization. Keep in mind the dilemma of conflicting role obligations as we discuss major roles in the system of higher education.

Roles in Higher Education: The Clients

Without students there would be no institutions of higher education, and most professors would be out of work. Students are clients of the system, buying a service, and members of the system, playing an integral part in its functioning. At different times students have held different degrees of power in the system, from an ineffectual group that comes and goes and has little real power, to a group that, by their choices, determines which faculty members, programs, and even universities will survive.

The students of the 1950s were a cautious "silent generation." By the 1960s, students began to demand a major role in the governance of universities and other institutions and to create pressures for change. This politically active student population flexed its muscles with the Free Speech Movement at Berkeley; it went on, in greater strength, to the Vietnam War protests in the late 1960s and 1970s. What was remarkable about the revolt of the 1960s was that the youth culture profoundly impacted other members of the higher-education community with the ideas and practices adopted by adults. Changes initiated by students affected all members of higher education because of their reciprocal role involvements.

Through the baby-boom years, college enrollments expanded dramatically; then came the bust and retrenchments. Between 1979 and 1985, the number of 18-year-old high school graduates decreased by a half-million. Colleges feared that there would not be enough students to sustain them, but increasing recruitment among nontraditional students, a recession that kept students nearer their home institutions, and increases in the number of high school graduates attending colleges forestalled disaster for many small institutions. College marketing budgets have increased dramatically, using direct mail, videos, telephone contacts, invitations to visit, and scholarships to academically talented students for recruitment. Ironically, at a time when it seems that underrepresented groups might have an advantage, many colleges did not lower but increased their admissions requirements and expectations, recruiting students with high SATs and those from wealthier areas rather than poor, disenfranchised minority students.

More than 14.6 million students enrolled in higher education for the 1998–99 academic year, up 1.7 percent from the 1996–97 year. Private college enrollments were down 1 percent, and public institution enrollments were up 2.5 percent (*The Chronicle of Higher Education Almanac*, 1999). Fluctuations in enrollments are caused by many factors, including low numbers of college-age students in the population, but high enrollments of certain groups. For students of college age, 1996 was a record low year in the 1990s, but future enrollments should continue to increase and are expected to surpass 16 million by 2005 (*The Chronicle of Higher Education Almanac*, 1999, pp. 24–25).

The profile of the typical college student is becoming more diversified, with older nontraditional students, minority students, and married students attending college in greater numbers. In 1965, only 4.8 percent of all U.S. college students were African American. One percent of law students were African American. These numbers have changed dramatically over the past 30 years (Bowen and Bok, 1998). Today, African American enrollees make up close to 15 percent of college enrollments, an increase of 21 percent from 1990 to 1996, wheras Hispanic enrollees increased by 49 percent for the same period (*The Chronicle of Higher Education Almanac*, 1999, p. 24). Native American enrollments also rose, and today there are 24 tribally controlled colleges in the United States.

At 28 selective colleges, 75 percent of African American students graduated within six years, and 4 percent more graduated from schools to which they had transferred. These percentages are higher than for many other groups. Ninety percent of African Americans in professional schools complete their training and earn twice what African American men with bachelor's degrees earn. Despite the success of some students who would not have been admitted without affirmative action, the courts are changing the laws to deny special consideration.

Gender and Race in Higher Education

The number of women attending college in the United States has doubled since the 1970s. In fact, in 1996 college women outnumbered men by 7.96 million to 6.3 million. Part of the increase results from nontraditional-age women returning to college. There is evidence, however, that women's participation in higher education in noncore developing nations is being hindered by multinational corporations, which hire men in high-status occupations, thus creating less demand for educated women (Clark, 1992).

Women earn more graduate degrees in the humanities, social and behavioral sciences, education, and health professions, and men earn more in natural sciences, computer sciences and engineering, and business management. The differences are particularly significant in engineering and computer science (National Center for Education Statistics, *Digest*, 1999, p. 306, Table 268; Olsen, 1999). Women's achievement in math and science courses at all levels of education continues to occupy the efforts of researchers. In college, women's and men's grades are similar in math courses through calculus (Bridgeman and Wendler, 1991, p. 283).

The median annual income of year-round, full-time male workers 25 years and over in 1997 with a bachelor's degree was $48,616; those with associate college degrees averaged $38,022. Women in the same categories averaged $35,379 with bachelor's degrees and $28,812 with associates degrees (National Center for Education Statistics, *Digest*, 1999, p. 434, Table 380). Though factors such as time out for childrearing can be taken into consideration, women continue to receive lower income for similar levels of education.

A hope for some institutions of higher education with dropping enrollments lies in attracting women from nontraditional-age categories. In recent years, this group has been a target for admissions officers. These women are already entering, or returning to, college in large numbers. There are more than one million "reentry women" in higher education. Many reentry women are attempting to fulfill two sets of expectations: family roles and educational roles. Changes in family status often require that they go back to school. Survey data indicate that most reentry women are committed to their studies and have confidence and energy. Several colleges, including elite women's colleges, admit reentry women as a percentage of their college classes and provide special programs for them (see Box 10–2).

Most women students seem reasonably satisfied with their college experience, including professors, other students, and classroom and study conditions. Students at all-women's colleges tend to be very satisfied with their experiences. They perceive their ability to acquire skills high, and educational aspirations, including the likelihood of attending graduate school, are also high (Smith, 1990, p. 181).

Many colleges are offering more nondegree courses for adult men and women through continuing education or lifelong learning programs. Not only do these programs enable interested adults to learn for pleasure, but they also help offset budget deficits in programs being run at a financial loss. Courses are taken by a wide range of adults—"do-it-yourselfers"; senior citizens; those who have a specific motivation, such as learning a language for a holiday trip

◆◆Box 10–2 *Case of a Reentry Woman*

The case of Anne Martindell, former state senator and ambassador, illustrates some of the many challenges and conflicts that faced women who tried to get college educations.

> Martindell has left the political pioneering to a younger class of legislators. Still, that doesn't mean she has stopped breaking barriers. At the age of 85, she has come back to Smith College as an Ada Comstock Scholar to finish an education that was cut short more than 60 years ago when her father forbade her to return to campus, fearing that an educated woman would never marry. In returning now, Martindell has earned the title of Smith's oldest student and has been teaching fellow students and faculty a few things about getting older . . . Martindell's academic advisor [says] "She is voracious in her interests and wants to learn as much as she possibly can. I hope that what students can see by her example is that life goes on and people, whatever their age, can continue to learn and be active participants in the classroom." (MacMillan, 2000, pp. 1, 14ff.)

abroad; those who wish to prepare for college reentry, to have contact with others, to increase mental stimulation, or just to have fun (survey by author of students in continuing education classes).

By and large, women are gaining ground in academic settings though they are less segregated within institutions where there are higher percentages of women students and administrators and less emphasis on research (Kulis, 1997). However, the story for other minorities is mixed. By 2010, almost one-third of the nation will be African American or Hispanic. By 2050, the non-Hispanic white population is projected to be 52.8 percent of the total U.S. population (U.S. Census Bureau, 2000). Yet the numbers of minority groups in higher education do not reflect this diversity. Because statistics on enrollments are two years old, they do not yet reflect the impact of court affirmative action decisions in California and Texas, decisions which could cause reductions in the number of minorities in higher education. There are many plans to increase the numbers, but only time will determine their success (see Figure 10–3).

Factors Related to Minority Student Success or Failure. Student success in higher education is based not only on individual goals, motivations, and abilities but also on social class, race, sex, and early labeling. "Success" or "failure" begins early in life with the labeling of children. By the high school years, teachers, counselors, students, and parents have a fair idea of the student's academic ability. Tracking into college-preparatory or vocational courses is often an easy decision. Conflicts arise for those who have high aspi-

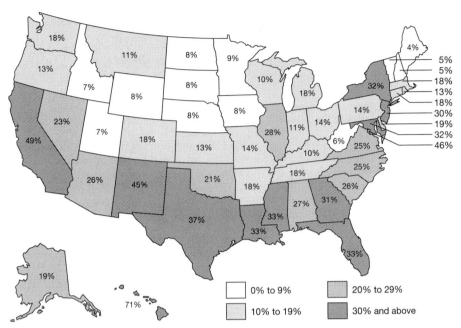

FIGURE 10–3 Proportion of college students who are minority-group members, fall 1996.

Source: The Chronicle of Higher Education, Dec. 17, 1999, p. A53.

rations but little support in the form of teacher recommendations, test results, counselor evaluations, and parental encouragement.

The system provides for open competition and rewards high achievers with acceptance to the better academic institutions. This has been referred to as "contest mobility." However, "sponsored mobility" removes some of those slots from open competition, because it singles out some favored or elite students and trains them for particular positions in society (Turner, 1960).

Other students are not prepared for the college experience. Basic skills in reading, writing, and math, plus lack of college-preparatory curricula, put students "at risk" in college. Early diagnosis and remedial action to build basic skills of students while they are still in high school can help students achieve, and many colleges are offering special services in remedial and developmental education.

Students with limited economic means are eight times less likely to graduate from college than other students (Levine, 1995), and options for funding are becoming more limited with government and campus cutbacks ("The Widening Gap . . .," 1996). Many of those affected are also minority students who make up 23.4 percent of higher-education enrollments. Sixteen percent of African American students and 13 percent of Hispanic students with high school degrees have earned four-year college degrees or more. This is compared with 30 percent of white students. The difference often begins in earlier years of schooling, and many universities find themselves offering remedial courses for low-achieving students with weak skills. Urban universities in particular are being hit by underfunding and cutbacks in services, making them unable to respond effectively to many minority students' needs. Many minority students who enter college fail to complete their degree work, not because of ability level, but because of poor academic preparation and campus climates. As an example, Latino college students who had memberships in religious or social organizations and who had contact with other students outside of class in their first two years of college were more likely to continue in college, compared to those who faced a hostile racial climate (Hurado and Carter, 1997). Those who do graduate have lower grades and less chance of going on to graduate school (Steele, 1992). The number of Ph.D.'s granted to African Americans rose slightly between 1977 and 1997, to 4.8 percent of all doctorates (*The Chronicle of Higher Education Almanac*, 1999, p. 29). The percentage of doctorates earned by other minority groups is shown in Table 10–4.

Even with adequate preparation, many minority students feel undervalued, stigmatized, and vulnerable. It is as though others look for reasons to "confirm" racial inferiority (Steele, 1992). College is an impersonal, unfamiliar (Thompson and Fretz, 1991), even hostile world for many. It challenges self-respect and self-esteem, especially if one is insecure about one's ability to cope with college work and believes that others are questioning that ability too (Kraft, 1991). Recent racial incidents on campuses hinder efforts to integrate African Americans and other minorities and to improve their self-esteem. One explanation is that these incidents are sparked by the competition for scarce resources—grades, acceptance to competitive programs, graduation, and ultimately jobs and income.

TABLE 10–4 Characteristics of Recipients of Doctorates, 1996 (all fields)

Total Doctorates	44,652
American Indian	153
Asian	2,492
African American	1,563
Hispanic	950
White	26,363
Non-resident aliens	11,450
Race unknown	1,681

Source: *The Chronicle of Higher Education Almanac*, August 27, 1999, p. 32.

Student Subcultures or Peer Groups. Students belong to peer groups, which have great influence on their activities, interests, and academic success. Some years ago, a typology of student subcultures or peer groups was developed by Burton Clark and Martin Trow (1966). Students were categorized into one of four types:

1. *Collegiate*—sports, dates, fun, fraternities and sororities, "Joe College," some money
2. *Vocational*—job preparation, no-nonsense attitude, financially less well-off, often working, married
3. *Academic*—intellectual, identification with faculty, time spent in library and lab, planning graduate and professional training
4. *Nonconformist*—several types: the aggressive intellectual, the student seeking personal identity, and the rebellious student

With the radical student movements of the 1960s, new student types emerged that did not fit clearly into these categories. Although these types may have altered, the concept of a "reference group" that provides both a sense of belonging and a model for behavior has not changed.

Fraternities and sororities function to provide group identity for some students in higher education. These "formalized" peer-group relationships generally fall into the collegiate subculture. They provide an alternative to the academic side of college life. Although Greek organizations declined in number during the 1960s, since the mid-1970s they have increased in strength and number on many campuses. This peer-group pressure has led to some serious charges, from hazing of pledges in sororities and fraternities (Nuwer, 1990) to date rape and even gang rape (Sanday, 1990), sometimes linked with alcohol usage. Though many college officials have strict policies and states have criminal laws that cover Greek activities, critics argue that these laws are ineffective and problems continue (Gose, 1997). The good news is that drug and alcohol use is down somewhat on campuses, and some fraternities are eliminating drinking parties (see Box 10–3).

The vocational subculture dominates on some campuses because of economic pressures, competition for jobs, and many first-generation college students trying to improve their chances for upward mobility.

The Graying of College Graduates

During the 1980s, the traditional college-age population of 18- to 22-year-olds dropped by 2.7 million students. However, the overall number of college students rose by 1.8 million. Why? The increase in the number of students over age 25 rose significantly; the Census Bureau reports that college enrollments were made up of 38.2 percent of students age 25 and older in the United States in

---

◆◆**Box 10–3** *The Antirape Movement on Campus*

The campus antirape movement, rooted in both the feminist and victim's rights movements, can be considered a "new social movement" because the social base transcends social class structure and represents such groups as youth, gender, or sexual orientation (Johnson, Larana, and Gusfield, 1994, p. 6). Participants are a diverse group. Though there is agreement on the general goals of preventing and eliminating rape on campuses and ending sexual violence, there are conflicting ideas about how to accomplish the goals.

Debates cover a range of areas some of which include: What should be the content of rape awareness education? Who should conduct education and who should be the target audience? How should allegations of sexual assault be handled and what are appropriate punishments? What support services should be provided by campuses and available for victims? What are individual and institutional responsibilities?

The movement helped develop a shift in the media and the public attitudes from rape as a sexual act to rape as a crime of violence. A database documenting the amount and consequences of sexual violence, dispelling myths about rape, and developing services for victims are also accomplishments of the movement.

Concern about date or acquaintance rape on campus gained attention in the late 1980s and early 1990s with many programs and counseling services. Laws require that colleges keep track of crimes committed on campus and make that information available to students.

From an issue that received little attention a decade ago to a concern on most campuses, the antirape movement has made significant progress in bringing the issue to the attention of campuses. Most participants in the movement share feelings of injustice to rape victims, and though there is little national coordination of the movement, changes in policies and legislation are likely to continue.

1997 (*The Chronicle of Higher Education Almanac*, 1999, p. 24). The older, nontraditional students are upgrading their job skills, changing careers, and seeking personal improvement by taking classes for credit or audit. Education becomes important in retooling for the paid labor force that many older people enter. Financial aid, including federal and state assistance, is available to help older citizens pay for schooling, and senior citizens often attend for free.

This demographic shift is having an impact on curricula and on campus life. Evening and weekend classes have increased; more convenient off-campus sites have been established, especially in metropolitan areas; much of the course work can be done at home; and some universities provide transitional programs for older students.

Many older students accept the stereotypes imposed on them, however, fearing to go back to school after so many years. They fear that they might prove to themselves or others that they are unable to cope with the college crowd, the work, the new and demanding environment, or the stress. Although there may be some performance decline with age, many older people remain highly productive and enjoy college life. Older people make good students, and they are highly motivated and dependable (Cox, 1996).

The postwar baby boom increased the number of births from 2.75 million in the 1940s to 4.35 million in the 1960s. The population of people age 65 and over is projected to increase from 39 million in 2010 to 69 million in 2030, using middle series projections. About 20 percent of the total population would be over 65 by 2030, compared to 13 percent in the late 1990s (Current Population Reports, 1996). This group also will be living longer because of continuing medical advances. As this group ages, it will be more active than its predecessors. Although ageism has historically plagued older cohorts, the baby-boom generation will probably defy most of the age-related stereotypes because of its proportion of the population. Federal and state legislation addressing the needs of older people has also been passed in some countries, including the United States, ensuring educational opportunity for all citizens "without regard to restrictions of previous education or training, sex, age, handicapping condition, social or ethnic background, or economic circumstances."

For example, all state-funded colleges and universities in Ohio must provide free enrollment, on a space-available basis, to those 60 years and older (Ohio Revised Code). Countries that educate and make use of their older citizens can enhance their economic and social systems.

The profile of clients of higher education is changing, and their needs must be taken into consideration. Institutions will see a more diverse student body with a variety of goals and interests. It will take a flexible faculty to meet the changing needs.

*A*pplying Sociology to Education: What role(s) do you play in the higher-education system, and how do(es) your role(s) compare with those of others around you in higher education?

Roles in Higher Education: The Faculty

Universities expect professors to teach well, be knowledgeable and current in their disciplines, and produce work that will be influential and prestigious. The institution thus gains prestige, which in turn produces resources. Students, parents, and others in the institution's environment also hold certain expectations of faculty. The following section deals with some specific aspects of this role.

Characteristics of Faculty. Sociologists identify groups of people in part by the characteristics they have in common. Faculty are no exception. They can be characterized by their race, sex, type of institution, and academic discipline (see Table 10–5). In 1940, 15,000 people were employed on the faculties of U.S.

colleges and universities. The 1960s brought a tremendous increase in numbers of faculty along with increases in the student body, and by the 1970s faculty numbered more than 600,000. By 1992, the number of faculty had dropped to 526,222, and in 1995 had risen slightly to 550,822, with 380,884 part time faculty (*The Chronicle of Higher Education Almanac*, 1999, p. 38).

The proportion of females and males on the faculty varies depending on the program. In nursing, women make up nearly 100 percent of the faculty, but in engineering and agriculture they constitute less than 1 percent of faculty ranks. Women were found most frequently in teaching rather than research institutions and in departments with low prestige. Their total numbers were 190,672 out of 550,822 total faculty.

There has been little change in the number of full-time African American faculty in institutions of higher learning in the United States in the past four decades, with 26,835 in 1995. Recent figures indicate that the proportions of female and minority professors are growing, but slowly. However, those faculty are less likely to be tenured or in tenure-track positions, and to be U.S.-born citizens (Finkelstein, Schuster, and Seal, 1995). One-third of the professoriate are in their first seven years of teaching. Only 43 percent of this new cohort of faculty are native-born, white males, compared with 59 percent of the senior cohort. Women make up about 41 percent of the new cohort, compared with 28 percent of senior faculty, but they are not concentrated at research institutions. Nearly 17 percent of the new cohort are minority faculty, compared with 11 percent of senior professors; the most significant gains are among Asian Americans, especially men.

To have increases in the number of faculty, more students must be coming through the system. We have already seen that there has been little increase in the number of African Americans going to graduate school and receiving Ph.D.s. The same is true for students coming from manual or blue-collar backgrounds, but they receive no special consideration because they are not considered an "official" category (*The Chronicle of Higher Education Almanac*, 1995, p. 29). Faculty representation from Catholic and Jewish backgrounds about doubled in the first half of the twentieth century, but has leveled off or dropped in recent years.

Faculty Issues in Higher Education

Three issues related to the role of faculty in higher education have been particularly important: professionalism, collective bargaining, and status of women faculty and staff in higher-educational institutions.

Professionalism and Orientation: The Faculty Role. Faculty members go through several years of intense training in order to become professionals. The primary mark of acceptance into professional status is the highest degree in the

TABLE 10-5 Characteristics of Full-Time Faculty Members with Teaching Duties, Fall 1992

	Full-Time Faculty Members	American Indian		Asian		African American		Hispanic		White	
		Men	Women	Men	Women	Men	Women	Men	Women	Men	Women
Total	526,222	0.3%	0.2%	4.0%	1.3%	2.6%	2.3%	1.7%	0.8%	58.9%	27.9%
Type of Institution											
Public research	108,493	0.1	0.1	5.7	1.3	1.5	1.2	1.4	0.5	68.7	19.7
Private research	32,350	0.2	—	6.7	2.4	2.8	1.9	1.2	0.7	59.2	25.0
Public doctoral[a]	54,433	0.6	0.2	4.9	1.4	1.6	1.3	1.7	0.6	62.1	25.7
Private doctoral[a]	25,397	0.1	0.1	5.1	1.4	2.9	1.2	2.3	1.0	66.5	19.4
Public comprehensive	96,350	0.2	0.3	4.1	1.0	4.9	3.9	1.8	0.8	55.5	27.5
Private comprehensive	36,548	—	0.1	2.5	0.9	1.4	1.6	1.0	0.6	60.5	31.3
Private liberal-arts	37,560	0.3	0.1	1.9	0.9	3.7	1.8	0.9	0.5	54.2	35.8
Public 2-year	109,551	0.7	0.3	1.9	1.4	2.5	3.6	2.5	1.6	47.8	37.7
Other[b]	25,540	0.3	0.2	3.7	0.9	1.6	1.2	0.8	0.4	67.3	23.6
Academic Discipline											
Agriculture and home economics	11,466	—	0.7	1.0	1.8	2.2	1.5	1.6	0.2	71.3	19.6
Business	39,848	0.6	0.3	4.0	0.8	1.9	2.0	0.9	0.4	62.3	26.6
Business	10,344	0.9	0.3	4.3	1.2	2.8	2.8	1.6	—	56.3	29.8
Communications	36,851	0.7	0.3	0.5	1.1	3.9	5.1	0.9	2.4	43.9	41.2
Education	24,680	0.7	—	15.6	1.3	2.1	0.6	2.8	0.2	73.0	3.8
Engineering	31,682	0.3	0.2	1.2	1.6	3.8	1.8	2.1	0.3	60.4	28.3
Fine arts	77,996	0.1	0.1	4.0	2.0	2.0	3.2	1.3	0.7	43.1	43.5
Health sciences	74,086	0.3	0.1	1.3	1.9	2.1	2.0	2.0	2.0	53.5	34.8
Humanities											

Law	7,337	—	—	0.2	0.7	5.8	2.9	1.3	1.1	57.8	30.0
Natural sciences	101,681	0.2	0.1	7.2	0.9	2.5	0.9	1.5	0.3	69.0	17.4
Social sciences	58,526	0.3	0.2	2.6	0.7	2.9	2.9	1.9	0.8	65.4	22.3
Occupationally specific programs	15,395	0.5	0.2	1.9	0.2	3.5	0.9	3.1	0.3	75.9	13.5
Other	27,466	—	0.1	2.3	0.6	2.8	3.3	2.0	0.7	58.1	30.1

—Too few cases for a reliable estimate.

[a]Includes medical schools.

[b]Includes public liberal-arts, private two-year, religious, and other specialized colleges and excludes medical schools.

Note: The figures are based on responses to a survey conducted in 1992 and 1993 of 25,780 full- and part-time faculty members and other instructional personnel at 817 colleges and universities. The survey covered employees whose regular assignment included instruction; people with faculty status whose regular assignment did not include instruction; temporary and permanent employees that had any instructional duties; and faculty members and instructional personnel on sabbatical leave. The survey excluded graduate teaching assistants, among others. The sample was weighted to produce national estimates. This table is limited to only those members and other personnel who did at least some teaching. Details may not add to totals because of rounding.

Source: The Chronicle of Higher Education Almanac, August 27, 1999, p. 36.

field: the Ph.D. (Doctor of Philosophy), L.L.D. (Doctor of Laws), M.D. (Doctor of Medicine), and so on. During the education period, intensive training and professional socialization take place as the graduate students learn not only their subject areas but also the appropriate attitudes, behaviors, and ethics of their discipline. Typically, graduate school training for a Ph.D. involves three or four years of course work, followed by comprehensive examinations and a major work of original research—the dissertation. Having been through an intense common experience, graduates become part of a "fraternity" protecting the entrance gates of the discipline by maintaining the traditions. These traditions are most highly protected in the most prestigious professions, such as medicine. This socialization process has had its critics. Some graduate students complain that their training lacks relevance to the professional tasks they will be performing. Some have limited practical experience. Others claim that they receive little or no training in teaching techniques, and that their research focus is usually very narrow. Full-time faculty spend, on average, between 47 and 57 working hours each week (Magner, 1995). Faculty report spending 54.4 percent of their time in teaching activities, 17.6 percent in research and scholarship, and 13 percent in administrative duties.

The Association of American Colleges and Universities and the Council of Graduate Schools started a project in 1993 called "Preparing Future Faculty." A number of institutions do provide training for future university teachers, and many provide ongoing professional development for faculty (Cage, 1996, p. A19). Seminars for teaching assistants (TAs) and faculty are offered at a number of universities. More institutions are emphasizing the importance of quality teaching as student populations have become less stable.

Once on the job, faculty members face differing role expectations. Teaching is the primary task at the two-year institutions and at the four-year liberal arts colleges, whereas research takes a large percentage of faculty time at most universities. The orientation of faculty is also related to the type of institution. "Cosmopolitan" faculty—those who have attachments and professional interests outside their institution—develop their research and writing in relation to a wider audience; they attract more grant money and prestige. "Local" faculty focus their attention within the institution, are active and concerned about institutional matters, and tend to be more loyal to the institution. Though both types are found at all institutions, higher percentages of "local" faculty are likely to be found at two- and four-year colleges.

The most prestigious institutions, which attract the most prominent faculty members, also have problems retaining them. These faculty teach less, and spend a great deal of time consulting, lecturing, attending conferences, or working at other institutions as visiting scholars or lecturers. Committee assignments and teaching often fall to younger faculty members. Universities tolerate this because having respected, well-known faculty enhances the prestige of the university and may attract other top scholars and students as well as more funds.

A difficult problem for many faculty is the incongruity between the demands of teaching and research. This dilemma often hits young scholars hardest; they must "prove themselves" in order to be retained and given tenure. This means performing well not only in teaching and university service but also in research and publishing, which are seldom listed as part of the "job requirement." Young faculty members with family responsibilities may be forced to make hard decisions between family and career. Some argue that faculty have been pushed to "get it written rather than get it right." Thus, college faculty are hired to teach students, but are often expected to publish—or perish. Despite the pressures, professors are generally pleased with their careers, with 65 percent of males and 59 percent of females indicating they would pursue an academic career again if given the choice (Leatherman, 2000).

Professionals, Unions, and Collective Bargaining. Academic professionals are characterized by belief in academic freedom, autonomy over decisions related to their discipline and educational process, and service to the community. The American Association of University Professors (AAUP) has traditionally represented faculty interests, setting down guidelines for salaries, promotions, and policies. AAUP's "clout" with institutions has been the backing of the membership and the threat to blacklist an institution so that faculty would resist taking employment there.

Support for union representation among faculty varies considerably. Many faculty members are reluctant to address their grievances to the administration through a mediating union, preferring instead to retain control over problem solving. At two-year institutions, faculty are more likely to consider themselves "employees," to follow more closely the secondary school model, and to expect to gain by union representation. Faculty at prestigious universities are less likely to "stoop" to use union bargaining agents because they have less to gain by being represented. Many already have high salaries relative to others, and they have the flexibility to relocate if they are dissatisfied. Yet, many faculty members do belong to representative organizations—professional associations and the AAUP—and the idea of organizational membership is an established one. (In fact, on unionized campuses today AAUP represents faculty interests in such areas as due process and faculty salaries.) The American Federation of Teachers (AFT) and the National Education Association (NEA) are unions that have been trying to attract college faculty.

In recent years, faculty unions and collective bargaining have begun to look more attractive to large segments of the academic community. Higher education has expanded rapidly, especially at the two-year college level, which has fewer faculty members with terminal Ph.D. degrees. Economic problems have caused an uncertain job market in academia. Administrative decision making has become further removed from faculty, and young faculty members come from more varied backgrounds, providing a large core of faculty open to collective bargaining as a tactic (Morgan, 1992, pp. 2719–20).

Gender Issues in Higher Education. Women are more heavily concentrated in the two-year institutions than in universities, and in all institutions the percentage of women with tenure is lower than their percentage of the total faculty, meaning that women are concentrated in the lower ranks. One reason for this pattern, according to women's studies scholars, is the long tradition of male-dominated academic institutions. Traditional approaches to research are based on the male life cycle, following an established series of steps to success (Gilligan, 1979). Women, however, may pursue research with different career assumptions, such as entry into professions after childbearing years or shared academic positions. There is little recognition that other patterns also can lead to success, an attitude that has penalized women who are competent and effective—with consequent loss to the academic community.

"Women working on campuses face hostile environments," concludes a recent study of conditions facing women in academia. Not only is sexual harassment a continuing problem, but discrimination in the form of less pay for the same job, lower positions, and fewer promotions is common (Blum, 1991, p. A1; Lomperis, 1990, p. 643). African American women sometimes feel they must "outshine, outthink, and outperform their minority counterparts [white women in academia] to achieve legitimacy within the academy," and they often feel a sense of intense isolation (Fontaine, 1993, p. 121).

The proportion of female faculty has grown slowly in recent years, with women making up 34.6 percent of full-time faculty members: 17.8 percent of full professors and 50.4 percent of assistant professors. There are fears, however, that few women will be tenured and promoted, but they will disproportionately occupy lower ranks, part-time positions, and nontenure-track positions (Greenberg, 1995, pp. 35–36).

Women are dismissed in disproportionate numbers when faculty and staff are laid off. Women and minorities are less frequently hired in positions from which they have been excluded in the past, such as administrative positions. Also, women faculty are found disproportionately in female-dominated fields and lower-paying, lower-prestige institutions.

Roles in Higher Education: Administrators

Administrators must be jugglers, maintaining a delicate balance of goodwill between the environmental factors crucial to the institution and the academic interests of faculty and the student body.

In public institutions, primary authority over fiscal matters and programs falls to a state (or local) board of trustees or regents, and may depend on the attitudes and prejudices of state legislators and governors, who in theory reflect the mood of the public.

At private institutions, administrators depend in part on support from private funds, often from alumni. But again, this funding is tenuous and depends on retaining the goodwill of donors. In the case of one prestigious institution, pressure from alumni influenced decision making. The alumni newsletter reported various impending changes in the traditional structure of the university: admitting women to the formerly all-male school; opening the doors to more minority students; and reconsidering the practice of giving preference in admission to relatives of alumni. Cries of outrage were heard from alumni who threatened to or actually did cease to contribute. The issues became policy, but in modified forms more acceptable to alumni.

Critics of the increased role of administrators argue that the university has become "top heavy" with high paid administrators who see the university as falling into the business model of a competitive and profit-making institution. They also point out the high salary increases received by administrators in many institutions. For instance, in 1998 the average salary was 5 percent higher than in 1997, and salaries have outpaced inflation for the past six years. In 1999, the average increase was 4.5 percent, and in 1998, 4.6 percent (Lively, 2000).

The system of higher education cannot be understood without referring to the environment such as alumni. The next section in our chapter considers some examples of the higher-education environment.

ENVIRONMENTAL PRESSURES ON HIGHER EDUCATION

Environmental pressures affecting the higher-education system come from government, the courts, teacher organizations, publishing companies, churches, community, parents, and other interest groups (see Figure 10–4). Institutions of higher education are playing a game of survival; whatever parts of the environment are most crucial to that survival will have the greatest impact on decision making and changes that take place. Let us consider several key sources of environmental influence on higher education.

Government Influence on Funding of Higher Education

Government has a degree of power over institutions of higher education through the control of money. The combined federal, state, and local government funding for higher education made up approximately half of public institutions' budgets in the 1992–93 academic year (see Table 10–6, p. 308).

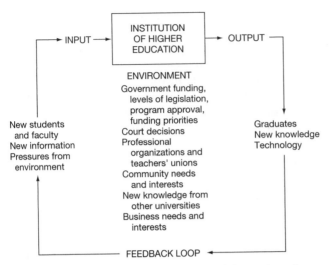

FIGURE 10-4 Open systems model of higher education.

Government influence over public institutions is greater, though private institutions often depend on governmental support for research and special programs. Tuition and fees play the largest role in most private institutions. Religiously affiliated institutions are generally least dependent on and influenced by government. The largest expenditures in higher education are for institutions.

If priorities for funding programs and research are established by the government in AIDS and cancer research or mental retardation, for example, then researchers are drawn to these areas to seek support funding. Some fields have higher funding priorities than others and, in fact, may be sustained by funding. Change in the funding priorities can bring about change in the number of faculty and staff in an academic department. Those staff on "soft money," or funded projects, may be cut back or not renewed. Laboratory or other facilities, faculty teaching loads, number of students attracted to a department as majors, and even a department's or institution's chances for survival can rest on levels of government support.

Colleges also receive funding from alumni, corporations, foundations, and religious organizations. Monies are often earmarked for special projects. These contributions rose 38 percent between 1989 and 1994, with alumni-giving up significantly because of aggressive fund-raising drives. In the early 1990s, most institutions experienced lean times, trimming their expenditures and raising tuition and fees to cover costs (see Table 10–7, p. 310). In some cities, businesses are providing funds to send inner-city students who graduate from high school to college.

The cost of financing a student's education is resting more heavily on families as tuition costs increase. A recent study looked at the effect of female and male siblings in a family on the financing of college. Having a number of sons in a family is more of a liability for parents than having daughters, partly because parents are more likely to encourage sons to enroll in college; if a daughter attends, they support her as well, but more effort goes into finding money for males (Powell and Steelman, 1989).

The federal government provides grants and loans for students with financial need to help them meet the costs of college. Controversy erupted in late 1990 when the U.S. education secretary announced a ban on scholarships based exclusively on race; race could be used as only one factor in awarding scholarships in order to increase diversity on campuses, or used to remedy proven discrimination. By 1995 the Supreme Court upheld a similar case, striking down race-based scholarships (Myers, 1995, p. A13).

Higher education has socioeconomic implications beyond the individuals who attain an education. The private economy in capitalist states is stimulated by government spending on higher education—especially on research—more than spending in general. Spending on research activities has long-lasting effects on private production. This is especially true because the university is a primary location for pure research, whereas industry in the United States spends money on applications of research findings. With government and family working together to help finance higher education, we have another example of the impact of environment and the interdependence of institutions. Government has also worked with schools in developing and funding curricula to meet national priorities.

The Courts and Affirmative Action

The law generally prohibits discrimination on the basis of race, sex, color, religion, ancestry, national origin, age, disability, veteran status, or sexual orientation by public institutions and those that receive federal funds. Federal law also requires universities to take "affirmative action" to eliminate or correct the effects of past discrimination, intentional or not. At the same time, the courts have issued some contradictory decisions as in the previously mentioned *Hopwood* v. *Texas* ruling.

Affirmative action includes a broad range of activities, such as publicly advertising vacant faculty positions instead of filling them through the "old-boy network" or by "word-of-mouth" connections. Other basic affirmative actions include eliminating inappropriate barriers that tend to exclude certain groups disproportionately and ensuring that admission and employment decisions are actually based on the announced criteria.

The types of affirmative action that often cause controversy are (1) consideration of race or sex as a criterion in admission or employment decisions for the purpose of increasing the presence of minorities or women to reflect their relative availability in the pool of qualified potential applicants, and (2) estab-

TABLE 10-6 Revenues and Expenditures of Colleges and Universities, 1995-96

	Public Institutions		Private Institutions	
	Amount	Percentage of Total	Amount	Percentage of Total
Revenues				
Tuition and fees	$23,257,454,000	18.8%	$32,002,839,000	43.0%
Federal government				
Appropriations	1,826,738,000	1.5	210,210,000	0.3%
Grants and contracts	11,595,201,000	9.4	6,770,274,000	9.1
Independent operations	250,529,000	0.2	3,286,124,000	4.4
State governments				
Appropriations	40,081,437,000	32.5	241,864,000	0.3
Grants and contracts	4,161,109,000	3.3	1,208,263,000	1.6
Local governments				
Appropriations	4,397,098,000	3.6	3,643,000	—
Grants and contracts	677,412,000	0.5	529,754,000	0.8
Private gifts, grants, and contracts	5,089,344,000	4.1	6,813,782,000	9.1
Endowment income	721,079,000	0.6	3,841,091,000	5.2
Sales and services				
Educational activities	3,528,610,000	2.9	2,002,153,000	2.7
Auxiliary enterprises	11,595,408,000	9.4	7,272,132,000	9.8
Hospitals	12,275,778,000	9.9	6,335,792,000	8.5
Other sources	4,043,955,000	3.3	3,954,162,000	5.3
Total current-fund revenues	$123,501,152,000	100%	$74,472,083,000	100%

Expenditures

Instruction	$38,653,245,000	32.3%	$19,156,788,000	27.0%
Research	12,076,357,000	10.1	5,441,530,000	7.7
Public service	5,321,014,000	4.5	1,686,399,000	2.4
Academic support	9,004,113,000	7.5	4,292,950,000	6.1
Student services	5,810,403,000	4.9	3,820,174,000	5.4
Institutional support	10,710,279,000	9.0	7,545,490,000	10.6
Operation and maintenance of plant	8,005,101,000	6.7	4,325,784,000	6.1
Scholarship and fellowships	5,084,653,000	4.3	8,110,450,000	11.4
Mandatory transfers	1,420,459,000	1.2	980,417,000	1.4
Auxiliary enterprises	11,309,031,000	9.5	6,290,030,000	8.9
Hospitals	11,878,939,000	9.9	6,062,047,000	8.5
Independent operations	250,906,000	0.2	3,239,604,000	4.6
Total current-fund expenditures	$119,524,500,000	100%	$70,951,662,000	100%

Note: A dash indicates less than 0.1%. Because of rounding, details may not add to totals.

Source: The Chronicle of Higher Education Almanac, August 27, 1999.

TABLE 10–7 Average College Costs, 1998–99

	Public Colleges		Private Colleges	
	Resident	Commuter	Resident	Commuter
Four-Year Colleges				
Tuition and fees	$3,243	$3,243	$14,508	$14,508
Books and supplies	662	662	667	667
Room and board[a]	4,530	2,098	5,765	2,101
Transportation	612	1,011	547	861
Other	1,411	1,491	1,046	1,233
Total	$10,458	$8,505	$22,533	$19,370
Two-Year Colleges				
Tuition and fees	$1,633	$1,633	$7,333	$7,333
Books and supplies	624	624	663	663
Room and board[a]	—	2,039	4,666	2,163
Transportation	—	978	562	880
Other	—	1,171	998	1,162
Total	—	$6,445	$14,222	$12,201

[a]Room not included for commuter students.
—Insufficient data.

Note: The figures are weighted by enrollment to reflect the charges incurred by the average undergraduate enrolled at each type of institution.

Source: The Chronicle of Higher Education Almanac, 1999, p. 46

lishment of numerical goals to measure progress in increasing the presence of minorities or women. One objection to the use of *goals*, which are defined as *targets* to be pursued by good-faith efforts, is that sometimes goals are interpreted to mean *quotas* (i.e., numbers that must be achieved in order to avoid some penalty). The result of establishing quotas would be that failing to base decisions on race or sex could result in loss of all federal funding, including grants, research contracts, and even student loan receipts.

Affirmative action has existed for one-third of a century, since Executive Order 11246 was issued in 1965; it has also been resisted for that amount of time. Great progress has been made toward eliminating discrimination based on race, sex, and various other criteria in educational and employment opportunities, but achieving equal opportunity will require additional effort.

In 1995, the U.S. Supreme Court ruled that government affirmative action programs that provide benefits on the basis of race or ethnicity must be subjected to "strict scrutiny" by the courts. That means such programs must be "necessary" to achieve a "compelling state interest" (i.e., government purpose). It is not yet known whether efforts to increase the diversity of a university's workforce or student body in order to enhance the diversity and richness of the educational process itself will be held to constitute a "compelling" interest. (*Note*: Information in this section was supplemented by Juanita Wehrle-Einhorn, affirmative action officer, Wright State University.)

Environmental Feedback and Organizational Change

"On September 30, 1964, five students concerned with civil rights were cited by the dean of men at the University of California, Berkeley, for violating rules which prohibited political propagandizing on campus" ("Ten Years Later," 1974, p. 1149). According to Neil Smelzer's theory of collective behavior (Smelzer, 1962), this was the "precipitating factor" that stimulated the confrontations between students and university administrators that lasted for four months and set an example for student protests at other campuses around the world. Such events as the following occurred:

> On December 2, 1964, 1,000 students, their morale bolstered by folk singer Joan Baez, occupied the administration building [at Berkeley]. What ensued was the sensational spectacle of some 700 police and sheriff's deputies bodily removing the unrelenting demonstrators. Instantaneously and spontaneously the number of sympathizers and collaborators multiplied. ("Berkeley Student Revolt," 1965, p. 51)

A university is concerned with its public image because of the effect image has on the public and private monies it receives and on the students it attracts. The Berkeley Free Speech Movement changed both the environmental image and the decision-making structure of the University of California. Many attempted to analyze the events. Some argued that the movement was the result of students trying to seize power in the educational system; others argued that they were responding to such concrete deprivations as lack of freedom of speech ("Berkeley Student Revolt," 1965, p. 51). In the years following the uprisings, there were intense debates over the purpose of the university, and pressures for change were felt by most institutions of higher education. In some cases, the institutions incorporated more students into the decision-making structure or were more tolerant on the issue of free speech. Other institutions reacted in the opposite way, tightening control over decision making in response to community pressures.

This example indicates that feedback from the primary environment—the students viewed as clients—and from the secondary environment—the community—bring about alterations and change. The dramatic and intense reaction at Berkeley was a form of feedback demanding attention and action, which led to change and long-term searching for alterations and improvements in the system.

The variables affecting change in each situation will differ, but the process of constant change can be traced and studied through the open systems model. Using this approach, the organization does not appear static—a criticism frequently made of functional analysis of organizations; nor will change necessarily be seen as resulting from continuous power struggles between factions or interest groups—as in conflict theory. Rather, change can be seen as a natural part of organizational process and function. Change is an ongoing, dynamic process in any system; organizations must rely on feedback from the environment and must constantly adapt and alter to meet changes in environmental demands if they are to survive.

> *A*pplying Sociology to Education: What are some environmental pressures on your institution of higher education? How is the institution dealing with these pressures? ◆

OUTCOMES OF HIGHER EDUCATION

Higher Education: Attitudes, Values, and Behaviors

What effect does college education have on the students who attend? This is the key question in studies of changes in students' political, religious, and moral attitudes and values over time. In the annual survey of first-year students conducted by the Higher Education Research Institute, changes over the past 29 years have been recorded; in 1966, for instance, 57.8 percent of students indicated that "keeping up with political affairs was important." This figure has declined over the years, reaching the lowest point in 1994, with only 31.9 percent saying this was important to them. An issue of concern in the mid-1990s was the environment, with 84 percent indicating the need for greater efforts to protect it (*The American Freshman*, 1995).

Over the years, undergraduates revealed substantial changes in attitudes and beliefs. The largest positive changes relate to supporting feminism, making a commitment to clean up the environment and to promote racial understanding, developing a meaningful philosophy of life, and supporting legal abortion. Declines are seen in the emphasis on being well-off financially.

A notable finding in the fall 1999 survey is that almost one-third of first-year students feel high degrees of stress; many must work to make ends meet, and they express concern about competition. Women tend to feel more stressed about concern over money. Women also spend more time studying, doing volunteer work, participating in student activities, and doing housework or taking care of children than men. Men report spending more time on leisure activities.

Greater numbers of students report being bored in class—about 40 percent in 1999, compared to a low of 26 percent in 1985. Students also spend less time on homework, a consequence of which may be the growing numbers of students requiring remedial work in high school.

Other trends indicate that drinking and smoking continue to decline; only half of incoming first-year college students say they drank beer frequently in the past year. The percentage of students who smoke is 14.2 percent, down from 15.8 percent in 1998 (Sax et al., 1999).

The Value of a College Education

Do higher-education credentials lead to higher occupational status and higher future earnings? College graduates earn up to 52 percent more than high school graduates, but that gap may narrow as college degrees become more common. Other factors such as the college attended and major may become more important, more so than college grades or job performance in predicting future status and earnings ("Costs and Benefits," 1993, p. 2; Hurn, 1978). (See Figure 10–5.)

Students who have gone to a prestigious school have greater chances for higher earnings than those who attend less selective colleges; however, students who go to institutions with equivalent standardized test scores earn as much as those at the Ivys, attributed to their motivation, maturity, and ambition (Gose, 2000).

Many students are accepting jobs in areas unrelated to their majors. This and the reduced economic advantages of college are causing young people to ask if college is worth the time and money. Consider Figure 10–5. The comparison shows that college graduates earn more than high school or elementary graduates but that these figures have declined in recent years, and the gap between groups is narrowing.

College type and quality are important determinants of returns from education in terms of salary and prestige. When students' ability and socioeconomic status are held constant, the findings are less conclusive, but still important.

The less tangible results of college have been summed up by Alexander Astin in his book *What Matters in College? Four Critical Years Revisited* (1993, p. 211). College helps students develop a positive self-image and great interpersonal and intellectual competence. They adopt more liberal political views and attitudes (which may or may not last) toward social issues. And their religious orientation decreases.

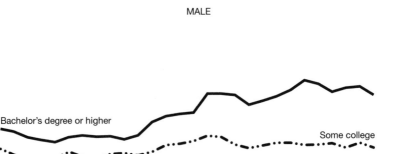

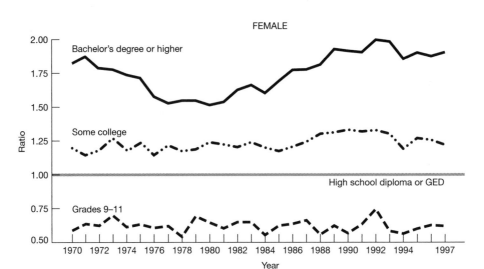

FIGURE 10–5 Ratio[a] of median annual earnings of all wage and salary workers ages 25 to 34 whose highest education level was grades 9 to 11, some college, or a bachelor's degree or higher, compared with those with a high school diploma or GED, by sex, 1970–97.

> [a]This ratio is most useful when compared with 1.0. For example, the ratio of 1.50 in 1997 for males whose highest education level was a bachelor's degree or higher means that they earned 50 percent more than males who had a high school diploma or GED. The ratio of 0.71 in 1997 for males whose highest education level was grades 9 to 11, means that they earned 29 percent less than males who had a high school diploma or GED. Data for 1994, 1995, and 1996 are revised from previously published figures.

Note: The Current Population Survey (CPS) questions used to obtain educational attainment were changed in 1992. In 1994, the survey instrument for the CPS was changed and weights were adjusted.

Source: U.S. Department of Commerce, Bureau of the Census, March Current Population Surveys.

Applying Sociology to Education: Is college worth the time and money? Why or why not? ◆

PROBLEMS AND REFORM IN HIGHER EDUCATION

With the increasing pressure on the educational system for accountability, higher education is in the critical eye of the public and policymakers. The ivory tower is facing more challenges, and many institutions are responding to problems: improve quality of teaching, evaluate the educational program, increase access for minority students, and prepare students with knowledge and skills for a good future.

Colleges are also criticized for certain "unethical" practices, and many are addressing these problems. Grade inflation between the 1960s and 1970s was rapid, but has leveled off; cheating by students is being firmly addressed in many institutions, with misconduct policies and procedures in place; curriculum and credit given for courses is undergoing both internal and external review. Reports of misuse of funds are being investigated, and curriculum reform is a constant process.

All organizations have their critics; higher education is no exception. Some critics have an ideology to back their reformist critiques. In recent years several authors have made sweeping criticisms of higher education, especially of humanities and social sciences. The conflict centers on views about the correct way to learn and the correct knowledge to learn. Issues of "political correctness" on campuses, stimulated in part by these critics, has brought about changes in curriculum and dominant issues on campuses. The conflicts represent an underlying tension between privilege and patriarchy on the one hand, and affirmative action and cultural diversity issues on the other (Wilkinson, 1991, pp. 550–51).

Not all views are negative. Positive aspects of ethical conduct in higher education include the following: There is expanded equality of opportunity; the university is serving as a forum for discussion of national issues; many students are serious about school, are satisfied with their instruction and academic programs, trust their teachers and feel they are available, and are learning as much as ever.

Colleges of education are particular targets because their products are visible and measurable. Some commission reports push for increasing the status of education as a major, whereas others argue that students should major in a subject area and take education during a fifth year (Astin, 1993).

The conventional wisdom is that universities are for the conservation, advancement, transmission, and interpretation of knowledge. The permanence of purpose implied by the almost universal acceptance of the definition throughout most of the twentieth century does not necessarily require permanence of method or curriculum content. Far from being detached from society, universities are very much a part of their environment, and their staff and students experience the societal tensions and strains caused by rapid economic and technological changes.

◆ Summary

There is no one system of higher education. To the extent that generalizations can be made across systems, we have discussed some common characteristics and problems: the development and meaning of higher education; access to the system; the structure, process, and role relationships within the system; the environmental pressures toward change; and some outcomes and reforms in higher education.

I. History and Development of Higher Education

Organized higher education dates back to the twelfth and thirteenth centuries. Over time, its structure and functions have changed dramatically. It now has a two-part structure—administration and faculty—and has taken on several additional functions such as research and service. The twentieth century brought the two-year college, and with it new structures and functions.

II. Theoretical Approaches to Higher Education

We can gain a better understanding of how sociologists view higher education through functional and conflict theories. The systems model helps integrate aspects of higher education for a more comprehensive view. The issue of access to higher education, who gets in and why, is of major concern to educational theorists. They focus particularly on the admissions process and testing, and public versus private institutions. There have been legal challenges to admissions decisions to professional schools, with unclear outcomes.

III. Characteristics of Higher Education in the United States

Institutions vary depending on sponsorship, student composition, types of programs, and degrees offered. The rapid growth of higher education threatened to weaken the value of college. Changing enrollments and economic patterns also forced cuts in programs and staff.

IV. Functions of the Higher Education System

The university can be viewed as a large community. With growth has come controversy over functions of the university: the form curriculum should adopt; the relationship between research and teaching; and the role service should play in the community. Controversy over the academic function of the university is illustrated by the role of "big business" sports on some campuses and the type of curriculum the university should have.

V. Higher Education as an Organization

Higher education has been administered using a bureaucratic model, which many argue is not appropriate for the unique composition of the university. Decision making varies by constituency in the university, as do areas of decision-making responsibility. For instance, faculty generally retain control of curriculum matters.

VI. Roles in Higher Education

Students are becoming a more diversified group, with older students, minorities, and married students attending college in greater numbers. More women students are moving through the system and into graduate school today, assuming multiple roles, than in the past. Colleges wrestle with the problem of underprepared students who lack necessary skills to complete college.

Three issues facing faculty are discussed: professionalism, collective bargaining, and gender issues.

VII. Environmental Pressures on Higher Education

Several issues related to the environment of higher education were used to illustrate its importance: funding of higher education, court actions, and community pressure on programs.

VIII. Outcomes of Higher Education

Outcomes of higher education include the value, attitude, and behavioral changes that take place and the financial outcomes of having a college education.

IX. Problems and Reform in Higher Education

Finally, some problems and reforms in the areas of challenges to the higher-education system and ethics are briefly discussed, including several critiques of faculty and curriculum. Proposals for reform are considered.

◆ *Putting Sociology to Work*

1. List the institutions of higher education in your geographical area.
   a. What is the purpose served by each? (What courses and degrees are offered, who is served?)
   b. What sorts of students go to each?
   c. What did your high school classmates do after graduation? college? work? other?
   d. Are there individuals who have not been accommodated by higher education in your area after high school?
   e. Do you see any gaps in the system of higher education in your area?

2. Think of a recent controversy in your institution. Put yourself in the place of other students who represent different viewpoints on the controversy; of a faculty member (or members); of an administrator involved with the controversy. How do they differ in their perspectives on the controversy? It may be useful to interview those involved.

3. Consider several issues in higher education that were raised in the text or others that are of concern to you. Explain how a functionalist and conflict theorist would interpret these issues differently.

4. What problems do you see in the program or curriculum of your institution or in your major area? Designate alternatives to the present system at your institution that could help solve the problems.

5. Who holds formal power and decision-making rights in your institution in various areas? Who holds informal power? Give some examples. It may be useful to interview others on this question.

6. With what areas of the environment must your institution interact? Talking with an administrator about pressures on the university would be informative here.

CHAPTER 11

Educational Systems Around the World

A Comparative View

In a rural village in West Africa, a few children sit under a tree, some with slates and chalk. A book is shared, and there are no paper, pencils, or other supplies. The teacher who has only a sixth grade education himself tries to help the children focus on learning to read. Several thousand miles to the north children sit at desks in a classroom well equipped with materials for their education. Let us visit two individual children in these systems and observe how their educations and life chances differ.

Aminu is eight. He falls somewhere in the middle of nine brothers and sisters. He and his family live in a small, rural village in West Africa, in the northern part of his country. Farming is the primary occupation of the villagers, with each family tilling their own plot. Aminu's family uses a hand plow in the fields; it is not an easy life, but the family generally has enough to eat—mostly a starchy diet of millet, cassava roots, bananas, and some bits of meat. Aminu has other relatives living in the village too—cousins, aunts and uncles, and grandparents.

From an early age Aminu helped the family in the fields; his father taught him about farming and his grandfather about his family and religion. Although he was one of many children, there was always some relative to whom he could turn for help. His life was secure and happy.

Schooling around the world takes place in many settings.

At age six, he began attending the village school. All the children went there from ages six to nine, as mandated by the central government. Aminu didn't much mind; he saw his friends there and could play during free time. The teacher was a young local man who had been away to secondary school and came back to take charge of the one-room schoolhouse located in the village meeting hall. Molam Hassan seemed a nice man but was very strict and frequently resorted to striking pupils or punishing them by making them stand in a corner. With older and younger children in one class, it was difficult to teach materials pertinent to all. Aminu learned basic mathematical functions, which he rather enjoyed doing, though he saw no use for them. He could read simple books. They were about English boys and girls going on picnics with their dog. Aminu studied the Koran and learned to recite passages. He disliked being called on to stand in front of the class and recite, for if he forgot, he would be punished. He had no time, peace, or quiet to sit down at home and learn the recitations. But writing was worse. The children were required to write down dictations, and Aminu could never get it right.

When planting and harvest time came, Aminu and his brothers stayed away from school to help with the farming. When anyone was sick, the children took turns staying home and helping. One time Aminu missed a month of school to help his father and travel with him to the big town 20 miles away.

At the end of this school year, Aminu will leave school along with most of his friends. Only two boys are considering going on to the secondary school in the big town, the two top boys in the school. One has relatives in town with whom he can live. But the other is doubtful about going; his father needs his help and cannot afford the additional money his son would need to live away from home, though the education is free. Besides, many of the villagers are critical of boys who have left to study; they seldom return, and when they visit, they seem to have a superior air.

Joan is ten. She lives in an urban area in Britain. Her parents have a nice home in a residential section of town from which her father commutes to his business each day. Joan began school at age three in a private nursery, where she learned her letters, numbers, and nursery rhymes, and to follow rules, routines, and schedules. Then she went to infant school and primary school near her home, and she is to enter a girls' public school next fall. ("Public school" in Britain is equivalent to private school in the United States. Tuition must be paid. Attending public school is generally considered to be preparatory to getting into a good university.) Here she will study the regular academic subjects, including Latin and French, plus horseback riding and a musical instrument. She particularly likes drawing and will have private lessons. Joan's parents stress education; she studies or reads for at least one hour each evening and is rewarded when her reports are good. Her parents both read a great deal and have many books, magazines, and newspapers in the home. Her mother was trained as a teacher; her father studied mathematics at Oxford and is a successful businessman. She has one brother, who is at a public school for boys.

Joan is a good student and applies herself. When she completes public school she thinks she would like to go on to the university, and she probably will.

These two scenarios provide a glance at two educational systems representing two worlds children are experiencing. The division is not only between two children, but between two educational systems, two countries and two worlds: one rich and developed, the other poor and developing. This distinction must be kept in mind as we consider the world system of education. As different as they are, there are also commonalities in these two educational systems. In this chapter we explore some of these commonalities and differences.

We begin with a consideration of the global educational system: first, the field of comparative education, cross-cultural educational studies, and approaches used to study education across cultures. Then we look at various theoretical views and typologies in comparative education. This is followed by a discussion of the interdependence of institutions within and among societies. In Chapter 12 we present examples of educational systems in the world.

CROSS-CULTURAL EDUCATIONAL STUDIES

Cross-cultural research in sociology of education provides new insights, ideas, and perspectives on one's own society. It provides information on what is unique in educational systems and what is universal. Cross-cultural research is not always easy to do because systems of education are difficult to compare and have different underlying ideologies and goals. Sociologists have been major contributors to the field of comparative education—developing useful methodologies, identifying key variables, constructing analytical models, and carrying out research projects. Most of this research can be used for applied, practical purposes (Farrell, 1997).

Comparative Education as a Field of Study

> More than 6,000 languages in the world, many of them not written. Cultures using very old technologies alongside those using the most modern. Discriminated minorities without access to an acceptable quality of life. Feelings of rejection. High rates of unemployment among disadvantaged minorities. The loss of traditional knowledge and culture. Religious problems. Intolerance. . . . ("The Challenge of Multicultural Education," 1994, p. 2)

These are some of the variables that make the study of comparative education a challenge for researchers.

The field of comparative education has moved from primarily descriptive data and case studies of specific problems in selected countries to an interdisciplinary field that looks at education in cross-cultural context using a variety of methodologies (Cummings, 1999; Epstein, 1988; Altbach, 1986). Research in the field ranges from studies using descriptive anthropological and ethnographic methods to large-scale achievement studies. Today many methods and theories are employed, including feminist, poststructural and postmodern theories, historical comparisons of development of educational systems, content analyses of curricula, large-scale studies based on international data sets, and area or regional studies using a variety of techniques from observation to interviews and questionnaires. Although most social research techniques have been used by comparative researchers, with the exception of experimental designs, a significant proportion of studies still do not use comparative research techniques, but rather "foreign education"—descriptive or case studies (Cummings, 1999; Rust et al., 1999).

William Cummings (1999) describes the field as having progressed through several historical phases of development:

1. Mid-nineteenth century: "Borrowers" and "predictors" used comparative inquiry to perfect and advance their own systems.

2. Mid-1950s: Classification of facts led to historical and area studies.
3. 1960s: Focus on education's role in transforming newly emerging developing nations.
4. Early 1970s: Relative neglect of comparative studies because of the idea that the United States was the leading society with little to learn from other countries.

In the past two decades several themes, influenced by international organizations (McNeely, 1995) and worldwide trends and issues, have dominated cross-cultural studies in education: curricula, per pupil expenditures, textbooks, and teacher training (Benavot, 1992). Three of these themes are discussed in this chapter: curriculum issues, international tests, and legitimacy of knowledge. Theoretical approaches—Marxist, neo-Marxist, correspondence, resistance and reproduction theories, dependency theory, feminist theory, and postmodern theories—have been added to existing theories to enrich the field (Paulston, 1999; Heyneman, 1993; Hall, 1990).

Although the United States has played a major role in the development of the field of comparative education, other countries have specific motivations for conducting studies as well; for instance, mainland China conducts comparative studies of Soviet theory and experiences in education, macroeducational systems, and higher education in order to absorb new ideas into its own system (Chen, 1994).

As the field has developed, so have differences of opinion on the focus of comparative education. Consider the following four opinions:

1. The process of developing an educational system is key for each country, and this should be done by "local cultural authorities," not external countries or organizations.
2. Single solutions are the key to educational success: technology, vouchers, distance teaching and learning, and so forth.
3. Universal standards of excellence developed by international organizations are unacceptable and should not be used to develop educational systems, even when based on research and funded.
4. Cross-cultural models of education should guide development of educational systems.

In actuality, none of these views is always right, but each has been proposed for some situation (Heyneman, 1993, pp. 383–84).

Many dimensions of education have been compared cross-culturally: quality and quantity of education, internal structure of systems, educational goals, educational materials, educational finance, teaching techniques, effectiveness of education, curricula, control of education, demographic groups, level of analysis, and so forth (Bray and Thomas, 1995, p. 1). Methodological problems such as differences in school starting ages, curricula, types of schools, testing and record-keeping techniques, and the expense of cross-cultural research all complicate efforts to find standard comparative techniques and data. As an example, in an extensive comparative study of 19 countries, the survey instruments had to be constructed in many different languages to obtain the information needed (Baker and Jones, 1993; Hambleton, 1993).

To help standardize data collection, the United Nations has established some common measurement techniques of education to be used by member countries, and as these techniques are adopted, comparative analysis is expanding with the help of more reliable data and government interest in international studies. This leads to a variety of new research questions, theoretical approaches, and methodologies.

Comparative Education and the Systems Approach

We cannot ignore the impact that countries have on each other and the interaction between education and other institutions in societal systems. The systems approach is again useful for piecing together these dynamics. Using the open systems approach helps us conceptualize the world context within which each country exists (Figure 11–1). From this perspective the world system is the environment for individual countries. How they interact economically and politically and their level of development within the world system influence the type of educational system they develop.

APPROACHES TO CROSS-CULTURAL STUDIES OF EDUCATIONAL SYSTEMS

What do we wish to compare, and how should we do it? Recent comparative studies show the diversity in research: gender issues, in-school variables, dysfunctional aspects of schooling, the role of the state, curriculum and textbook issues, comparative test results, and a variety of other themes (McAdams, 1993; Altbach, 1991, p. 506). These underlying questions lead to the following five approaches, which are by no means exhaustive of the approaches that exist:

FIGURE 11–1 The world educational system shows interdependence among countries.

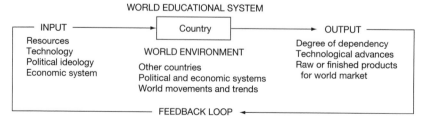

1. Models comparing countries on specific aspects of education such as subject-area achievement
2. Approaches identifying key elements in the internal structure of educational systems that can be compared cross-culturally
3. Societal system "strategies" or approaches to the development of educational systems to meet the needs of society
4. Models showing the link between mass education curricula and expansion of nation-state and standard curricula and structures (Benavot et al., 1991)
5. Models showing the interrelationships between societal institutions and the environment

Many approaches to cross-cultural studies present models or typologies. A model is like the frame of a house: It provides the foundation and supports for each unique unit. We vary the rooms, the decor, the outside covering. Yet each house has a foundation based on common principles of construction. Likewise, a model provides a framework for developing or studying the same types of systems; in this case, educational systems. A model is useful insofar as it reflects reality when matched against actual cases. Models commonly relate to either specific aspects of education or comparisons of systems. As methodologies become more sophisticated, so do models for cross-cultural studies. The model presented in Figure 11–2 shows three dimensions for analysis used in most studies today: aspects of education and of society, geographical/locational levels (levels of analysis), and nonlocational demographic groups.

The model presented in Figure 11–3 shows variables that can be compared across cultures in studies of achievement. An example of a "specific aspect" study may help clarify; in this case the specific aspect for study is achievement.

Comparative International Studies of Achievement

The educational level of the workforce in industrialized countries gives an idea of the skills available in that country. Though secondary school completion levels are similar in top industrial countries, the percentage of the population completing a bachelor's degree is highest in the United States (see Figure 11–4).

International comparative studies of academic achievement provide cross-cultural data on reading proficiency, mathematics, and science achievement. Use of international studies is increasing because of their value in providing alternative perspectives on educational practices, school curricula, school policies, student backgrounds, and other sociocultural variables that affect teaching and learning (Fletcher and Sabers, 1995, p. 455).

The International Association for the Evaluation of Educational Achievement carried out the most extensive cross-cultural research endeavor ever. The

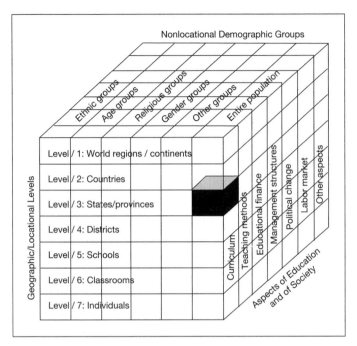

FIGURE 11-2 A framework for comparative education analyses.

Source: Figure 1, p. 475, from Bray, Mark, and Thomas R. Murray, "Levels of Comparision in Educational Studies: Different Insights from Different Literatures and the Value of Multilevel Analyses," *Harvard Educational Review* 65:3, pp. 479–490. Copyright © 1995 by the President and Fellows of Harvard College. All rights reserved.

original study is destined to become a classic in the field, not only because of its extent and its advanced cross-cultural methodological techniques, but because such a multimillion-dollar project may never again be possible (Passow et al., 1976, pp. 12–13). A number of volumes based on the data have resulted, with topics ranging from the significance of the study to methodology to comparative findings. Follow-up studies have provided additional data for comparisons.

A primary purpose of the study was to identify key characteristics affecting national systems of education and relate them to outcomes of learning (Passow et al., 1976, p. 12). The study analyzed school subjects—math, science, reading comprehension, literature, civic education, and French and English as foreign languages. Test results were compared for 10–year-olds and 14–year-olds, and for the year before students left school. Key variables included age of school entry and leaving, size of school and classroom, proportion of total age

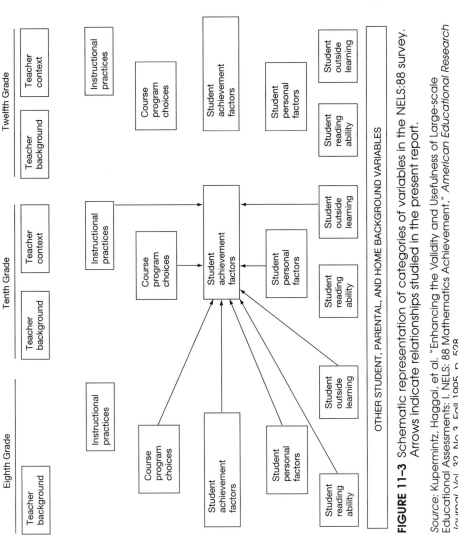

FIGURE 11-3 Schematic representation of categories of variables in the NELS:88 survey. Arrows indicate relationships studied in the present report.

Source: Kupermintz, Haggai, et al. "Enhancing the Validity and Usefulness of Large-scale Educational Assessments: I. NELS: 88 Mathematics Achievement," *American Educational Research Journal*, Vol. 32, No.3, Fall 1995, p. 528.

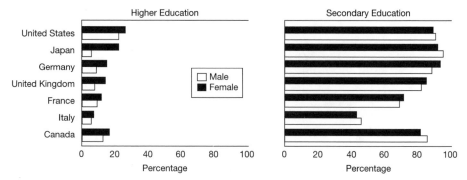

FIGURE 11–4 Percentage of 25- to 34-year-olds in large industrialized countries completing secondary and higher education, by sex and country, 1992.

Note: In the United States, completing secondary education is defined as graduating high school or earning a GED; completing higher education is defined as earning a bachelor's degree or more.

Source: Organization for Economic Cooperation and Development, Indicators of Education's Systems, *Digest of International Education Statistics*, 1995. Reprinted in "International Comparison of Educational Attainment," *The Pocket Condition of Education 1995* (Washington, DC: U.S. Department of Education, 1995).

cohort in school at termination time, specialized versus comprehensive curricula, student socioeconomic status, and sex differences.

Such a vast amount of data was collected and processed and so many hypotheses were tested that it is impossible to summarize the findings. However, this much can be concluded from the data analysis: After a country reaches a "critical threshold," educational efficiency between nations is similar. Differences between developed countries are probably best explained by how many resources are put into what aspects of education.

The IEA studies show only modest differences in achievement among advanced, primarily European, countries, though the range between subject areas such as math, science, and reading comprehension varies greatly. Differences that do exist have been explained by differences in school structure or curriculum (Elley, 1994). Figure 11–5 shows comparative findings for fourth- and eighth-grade mathematics and science achievement in 41 countries (Martin et al., 1999; National Center For Education Statisics, *Conditions*, 1999, p. 7).

If one compares schools in less developed countries with those in advanced ones, the differences are great as illustrated in the opening example. One suggested reason for the discrepancy is that children in less developed countries "arrive at school with substantially less development of the skills most relevant to school performance" (Inkeles, 1982, p. 228). The schools are unable to compensate for the deficits. However, when researchers control for the differences in facilities, teachers, and students, the schools' achievement level is about the same as in advanced countries. Comparing 19 countries on

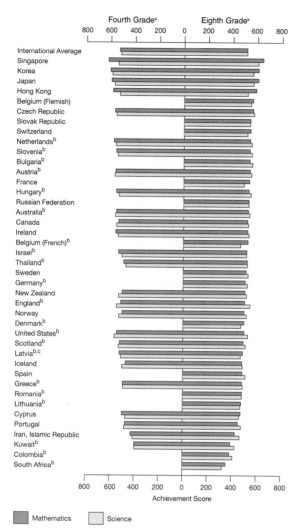

Fourth Grade[a]   Eighth Grade[a]

Mathematics   Science

[a]Fourth or eighth grade in most nations.

[b]Country did not satisfy one or more of the sampling or other guidelines for either the fourth- or eight-grade assessment.

[c]Latvian-speaking schools.

Note: Nations are sorted from highest to lowest average mathematics scores for eighth grade. Only 26 nations participated at the fourth-grade level of the 41 nations participating at the eighth-grade level.

FIGURE 11–5 Average mathematics and science performance scores, by grade and country, 1995.

Source: International Association for the Evaluation of Educational Achievement. TIMSS International Study Center, *Mathematics Achievement in the Primary School Years, Science Achievement in the Primary School Years, IEA's Third International Mathematics and Science Study,* 1997; *Mathematics Achievement in the Middle School Years, Science Achievement in the Middle School Years, IEA's Third International Mathematics and Science Study,* 1996.

math performance, a main variable accounting for differences in achievement levels was gender stratification, that is, the opportunities for women in higher education and work (Baker, 1993).

Another large comparative assessment, the National Assessment of Educational Progress (NAEP), found that U.S. test-takers ages 9 and 13 lag behind their peers in international rankings. American students performed well in reading, less well in science, and poorly in mathematics (Griffith et al., 1994). Of the 15 mostly industrialized countries recorded, math and science scores of 13–year-olds were highest in Korea and Taiwan, and lowest in Jordan, the United States, and Spain. Studies comparing Chinese, Japanese, and American eleventh graders showed Americans spend less time on academic endeavors and more time on working and socializing (Fuligni and Stevenson, 1995). In the most effective schools, students watched less TV, stayed in the same school longer, took more advanced courses including mathematics, and felt positive about academics (Mullis et al., 1994). No clear correlation was found between length of the school day or year, money spent, or use of innovative instructional techniques. However, findings did indicate that high expectations, rigor of the curriculum, and quality and content of instruction produced high achievement (Griffithe et al., 1994; Educational Testing Service, 1992.)

THEORETICAL PERSPECTIVES AND TYPOLOGIES IN COMPARATIVE EDUCATION

Education is viewed by much of the world's population as a gateway to opportunity. Many bright, eager Third World children beg foreign visitors to help them get more education, whereas children in many developed countries think they would like nothing more than to be free of the compulsory burden. But what can education actually do for the people of a nation? There is no clear-cut answer to this question; it is riveted with ideological differences of opinion that permeate the field of comparative education. What is needed is to recognize ideological differences and work with them to gain a deeper understanding of education's role in world development.

Some of the major ideological differences are presented in Figure 11–6, showing major theories and subtheories. The following section deals with subtheories from the functionalist and radical (conflict) perspectives. If our view holds that educational systems are the great "levelers" of society, providing individuals with opportunities to get ahead, and providing society with the skilled human power needed for economic development, our perspective will be functional. If, however, we believe that systems of education reflect the desires of capitalists and the elite in society, and are organized to perpetuate their status, our discussion of comparative education will have a conflict per-

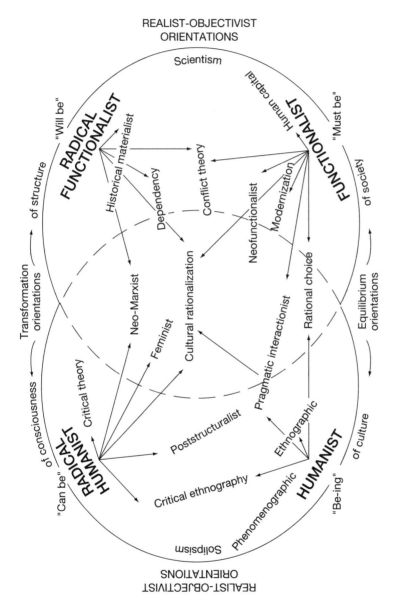

FIGURE 11–6 A macromapping of paradigms and theories in comparative and international education opens to all claimants room for inclusion in the social milieu.

Source: Paulston, Rolland G., and Martin Liebman, "An Invitation to Postmodern Social Cartography," *Comparative Education Review*, Vol. 38, No.2, May 1994, p. 224.

spective. Either perspective might be used, depending on the view of the researcher and the nature of the research questions being asked.

Modernization and Human Capital Perspectives

Many researchers look at the relationship between education and economic growth and development. Modernization and human capital perspectives, which dominated theory in the comparative field in the 1960s and early 1970s, pointed to the importance of education in transforming individuals' beliefs, values, and behaviors into those necessary for economic modernization—diligence, rational calculation, orderliness, frugality, punctuality, and achievement orientation (Slomczynski and Krauze, 1986)—and new social values such as meritocracy—getting ahead because of one's own ability (Becker, 1993).

Although it is clear that there is a relationship between the global economy and the role of education, this approach has been criticized for several reasons:

1. Meritocracy is an ideal reached in few countries. Review of data from 20 countries representing different types of political-economic systems shows that former "Eastern European nonmarket economies" (Poland, Czechoslovakia, Hungary, the former USSR) were closer to ideal meritocracy than the industrial market economies of Western Europe (France, Great Britain, Switzerland, Netherlands, Germany, Finland, Sweden). Contrary to widespread beliefs, Japan and the United States are very far from ideal meritocracy—much farther than some less developed countries (Kerbo, 2000).

2. There is a built-in "ethnocentric" assumption that all nations will emulate the Western model of development. In fact, countries do not always lose their indigenous educational systems even if they adopt Western ones; countries may tailor models from other countries to meet their own needs (Brown, 1999). In one case study, traditional Islamic schooling was maintained along with the increase in Western influence on schooling (Morgan and Armer, 1987).

3. Making individuals "modern" through education may not result in a modern society (Benavot, 1987). Lack of jobs, gender inequality, and low wages for the educated may cause discontent and some "brain drain." In fact, a relatively new structure of international mobility is creating a "brain circulation" in which "highly skilled personnel" move from one country to another, but may not stay long in their home countries (Cao, 1996).

4. The need for workers with greater skill levels has been overrated as most new jobs are in the service and sales sectors and require training. There is little evidence that new skilled jobs will be created as workers receive increased training (Redovich, 1999).

Two alternative views, world systems perspective and dependency theory, challenge the claim that education is a positive force in economic development.

Dependency and world system scholars argue that: (1) the global capitalist economy is a holistic system characterized by structural inequalities both between and within nation-states; (2) the economies of Third World nations were systematically plundered and underdeveloped in earlier historical epochs and now constitute a peripheral component of the global system which continues to supply raw materials and cheap labor to the industrial centers; (3) the expropriation of profit and surplus value by core nations and multinational corporations depended upon the complicity and power of national elites who were usually educated in Western school systems; and (4) by seeking to maximize returns to foreign investments and by setting national priorities according to foreign standards, the actions of the national bourgeoisie have intensified internal inequalities, reinforced the dependency of Third World nations, and retarded long-term economic development. (Benavot, 1992, p. 8)

These theorists look instead to "a nation's structural position in the world economy, trade flow, dependence on primary product exports, state strength, degree of foreign investment, and the presence of multinational corporations" (Benavot, 1992, p. 8). Education plays a small role in determining or influencing economic development, according to these views.

More recently, some reproduction theorists have argued that education *does* affect development: Western-educated Third World leaders have perpetuated former colonial patterns that keep their countries in dependent positions. Education systems in peripheral nations have reproduced and reinforced the class structure, strengthening the position of national elites (Carnoy, 1982). Although some economic growth has taken place, the profits go outside the country and the masses see little change.

"Legitimation of Knowledge" Perspective

The study of comparative educational knowledge has gone through two broad phases of development, according to Welch (1991). The first was to study the process whereby educational knowledge becomes "legitimate" (that is, accepted by the citizens), and how that knowledge base changes over time. The second was to consider the relationship between the legitimation of educational knowledge and power relations in the modern state. Conflict or "critical" theorists have taken the lead in these discussions. They use as a foundation writings by Max Weber, Karl Marx, Jurgen Habermas, and others.

In the 1970s, with the advent of the "new" sociology of education, Michael Young (1971) and others no longer assumed that education represented the social consensus or agreement of citizens of a country; in fact, "critical" sociologists questioned every assumption and structure. Some viewed education as a form of "ideological domination" by those in power to control the knowledge taught and to stay in power.

Three central questions are related to the issue of legitimate knowledge: How does certain knowledge become legitimate? Under what circumstances does it become changed? And what does a cross-national comparison of such processes tell us (Welch, 1991, p. 515)? The hypothesis underlying these questions was that in the process of knowledge transfer (education of children), some groups in society may be left out of decision making about curricula.

The underlying theme in much of the recent writing is that curriculum and acceptable knowledge transmission are not neutral, but rather are driven by social elements such as who is in power and who has economic control (Archer, 1979; Habermas, 1978). Some argue that the form schooling takes, such as "comprehensive school structure" in Europe, is influenced by the needs of capitalist labor markets (Levin, 1978). Another influence is international organizations that "define and promote overall world-level principles and ideas that then are used to guide state policy behavior . . . national policy aims tend to be consistent with international organization decisions and policies" (McNeely, 1995, p. 504).

Even the day-to-day routines that take place in schools around the world have been studied for hidden messages children receive from external influences such as international organizations. This "hidden curriculum" is exemplified in the African thought process. Science education is more closely associated with a Western cause-effect view of the world than with a worldview from traditionally agricultural, religious countries. As science becomes an integral part of most countries' basic curriculum, these new Western worldviews are transmitted. Some argue that these "hidden messages" lead to a more rapid increase in a country's standard of living (Benavot, 1991). But such a worldview may also perpetuate stratification systems by giving some members of society more access to elite education.

Despite the conflicting views over the role of education in societies, all nations have some form of formal education. In the next section we consider cross-national studies in comparative education: rich versus poor countries, studies of internal structure of educational systems, and societal strategies for education.

Rich versus Poor: An Educational Typology

Nepal is one of the poorest countries of the world, with a gross national product per capita of $220; it is better off than many African countries including Ethiopia ($110), Mozambique and Burundi ($140), and Sierra Leone ($160); and only slightly ahead of Niger ($200), Tanzania, Malawi, and Rwanda ($210) (United Nations, 1999). The vast majority of the 24 million citizens (81 percent) engage in agriculture, most subsistence-level. Infant mortality rate (birth to one year) is a high 73.6 per thousand live births, and almost half of the infants are underweight (*The Time Almanac 2000*, 1999). Many children are undernourished or suffer from severe malnutrition. Life expectancy is less than 60 years of age. Population growth does not help the situation. Education rates often provide an indicator of a country's position in the world system. In Nepal, 89 percent of the women and 46 percent of the men are illiterate, though the gender gap is decreasing (United Nations, 1999). The poorest citizens have the lowest literacy.

Despite various government programs to improve the basic health, welfare, and educational level, many barriers must be overcome. Subsistence agriculture demands that all hands work, so children have little time for schooling and little opportunity to be educated however much they may value education. The population growth requires that the government spend money just to keep up with the additional children; girls are involved in household chores and child care; and long distances from school make attendance difficult. Teacher quality also affects attendance rates. The government, by implementing a vast system of adult education that is reaching thousands, hopes to break the cycle of illiteracy. This is but one example of a country's barriers to formal education in developing countries.

Learning takes place in many ways and settings: For the rich, much learning is formal, in classrooms and specially designed buildings. For the poor, there may or may not be a classroom. Often formal learning is a small part of the poor child's education; mostly he or she learns informally through imitating elders and learning the family trade. An anthropology professor once warned that before we scoff at informal learning we should consider its impact. He asked us to imagine ourselves transferred to the Kalahari Desert. How would we survive? Where would we find food and water? Without help we would be likely to perish. Yet the Hottentots and Bushmen survive and flourish there; they have been learning survival techniques, passed on through the generations, from early childhood. The film *The Gods Must Be Crazy* shows the contrasts between the lives of Europeans and Bushmen.

In 1995, there were more than one billion primary and secondary school students in the world (National Center for Education Statistics, *Digest*, 1999, p. 445) and 52 million professional teachers (National Center for Education Statistics, *Digest*, 1995, p. 451). Yet this is not the whole picture, for the proportion of children at primary school in Bhutan is 13.2 percent; in Haiti, 19.4 percent; and in Niger, 24.4 percent (United Nations; 1999, pp. 178–79, Indicator 10), whereas in rich Western countries it is 100 percent. The number of children in school in any country is closely related to that country's wealth and level of economic development. Illiteracy and economic development are related; Third World countries that are struggling economically also have the highest illiteracy rates, with up to two-thirds of women and one-third of men illiterate ("The World's Women," 1995). World adult literacy is 81 percent for men and 65 percent for women (UNICEF, 2000). (Illiteracy rates for men and women in selected regions are listed in Figure 4–1.)

Unfortunately, the quality of schools in many of the poorest Third World countries is eroding, and public spending per pupil is dropping. Although middle-income countries show a rise in school quality, the overall differences in comparisons of Third World countries with industrial nations is great and the gap is widening. Why the differences? The reasons are many, but they center on the position of Third World countries in the world system. Influencing the educational situation are the level of wealth in a country; the rapid growth in enrollments, which forces limited resources to be spread even thinner; and other factors related to dependent and debtor nations (Gallagher, 1993; Fuller, 1986). Unfortunately, rapid population growth in some of the poorest regions will only exacerbate the problems (see Figure 11–7).

Within many countries there are unofficially two educational systems: one in rural areas and the other in urban areas (Hannum, 1999). Some urban education is elite education. Village schools, as seen in the opening scenario in this chapter, have fewer resources, often less qualified teachers, and less parental support. They may be state-run or attached to a local temple, mosque, or mission; religious education may be the main emphasis. Urban schools in developing nations are usually organized and run on a Western or colonial model, often patterned after the English or French forms of education; many serve the nation's elite population. Within the poor nations are families who

FIGURE 11–7 Population of major areas, medium series, 1950–2150.

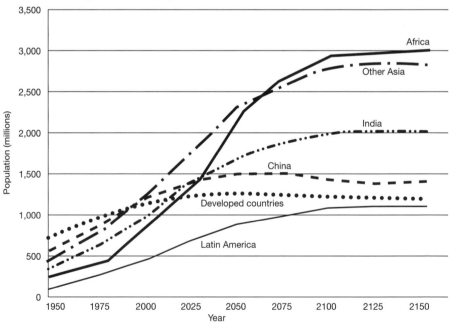

Source: "The UN Long-Range Population Projections" (Washington, DC: Population Reference Bureau, 1995), p. 15.

cannot afford to take advantage of available preschool and elementary education because their children are needed to help with the farm work; survival has priority over schooling. In some countries (such as Latin American countries), however, early-childhood intervention programs are available and provide useful information, services, and support to the family and child. This provides one method for governments to increase the health and nutritional awareness of families.

Many of the cross-cultural analyses of elementary school curricula show worldwide standardization in major subject areas, reflecting ideologies, rules, and customs that are transnational in character, cutting across regions and economic systems. Instead of individual countries or regions determining content, a world system based on scientific values guides the process of curriculum development (Meyer et al., 1992; Benavot et al., 1988). As mentioned, standardization usually reflects Western models that are not always most relevant for developing countries. Some theorists disagree with the indicators of a world system of education, but similarities in systems have been supported.

Secondary curricula, too, show homogeneity across cultures. In a study of 120 countries comparing curricula for students preparing for university, standard world models were apparent, although in secondary schools distinct curricular types, such as tracks in the arts and humanities or in math and science, were found (Kamens, Meyer, and Benavot, 1996). Secondary education is more elusive than primary education for rural children of developing nations, for they may be required to pay for transportation, boarding, books, or clothes that often make education impossible.

The educational system often serves to perpetuate inequality by being available only to elites, usually those from urban areas. Inequality is found in wealthy, developed, industrial societies as well as poor, emerging, developing, and modernizing ones. The inequalities between individuals are related to class, race, sex, and religion as well as to rural versus urban residence. Even the age at which children start school and the preprimary enrollment rates vary by country. For instance, in Finland and Norway, many children do not start school until age seven, whereas in Spain, Belgium, France, and the Netherlands, more than 90 percent of four-year-olds are in school ("Preprimary Enrollment Rates," 1992, p. 7).

World System Analysis

This global critical (conflict) perspective views stratification between world countries just as conflict theory studies stratification within race, class, and gender in countries. World system analysts consider education within the transnational social structural system, and observes the effects of this system on subunits, or nation-states (Wallerstein, 1974). Both ideological systems and organization (political, economic, religious) affect the direction of educational development. States or national governments are the means by which capitalists control the world market, including educational systems (Chase-Dunn, 1980). For instance, most countries are caught up in the "myth of progress" (Ramirez and Boli-Bennett, 1987, p. 18). Because all states respond to this common global ideology, educational developments have been similar, with the underlying assumption that growth is good for society and the individual. "Core" (developed capitalist) states are often involved in the educational development of "periphery" (developing) states, a factor some argue serves the core states by returning capital to the core (Clayton, 1998).

An example of world system analysis is seen in the theoretical model developed by Robert Arnove (1994; 1980, p. 49), who uses "dependency theory" to explain the relationships between societies and education. A chain of exploitation exists at several levels: metropolitan (developed) countries and world organizations over peripheral (developing) countries; centers of power in Third World countries over peripheral rural areas; and so on down to the village level. In this system, the peripheral areas may gain by getting needed resources, but the price is domination (by the metropolitan or center areas) over local affairs—curricula, texts, and reforms, for example.

To illustrate the world system of education, scholars (Meyer, Kamens, and Benavot, 1992; Ramirez and Boli, 1987) point to the many international organizations coordinating education worldwide: the Ford and Rockefeller foundations, the World Bank, UNESCO, UNICEF, and so on (McNeeley, 1995; Samoff, 1993; Meyer, Ramirez, and Soysal, 1992). These organizations have the power and money to promote ideas and programs around the world, and models advocated by international agencies have spread around the world. Some of these programs are successful, others disappointing—as in the case of rural India, where emphasis on "nonformal education" gave the government an excuse not to provide classrooms for students. Faculty in higher-education institutions in Third World countries have been sponsored by organizations such as the Rockefeller Foundation. To some this seems like philanthropy at its best, but to conflict theorists, this exemplifies international organizational philanthropy spreading capitalist ideologies and shaping Third World educational systems to meet the needs of international, multinational, and American corporate needs. They point out that the World Bank is financed by wealthy capitalist countries to give advice to developing nations.

Theorists moving away from the traditional world system theory contend that subordinates in periphery states are often aware of their status in relation to others and do act in relation to their knowledge, often by resisting dominance of core countries. In some countries this is taking the form of controlling development of their own educational systems. Moving from macrolevel analysis to postmodern interpretations, which include a consideration of periphery states as conscious actors in the process, parallels developments in conflict theory (Clayton, 1998). Not all theorists agree that the world system is bringing educational systems more in line with each other (Cummings, 1999; Carnoy and Samoff, 1990).

Each societal system of education is influenced by the larger world system. Few societies in today's interdependent world can be studied without careful consideration of the world community. Yet this is not an easy task, because comparing complex and different systems presents methodological difficulties.

Whatever theoretical perspective one holds, it can be agreed that education does not stand alone in society. Education must be considered in relation to other institutions in the society, and in relationship to that society's international environment. This is particularly important in the case of developing nations, many of which are in a postcolonial period and have inherited the educational system of former colonial powers. In the following section, examples of institutional interdependency models are discussed.

GLOBAL INSTITUTIONAL INTERDEPENDENCE

Every society shares a set of common institutions: family, education, religion, politics, economics, and health systems. As the world shrinks with the aid of technology, communication networks, and transportation systems, institutional models influence each other and become similar around the globe. However, political systems, economic systems, and religious beliefs are also major variables separating countries. For instance, a rough separation in world countries divides the northern and southern hemispheres, with those countries in the southern hemisphere more often part of the developing world, characterized by recent independence (since 1945), legacies of colonialism, and debt to wealthier countries. Problems of poverty, disease, hunger, rapid population expansion, and illiteracy occupy governments and force educational issues into the background in poor countries. News reports tell us of death and suffering in a constant string of wars, famines, epidemics, and refugee crises.

Approaches to institutional interdependence can be *global*, as in the case of the "world system perspective" (Wallerstein, 1974); *cross-national*, as in the case of Williamson's economic-political typology of societies or studies of curricula, knowledge, or tests (Williamson, 1979); *institutional*, focusing on the institution of education in relation to other institutions (Benavot, 1997); or *national*, with applicability to comparative studies. In the global approach, the world is conceptualized as a system with interdependent units. Internal and external change is linked to relationships between countries. Much research related to this theory has dealt with economic and political institutional characteristics, though cultural and ideological elements have been examined as well. More recently, this approach has been expanded to take an international view of forces that produce similar patterns of social change across societies.

Several themes are common in the relatively new institutional approach to the study of education:

> First, it focuses on the origins and expansion of modern, secular mass systems of schooling in Europe and North America and their worldwide institutionalization during the twentieth century. Second, it analyzes the institutional underpinnings of education in society. . . . Third, this approach examines the ways in which mass and elite education alter important social constructions and institutional arrangements in society. (Benavot, 1997, p. 340)

From this perspective, institutionalists see education as creating a redistribution of political and economic power in national societies.

Education and the Institution of Religion

Within one country—even within one village—the relationship between education and religion is complex and sometimes contradictory. A few examples may clarify:

◆ *Northern Nigeria.* A Koranic school for boys stresses traditional religious beliefs, attitudes, and behavior patterns, and is not supportive of change. It exists next to a state-run village school, formerly run by Christian missionaries, which stresses "modern" attitudes and the importance of education in "getting ahead."

◆ *Northern Ireland.* The Catholic parochial schools and the state schools attended primarily by Protestants protect and perpetuate a distinction between segments of the society, and the hostilities between the two religious groups.

◆ *Iran.* Fundamentalist Muslim schools support the status quo and reflect the leadership and views of Muslim imams, or religious leaders.

◆ *United States.* Fundamentalist Christian schools stress some values opposed to the constitutional separation of church and state; they express the group's alienation from the technological society. Examples of the latter are controversies about textbooks and the questioning of certain scientific teachings on evolution.

◆ *Israel.* Religion and education work hand in hand to accomplish the goals of the state. Hebrew language and religious training provide unifying themes in an otherwise heterogeneous society. Religion and political beliefs blend in many cases, however, as seen in the murder of Israeli Prime Minister Yitzhak Rabin in 1995 by a militant religious student.

Religion is often closely linked to a group's ethnic, racial, or national origins; therefore, it may provide for the group a point of stability in a time of rapid and confusing change in which norms break down—a situation sociologists refer to as "anomie." Attitudes toward change are reflected in religious schools, or in state schools where the religion is represented. If a change is consistent with the principles of the religion, the church may in fact be a leader in that change. Religion may also serve to retard change, however, especially if the change threatens the principles of the belief system.

Family, Social Class, and Education

The family is the primary social bond and purveyor of values. In the family we develop an attitude toward ourselves and what we can become; we develop expectations concerning our education. It is in the environment created by the family that we receive informal education, and also encouragement, support, and behavior models for formal educational pursuit. Deviation from this early influence probably means that some alternative model is available to us and is seen as realistic: The child may be influenced by a teacher, minister, or older child; the community may require children to attend school and encourage the brightest to continue, perhaps even providing support.

In developing "peripheral" communities, some families may be too poor to take advantage of educational opportunities; formal education may not be a realistic part of their lives. Thus, the cycle of poverty for some and great opportunity for others—both in individual countries and in the world— is perpetuated. Paulo Freire, a Brazilian who is minister of education for the state of Sao Paulo and has worked with developing education for the poor, has written about what he sees as the hopelessness of the poor classes, caused in part by their inability to see beyond immediate problems and to look at the world critically. This inability allows a system of educationally elite landowners to dominate rural, uneducated peasants (Torres, 1994; Freire, 1987, 1973, 1970). The peasants adopt a fatalistic attitude about life, supported by supernatural religious beliefs, which serves to hold them in their inferior places.

As a society becomes more literate, certain attendant changes occur: urbanization, mobility, and modernization. These have a direct bearing on the family. Extended families begin to break down; the birthrate decreases and urbanization increases; it is difficult to house and feed a large family in an urban, mobile society. Women's status often changes with entry into urban life as many women enter the industrial workforce and have fewer children. Again, changes in one part of society inevitably affect other parts. The position of one's family in the social structure affects both one's chances for education and one's place in an educational system.

In a well-known typology, Turner (1960) suggested that the pattern of upward mobility shapes the school system. He has compared English and American schools, concluding that the values in England support what he calls the "sponsored" form of mobility, where elites select elites and perpetuate themselves. This compares with "contest" mobility in America, where an individual's abilities are more important in placement. These values underlie the institution of education in each country.

Parents in developed countries generally want to have a say in their children's education, to "manage" their school careers. For instance, in American schools, parents who manage the daily activities of their children raise the academic standing of their children. In Germany, parental management differs by the type of secondary school the child attends. In Japan, parents support schooling activities outside of the formal setting by tutoring their children and providing extra classes, which enhances examination preparation and future opportunities (Baker and Stevenson, 1989, p. 348). Parents want to choose the school their children will attend, including the religious affiliation, pedagogy, and curriculum. Minority and immigrant parents may make special efforts to influence their children's education (Baker and Stevenson, 1990; Glenn, 1989). The importance of one's family background for educational achievement is discussed in other chapters throughout the book.

The interdependence between education and other institutions in society helps us to focus on important variables as we attempt to understand very different educational systems.

Education and Economic Institutions

Most countries believe that there is a relationship between education, economic development, and modernization. Governments act on this premise even though the facts do not always uphold it. They invest in education, and thus education reflects the political philosophy of a country and the goals of the group in power. Many governments have the power to adopt or reject educational programs, or even to totally revamp the educational system, as in China and Cuba during the communist revolutions. If the government establishes certain priorities for the society, the educational system is likely to reflect these in curriculum, texts, and other aspects of the program.

In order to meet a country's goals, trained personnel are needed. Human capital theorists argue that individuals are like pieces of machinery—a capital good—and can increase their value in the labor market by increasing their education, especially training in occupational skills (Becker, 1993; Bowles, 1976). (This argument is challenged by Samuel Bowles and Herbert Gintis, 1976, among others, who contend that individuals are labor, not capital.) However, the system of supply and demand of educated persons does not always work perfectly for several reasons. Illiteracy and low levels of schooling are the major social problems confronting the Third World, problems that can inhibit economic growth and political stability. For instance, those from developing countries who receive a higher education will be among the elite. But the prestigious fields for which their training prepares them are not necessarily those where the country's needs lie. India, for instance, has many trained lawyers and engineers who cannot be absorbed into the system. This has caused a number of highly skilled individuals to leave India. China is experiencing a similar phenonenon as many students go abroad to study. In 1998, the People's Republic of China had the second greatest number of foreign students studying in the United States, with Japan being first (*The Chronicle of Higher Education Almanac*, 1999, p. 29). Of the 80,000 students sent abroad between 1978 and 1993, only 20,000 returned to China, causing concern about a "brain drain" of talent. China tries to lure the talent back with promises of higher wages and better social, political, and economic status, but the crackdown on prodemocracy students at Tiananmen Square in Beijing did not help in the process (Broaded, 1993).

Unfortunately, much of the supply-demand problem has arisen because of unsuitable models of education. Some have been adopted from or left by colonial powers; others are copies from Western science and technology. China has studied Western systems in attempts to modernize its educational system, but this creates the problem of trying to develop a system that is suited to China's needs by studying Western education (Chen, 1994). Structures left from the colonial period still influence power relationships, as seen in the case of the lower status of women in former colonial societies (referred to as "gender colonization"). Until these relationships are altered, countries cannot use their human resources, especially women, to the fullest (Acosta-Belen, 1990). Some multinational corporations hire large numbers of workers in Third World countries, especially women, but often for unskilled jobs that need little education (Fisher, 1990). When both the host countries and the multinational corporations see the value of economic development in education, women's progress may be enhanced.

Various countries are breaking this unproductive mold and developing different definitions and forms of education, recognizing the diversity between national needs. Educational reforms relate to religious, social, economic, and political ideologies. Countries as varied as Iran, Nicaragua, and Tanzania have moved away from Western models. Many comparative educationists advocate programs of education based on the countries' needs. Tanzania received attention in this respect in the 1970s and 1980s for its program called "education for self-reliance," advocated by President Julius Nyerere from 1964 to 1980, to train people in needed skills; Kenya's harambee school movement, started by leader Kenyatta after independence, encouraged local areas to form schools to meet local needs. Unfortunately, these schools have become less respected than government-run secondary schools.

Stages of Economic Development and Educational Change. The development of educational systems can be related to three technological stages. In the first stage only a limited number of people, a privileged few, are involved in education—cloistered monks, for example. The second stage involves education that reaches further, training a core of the population for factory work and the civil service and to be leaders of business, industry, and government. Third is the training required for the technological age, for the "communication society," where education, work, and society are closely interrelated (King, 1979; Bell, 1973).

Education for Modernization—"Modern Man." As a society moves through these stages, changes besides those in skill education and literacy take place. The values of the population and attitudes toward education and development also change, according to Alex Inkeles and David Smith's functional perspective of the modernization process. A society that places emphasis on economic development needs what they call "modern man." Modern man has "those personal qualities which are likely to be inculcated by participation in large-scale modern productive enterprises such as the factory . . . if the factory is to operate efficiently and effectively" (Inkeles and Smith, 1974). These personal qualities include

1. Openness to new experience
2. Readiness for social change
3. Growth of opinion, disposition to hold or form opinions, awareness of diversity of opinions, and the placing of positive value on variations in opinion
4. Interest in acquiring facts and information
5. Acceptance of fixed schedules, punctuality, present-time orientation
6. Belief that man can exert control over the environment and advance goals
7. Long-term planning in public affairs and private life
8. Calculability or trust in the world and others
9. Valuing technical skill
10. Educational and occupational aspirations
11. Awareness of and respect for the dignity of others
12. Understanding of production and the decision-making process

These 12 personal qualities were closely related to other factors in the individual's background experience and society: kinship and family, women's rights, religion, the role of the aged, politics, communications, consumerism, social stratification, and work commitment. This "modern man" places a high value on formal education and schooling in skills such as reading, writing, and mathematics, and has the skills and attitudes needed for economic development.

The Challenge of Becoming Modern. The Industrial Revolution was a simple, gradual transition in its early stages. One development led naturally to another and to the increased investment of capital. Today, developing countries face pressures to make that transition rapidly. The technology is available, but economic development requires a change in the whole structure and value system of society. Subsistence agricultural societies must make enormous transitions to become "modern." Imagine for a moment a traditional, largely rural, agriculturally based country, its internal structure reliant as much on extended family relationships as on any central or even regional government. In order to modernize, leaders must gain support for massive and rather rapid changes involving all institutions in the society. Some religious and political systems make the transition easily. Others resist change. Transportation and communication, health systems, economic planning, capital to build, an educational system for many levels and types of knowledge and skills will all be needed. Developing the human capital necessary to carry out the economic development requires willingness to modernize and be mobile, motivation to pursue the education or training needed, and cooperation with the goals set by those in power. In other words, economic development depends on the attitudes and values of the population quite as much as on the technological machinery and necessary capital.

Dependency on rich nations may occur in the development process, for it takes massive input of capital and expertise for such a mobilization. Countries often bargain for aid from the developed world—socialist or capitalist—with the implicit understanding that they owe some degree of allegiance to the provider. International organizations, including the World Bank and the International Monetary Fund (IMF), have become involved in the global economy, playing a role in the development of Third World countries that is criticized for perpetuating debt and dependency status.

Political-Economic Divisions Between Societal Systems

Sociologists have laid out major political-economic divisions among societies and broad generalizations about the implications of those divisions for educational systems. For instance, socialism ranges from Marxism to social democracy, capitalism from free market economies to state-regulated capitalism and the welfare state. Socialist models put special emphasis on "egalitarian and relevant" education, as we shall see in the case on China presented in Chapter 12; capitalist models, predominant in Western Europe and the United States, tolerate inequality and stress "classical" as well as "practical" subjects in the curriculum, as we shall see in the case on Britain. Generally, educational systems reflect the position of the dominant group in society.

With many countries in Latin America, Asia, and Eastern Europe moving toward more representative democratic forms of government in the past quarter century, scientists have raised questions about education's role in both the emergence and stability of these new political systems. Modernization theorists argue that mass education prepares the population for the responsibilities of living in a democracy where participation is expected, and thus see education as preparation for successful democracies. Conflict theorists see the potential for directing the mass population into desired positions to perpetuate the existing power structure, even in democracies. Through the institutional perspective, researchers are considering the impact of higher education on the development and stability of democracies (Benavot, 1996).

In a systems model that illustrates the interdependence of institutions, Williamson (1979) combines elements from the political and economic institutions. He contends that the educational system reflects the political structure and distribution of power in society. It is also important to understand the historical comparative context of a country in order to encompass its past, present, and future environments. This is especially important in cases of postcolonial educational systems. Williamson divides the world into four predominant types of societies (see Figure 11–8).

Developed Socialist Societies. The former USSR and some other Eastern European societies can be understood as socialist societies whose special features flow historically from the programs of industrial development followed by Lenin and Stalin. The Soviet system provided the model for the development of a number of Third World agricultural countries.

Underdeveloped Socialist Societies. Peasant societies try to build socialist societies. Because most are predominantly agricultural, accumulating capital for industrialization is difficult. This has forced them into a dependency role in relation to other societies. Underdeveloped socialist societies face the structural problem of involving peasants and rural workers in revolutionary change; they must satisfy both immediate demands for a better life and longer-term demands for capital accumulation, which involves sacrifice and deferred consumption.

Advanced Capitalistic Societies. Capitalism has been described in many ways and has undergone many changes over the years. The main features of capitalism as described in classical theory include the following:

1. Private ownership of the means of production
2. A free market in labor
3. The concentration of production into factories and the incorporation of agriculture into the capitalist market
4. Production geared to a market and aimed at realizing profit
5. The rationalization of economic life to principles of clear capital accounting
6. Production geared to a world market

In today's world, multinational conglomerates spread across the globe, competing for cheap raw products, labor, and world markets.

Dependent Societies. Dependent societies are characterized by an "interdependence of poverty, low income, low productivity, high mortality rates, urban squalor, economic dependence, political corruption and illiteracy"

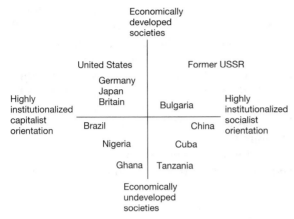

Economically
developed
societies

United States		Former USSR
Germany		
Japan		
Highly institutionalized capitalist orientation · Britain · Bulgaria · Highly institutionalized socialist orientation

Brazil · China

Nigeria · Cuba

Ghana | Tanzania

Economically
undeveloped
societies

FIGURE 11–8
Models of development
and type of economy.

Source: Williamson, Bill,
*Education, Social Structure, and
Development* (London:
Macmillan, 1979), p. 36. Used
with permission.

(Williamson, 1979, p. 39) and account for about two-thirds of the world's population. In Williamson's view, economic backwardness is the result of poor societies having had their economic and social systems distorted by the overseas expansion of capitalist enterprises. Thus, poverty is not intrinsic to these societies but results from historical factors such as colonialism. These societies often must become dependent on Western aid and expertise in their efforts to modernize, thus perpetuating their dependent status in the world economy.

From this economic-political typology comes the model shown in Figure 11–8, combining the level of economic development and the political orientation of sample countries. Williamson (1979) argues that education is not a product for sale, but a program of action in that it has political and ideological dimensions. These help explain variations in educational form and content between countries. Models of change or development in education reflect these political-ideological underpinnings and define what a society is about and what actions it takes. Of course, there are varying degrees of support for the ideology of political groups in control, and this may in turn influence the support for educational systems reflecting the dominant ideology. If a group in society feels that it is not receiving its share of resources, it may oppose the existing system.

This and similar typologies based on institutional interdependence are closely related to the open systems approach; they make paramount the relationship between the institution of education and other institutions in the national system and international environment. As societies change, these models will need to be adapted.

Higher Education Around the World

In 1989, students in China occupied Tiananmen Square in a fight for democracy in that communist stronghold. The government routed out the dissidents; some leaders were imprisoned, others went underground. Students at the universities are now closely watched, and new students must go through intensive political indoctrination. Yet underneath the surface, the democratic movement still festers (Lin, 1992). Institutions around the world, from China to South Africa, experience student activism over issues of concern. They also share common trends: rapid growth in the demand for higher education, rising expectations, increased financial support for students, growing involvement of research and continuing education, diversification of the types of education offered, gender equity issues, and concern about dropouts; any of these issues may lead to student activism and disorder (Rubin, 1996).

Some common themes encircle the world's higher-education institutions. As outlined by Altbach and Davis (1999), these themes include the following:

1. Access and equity
2. The link between education and work
3. The transition from school to work
4. Effects of technological developments
5. Transfer of talent across borders
6. Expansion of graduate education
7. Privatization of higher education
8. Crisis in academic professions
9. Access and equity
10. Accountability

These common themes permeate the world system of higher education. Consider the first point, access to higher education. People around the globe see higher education as the key to future jobs, but countries vary greatly in their ability to meet the demand. In China and India, only about 5 percent of recent high school graduates attend college, and in most of Africa only a fraction have access. Higher-education systems face change from elite to mass to universal access, thus providing access to a wider range of students.

With additional access comes the question of funding the additional students. Should countries invest in citizens' higher education, taking funds from other essential services including education at lower levels? Should citizens pay for their higher education, making it available to a limited number in the population and perpetuating an elite educational system? Or should financial support come from external sources, including international organizations, businesses, and private contracts, resulting in higher education being influenced by these sources? Each of these plans has advantages and disadvantages that impact these issues and themes.

In some regions higher-education institutions are creating links. For instance, the united European Community is resulting in more collaboration and internationalizing of higher education in European countries (Cerych, 1990; Woodhall, 1991, p. 30). Student exchanges also create links between institutions and countries, with more than one million students studying outside their borders (Altbach and Davis, 1999). Table 11–1 shows the number of foreign students studying in the United States, and the United States sends thousands of students abroad to study in countries around the world (see Figure 11–9). Study results of exchange students who go from the United States to other countries indicate that they return more interested in current events and international affairs and have an increased appreciation for foreign cultures

TABLE 11–1 Foreign Students' Studying in the United States—Countries of Origin, 1997–98

Country or Territory	Students	1-Year Change	Country or Territory	Students	1-Year Change
Japan	47,073	+1.7%	Argentina	2,473	+8.7%
China	46,958	+10.5	Nigeria	2,436	+11.5
South Korea	42,890	+15.5	Norway	2,316	+2.1
India	33,818	+10.4	Australia	2,308	+4.6
Taiwan	30,855	+1.2	Bulgaria	2,265	+25.5
Canada	22,051	−4.1	United Arab Emirates	2,225	+4.3
Thailand	15,090	+11.9	Peru	2,127	−3.5
Malaysia	14,597	+0.5	Jordan	2,027	−3.2
Indonesia	13,282	+6.6	Cyprus	2,026	+12.2
Hong Kong	9,665	−11.7	Romania	1,951	+16.9
Mexico	9,559	+6.5	Netherlands	1,938	+2.9
Germany	9,309	+3.5	Trinidad and Tobago	1,927	−13.3
Turkey	9,081	+11.8	Bahamas	1,917	−6.9
Britain	7,534	+2.4	Iran	1,863	−12.5
Brazil	6,982	+13.2	Sri Lanka	1,852	+2.0
Russia	6,424	+3.6	Switzerland	1,850	0.0
France	5,992	+5.3	Poland	1,844	+8.0
Pakistan	5,821	−4.5	Egypt	1,831	+18.9
Venezuela	4,731	+3.1	South Africa	1,809	−2.3
Saudi Arabia	4,571	+7.2	Nepal	1,697	+21.2
Sweden	4,412	+7.7	Ecuador	1,643	+8.4
Spain	4,371	−6.5	Former Yugoslavia	1,498	+5.6
Kenya	4,346	+16.7	Ghana	1,494	+12.6
Colombia	4,345	+19.5	Ukraine	1,402	+7.4
Singapore	3,843	+3.1	Lebanon	1,321	−3.6
Bangladesh	3,458	0.1	Panama	1,286	0.0
Italy	3,090	+8.8	Vietnam	1,210	+24.1
Greece	3,065	+1.8	Morocco	1,168	+10.9
Kuwait	2,810	3.9	Chile	1,156	+17.0
			Denmark	1,063	+5.7

Source: The Chronicle of Higher Education Almanac, 1999, p. 29.

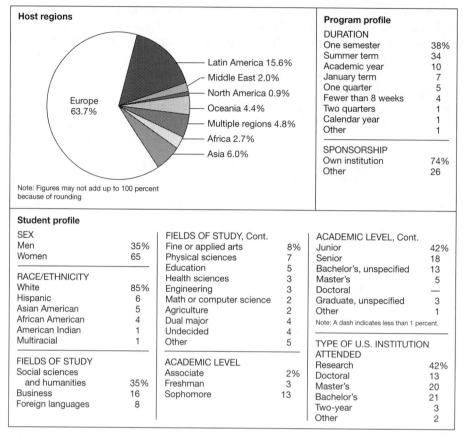

FIGURE 11-9 Study abroad by U.S. students, 1997–98.

Source: The Chronicle of Higher Education, December 10, 1999, p. A61.

(Kraft and Ballantine, 1994; Carlson, 1990). In addition, increased Internet communication is resulting in contact and research among scholars.

Some countries are losing their best and brightest in the "brain drain" as record numbers of students go abroad for education and job opportunities. Again refer to Table 11–1 which shows the numbers of international students from various countries studying in the United States. Thirty-five percent of doctorates granted in 1997 were awarded to non–United States citizens *(The Chronicle of Higher Education Almanac,* 1999, p. 29). There has been a drop in the number of doctorates awarded to Americans compared with doctorates granted by U.S. universities to foreign students.

For many countries struggling to advance, some forms of higher education may be inappropriate. These societal needs and institutional demands could change the structure of higher education as it exists today. Until developing countries can absorb their graduates, the brain drain will remove some of the young talent. Many students, even in developed countries, are demanding a more vocationally oriented, practical education to help them get jobs.

In order to provide examples of educational systems in the world, Chapter 12 presents countries falling into three quadrants of Williamson's typology: United Kingdom in the economically developed, capitalistic orientation; China, in the socialistic orientation, developing societies quadrant; and West Africa, especially Ghana, in the developing societies that lean more toward capitalism. Only a few countries fall into the fourth quadrant, developed and socialist. We are ready to explore the educational systems of these countries.

*A*pplying Sociology to Education: What are the advantages and disadvantages of studying abroad? ◈

◈ Summary

This chapter is about education around the world. It discusses issues facing educational systems, covers theoretical approaches, typologies to understand similarities and differences among systems.

I. Cross-Cultural Educational Studies

The field of cross-cultural educational studies has been largely descriptive in the past, using case studies of selected countries. Theories and typologies are advancing our knowledge of the area. The systems approach helps us conceptualize the links between countries. One approach to comparative studies has been assessment of achievement in different subject areas across societies.

II. Approaches to Cross-Cultural Studies of Educational Systems

Institutional interdependence means that each institution is affected by each other institution. A change in one means that adaptations will be necessary in others. World system analysis stresses the interdependence of nations of the world, with "metropolitan" centers and nations dominating over "peripheral" areas.

In comparing nations, most emphasis has been put on political-economic systems as they influence educational systems. Williamson's typology illustrates this point. Relationships of education to religion and family were discussed. Examples of "world environment" were given.

Higher-education structures have ranged from Western forms to indigenous models. A problem faced by some countries is that elite students are educated in foreign countries and bring back Western political and legal models; these models are not necessarily best for countries struggling with development and literacy. Also, some of the educated elite may not find need for their skills in their developing countries and may become alienated.

III. Theoretical Perspectives and Typologies in Comparative Education

Recent theoretical approaches contrast functional and conflict theoretical approaches; several of these focus on the relationship between educational and economic growth and development. Earlier theories focused on changing individuals to fit modern society. Human capital, legitimation of knowledge, rich versus poor countries, and world systems analysis are reviewed.

World system analysis stresses the interdependence of nations of the world, with "metropolitan" centers and nations dominating over "peripheral" areas. Cross-cultural studies all fit into several types: contrasting rich and poor nations, studying the internal structures of educational systems, and studies of institutional interdependence.

IV. Global Institutional Interdependence

Institutional interdependence means that each institution is affected by each other institution. A change in one means that adaptations will be necessary in others.

In comparing nations, relationships of education to religion and family were discussed. Examples of "world environment" were given. Most emphasis has been put on political-economic systems as they influence educational systems. Williamson's typology illustrates this point.

Higher-education structures have ranged from Western forms to indigenous models. A problem faced by some countries is that elite students are educated in foreign countries and bring back Western political and legal models; these models are not necessarily best for countries struggling with development and literacy. Also, some of the educated elite may not find the need for their skills in their developing countries and may become alienated.

◆ *Putting Sociology to Work*

1. Talk to several international students about educational systems in their countries. Ask about the structure, access for various groups and classes of students, and how their systems differ from that in the United States.
2. Find out how you would be educated in your major field if you were studying in another country of your choice.
3. Select two developing countries, one capitalist, the other socialist. How do their educational systems differ? Can this be attributed to their political ideologies?
4. Put yourself in the position of a minister of education in a developing country. What would be your primary concerns in planning the educational program?
5. Pose a question about cross-cultural educational systems. Which of the theoretical approaches would be useful in dealing with your question?

CHAPTER 12

Educational Systems Around the World

Case Studies

Education provides for a trained labor force and gives unity and identity to nation-states, qualities needed for individual and national progress (Benavot, 1992). Educational systems in newly developed nation-states often develop along Western models. But not always! Ramirez and Boli argue that economic competition between states has caused the pressure for all nations to organize educational systems in similar ways, leading to the universality of state schooling and similarities between systems. Pressures from the economically integrated and dependent developed world have caused newer nations to commit themselves to state-funded mass educational models as part of nation building (Ramirez and Boli, 1987). Commonalities in national curricula exemplify this trend.

The worldwide trends in education include increased enrollments; the establishment of educational ministries; compulsory education laws; increasing state funds; educational opportunity for all, including women and minorities; and schools serving the purpose of socializing agents for the nation.

Despite this world interrelationship, social scientists must be cautious not to assume that all systems are similar because of cross-national pressures and dominant powers. Even though education may be influenced by colonial models and world trends (Archer, 1987), each system brings its own country's unique culture into education. As discussed in Chapter 11, some nations or groups within nations actively resist adopting Western models.

Women's opportunities for education are increasing in most parts of the world.

In the following case examples we see both the similarities and the differences in educational systems. These case studies represent systems that fall into different sectors (see Figure 11–8) of Williamson's (1979) political-economic typology. Britain is located in the economically developed countries' sector, with a political system more clearly capitalistic than socialistic in orientation. China represents a system in the socialist tradition. Finally, Ghana, a former colony of Britain, is economically dependent and developing along capitalistic political lines.

Discussions of each country will include the historical background leading up to the present system; the national goals for the educational system; structural aspects of education, such as the number of years of schooling and type of curriculum; equality or inequality in the educational system; and higher education.

EDUCATION IN BRITAIN

Development of Education in Britain

Britain is the land of monarchy, peerages and nobility, pomp and circumstance, a land that once ruled one-third of the world. It is also a land that was devastated by two world wars, that experienced extreme poverty in the wake of industrial prosperity, and that has a legacy of immigrants from former colonies who have moved to Britain and must be educated and integrated into the society.

Britain was one of the early industrialized and urbanized countries. The process of creating an educational system took place gradually, aided by a mobile peasantry able to provide the needed labor, and by an international trade market anxious to buy goods. During this evolution, the rigid class structure in Britain was strengthened and was reflected in the educational system.

Marxist interpreters have described the development of education in Britain as serving the needs of the elite. An educated mass was needed for the expansion of capitalism, with a trained labor force for various levels of industry. Morality, obedience, and frugality could be taught through the schools, and these goals were reflected in curricula. The subordination of the lower orders had several aims—political control, the suppression of crime and drunkenness, the propagation of Christian morality, and preparing the lower orders for a life of industry and toil (Williamson, 1979, p. 55).

As the working classes grew and became more organized, they demanded greater access to education, among other rights. This was to the advantage of the elite, who needed an ever more sophisticated and skilled labor force. First, secondary education opened to the working class, and compulsory attendance, beginning at age five, was eventually extended to age 11. Parents were and are required to see that their children receive an education for this period. After five years of secondary education, about age 16, students take the General Certificate of Secondary Education.

During the period after World War II, education was free for all—even university, if one qualified. But the school divisions still perpetuated class distinctions: grammar schools; secondary comprehensive schools with academic programs; and secondary technical schools representing trade-training programs. Increased access to higher education took place in the 1960s with the establishment of additional universities, polytechnics and "red-brick universities" (now part of the university system), colleges, and the Open University for those who might not otherwise be able to attend an institution of higher education.

The official goals for British education, as stated in the Education Reform Act of 1988 and other education acts which have followed, are to raise standards at all ability levels; give parents a wider choice of schools and improve the partnership between schools and parents; make further and higher education more economically relevant and available to larger numbers; and obtain good value for money from the educational service as a whole (Education in Britain, 1995).

Education for the elite and middle class is a different matter. English "public schools," similar to private schools in many countries and too expensive for the commoner, served those who wished to retain a social distinction, and they still do. These schools provide both excellent academic foundations and also training in the art of being "ladies and gentlemen," fostering the mannerisms and speech patterns typical of the elite. They give the well-rounded education necessary to pass entrance exams for elite universities such as Oxford and Cambridge. A large number of senior civil servants and business and professional leaders were and are drawn from these schools, although highly qualified students from lower classes have some chance to attend elite schools as scholarship students.

Because of high unemployment, especially among the young who leave school at age 16, two-year, "postcompulsory," sixth-form education, or "A-levels," prepares young adults for a vocation or to continue college training. Work-study plans also have been proposed. There are government-sponsored training programs, but only a small proportion of those in need can be accommodated. Thus, large numbers of youth are leaving school disillusioned and with little hope of employment.

Control and Decision Making in Education

Historically, local control has been valued in Britain, and it still is. The 1988 Education Reform Act, however, gave control to the national government to carry out national research and planning, recommend major revisions in the structure of education, and determine the basic national curriculum. Students are required to take a nationally mandated curriculum. The day-to-day decisions and running of the school are retained by local communities through the Local Education Authorities (LEA); these bodies have wide-ranging power and duties. Each school has a governing body ideally consisting of equal numbers of local authority representatives, school staff including the head teacher, elected parents, students in older classes, and community representatives. LEAs have responsibility for the management of schools and the proper conduct of administrators. Both county (state-supported) and voluntary (usually church) schools are under the jurisdiction of LEAs. Teachers feel the changes in less autonomy at the local level and more paperwork with assessment of students required by the government (Poppleton, Gershunsky, and Pullin, 1994, p. 346).

Structure of the Educational System

State-supported British infant and primary schools have received a great deal of attention, and they have provided models for many elementary schools in the United States and around the world. The widely read Plowden Report, Children and Their Primary Schools (Central Advisory Council for Education, 1967), detailed a system of British primary education; these schools are noted for their informal and open approaches to education. The visitor to a British primary school has the feeling of entering a child's world. From the ceiling hang mobiles; the walls are covered with artwork; books and educational toys line the walls. Classroom activities are minimally structured, with emphasis on individualized work. Curricula include plenty of active time, music, art, time for special projects, and a range of opportunities for TV education, theater trips, and museum visits.

The structural levels of British education have been undergoing changes in recent years at the upper-secondary and higher-education levels. Comprehensive schools were formed in the 1970s to counter the streaming of children into elite and working-class schools. They combine what were formerly grammar (more academic) and secondary-modern schools. Today 3.7 million children attend secondary schools, some of which specialize in technology, language, sports, or the arts. Approximately 10 percent of high school students go to "public" schools (Whitaker, 1999). Within secondary schools there may be some differentiation between students on the basis of academic versus vocational tracks, but the stated goal is to identify talent and allow children to develop their capabilities.

"Public" schools—such as Eton, Harrow, Rugby, Winchester, and other elite secondary schools—serve a unique role. Eton, for instance, is set in a small town a short distance from Windsor Castle. The young men can be seen walking purposefully, surrounded by stately old buildings resonant with English tradition. "You are destined to be a statesman and gentleman," Eton seems to suggest to its inhabitants. Following rigid rituals and ceremonies and dressed in their uniform of black-and-white pin-striped trousers, white bow ties, black vests and waistcoats, and braided tailcoat, an Eton lad would never be mistaken for a comprehensive school student (London Sunday Times Magazine, 1980, p. 94).

Composition of British Schools

In 1999, there were almost 60 million people in the United Kingdom (including Northern Ireland), an area the size of the state of Oregon. Of this population, 8.9 million were schoolchildren attending approximately 30,500 secondary schools and 2,500 independent schools; nursery and primary students accounted for 5.2 million students. About 1.5 million students age 16 and older are full-time students or "sandwich" students, both working and going to school. (For Europe as a whole, this is a relatively low number of students attending school at this age.)

The Education Reform Act of 1988 reflects international pressures for change. The primary impact is that all schools are to follow a common curriculum, prescribed by law, in ten subjects: English, mathematics, science, technology, a modern foreign language, history, geography, art, music, and physical education (Davies, 1991, p. 28). The national Department of Education, which determines the national curricula, published new subject criteria in 1995 and new syllabi in 1998; these outline the objectives for each course, the content, and assessment measures. The guidelines also provide the basis for the General Certificate of Secondary Education (GCSE) exam that all students take before they leave school.

Effective schools in Britain share many characteristics with effective schools in other countries. A study conducted in London singled out characteristics of effective primary schools: small school and class size, teacher planning periods and involvement in curriculum planning, lesson plans, progress reports on each child, low turnover of all school personnel and students, and an orderly work environment (Mortimore et al., 1988).

Exams and Credentials

Britain is a highly "credentialed" society, placing great emphasis on exams and certificates. It also claims a 99 percent literacy rate. Exams are given in subject areas. At about age 16, students take the GCSE exam in major subjects such as mathematics and literature; following two more years of study, students take Advanced or A-level exams. Between these two are the AS exams, equivalent to two General Certificate of Education exams or one A-level exam. Universities generally require three A-level exams for entrance (Whitaker, 2000).

There is yet another very prestigious exam—the International Baccalaureate—taken by sixth-form (16- to 18-year-old) students and requiring competence in six subject areas: one's native language, a foreign language, the study of man (history, geography, social science, or philosophy), experimental science, mathematics, and an art or advanced work in one area.

Critics argue that those who can afford the "elite" education are best prepared for A-levels and elite-university entrance exams, and that the exam system helps perpetuate the class system.

Inequality in Education and Occupational Mobility

Several British sociologists have written about the resistance to schooling found among some young British adolescents. This "counterculture of resistance" among working-class males in particular is seen in patterns of behavior—dress, truancy, smoking, vandalism, rudeness—and represents their view that school is irrelevant to the life they will enter (Lees, 1994, p. 86; Willis, 1983; Corrigan, 1979). Great strides have been made toward providing opportunity for students of all social backgrounds to move as far as possible in the educational system. However, there are at least two kinds of problems encountered in this endeavor. The Plowden Report and more recent studies point up the special problems of deprived neighborhoods such as inner-city areas where health and housing standards are low and child mortality high. Living in these areas are many from immigrant groups and those who fall into the poorest classes of society. The Plowden Report recommended that schools in these blighted areas be given extra funds from the 7 percent national educational budget, though the report also said that educational disadvantage cannot be solved in schools alone (Garner, 1991, p. 251).

Another problem inhibiting mobility is the distinction between "public" schools and state-supported schools. With the tradition behind the elite schools and the excellent education they provide, plus the tendency for elite universities and government and industry to fill their top ranks with graduates of these schools, mobility at the top remains the prerogative of a limited, select group. Education reflects the history and traditions built up over long periods in Britain. Complete equality seems impossible without altering the basic structure of the educational system.

What does educational inequality mean for occupational attainment? Depending on the measures used, we can generally say that one's class origins are more important in Britain than in the United States in occupational attainment. In the United States, educational attainment is more important, especially for one's first job placement (Kerckhoff, 1989). Though the process of career mobility in the two countries differs, the degree of openness or mobility is about the same when we look at occupational status 10 to 20 years after labor force entry.

Higher Education in Great Britain: Elite versus Mass Education

Oxford and Cambridge universities—prestigious institutions with spires, courtyards, and long traditions—have been the models for educational systems around the world. Classical, traditional education can be obtained from robed dons behind the cloistered walls. Students are affiliated with a college in the university.

For centuries these universities provided access to high positions and perpetuated the intellectual elite. With the worldwide trend toward more access to all levels of education by all groups in society, and the need for a more educated populace to fill the technical positions in an industrialized society, several changes have occurred: The great universities opened their doors a crack to let in larger numbers of qualified students from state-supported schools, and other institutes and colleges were developed to meet growing needs for trained personnel. University access is still limited, and children of professionals stand a much better chance of acceptance than do those from lower socioeconomic levels. The government, however, is expanding access to many universities for the three-year degree courses; the goal was to have 31 to 33 percent of the 18- and 19-year-olds in one of the 88 institutions of higher education, and in 1998, 34 percent were enrolled (Whitaker, 2000). Institutions of higher education give access to those who fail university entrance exams for the most prestigeous universities or who wish to pursue specialized studies. There are also differences in treatment of female and male faculty at universities. In 1991, women were paid an average of $3,520 less than men, regardless of age and discipline ("Female Professors in Britain," 1991, p. A46).

A number of polytechnics were developed, beginning in 1966, to meet the need for trained engineers, technical experts, and technicians. They are closely associated with business and industry. Another development in British higher education is the Open University. Begun in 1971 to give opportunities to people who might not otherwise be able to attend university (e.g., teachers, those working, those at home) the idea caught on to the extent that, by 1976, the Open University received about 53,000 applications and was enrolling up to 20,000 students a year. The Open University currently enrolls about 24,500 new students a year, including 5,900 master's and 625 doctoral students (Walker, 1991, p. A25). Open University students pay tuition and sign up for courses. They tune in to lectures on British Broadcasting Corporation (BBC) radio or TV. Texts are developed for the courses, and assignments are sent to tutors who correct and return them. At the end of the year students take examinations. A wide range of courses are offered through the Open University, with most degrees being given in general arts and science. The average student takes six years to complete a degree, compared with three or four years for students in residence on a campus, and the dropout rate is higher than at campuses.

The number of Open University students is growing rapidly as the program enters its third decade; it enrolled 95,000 undergraduates in 1996, 50 percent of whom were women. Open University has graduated well over 100,000 students, mostly adult homemakers and full-time employees wishing to upgrade credentials (Walker, 1991).

Part of the recent growth in higher-education enrollments is because of reduced job opportunities in society. Changes being initiated to help cope with the increased demand are familiar: larger classes, use of teaching assistants, and availability of intensive "24-month degrees" in some fields of study that normally take three years to complete (Walker, 1991, p. A51). In the future, Britain will face pressures to open its educational system further and provide opportunities for the many unemployed working-class and immigrant members of society.

EDUCATION IN THE PEOPLE'S REPUBLIC OF CHINA

China's closed-door policy kept the West out for many years. In recent years, however, China has opened its doors again to the West. This huge country's population in 1999 was more than 1,246,872,000 and is estimated to reach more than 1.5 billion by 2025. The territory covers almost a quarter of the world's land surface. Its Communist government officials are selectively allowing its officials and scholars to make forays into the world outside and now admit both curious tourists and foreign scholars into its vast reaches. In fact, the second largest number of foreign students in the United States are now from China (*The Chronicle of Higher Education Almanac*, 1999, p. 29).

Recent Historical Events Affecting Education

Several key dates mark major transitions in China: In 1949, the Chinese Communist Party won national power and declared the founding of the People's Republic of China. At this time the borders closed to the outside world. China closed 2,200 private schools, about 4 percent of the nation's schools. In 1976, Chairman Mao (Mao Tse-tung) died; this event ushered in a new era of changing policies and programs and opened China's borders to the outside world. Since the adoption of market socialism in 1978, more than 60,000 private schools have reemerged. These are referred to as "society-run" or "people-run" schools and are privately owned proprietary institutions with few government ties (Kwong, 1997).

In 1989, protests led by university students were forcefully repressed, and contacts with Western countries were curtailed. The situation has eased recently. Though the Chinese have some suspicions about the motivations of Westerners, most exchanges have returned to prerevolution levels. Social science research, however, has been restricted because of China's suspicions that the West is spying on China's social situation ("Chinese Academy Considering New Restrictions," 1991, p. A27).

No period can be ignored in reviewing Chinese education; each has been a reaction to the previous era, yet each reflects the changing political-economic scene of that time.

The Drive Toward Modernization

China's Confucian educational legacy has served the interests of China's power elite with its subtle underlying antiegalitarian political ideology, justifying elite privileged education (Hayhoe, 1992). But in recent years, the growing realization of the need to modernize has gained popularity; in addition, there has been a realization that national development and modernization go hand in hand with basic education for all. Fundamentally, education is "intended to meet basic learning needs": foundation-level education, early childhood and primary education, literacy, and general knowledge and life skills ("Meeting Basic Learning Needs," 1990, p. ix). China has made some progress on population literacy. The issue has become how to mediate between competing views and modernization.

Tensions exist between four competing purposes of education in China: "to modernize the economy, to provide sources for education as a universal citizen right, to establish paths for the recruitment and circulation of elites, and to share a political ideology that reformulates varying political interests" (Robinson, 1991, p. 177). The move to modernize has come from both internal sources and external forces: the international context, market forces, and sensitivity to social and political demands (Law, 1995) are all believed to be necessary for growth and prosperity (Hayhoe, 1992).

Deng Xiaoping became leader of China in 1977, and with his leadership the Communist ideology was reinterpreted and economic changes put in motion. Western technology and management techniques were introduced to speed up modernization. With these changes came reform of the educational system.

Some degree of decentralized educational authority and reduction in rigid central governmental policies is needed at all levels of the educational system for modernization reforms to take place (Du, 1992). The central government is giving more autonomy to communities and to private schools, a necessity for reform. Of private schools started in the late 1980s, about half are trade schools and half academic; they are responding to the demand for education that cannot be met by the government, and they do meet part of that need. Though the government believes it should control all education, it also realizes it cannot meet all needs and has allowed the private schools to be established. These schools are not ethnic or religious, but are for-profit in the market socialism system.

Educational systems reproduce, maintain, and perpetuate the existing social order, especially where they are government controlled. However, when the society is in transition, the education system will experience change as well. The Chinese government faces several dilemmas: how much decentralization the Communist government can allow, the potential "brain drain" from allowing scholars to travel abroad, and the methods used to teach students such as rote memorization—methods not conducive to preparing decision makers for modernization (Hayhoe, 1992). Decentralization is creating a latent effect—elitism—with those who can afford private education receiving it (Kwong, 1997). Scholars studying and traveling abroad are bringing back new ideas, and preparing teachers and students for the competitive world market requires new techniques (Kelly and Liu, 1998).

Who receives the best educations in China has been shaped by political processes, and these processes have differed over time depending on who was in power and the policies of that group. Sometimes family status mattered and sometimes political priorities mattered. Immediately following the Cultural Revolution, having a father with high-rank status was a significant positive, though all schooling was limited during this time. At other times family status was not significant or was of benefit to those in favor. In the period from 1978 to 1994, China experienced increased educational inequality with rapid economic growth and reform. The rise of private schools, for instance, has given access to those with money. Those who are benefiting most from changes are urban residents from high-ranking cadres, professionals, and men (Zhou, Moen, and Tuma, 1998).

Status and Structure of Education in China

A typical day in a Chinese elementary school includes courses in Chinese, math, physical education, music, drawing, painting, and moral (political) education. Language study takes up to one-third of the day. The day starts with an exercise period, followed by four periods in the morning. There is a two-hour break for lunch and rest, followed by three more periods. After school, which ends about 4:00 P.M., some students stay for special help. After school on Saturday morning there are organized activities such as sports (Hauser, 1990, pp. 44–45). Foreign language study begins in third grade; history, geography, and science begin in fourth through sixth grade. Classes range in size from 40 to 55 students.

According to Chinese statistics, 98 percent of primary-age children, 136 million students, attend 646,000 primary schools (Turner, 2000). Forty percent of secondary-age children attend school, with boys outnumbering girls by a small percentage (The World Bank, 1990, pp. 234–35). About 3.2 million students attend institutions of higher education at 1,032 institutions, one-third in engineering. These students compete for scholarships to pay for their education.

China is also concerned about improving adult literacy, believing this is essential for economic growth (Stites and Semali, 1991). As far back as 1949, Chairman Mao said:

> Sweeping away illiteracy from 80 percent of the population is an important mission for New China. We must work energetically to realize this goal, so that workers and peasants can easily grasp scientific learning [and] become weapons for [class] struggle and [socialist] construction—complete and developed weapons for the people's democratic dictatorship. (Stites and Semali, 1991, p. 73)

His goal has been accomplished, with an 82 percent literacy rate. Schools in China have been the site for political indoctrination (Kwong, 1988), and at times the secondary curriculum focused on industrial and agricultural courses.

Authority structures in Chinese schools are based on personal ties and networks and on loyalty to authority and the political system. Because the party leadership perceived weaknesses in education that could prevent modernization, structural changes are taking place in the educational system. These include the growing importance of local districts' obtaining their own financial resources for schools, expansion of vocational and technical learning, and demands for new teaching techniques to improve creativity and independence (Delany and Paine, 1991). "The political climate of the early 1990s formally reasserts the authority of the Party, including its role in running the schools. Yet the economic and demographic pressures that prompted changes in authority relations have not subsided" (Delany and Paine, 1991, p. 43).

Recent changes in government policy concerning education muddle the picture. For instance, with the move toward individual rather than collective responsibility has come an emphasis on rural self-sufficiency, including local funding of rural schools. But many children have left school to participate in individual family money making ventures.

Higher Education in PRC

Chinese higher education dates back more than 3,000 years; before modern time it was dominated by Confucian ideas and served primarily to prepare government officials. China has long held the belief that education and the economy are integrally linked. Hence, most changes have reflected this belief and current thinking along these lines. Higher education is undergoing radical change, with increased emphasis on science, applied research, foreign languages, the emergence of business schools, and restructuring of the management of education in the form of a Western model of scientific management. How long these measures will last is uncertain in the rapidly changing environment of Chinese education.

During the Cultural Revolution the Ministry of Education in China was dismantled; it was reestablished in 1975. Major changes began in 1976, with the separation of politics and higher-education decision making—putting education in the hands of academics, the Ministry, and local committees. The Ministry controlled programs, curricula, and admissions. In May 1985, a State Council Education Commission replaced the Ministry to allow for closer regional control and to reflect the needs of regions (Kwong, 1987).

Universities have been under the strictest controls and intense political indoctrination since restrictions after the fall of the Maoist Gang of Four in 1976 (Sautman, 1991). Since the rebellious "counterrevolutionaries" protested at Tiananmen Square, students have been required to study ideology and be repoliticized (Robinson, 1991). First-year students at Beijing University are required to serve in the military for one year ("Forcing Bejing University Students," 1991, p. A51). Unhappy students have been sent to remote factories to gain socialist experience (Lubman, 1990, p. A37). In recent years, the State Education Commission and "president's responsibility" at institutions have made reform more possible; reform of higher education has focused on two areas of concern: management and structure, and curriculum and instruction (Du, 1992). This involves increasing the credentials of faculty and expanding access to higher education. For instance, in 1995 higher education served about 3.5 percent of university-age students. By the year 2000, that number was close to 8 percent, with rapid increases predicted thereafter. Again, economic, social, and political changes in China have stimulated the new State Education Commission's comprehensive plan (Hayhoe, 1995, p. 299), and private institutions are increasing opportunity for higher education.

Emphasis on applied research has led to a professorate concerned with contract research more than pure research or teaching. Some have pointed out the danger of this shortcoming. Joint university projects with other countries, such as the United States, Canada, Japan, and Western Europe, are often initiated by the Chinese and generally involve mutual sharing and respect rather than control by the industrialized nations; yet there is concern that the "foreigners" do not understand the culture with which they are interacting (Hayhoe, 1986).

Efforts to contain Western influence take the form of curtailed exchanges, often available only after five years of work; repoliticalization programs; and limits on the type of research allowed. The government is trying to seek a balance between the need for scholars and Western knowledge, and the need for loyalty and indoctrination; one still sees patterns of patron-client relations, where political rulers offer prestige, privilege, and protection in return for support from scholars ("Forcing Beijing University Students," 1991). It remains to be seen whether allowing intellectuals freedom to pursue their research is compatible with repressing independence and democracy.

China has had a period of independence from the influence of other nations; however, much of Africa labors under a colonial legacy that has major implications for education.

FORMAL EDUCATION IN COLONIAL AFRICA

In the nineteenth and early twentieth centuries, Europeans conquered most of Africa. Ostensibly the purposes were ending the slave trade, spreading Christianity and civilization, and opening the area for trade. Hardly mentioned were the expansion to new lands and the wealth of raw products that the colonial powers enjoyed.

Early in the colonial period, missionaries set up schools to teach Christianity and Bible studies. Colonial governments also organized schools according to the mother country's system of education. Their purpose was to teach the language of the colonizing power and develop a cadre of Africans to help fill lower posts in colonial administration, as well as to develop understanding and acceptance of European-style law and order. Many Europeans wanted to limit African education to technical, vocational, and agricultural skills, which would be helpful to them in exploiting the resources of the countries. However, Africans saw this type of training as an attempt to keep them in their places, and they sought the academic education of the

Western elite. Some went abroad to receive this training, with European encouragement.

Those few Africans who moved up the colonial education ladder adopted European views and worked for the colonial administrations. They were often alienated from their own people and traditions, strangers in their own lands. With independence, some of these same European-educated Africans became postcolonial leaders; their proposals were often greeted with skepticism by the people.

History of Ghanaian Education

The Portuguese, the Dutch, the Danes, and then the British ruled the "Gold Coast," as Ghana was called. It was a prize colony, rich in mineral resources and later valued for its cocoa plantations. British rule began in 1820; in the period of their rule from 1844 to 1957, the British developed trade relations with other countries. Thus, when Ghana achieved independence in 1957, it was economically stable and its institutions were based on British models. Since independence, however, several different governments have ruled and been overthrown. In 1961–66 there was a period of rapid expansion of education at all levels in Ghana. After 1966, however, enrollment in public primary schools in many parts of the country declined steadily (McWilliam and Kwamena-Poh, 1975, p. 116).

The early rapid growth was curtailed when a military government took over in 1966. The government ordered a study of the system, which resulted in the following recommendations: "reorganizing and adopting new approaches to teacher training; creating new places at secondary Form I level and strengthening the secondary base in advance of university expansion; and considering the country's needs in the development of technical education" (McWilliam and Kwamena-Poh, 1975, p. 117). Despite the studies and recommendations, however, for many years following 1966 there was little change in the educational system. Political instability led to coups in 1979 and 1981. This could be related to mistrust of the government by the people, the rich-poor division in the population, lack of opportunity, or the government's lack of movement in the area of education. Enrollments peaked at 66.8 percent in 1965 for children from 6 to 11 years old, followed by a drop of almost 14 percent for this age group in a seven-year period to 1972.

In 1974 the government designed an experimental structure for education. Ninety percent of students, however, followed the old system. By 1983 the primary school enrollment during the first six years of school was 79 percent (89 percent of boys, 70 percent of girls); middle schools enrolled 38 percent of the school-age children (48 percent of boys, 28 percent of girls). Elections in both 1992 and 1996 resulted in Jerry Rawlings being selected, providing for a period of stability in a country that has seen its share of political instability. By 1990, 75 percent of primary school students and 39 percent of secondary school students were enrolled in school (Turner, 2000). Approximately 71 percent of boys and 63 percent of girls were enrolled in primary school (40 percent) and in secondary school (32 percent). Only 2 percent went on to higher levels of education; these figures are higher than those for many other African countries (The World Bank, 1990, p. 234).

The illiteracy rate in Africa is 52.7 percent, but for Ghana it is 36 percent (25 percent for men and 47 percent for women). With overwhelming problems of poverty and hunger in much of Africa, increasing the literacy rate has a low priority. Third World countries cannot compete with developed countries, however, if their populations are illiterate. Some countries have had the elimination of illiteracy as part of their educational goals. For instance, in Tanzania, motivation to reduce illiteracy has produced both political and economic goals (Stites and Semali, 1991).

Forms of Education

Education existed in Ghana and other African nations long before modern boundaries and European systems were introduced. It is important to distinguish, therefore, between traditional and formal education in many African countries.

> There were systems of education in Africa before the colonial period; for every community must have a way of passing on to the young its accumulated knowledge to enable them to play adult roles and so ensure the survival of their offspring, and the continuity of the community.
>
> In African communities, the older generation passed on to the young the knowledge, the skills, the mode of behaviour and the beliefs they should have for playing their social roles in adult life.
>
> The young were taught how to cope with their environments; how to farm, or hunt, or fish, or prepare food, or build a house, or run a home. They were taught the language and manners, and generally the culture of the community. The methods were informal, the young learnt by participating in activities alongside their elders. They learnt by listening, by watching, by doing. In many practical ways they learnt how to live as members of their community. (Busia, 1964, p. 5)

Many educators are asking how traditional systems can be used as a base for meeting the educational needs of modernizing countries. Options range from continuing French, English, or other colonial models, to developing completely new indigenous types of education. Formal schooling is still primarily for the urban elite. The question becomes this: What kind of education should be offered in rural peasant communities?

"Nonformal" education and "basic" education have received the attention of many African educators. They are distinguished from "formal school" by the following facts:

1. [Formal] schooling is just a part of education.
2. Education cannot be conceived of as taking place at certain ages, stages, times and places. It is always unfinished business.
3. Educational opportunities, formal and nonformal, must relate to each other both horizontally (e.g., school, home, mosque, media, work experience) and vertically throughout the different stages of a learner's life.
4. There are many paths to learning, no one path being better or worse than another, only more efficient or more appropriate.
5. Methods, materials, and delivery systems must also vary to suit purposes and means available. (Hawes, 1979, p. 163)

"Nonformal" and "basic" education seem to work together. Neither puts age or time strictures on education; both provide many varied paths to education, individual attainment of goals, and lifelong learning; and both involve various agencies—family, school, community. Subjects range from functional literacy to knowledge of processes, such as health and sanitation; crops and animals; and household skills, including caring for the sick, making clothes, and civic knowledge. An attempt at nonformal, grassroots education is seen in the Community Development experiment, which has been tried in several communities. Informal courses or training in preventive medicine, health, nutrition, cooking, sewing, and other skills are made available to any person in the villages. Another example of nonformal education is the Mancell Girls' Vocational Institute in Kumasi for women ages 13 to 28. More than 1,000 students have been enrolled in one-year courses in "skills required for self-development and for jobs in laundry, baking, sewing, dressmaking, designing, and catering" (Sine, 1979). Other programs have been developed to preserve African ways but teach Western thought.

A related curriculum issue has to do with the language used for teaching. If the former colonial power's language is used, some feel that it imposes "linguistic imperialism on the country"; but if a native tongue is used, one group might gain dominance over another. Therefore, several countries are promoting learning for each group in its mother tongue to preserve cultural diversity and avoid conflicts (Akinnaso, 1991, p. 89).

This question remains: Will "basic" or "nonformal" education and mother-tongue teaching meet the needs of individuals and countries, or will their implementation perpetuate the rich-poor dichotomy without significantly raising the developing countries from the poverty level? For many countries, the question is how to maximize development and still preserve national cultures and traditions.

In many Third World countries, such as those in West Africa, international funding agencies have attempted to direct the development of education, as mentioned. However well-intentioned the efforts, these too may cause problems because the policies tend to emphasize agency goals and political agendas rather than country needs.

One example is the World Bank. In the process of carrying out research on development and providing development funding, the development expertise and experience of the organization "manages the creation of knowledge and, in doing so, sets the standards for what has come to be called knowledge production." Some courses of action become favored, others dismissed though they may have merit for the citizens of a country (Samoff, 1993, p. 181).

Structure of the Ghanaian Educational System

Children in Ghana enter school at age six. Some go on to secondary school at age 12, which lasts five years. The stated goal is compulsory education for ten years, but Ghana has a long way to go to achieve that level of schooling.

The subjects taught in secondary schools generally follow the British model: language, mathematics, general science, social studies, religious education, and physical education. The exception is "cultural and practical activities," which focus on African heritage and necessary skills for daily life. Examinations also follow the British model. Institutions for higher education include universities, technical and craft institutes, polytechnics, and vocational school. Vocational training is also provided in some communities outside the formal school setting.

Equality of Opportunity in Ghanaian Education

Sons and daughters of the urban elite have a disproportionate share of places in education as one progresses upward through the system; this includes places as teachers. However, there is now an economic motivation for basic education for all—to be competitive in the world and achieve social equality (Stites, 1991, p. 74).

Families in Ghana, as in other countries, make educational choices for their children based on a number of factors. These include cost to the family, school quality, travel time, and anticipated return on cost. Of those children who enroll in school at the appropriate age and stay in school, those with higher ability do have more opportunity to attend good schools and move ahead (Glewwe, 1994; Glewwe and Jacoby, 1992).

Differences in opportunity for education between the elite and the masses, however, persist in most African countries. In Ghana, these differences are to some extent regional. For instance, in northern Ghana many of the people have never been to school. One final point on the topic of equality: Ability to speak the English language has become a potent force of "academic colonialism," separating the educated elite from the rural illiterate (Sherman 1990, p. 363).

Although each African system is unique, some general observations apply to many postcolonial countries. Education was seen as a high priority following independence from colonial control, for it was thought that, through education, countries could become truly independent of foreign domination and provide the indigenous leadership needed for technological development, industrialization, business, and politics in the long push toward modernization. The educated elite of these countries could afford to send their children abroad, where they often pursued prestigious fields such as engineering or law (but also Greek and Latin, less directly useful in modernizing a country). Returning students brought with them not only their expertise but also foreign ideologies and models for curricula. However, the development of technical and agricultural skills, emphasis on preventive medicine within the context of traditional tribal medicine, and integration of new knowledge with existing values and traditions may be more relevant to the needs of the nations than European models of education.

Some members of the African elite rejected their own countries' traditional values, cultural uniqueness, and tribal ties in favor of Western models. Others became dissatisfied and alienated because they were overeducated for the available jobs. There is high prestige in being a lawyer or an engineer, but a developing country can absorb only a limited number of them. It might be better able to use schoolteachers and agricultural technicians.

Higher Education

Africa has many fine universities, some of which have difficulty integrating their programs into life on the continent (Sherman, 1990, p. 363). Others offer a combination of indigenous and Western education. For instance, Ghana has two universities with 11,225 students; the University of Ghana at Accra offers some excellent programs in traditional African arts, music, dance, and oral traditions in literature, as well as courses of study patterned after European models. In Nigeria, the plan is to improve the technological base by providing an appropriate mix of students, with 60 percent in sciences and 40 percent in arts, but reality is far from these figures. Some universities are centers of political activity, spearheading prodemocracy drives that sometimes result in violence (Morna, 1990, pp. A1, 40). Meanwhile, a high percentage of university graduates are disillusioned because they cannot find jobs (Chuta, 1986).

Several problems plague many African universities. In a report on higher education in sub-Saharan Africa, the experts reviewing the situation found rapidly growing enrollments and demand for higher education, poor revenue and expenditure patterns, declining quality, and insufficient relevance to needs of the countries being served; the results were systems severely strained. The report makes suggestions that directly address these problems (Saint, 1992; United Nations Development Program, 1992).

In the future, African leaders searching for ways to improve standards of living will be looking at new models of education. Although political factors may prevent rapid changes in educational systems, there is greater awareness of the problems, and alternative educational models are becoming more prevalent.

The three systems discussed in this chapter, the United Kingdom, China, and Ghana and other former colonial African countries, fit into three quadrants of the Williamson's political-economic model discussed in Chapter 11. Whether we divide the countries of the world into these political-economic quadrants, or core and periphery countries, or northern and southern, or rich and poor, or postindustrial and agricultural, or developed and developing, the fact remains that children are receiving very different educations and are prepared for very different lives. Most children around the world receive some formal education, but the amount and circumstances vary greatly depending on the country's culture and place in the world political-economic system.

◆ Summary

All countries provide some form of education to their citizens. These forms differ depending on the level of development and other issues facing government.

I. Education in Britain

Education in Britain originated to prepare the elite to lead. With the need for skilled workers, education filtered to the masses, first as training for trades, and eventually as primary and secondary schooling for everyone. Though elite "public schools" still prepare a select group of students, opportunities for most young people have increased greatly at all levels of education.

II. Education in the People's Republic of China

Beginning with the Confucious philosophy, education has always been valued in the PRC. During the Cultural Revolution in 1949, the educational system was in shambles. By the 1970s, education was under firm government control and had spread throughout the country. One recent change has been in the number of private schools that have been created to fill a demand for education, especially higher education. Today China claims 82 percent literacy in its vast territories and is increasingly establishing educational links with other countries.

III. Formal Education in Colonial Africa

Formal education in colonial Africa was established and controlled by European colonists. With independence, African countries have had to struggle with what type of education is best for their varied cultures. In some cases the new hybrid educational systems are combinations of European and indigenous systems. Ghana is a case in point. The discussion traces issues and problems faced by Ghana in establishing a modern educational system that meets both internal needs and prepares Ghanaians for the future.

◆ Putting Sociology to Work

1. Interview someone from another country about their educational system: its history, access and equity, funding, curriculum, and preparation of the population for the twenty-first century.
2. In this chapter you have read about the experience of Ghana as a former colonial country. Read about another former colonial country and compare the differences.
3. Some countries have centralized control of education (China). Others allow more local control of schools (United States and Britain). What are the advantages and disadvantages of each?
4. Chapter 12 does not provide an example of a country falling into the fourth quadrant—socialist and developed. Research the educational system in a country in this quadrant.

CHAPTER 13

Educational Movements and Reform

Which school is more effective: a traditional school, with stress on basic skills and discipline; or an alternative "open" school, with freedom of movement, less structural rigidity, and greater student participation in decision making? In which school would you learn the most: one with group instruction and students progressing through the same material at the same rate, or one with individual instruction and students progressing at their individual rates? These kinds of questions underlie this chapter on educational movements and reform.

Since the early 1980s, numerous commissions, task forces, and individuals have produced documents lamenting the condition of education in the United States and arguing the need for reform. States have followed suit with hundreds of reports and proposals for reform, many of which are in operation. One notable area is in that of accountability; more than 35 states now require prospective teachers to pass a test before entering the classroom, and many others require students to pass achievement tests at various levels before they can move to the next level or be graduated. As you read, consider how the major educational movements discussed have affected your own educational experience. Such movements are common in countries that lack centralization of decision making in the educational system because influencing education at the local level is easier. Each school district has ultimate jurisdiction over its own educational decision making, a factor that encourages many points of view on education. The United

States takes pride in local control of schools, a plan originated to take into account the diverse local population needs. Countries with more centralized educational decision making and more homogeneous populations have less diversity in educational programs and fewer popular movements for change.

In recent years, demands for accountability and court cases on desegregation, censorship, separation of church and state, and financing have led U.S. state legislatures and boards of education to play a greater role in educational decisions that affect the local level. Societal attitudes swing like a pendulum, from right to left and back again (see Figure 13–1). Education is but one area of society, and the educational pendulum reflects broad societal trends, movements, and attitudes as we shall find in our discussion of movements.

Theoretical approaches also enter into an understanding of movements. Some conflict theorists argue that attempts by conservatives and minority groups to stress basics will only widen the gap in the opportunity structure. The argument is this: The more fundamentals, rigidity, and discipline the schools stress, the more compliant will be the future laborers. This in turn perpetuates the unequal class structure by creating a well-trained workforce—exactly what those in power need to perpetuate the class differences. Conflict theorists argue that only a restructuring of the obsolete educational and economic systems can lead to expansion of the opportunity ladder. If one accepts this theory, it seems ironic that many persons in those very groups that would be most hurt by stress on basics and discipline—minorities—are among those pushing for changes in this direction.

The role of schools in preparing young people for the workplace has been in the forefront of educational reform movements, and there is a correspondence between schools and workplaces. However, conflict theorists are concerned that schools are controlled by the state; schools also produce the workers for the capitalistic system. Strong democratic social movements for equal opportunity in schools and society can help counter what conflict theorists see as reproduction of the social class system (Carnoy and Levin, 1986).

The view of functionalist theorists is very different. They believe that more stress on basics, discipline, and accountability will help people achieve a niche in the competitive society. Education in the basics would provide oppor-

FIGURE 13–1 The pendulum of attitudes swings from right to left and back.

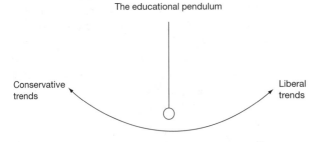

The educational pendulum

Conservative trends

Liberal trends

tunity, even though it is unlikely to create a fundamental change in the stratification system of society.

THE NATURE OF EDUCATIONAL MOVEMENTS

Systems change because of constant internal and external pressures from many sources. Figure 13–2 notes some sources of change in educational systems. You can undoubtedly think of more.

When change is brought about in one system or subsystem of society, such as education or politics, it will affect other systems. Social movements are one major indication of the direction in which a society is moving and of the constant pressure for change on parts of the system.

The concept of social movement has been used to refer to numerous collective efforts for change—women's rights movement, civil rights movement, prohibition movement, antiwar movement, right-to-life movement. Movements arise because large groups of people are dissatisfied with existing conditions. They focus on a general guiding ideology or philosophy, a strong idealism and dedication to this ideology on the part of adherents, and some form of action.

There has never been a time when all members of a society were content with the society or its educational system. The supporters of a movement are generally attempting to bring about or resist some change in society; their motives for involvement in a movement vary from idealism to the personal satisfaction of belonging to a group of believers and having a "cause." Problems in society may first come to light because of a growing social movement. If a movement "catches

FIGURE 13–2 Sources of change in the school system.

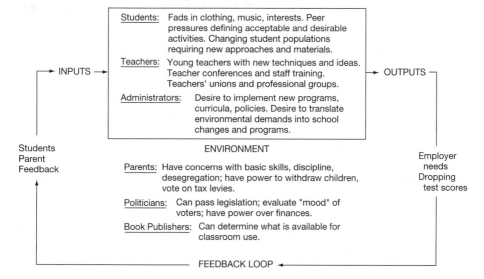

on" and attracts large numbers of adherents, it is likely to have a direct impact on the existing system. It often starts out as a small fringe group bucking the general trends; with the development of leadership and a communication network such as a newsletter, and with the attention of the media, more people are attracted to the movement. Eventually ideas from the movement may be adopted by schools or other institutions and become "institutionalized," that is, accepted as integral parts of society. Some social movements attract few followers and eventually die. These are often groups pushing for ideas that are not easily integrated into the existing system. Any large social movement is likely to include splinter groups or smaller groups of reformers or radicals supporting specific, related ideologies and causing internal dissent as supporters quarrel over means and ends.

Movements may be organized, or they may be unstructured and without clear leadership, as in the case of the counterculture movement from which free schools were spawned. However, individuals or books presenting common threads or ideologies, such as the desire for individuality and freedom, hold movements together. Leaders who have written influential books that generate and espouse the movements' philosophy and ideological bases provide common focal points.

Several typologies of movements have been constructed. Following is a summary of those types of social movements most relevant to our discussion:

1. *Reform movements* believe that certain reforms are necessary, usually in specific areas of society.
2. *Regressive movements* aim to "put the clock back," reverse current trends, and return to a former state of affairs.
3. *Revolutionary movements* are deeply dissatisfied with the existing order and seek to reorganize society.
4. *Utopian movements* include "loosely constructed collectivities that envision a radically changed and blissful state," such as the 1960s counterculture movement. (Robertson, 1989, pp. 383–84)

From the counterculture movement of the 1960s emerged the free school movement. This movement developed as a reaction to structured, authoritarian schools and led to the development of schools with freedom of choice and little structure. Initially, this was a fairly isolated, utopian movement. As more people learned about it and its ideology, several things happened (see Figure 13–3). (1) Some were attracted and joined. (2) Others were intrigued, but rather than join the movement and give up their positions in the society or educational system, they adopted a middle-ground or compromise position and accepted some ideas that could be adapted to fit within the existing system without major structural change. These people acted as change agents in what now took on reform movement elements. (3) The educational system faced pressures from the educational movements without, and from persons within who wished to adopt the movements' ideas.

Demands for change range from "throw the whole system out and start over" to "there is always room for reform within the existing framework." Most

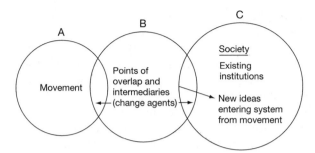

FIGURE 13–3 Educational movements can bring about change in systems.

educational policymakers take a cautious middle ground when it comes to changes because gradual change makes planning and adaptation possible without much disruption to the existing system. However, this approach appears unresponsive to some who want major structural and ideologic change.

Caution must be exercised in using the label "movement" when referring to very specific or short-term changes. For example, many technological "fads" such as reading machines, talking typewriters, and programmed texts brought about significant structural change in many schools, but they would probably not be considered movements. They might be subsumed under a larger "movement" such as "classroom technologies."

The purposes of the remainder of this chapter are twofold: to stress the impact of educational movements on school systems, and to discuss some major educational movements that have influenced education in the United States. Because the ideology behind education helps determine its structure, functioning, and change in the system, an understanding of these major movements is important.

*A*pplying *Sociology to Education:* What are some specific examples of sources of change in the schools in your district? ◆

EDUCATIONAL MOVEMENTS THROUGHOUT HISTORY

Early European Education: Purpose and Function for Society

Education has always been a part of a society's way of acculturating its young, of teaching a child to become a member of a society. Education is both informal and formal: It is informal in that a child learns the ways of his or her culture by being a member immersed and participating in that society; it is formal in that a child is taught by a teacher about certain aspects of his or her culture in a specific place, such as a school.

In ancient Greece and Rome, boys (seldom girls) were educated by wandering teachers called *Sophists* who taught youngsters the skills needed to develop their reasoning power and rhetoric; that is, the art of persuasion. This "formal" education met the needs of the society and times. Philosophers and great teachers such as Socrates, his student Plato, and Aristotle are still studied for their concepts of the educated person, freedom of thought, and rational inquiry.

After the fall of the Roman Empire and the decline of the ancient, classical civilization, formal education was found in only a few places, such as religious institutions. Many towns in Europe had monastic schools that conducted elementary education, but at the secondary level, only monasteries offered any kind of educational opportunities. Societies at this time did not rely on a formally educated class to perform necessary functions. Education of a formal type, however, could be found at the castles of great lords where young knights were trained in the skills of military tactics and the code of chivalry. Also, merchant and craft guilds maintained means of instructing apprentices for trade. Universities evolved during the Middle Ages.

One influence from the education of the Middle Ages on today's educational movements is the concept of human depravity. Because lust was considered a sin, all children were conceived in sin and, thus, were born depraved. Early religious leaders, such as St. Augustine, and later John Calvin and Martin Luther, stressed that corruptive weakness could be corrected by a strong teacher who used authoritarian methods. Similarly, in the early colonies of New England "Old Deluder Satan Acts" were legislated to save children from the temptation of straying from the faith. Many today still advocate the use of authoritarian methods in the classroom.

During the Renaissance in Europe the concept of the well-rounded and liberally educated person was developed. There was great interest in the humanistic aspects of Greek and Latin classics. In contrast to the sectarian education of the Reformation, with its God-centered worldview, the secular education of the Renaissance focused on the earthly experience of human beings. These views continue to influence curriculum movements, especially in higher education, which focuses on developing well-rounded students.

Another period of European history that had an effect on American education was the Enlightenment of the eighteenth century. It was believed that people could improve their lives by reason, by using their minds to solve problems; education would enable society to progress toward a new and better world, and schools were believed to be instruments for cultivating the reasoning powers of youth.

Educational Movements in the United States

The Public School Movement. Until the early nineteenth century, many children in the United States attended only primary schools. Schools at the secondary level were for the elite children, who were sent there to prepare for university, which would lead to occupations in the church or in commerce. This pattern perpetuated an elite and commercial class.

Several concerns have led to movements for increased opportunity for schooling:

1. With the industrialization of the northeastern United States, many people were concerned about the well-being of children; school provided one alternative to working long hours in the factories.
2. Industrialists sought ways to educate and urbanize those coming to towns from rural areas to make them reliable, compliant workers.
3. Many wanted to Americanize and assimilate immigrants.

The school appeared to be the institution that could solve these problems.

Horace Mann, a member of the Massachusetts legislature during the late 1820s and 1830s, was the most forceful advocate and leader of the public school movement. It was Mann who pushed for the establishment of schools for all children free of charge, without religious teaching, and financed through public taxation. He said, "Let the home and the church teach faith and values, and the school teach facts" (Blanchard, 1971, p. 88). He also advocated locally elected boards of education to remove control of the schools from conservative church ministers and schoolmasters. Local districts were supervised by and under the influence of a centralized bureaucracy—the state board of education. Mann himself was appointed head of this agency in Massachusetts.

Another innovation of Horace Mann's was the professionalization of teachers: Teacher training colleges, or "normal schools," were established; higher salaries were paid to attract better-qualified teachers; and scientific methods were used for the evaluation of teachers. This reform movement came at a time when societal needs favored development of mass education. Following Massachusetts's lead, people in other states pressed for laws establishing universal, free, primary education. This movement also extended to secondary education, but it was not until after the Civil War, with the need for a highly-educated labor force, that the cry of "more education for more people" really made an impact.

The Progressive Education Movement. Just as the movement for public education during the first half of the nineteenth century paralleled the wider social trend to integrate newcomers into an industrial society, the progressive education movement extending into the 1920s and 1930s paralleled the political progressive movement of the 1890s.

Controversy exists today over an offshoot of progressive education philosophy: "life skills." Courses in sex and drug education, marriage, parenting, death and dying, values clarification, money management, consumer knowledge, house buying, insurance, and other practical skills are seen by some as essential skills for students to have before leaving high school. Others believe that schools should concentrate on basic skills and that life skills should be taught at home.

The Essentials. Theodore Brameld (1977, pp. 118–20), who has written extensively on the various movements in American education, has used the term *essentialist* to describe those involved in a 1950s movement opposing progressive education. Essentialists were particularly vexed about an offshoot of progressive education called the life adjustment movement, which they believed reduced education to teaching survival skills such as home economics, driver education, and hygiene—ignoring the intellectual mission of schooling to teach disciplines.

Essentialist critics, such as Arthur Bestor and Robert Maynard Hutchins, decried the "intellectual flabbiness and soft-headedness" of the schools. Navy Admiral Hyman Rickover complained that he could not find enough scientists and technicians to build and run the Navy's nuclear submarines; and many church leaders and their followers deplored the teaching of cultural relativism and the ignoring of the eternal truths. Politically, the decade of the 1950s was a time of fear; Joseph McCarthy stressed the communist threat, with communists lurking in the teachers' lounges and superintendents' offices of the nation's schools. Some saw progressive education as a movement to weaken educational institutions.

Humanistic Education. American education in the twentieth century follows the pendulum-swing theory. Progressivism was in many ways a reaction to the crimping, stultifying schools of Victorian authoritarianism; essentialism was a reaction against progressivism; and the humanistic education movement of the 1960s and 1970s was in reaction to the authoritarianism that had never been given up by the schools. It was a rediscovery of the teachings of the child-centered progressives.

Leaders of the humanistic movement said that schools should eliminate coercive rules and regulations. More opportunities should be created for students to participate in shaping educational goals, especially at the secondary level. This movement was greatly influenced by the client-centered therapies of such psychologists as Carl Rogers and Abraham Maslow. In practice, educators such as Sidney Simon (Values Clarification) and Lawrence Kohlberg (Stages of Moral Development) presented teachers with a variety of techniques to clarify the values and develop the moral base of their students. Charles Silberman's *Crisis in the Classroom* (1970) was a keynote book on humanistic education. His analysis of American education described the schools as overly formal, devitalized, and often inhumane. He looked at the informal classroom of the English primary school as a model for reform. A number of teacher training colleges, most notably the University of North Dakota, adopted the practices of English primary schools and provided learning experiences whereby prospective teachers were trained to sense their pupils' needs and interests and to follow these in the classroom. Humanistic educators insisted that greater attention should be placed on developing the "affective domain," or emotions and feelings, of a child, not just the "cognitive domain," or intellect. Emotions, intellect, and psychomotor skills all need attention.

From the humanistic education movement came interest in an area of "preparation for life" called *moral education,* also known by such terms as *moral development, civic education, citizen/moral education, moral sensibility, moral reasoning,* and *values clarification.* Moral education does not "teach" morals; rather, through the use of classroom exercises, it helps children deal with ethical issues that affect them and the world in which they live, and that will be involved in their decision-making processes (Simon, 1972).

The whole idea of values clarification is not to instill or introduce any particular values, new or old, but to help students discover those they already have. Moreover, the theory stresses that "exercising" one's values via such paper-and-pencil exercises will help students hold on more firmly to their values (Etzioni, 1977).

Critics of humanistic education argue that we should be more directive and absolute, not morally neutral, in teaching values. They also question whether teachers can remain neutral or hide their values in the teaching process (Etzioni, 1977).

ALTERNATIVE EDUCATION AND RELATED MOVEMENTS

From the humanistic philosophical perspective came the origins of the alternative education movement, with its emphasis on the whole child. It is impossible to speak of one philosophy that all in the movement share, but terms used to describe the schools loosely adhere to philosophical tenets including *free, open, innovative, experimental, new,* and *radical.* Many of these philosophical underpinnings have been spelled out in books that have become the "Bibles" of alternative school advocates.

Free schools refer to schools that give people freedom and choice; reflect qualities of openness, informality, flexibility, parental and community involvement, and integration in contrast to segregation; stress intellectual, social, and emotional development; encourage self-knowledge, independence, and interdependence; stimulate creativity in an environment of shared responsibility; and minimize failure, competitiveness, authoritarianism, top-down administration, expensive facilities, and labels.

Summerhill is a small residential school set in a village in England; it advocates a totally free learning environment and unrestrained spontaneity. The late A.S. Neill (1960), who founded Summerhill in 1921, believed that to become fulfilled adults, children must be allowed to have a "free" experience, unfettered by rules. The few rules of the school are established by the whole community in a democratic way. Although regular classes from primary through secondary levels are offered, attendance is voluntary (Hart, 1970).

Some free schools in the United States have been patterned specifically on the Summerhill model; others have adopted aspects of the model.

The free school movement was not, however, simply a reaction against repressive school structures, outdated curricula, or ineffective teaching methods, but one against the school as an instrument of the mainstream culture. Many, though not all, free school advocates were motivated by the philosophy that education should be regarded as a means to a political end.

The largest group of students in free schools are bright children seeking escape from the anxiety and boredom of more traditional schools. They also include students who have experienced academic failure and are potential dropouts. For both of these types of students, free schools meet a need.

Third World Alternative Educational Movements

Changing the educational power structure was also the goal of some Third World educators. In *Pedagogy of the Oppressed* (1970), Brazilian educator Paulo Freire asserted that literacy among oppressed peasants could be increased by leading these people to an awareness of their cultural reality (the powers that oppress them) and thus giving them the knowledge and its attendant power to fight back against the oppressor. Freire devised a new method of teaching reading that achieved considerable success among the people of poverty-stricken northeastern Brazil. The result was an increased politicalization of the peasantry, which was perceived as a threat by the government. Freire was jailed and eventually forced into exile. Ivan Illich (1971), a former priest and reformer who worked in Mexico, viewed schools as among several institutions that are coercive, discriminatory, and destructive to the individual. He claimed that by disengaging education from "schooling," deinstitutionalization of the social order would occur, allowing for change. Illich also argued that one does not have to go to school to get an education and that schools can actually inhibit education.

English Primary Schools

The open primary school model of English Primary Schools features a commitment to individualized education and stresses the basics—reading, writing, and mathematics. In this system, children work at their own level in basic skills, which are taught in conjunction with other subjects such as history, science, music, and art. Evaluations of this system indicate the following:

> The back-to-basics movement in America and in Britain seems to assume that if children will spend longer periods of time working in a narrower way at basic skills they will achieve more. Our major national survey suggests that the opposite is true. If the basic skills are embedded in a web of direct experience on the part of the child that engages the many facets of his personality and being, then basic skills grow most strongly. ("A British Administrator," 1979, p. 61)

The impact of the alternative education movement can be seen in many school systems and classrooms where students are taught in less traditional ways, and in school districts where alternative types of schools or classrooms are available.

Many public school systems established "alternative public schools" for those students who were potential dropouts and could not function effectively within the traditional high school system. These "fringe" public high schools included many of the features of private alternative or free schools. They were informal and small, with personalized learning, student involvement in decision making, innovative learning techniques, and community involvement. Some major cities have retained alternative high schools for limited numbers of students.

Open Classrooms

"Open classrooms" have their roots in the progressive education movement. Sometimes called *open classrooms, open education, open schools,* and *open space,* they are characterized by the following:

1. Concern over quality of teacher–child interaction; warmth, acceptance; children's thoughts taken seriously
2. Emphasis on cooperation, not competition; few behavioral problems
3. Freedom of movement and use of materials, within certain boundaries; communication among children
4. Other factors related to positive self-image and willingness to take risks and persist

The teacher is available to facilitate learning and to help students in their activities. The teacher's role is supportive, guiding, and child-centered. The physical environment presents an atmosphere of informality. Desks are grouped, and different activities are available in different areas of the room. Open classrooms are most commonly found in elementary schools (see Figure 13–4).

Parents tend to be involved in open classrooms, volunteering help or bringing in projects for the children. Open education results in different

FIGURE 13–4 Open classroom.

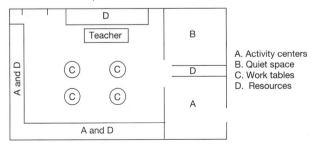

interaction patterns in the classrooms; there is generally more interaction among students and less formal teacher–student interaction. Open education is particularly beneficial for some students, such as Native American children, who come from a culture that holds values similar to those of open education— cooperation, sharing, and individual responsibility for decision making.

In times of back-to-basics movements, open education classrooms have come under attack as "schools without failure," automatically promoting children without identifying lack of achievement. Some open education structures have been replaced by more traditional classrooms with desks and chairs in rows, but many teachers have retained some semblance of the open education atmosphere in their classrooms.

Back to Basics

From the alternative education movement, the swing of the pendulum moved to the conservative side. The movement, referred to as *back to basics*, features good, old-fashioned readin', writin', and 'rithmatic with a good dose of discipline thrown in and none of the "frills" such as humanistic education and the arts. Supporters of basic-skills education argued that schools should be guided by essentialist principles, including the following:

1. The elementary school curriculum should aim to cultivate basic tool skills that contribute to literacy and mastery of arithmetical computation.
2. The secondary curriculum should cultivate competencies in history, mathematics, science, literature, English, and foreign languages.
3. Schooling requires discipline and a respect for legitimate authority.
4. Learning requires hard work and disciplined attention. (Donohue, 1976)

Having completed such a school curriculum, the students should be able to apply their knowledge to solve many problems. Some argue, however, that they also will have learned their place in the class structure. Back to basics places more emphasis on basic skills; initially the pressure came from parents concerned about their children's skill levels. Additionally, pressure comes from commission reports, state legislators, and concerns of the public about the decline in achievement test scores.

Our historical summary shows that back-to-basics education is not new. In Puritan times most schools were set up to teach basic skills and religion so that children could develop an understanding of morals, religion, and law. Young boys from elite homes attended grammar schools where Greek and Latin literature were taught; always the emphasis was on basic skills. As the colonies expanded, different types of schools were founded to meet the differing needs of students and society, but always stressing basic skills. McGuffey Readers reigned as the primary texts used in classrooms for almost a century, from 1836 to the 1930s. In addition to basic skills, the texts stressed morals and manners, see Box 13–1, which provides a clear example of cultural transmission of dominant values.

The Council for Basic Education, founded in 1956, acted as a liaison group for those interested in basic education, or basic skills. Proponents of basic education today have a variety of interests and motives. Some advocate use of the paddle and stress truth, virtue, justice, religious principles, and dress codes as the primary focus of schools. Others mainly want to be assured that the three Rs are being mastered.

Reaction to the failures of promised miracles, to desegregation, and to the ban on Bible-reading and prayers in classrooms; a "break-down in the moral fiber of society"; and a need for "patriotism, morality, manners, adult authority, discipline, order, and quality education" have provided the main uniting ideologies for back-to-basics proponents (Egerton, 1976).

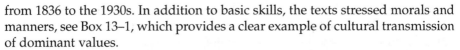

◆◆**Box 13–1** *Excerpt from a McGuffey Reader: Things to Remember*

1. When you rise in the morning, remember who kept you from danger during the night. Remember who watched over you while you slept, and whose sun shines around you, and gives you the sweet light of day.
2. Let God have the thanks of your heart, for His kindness and His care. And pray for His protection during the wakeful hours of day.
3. When you are at the table, do not eat in a greedy manner, like a pig. Eat quietly, and without noise. Do not reach forth your hand for the food, but ask someone to help you.
4. Avoid a pouting face, angry looks, and angry words. Do not slam doors. Go quietly up and down stairs; and never make a loud noise about the house.
5. Be kind and gentle in your manners; not like the howling winter storm, but like the bright summer's morning.
6. Do always as your parents bid you. Obey them with a ready mind, and with a pleasant face.
7. Never do anything that you would be afraid or ashamed that your parents should know. Remember, if no one else sees you, God does; from whom you can not hide even your most secret thought.
8. We must do all the good we can to all men, for this is well pleasing in the sight of God. He delights to see his children walk in love, and do good, one to another.

Exercises—What should you remember in the morning? Whom should you thank, and for what should you pray? How should you behave at the table? What should you avoid? How should you behave to your parents? What should you do at night? Whom should you always trust?

Source: McGuffey, William H., *Third Eclectic Reader* (Cincinnati: Wilson, Hinkle, 1857; 2nd ed., 1965), pp. 55–57.

What did this mean in terms of changes in the schools? Many open class-rooms were eliminated. Courses other than basics were questioned or elimi-nated, including art and music appreciation, sex and drug education, physical education, and drivers' education, as were emphases on the well-being of the whole child and use of counselors and other social service programs. Discipline and basic skills took their place. In recent years we have seen a swing of the pendulum back with the slow return of some social programs and additional courses.

Private Schools

The booming private school business owes a great deal to back-to-basics pro-ponents. Private schools thrive on the discontent of frustrated parents who want a reprieve from the conflicts over desegregation, the perceived lack of dis-cipline, and apparent lowering of standards.

Categories of private schools include the following: elite preparatory schools such as Choate, Phillips-Andover, Groton, and Lawrenceville, which cater to the wealthy who plan to go to elite colleges; special schools for the disabled, gifted, or retarded; military academies; and religious, sectarian day schools sponsored by Catholic, Jewish, Baptist, Lutheran, Quaker, fun-damentalist Christian, and other religious groups. These private schools meet the preferences of many different people holding various beliefs about the role of education.

One type of private school that experienced tremendous growth in the 1970s was the fundamentalist Christian school. Some of these schools were established in reaction to a sense of negativity about the public schools, others in response to integration of schools. At the core of this movement is a distrust of the educational system, which seems to some to be imposing an alien value system on their own.

Fundamentalist Christians believe that education and Christian teachings cannot be separated. They object to public school teachings that include such ideas as humans having evolved from lower forms of life, denying the literal biblical interpretation of the Creation; the idea that humans are animals, implying that humans do not have a soul; and other specific teachings. Reaction to such teachings in public schools has led to an upsurge of interest in Christian schools. In this, as in other movements, one senses an in-group–out-group or we-they tone. "They" are destroying our children's faith in God, implanting alien ideas in their minds.

Since 1991, private school education has received a boost from the gov-ernment in the form of a push for "choice" systems. This would allow parents to select from various schools, which in turn would receive funds for each student enrolled (*America 2000*, 1991). Thus, more students might be able to attend private schools.

*A*pplying Sociology to Education: Should parents and students be able to select the school of their choice? What are the pros and cons? ◆

Accountability Movements

Accountability refers to a means of controlling educational standards of competency and measuring outcomes against expenditures. The accountability movement arose in reaction to the humanistic emphasis in education. Of paramount concern was the attempt to account for dollars spent and to hold someone responsible, usually teachers, for the output of schools, as measured by student achievement. Some educational writers arguing for reforms in the schools supported the idea of accountability. Nat Hentoff, for one, urged parents to speak up against the "great consumer fraud" and demand competent teachers, though he indicated that teachers are almost never fired for incompetence (Hentoff, 1978, pp. 3–8). In order to try to ensure accountability, many proposals have been set forth for measuring teachers' performance, from student performance on standardized tests to the National Teacher Exams. For instance, competency-based education (CBE) in teacher training institutions requires students to master certain skills before graduation.

Low student test scores, violence in schools, and high dropout rates are cited as reasons for recent calls for accountability. Many states are requiring students to pass exams at one or more points in their school careers. Some states and local school districts have proposed that teacher pay be tied to student test results. This practice is likely to reduce creativity in classrooms, as teachers teach to the tests. Movements for accountability have increased the power and influence of testing agencies in the school environment. School districts desiring to evaluate their student populations compared with state or national norms rely on standardized tests. A decline in standardized test scores on the College Boards or SAT, put out by the Educational Testing Service (ETS), and on the ACT was cited as a major reason for the back-to-basics drive in the late 1970s and early 1980s.

Humanists point out that accountability may turn the schools from humane, spontaneous, creative places that encourage positive self-concepts and success, to cold, formal places with measurement procedures and clearly delineated objectives, allowing for little spontaneity and creativity.

According to the systems approach, problems in education cannot be attributed to only one source. Teachers are not the only villains, nor are the students. Perhaps the schools are scapegoats, blamed because of expectations that they can solve all of society's problems. Government at all levels is involved, as are all those who serve the school. And families also play a role in school achievement.

Some critics of the accountability movement argue that there are numerous causes for educational problems besides the teacher or school administrators, including parents, community residents, school board members, taxpayers, and most important, the students themselves. Recently, families and teacher education programs have faced their share of criticism for school failures. Numerous people play a role in educating the child. Concentrating on only one aspect of the system and the environment will produce a "bandage effect," but it probably will not result in solutions to problems.

The testing controversy is complex, and many factors entered into the decline in scores. Change in the number and type of students taking the test and student motivation are only two. In fact, some critics argue that tests should not be used at all for placement and college entrance because they are the greatest single barrier to equal opportunity in the sphere of education.

Effective Schools and Educational Reform

A recent buzzword in the halls of education is *effective schools*. Exactly what is meant by this term varies, but common themes include schools in which students are achieving at a high level or in which achievement has risen significantly. Drawing from multiple studies of effective schools, we can summarize the characteristics that enable students to achieve at a high level:

1. Professional staff holds high expectations and believes all students can reach these.
2. Students understand high expectations, have high self-concepts, and have low sense of academic futility.
3. Role expectations of teachers and students include high achievement.
4. The school reward structure is centered on achievement.
5. Stratification of students and differentiation of instructional programs is minimal.
6. School goals and objectives are shared.
7. The school climate is conducive to learning. (Brookover, Erickson, and McEvoy, 1996)

How to achieve effective schools is the subject of even more studies and reports. The highest rates of improvement in school achievement have been reported when there is clear articulation of grade-level expectations and standards in each area, clear homework policies throughout the school, and all students are taught the curriculum for their grade level. Other findings focus on instructional techniques, classroom expectations, and rules; how students are grouped for subjects; and other specific recommendations, some of which are discussed in earlier chapters (Talbert, 1995).

There is the danger in reform movements, such as effective schools, that schools, districts, or states will simply attempt to institute a "list" of reforms rather than consider carefully what is best for each school. Some influential reformers argue that the individual school must be the center for efforts to improve schools. In a large research project based on extensive descriptive data from 38 schools in 13 diverse communities, Goodlad (1984) investigated the following aspects of schools: school functions, the relevance of schools to students, how teachers teach, circumstances surrounding teaching, curriculum, distribution of resources for learning, equity, hidden curriculum, satisfaction with school quality, and the need for school data collection. He argues that school reform must take place at the individual school and classroom level, not at some distant central location. Uniformity imposed from a central office hinders real change, and decentralization of decision making is essential. The strong leadership of a principal who gives teachers power and works with them will have the greatest impact on achievement in the school (Bernhardt and Ballantine, 1995).

The risk with back to basics, accountability, and effective schools is that some of the ever-growing number of disadvantaged students who fall in the bottom half will be left farther behind and eventually drop out.

STRUCTURAL AND CURRICULAR CHANGES IN THE SCHOOLS

Changes introduced in educational systems affect structure and role relationships. When movements produce new ideas, concerns, and programs, there are often efforts to incorporate them into the existing system. This requires adaptation of the physical and role structure of schools. Structural changes can take place at the system level (for example, magnet schools, voucher systems, or charter schools); the school level (for example, tracking students, integrating the disabled, programming for gifted children, installing architectural alternatives); and the classroom level (for example, alternative curriculum models, team teaching, open classrooms).

The "School Choice" Movement

Several educational movements advocate options and choices for students and parents. They fall into four categories: charter schools, home schooling, open enrollemnt, and vouchers. School choice is a fast-growing innovation in public education with almost one in ten public school students in the United States participating in some form of choice. Charter schools are increasing in popularity in many states, though court cases are limiting their expansion. Home schooling allows parents to arrange for their children's schooling. Open enrollment gives parents the option to choose where their children go to school, generally within a district. Vouchers also allow parents to send their children to any of a number of schools, depending on their preference (Education Commission of the States, 1999).

Though the idea has been practiced in some cities for many years, only recently have districts formally adopted magnet school policies to desegregate and integrate, which often leads to systemwide change. These were established in some cities to distribute students and desegregate schools on the basis of special interests or talents: science, mathematics, art and music, and vocational education. The plan is in place in some cities, sometimes as part of a busing-desegregation plan. In 1992, there were 5,000 magnet schools nationwide, and the number was growing until districts began to explore other alternatives. Research indicates that magnet schools can improve the choices for students, help in desegregation efforts, and improve the quality of education (Blank and Archibald, 1992).

Charter schools are a more recent innovation; they also allow for choice and are similar in some ways to magnet schools. By the end of 1998 there were 1,050 charter schools operating in 27 states (Berman et al., 1999), and though most had been in operation only a short time, some were already closing. Charter schools can be part of the public school system or for-profit, and they can be newly created schools or converted public schools (Schneider, 1999). New charter schools can arise to serve at-risk or minority children or to meet concerns of parents. Any time choice is involved, however, some families are going to forego that choice, and this lack of choice may lead to greater inequality for some (Wells et al., 1999).

Community schools are similar to charter schools, but often integrate social welfare services such as health and emotional needs (Coltoff, 1998). Similar to charter schools, they focus on a particular method, theme, or curriculum; they are publicly funded but give parents and students autonomy in governance (Bennett, deMarrais, and LeCompte, 1995, p. 298). Critics concerned about for-profit charter schools may cut corners to be cost efficient or establish bureaucracies that limit teacher creativity and freedom (Dykgraaf and Lewis, 1998).

Voucher systems also produce systemwide changes. School districts establish schools with a variety of philosophies, educational programs, kinds of discipline, and services. Theoretically, communities and parents become involved in both the selection and the operation of schools. Each family receives money vouchers for school-age children. The vouchers are good for a year of education at the school of their choice.

Each of these options falls into the category of school choice. Choice-movement leaders have advocated parental and student free choice of schools so that parents can select between educational philosophies and curricula. One argument for these programs is that competition between schools for student enrollment and voucher money could raise standards. In each case, a major goal is to involve parents in the educational decisions regarding their children.

Opponents of choice have several key concerns: urban public schools might become the dumping ground for students not enrolled in other schools; and private schools supported in part by public funds might create further divisions in society by becoming more selective about their student bodies. Some have predicted the demise of public school education and heterogeneous grouping in schools. An early evaluation of Milwaukee's voucher plan, however, indicates that the parental choice program is attracting some students who are more likely to have behavioral problems, and that these parents are more involved in and satisfied with their children's education than those not involved in the plan (Olson, 1991, p. 12).

The message is unclear about whether choice systems improve schooling for low-income youth. On the one hand, it could encourage more youth and family involvement and give the children alternative school options. On the other hand, it could perpetuate the gap between wealthy and poor youth because high-income youth would continue to receive better educations than poor youth because of their choices (Wells et al., 1999; Manski, 1992, p. 1).

*A*pplying *Sociology to Education:* What are some effects of recent choice movements on your district's schools? ◆

"Multiculturalism" and "Political Correctness"

Multicultural curriculum refers to teaching history and literature, among other subjects, in ways that accurately reflect the different cultural strands in our society and world (Ravitch, 1990). Integration of multicultural materials into existing curricula involves inclusion of reading materials by and about minority groups, history that integrates all groups, and other broadened themes that promote understanding of all segments of multicultural society in the United States and around the world.

"Hey, hey, ho, ho, Western culture's got to go," was the cry at Stanford University in 1987. The next year saw changes in the required course in Western culture at Stanford and also saw the debate over what is taught in schools and universities intensify.

On one side are those who feel universities' curricula and admissions standards are being "dumbed down," that a common core of knowledge, sometimes referred to as "the Canon," is being disgarded in the wave of multicultural rhetoric, and that campuses are facing "anti-Western zealotry" and witch hunts in the name of multiculturalism (Sacks and Thiel, 1995).

Arguments on the other side range from reasoned plans for new curricular content to radical plans to overturn university content and teaching as we know it. Diverse democratic societies need educated citizens who accept democratic ideas and move beyond nations divided along racial, ethnic, class, and cultural lines (Banks, 1999).

Some educators feel that to accomplish real multiculturalism in curricula and classrooms, we need to strengthen diversification (Cope and Kalantzis, 1997). Revolutionary multiculturalism argues for reanalysis of power and privilege in the capitalist system that is linked to the Western Canon of ideas, where what whiteness means would be a topic of study (McLaren, 1997a, 1997b).

Political correctness refers to fair and accurate inclusion of minorities and women in discussions of history, literature, and other subjects. The movement has served to sensitize the many segments on campus to issues of racism, sexism, and other delicate areas. The widespread and often acrimonious debate about "PC" centers on what is fair and accurate, and whether traditional values of academic freedom are being threatened by pressure to revise "traditional" curricula.

With the movement toward broadened curricula has come criticism of some educators for teaching traditional curricula or using "outdated" terms or explanations. A backlash began, based in Princeton, New Jersey, and known as the National Association of Scholars. Originally made up of conservative scholars, the organization has become more diverse over the years as more scholars have become concerned about issues of academic freedom (Mooney, 1990).

Dinesh D'Souza, one of the most controversial figures in the debate over the "politically correct" movement, argues that the

> issue is not the inclusion of more works by women, or more works by blacks, or more works from outside the Western tradition; that broader representation is proper and justified has been conceded. The real issues—the ones underlying a wide range of campus debates—include the assumption by many that Western values are inherently oppressive, that the chief purpose of education is political transformation, and that all standards are arbitrary. (D'Souza, 1991)

When the controversy subsides, we should see some new and innovative approaches combining traditional and newer approaches to core curriculum in both public schools and higher education.

Technology and the Classroom

Concern over declining achievement scores brought a flood of cure-alls beginning in the late 1950s. Teaching machines, reading programs, talking typewriters, educational television, tape-cassette machines, and other technological innovations were introduced into classrooms across the nation. Proponents of the new technology argued that schools should take advantage of the technological revolution, just as business and other institutional sectors were doing. "Traditional" classrooms could be changed into individualized instructional centers to meet a wide variety of learning styles and interests. Potential for linking home and school learning excited educators. Computers in the classroom and computer-assisted instruction (CAI) began in the late 1960s.

Though the specific types of technology in the classroom have changed, the new forms are here to stay. As new capabilities develop, new uses for technology will be implemented. We have only seen the beginning of this far-reaching movement as we move through the twenty-first century. Classrooms and the role of teacher may be very different in the future. Information retrieval using electronic means will be key, and distance learning will bring unlimited learning potential around the world. This is one example of a trend that is likely to have a lasting impact because of its importance to future jobs in society. Technology has its skeptics, however, in those who fear the loss of the human side of education and learning, which involves using the senses and learning through contact with others (Jones and Smart, 1998).

Other Movements, Reforms, and Fads

"In the last decade hundreds of expensive reports and thousands of articles by social scientists and journalists have documented the shortcomings of America's schools. There has been general agreement over the need for change; there has been bitter disagreement over the content and philosophy of that change" (Ewen, 1990, p. 1).

Educational reforms have been proposed to solve everything from major educational concerns to small problems. Some ideas have been tried, succeeded, and been integrated into the system as permanent features; others have failed

One alternative educational movement is home schooling.

for lack of interest and support. New ideas vary in their rate of acceptance based on a number of factors, including political climate, economic conditions, sources and pressures for change, change in routine required at the school and classroom level, and support of classroom teachers. For example, a recent innovation that may be short-lived or become widely adopted is "block scheduling." Initial research shows improved school climates, increased attendance, achievement in reading and math, and higher standardized test scores; teachers prefer this format as well (Rettig and Canady, 1999; Thayer and Shortt, 1999).

The language of school reform has changed dramatically over the past 30 years, from concepts like "innovation" to systematic ideas of "restructuring and transformation" (Hartoonian, 1991). The problems that stimulate efforts to change are the growing numbers of low-income and minority children, dropouts, and failures.

Observers worry that current efforts to reform education are not based on research findings or an overall plan, and are likely to intensify problems rather than begin to solve them ("Research and the Renewal," 1991). Little dialogue occurs between educational researchers and policy experts and opinion leaders who have influence over action taken (Gardner, 1992). Educators agree on many causes of school difficulties, but without influence, their advice often goes unheeded.

Though some would have us return to "the good old days" of education, no period in history has been free of educational critics and problems in schools, including high dropout rates, nonreaders, boredom, violence, and undisciplined students. We can predict that the pendulum will continue to swing.

Using the open systems approach helps make clear that one integrated approach to educational policymaking is difficult to accomplish in a system with such diverse environmental pressures and movements. It must take into account the many interdependent parts of the system. Schools are vulnerable to environmental pressures and to the moods of the time; a balanced program is difficult to achieve when each new fad creates upheaval in the system, altering its structure and role relationships.

*A*pplying Sociology to Education: What kinds of changes do you predict in schools as we move through the twenty-first century? ◆

◆ Summary

Social and educational movements reflect the diversity of opinion present in a society. They reflect the range of perceived options. Systems experience pressure to change from movements in society; change may involve minor modifications in existing programs or major structural and curricular changes. Movements are only as effective in changing societal institutions as the attention they attract and the feasibility of the programs they propose and stimulate. Some movements seek separation from the existing structure. In this chapter we have reviewed theory of movements; the educational periods that have influenced today's education; movements in the United States, with specific examples; and trends in movements.

I. The Nature of Educational Movements

Educational movements come and go like the swing of a pendulum, reflecting the mood of the times. They influence educational systems as pressure groups from the environment. Some movements stimulate schools outside the traditional or public school system; others press for reform within the system.

II. Educational Movements Throughout History

Three influences from early European education on educational movements and systems today include:

1. Influential methods of teaching such as "reasoning power, rhetoric, and the art of persuasion" and rational inquiry
2. Human depravity of children, which encouraged authoritarian methods
3. The Renaissance concept of well-rounded, liberally educated persons

Several movements have dominated educational history in the United States: the public school movement, progressive education, essentialism, and humanistic education.

III. Alternative Education and Related Movements

The alternative education movement came at a time when all institutions in our country were being challenged. It focused on what adherents felt was the oppressive nature of schools. Influential in movement philosophy were Summerhill and the English primary schools. From the movement came free schools outside the existing system, and alternative schools and open classrooms within.

IV. Structural and Curricular Changes in the Schools

The back-to-basics movement is a backlash against the "permissiveness of alternative education." It stresses basic skills and places less emphasis on "nonessentials." It gave rise to private schools, competency-based education, and other submovements, such as accountability.

Accountability has meant many things, but it usually includes teachers' concerns for competency and schools' assessment of outcomes of the educational process while considering expenses.

Effective schools are concerned with how to help students achieve, and studies point out variables that schools should consider to raise levels of achievement.

Some movements have a lasting effect; others, thought to be cure-alls, fizzle. Some forms of educational technology and performance contracting did not live up to expectations. Vocational education and some structural changes—magnet schools and voucher systems—have had mixed success. Open education has left a permanent, if limited, mark.

Societal movements are reflected in higher-education systems through curriculum and structural changes. Some institutions have produced alternative educational models.

Change related to educational movements has been reflected in proposed innovations, radical reforms, and other alternatives. Many concerns of individual groups are reflected in these changes. Predictions are that concerns for equal education will continue and that practical education will be a focus because of economic conditions.

◆ Putting Sociology to Work

1. Find out what alternatives in primary and secondary education exist in your community.
2. Have any of the "fads" mentioned in this chapter been tried in schools in your community? Are they still in use? What has been their success or failure record?
3. Design a hypothetical school at any level of the system of the type you would like to attend. Include features of systems discussed in this chapter and others you would like to add.
4. Conduct an informal survey of parents in your neighborhood about their attitudes toward education for their children and toward alternative versus basic education.
5. Spend some time observing in two local schools or classrooms that represent different philosophies.

CHAPTER 14

Change and Planning in Educational Systems

This book presents the story of a dynamic system. It is a system that does not and cannot remain stagnant, for there are constant pressures for change. Recall our systems model of the school (see Figure 14–1). Everyone in our society is affected by that system. A large segment of our population has a primary involvement with the school system, including those who are educated by it or employed by it. It touches the lives of all taxpayers, parents, and students.

Schools face constant challenges from within the system and from the environment. Flexibility and adaptation are necessary if an open system such as a school is to survive; it is dependent on the support of both internal and external individuals and groups in order to maintain a viable program and meet needs. Change affects all aspects of educational systems. Some pressures for change have focused on "loosening" the social structure and allowing students more flexibility and freedom of choice; other pressures call for tightening requirements. Experiments with physical space and learning have been seen in "open space" schools and alternative classrooms. In this final chapter we explore the process of change in educational systems and some methods that have been proposed to bring about change.

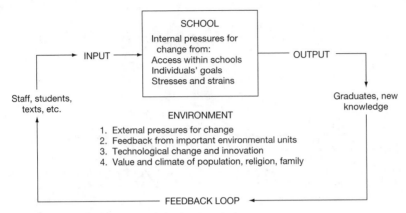

FIGURE 14–1 Systems model of school change.

THE DYNAMICS OF CHANGE

Change is ever present. It takes place in societies, organizations, groups, and individuals. The difficulty lies in coming up with one definition that fits all levels and types of change, planned and unplanned. Here is one definition of change: It is "the process of planned or unplanned qualitative or quantitative alterations in social phenomena" (Vago, 1989, p. 9). Also, "planned social change refers to deliberate, conscious, and collaborative efforts by change agents to improve operations of social systems" (Bennis, Benne, and Chin, 1985, p. 280). Let us consider several components of the change process:

- ◆ *Identity* of change refers to a specific social phenomenon undergoing transformation.
- ◆ *Level* of change delineates the location in a social system where a particular change takes place.
- ◆ *Duration* refers to the question of how long a particular change form endures after it has been accepted.
- ◆ *Direction* of change may indicate development or decay, progress or decline.
- ◆ *Magnitude* may be based on a three-part scheme of incremental or marginal, comprehensive, and revolutionary change.
- ◆ Rate of change may be based on an arbitrary scale such as fast or slow. (Vago, 1989, p. 9)

The process can take place in rapid spurts or it can be gradual and almost evolutionary. It can be planned or unplanned. Planned change often takes place as a result of the "manifest functions" or stated purposes of a system. Unplanned change, in some cases referred to as "latent functions," may result from unanticipated consequences of planned change.

The impetus for change comes from the internal functioning of schools or from the environmental influences on schools. For example, we can consider snapshots capturing one moment. Tomorrow's snapshot will be different from today's, for this is the nature of the unending process of change, a process that has been an underlying theme throughout this book (Hall, 1991).

Change is often seen as a positive, productive process improving our lives. Yet it can also be a threatening, frightening, and conflict-producing force pushing and pulling people with its constant motion. Change often upsets the routines we have established, and as creatures who need some stability, we find this unsettling. The term *future shock*, coined by Alvin Toffler, refers to extreme cases of inability to adjust or adapt to rapid social-cultural change (Toffler, 1970). Routines are important. They give us familiar benchmarks; take them away and there is no structure within which to move from one activity to another. It is within this process framework that we look at change in educational institutions.

Applying Sociology to Education: Outline the components of a planned change that has taken place in your schools or community. ◆

Change and Levels of Analysis

When we think of change, we must visualize a complex and ubiquitous process. It is useful to be aware of the level at which change is occurring when we are proposing and implementing change and studying its impact. Social scientists generally conceptualize four "levels of analysis" when referring to change in systems such as schools:

1. The *individual level* refers to change that is initiated by or directed toward persons holding roles within the system—teachers, students, or others. For instance, there might be attempts to change teacher attitudes toward a new program.
2. The *organizational level* refers to change within a school. Perhaps a new curriculum model is introduced that will require changes in the physical and role structures of the school.
3. The *institutional* or *societal level* refers to large systemwide change. This is usually related to changes in other parts of society. For instance, change in the political institution and structure of a nation will often result in changes in educational policy.
4. The *cultural level* refers to change in societal attitudes and values. These are often the slowest to change, lagging behind technological innovations.

Change occurs at each level of analysis, and major change affects all levels. When considering levels of analysis, we can use several types of strategies, depending on whether the change is short- or long-term (see Table 14–1) (Vago, 1989, pp. 281–82; Zaltman and Duncan, 1977, p. 11). At the micro- or individual level, there may be short-term changes in attitudes and behavior (Type 1). An example of this change would be the use of sensitivity training to alter a person's attitudes. A longer-term change at the microlevel (Type 2) is the training and socialization process of new recruits in an institution. Priests, for example, when they start their training program, learn a new set of attitudes and behavior that affects their entire life. At the group or intermediate level of short-term change, normative or administrative change may be introduced. Normative changes take place when a group alters its norms temporarily to experiment with an innovation (Type 3). For example, in a corporation a team sets up a novel computerized information bank. Team members are given freedom to experiment, and they can bend established organizational rules. The change agent (in this case, the manager responsible for the innovation) encourages the team. Once the innovation has been tried and found useful, it is institutionalized (Kanter, 1991, 1985). At this point, it will become a more long-term change (Type 4) at the organizational level. The original participants in the change effort will be rewarded; this process then provides incentives for others to experiment.

At the societal level of change, short-term (Type 5) change is often the result of innovations or inventions. For example, the introduction of birth-control technology in a receptive society can alter birthrates and population size in a relatively short time period. In the long run, these changes could result in major changes in the social structure of the society. The long-term consequences are (Type 6) sociocultural change—for instance, the facilitation of the modernization process in an underdeveloped nation.

TABLE 14–1 Time Dimensions and Target Levels

	Level of Society		
Time Dimension	Micro (Individual)	Intermediate (Group)	Macro (Society)
	Type 1	Type 3	Type 5
Short-term	(1) Attitude change (2) Behavior change	(1) Normative change (2) Administrative change	Invention-innovation
	Type 2	Type 4	Type 6
Long-term	Life-cycle change	Organizational change	Sociocultural evolution

Source: Zaltman, Gerald, and Robert Duncan, *Strategies for Planned Change* (New York: Wiley, 1977), p 11. Reprinted by permission of John Wiley & Sons, Inc.

Learning takes place in many settings and many ways.

A national study of "effective schools programs" and other educational reforms, "Improving Schools from the Bottom Up," presents information on successful reforms to solve problems in schools, improve teaching, and increase student learning. Successful reform generally took place at individual schools in which teachers worked collaboratively, had a voice in decision making, and had a sense of ownership in the change process, but also involved administrators in the districts. The reforms balanced top-down and bottom-up decision-making structures (Shields et al., 1995).

By recognizing where the change is taking place, we can better understand the process and deal with its consequences.

Sources of Change

Stresses and strains in school systems are major sources of change. Stresses, which Olsen (1968, pp. 141–42) describes as "sources external to an organization" and which are part of the system's environment, fall into four main categories:

1. *Population size and composition.* In the early 1960s, there was a need for more teachers to meet the demand of increased student populations from the baby boom; yet now many schools have been forced to close, and there is a teacher glut because of the drop in student population. Although these trends can hardly be controlled, they can be predicted with some degree of accuracy for future planning.

2. *The human factor.* Individuals in positions of power can bring about change in the climate or structure of the classroom or school system through their personality. For instance, the classroom teacher often initiates change at this level. Individuals holding positions in the system must be considered whether change is being planned, implemented, or analyzed.

3. *Material technology.* There are always new ideas and new materials that could be integrated into the educational system. Whether an invention be major or minor, involving materials or techniques, educators are challenged to integrate the new technology into the system and pass it on through the process of learning.

4. *Natural environment* (including such factors as "climatic adaptation," depletion of vital natural resources, natural disasters, epidemics, and weather conditions). Some schools were required to close their doors because of fuel shortages during the coldest days of the extreme winters of 1977 and 1978. Blizzards and ice also affect school days and alter schedules. These are examples of natural environment influences.

In addition to the four sources mentioned by Olsen, there are major trends in societies that stimulate change in all institutions: movement toward urbanization, industrialization, modernization, and postindustrial, technocratic society. Yet another source of change comes from attitudes of the public and educators at any particular time stimulated by social movements reflecting societal concerns. Major sources of change for schools include legislation, mandates, or accreditation requirements (Adams, 1997).

Strains are sources of conflict and pressure that develop within the internal organization. Many examples of change in the literature focus on strains, though it is important to keep in mind that change in the internal organization is also affected by what is happening in its environment. Let us consider several examples of internal strain in educational systems:

1. *Individuals or subgroups within the organization.* Goals of individuals or subgroups within the organization may be supportive of system goals, or they may contradict them. Conflict can occur when goals differ. If the individual or subgroup is influential or holds a position of power and favors change, then change is likely to result from the conflict. However, as in the case of minorities in the system, success defined as individual gain and upward mobility assumes that these are equally available to all and that all share these goals. This assumption may also lead to conflict (Sleeter and Grant, 1988).

2. *"Deviant" individuals or groups within the organization.* Students who are rebellious, have behavioral problems, or are potential dropouts create strain in the system because they are not working toward system goals. Therefore, the educational system will frequently devote human and financial resources to reducing or eliminating the strain. "Deviant" teachers who propose alternative methods or structures that would force the system to change can also create strain.

3. *Ideology, goals, structure, and resources.* Strain can develop as a result of incongruencies between a system's ideology and goals, the structure within which the system must function, and the resources available to the system. "Open space" schools or schools without walls, built in the late 1960s and early 1970s, are sometimes seen as a hindrance to more rigid programs.

*A*pplying Sociology to Education: Referring to Table 14–1, fill in the cell types with examples. ◈

PERSPECTIVES ON CHANGE

Imagine that we have an assignment to outline a process for bringing about change in a school. One important aspect of this process is to identify our perspective on change. When sociologists consider the process of change, two theoretical perspectives dominate the literature. Structural-functional theory sees change as a gradual adjustment of a system to stresses and strains. Conflict theory sees change as occurring through conflict or more dramatic revolution (see Table 14–2).

Structural-Functional Approach to Change

The educational system attempts to maintain order and integration among its principal parts. The system is basically in a state of equilibrium; social control mechanisms help maintain stability and adjustment. Threats to this equilibrium in the form of pressures for change are likely to be perceived as dysfunctional or negative for the system, but balancing is a continual process. "Dysfunctions," tensions, and deviance exist and persist in systems, but tend to become part of the ongoing system, or to become "institutionalized." The system tries to achieve and maintain equilibrium and integration. Change is believed to occur in a gradual, adaptive fashion; sudden changes leave the core structure unchanged. From this point of view, change stems from three sources: adjustment of the system to environmental demands, growth of the system, and inventions or innovations of group members.

Critics of structural-functional theory point out that the theory does not give a complete view of change. For instance, it cannot account for sudden or revolutionary change, and for systems that are not integrated. What may be functional change for one group may be harmful to another (Eisenstadt, 1985). Later in this chapter we discuss several of the strategies for bringing about change through a functionalist approach that maintains order and attempts to achieve change with the least disruption to the system.

TABLE 14–2 Summary of Sociological Theories of Education and Implications for Planning

Theoretical Approaches	Theory of Society	Theory of Education	Policy Priorities	Planning Strategies
Functionalist-Consensus	Integrated social institutions Social order based on consensus Homeostasis, i.e. balance-seeking among institutions	Education integrated with other institutions Socialization function Selection and allocation functions Creation of new knowledge "Babysitting" functions, i.e., keep youth off streets and postpone entry to job market	Equal opportunity/meritocracy; each can rise to their level of competence Maximize use of talent Closer links with other sectors of society	Selective educational systems/late selection Human capital, "rates of return" planning Educational expansion as investment Compensatory education programs Remove barriers to social mobility
Conflict (Marxist and non-Marxist)	Conflict and exploitation Power and force to maintain order Constant struggle between dominant and subordinate groups	Education as extension of dominant group power/doubtful autonomy Education reproduces social order	Break correspondence between school organization/structure and the needs of the economy Consciousness-raising and resistance taught in schools	Change structure of schools/work/society Replace dominant ideology in curriculum Education expansion as liberation

404

Interactionist	Social reality as negotiated and defined by actors Social order result of shared symbols and values	Education as process of definition of reality Classroom interaction the center of education process Classroom as self-fulfilling prophecy	Remove bias from classroom interaction Equality of opportunity and treatment in the classroom	Teacher training—expose teacher bias Focus on positive student self-identity and self-confidence Restructure classroom setting to eradicate "labeling" Reduce emphasis on examinations and class competition
Critical Theory	Oppression by dominant class and dominant ideology, maintained by hidden agenda and hidden curriculum	Education serves to maintain oppression	Remove oppression through empowerment skills	Curriculum reform Critical enquiry

Source: Saha, Lawrence J., "Bringing People Back In: Sociology and Educational Planning," in A. Yogev (ed.), *International Perspectives on Education and Society,* Vol. 5 (Greenwich, CT: JAI Press, 1996).

Conflict Approach to Change

Change is seen by conflict theorists as inevitable, ever present, and part of the nature of events. Change is the essential element of social life.

Conflict between competing interest groups in modern society accentuates the pressure for change in schools and the community. Dominant groups or power-holders attempt to protect the system from change that will alter their status or threaten vested interests, such as an educational system that favors certain groups. When change does occur it may be the result of a crisis, a conflict over power and decision making. The current conflict over curriculum content provides a case in point. Significant change in schools is unlikely to come about as a result of additional resources, but rather it will require change in the structure, roles, and power relationships within schools, according to conflict theorists. Fewer stated strategies for change in educational systems have been developed from the conflict perspective, but change does occur through disruptions, and there is ever-present potential for conflict in the system.

Table 14–2, taken from an article by Lawrence Saha (1996), summarizes conceptual and theoretical frameworks of change and their relationship to educational change. Note that the strategies for planning, as well as the outcomes, depend on the theory employed. The items under each column of the table represent a cluster and are not intended to be linked with particular items in adjacent cells.

When social scientists are studying change, their theoretical perspectives influence their interpretations. For instance, note the difference between the "rationales for educational change" of the structural-functionalists focusing on "system needs" and the neo-Marxist focus on "social justice and equality."

> **A**pplying Sociology to Education: Think of a specific example of change in your school district. How would this example be explained by different theoretical approaches? ◆

Open Systems Approach to Change

The open systems approach is based on the assumption that change, whether evolutionary or revolutionary, is inevitable and ever present in systems. Systems are constantly in the process of change because of their adaptation to feedback from the environment. The systems approach provides us with a framework for viewing the total system, locating the impetus for change, and tracing the repercussions of change throughout the system. The theoretical perspectives on change discussed previously both have limitations. The open systems approach to change removes the emphasis from stability and equilibrium and examines the system from a different perspective. It is not locked into a specific theoretical perspective and, therefore, can help us analyze the type, speed, location, and effects of change on the total system. It does not assume equilibrium or disruption related to change. Systems are not viewed as intransigent or in crisis; rather, change is seen as a normal part of the system, whether it is planned or unplanned. Theories of change can be used in combination with the systems approach to better understand the total impact of the process of change.

Viewed from an open systems approach, change may emanate from inside a school system or a subsystem or may come from environmental sources outside. The environment has a constant impact on the school. Inputs into the school system, such as legal requirements, financial resources, and community attitudes, change constantly, requiring the system to adapt. The change may be rapid, such as that caused by a student movement or fad, or it may be slower, as in rising or dwindling student or teacher populations (Morris, 1996).

Consider an example: For teachers, the educational contexts that matter most are not only those defined by formal policy but other formal and informal organizations as well. Each of these parts of the system can facilitate or constrain systemic change. Figure 14–2 shows parts of the system that affect the process of change (McLaughlin and Talbert, 1993, p. 17).

The school system relies on feedback from the environment in adapting its programs. If, for instance, a goal is to produce students who can find jobs, the school system must be aware of the changing demands for skills. It may even attempt to influence the job market by interacting with business and the community. The school system may attempt to control aspects of its environment. For instance, funding and finances are essential to continue programs. In order to increase security and stability, school systems may become involved in public relations efforts to "sell" themselves to the public. This is especially true with efforts to justify expenditures and get levies passed. There is give and take between the school and its environment, but schools must adapt to environmental demands, which often necessitate change.

The systems approach most often focuses on the organizational level of structure and roles, and gives an overview of the system and its parts. Potential exists for bringing the numerous studies of system change under one umbrella, thus obtaining a view of the whole that is closer to reality than an individual study can provide.

For an outsider looking in or an insider trying to get some perspective on the organization, the open systems approach can help locate elements of particular interest for change in the organization or its environment. This ability to see the relationship of parts to the whole can be crucial in assessing accurately

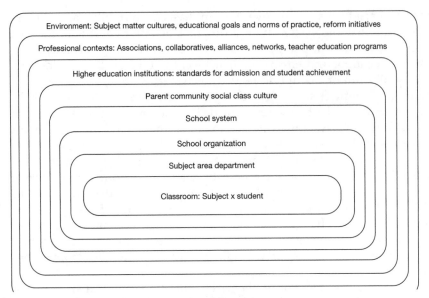

FIGURE 14-2 Embedded contexts of teaching.

Source: McLaughlin and Talbert, "Contexts That Matter for Teaching and Learning," Center for Research on the Context of Teaching. Stanford, CA: Stanford University School of Education, March 1993, p. 17.

the potential problems in the process and need for change. The open systems approach also aids in the planning of change and thus is more effective than haphazard response to transitory social movements.

BRINGING ABOUT CHANGE

One gets the feeling of a force, a perpetual-motion machine, when viewing change in the educational system. Resistance from participants and caution on the part of decision makers, however, keep the change process from rushing forward headlong. These hinderances cannot stop the system, but they can slow it. Every part of the educational system is caught up in change, for no part is totally autonomous. What are some of the factors involved in the push toward change? Most of the factors have their roots in organizational or structural rather than individual attributes.

Any time we introduce a major change, we must consider the impact on the whole system, for every part of the system experiences stresses and strains. The impetus for change comes from environmental pressures and educational hierarchies, and is often mandated by a central office. Superintendents have the power and resources unavailable at the local district level to bring about change.

But it is the individual school and teachers who must carry out the change. Without their support change is likely to fail.

Individuals in the System

The individuals who hold positions in educational systems influence the rate of change by their initiation, acceptance, or resistance to it. Let us consider examples of administrators and teachers. Impetus for change from administrators has come in such areas as court-ordered busing or integration of teaching staff, mainstreaming of disabled students, measures to cut budgets, new programs such as computer technology and computer-assisted instruction (CAI), restructuring of classrooms for homogeneity or heterogeneity, and reading or testing programs. Generally, initiation for change comes from the more powerful units because they control the resources. Those with less power either will be persuaded to agree, will feel neutral about the change, or will be unable to mount substantial resistance if they oppose the change. Although it is recognized that school administrators, especially superintendents, play a significant role in innovation and change, study results differ as to the degree of their influence; some administrators are believed to be preservers of the status quo and others as forces for change.

Impetus for change also may come from the classroom teacher. Teachers are bombarded with new technology and materials from the environment that promise to improve their teaching and ease their teaching load, such as new texts, innovative classroom arrangements, rearrangement of students for better interaction, and new technological advances. Sometimes teachers' roles in initiating change have been downplayed because of their subordinate position in the structure. Many teachers remember good ideas they had that never came to fruition because of resistance from administrators, the school board, or parents.

Change at the School Level

Proposals for school-level change involve teachers, administrators, boards, and sometimes parents or other outside agents in decision making. Consider the following two examples, one emanating from the school district of Philadelphia, Pennsylvania, the other from the national level.

The cluster initiative program in Philadelphia—PATHS/PRISMS—has the goal of "bringing about systemic change in schools serving low-income students" (Useem, 1994). The successful programs were those involved in implementing the program through shared decision making and action:

> Ingredients of Success: The initiative succeeded in schools where (a) there was a history of reasonably respectful relations between the faculty and principal and among the faculty themselves; (b) one or more highly capable and committed

teachers or administrators took on the task of following up on plans and ideas; (c) the principal was supportive; (d) a committee structure was established that included the entire staff; (e) one or more staff had a previous record of involvement with PATH/PRISMS programs.(p. 3)

Goal 7 of the National Education Goals states: "By the year 2000, every school in the United States will be free of drugs, violence and the unauthorized presence of firearms and alcohol, and will offer a disciplined environment conducive to learning" (The National Education Goals Panel, 1995). Another report outlines strategies to accomplish this and other goals in schools. It states that any successful strategy must be comprehensive—encompassing peer groups, families, schools, media, community organizations, and religious and law enforcement agencies to develop life skills and change community policies and norms ("Reaching the Goals," 1993, p. 2).

Again, the key point in these examples reinforces our systems theory—change is unlikely to be effective unless it takes place at all levels of the system.

> *A*pplying *Sociology to Education:* What is a change you would like to see implemented in a school in your district? What factors need to be taken into consideration when planning for change? ◆

STRATEGIES FOR SCHOOL CHANGE

In order for major change to be made, the whole school system and often the community must be involved in it. In the 1960s and 1970s, change agents emphasized a bottom-up approach to involve teachers and create in them a sense of ownership of the changes. The emphasis in the 1980s and 1990s has shifted to stress top-down and external impetus (Levine and Levine, 1996, p. 445). This approach must be accompanied by support from the internal and external constituencies, however, or it is unlikely to be successful (Shields, 1995; Fullan and Miles, 1992). First, community concern about an issue can stimulate change because the community supplies feedback and financial support. Second, there must be support from the school district, which provides money, programs, and extra personnel to assist in implementing change. Third, the school principal must provide leadership throughout the process. Fourth, teachers must be willing to support the change. During the change process, some teachers become "early adopters"; after they are recognized as such, other teachers follow. Implementing change goes through stages in which some teachers learn what to do, how to do it, and then expand the change process to a wider group, and finally institutionalize the change (Shachar, 1996). It is not always necessary for the entire staff to support an innovation, but it seems essential to have "early adopters" who are willing to take the risk involved in the process. Finally, students affected by the change can facilitate its adoption or rebel against the new plans.

Types of Strategies

Educators and social scientists differ in their views concerning the strategies most effective for implementing change. In a classic book on change in educational systems, Baldridge and Deal (1975, pp. 25–33) outline five key perspectives that have been commonly proposed for bringing about change, and that correspond with our levels of analysis.

Individual Perspective. The individual perspective focuses on the individual and small-group approach, which is greatly influenced by psychological and social-psychological research. The individual is believed to propose, adopt, or reject change. Because attitudes toward change are influenced by the individual's value system, the underlying assumption is that organizational change can occur by changing individual attitudes and thus individual actions.

Implementing change depends on changing the person(s) who will be installing and utilizing the innovation or invention. Organizational members are selected for their reliability and accountability, factors that can lead to inertia.

The problem with conceptualizing and planning change by emphasizing individuals holding positions in schools, however, is that it ignores the characteristics of the system within which change is to take place.

Goals and Saga Perspective. Goals are often the focal point of educational change. Despite difficulties in clarifying vague and diffuse goals, this perspective is important because goals establish reasons for an organization's existence and a common ground from which participants can direct their efforts. A saga is a myth or belief system rooted in the organization's history. It justifies an organization's existence and reduces the time and energy needed to maintain the system. An organization with a deep-rooted saga will be difficult to change. In crisis circumstances, however, it may be possible to develop a new saga and so produce long-lasting changes. Goals and sagas are crucial elements to consider when managing organizational change.

Technological Perspective. The technology of a system or organization is the nature of the work the organization performs, and the procedures, processes, activities, and devices that assist it in accomplishing its goals and objectives. Technology changes for several reasons. Sometimes the environment places new demands on the organization, or new inventions are developed. Sometimes organizational participants themselves devise new ways of doing things. Technological changes must be assessed in terms of the demands they make on the structure. For example, implementing new individualized instructional devices might involve organizing teachers into teams and increasing their ability to deal with individual students (a structural change). Technological innovations require new roles, more coordination and problem solving, and increased interdependency, all of which involve structural changes.

Environmental Perspective. The school environment includes not only parents, students, teachers, and the local community, but also the teachers' unions; state, local, and federal government agencies; other educational agencies; and the professional and educational climate. All educational systems depend on their environment for financial and moral support. The environment can be both a stimulator of and a barrier to educational change. It must be taken into consideration constantly when attempting to implement change.

Structural Perspective. Structural elements include individual jobs; subunits (departments/divisions); and the organization's hierarchy, rules, goals, and plans. An organization's structure can be viewed as a consequence of change (a change in instructional devices could place new demands on the structure) or as a facilitator of innovation. Collaboration between two organizations requires a balancing of interests and tensions between the two units (Osguthorpe and Patterson, 1998).

Many social scientists contend that long-lasting organizational change can come about only through manipulation of organizational variables (authority structure, reward systems, technological and environmental relations). Though the individual and small groups are necessary to implement change, structural aspects of the system must be part of planning. Basic structural reorganization is often necessary for schools to accomplish goals, monitor and influence the environment, and successfully adopt new technology. Strategies fall into four general categories:

1. *Facilitative strategies* make the implementation of changes easier by and/or among the target group (Zaltman and Duncan, 1977, p. 90).
2. *Reeducative strategies* are used when time is not a pressing factor. The relatively objective presentation is intended to provide a rational justification for action.
3. *Persuasive strategies* try to bring about change through bias in the way in which a message is structured and presented.
4. *Power strategies* involve the use of coercion to secure the target's compliance (Vago, 1989, pp. 289–90).

From our open systems perspective, a system that involves primary participants in change-oriented activities, that takes into consideration the organizational structure, and that develops an internal process to bring about change while being responsive to environmental pressures, is likely to be responsive to the many internal and external organization demands (Goodlad, 1975).

We are all familiar with great ideas that failed. Reading machines and satellite education that were purchased but never quite integrated into the classroom are examples. Why do such ideas fail?

Actual change in a school should involve the key participants in the planning. If the change will affect the classroom, involving teachers from the beginning of the planning can reduce resistance to the change. Training is a crucial element in the success formula; new programs are unlikely to be adopted if teachers are unclear on any details. Support from the leadership is also critical in successful implementation (Goodlad, 1984). The key principles are that change at one level and part of the organization will affect other levels and parts—it does not occur in a vacuum—and change is more likely to be successful if key participants are involved in the process of planning and implementing change.

The degree to which an innovation is implemented also depends on the extent to which certain conditions are present during implementation: clarity of goals and plans, capabilities of administrators and staff, availability of resources, compatibility of the organizational structure with the proposed changes, and willingness of those involved to expend time and effort. The extent to which these conditions are met depends on the performance of the administrators during the period of implementation. Key participants—for example, teachers and students—can ensure that changes proceed smoothly. However, they can also act as barriers to change.

Applying *Sociology to Education:* In your proposed change, how is each of the preceding perspectives relevant? ◆

Obstacles and Resistance to Implementation of Change

Obstacles to change often seem overwhelming to those involved in the implementation process. Vested interests in the status quo, opposing values and goals, apparent deficiencies and inadequacies in the proposed alteration, perceived intolerable consequences, and sheer human inertia can themselves limit change or allow for opposition to form and block change.

The toughest barrier to overcome is resistance from within the educational system, especially from the teachers who may feel vulnerable. Their fears may stem from perceived threats of being considered inadequate in their job performance. Teachers have their set routines and work patterns, and there must be compelling reasons for them to abandon those patterns and take a chance on new ones. Teachers, especially older experienced ones, may believe the proposed change is a bad one. Respect for their views and working to include them in decision making can reduce barriers (Rusch and Perry, 1999).

Ideas, values, traditions, and beliefs are the bases of our nonmaterial culture and the institutions it comprises. Although the material culture is changing rapidly, the nonmaterial culture lags behind, sometimes resisting change. Scientists developed satellite TV, which will, we are told, solve the world's literacy and basic skills problems by beaming education to stations at home and abroad. But compare the process of invention to the complexity of gaining approval and implementing the "cure-all" into classrooms and communities; ideas change slowly.

In summary, implementation of change must take into account several factors:

1. A serious assessment of the needs of the organization must be taken.
2. The proposed change must be relevant to the organization.
3. The environment must be taken into account.
4. Both the organizational structure and individual attitudes must be considered.
5. The change must be directed at manipulable factors.
6. The change must be both politically and economically feasible.
7. The change must be effective in solving the problems that were diagnosed. (Baldridge and Deal, 1975, pp. 14–18)

Once these considerations are taken into account, change is more likely to be successfully implemented.

THE SOCIOLOGIST'S ROLE IN EDUCATIONAL CHANGE AND POLICY FORMATION

In the civil rights movement, the desegregation battles, the integration and busing controversies, affirmative action issues, minority-based scholarship controversies, and other major issues of our time, sociologists were there. They were there in a variety of capacities, filling many roles. In this final section, let us consider some of these roles and the controversy about what is an appropriate role for sociologists.

Sociologists do *basic research*. They conceptualize school systems within theoretical frameworks, collect data, and analyze aspects of the systems. They may use, as a basis, Weber's bureaucratic model, a Marxist conflict theory, or many other approaches. Studies focus on a number of aspects of schooling such as those discussed in this book.

Basic research provides knowledge about the system of education not available elsewhere. Knowledge is used by investigative committees, the legal system, school boards, administrators, and teachers to make planning decisions. Some research is commissioned or funded, such as analysis of survey data about education by sociologists.

Problem research and integration is another major role carried out by sociologists of education. This involves the following tasks:

1. *Collecting data for a specific purpose.* A researcher may be presented with a specific question or problem, such as declining enrollments, and be expected to collect relevant data and interpret them to shed light on the problem.
2. *Working with existing data.* The sociologist may consider existing data from one or more sources, such as the census or school testing results, and may analyze and interpret the data within a theoretical framework to discover existing trends.

Teaching is a role carried out by the majority of sociologists. In this role as teachers and advisers, many faculty are aware of changing student body composition and needs, and they must be able to train students to cope with lifelong learning and solve complex problems (Ewens, 1987). In this capacity, knowledge about educational systems is disseminated to future sociologists, educators, and citizens. Implicit in this role is the decision of what theoretical perspective to use and what information to teach.

Evaluation research is receiving increased attention because of recent pressure for accountability; evaluation can be used as a strategy for producing and controlling innovations and reforms in educational systems. The purpose of evaluation is to learn how well a program or innovation is reaching its goals. In practice, evaluation is most often used to help with decisions about adopting, improving, or discontinuing a program. Evaluation can demonstrate three things:

1. The need for change
2. Whether change has taken place
3. The outcome of any particular change or innovation (Ballantine, 1992)

In the past, evaluation research has been used to its full potential in supporting or discouraging educational innovations because educational systems have shown resistance to unwanted or negative information—and unwanted change. But because the importance of accurate evaluation is being recognized in the educational arena, and accountability is required by many funding agencies, it will probably be used to a greater extent and even be required as a strategy for change in the future.

Policy formation and advocacy is the most controversial role. The controversy revolves around whether sociologists should become involved in areas outside their research training, thus moving into "nonobjective" arenas. The controversy became heated in the 1950s, when C. Wright Mills (1959) advocated a more active role for sociologists. He argued that sociologists cannot remain neutral and detached when they have knowledge that, if implemented into policy, could improve conditions for many people. Many sociologists chose a middle ground, thereby making a valuable contribution to education and change.

The dynamic system of education will continue to change. We can deal with that change in a logical and consistent manner only if we have research capabilities, an understanding of the change process, and a clear concept of the educational system.

Whether you are or will be a student, a taxpayer, a parent of a school-age child, a member of the PTA, a school board member, or an educator, an understanding of the complex elements that make up the educational system will help you deal effectively with its problems.

◆ Summary

In this final chapter we have analyzed the pervasive process of change.

I. The Dynamics of Change

Change is a dynamic process, and an integral part of the concept of an educational system. It can occur at any level of analysis—individual, organizational, societal, or cultural—or it can affect all levels if it is major change. The process originates because of stresses or strains within or outside the system.

Change comes from stresses external to the system, such as population size and composition; individuals who affect the system; material technology and the natural environment; or from strains within the system. These can come from conflicting goals of individuals or subgroups, deviant individuals or groups, or incongruencies between ideology and goals.

II. Perspectives on Change

Change can be seen from a number of theoretical perspectives. The structural-functional approach views the system as in equilibrium and tending toward stability. Major change can threaten this equilibrium. Most change, however, is gradual and the system adapts to it. The conflict approach views change as inevitable and often disruptive. The open systems approach views change as a part of the system; it can be disruptive, or it can help the system adapt to changing environmental demands.

III. Bringing About Change

Most important in bringing about change is working with all levels of the system. For those trying to implement change, certain conditions are necessary: an understanding of the system, familiarity with strategies for bringing about change, and experience in the process. Administrators, teachers, and students serve as catalysts for change. An organization ideally should possess certain characteristics to be receptive and successful in change efforts. The health of an organization may determine whether change will be successful.

Key participants need to be informed and involved if the process is to proceed smoothly. There are, however, often obstacles that must be addressed before change can be implemented.

IV. Strategies for School Change

Strategies for change range from minor programmatic changes to reform strategies, to total system overhaul. Most plans are for implementation of program changes. Though planned and controlled change is the ideal, in reality the process does not always work smoothly. Strategies focus on different levels and parts of the system.

Resistance to change may come from any part of the system or environment. It is most important that classroom teachers are involved in planning for the change or it cannot be successful.

The systems theme of this book suggests that no one level is enough to implement change successfully. Several cases of organizational change were discussed as examples. Some reasons for failure to implement change were discussed.

V. The Sociologist's Role in Educational Change and Policy Formation

Sociologists play several roles in the process of change: basic researchers, problem researchers and interpreters, teachers, evaluators, policymakers, and advocates.

◆ *Putting Sociology to Work*

1. Imagine yourself in any position in the school system: student, teacher, or administrator. Now imagine a major change in the school, let us say a change to an open classroom (school without walls) from a formal, closed classroom structure. In your imagined position, what feelings are you experiencing? Are there conflicts in your role because of this change? Why?

2. Investigate the history of a program that has been implemented at a public school or college. Find out about the stages leading up to implementation. What is the current status of the program?

3. Trace the history of a program or project that failed or was not implemented. Why did this happen?

4. Design a project that you would like to see implemented. What steps would you take to plan implementation?

5. Interview administrator(s) and teacher(s) about their techniques for introducing new ideas. What effect, if any, does their status have on the success of an idea?

Schools in the Early Twenty-First Century

Planning for change assumes knowledge of educational systems and future trends. Demographers provide us with relevant information: population projections, migration patterns, and social trends. Other social scientists also study educational systems. Proposals for reform and innovation come both from within the educational organization and from its environment— political, economic, and technological dimensions as well as world and national trends (Tedesco, 1995, p. 1). In this final section, we will provide examples of some trends and projections that affect education, and some policy implications.

DEMOGRAPHIC TRENDS

The rapid growth of education through the 1960s in the United States and many other countries created a boom mentality: There was an expansion of teacher training programs, new facilities were built, monies became available, and innovations were implemented. With the end of the boom came the prophets of doom, loss of jobs, boarded-up schools, and dropping financial bases.

The birthrate has been in decline since the 1960s, with only temporary upswings. The low point for enrollments was in 1983; since that time there has been a gradual increase each year into the mid-1990s. High schools were at their low in 1990. Table E–1 shows actual and projected enrollments to the year 2009.

FAMILY, ECONOMIC, AND SOCIAL TRENDS

Change in the social class composition of the school-age population is taking place because minority groups, many of whom fall disproportionately at the lower end of the educational achievement scale, are the fastest-growing populations in the United States. They also have the highest percentage of children

TABLE E–1 **Enrollment in All Public and Private Elementary and Secondary Schools, by Organizational Level, with Projections, Fall 1984–2009**

Year	Total		
	K–12[a]	Elementary	Secondary
1985	44,979	28,330	16,649
1990	46,448	31,145	15,304
1995	50,502	33,894	16,608
2000[b]	53,539	35,438	18,101
2005[b]	54,477	35,075	19,403
2009[b]	54,174	34,844	19,330

[a]Includes most kindergarten and some nursery school enrollment.
[b]Projected.

Note: Historical numbers may differ from those in previous editions. . . . Designation of grades as elementary or secondary varies from school to school. Projections are based on data through 1996. Because of rounding, details may not add to totals.

Source: U.S. Department of Education, National Center for Education Statistics, *Statistics of Public Elementary and Secondary Schools;* Common Core of Data surveys; *NCES Bulletin,* December 1984; 1985 Private School Survey; "Key Statistics for Private Elementary and Secondary Education: School Year 1988–89," *Early Estimates;* "Key Statistics for Private Elementary and Secondary Education: School Year 1989–90," *Early Estimates;* "Key Statistics for Private Elementary and Secondary Education: School Year 1990–91," *Early Estimates;* "Public and Private Elementary and Secondary Education Statistics: School Year 1991–92," *Early Estimates;* "Public and Private Elementary and Secondary Education Statistics: School Year 1992–93," *Early Estimates; Private School Universe Survey, 1995–96;* and National Elementary and Secondary Enrollment Model.

living in poverty (see Figure E–1) (Levine and Levine, 1996, p. 28). (Box E–1 outlines factors that make teaching and learning difficult for many students.)

The Hispanic population is the fastest-growing ethnic group in the United States (National Center for Education Statistics, 1999), and more than one-third attend schools that are 90 to 100 percent minority. The dropout rate is double that of other groups. These figures indicate that schools will be teaching an increasing number of children from poor backgrounds and non-native-English-speaking households.

An increasing proportion of the minority population will be Asian refugees, immigrants, and illegal aliens; this is having a great impact in some states, such as California, where English as a second language is an important part of the curriculum. Because the percentage of children from poor families in urban areas is increasing, city tax bases are declining, causing increased financial problems. In addition to class and race composition, family structure is undergoing alterations; many children will live in single-parent households part of the time before their eighteenth birthday (see Figure E–1). An increasing number of mothers of school-age children are working, creating a need for after-school care.

FIGURE E–1 Percentage of children under eighteen years of age in poverty, by race/ethnicity and family type, 1990.

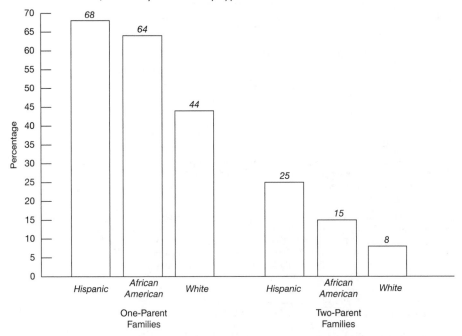

Source: U.S. Bureau of the Census; reprinted in Levine, Daniel U., Rayna F. Levine, Society and Education, 9th ed. (Boston: Allyn and Bacon, 1996), p. 28.

◆◆Box E–1 *Barriers to Student Success*

- ◆ Nearly 13 million children live in poverty, 2 million more than a decade ago.
- ◆ At least one in six children has no health care at all.
- ◆ Only slightly more than half of U.S. preschoolers have been fully immunized.
- ◆ On any given night, at least 100,000 children are homeless.
- ◆ Every year, more than a million young people join the ranks of runaways.
- ◆ The overall percentage of students graduating from high school between 1985 and 1990 decreased for whites, African Americans, and Hispanics.
- ◆ Dropouts are 3.5 times more likely to be arrested than high school graduates. [Secretary Riley (1995) says that 82 percent of all people behind bars are high school dropouts.] Dropouts are six times more likely to become unmarried parents.
- ◆ Every year, approximately one million teenage girls become pregnant. Births to single teens increased 16 percent from 1986 to 1991.
- ◆ The juvenile *violent* crime arrest rate increased by 300 percent from 1960 to 1988.
- ◆ 135,000 American students bring guns to school every day.
- ◆ Driving after drinking remains the number one killer of adolescents.
- ◆ Suicide is now the second leading cause of death among adolescents, and has almost tripled since the 1960s.
- ◆ Homicide is now the leading cause of death among minority youth ages 15 to 19 and is increasing for white youths.
- ◆ Reported child abuse increased 48 percent from 1986 to 1991.
- ◆ Fifty percent of America's adults are functionally illiterate.

Source: Stallings, Jane A., "Ensuring Teaching and Learning in the 21st Century," *Educational Researcher*, Vol. 24, No. 6, August–September, 1995, p. 4.

Many of those in poverty fail to achieve because of dropout rates and lack of access or funds to continue education. The number of service sector and skilled high-tech jobs in society is increasing, but the skills needed will change frequently because of new technologies, in turn requiring reeducation. Those who have not finished high school will lack skills and have difficulty training for the new jobs.

As our society moves into the postindustrial information age, knowledge creation and processing becomes a primary commodity. Service sector jobs in health, education, and other service areas are growing rapidly, whereas jobs in primary sectors of fishing, forestry, agriculture, and manufacturing are declining as white-collar jobs outstrip blue-collar jobs (Judis, 1994). The growth sectors will require information-processing skills, especially the ability to use computers and related technologies. Thus, job growth will be in areas requiring high levels of education; high school dropouts and less educated citizens will have increasing difficulty competing, and some will be left behind.

SCHOOLS IN THE NEW CENTURY

Predictions are always problematic; technologies are changing at such a rapid rate that tomorrow is uncertain. However, a number of futurologists have attempted to draw scenarios of the schools of tomorrow using knowledge of socioeconomic conditions, predicted new technologies, recommendations from more than 30 commission and task force reports, knowledge of demographics, and other sources. *Schools of the Future: Education into the 21st Century* (Cetron et al., 1985) presents the following concepts: shorter workweeks and longer school weeks; an earlier start in education, more education, and reeducation of the total workforce, for the rapidly changing work world; expansion of the school year to at least 210 days; more education in the home using new technologies; business involvement with schools; higher pay for teachers; computer software to replace some textbooks; and students placed in businesses for job training.

Futurologists predict that technology will play an increasing role in the educational process both in classrooms and in information retrieval out of classrooms. Teachers are likely to become more involved with their students, adding a human touch to education; more class time will be devoted to group discussions; field trips will become more frequent; demonstrations, investigative projects, and hands-on lab experiences will increase; and education will become more individualized. Lifelong learning will be a regular part of the adult experience and will take place in many settings. Structures of schools may also change, including smaller schools; more private schools, especially if a voucher system is enacted; and more hours of operation including after-school and evening programs.

Most of these plans sound plausible, but we must keep several factors in mind; first, money. Most of the suggestions for school changes require money, and at a time when many districts are struggling to hold on to the programs and teachers they have without making major cutbacks, this appears problematic. So far the public record on passage of levies for additional monies has not been promising.

In addition, some groups in American society may not participate in the new educational and economic state. The knowledge and skill gap that exists today is likely to widen the gap between socioeconomic groups and leave an even more pronounced underclass.

REFORM AND POLICY IN EDUCATIONAL SYSTEMS

Throughout this book we have discussed issues facing education today. In some cases, such as desegregation and early childhood education, policies have been formulated and programs implemented to deal with problems. In other existing and emerging areas, such as world systems of education, problems are beginning to receive attention. The sociologist has a role to play at several stages in research, policymaking, and change process. Every organization needs to have built-in, ongoing data-collection mechanisms. Sociologists can help develop procedures for collecting and analyzing data. Specific information may be sought for which methodological techniques and data gathering are important. Programs often require evaluation to determine whether goals are being met, and sociologists are frequently called on to provide these program evaluations. Data sociologists contribute to our understanding of educational systems by studying how systems work and how the parts fit together. Viewing education as a total system helps us visualize the dynamic organization that is education.

We have examined some sources of tension, strain, and change both from inside and outside the organization that provide impetus for change; yet many reformers are pessimistic about changing the "self-preserving, flexible" educational system in more than a superficial way. The implications of our discussions are that educational systems are vulnerable to pressures from within the system and from the environment. If those who implement change take into consideration the total context of the educational systems and their members, reform is possible—with the ever-present possibility of unanticipated consequences. To bring about reform, then, an understanding of individuals, organizations, and environment is essential.

The National Education Goals

Goals for the year 2000 represented the work of the Bush and Clinton presidencies in the United States and the nation's governors. The six national goals for education (see Box E–2) were an attempt to lead the educational system out of a morass in which one in ten students do not complete high school and 50 percent do not feel safe in school. Many other problems exist. A Gallup poll asked the public to indicate the importance of each goal. Highest priority was assigned to ridding the schools of drugs and violence and offering a disciplined environment to students in schools (Rose and Gallup, 1999). Whether these goals can be achieved is a matter of debate, but most educators do not feel that current policies will turn the system around enough to see major progress, and, in fact, some predict that the educational statistics will only regress ("How're We Doing," 1991).

Box E-2 *The National Education Goals for the Year 2000*

◆ All children in America will start school ready to learn.
◆ The high school graduation rate will increase to at least 90 percent.
◆ American students will leave grades 4, 8, and 12 having demonstrated competency in challenging subject matter, including English, mathematics, science, history, and geography; and every school in America will ensure that all students learn to use their minds well, so they may be prepared for responsible citizenship, further learning, and productive employment in our modern economy.
◆ American students will be the first in the world in science and mathematics achievement.
◆ Every adult American will be literate and will possess the knowledge and skills necessary to compete in a global economy and exercise the rights and responsibilities of citizenship.
◆ Every school in America will be free of drugs and violence and will offer a disciplined environment conducive to learning.

Source: National Education Goals Panel, "The National Education Goals Report: Building the Best" (Washington, D.C.: NEGP Communications, 1993), p. 3.

SOME THINGS WE HAVE LEARNED

It is clear that schools cannot solve societal problems. Although many once held out hope that inequality in society could be reduced through equal educational opportunities, we are now more realistic about the limitations of schooling. Although schooling may enhance some individuals' societal status and opportunity in societal institutions, schools can also perpetuate inequality through their structure, expectations, and other practices.

We have learned about the structure of schools, roles that individuals perform, and dysfunctions within these structures. For instance, we know that bureaucratic structures often produce conflict for professionals, and that decision making in educational systems is complicated by bureaucracy.

We have learned how classrooms and school climates affect learning. We know that the hidden curriculum plays a crucial role in the experience of students and teachers, that the value climate resulting from student backgrounds and other factors is important in student achievement, and that power relations and other interaction patterns between students and teachers in classrooms affect achievement.

We have learned that the environment can both promote and hinder or prevent educational systems from engaging in activities and decision making. Questions concerning control of school resources and decision making relate to environmental control. The home environment is a critical determinant of school success, because the child learns linguistic patterns and behavior codes at home that influence success in school. In addition, the type and level of community commitment and support is important in school functioning.

We have learned that educational systems differ greatly among countries of the world. We have discussed some of the variables that relate to these differences; they include economic and political systems that force countries into independent or dependent status, and colonial histories.

We have learned that educational movements come and go, that some new ideas are favorably received and integrated into the structure whereas others are discarded because they lack acceptance or are difficult to implement. This was exemplified by the free and alternative school movements, the back-to-basics movement, and choice movements. Educational systems are constantly responding to changes in the environment. Given proper conditions, change can be planned and implemented. Knowledge of the system and its environment can mean achieving planned change.

References

ACHILLES, C. M., PATRICK HARMAN, and PAULA EGELSON "Using Research Results on Class Size to Improve Pupil Achievement Outcomes," *Research in the Schools*, Vol. 2, No. 2, Fall 1995, pp. 25–30.

ACOSTA-BELEN, EDNA "From Structural Subordination to Empowerment: Women and Development in Third World Contexts," *Gender and Soceity*, Vol. 4, No. 3, September 1990, pp. 199–320.

ADAMS, FRANK G. "Guiding Institutional Change," *ATEA Journal*, Vol. 25, No. 1, October-November 1997, pp. 12–14.

ADAMS, MIKE S., and T. DAVID EVANS "Teacher Disapproval, Delinquent Peers, and Self Reported Delinquency: A Longitudinal Test of Labeling Theory," *Urban Review*, Vol. 28, No. 3, September 1996, pp. 199–211.

ADLER, PATRICIA A., and PETER ADLER *Backboards and Blackboards: College Athletes and Role Engulfment* (New York: Columbia University Press, 1991).

ADLER, PATRICIA A., STEVEN J. KLESS, and PETER ADLER "Socialization to Gender Roles: Popularity Among Elementary School Boys and Girls," *Sociology of Education*, Vol. 65, No. 3, July 1992, pp. 169–87.

AGUIRRE, ADALBERTO, JR. , and JONATHAN H. TURNER. *American Ethnicity: The Dynamics and Consequences of Discrimination*, 3rd ed. Boston: McGraw-Hill, 2001.

AKINNASO, F. NIYI "On the Mother Tongue Education Policy in Nigeria," *Educational Review*, Vol. 43, No. 1, 1991, p. 89.

ALEXANDER, KARL L. "Public Schools and the Public Good," *Social Forces*, Vol. 76, No. 1, September 1997, pp. 1–30.

ALEXANDER, KARL L., GARY NATRIELLO, and AARON M. PALLAS "For Whom the School Bell Tolls: The Impact of Dropping Out on Cognitive Performance," *American Sociology Review*, Vol. 50, June 1985, pp. 409–20.

ALEXANDER, KARL L., and A. M. PALLAS "Private Schools and Public Policy: New Evidence on Cognitive Achievement in Public and Private Schools," *Sociology of Education*, Vol. 56, 1983, pp. 170–82.

ALEXANDER, KARL L., and A. M. PALLAS "In Defense of 'Private Schools and Public Policy': Reply to Kilgore," *Sociology of Education*, January 1984, pp. 56–58.

ALEXANDER, KARL L., and A. M. PALLAS "School Sector and Cognitive Performance: When Is a Little a Little?" *Sociology of Education*, Vol. 58, April 1985, pp. 115–28.

ALTBACH, PHILIP G. "Trends in Comparative Education," *Comparative Education Review*, Vol. 35, No. 3, August 1991, pp. 491–507.

ALTBACH, PHILIP G., and TODD M. DAVIS "Global Challenge and National Response: Notes for an International Dialogue on Higher Education," *CIES Newsletter* (New York: Institute of International Education. January 1999), No. 120, P. 1+.

ALTBACH, PHILIP G., and GAIL P. KELLY (eds.) *New Approaches to Comparative Education* (Chicago: University of Chicago Press, 1986).

"Alternatives, Yes; Lower Standards, No: Minimum Standards for Alternative Teacher Certification Programs" (Reston, Va.: Association of Teacher Educators, 1989).

America 2000: An Education Strategy (Washington, D.C.: U.S. Department of Education, 1991).

American Association of University of Women "Gender Gaps: Where Schools Still Fail Our Children" 1998.) www.aauw.org/2000/ggbod.html

American Association of University Women "Hostile Hallways: The AAUW Survey on Sexual Harassment in America's Schools (1993)" www.aauw.org/2000/hhbod.html, 2000.

American Freshman: National Norms for 1986 (Los Angeles: Higher Education Research Institute, UCLA, 1986).

The American Freshman: National Norms for Fall 1994 (Los Angeles: Higher Education Research Institute, UCLA, January 1995).

American Library Association. "The Most Frequently Challenged Books of 1999." Copyright 2000. Available: http://www.ala.org/bbooks/challeng.html#mfcb (Access Date: March 1, 2000.)

"The American Research University," *Daedalus*, Fall 1993.

American School Counselor Association "Role Statement." Approved June 1999.

AMES, NANCY L., and EDWARD MILLER *Changing Middle Schools: How to Make Schools Work for Young Adolescents* (San Francisco: Jossey-Bass, 1994).

ANDERSON, RICHARD C., ET AL. *Becoming a Nation of Readers: The Report of the Commission on Reading* (Washington, D.C.: National Institute of Education, National Academy of Education, 1985).

ANDERSON, RONALD D. "Curriculum Reform: Dilemmas and Promise," *Phi Delta Kappan*, September 1995, pp. 33–36.

ANDREWS, RICHARD L., and MARGARET R. BASOM "Instructional Leadership: Are Women Principals Better?" *Principal*, Vol. 70, No. 2, November 1990, p. 38.

ANYON, JEAN "Social Class and the Hidden Curriculum of Work," *Journal of Education*, Vol. 162, 1980, pp. 67–92.

ANYON, JEAN "Social Class and School Knowledge," *Curriculum Inquiry*, Vol. 11, 1981, pp. 3–42.

APPLE, MICHAEL W. "Analyzing Determinations: Understanding and Evaluating the Production of Social Outcomes in Schools," *Curriculum Inquiry*, Vol. 10, 1980, pp. 55–76.

APPLE, MICHAEL W. *Teachers and Texts* (New York: Routledge, 1988).

APPLE, MICHAEL W. *Official Knowledge* (New York: Routledge, 1993), p. 215.

APPLE, MICHAEL W. "The Politics of Official Knowledge: Does a National Curriculum Make Sense?" *Teachers College Record*, Vol. 95, No. 2, Winter 1993, pp. 222–41.

APPLE, MICHAEL W. "Power, Meaning and Identify: Critical Sociology of Education in the United States," *British Journal of Sociology of Education* Vol. 17, No. 2, June 1996, pp. 125–44.

APPLE, MICHAEL W. "Justifying the Conservative Restoration: Morals, Genes, and Educational Policy," *Educational Policy*, Vol. 11, No. 2, June 1997, pp. 167–82.

APPLE, MICHAEL W., and LOIS WEIS "Seeing Education Relationally: The Stratification of Culture and People in the Sociology of School Knowledge," *Journal of Education*, Vol. 168, No. 1, 1986.

ARCHER, MARGARET *The Social Origins of Educational Systems* (London: Sage, 1979).

ARCHER, MARGARET "Cross-National Research and the Analysis of Educational Systems," paper presented at American Sociological Association meetings, Chicago, August 1987.

"An Architectural Revolution Is Going on Inside Schools," *The American School Board Journal*, August 1990, p. 9.

ARNOLD, ANITA C. "Designing Classrooms with Students in Mind," *English Journal*, Vol. 82, No. 2, February 1993, pp. 81–83.

ARNOVE, ROBERT F. "Comparative Education and World-Systems Analysis," *Comparative Education Review*, Vol. 24, 1980, p. 49.

ARONSON, RONALD "Is Busing the Real Issue?" *Dissent*, Vol. 25, 1978, p. 409.

ASTIN, ALEXANDER W. *What Matters in College?: Four Critical Years Revisited* (San Francisco: Jossey-Bass, 1993).

ASTONE, NAN MARIE, and SARA S. MCLANAHAN "Family Structure, Parental Practices and High School Completion," *American Sociological Review*, Vol. 56, No. 3, June 1991, pp. 318–19.

AYRES, ROBERT, ERIC COOLEY, and CORY DUNN "Self-Concept, Attribution, and Persistence in Learning-Disabled Students," *The Journal of School Psychology*, Vol. 28, No. 2, Summer 1990, pp. 153–62.

BABAD, ELISHA, FRANK BERNIERI, and ROBERT ROSENTHAL "Students as Judges of Teachers' Verbal and Nonverbal Behavior," *American Educational Research Journal*, Vol. 28, No. 1, Spring 1991, pp. 211–34.

BAKER, DAVID P., and DEBORAH PERKINS JONES "Creating Gender Equity: Cross-National Gender Stratification and Mathematical Performance," *Sociology of Education*, Vol. 66, No. 2, April 1993, pp. 91–103.

BAKER, DAVID P., and DAVID L. STEVENSON "Mothers' Strategies for Children's School Achievement: Managing the Transition to High School," *Sociology of Education*, Vol. 59, July 1986, pp. 156–66.

BAKER, DAVID P., and DAVID L. STEVENSON "Parents' Management of Adolescents' Schooling: An International Comparison," Chapter 20 in Klaus Hurrelmann and Uwe Engel (eds.), *The Social World of Adolescents* (New York: Walter de Gruyter, 1989), p. 348.

BAKER, DAVID P., and DAVID L. STEVENSON "Institutional Context of an Adolescent Transition: Going from High School to College in the United States and Japan," *Journal of Adolescent Research*, Vol. 5, No. 2, April 1990, pp. 242–53.

"Balancing the Tensions of Change: Eight Keys to Collaborative Educational Renewal." ERIC: ED424590, 1998.

BALDRIDGE, J. VICTOR, and TERRENCE E. DEAL (eds.) *Managing Change in Educational Organizations* (Berkeley: McCutchan, 1975).

BALLANTINE, JEANNE H. "The Role of Teaching Around the World," *Teaching Sociology*, Vol. 17, No. 3, July 1989, pp. 291–96.

BALLANTINE, JEANNE H. "Market Needs and Program Products; The Articulation Between Undergraduate Applied Programs and the Marketplace," *Journal of Applied Sociology*, Fall 1992.

BAMBURG, JERRY "Raising Expectations to Improve Student Learning," North Central Regional Educational Laboratory Monograph, 1994.

BANKS, JAMES A. "Multicultural Education in the New Century," *School Administrator,* Vol. 56, No. 6, May 1999, pp. 8–10.

BARR, REBECCA, and ROBERT DREEBEN *How Schools Work* (Chicago: University of Chicago Press, 1983).

BARTON, PAUL E., and RICHARD J. COLEY "America's Smallest School: The Family," Policy Information Report (Princeton, N.J.: Educational Testing Service, 1992).

BAUER, SCOTT C. "Designing Sote-Based Systems, Deriving a Theory of Practice," *International Journal of Education Reform* Vol. 7, No. 2, April 1998, pp. 108–21.

BAUMAN, KARL E., and SUSAN T. ENNETT "Peer Influence on Adolescent Drug Use," *American Psychologist,* Vol. 49, No. 9, September 1994, pp. 820–22.

BECK, E. M., and GLENNA COLCLOUGH "Schooling and Capitalism: The Effect of Urban Economic Structure on the Value of Education," in George Farkas and Paula England (eds.), *Industries, Firms and Jobs: Sociological and Economic Approaches* (New York: Plenum Press, 1987).

BECKER, GARY S. *Human Capital: A Theoretical and Empirical Analysis with Special Reference to Education,* 3rd ed. (Chicago: University of Chicago Press, 1993).

BECKER, HOWARD S. "The Career of the Chicago Public Schoolteacher," *American Journal of Sociology,* Vol. 57, 1952, pp. 470–77.

BECKER, HOWARD S. "The Teacher in the Authority System of the Public Schools," *Journal of Educational Sociology,* Vol. 27, 1973, pp. 128–41.

BEGLEY, SHARON "Your Child's Brain," *Newsweek,* Feb. 19, 1996, p. 55.

BELL, TERREL *A Nation at Risk,* National Commission on Excellence in Education, April 1983 report, p. 5.

BELLAS, MARCIA L. "Faculty Salaries: Still a Cost of Being Female?" *Social Science Quarterly,* Vol. 74, No. 1, March 1993, pp. 62–75.

BELLISARI, ANNA "Male Superiority in Mathematical Aptitude: An Artifact," *Human Organization,* Vol. 48, No. 3, Fall 1989, pp. 273–79.

BELLISARI, ANNA "Cultural Influences on the Science Career Choices of Women," *Ohio Journal of Science,* Vol. 91, No. 3, 1991, pp. 129–33.

BEN-DAVID, JOSEPH *American Higher Education* (New York: McGraw-Hill, 1972).

BENAVOT, AARON "Education and Economic Growth in the Modern World System, 1913–1985," paper presented at American Sociological Association meetings, Chicago, 1987.

BENAVOT, AARON "Curricular Content, Educational Expansion, and Economic Growth," *Comparative Education Review,* Vol. 36, No. 2, May 1992.

BENAVOT, AARON "Educational and Political Democratization: Cross-National and Longitudinal Findings," *Comparative Education Review,* Vol. 40, No. 4, November 1996, pp. 377–403.

BENAVOT, AARON "Institutional Approach to the Study of the Education," in Lawrence J. Saha, (ed.), *International Encyclopedia of the Sociology of Education.* (Oxford, England: Elsevier Science Ltd., 1997), pp. 340–45.

BENAVOT, AARON, DAVID KAMENS, SUK-YING WONG, YUN-KYUNG CHA, and JOHN MEYER, "World Culture and the Curricular Content of National Educational Systems, 1920–1985," paper presented at American Sociological Association meetings, Atlanta, August 1988.

BENAVOT, AARON, ET AL. "Knowledge for the Masses: World Models and National Curricula: 1920–1986," *American Sociological Review,* Vol. 56, No. 1, February 1991, pp. 85–100.

BENBOW, CAMILLA PERSSON, and LOLA L. MINOR "Mathematically Talented Males and Females and Achievement in the High School Sciences," *American Educational Research Journal,* Vol. 23, No. 3, 1986, pp. 425–36.

BENBOW, CAMILLA PERSSON, and JULIAN C. STANLEY "Sex Differences in Mathematical Reasoning Ability: More Facts," *Science,* December 2, 1983, pp. 1029–31.

BENHAM, BARBARA J., PHIL GIESEN, and JEANNIE OAKES "A Study of Schooling: Students' Experiences in Schools," *Phi Delta Kappan*, Vol. 61, January 1980, p. 339.

BENNETT DEMARRAIS, KATHLEEN, and MARGARET D. LECOMPTE *The Way Schools Work: A Sociological Analysis of Education*, 2nd ed. (White Plains, N.Y.: Longman, 1995).

BENNIS, WARREN G., KENNETH D. BENNE, and ROBERT CHIN (eds.) *The Planning of Change*, 4th ed. (New York: Holt, Rinehart and Winston, 1985).

BERGAN, JOHN R., ET AL. "Effects of a Measurement and Planning System on Kindergartners' Cognitive Development and Educational Programming," *American Educational Research Journal*, Vol. 28, No. 3, Fall 1991, pp. 683–714.

"Berkeley Student Revolt," ed. S. M. LIPSET and S. S. WOLIN, Review. *Newsweek*, 66:51, Sept. 6, 1965.

BERMAN, EDWARD H. "The Foundation's Role in American Foreign Policy," in Robert Arnove (ed.), *Philanthropy and Cultural Imperialism: The Foundations at Home and Abroad* (Boston: G. K. Hall, 1980).

BERMAN, PAUL, ET AL. "The State of Charter Schools: National Study of Charter Schools. Third Year Report" (Washington, D.C.: National Institute on Student Achievement, Curriculum and Assessment, June 1999).

BERNARD, HAROLD W., and DANIEL W. FULLMER *Principles of Guidance*, 2nd ed. (New York: Thomas Y. Crowell, 1977).

BERNDT, THOMAS J., JAQUELINE A. HAWKINGS, and ZIYL JIAO "Influences of Friends and Friendships on Adjustment to Junior High School," *Merrill-Palmer Quarterly*, Vol. 45, No. 1, January 1999, pp. 13–41.

BERNHARDT, GREGORY, and JEANNE BALLANTINE "General Education and the Education of Educators," *Record in Educational Leadership*, Vol. 14, No. 2, Spring/Summer 1994.

BERNSTEIN, BASIL "Social Class and Linguistic Development: A Theory of Social Learning," in A. H. Halsey, J. Floud, and C. A. Anderson, *Education, Economy and Society* (New York: Free Press, 1961), pp. 288–314.

BERNSTEIN, BASIL "Social Structure, Language, and Learning." *Educational Research*, Vol. 3, 1961, pp. 163–76.

BERNSTEIN, BASIL "Sociology and the Sociology of Education: A Brief Account," in John Rex (ed.), *Approaches to Sociology* (London: Routledge, 1974), pp. 145–59.

BERNSTEIN, BASIL *Class, Codes and Control*, Vol. 3 (London: Routledge, 1975).

BERNSTEIN, BASIL "Codes, Modalities and the Process of Cultural Reproduction: A Model," *Language and Society*, December 1981.

BERNSTEIN, BASIL *Class, Codes and Control: Vol. 4. The Structuring of Pedogogic Discourse*. London: Routledge, 1990).

BERNSTEIN, BASIL *Pegogogy, Symbolic Control and Identity: Theory, Research, Critique* (London: Taylor and Francis, 1996).

BERNSTEIN, RICHARD J. *The New Constellation* (Cambridge: MIT Press, 1993.)

BIAGI, SHIRLEY *Media/Impact: An Introduction to Mass Media*, 3rd ed. (Belmont, Calif.: Wadsworth, 1998).

BIDWELL, CHARLES E. "The Sociology of the School and Classroom," paper presented at American Sociological Association meetings, Boston, August 1979.

BINDER, FREDERICK M. *The Age of the Common School, 1830–1865* (New York: Wiley, 1974), pp. 94–95.

BJORKLUN, EUGENE C. "School Book Censorship and the First Amendment," *The Educational Forum*, Vol. 55, No. 1, Fall 1990, pp. 37–38.

BLACK, SUSAN "Less Is More," *American School Board Journal*, Vol. 186, No. 2, February 1999, pp. 38–41.

BLAIR, SAMPSON LEE, and ZHENCHAO QIAN "Family and Asian Students' Educational Performance: A Consideration of Diversity," *Journal of Family Issues*, Vol. 19, No. 4, July 1998, pp. 355–74.

BLAKE, JUDITH "Sibship Size and Educational Stratification: Reply to Mare and Chen," *American Sociological Review*, Vol. 51, 1986, p. 416.

BLAKE, JUDITH "Number of Siblings and Personality," *Family Planning Perspectives*, Vol. 23, No. 6, November 1991, pp. 272–74.

BLALOCK, GINGER "Paraprofessionals: Critical Team Members in Our Special Education Programs," *Intervention in School and Clinic*, Vol. 26, No. 4, March 1991, pp. 200–14.

BLANCHARD, JOHN F., JR. "Can We Live with Public Education," *Moody Monthly*, October 1971, p. 88.

BLANK, R. K., and ARCHIBALD, D. A. "Magnet Schools and Issues of Educational Quality," *The Clearinghouse*, Vol. 82, No. 2, 1992, pp. 81–86.

BLOOM, BENJAMIN S. *All Our Children Learning* (New York: McGraw-Hill, 1981).

BLOOM, BENJAMIN S. *Human Characteristics and School Learning* (New York: McGraw-Hill, 1976).

BLUM, DEBRA E. "Environment Still Hostile to Women in Academe, New Evidence Indicates," *The Chronicle of Higher Education*, October 9, 1991, p. A1.

BLUM, DEBRA E. "Athletes' Graduation Rates," *The Chronicle of Higher Education*, July 7, 1995, p. 34.

BOE, ERLING E., SHARON A. BOBBITT, LYNNE H. COOK, GEMA BARKANIC, and GREG MAISLIN. "Teacher Turnover in Eight Cognate Areas: National Trends and Predictors" (Washington, D.C.: Department of Education, October 5, 1998).

BONETARI, D. "The Effects of Teachers' Expectations on Mexican-American Students," paper presented at the annual meeting of the American Psychological Association, New Orleans, April 1994.

BORMAN, KATHRYN M., PETER W. COOKSON JR., ALAN R. SADOVNIK, and JOAN Z. SPADE *Implementing Educational Reform: Sociological Perspectives on Educational Policy* (Norwood, NJ: Ablex Publishing Corp., 1996).

BOURDIEU, PIERRE "Cultural Reproduction and Social Reproduction," in J. Karabel and A. H. Halsey (eds.), *Power and Ideology in Education* (New York: Oxford University Press, 1977), pp. 487–511.

BOURDIEU, P., and J. C. PASSERON *Reproduction in Education, Society and Culture* (London: Sage, 1977).

BOWDITCH, CHRISTINE "Getting Rid of Troublemakers: High School Disciplinary Procedures and the Production of Dropouts," *Social Problems*, Vol. 40, November 1993, pp. 493–509.

BOWEN, WILLIAM G., and DEREK BOK *The Shape of the River: Long-term Consequences of Considering Race in College and University Admissions* (Princeton, N.J.: Princeton University Press, 1998).

BOWLES, SAMUEL "Unequal Education and the Reproduction of the Social Division of Labor," in Jerome Karabel and A. H. Halsey (eds.), *Power and Ideology in Education* (New York: Oxford University Press, 1977), p. 137.

BOWLES, SAMUEL, and HERBERT GINTIS *Schooling in Capitalist America: Education and the Contradictions of Economic Life* (New York: Basic Books, 1976).

BOYER, ERNEST L. *College: The Undergraduate Experience in America* (New York: Harper & Row, 1987).

BRACEY, GERALD W. "Test Scores of Nations and States," *Phi Delta Kappan*, Vol. 80, No. 3, November 1998.

BRAMELD, THEODORE "Social Frontiers: Retrospective and Prospective," *Phi Delta Kappan*, October 1977, pp. 118–20.

BRAY, MARK, and R. MURRAY THOMAS "Levels of Comparison in Educational Studies: Different Insights from Different Literatures, and the Value of Multilevel Analyses," *Harvard Educational Review*, Vol. 65, No. 3, 1995, pp. 479–90.

BRIDGEMAN, BRENT, and CATHY WENDLER "Gender Differences in Predictors of College Mathematics Performance and in College Mathematics Course Grades," *Journal of Educational Psychology,* Vol. 83, No. 2, June 1991, p. 283.

BRINKLEY, ELLEN HENSON *Caught Off Guard: Teachers Rethinking Censorship and Controversy* (Boston: Allyn & Bacon, 1999).

BRINT, STEVEN, and JEROME KARABEL *The Diverted Dream: Community Colleges and the Promise of Educational Opportunity in America, 1900–1985* (New York: Oxford University Press, 1989).

"A British Administrator Looks at British Schools" (interview with John Coe by Vincent Rogers), *Phi Delta Kappan,* September 1979, p. 61.

BROADED, C. MONTGOMERY "China's Response to the Brain Drain," *Comparative Education Review,* Vol. 37, No. 3, August 1993, pp. 277–303.

BROOKOVER, WILBUR B., and EDSEL L. ERICKSON *Sociology of Education* (Homewood, Ill.: Dorsey Press, 1975).

BROOKOVER, WILBUR B., FRITZ J. ERICKSON, and ALAN W. McEVOY *Creating Effective Schools: An In-Service Program for Enhancing School Learning Climate and Achievement* (Holmes Beach, Fla.: Learning Publications, 1996).

BROPHY, JERE "Interactions of Male and Female Students with Male and Female Teachers," in *Gender Influences, Classroom Interactions* (Madison: University of Wisconsin, 1985).

BROPHY, JERE E., and THOMAS L. GOOD *Teacher-Student Relationships: Causes and Consequences* (New York: Holt, Rinehart and Winston, 1974).

BROWN, B. BRADFORD, ET AL. "Parenting Practices and Peer Group Affiliation in Adolescence," *Child Development,* Vol. 64, No. 2, April 1993, pp. 467–82.

BROWN, FRANK, and CHARLES J. RUSSO "Single-Sex Schools and the Law," *School Business Affairs,* Vol. 65, No. 5, May 1999, pp. 26–31.

BROWN, TONY "Challenging Globalization as Disclosure and Phenomenon," *International Journal of Lifelong Education,* Vol. 18, No. 1, January-February 1999, pp. 3–17.

BURD, STEPHEN "Who Has the 'Ability to Benefit'?" *The Chronicle of Higher Education,* January 12, 1996, p. A25.

BURNETT, GARY "Alternatives to Ability Grouping: Still Unanswered Questions." New York: ERIC Clearinghouse on Urban Education, December 1995. ED390947, Digest Number 111.

BURNETT, GARY, and GARRY WALZ "Gangs in the Schools" (Washington, D.C.: Office of Educational Research and Improvement, July 1994).

BUSIA, K. A. *Purposeful Education for Africa* (London: Moutin, 1964).

BYRNE, JOHN J. "Teacher as Hunger Artist: Burnout: Its Causes, Effects, and Remedies," *Contemporary Education,* Vol. 69, No. 2, Winter 1998, pp. 86–91.

CAGE, MARY CRYSTAL "Learning to Teach," *The Chronicle of Higher Education,* February 9, 1996, p. A19.

"California Student Sues School: Poor Reader Fault of System," *Library Journal,* Vol. 98, 1973.

"California and Texas Enter Textbook Deal," *The American School Board Journal,* August 1991, p. 11.

CANADA, KATHERINE, and RICHARD PRINGLE "The Role of Gender in College Classroom Interactions: A Social Context Approach," *Sociology of Education,* Vol. 68, July 1995, pp. 161–86.

CAO, XIAONAN "Debating the 'Brain Drain' in the Context of Globalization," *Compare,* Vol. 26, No. 3, October 1996, pp. 269–85.

CAPLAN, N., M. H. CHOY, and J. K. WHITMORE "Indochinese Refugee Families and Academic Achievement," *Scientific American,* 1993, Vol. 266, No. 2, pp. 36–42.

CARELLI, RICHARD "Divided Supreme Court Hears Arguments on School Prayer," *Texas News,* March 30, 2000.

CARLSON, JERRY S., BARBARA B. BURN, JOHN USEEM, and DAVID YACHIMOWICZ *Study Abroad: The Experience of American Undergraduates* (New York: Greenwood Press, 1990).

Carnegie Commission on Science, Technology, and Government, "In the National Interest: The Federal Government in the Reform of K–12 Math and Science Education," 1991.

The Carnegie Corporation, "Education That Works: An Action Plan for the Education of Minorities," 1990.

Carnegie Task Force on Education of Young Adolescents, *Turning Points: Preparing American Youth for the 21st Century* (Washington, D.C.: Carnegie Council on Adolescent Development, 1989).

CARNOY, MARTIN *Education as Cultural Imperialism* (London: Longman, 1974).

CARNOY, MARTIN "Is Compensatory Education Possible?" in M. Carnoy (ed.), *Schooling in a Corporate Society* (New York: McKay, 1975).

CARNOY, MARTIN "Education for Alternative Development," *Comparative Education Review*, Vol. 26, 1982, pp. 160–77.

CARNOY, MARTIN, and HENRY M. LEVIN "Educational Reform and Class Conflict," *Journal of Education*, Vol. 168, No. 1, 1986, pp. 35–46.

CARNOY, MARTIN, and JOSEPH SAMOFF *Education and Social Transitions in the Third World* (Princeton, N.J.: Princeton University Press, 1990).

CARTER, R. L. "The Unending Struggle for Equal Educational Opportunity," *Teachers College Record*, Vol. 96, No. 4, Summer 1995, pp. 619–26.

Central Advisory Council for Education, *Children and Their Primary Schools* (London: H.M. Stationery Office, 1967).

CERYCH, LADISLAV "EC '92: What Will It Mean for Higher Education?" *Educational Record*, Spring 1990, pp. 38–41.

CETRON, MARVIN J., BARBARA SORIANO, and MARGARET GAYLE *Schools of the Future: Education into the 21st Century* (New York: McGraw-Hill, 1985).

CHADDOCK, GAIL RUSSELL, ET AL. "A Challenge for Public Schools: Educating Minds and Hearts," *The Christian Science Monitor*, May 4, 1999.

"The Challenge of Multicultural Education," *Educational Innovation and Information*, September 1994, p. 2.

CHARLES, C. M. *Building Classroom Discipline* (New York: Longman, 1999).

CHASE-DUN, CHRISTOPHER "Socialist States in the Capitalist World-Economy," *Social Problems*, Vol. 27, June 1980, p. 506.

CHAVERS, DEAN "Indian Education: Dealing with a Disaster," *Principal*, Vol. 70, No. 3, January 1991, pp. 28–29.

CHEN, SHU-CHING "Research Trends in Mainland Chinese Comparative Education," *Comparative Education Review*, Vol. 38, No. 2, May 1994, pp. 233–52.

CHEN, XIANGLEI "Students' Peer Groups in High School: The Pattern and Relationship to Educational Outcomes" [Washington, D.C.: NCES. ERIC (ED410518, 1997)].

CHERRYHOLMES, C. *Power and Criticism: Poststructural Investigations in Education* (New York: Teachers College Press, 1988).

Children's Defense Fund, *A Children's Defense Fund Budget* (Washington, D.C.: Children's Defense Fund, 1996).

"Chinese Academy Considering New Restrictions on Joint Research," *The Chronicle of Higher Education*, Vol. 37, No. 42, July 3, 1991, p. A27.

The Chronicle of Higher Education, June 19, 1991, p. A25.

The Chronicle of Higher Education, Vol. 11, No. 12, November 20, 1991, p. 15.

The Chronicle of Higher Education Almanac, August 28, 1991; September 1, 1995; August 27, 1999.

CHUBB, JOHN E., and TERRY M. MOE *Politics, Markets and America's Schools* (Washington, D.C.: The Brookings Institution, 1990).

CHUTA, E. J. "Free Education in Nigeria: Socioeconomic Implications and Emerging Issues," *Comparative Education Review*, Vol. 30, No. 4, 1986, pp. 523–31.

CLARK, BURTON R. "The Cooling-Out Function in Higher Education," *The American Journal of Sociology*, Vol. 65, 1960, pp. 569–76.

CLARK, BURTON R. "Structure of Academic Governance in the United States," working paper, Institute for Social and Policy Studies (New Haven, Conn.: Yale University, 1976).

CLARK, BURTON, and MARTIN TROW "The Organization Context," in Theodore Newcomb and Everett Wilson (eds.), *College Peer Groups: Problems and Prospects for Research* (Chicago: Aldine, 1966), pp. 17–70.

CLARK, ROGER "Multinational Corporate Investment, and Women's Participation in Higher Education in Noncore Nations," *Sociology of Education*, Vol. 65, No. 1, January 1992, pp. 37–47.

CLAYTON, THOMAS "Beyond Mystification: Reconnecting World-System Theory for Comparative Education," *Comparative Education Review*, Vol. 42, No. 4, November 1998, pp. 479–496.

CLEWELL, BEATRIZ CHU, ET AL. *Breaking the Barriers: Helping Female and Minority Students Succeed in Mathematics and Science* (San Francisco: Jossey-Bass, 1992).

CLINTON, WILLIAM J. "Remarks on Signing the National Child Protection Act of 1993," December 20, 1993.

COHEN, ARTHUR M. "The Transfer Rate: A Model of Consistency" (Los Angeles: Center for the Study of Community Colleges, July 1997).

COHEN, JERE "Parents as Educational Models and Definers," *Journal of Marriage and the Family*, Vol. 49, May 1987, pp. 339–51.

COHEN, MURIEL "Gender Bias: A Textbook Case," *The Boston Globe*, March 1, 1992. p. A1.

COLCLOUGH, GLENNA, and E. M. BECK "The American Educational Structure and the Reproduction of Social Class," *Sociological Inquiry*, Vol. 56, No. 4, Fall 1986, pp. 456–73.

COLEMAN, JAMES S. *Equality and Achievement in Education* (Boulder, Colo.: Westview Press, 1990).

COLEMAN, JAMES S., THOMAS HOFFER, and SALLY KILGORE *Public and Private Schools, Report to the National Center for Education Statistics* (Chicago: National Opinion Research Center, 1981).

COLEMAN, JAMES S., ET AL. *Equality of Educational Opportunity* (Washington, D.C.: U.S. Department of Education, 1966).

COLEMAN, JAMES S., ET AL. *Youth: Transition to Adulthood* (Chicago: University of Chicago Press, 1974).

COLLIER, PAUL, and COLIN MAYER "An Investigation of University Selection Procedures," *Supplement to the Economic Journal*, Vol. 96, 1986.

COLLINS, RANDALL *The Credential Society* (New York: Academic Press, 1978).

COLTOFF, PHILLIP "Community Schools: Education Reform and Partnership with Our Nation's Social Service Agencies" (Washington D.C.: Child Welfare League of America, 1998).

"Comparing Two Plans for Education," *The New York Times*, March 29, 2000, p. A18.

COOK, RONALD J. "The Religious Schools Controversy." *America*, Vol. 172, No. 5, February 18, 1995, pp. 17–19.

COOKSON, PETER W., JR. *School Choice: The Struggle for the Soul of American Education* (New Haven, Conn.: Yale Univeristy Press, 1994).

COOKSON, PETER W., and CAROLINE H. PERSELL "English and American Residential Secondary Schools: A Comparative Study of the Reproduction of Social Elites," *Comparative Education Review*, August 1985, pp. 283–84.

COON, H., ET AL. "Influence of School Environment on the Academic Achievement," *Intelligence*, January/March 1993, pp. 79–104.

COOPER, HARRIS, and CONSWELLA J. MOORE "Teenage Motherhood, Mother-only Households, and Teacher Expectations." *Journal of Experimental Education*, Vol. 63, No. 3, Spring 1995, pp. 231–48.

COPE, BILL, and MARY KALANTZIS "White Noise: The Attack on Political Correctness and the Struggle for the Western Canon," *Interchange*, Vol. 28, No. 4, October 1997, pp. 283–329.

CORD, ROBERT L. "Church, State and the Rehnquist Court," *National Review*, Vol. 44, No. 16, August 17, 1992, pp. 35–37.

CORRIGAN, PAUL *Schooling the Smash Street Kids* (London: Macmillan, 1979), p. 92.

CORSARO, WILLIAM A. "Discussion, Debate and Friendship Processes: Peer Disclosure in U.S. and Italian Nursery Schools," *Sociology of Education*, Vol. 67, No. 1, January 1994, pp. 1–26.

CORSARO, WILLIAM A., and DONNA EDER "Children's Peer Cultures," *Annual Review of Sociology*, Vol. 16, 1990, pp. 197–220.

"The Cost and Effectiveness of Educational Technology" (Washington, D.C.: Department of Education, November 1995).

"Costs and Benefits of Higher Education," *Society*, Vol. 30, No. 2, January 1993, p. 2.

COTTON, KATHLEEN "The Academic and Social Effectiveness of Small-Scale Schooling," *Journal of Early Education and Family Review*, Vol. 6, No. 1, September-October 1998, pp. 25–28.

COUGLAN, SEAN "Lessons from on High," *Times Educational Supplement*, June 30, 1995.

COX, HAROLD G. *Later Life: The Realities of Aging*, 4th ed. (Englewood Cliffs, N.J.: Prentice Hall, 1996).

CRAWFORD, JAMES "Chapter 2 Limits Set in Suit Settlement," *Education Week*, September 17, 1986, p. 15.

CROWLEY, CAROLYN L., BARBARA LAVERY, ALEXANDER W. SIEGEL, and JENNIFER H. COUSINS "Moving Beyond Labels: Approaching Gang Involvement through Behavior." ERIC 417240, 1997.

CUMMINGS, WILLIAM K. "The Institutions of Education: Compare, Compare, Compare!" *Comparative Education Review*, Vol. 43, No. 4 (1999) pp. 413–37.

CUSICK, PHILIP A. *Inside High School: The Student's World* (New York: Holt, Rinehart and Winston, 1973).

D'SOUZA, DINESH *Illiberal Education: The Politics of Race and Sex on Campus* (New York: Free Press, 1991).

DANDY, EVELYN B. "Increasing the Number of Minority Teachers: Tapping the Paraprofessional Pool," *Education and Urban Society*, Vol. 31, No. 1, November 1998, pp. 89–103.

DARLING, NANCY "Parenting Style and Its Correlates." ERIC #ED427896, March 1999.

DARLING-HAMMOND, LINDA "Performance-based Assessment and Equation Equity," *Harvard Educational Review*, Spring 1994, Vol. 64, pp. 5–30.

DARLING-HAMMOND, LINDA, and MILBREY W. MCLAUGHLIN "Policies That Support Professional Development in an Era of Reform," *Phi Delta Kappan*, April 1995, pp. 597–604.

DAVIES, MARTIN R. "The English National Curriculum: A Landmark in Educational Reform," *Educational Leadership*, Vol. 48, No. 5, February 1991, p. 28.

DAVIS, KINGSLEY, and WILBERT MOORE "Some Principles of Stratification," *American Sociological Review*, Vol. 10, 1945, pp. 242–49.

DAYTON, JOHN "An Examination of Judicial Treatment of Rural Schools in Public School Funding Equity Litigation," *Journal of Education Finance*, Vol. 24, No. 2, Fall 1998, pp. 179–205.

DEAL, T. E., and K. D. PETERSON *The Principal's Role in Change: Technical and Symbolic Aspects of School Improvement* (Madison: University of Wisconsin, Wisconsin Center for Educational Research, National Center for Effective Schools, 1993).

DELACY, DAN R. "Unitary Status," *American School Board Journal*, Vol. 184, No. 12, December 1997, pp. 22–24.

DELANY, BRIAN, and LYNN W. PAINE "Shifting Patterns of Authority in Chinese Schools," *Comparative Education Review*, Vol. 35, No. 1, 1991, pp. 23–44.

DERIDDER, LAWRENCE M. "How Suspension and Expulsion Contribute to Dropping Out," *Educational Horizons*, Spring 1990, pp. 153–57.

DEWEY, JOHN *Democracy and Education* (New York: Free Press, [1916] 1966).

DIAMOND, J. "Speaking with a Single Tongue," *Discover*, 1993, Vol. 14, No. 2, pp. 78–85.

DIAZ, IDRIS M. "What's at Stake: The Court Decisions Affecting Higher Education and Diversity," *Black Issues in Higher Education*, Vol. 14, No. 22, December 25, 1997, pp. 19–21.

DIETRICH, LISA C. "Chicana Adolescents: Bitches, 'Ho's,' and Schoolgirls." 1998 ERIC #ED425036.

DIETZ, TRACY L. "An Examination of Violence and Gender Role Portrayals in Video Games: Implications for Gender, Socialization and Aggressive Behavior," *Sex Roles: A Journal of Research*, Vol. 38, Nos. 5–6, March 1998, pp. 425–42.

DODGE, SUSAN "More College Students Choose Academic Majors That Meet Social and Environmental Concerns," *The Chronicle of Higher Education*, December 5, 1990, p. A31.

DORNBUSCH, SANFORD M., and PHILIP L. RITTER "Home-School Processes in Diverse Ethnic Groups, Social Classes and Family Structures," in Sandra Christenson and Jane C. Conoley (eds), *Home-School Collaboration* (Silver Spring, Md.: National Association of School Psychologists), 1992, pp. 111–25.

DOUGHTERY, KEVIN J. "The Community College: The Impacts, Origins and Future of a Contradictory Institution," in Jeanne H. Ballantine and Joan Z. Spade, (eds.) *Schools and Society* (Belmont, Calif.: Wadsworth, 2000).

DOUGHTERY, KEVIN J., and MARIANNE F. BAKIA "Community Colleges and Contract Training: Content, Origins, and Impacts," *Teachers College Record*, Vol. 102, February 2000, pp. 198–244.

DRAKE, DANIEL D. "Student Diversity: Implications for Classroom Teachers," *Clearing House*, Vol. 66, No. 5, May 1993, pp. 264–66.

DREEBEN, ROBERT *On What Is Learned in School* (Reading, Mass.: Addison-Wesley, 1968).

DREEBEN, ROBERT "The School as a Workplace," in R. Travers (ed.), *Second Handbook of Research and Teaching* (Skokie, Ill.: Rand McNally, 1973), pp. 450–73.

DRINAN, ROBERT F. "The Constitution and Handicapped Hasidim Children." *America*, Vol. 170, No. 7, February 26, 1994, pp. 8–11.

DRONKERS, JAAP "The Changing Effects of Single-Parent Families on the Educational Attainment of their Children in a European Welfare State," presented at meetings of Social Stratification and Mobility, International Sociological Association, Trento, Italy, Spring 1992.

DU, RUIQUIG *Chinese Higher Education: A Decade of Reform and Development (1978–1988)* (New York: St. Martin's Press, 1992).

DUNN, SAMUEL "The Virtuality of Education," *The Futurist*, March/April, 2000, pp. 34–38.

DURKHEIM, EMILE *Education and Sociology* (trans. Sherwood D. Fox) (Glencoe, Ill.: Free Press, 1956), p. 28.

DURKHEIM, EMILE *Moral Education* (trans. Everett K. Wilson and Herman Schnurer) (Glencoe, Ill.: Free Press, 1961).

DURKHEIM, EMILE *The Evolution of Educational Thought* (trans. Peter Collins) (London: Routledge, 1977).

DWORKIN, ANTHONY GARY *When Teachers Give Up: Teacher Burnout, Teacher Turnover and Their Impact on Children* (Austin: University of Texas, 1985).

DWORKIN, ANTHONY GARY, and C. ALLEN HANEY "Fear, Victimization, and Stress Among Urban Public School Teachers," *Journal of Organizational Behavior*, Vol. 9, 1988, pp. 159–71.

DWORKIN, ANTHONY GARY, and MERRIC LEE TOWNSEND "Teacher Burnout in the Face of Reform: Some Caveats in Breaking the Mold," in Bruce Anthony Jones and Kathryn M. Borman (eds), *Breaking the Mold: Alternative Structures for American Schools* (Norwood, N.J.: Ablex, 1993).

DWORKIN, ANTHONY GARY, ET AL. "Stress and Illness Behavior Among Urban Public School Teachers," *Educational Administration Quarterly*, Vol. 26, No. 1, February 1990, pp. 60–72.

DYE, THOMAS R., and HARMON ZEIGLER *The Irony of Democracy: An Uncommon Introduction to American Politics*, 10th ed. (Belmont, Calif.: Wadsworth, 1997).

DYKGRAAF, CHRISTY LANCASTER, and SHIRLEY KANE LEWIS "For-Profit Charter Schools: What the Public Needs to Know," *Educational Leadership*, Vol. 56, No. 2, October 1998, pp. 51–53.

EARTHMAN, GLEN I., and LINDA LEMASTERS "Review of Research on the Relationship Between School Buildings, Student Achievement, and Student Behavior," paper presented at the annual meeting of the Council of Educational Facilities Planners, International, Tarpon Springs, Fla., October 8, 1996.

EASTON, DAVID *A Systems Analysis of Political Life* (New York: Wiley, 1965).

EATON, JUDITH S. "Minorities, Transfer, and Higher Education," *Peabody Journal of Education*, Vol. 66, No. 1, Fall 1990.

ECCLES, JAQUELYNNE "Does Junior High Itself Create Those 'Monsters'?" *Institute for Social Research Newsletter*, Vol. 18, 1994, p. 10.

ECKERT, PENELOPE *Jocks and Burnouts: Social Categories and Identity in High School* (New York: Teachers College Press, 1989).

EDER, DONNA "The Cycle of Popularity: Interpersonal Relations Among Female Adolescents," *Sociology of Education*, Vol. 58, No. 3, 1985, pp. 154–65.

EDER, DONNA, ET AL. School Talk: Gender and Adolescent Culture (New Brunswick, N.J.: Rutgers University Press, 1995).

Educational Testing Service, "Learning Mathematics" and "Learning Science" (Princeton, N.J.: Center for the Assessment of Educational Progress, 1992).

Education in Britain (London: Foreign and Commonwealth Office, 1995).

Education Commission of the States, "New Strategies for Producing Minority Teachers" (Denver, Colo.: Education Commission of the States, 1990).

Education Commission of the States "School Choice." *The Progress of Education Reform 1999–2001*. May 1999.

Education Commission of the States "Youth Violence. The Progress of Education Reform 1999–2001," *The Progress of Education Reform 1999–2001*, Vol. 1, No. 2, July-August 1999, p. 5.

"The Educational Progress of Hispanic Students," *The Condition of Education*, 1995, U.S. Department of Education, NCES 95–767.

"The Educational Progress of Women." Findings from *The Condition of Education, 1995* (Washington, D.C.: U.S. Department of Education, 1995), p. 13.

Effective School Practices: A Research Synthesis, 1990 (Portland, Ore.: Northwest Regional Educational Laboratory, 1990).

"Effective Schools: What Makes a Public School Work Well?" *Our Children*, Vol. 24, No. 1, August-September 1998, pp. 8–12.

EGERTON, JOHN "Back to Basics," *The Progressive*, September 1976, p. 21–24.

EISENSTADT, S. N. "Macro-Societal Analysis—Background, Development and Indication," in S. N. Eisenstadt and H. J. Heile (eds.), *Macro-Sociological Theory: Perspectives on Sociological Theory*, Vol. 1 (London: Sage, 1985), pp. 7–24.

ELAM, STANLEY M., LOWELL C. ROSE, and ALEC M. GALLUP "The 27th Annual Gallup Poll of the Public's Attitudes Toward the Public Schools," *Phi Delta Kappan*, September 1995.

ELIAS, MAURICE J. "Preventing Youth Violence," *Education Week*, August 2, 1995, pp. 54, 56.

ELKIND, DAVID "Educational Reform: Modern and Postmodern," *Holistic Education Review*, 1994, pp. 5–13.

ELLEY, WARWICK B. (ed.) *The IEA Study of Reading Literacy: Achievement and Instruction* (Oxford: Pergamon Press, 1994).

ELLIOTT, MARTA "School Finance and Opportunities to Learn: Does Money Well Spent Enhance Students' Achievement?" *Sociology of Education*, Vol. 71, No. 3, July 1998, pp. 223–45.

"Enforcing the ADA: Fifth Anniversary Status Report" (Washington, D.C.: Department of Justice, July 26, 1995).

ENTWISLE, DORIS R., and KARL L. ALEXANDER "A Parent's Economic Shadow: Family Structure vs. Family Resources as Influences on Early School Achievement," *Journal of Marriage and the Family*, Vol. 57, No. 2, May 1995, pp. 399–409.

EPPERSON, AUDREY I. "The Community Partnership: Operation Rescue," *Journal of Negro Education*, Vol. 60, No. 3, 1991.

EPSTEIN, ERWIN H. "The Problematic Meaning of 'Comparison' in Comparative Education," in Jurgen Schriewer and Brian Holmes (eds.), *Theories and Methods in Comparative Education* (Frankfurt am Main: Peter Lang, 1988), pp. 3–23.

EPSTEIN, JOYCE "Single Parents and the Schools: The Effect of Marital Status on Parent and Teacher Evaluations," Report 353 (Baltimore: Johns Hopkins University, Center for Social Organization of Schools, March 1984).

EPSTEIN, JOYCE "Target: An Examination of Parallel School and Family Structures That Promote Student Motivation and Achievement," Report 6 (Baltimore: Johns Hopkins University, Center for Research on Elementary and Middle Schools, January 1987).

EPSTEIN, JOYCE "Toward a Theory of Family-School Connections: Teacher Practices and Parent Involvement Across the School Years," in Klaus Hurrelmann and Franz-Xavier Kaufman (eds.), *The Limits and Potential of Social Intervention* (Berlin/New York: Aldine de Gruyter, 1987).

EPSTEIN, JOYCE "Effects on Student Achievement of Teachers' Practices of Parent Involvement," in S. Silvem (ed.), *Literacy Through Family, Community, and School Interaction* (Greenwich, Conn.: JAI Press, 1988).

EPSTEIN, JOYCE L. "School/Family/Community Partnerships." *Phi Delta Kappan*, May 1995, pp. 701–12.

EPSTEIN, JOYCE L., and SUSAN L. DAUBER "School Programs and Teacher Practices of Parent Involvement in Inner-City Elementary and Middle Schools," *The Elementary School Journal*, Vol. 91, No. 3, 1991, p. 289.

EPSTEIN, JOYCE, and KAREN SALINAS "New Directions in the Middle Grades," *Childhood Education*, Annual Theme 1991.

ESTRICH, SUSAN "Single-sex Education Deserves a Real Chance," *USA Today*, September 15, 1994, p. A11.

ETZIONI, AMITAI "Can Schools Teach Kids Values?" *Today's Education*, September/October 1977.

EVALDSSON, ANN CARITA, and WILLIAM A. CORSARO "Play and Games in the Peer Cultures of Preschool and Preadolescent Children: An Interpetive Approach," *Childhood: A Global Journal of Child Research*, Vol. 5, No. 4, November 1998, pp. 377–402.

EVANGELAUF, JEAN "Enrollment Projections Revised Upward in New Government Analysis," *The Chronicle of Higher Education*, January 22, 1992, p. A1.

EWEN, LYNDA ANN "Turning Around the American Dream: The Social Implications of the Changes in Education," paper presented at American Sociological Association meetings, Washington, D.C., August 1990.

EWENS, WILLIAM "Sociology and Social Change in the Coming Century," paper presented at American Sociological Association meetings, Chicago, August 1987.

FARNUM, RICHARD "Elite College Discrimination and the Limits of Conflict Theory," *Harvard Educational Review*, Vol. 67, No. 3, Fall 1997, pp. 507–30.

FARRELL, EDWIN *Hanging In and Dropping Out: Voices of At-Risk High School Students* (New York: Teachers College Press, 1990).

FARRELL, JOSEPH P. "A Retrospective on Educational Planning in Comparative Education," *Comparative Education Review* Vol. 41, No. 3 (1997) pp. 277–313.

FEENEY, STEPHANIE *Early Childhood Education in Asia and the Pacific: A Source Book* (New York: Garland, 1992).

"Female Professors in Britain Paid Less Than Males, Study Finds," *The Chronicle of Higher Education*, Vol. 38, No. 5, September 25, 1991, p. A46.

FENNEMA, ELIZABETH, and G. C. LEDER (eds.) *Mathematics and Gender* (New York: Teachers College Press, 1990).

FERDMAN, BERNARDO M. "Literacy and Cultural Identity," *Harvard Educational Review*, Vol. 60, No. 2, May 1990, p. 201.

FINCH, MICHAEL D., ET AL. "Work Experience and Control Orientation in Adolescence," *American Sociological Review*, Vol. 56, No. 5, October 1991.

FINKELSTEIN, MARTIN J., JACK H. SCHUSTER, and ROBERT K. SEAL "The American Faculty in Transition: A First Look at the New Academic Generation," National Center for Education Statistics (Washington, D.C.: U.S. Department of Education, 1995).

FISCHER, CLAUDE S., MICHAEL HOUT, MARTIN SANCHEZ JANKOWSKI, SAMUEL R. LUCAS, ANN SWIDLER, and KIM VOS *Inequality by Design: Cracking the Bell Curve Myth* (Princeton, N.J.: Princeton University Press, 1996).

FISHER, GEORGE M. C. "World-Class Corporate Expectations of Higher Education," *Educational Record*, Fall 1990, pp. 19–21.

FISKE, EDWARD B. "Gender Issues in the College Classroom," in Paula S. Rothenberg (ed.), *Race, Class, and Gender in the United States*, 2nd ed. (New York: St. Martin's Press, 1992), pp. 52–53.

Fletcher, Todd V., and DARRELL L. SABERS "Interaction Effects in Cross-National Studies of Achievement," *Comparative Education Review*, Vol. 39, No. 4, November 1995, p. 455.

FLOUD, JEAN, and A. H. HALSEY "The Sociology of Education: A Trend Report and Bibliography," *Current Sociology*, Vol. 7, 1958, pp. 165–235.

FOERSTEL, HERBERT N. *Banned in the U.S.A.: A Reference Guide to Book Censorship in Schools and Public Libraries* (Westport, Conn.: Greenwood Press, 1994).

FONTAINE, ANNE MARIE "Achievement Motivation and Child Rearing in Different Social Contexts," *European Journal of Psychology of Education*, Vol. 9, No. 3, September 1994, pp. 225–40.

FONTAINE, DEBORAH C. "Black Women: Double Solos in the Workplace," *Western Journal of Black Studies*, Vol. 17, No. 3, Fall 1993, pp. 121–25.

"Forcing Bejing University Students to Serve a Year in the Military," *The Chronical of Higher Education*, Vol. 38, No. 8, October 16, 1991, p. A51.

FORDHAM, SIGNITHIA *Blacked Out: Dilemmas of Race, Identity, and Success at Capital High* (Chicago: University of Chicago Press, 1996).

Four Years After High School: A Capsule Description of 1980 Seniors, Office of Educational Research and Improvement, Center for Education Statistics (Washington, D.C.: U.S. Department of Education, August 1986).

Fox-Genovese, Elizabeth "For Women Only," *The Washington Post*, March 26, 1995, p. C7.

Fraser, Steven (ed.) *Bell Curve Wars: Race, Intelligence, and the Future of America* (New York: Basic Books, 1995).

Freeman, Jesse L., Kenneth E. Underwood, and Jim C. Fortune "What Boards Value," *The American School Board Journal*, January 1991, pp. 32–39.

Freire, Paulo *Pedagogy of the Oppressed* (New York: Herder & Herder, 1970).

Freire, Paulo *Education for Critical Consciousness* (New York: Herder & Herder, 1973).

Freire, Paulo *A Pedagogy for Liberation: Dialogues on Transforming Education* (South Hadley, Mass.: Bergin & Garvey, 1987).

Friedman, Debra "The Academy," *Contemporary Sociology*, Vol. 24, No. 6, November 1995, p. 746.

Friedman, Isaac A. "High- and Low-Burnout Schools: School Culture Aspects of Teacher Burnout," *Journal of Educational Research*, Vol. 84, No. 6, July/August 1991, pp. 325–31.

Fuligni, Andrew J., and Harold W. Stevenson "Time Use and Mathematics Achievement Among American, Chinese, and Japanese High School Students," *Child Development*, Vol. 66, No. 3, June 1995, pp. 830–42.

Fuller, Bruce "Is Primary School Quality Eroding in the Third World?" *Comparative Education Review*, Vol. 30, No. 4, 1986, pp. 491–508.

Fullon, M. G., and M. B. Miles "Getting Reform Right: What Works and What Doesn't," *Phi Delta Kappan*, Vol. 73, No. 10, 1992, pp. 745–52.

Fulton, Mary, and David Long "School Financial Litigation: A Historical Summary" (Denver, Colo.: Education Commission of the States, April 1993).

Gallagher, Mark "A Public Choice Theory of Budgets: Implications for Education in Less Developed Countries," *Comparative Education Review*, Vol. 37, No. 2, May 1993, pp. 90–106.

Galton, Maurice "Class Size and Pupil Achievement," *International Journal of Educational Reasearch*, Vol. 29, No. 8, 1998 Theme Issue, pp. 687–818.

Gamoran, Adam, and Robert Dreeban "Coupling and Control in Educational Organizations," in Jeanne H. Ballantine (ed.), *Schools and Society: A Unified Reader*, 2nd ed. (Mountain View, Calif: Mayfield, 1989), pp. 119–38.

Gamoran, Adam et al. "An Organizational Analysis of the Effects of Ability Grouping," *American Educational Research Journal*, Vol. 32, No. 4, Winter 1995, pp. 687–715.

Garcia, Anita, and Cynthia Morgan "A 50–state Survey of Requirements for the Education of Language Minority Children." Research and Policy Brief, Institute, November 1997.

Garcia, E. E. "Language, Culture and Education," in Linda Darling-Hammond (ed.), *Review of Research in Education* (Washington, D.C.: American Educational Research Association, 1993).

Gardner, Howard "The Theory of Multiple Intelligences," *Annual Dyslexia*, Vol. 37, 1987, pp. 19–35.

Gardner, Howard "The Two Rhetorics of School Reform: Complex Theories vs. the Quick Fix," *The Chronicle of Higher Education*, May 6, 1992, sec. 2, pp. 1–2.

Gardner, Howard *Intelligence Reframed: Multiple Intelligences for the 21st Century* (New York: Basic Books, 1998).

Gardner, John W. *Excellence* (New York: Harper & Row, 1984).

Garner, Catherine L., and Stephen W. Raudenbush "Neighborhood Effects on Educational Attainment: A Multilevel Analysis," *Sociology of Education*, Vol. 64, No. 4, October 1991, pp. 251–62.

Gavora, Jessica, and Kimberly Schuld "Title IX Didn't Score the Winning Goal" *Wall Street Journal*, July 15, 1999.

GEEWAX, MARILYN "Meeting Puts Focus on Girls," *Dayton Daily News*, September 17, 1995, p. 16A.

General Accounting Office "School Facilities: Profiles of School Condition by State" (Washington, D.C.: Health, Education and Human Services Division, June 1996).

The General Social Surveys, 1972–1988: Cumulative Codebook (Chicago: National Opinion Research Center, 1998), pp. 123–41, 1223–41.

GENZEN, HOLLY "The Changing/Challenging Roles of the Principal." *The AASA Professor*, Vol. 23, No. 2, Winter 2000.

GEORGE, PAUL S., ET AL. *The Middle School and Beyond* (Alexandria, Va.: Association for Supervision and Curriculum Development, 1992).

GEORGIOU, STELIOS N. "Family Dynamics and School Achievement in Cyprus," *Journal of Child Psychology and Psychiatry and Allied Disciplines*, Vol. 36, No. 6, September 1995, pp. 977–91.

GERTH, H. H., and C. WRIGHT MILLS (eds.) *From Max Weber: Essays in Sociology* (New York: Oxford University Press, 1946).

GILLIGAN, CAROL "Women's Place in Man's Life Cycle," *Harvard Educational Review*, Vol. 49, 1979, pp. 431–46.

GILLIGAN, CAROL, NONA P. LYONS, and TRUDY J. HANMER (eds.) *Making Connections* (Cambridge, Mass.: Harvard University Press, 1990), p. 26.

GILMORE, MICHAEL J., and JOSEPH MURPHY "Understanding Classroom Environments: An Organizational Sensemaking Approach," *Educational Administration Quarterly*, Vol. 27, No. 3, August 1991, pp. 392–429.

GIPP, GERALD E., and SANDRA J. FOX "Promoting Cultural Relevance in American Indian Education," *National Forum*, Vol. 71, Spring 1991, pp. 2–4.

GIROUX, H. A. *Teachers as Intellectuals: Toward a Critical Pedagogy of Learning* (Hadley, Mass.: Bergin and Garvey, 1988).

GIROUX, H. A. *Postmodernism, Feminism, and Cultural Politics: Redrawing Educational Boundaries* (Albany: State University of New York Press, 1991).

GIROUX, H. A. "Educational Reform and the Politics of Teacher Empowerment," in Joseph Kretovics and Edward J. Nussel (eds.), *Transforming Urban Education* (Boston: Allyn & Bacon, 1994.)

GLENN, CHARLES L. "Personal Reflections," from *Choice of Schools in Six Nations* (Washington, D.C.: U.S. Department of Education, December 1989).

GLENN, NORVAL "Television Watching, Newspaper Reading, and Cohort Differences in Verbal Ability," *Sociology of Education*, Vol. 67, No. 3, July 1994, pp. 216–30.

GLEWWE, PAUL "Student Achievement and Schooling Choice in Low-Income Countries: Evidence from Ghana," *Journal of Human Resources*, Vol. 29, No. 3, Summer 1994, pp. 843–64.

GLEWWE, PAUL, and HANAN JACOBY "Estimating the Determinants of Cognitive Achievement in Low-Income Countries: The Case of Ghana," Living Standards Measurement Study Working Paper no. 91 (Washington, D.C.: World Bank, 1992).

GLUCKMAN, IVAN B. "Dress Codes and Gang Activity" (Reston, Va.: National Association of Secondary School Principals, March 1996).

Goals 2000: Educate America Act (Washington, D.C.: U.S. Department of Education, 1994).

GOODLAD, JOHN I. *The Dynamics of Educational Change Toward Responsive Schools* (New York: McGraw-Hill, 1975), pp. 175–84.

GOODLAD, JOHN I. *A Place Called School* (New York: McGraw-Hill, 1984).

GOODLAD, JOHN I. *Educational Renewal: Better Teachers, Better Schools* (San Francisco: Jossey-Bass, 1998).

GOODMAN, J. L. "Reading Toward Womanhood: The Baby-Sitters Club Books and Our Daughters," *Tikkun*, Vol. 8, No. 6, (1993), pp. 7–11.

GOSE, BEN "Test Scores and Stereotypes," *The Chronicle of Higher Education*, August 18, 1995, p. A31. (Refers to paper by Claude M. Steele, presented at the American Psychological Association meetings, New York, April 1995.)

GOSE, BEN "A 'First' for Scholarships," *The Chronicle of Higher Education*, Vol. 41, No. 24, February 24, 1995, pp. A37–38.

GOSE, BEN "Efforts to End Fraternity Hazing Have Largely Failed, Critics Charge," *Chronicle of Higher Education*, Vol. 43, No. 32, April 18, 1997, pp. A37–38.

GOSE, BEN "Measuring the Value of an Ivy Degree," *Chronicle of Higher Education*, Vol. 46, January 14, 2000, pp. A52–3.

GOTTFREDSON, DENISE C. *School Size and School Disorder*, Vol. 21, No. 2 (Washington, D.C.: National Institute of Education, February 1986).

GOULDNER, ALVIN *The Coming Crisis of Western Sociology* (New York: Avon Books, 1971).

GOULDNER, HELEN R. *Teacher's Pets, Troublemakers and Nobodies: Black Children in Elementary School* (Westport, Conn.: Greenwood Press, 1978).

GOYETTE, KIMBERLY, and YU XIE "Educational Expectations of Asian American Youths: Determinants and Ethnic Differences." *Sociology of Education* 72, no. 1 (1999), pp. 22–36.

GRACEY, HARRY L. "Learning the Student Role: Kindergarten as Academic Boot Camp," in Dennis Wrong and Harry L. Gracey (eds.), *Readings in Introductory Sociology* (New York: Macmillan, 1967).

GRASHA, ANTHONY F. "Grasha-Reichmann Student Learning Styles Questionnaire," *Faculty Resource Center* (Cincinnati, Ohio: University of Cincinnati, 1975).

GREENBERG, MILTON "Considering Tenure—It's Not Holy Writ," *Educational Record*, Vol. 76, No. 4, Fall 1995, pp. 35–36.

GREENWOOD, GORDON E., and CATHERINE W. HICKMAN "Research and Practice in Parent Involvement: Implications for Teacher Education," *The Elementary School Journal*, Vol. 91, No. 3, 1991, p. 287.

GREIM, CLIFTON, and WILLIAM TURNER "Breathing Easy Over Air Quality," *The American School Board Journal*, November 1991, p. 29.

GRIFFITH, JAMES "An Empirical Examination of a Model of Social Climate in Elementary Schools," *Basic and Applied Psychology*, Vol. 17, No. 1–2, August 1995, pp. 97–117.

GRIFFITH, JEANNE, ET AL. "Understanding the Performance of U.S. Students on International Assessments," National Center for Education Statistics report NCES-94-240, 1994.

GRIFFITHS, D. "Systems Theory and School Districts," *Ontario Journal of Educational Research*, Vol. 8, 1965, p. 24.

GROSS, NEAL, and ANNE E. TRASK *The Sex Factor and the Management of Schools* (Ann Arbor: University of Michigan Press, 1991).

GRUBAUGH, STEVE, and RICHARD HOUSTON "Establishing a Classroom Environment That Promotes Interaction and Improved Student Behavior," *Clearing House*, April 1990, Vol. 63, pp. 375–78.

GRUBB, W. NORTON "The Decline of Community College Transfer Rates: Evidence from National Longitudinal Surveys," *Journal of Higher Education*, Vol. 62, No. 2, March/April 1991, pp. 194–217.

HABERMAS, JURGEN *Knowledge and Human Interests*, 2nd rev. ed. (London: Heinemann, 1978).

HALABY, CHARLES N. "Overeducation and Skill Mismatch," *Sociology of Education*, Vol. 67, January 1994, pp. 47–59.

HALE, NOREEN *The Older Worker* (San Francisco: Jossey-Bass, 1990).

HALL, RICHARD H. *Organizations: Structures, Processes, and Outcomes* (Englewood Cliffs, N.J.: Prentice Hall, 1991).

HALL, W. D. (ed.) *Comparative Education: Contemporary Issues and Trends* (London: Jessica Kingsley, 1990).

HALLINAN, MAUREEN T. "Friendship Patterns in Open and Traditional Classrooms," *Sociology of Education*, Vol. 49, 1976, pp. 254–65.

HALLINAN, MAUREEN T. "Structural Effects on Children's Friendship and Cliques," *Social Psychological Quarterly*, Vol. 42, 1979, pp. 43–54.

HALLINAN, MAUREEN T. "The Effects of Ability Grouping in Secondary Schools: A Response to Slavin's Best-Evidence Synthesis," *Review of Educational Research*, Vol. 60, No. 3, Fall 1990, pp. 501–4.

HALLINAN, MAUREEN T., and RICHARD A. WILLIAMS "Students' Characteristics and the Peer-Influence Process," *Sociology of Education*, Vol. 63, No. 2, April 1990, pp. 122–32.

HALSEY, A. H. "Education Can Compensate," *New Society*, January 24, 1980, pp. 172–73.

HAMBLETON, RONALD K. "Translating Achievement Tests for Use in Cross-National Studies," *European Journal of Psychological Assessment*, Vol. 9, No. 3, 1993, pp. 233–41.

HAMMACK, FLOYD M. "From Grade to Grade: Promotion Policies and At-Risk Youth," in Joan Lakebrink (ed.), *Children at Risk* (Springfield, Ill.: Charles C. Thomas, 1990).

HAMMERSLEY, MARTYN, and GLENN TURNER "Conformist Pupils?" in Peter Woods (ed.), *Pupil Strategies: Explorations in the Sociology of the School* (London: Croom Helm, 1980) pp. 24–49.

HAMMERSLEY, MARTYN, and PETER WOODS *Teacher Perspectives* (Milton Keynes, England: Open University Press, 1977), p. 37.

HANNAWAY, JANE *Decentralization and School Improvement: Can We Fulfill the Promise?* (San Francisco: Jossey-Bass, 1993).

HANNAWAY, JANE "Political Pressure and Decentralization in Institutional Organizations: The Case of School Districts," *Sociology of Education*, Vol. 66, No. 3, July 1993, p. 147.

HANNUM, EMILY "Political Change and the Urban-Rural Gap in Basic Education in China, 1949–1990," *Comparative Education Review*, Vol. 43, No. 2, May 1999, pp. 193–211.

HANSON, SANDRA L., and REBECCA S. KRAUS "Women, Sports, and Science: Do Female Athletes Have an Advantage?" *Sociology of Education*, Vol. 71, No. 2 (1998), pp. 93–110.

HANUSHEK, ERIC A. "The Trade-Off Between Child Quantity and Quality," *Journal of Political Economy*, Vol. 100, No. 1, February 1992, pp. 84–117.

HARDY, LARENCE "A Private Solution," *American School Board Journal*, Vol. 186, No. 4, April 1999, pp. 46–48.

HARGREAVES, ANDY "Experience Counts, Theory Doesn't: How Teachers Talk About Their Work," *Sociology of Education*, Vol. 57, October 1984, pp. 244–53.

HARGREAVES, D. *Social Relations in a Secondary School* (London: Routledge, 1967).

HARGREAVES, D. "Power and the Paracurriculum," in C. Richards (ed.), *Power and the Curriculum: Issues in Curriculum Studies* (London: Driffields Nafferton Books, 1977), pp. 126–37.

HART, HAROLD H. *Summerhill: For and Against* (New York: Hart, 1970).

HARTOONIAN, MICHAEL "Good Education Is Bad Politics: Practices and Principles of School Reform," *Social Education*, Vol. 55, No. 1, January 1991, pp. 22, 65.

HASTINGS, NIGEL "Seats of Learning?" *Support for Learning*, Vol. 10, No. 1, February 1995, pp. 8–11.

HAUSER, MARY, CURTIS FAWSON, and GLENN LATHAM "Chinese Education: A System in Transition," *Principal*, January 1990, pp. 44–45.

HAUSER, ROBERT M., and DOUGLAS K. ANDERSON "Post-High School Plans and Aspirations of Black and White High School Seniors: 1976–1986," *Sociology of Education*, Vol. 64, No. 4, October 1991, p. 272.

HAUSER, ROBERT M. "Symposium," *Contemporary Sociology*, Vol. 24, No. 2, March 1995, pp. 149–61.

HAWES, HUGH *Curriculum and Reality in African Primary Schools* (Harlow, Essex, England: Longman, 1979), p. 163.

HAWORTH, KARLA. "Graduation Rates Fall for Athletes," *The Chronicle of Higher Education*, Vol. 45, No. 13, November 20, 1998, pp. A41–42.

HAYES, CONSTANCE "Channel One's Mixed Grade," *The New York Times*, December 5, 1999.

HAYHOE, RUTH "Penetration or Mutuality? China's Educational Cooperation with Europe, Japan and North America," *Comparative Education Review*, Vol. 30, No. 4, 1986, pp. 532–59.

HAYHOE, RUTH (ed.) *Education and Modernization: The Chinese Experience* (Oxford: Pergamon Press, 1992).

HAYHOE, RUTH "An Asian Multiversity? Comparative Reflections on the Transition to Mass Higher Education in East Asia," *Comparative Education Review*, Vol. 39, No. 3, August 1995, pp. 299–321.

HAYWARD, PAMELA A. "When Novelty Isn't Enough: A Case Study of Students' Reactions to Technology in the Classroom," *College Student Journal*, Vol. 28, No. 3, September 1994, pp. 320–25.

HEALY, PATRICK "Affirmative Action Survives at Colleges in Some States Covered by Hopwood Ruling," *Chronicle of Higher Education*, Vol. 44, No. 33, April 24, 1998, pp. A42–A43.

HEGGER, SUSAN C. "Lawmakers Pushing Gender Equity Say 'Glass Ceiling' Starts in Schools," *The St. Louis Post-Dispatch*, September 16, 1993, p. A5.

HENRY, JULES *Culture Against Man* (New York: Vintage Books, 1963).

HENRY, MARY E. *Parent-School Collaboration: Feminist Organizational Structures and School Leadership* (Albany: State University of New York Press, 1996).

HENTOFF, NAT "The Great Consumer Fraud," *Current*, March 1978, pp. 3–8.

HERBERT, VICTOR "School-Based Collaborations in Dropout Prevention," *NASSP Bulletin*, September 1989.

HERNANDEZ, DEBRA GERSH "Supreme Court orders funding of religion-oriented student publication," *Editor and Publisher*, Vol. 128, No. 28. July 15, 1995, pp. 18–19, 39.

HERRNSTEIN, RICHARD "In Defense of Intelligence Tests," *Commentary*, February 1980, pp. 40–51.

HERRNSTEIN, RICHARD J., and CHARLES MURRAY *The Bell Curve: Intelligence and Class Structure in American Life* (New York: Free Press, 1994).

HESS, BETH B., ELIZABETH W. MARKSON, and PETER J. STEIN *Sociology*, 5th ed. (Boston: Allyn & Bacon, 1996), pp. 173–74.

HEYNEMAN, STEPHEN P. "Education of the World Market," *The American School Board Journal*, March 1990, p. 28.

HEYNEMAN, STEPHEN P. "Quantity, Quality, and Source," *Comparative Education Review*, November 1993, Vol. 37, No. 4, pp. 372–88.

HIBBARD, DAVID R., and DUANE BUHRMESTER "The Role of Peers in the Socialization of Gender-Related Social Interaction Styles," *Sex Roles: A Journal of Research*, Vol. 29, Nos. 3–4, August 1998, pp. 185–202.

HILL, HOWARD "Ideas and Programs to Assist in the Untracking of American Schools," in Harbison Pool and Jane A. Page (eds.), *Beyond Tracking* (Bloomington, Ind.: Phi Delta Kappa Educational Foundation, 1995).

HILL, PAUL T., and JOSEPHINE BONAN "Site-based Management: Decentralization and Accountability," in *Decentralization and Accountability in Public Education* (Santa Monica, Calif: The Rand Corporation, 1991).

HIRSCH, E. D. *Cultural Literacy: What Every American Needs to Know* (Boston: Houghton Mifflin, 1987).

"Hispanic Education Fact Sheet" (Washington, D.C.: National Council of La Raza, February 1999).

History of Miami County, Ohio, 1880 (Chicago: W. H. Beers; reproduction by Unigraphic, Inc., Evansville, Ind., 1973).

HODGES, LUCY "Ne'er the Twain Shall Meet," *The Times Educational Supplement*, March 24, 1995, p. 16.

HODGES, LUCY "Sinbins Revived for a Dangerous Age," *The Times Educational Supplement*, April 28, 1995, p. 17.

HOFFER, THOMAS, ANDREW M. GREELEY, and JAMES S. COLEMAN "Achievement Growth in Public and Catholic Schools," *Sociology of Education*, Vol. 58, April 1985, pp. 74–97.

HOFFER, THOMAS B., and DAVID H. KAMENS "Tracking and Inequality Revisited: Secondary School Course Sequences and the Effects of Social Class on Educational Opportunities," paper presented at American Sociological Association, Pittsburgh, Pa., August 1992.

HOFFERTH, SANDRA L., ET AL. *Access to Early Childhood Programs for Children at Risk* (Washington, D.C.: U.S. Department of Education, May 1994).

HOLLINGSHEAD, A. B. *Elmtown Revisited* (New York: Wiley, 1975).

HOLMES GROUP *Tomorrow's Schools of Education* (East Lansing, Mich.: Holmes Group, 1995).

HOLT, JOHN *How Children Fail* (New York: Pitman, 1968).

HOOKS, BELL, and CORNEL WEST *Breaking Bread: Insurgent Black Intellectual Life* (Boston: South End Press, 1991), chap. 9.

HORATIO ALGER ASSOCIATION. *The State of Our Nation's Youth*, 1999.

"How're We Doing on the National Goals?" *The American School Board Journal*, November 1991, pp. 10–21.

HOUSE, J. DANIEL "The Relationship between Self-Beliefs, Academic Background and Achievement of Adolescent Asian-American Students," *Child Study Journal*, Vol. 27, No. 2, 1997, pp. 95–110.

HUDLEY, C., B. BRITSCH, W. WAKEFIELD, T. SMITH, M. DEMORAT, and S. CHO "An Attribution Retraining Program to Reduce Aggression in Elementary School Students," *Psychology in the Schools*, Vol. 35, No. 3 (1998), pp. 271–82.

HUESMANN, L. ROWELL, and LAURIE S. MILLER *Long-Term Effects of Repeated Exposure to Media Violence in Childhood* (New York: Plenum, 1994).

HURADO, SYLVIA, and DEBORAH FAYE CARTER "Effects of College Transition and Perceptions of the College Racial Climate on Latino College Students' Sense of Belonging," *Sociology of Education* Vol. 70, No. 4, October 1997, pp. 324–45.

HURN, CHRISTOPHER J. *The Limits and Possibilities of Schooling: An Introduction to Sociology of Education*, 3rd ed. (Boston: Allyn & Bacon, 1993).

IDEA www.ed.gov/offices/OSERS.IDEA/OVERVIEW.HTML, 1997.

ILLICH, IVAN *Deschooling Society* (New York: Harper & Row, 1971).

"In Beijing, Big Brother Is the Anchorman," *U.S. News & World Report*, June 26, 1989, p. 37.

"Information and Decision Making," *Educational Innovation and Information*, No. 79, June 1994, p. 1.

INGERSOLL, RICHARD M. "Organizational Control in Secondary Schools," *Harvard Educational Review*, Vol. 64, No. 2, Summer 1994, pp. 150–72.

INGERSOLL, RICHARD M. "Teacher Turnover and Teacher Quality: The Recurring Myth of Teacher Shortages," *Teachers College Record*, Vol. 99, No. 1, Fall 1997, pp. 41–44.

INGERSOLL, RICHARD M. "The Status of Teaching as a Profession," in Jeanne Ballantine and Joan Spade, *Schools and Society* (Belmont, Calif.: Wadsworth Publishing Co., 2001).

INKELES, ALEX "National Differences in Scholastic Performance," in Philip G. Altbach, Robert R. Arnove, and Gail P. Kelly, *Comparative Education* (New York: Macmillan, 1982), pp. 210–31 (esp. p. 228).

INKELES, ALEX, and DAVID H. SMITH *Becoming Modern: Individual Change in Six Developing Countries* (Cambridge Mass.: Harvard University Press, 1974), pp. 19–32.

IRVINE, JACQUELINE JORDAN "Beyond Role Models: An Examination of Cultural Influences on the Pedagogical Perspectives of Black Teachers," *Peabody Journal of Education*, Vol. 66, No. 4, Summer 1989, p. 51.

JACKSON, PHILIP *Life in Classrooms* (New York: Holt, Rinehart and Winston, 1968).

JACKSON, PHILIP W., ROBERT E. BOOSTROM, and DAVID T. HANSEN *The Moral Life of Schools* (San Francisco: Jossey-Bass, 1993).

JENCKS, CHRISTOPHER, and DAVID RIESMAN *The Academic Revolution* (Garden City, N.Y.: Doubleday, 1968).

JENCKS, CHRISTOPHER, ET AL. *Inequality: A Reassessment of the Effects of Family and Schooling in America* (New York: Basic Books, 1972).

JENCKS, CHRISTOPHER, ET AL. *Who Gets Ahead? The Determinants of Economic Success in America* (New York: Basic Books, 1979).

JENKINS, MELVIN "Factors Which Influence the Success or Failure of American Indian/Native American College Students," *Research and Teaching in Developmental Education*, Vol. 15, No. 2, Spring 1999, pp. 49–53.

JENKINSON, EDWARD B. "Tactics Used to Remove Books and Courses from Schools," in John S. Simmons (ed.) *Censorship: A Threat to Reading, Learning, Thinking* (Newark, Del.: International Reading Association, 1994), pp. 29–38.

JENSEN, ARTHUR, R. "How Much Can We Boost IQ and Scholastic Achievement?" *Harvard Educational Review*, Vol. 30, 1969, pp. 1–123.

JOHNSON, D. "Gambling Helps Tribe Invest in Education and the Future," *The New York Times*, February 21, 1995, pp. A1, A12.

JOHNSON, WILLIAM L., ANABEL M. JOHNSON, DOUGLAS A. KRANCH, and KURT J. ZIMMERMAN. "The Development of a University Version of the Charles F. Kettering Climate Scale," *Educational and Psychological Measurement*, Vol. 59, No. 2, April 1999, pp. 336–50.

JOHNSTON, JEROME "Channel One: The Dilemma of Teaching and Selling," *Phi Delta Kappan*, February 1995, pp. 437–42.

JONES, JAMES D. "Tracking in the 1990s," paper presented at the American Sociological Association, New York, August 1996.

JONES, JAMES D, BETH E. VANFOSSEN, and MARGARET E. ENSMINGER "Individual and Organizational Predictors of High School Track Placement," *Sociology of Education*, Vol. 68, No. 4, October 1995, pp. 287–300.

JONES, STEVEN P. and KARLA J. SMART "Humanness Under Assault: An Essay Questioning Technology in the Classroom," *Bulletin of Science, Technology, and Society*, Vol. 18, No. 2, May 1998, pp. 87–95.

JORDON, ELLEN "Fighting Boys and Fantasy Play: The Construction of Masculinity in the Early Years of School," *Gender and Education*, Vol. 7, No. 1, March 1995, pp. 69–86.

JUDIS, J. B. "Why Your Wages Keep Falling," *The New Republic*, Vol. 210, No. 7, 1994, pp. 26–29.

JUSTIZ, MANUEL J., and MARILYN C. KAMEEN "Increasing the Representation of Minorities in the Teaching Profession," *Peabody Journal of Education*, Vol. 66, No. 1, Fall 1988.

KALEKIN-FISHMAN, DEVORAH "Latent messages: The Acoustical Environments of Kindergartens in Israel and West Germany," *Sociology of Education*, Vol. 64, No. 3, July 1991, pp. 209–22.

KALMIJN M., and GERBERT KRAAYKAMP "Race, Cultural Capital, and Schooling: An Analysis of Trends in the United States," *Sociology of Education*, Vol. 69, No. 1, January 1996, pp. 22–34.

KAMENS, DAVID H., JOHN W. MEYER, and AARON BENAVOT "Worldwide Patterns in Academic Secondary Education Curricula, 1920–1990," *Comparative Education Review*, Vol. 40, May 1996, pp. 106–20, 824.

KANTER, ROSABETH *The Change Masters: Innovation for Productivity in the American Coporation* (New York: Simon & Schuster, 1985).

KANTER, ROSABETH *The Challenge of Organizational Change: How People Experience and Manage It* (New York: Free Press, 1991).

KARABEL, JEROME, and A. H. HALSEY *Power and Ideology in Education* (New York: Oxford University Press, 1977).

KAREN, DAVID "Toward a Political-Organizational Model of Gatekeeping: The Case of Elite Colleges," *Sociology of Education*, Vol. 63, No. 4, October 1990, pp. 227–40.

KAREN, DAVID "Achievement and Ascription in Admission to an Elite College: A Political-Organizational Analysis," *Sociological Forum*, Vol. 6, No. 2, June 1991, pp. 349–80.

KASTL, TAMARA "Upward Bound Experience: Water, Wind and Wisdom, *Winds of Change*, Vol. 12, No. 4, Autumn 1997, pp. 71–72.

KATZ, SUSAN ROBERTA "Presumed Guilty: How Schools Criminalize Latino Youth," *Social Justice*, Vol. 24, No. 4, 1997, pp. 77–95.

KEITH, PATRICIA B., and MARILYN V. LICHTMAN "Does Parental Involvement Influence the Academic Achievement of Mexican-American Eighth Graders? Results from the National Education Longitudinal Study," *School Psychology Quarterly*, Vol. 9, No. 4. Winter 1994, pp. 256–73.

KELLY, DONALD P., and JUDITH LIU "Sowing the Seeds: Reproduction and Educational Reform in China," *Comparative Education Review*, Vol. 42, No. 2, May 1998, pp. 184–96.

KERBO, HAROLD R. *Social Stratification and Inequality: Class Conflict in Historical, Comparative, and Global Perspective* (Boston: McGraw-Hill, 2000).

KERCKHOFF, ALAN C., RICHARD T. CAMPBELL, JERRY M. TROTT, and VERED KRAUS "The Transmission of Socioeconomic Status and Prestige in Great Britain and the United States," *Sociological Forum*, Vol. 4, No. 2, 1989, pp. 155–77.

KEVAN, SIMON M., and JOHN D. HOWES "Climatic Conditions in Classrooms," *Educational Review*, Vol. 32, 1980, pp. 514–25.

KILGORE, SALLY B. "The Organizational Context of Tracking in Schools," *American Sociological Review*, Vol. 56, No. 2, April 1991, pp. 201–2.

KILGORE, SALLY B. "The Organizational Context of Learning: Framework for Understanding the Acquisition of Knowledge," *Sociology of Education*, Vol. 66, No. 1, January 1993.

KING, EDITH W. *Teaching Ethnic and Gender Awareness*, 2nd ed. (Dubuque, Iowa: Kendall/Hunt, 1990).

KING, EDITH W. *Looking into the Lives of Children: A Worldwide View* (Albert Park, Australia: James Nicholas Publishers, 1999).

KING, EDMUND J. *Other Schools and Ours: Comparative Studies for Today*, 5th ed. (London: Holt, Rinehart and Winston, 1979).

KINNEY, DAVID A. "From Nerds to Normals: The Recovery of Identity Among Adolescents from Middle School to High School," *Sociology of Education*, Vol. 66, No. 1, January 1993, pp. 21–40.

KOHL, PATRICIA T., WILBERT M. LEONARD II, WILLIAM RAU, and DONNA TAYLOR "Vocabulary and Academic Interest Differences of Athletes and Nonathletes," *Journal of Sports Behavior*, 1990, pp. 71–83.

KOZOL, JONATHAN *Savage Inequalities: Children in America's Schools* (New York: Crown, 1991).

KRAFT, CHRISTINE L. "What Makes a Successful Black Student on a Predominantly White Campus?" *American Educational Research Journal*, Vol. 28, No. 2, Summer 1991, pp. 423–43.

KRAFT, RICHARD, JEANNE BALLANTINE, and DANIEL E. GARVEY "Study Abroad or International Travel? The Case of Semester at Sea," *Phi Beta Delta International Review*, Vol. 4, Fall 1993/Spring 1994, pp. 23–62.

KULIS, STEPHEN "Gender Segregation Among College and University Employees," *Sociology of Education*, Vol. 70, No. 2, April 1997, 151–173.

KUNKEL, DALE, and JULIE CANEPA "Broadcasters' License Renewal Claims Regarding Children's Educational Programming," *Journal of Broadcast and Electronic Media*, Vol. 34, No. 4, Fall 1994, pp. 397–416.

KWONG, JULIA "In Pursuit of Efficiency: Scientific Management in Chinese Higher Education," *Modern China*, April 1987.

KWONG, JULIA *Cultural Revolution in China's Schools: May 1966–April 1969* (Stanford, Calif.: Hoover Institution Press, 1988).

KWONG, JULIA "The Reemergence of Private Schools in Socialist China," *Comparative Education Review*, Vol. 43, No. 3, August 1997, pp. 244–59.

KYMAN, WENDY. "Into the 21st Century: Renewing the Campaign for School-Based Sexuality Education," *Journal of Sex and Marital Therapy*, Vol. 24, 1998, pp. 31–137.

LABI, NADYA "Classrooms for Sale," *Time*, April 19, 1999, pp. 44–45.

LAKE, ROBERT "An Indian Father's Plea." *Teacher Magazine*, Vol. 2, September 1990, pp. 48–53.

LAM, SHI FONG "How the Family Influences Children's Academic Achievement." ERIC #ED411095, 1997.

LAREAU, ANNETTE "Social Class Differences in Family-School Relationships: The Importance of Cultural Capital," paper presented at American Sociological Association meetings, August 1985.

LAREAU, ANNETTE *Home Advantage: Social Class and Parental Intervention in Elementary Education* (London: Falmer Press, 1989).

LAREAU, ANNETTE, and ERIN MCNAMARA HORVAT "Moments of Social Inclusion and Exclusion: Race, Class, and Cultural Capital in Family-School Relations," *Sociology of Education*, Vol. 72, No. 1, January 1999, pp. 37–53.

LASHWAY, LARRY "School Size: Is Small Better?" *Research Roundup*, Vol. 15, No. 1, Winter 1998–1999.

LAW, WING-WAH "The Role of the State in Higher Education Reform: Mainland China and Taiwan," *Comparative Education Review*, Vol. 39, No. 3, August 1995, pp. 322–55.

LAWTON, MILLICENT "Schools' 'Glass Ceiling' Imperils Girls, Study Says," *Education Week*, February 12, 1992, p. 17.

LAZEAR, D. G. *Seven Ways of Knowing: Teaching for Multiple Intelligences* (Bloomington, Ind.: Phi Delta Kappa Educational Foundation, 1992).

Learning to Fail: Case Studies of Students at Risk (Bloomington, Ind.: Phi Delta Kappan, 1991).

LEATHERMAN, COURTNEY. "Despite Their Gripes, Professors Are Generally Pleased with Careers, Poll Finds," *The Chronicle of Higher Education*, Vol. 46, March 3, 2000, p. A19.

LECOMPTE, MARGARET, and ANTHONY GARY DWORKIN *Giving Up in School* (Newbury Park, Calif.: Sage, 1992).

LEDERMAN, DOUGLAS "Students Who Competed in College Sports Fare Better in Job Market Than Those Who Didn't, Report Says," *The Chronicle of Higher Education*, September 26, 1990, p. A47.

LEDERMAN, DOUGLAS "A Key Sports-Equity Case," *The Chronicle of Higher Education*, October 5, 1994, p. A51.

LEE, SEH-AHN "Family Structure Effects on Student Outcomes," *Resources and Actions: Parents, Their Children and Schools, Report to National Science Foundation and National Center for Education Statistics*, August 1991.

LEE, VALERIE "Effects of High School Restructuring and Size on Early Gains in Achievement and Engagement," *Sociology of Education*, Vol. 68, No. 4, October 1995, pp. 241–70.

LEE, VALERIE E., ROBERT R. DEDRICK, and JULIA B. SMITH "The Effect of the Social Organization of Schools on Teachers' Efficacy and Satisfaction," *Sociology of Education*, Vol. 64, No. 3, July 1991, pp. 190–208.

LEE, VALERIE E., and KENNETH A. FRANK "Students' Characteristics That Facilitate the Transfer from Two-Year to Four-Year Colleges," *Sociology of Education*, Vol. 63, No. 3, July 1990, pp. 178–93.

LEE, VALERIE E., CHRISTOPHER MACKIE-LEWIS, and HELEN MARKS "Persistence to the Baccalaureate Degree for Students Who Transfer from Community College," *American Journal of Education*, Vol. 102, No. 1, November 1993, pp. 80–114.

LEE, VALERIE E., and HELEN M. MARX "Who Goes Where? Choice of Single-Sex and Coeducational Independent Secondary Schools," *Sociology of Education*, Vol. 65, July 1992, pp. 226–53.

LEE, VALERIE E., and JULIA B. SMITH "Effects of High School Restructuring and Size on Early Gains in Achievement and Engagement," *Sociology of Education*, Vol. 68, No. 4, October 1995, pp. 241–70.

LEES, LYNN HOLLEN "Educational Inequality and Academic Achievement in England and France," *Comparative Education Review*, Vol. 38, No. 1, February 1994, p. 86.

LEVIN, HENRY "The Dilemma of Secondary School Comprehensive Reforms in Western Europe," *Comparative Education Review*, Vol. 22, No. 3, 1978, pp. 434–51.

LEVINE, ARTHUR, and JANA NIDIFFER Beating the Odds: How the Poor Get to College (San Francisco: Jossey-Bass, 1995).

LEVINE, DANIEL U., and RAYNA F. LEVINE *Society and Education*, 9th ed. (Boston: Allyn & Bacon, 1996).

LEVINE, DANIEL U., and LAWRENCE W. LEZOTTE "Effective Schools Research." Chapter 29 in the *Handbook of Research on Multicultural Education*, 1995, pp. 525–47, ERIC No. 383724.

LEVINE, DANIEL U., and A. C. ORNSTEIN "School Effectiveness and National Reform," *Journal of Teacher Education*, November/December 1993, pp. 335–45.

LEVINE, DANIEL U., and J. STARK "Instructional and Organizational Arrangements That Improve Achievement in Inner City Schools," *Educational Leadership*, Vol. 40, 1983, pp. 41–46.

LEVITAS, MAURICE *Marxist Perspectives in the Sociology of Education* (London: Routledge, 1974), p. 165.

LI, QING "Teachers' Beliefs and Gender Differences in Mathematics: A Review," *Educational Research*, Vol. 41, No. 1, Spring 1999, pp. 63–76.

LIN, BIH-JAW *The Aftermath of the 1989 Tiananmen Crisis in Mainland China* (Boulder, Colo.: Westview Press, 1992).

LINDJORD, DENISE "Smaller Class Size: Raising the Academic Performance of Children from Low- and Moderate-Income Families, *Journal of Early Education and Family Review*, Vol. 6, No. 2, Nov.-Dec. 1998, pp. 6–7.

LITTLETON, ROOSEVELT "Developmental Education: Are Community Colleges the Solution?" ERIC: ED414982, 1998.

LIVELY, KIT "Administrators' Pay Increase Is Biggest in 9 Years," *The Chronicle of Higher Education*, Vol. 46, February 25, 2000, p. A46.

LOEWEN, JAMES W. *Lies My Teacher Told Me: Everything Your American History Textbook Got Wrong* (New York: Touchstone Books, 1996).

LOMPERIS, ANA MARIA TURNER "Are Women Changing the Nature of the Academic Profession?" *Journal of Higher Education*, Vol. 61, No. 6, November/December 1990, p. 643.

London Sunday Times Magazine, December 14, 1980, p. 94.

"Louisiana Creationism Law: A 'Religious Purpose,' " *Education Week*, August 4, 1987, p. 23.

LUBECK, SALLY "Kinship and Classrooms: An Ethnographic Perspective on Education as Cultural Transmission," *Sociology of Education*, October 1984, p. 230.

LUBECK, SALLY *Sandbox Society: Early Education in Black and White America* (London: Falmer, 1985).

LUBMAN, SARAH "Facing Widespread Discontent, China May Relax Rules Limiting Graduate Education and Overseas Study," *The Chronicle of Higher Education*, Vol. 37, No. 2, September 12, 1990, p. A37.

LUCAS, SAMUEL R. "Secondary School Track Rigidity in the United States: Existence, Extension, and Equity," paper presented at the American Sociological Association meetings, Pittsburgh, Pa., August 1992.

LYONS, JAMES E. "How School Principals Perceive Their Roles, Rewards, and Challenges," *ERS Spectrum*, Vol. 17, No. 1, Winter 1999, pp. 18–23.

LYND, ROBERT S., and HELEN M. LYND *Middletown: A Study of American Culture* (New York: Harcourt Brace & World, 1929).

MACFARLANE, ANN G. "Racial Education Values," *America*, Vol. 17, No. 9, October 1, 1994, pp. 10–12.

MACIONIS, JOHN J. *Society: The Basics*, 5ᵗʰ ed. (Upper Saddle River, N.J.: Prentice Hall, 2000), p. 46.

MACIVER, DOUGLAS J., and JOYCE L. EPSTEIN "Responsive Education in the Middle Grades: Teacher Teams, Advisory Groups, Remedial Instruction, School Transition Programs, and Report Card Entries," Report No. 46 (Baltimore: Center for Research on Elementary and Middle Schools, The Johns Hopkins University, February 1990).

MACLEOD, JAY *Ain't no Makin' It: Aspirations and Attainment in a Low-Income Neighborhood* (Boulder, Colo.: Westview, 1996).

MACMILLAN, JOHN "A Junior at 85" (Northhampton, Mass.: Smith Alumini Quarterly, Spring 2000) pp. 1–14.

MANN, HORACE *The Twelfth Annual Report*, 1848, in *Life and Works of Horace Mann* (New York: C. T. Dillingham, 1891), Vol. IV.

MANSKI, CHARLES F. "Educational Choice (Vouchers) and Social Mobility," Institute for Research on Poverty (Madison: University of Wisconsin, June 1992).

MAGNER, DENISE K. "Wellesley Rethinks Its Multicultural Requirement." *The Chronicle of Higher Education,* Vol. 41, No. 33, April 28, 1995, pp. A45, 47–48.

MARKLEIN, MARY BETH "Fixing Classroom Gender Inequities," *USA Today*, March 18, 1992, p. D6.

MARTIN, MICHAEL O., et al. "School Contexts for Learning and Instruction: IEA's Third International Mathematics and Science Study" (Chestnut Hills, MAss.: TIMSS International Study Center.)

MASLOW, ABRAHAM H. *Toward a Psychology of Being* (New York: Van Nostrand Reinhold, 1962).

MCADAMS, RICHARD P. *Lessons from Abroad: How Other Countries Educate Their Children* (Lancaster, Pa.: Techomic, 1993).

MCCOLLUM, PAM, ALBERT CORTEZ, OANH H. MARONEY, and FELIX MONTES "Failing Our Children: Finding Alternatives to In-Grade Retention" (San Antonio, Tex.: Intercultural Development Research Association, 1999).

MCCORMICK, THERESA MICKEY *Creating the Nonsexist Classroom: A Multicultural Approach* (New York: Teachers College Press, 1994).

MCDILL, EDWARD L., ET AL. "Institutional Effects on the Academic Behavior of High School Students," *Sociology of Education*, Vol. 40, 1967, pp. 181–99.

MCDONALD, LAUREN E. "Boston Public School White Enrollment Decline: White Flight of Demographic Factors?" *Equity and Excellence in Education*, Vol. 30, No. 3, December 1997, pp. 21–30.

MCDONOUGH, PATRICIA M. "Choosing Colleges: How Social Class and School Structure Opportunity." ERIC #ED415323, 1997.

MCEVOY, ALAN "Interview with Dr. Edward McDill," *School Intervention Report*, Vol. 1, No. 5, February 1988, p. 7.

MCEVOY, ALAN "Children of Alcoholics and Addicts," *School Intervention Report*, Vol. 3, No. 6, June–July 1990, p. 1.

MCEVOY, ALAN "Confronting Gangs," *School Intervention Report*, February/March 1990.

MCEVOY, ALAN W. *When Disaster Strikes* (Holmes Beach, Fla.: Learning Publications, 1992).

MCEVOY, ALAN "The Revelance of Theory to the Safe Schools Movement," *Education and Urban Society*, Vol. 31, No. 3, May 1999, pp. 275–85.

MCEVOY, ALAN, and ROBERT WELKER "Antisocial Behavior, Academic Failure, and School Climate: A Critical Review," *Journal of Emotional and Behavioral Disorders*, June 2000.

MCGROARTY, MARY "The Societal Context of Bilingual Education," *Educational Researcher*, Vol. 21, No. 2, 1992, pp. 7–9.

MCLAREN, PETER L. "Decentering Whiteness: In Search of a Revolutionary Multiculturalism," *Multicultural Education*, Vol. 5, No. 1, Fall 1997, pp. 4–11.

MCLAREN, PETER L. "Unthinking Whiteness, Rethinking Democracy: Or Farewell to the Blonde Beast; Toward a Revoluntionary Multiculturalism," *Educational Foundations*, Vol. 11, No. 2, Spring 1997, pp. 5–39.

MCLAUGHLIN, MILBREY W., and JOAN E. TALBERT "Contexts That Matter for Teaching and Learning: Strategic Opportunities for Meeting the Nation's Education Goals" (Stanford University: Center for Research on the Context of Secondary School Teaching, March 1993), p. 17.

MCNABB, MARY, MARK HAWKES, and ULLICK ROUK "Report on the Secretary's Conference on Educational Technology: Critical Issues in Evaluating the Effectiveness of Technology," U.S. Dept. of Ed., available: www.ed.gov.

MCNEAL, RALPH B. "Are Students Being Pulled Out of High School? The Effect of Adolescent Employment on Dropping Out," *Sociology of Education*, Vol. 70, No. 3, July 1997, pp. 206–220.

MCNEELY, CONNIE L. "Prescribing National Education Policies: The Role of International Organizations," *Comparative Education Review*, Vol. 39, No. 4, November 1995.

MCPARTLAND, JAMES M., RUSSELL L. DAWKINS, JOMILLS H. BRADDOCK II, ROBERT L. CRAIN, and JACK STRAUSS "Three Reports: Effects of Employer Job Placement Decisions, and School Desegregation on Minority and Female Hiring and Occupational Attainment," Report 359, Center for Social Organization of Schools (Baltimore: Johns Hopkins University, July 1985).

MCPARTLAND, JAMES M., and EDWARD L. MCDILL "Control and Differentiation in the Structure of American Education," *Sociology of Education*, Vol. 55, No. 2/3, 1982, pp. 77–78.

MCPARTLAND, JAMES M., and SAUNDRA MURRAY NETTLES "Using Community Adults as Advocates or Mentors for At-Risk Middle School Students: A Two-Year Evaluation of Project RAISE," *American Journal of Education*, Vol. 99, No. 4, August 1991.

MCWILLIAM, H. O. A., and M. A. KWAMENA-POH *The Development of Education in Ghana* (Harlow, Essex, England: Longman, 1975).

"Meeting Basic Learning Needs" (New York: World Conference on Education for All, 1990), p. ix.

MEHAN, HUGH "Understanding Inequality in Schools: The Contribution of Interpretive Studies," in Jeanne H. Ballantine and Joan Z. Spade (eds.), *Schools and Society* (Belmont, Calif.: Wadsworth, 2001).

MEKOSH-ROSENBAUM, VICTORIA, JOAN Z. SPADE, and GEORGE P. WHITE "Effects of Homogeneous and Heterogeneous Groupings on Classroom Environment and Achievement in Middle Schools," unpublished manuscript, 1996.

METZ, MARY H. *Classroom and Corridors: The Crisis of Authority in Desegregated Secondary Schools* (Berkeley: University of California Press, 1978).

METZ, MARY "Real School: A Universal Drama Amidst Disparate Experience," in Douglas E. Mitchell and Margaret E. Goertz (eds.) *Education Politics for the New Century: The 20th Anniversary Yearbook of the Politics of Education Association* (London: Falmer, 1990), pp. 75–92. ERIC 319140.

METZ, MARY H. "Desegregation as Necessity and Challenge," *The Journal of Negro Education*, Vol. 63, No. 1, 1994, pp. 64–76.

MEYER, JOHN W., FRANCISCO RAMIREZ, and YASMIN N. SOYSAL "World Expansion of Mass Education, 1870–1980," *Sociology of Education*, Vol. 65, 1992, 128–49.

MEYER, JOHN W., and BRIAN ROWAN "The Structure of Educational Organizations," ch. 4 in Marshall W. Meyer and Associates, *Environments and Organizations: Theoretical and Empirical Perspectives* (San Francisco: Jossey-Bass, 1978), pp. 78–109.

MEYER, JOHN W., W. RICHARD SCOTT, and DAVID STRANG *Centralization, Fragmentation, and School District Complexity*, Stanford Policy Institute (Stanford, Calif.: Stanford University, February 1986).

MEYER, JOHN W., ET AL. *School Knowledge for the Masses: World Models and National Primary Curricular Categories in the Twentieth Century* (Washington, D.C.: Falmer Press, 1992).

MICKELSON, ROSLYN ARLIN, and ANNE E. VELASCO "Mothers and Daughters Go to Work: The Relationship of Mothers' Occupations to Daughters' Career Aspirations," paper presented at the annual meeting of the American Educational Research Assocation, San Diego, California.

MILLER, C. M. L., and M. PARLETT "Cue-Consciousness," in Martyn Hammersley and Peter Woods (eds.), *The Process of Schooling: A Sociological Reader* (London: Routledge, 1976), pp. 143–49.

MILLS, C. WRIGHT *The Sociological Imagination* (New York: Grove Press, 1959).

MOLITOR, FRED, and KENNETH WILLIAM HIRSCH "Children's toleration of real-life aggression after exposure to media violence: A replication of the Drabman and Thomas studies," *Child Study Journal*, Vol. 24, No. 3, 1994, pp. 191–207.

"Monitoring the Future Study, 1999" (University of Michigan, Survey Research Center, Institute for Social Research, 1999).

MONK-TURNER, ELIZABETH "Factors Shaping the Probability of Community vs. Four-Year College Entrance and Acquisition of the B.A. Degree," unpublished manuscript, 1992a.

MONK-TURNER, ELIZABETH "Is Going to a Community College Better Than Not Going to College at All?" unpublished manuscript, 1992b.

MOONEY, CAROLYN J. "Academic Group Fighting the 'Politically Correct Left' Gains Momentum," *The Chronicle of Higher Education*, December 12, 1990, p. A13.

MOORE, DAVID W. "Americans Support Teaching Creationism as well as Evolution in Public Schools." Princeton, N.J.: Gallup News Service, August 30, 1999.

MOORE, JOAN, and RAQUEL PINDERHUGHES (eds.) *In the Barrios: Latinos and the Underclass Debate* (New York: Russell Sage Foundation, 1993).

MOORE, JOHN P., and IVAN L. COOK "Highlights of the 1998 National Youth Gang Survey." *OJJDP Fact Sheet* 123, December 1999.

MOORE, ROB, and JOHN TRENWITH "The Intergenerational Dimension of Credentialisation and Its Implications for Vocational Change in Education." *Journal of Education and Work*, Vol. 10, No. 1, March 1997, pp. 59–71.

MORGAN, NEVILLE N. "Race and Gender Differences in Support of Collective Bargaining by College and University Faculty," *Dissertation Abstracts International*, Vol. 52 (7–A), January 1992, pp. 2719–20.

MORGAN, WILLIAM R., and J. MICHAEL ARMER "Islamic and Western Educational Expansion in a West African Society: A Cohort Comparison Analysis," paper presented at American Sociological Association meetings, Chicago, August 1987.

MORNA, COLLEEN LOWE "Africa's Campuses Lead Pro-Democracy Drives," *The Chronicle of Higher Education*, Vol. 37, No. 13, November 28, 1990, pp. A1, A40.

MORRIS, DON R. "Institutionalization and the Reform Process: A System Dynamic Perspective," *Educational Policy*, Vol. 10, No. 4, December 1996, pp. 427–47.

MORROW, ROBERT D. "The Challenge of Southeast Asian Parental Involvement," *Principal*, Vol. 70, No. 3, January 1991, p. 20.

MORTIMORE PETER, ET AL. *School Matters* (Berkeley: University of California Press, 1988).

MULKEY, LYNN M., ROBERT L. CRAIN, and ALEXANDER J. C. HARRINGTON "One-Parent Households and Achievement: Economic and Behavioral Explanations of a Small Effect," *Sociology of Education*, Vol. 65, No. 1, 1992.

MULLER, CHANDRA "Gender Differences in Parental Involvement and Adolescents" Mathematics Achievement," *Sociology of Education*, Vol. 71, No. 4, 1998, pp. 336–56.

MULLER, CHANDRA "Maternal Employment, Parent Involvement, and Academic Achievement: An Analysis of Family Resources Available to the Child," in *Resources and Actions: Parents, Their Children and Schools*, Report to the National Science Foundation and National Center for Education Statistics, August 1991.

MULLIS, INA V., ET AL "Effective Schools in Mathematics: Perspectives from the NAEP 1992 Assessment. Research and Development Report," National Center for Education Statistics, NAEP-23–RR-01, 1994.

MUNITZ, BARRY "California State University System and First Amendment Rights to Free Speech," *Education*, Vol. 112, No. 1, Fall 1991, p. 4.

MYERS, DAVID and ALLEN SCHIRM *The Impacts of Upward Bound: Final Report for Phase 1 of the National Evaluation* (Washington, D.C.: Department of Education, April 1999).

MYERS, KEN "Denial of Scholarship Case Leaves Some Officials Wondering," *National Law Journal*, Vol. 17, No. 41, June 12 1995, p. A13.

NASON, R. BETH "Retaining Children: Is It the Right Decision?" *Childhood Education*, Annual Theme 1991, pp. 300–304.

National Association for Women in Education, "The Chilly Classroom Climate: A Guide to Improve the Education of Women," 1996.

National Center for Education Statistics, *Second International Mathematics Study: Summary Report for the United States* (Washington, D.C.: U.S. Department of Education, May 1985).

National Center for Education Statistics, "States Requiring Testing for Initial Certification of Teachers, by Authorization, Year Enacted, Year Effective, and Test Used," 1990 and 1998.

National Center for Education Statistics, *Digest of Education Statistics 1991* (Washington, D.C.: U.S. Department of Education, November 1991), tables 140, 357–58, pp. 134, 135.

National Center for Education Statistics, *Science and Math Teacher Preparation* (Washington, D.C.: U.S. Department of Education, 1991).

National Center for Education Statistics, "Incidents of Student Infractions," *Digest of Education Statistics 1991* (U.S. Department of Education, 1991), p. 134.

National Center for Education Statistics, *National Dropout Statistics Field Test Evaluation* (Washington, D.C.: U.S. Department of Education, January 1992), p. xi.

National Center for Education Statistics, *The Conditions of Education 1987, 1991, 1992, 1993, 1994, 1995, and 1999* (Washington, D.C.: U.S. Department of Education, 1992–1999).

National Center for Education Statistics, *Digest of Education Statistics* (Washington, D.C.: U.S. Department of Education, 1991–1999).

National Center for Education Statistics, "Access to Early Childhood Programs for Children at Risk" (Washington, D.C.: U.S. Department of Education, May 1994), NCES 93–372.

National Center for Education Statistics, "Dropout Rates in the United States: 1993" (Washington, D.C.: U.S. Department of Education, 1994), table 21.

National Center for Education Statistics, "America's Teachers Ten Years after *A Nation at Risk,*" in *The Condition of Education 1994* (Washington, D.C.: U.S. Department of Education, 1995).

National Center for Education Statistics, *Digest of Education Statistics 1994*, table 77, in *The Condition of Education 1995* (Washington, D.C.: U.S. Department of Education, 1995), p. 410.

National Center for Education Statistics, *Digest of Education Statistics*, "Selected Characteristics of Public School Teachers: Spring 1961 to Spring 1996" (Washington, D.C.: Department of Education, 1999), p. 80, Table 70.

National Center for Education Statistics, "The Educational Progress of Women." Findings from *The Condition of Education 1995* (Washington, D.C.: U.S. Department of Education, 1995), NCES 96–768.

National Center for Education Statistics "Selected Characteristics of Public School Teachers: Spring 1961 to Spring 1996." Digest Educational Statistics, October 1997, p. 80.

National Center for Education Statistics, "Sources of Supply of Newly Hired Teachers." The Condition of Education, 1996. Indicator 56.

National Center for Education Statistics, "Student Victimization at School," p. 4; and "Student Strategies to Avoid Harm at School" (Washington, D.C.: U.S. Department of Education, October 1995), NCES 95–203 and 95–204.

National Center for Education Statistics, *Student Victimization at School* (Washington, D.C.: U.S. Department of Education, October 1995).

National Center for Education Statistics, *The Condition of Education*. "Remedial Education in Higher Education Institutions." 1999.

National Center for Education Statistics, *Projections of Educational Statistics to 2009*. 1999, pp. ix, 67.

National Center for Education Statistics, *Indicators of School Crime and Safety* (Washington, D.C.: National Center for Education Statistics, 1998) pp. 34–35.

National Center for Education Statistics, "Subsequent Educational Attainment of High School Dropouts." June 1998. NCES 98–085.

National Center for Education Statistics, *Indicators of School Crime and Safety*, 1998.

National Center for Education Statistics, *The Condition of Education* (Washington, D.C.: U.S. Department of Education, 1999), p. 85.

National Center for Education Statistics, "Statistics of State School Systems; Revenues and Expenditures for Public Elementary and Secondary Education, and Common Core of Data Surveys" (Washington, D.C.: U.S. Department of Education, 1999).

National Commission on Teaching and America's Future, *What Matters Most: Teaching for America's Future*, 1996.

National Council of La Raza, "The Decade of the Hispanic: A Sobering Economic Retrospective" (Washington, D.C.: National Council of La Raza, 1991a).

National Council of La Raza, "The State of Hispanic Americans, 1991: An Overview" (Washington, D.C.: National Council of La Raza, 1991b).

National Education Association, "Status of the American Public School Teacher, 1995–96" (Washington, D.C.: National Education Association, October 1997).

National Education Goals Panel, "The National Education Goals Report: Building the Best" (Washington, D.C.: NEGP Communications, 1993).

National Education Goals Panel, "The National Education Goals Report: Building a Nation of Learners (Washington, D.C.: U.S. Government Printing Office, 1995).

National Middle School Association, "NMSA Research Summary #1: Grade Configuration" (Washington, D.C.: NCES, Digest of Educational Statistics, 1999), p. 93.

National School Board Foundation, *Leadership Matters: Transforming Urban School Boards, 1999.*

National School Boards Association, *Violence in the Schools: How America's School Boards Are Safeguarding Your Children* (Alexandria, Va.: National School Boards Association, 1993).

National Science Foundation, *America's Academic Future*, January 1992, pp. 1–4.

NATRIELLO, A., E. McDILL, and A. PALLAS *Schooling Disadvantaged Children: Racing Against Catastrophe* (New York: Teachers College Press, 1990).

NATRIELLO, GARY "Failing Grades for Retention," *School Administrator*, Vol. 5, No. 7, August 1998, pp. 14–17.

NATRIELLO, GARY, and EDWARD L. McDILL "Performance Standards, Student Effort on Homework, and Academic Achievement," *Sociology of Education*, Vol. 59, January 1986, pp. 18–31.

NCAA Guide for the College-Bound Student Athlete, 1995–96," Overland Park, Kans., April 1995.

NEILL, A. S. *Summerhill: A Radical Approach to Child Rearing* (New York: Hart, 1960).

1999 NCAA Graduation Rates Summary www.ncaa/grad-rates, 1999.

NEPPL, TRICIA K. and ANN D. MURRY "Social Dominance and Play Patterns among Preschoolers: Gender Comparison," *Sex Roles: A Journal of Research*, Vol. 36, Nos. 5–6, March 1997, pp. 381–93.

"A New Divide Between Black and White," *Newsweek*, June 21, 1999.

New York City Board of Education, *2000 Annual Report.*

NEWPORT, FRANK "Media Portrayals of Violence Seen by Many as Causes of Real-life Violence." The Gallup Organization, May 10, 1999b.

NEWPORT, FRANK "Television Remains Americans' Top Choice for Evening Recreation." Gallup Poll www.gallup.com/pollreleases/pr990301a.asp/2000a.

NOGUERA, PEDRO A. "Preventing and Producing Violence: A Critical Analysis of Responses to School Violence," *Harvard Educational Review*, Vol. 65, No. 2, Summer 1995, pp. 189–212.

"Number of Colleges by Enrollment, Fall 1995," U.S. Department of Education, in *The Chronicle of Higher Education Almanac*, September 1, 1995, p. 12.

NUWER, HAND *Broken Pledges: The Deadly Rite of Hazing* (Marietta, Ga.: Longstreet Press, 1990).

NYE, B. A., C. M. ACHILLES, J. BOYD-ZAHARIAS, B. D. FULTON, and M. P. WALLENHORST "Small Is Far Better," *Better Research in the Schools*, Vol. 1, No. 1, Spring 1994, pp. 9–20.

OAKES, JEANNIE "Tracking, Inequality, and the Rhetoric of Reform: Why Schools Don't Change," *Journal of Education*, Vol. 168, No. 1, 1986, pp. 60–80.

OAKES, JEANNIE *Multiplying Inequalities: The Effects of Race, Social Class, and Tracking on Opportunities to Learn Mathematics and Science* (Santa Monica, Calif: The Rand Corporation, 1990).

OAKES, JEANNIE "Two cities' tracking and within-school segregation," *Teachers College Record*, Summer 1995, Vol. 96, No. 4, pp. 681–90.

OCHILTREE, GAY "Effects of Child Care on Young Children: Forty Years of Research," Childhood Study Paper No. 5 (Melbourne: Australian Institute of Family Studies, 1994).

Office of Bilingual Education and Minority Affairs. *General Questions on Bilingual Education* (Washington, D.C.: Government Printing Office, 1996).

OGBU, J. U. "Immigrant and Involuntary Minorities in Comparative Perspective," in M.A. Gibson and J.U. Ogbu, *Minority Status and Schooling: A Comparative Study of Immigrant and Involuntary Minorities* (New York: Garland, 1991), pp. 3–33.

Ohio Revised Code 3345.27, Amended Senate Bill 497.

OLSEN, KRISTEN "Despite Increases, Women and Minorities Still Underrepresented in Undergraduate and Graduate Science and Engineering Education" (Washington, D.C.: National Science Foundation, January 15, 1999).

OLSEN, MARVIN E. *The Process of Social Organization* (New York: Holt, Rinehart and Winston, 1968).

OLSEN, MARVIN E. *The Process of Social Organization: Power in Social Systems*, 2nd ed. (New York: Holt, Rinehart and Winston, 1978).

OLSON, CINDY "Two-Year Colleges: Serving Today's Students." *Connections,* Vol. 3, No. 4, Winter 1996, pp. 1 and 7.

OLSON, LYNN "Milwaukee Voucher Plan Found Not to 'Skim' Cream," *Education Week,* Vol. 11, No. 14, December 4, 1991, p. 12.

OPIE, IONA *The People in the Playground* (Oxford: Oxford University Press, 1993), p. 7.

ORFIELD, GARY A. *Public School Desegregation in the United States, 1968–1980,* U.S. Department of Education (Washington, D.C.: Joint Center for Political Studies, 1983), p. 4.

ORFIELD, GARY A., MARK D. BACHMEIER, DAVID R. JAMES, and TAMELA EITLE "Deepening Segregation in American Public Schools: A Special Report from the Harvard Project on School Desegregation, *Equity and Excellence in Education,* Vol. 30, No. 2, September 1997, pp. 5–24.

ORFIELD, GARY A., ET AL. "Status of School Desegregation: The Next Generation," Report to the National School Board Association (Alexandria, Va.: National School Board Association, 1992).

"Origin Theories Find Support for Schools," The Associated Press, March 11, 2000.

ORNSTEIN, ALLAN C. "Enrollment Trends in Big-City Schools," *Peabody Journal of Education,* Vol. 66, No. 4, Summer 1991, pp. 65–67.

ORNSTEIN, ALLAN C., and DANIEL U. LEVINE *An Introduction to the Foundations of Education,* 3rd ed. (Boston: Houghton Mifflin, 1985).

OROMANER, MARK "The Cooling Out Function and Beyond: Some Applications of Sociological Analysis to the Community College," in *ASA Resource Materials for Teaching* (Washington, D.C.: American Sociological Association, 1995).

OSGUTHORPE, RUSSELL T., and ROBERT S. PATTERSON. "Balancing the Tensions of Change: Eight Keys to Collaborative Educational Renewal." ERIC: ED424690, 1998.

OSTRANDER, KENNETH H., and KATHERINE OSTROM "Attitudes Underlying the Politics of Parent Involvement," *National Forum of Applied Educational Research Journal,* Vol. 3, No. 2, 1991, p. 37.

OTTER, JENNY *Women's Issues and Career Research Unit.* California State Framework Area: Social Studies, 1994.

OTTO, JEAN H. "Citizenship Literacy: No Longer a Luxury," *Social Education,* October 1990, p. 360.

PAGE, ANN L., and DONALD A. CLELLAND "The Kanawha County Textbook Controversy: A Study of the Politics of Life Style Concern," *Social Forces,* Vol. 57, 1978, pp. 265–81.

PALLAS, AARON M. "The Changing Nature of the Disadvantaged Population: Current Dimensions and Future Trends," *Educational Researcher,* June/July 1989, pp. 16–22.

PALLAS, AARON M., ET AL. "Ability-Group Effects: Instructional, Social, or Institutional?" *Sociology of Education,* Vol. 67, January 1994, pp. 27–46.

"Parent Involvement in Education" (Washington, D.C.: U.S. Department of Education, National Center for Education Statistics, 1994).

PARSONS, TALCOTT "Equality and Inequality in Modern Society, or Social Stratification Revisited," in Edward O. Lauman (ed.), *Social Stratification* (New York: Bobbs-Merrill, 1970), pp. 13–72.

PARSONS, TALCOTT "The School Class as a Social System: Some of Its Functions in American Society," *Harvard Educational Review*, Vol. 29, No. 4, 1959.

PASHAL, ROSANNE A., ET AL. "The Effects of Homework on Learning: A Quantitative Synthesis," *Journal of Educational Research*, Vol. 78, No. 2, 1984, pp. 97–104.

PASSOW, A. HARRY, ET AL. *The National Case Study: An Empirical Comparative Study of Twenty-One Educational Systems* (New York: Wiley, 1976).

PAULSTON, ROLLAND G. "Mapping Comparative Education After Postmodernity," *Comparative Education Review*, Vol. 43, No. 4, November 1999, pp. 438–63.

PEDERSEN, DARHL M. "Privacy Preferences and Classroom Seat Selection," *Social Behavior and Personality*, Vol. 22, No. 4, 1994, pp. 393–98.

PENA, ROBERT A. "Cultural Differences and the Construction of Meaning: Implications for the Leadership and Organizational Context of Schools," *Educational Policy Analysis Archives*, Vol. 5, No. 10, April 8, 1997.

People for the American Way, "Most Frequently Challenged Books, 1982–1987," *Education Week*, September 16, 1987, p. 3.

PERKINS, JAMES A. "Missions and Organizations: A Redefinition," in Perkins, *The University as an Organization: A Report for The Carnegie Commission on Higher Education* (New York: McGraw-Hill, 1973), p. 258.

PERSELL, CAROLINE HODGES, SOPHIA CATSAMBIS, AND PETER W. COOKSON, JR. "Differential Asset Conversion: Class and Gender Pathways to Selective Colleges," *Sociology of Education*, Vol. 65, No. 3, July 1992, pp. 208–25.

PERSELL, CAROLINE HODGES, and PETER W. COOKSON, JR. "Chartering and Bartering: Elite Education and Social Reproduction," *Social Problems*, Vol. 33, No. 2, December 1985.

PESCOSOLIDO, BERNICE A., and RONALD AMINZADE (eds.) *The Social Worlds of Higher Education* (Thousand Oaks, Calif.: Pine Forge Press, 1999).

PETERS, DONALD L. "Social Science and Social Policy and the Care of Young Children: Head Start and After," *Journal of Applied Developmental Psychology*, Vol. 1, 1980, pp. 14, 22, 24.

PETERS, WILLIAM *A Class Divided* (New York: Doubleday, 1971).

PHILLIPS, MARIAN B. and AMOS J. HATCH "Why Teach? Prospective Teachers' Reasons for Entering the Profession," paper presented at the 8th Reconceptualizing Early Childhood Education Conference, Columbus, June 27, 1999.

PINCUS, FRED L. "Customized Contract Training in Community Colleges: Who Really Benefits?," paper presented at American Sociological Association meetings, Washington, D.C., August 1985.

PINCUS, FRED L. "How Critics View the Community College's Role in the Twenty-first Century," in George A. Baker III (ed.), *A Handbook on the Community College in America: Its History, Mission, and Management* (Westport, Conn.: Greenwood Press, 1994).

"Poll: Origin Theories Find Support for Schools." The Associated Press, March 11, 2000.

POPPLETON, PAM, BORIS S. GERSHUNSKY, and ROBERT T. PULLIN "Changes in Administrative Control and Teacher Satisfaction in England and the USSR," *Comparative Education Review*, Vol. 38, No. 3, August 1994.

PORTES, ALEJANDRO, and LINGXIN HAO "E Pluribus Unum: Bilingualism and Loss of Language in the Second Generation," *Sociology of Education* Vol. 71, No. 4, October 1998, pp. 269–94.

PORTES, ALEJANDRO, and KENNETH L. WILSON "Black-White Differences in Educational Attainment," *American Sociological Review*, Vol. 41, 1976, pp. 414–31.

POWELL, BRIAN, and LAIA CARR STEELMAN "The Liability of Having Brothers: Paying for College and the Sex Composition of the Family," *Sociology of Education*, Vol. 62, No. 2, April 1989, pp. 134–47.

"Preprimary Enrollment Rates in Western Countries," *Education Week*, January 29, 1992, p. 7.

PROVENZO, EUGENE F.   *Religious Fundamentalism and American Education: The Battle for the Public Schools* (Albany: State University of New York Press, 1990).

PURCELL, P., and L. STEWARD   "Dick and Jane in 1989," *Sex Roles*, Vol. 22, 1990, pp. 177–85.

RABKIN, JEREMY   "The Curious Case of Kiryas Joel," *Commentary*, Vol. 98, No. 5, November 1994, pp. 58–60.

RADIN, NORMA   "Working Moms Are Positive Role Models," *USA Today: The Magazine of the American Scene*, August 1990, p. 5.

RAFFINI, JAMES P.   "Student Apathy: A Motivational Dilemma," *Educational Leadership*, September 1986, pp. 53–55.

RAMIREZ, FRANCISCO O., and JOHN BOLI-BENNETT   "Global Patterns of Educational Institutionalization," in Philip G. Altbach, Robert F. Arnove, and Gail Paradise Kelly (eds.), *Comparative Education* (New York: Advert, 1982) pp. 15–36 (esp. p. 18).

RAMIREZ, FRANCISCO O., and JOHN BOLI-Bennett   "The Political Construction of Mass Schooling: European Origins and Worldwide Institutionalization," paper presented at American Sociological Association meetings, Chicago, August 1987.

RAVITCH, DIANE   "Multiculturalism Yes, Particularism No," *The Chronicle of Higher Education*, October 24, 1990, p. A44.

RAYMOND, CHRIS   "Pioneering Research Challenges Accepted Notions Concerning the Cognitive Abilities of Infants," *The Chronicle of Higher Education*, January 23, 1991, p. A5.

RAYWID, MARY ANNE   "Separate Classes for the Gifted? A Skeptical Look," *Educational Perspectives*, Vol. 26, No. 1, 1989.

RAYWID, MARY ANNE   "Current Literature on Small Schools" (Charleston, W. Va.: ERIC Clearinghouse on Rural Education and Small Schools, January 1999), p. 4.

Reaching the Goals 6: Safe Disciplined and Drug-Free Schools (Washington, D.C.: U.S. Department of Education, February 1993).

REDDING, SAM   "Family Values, the Curriculum of the Home, and Educational Productivity," *School Community Journal*, Vol. 2, No. 1, Spring-Summer 1992, pp. 62–69.

REDOVICH, DENNIS W.   "The Education and Financial Systems of the World and the Big Con." Part One—World Education and Educational Reform in Europe. Report 10 Update. ERIC ED4326074.

REICH, R. B.   "Jobs: Skills Before Credentials," *The Wall Street Journal*, February 2, 1994, p. A16.

REIN, ANDREW S.   "The State of Municipal Services in the 1990s: Crowding, Building Conditions and Staffing in New York City Public Schools" (New York: Citizens Budget Commission, September 1997).

RENZETTI, CLAIRE, and DANIEL CURRAN   *Social Problems: Society in Crisis*, 5th ed. (Boston: Allyn and Bacon, 2000).

Report of the Board of Indian Commissions to the Secretary of the Interior (Meriam Report), 1928, pp. ii and 41.

"Research and the Renewal of Education: Executive Summary and Recommendations," *Educational Researcher*, Vol. 20, No. 6, August/September 1991, pp. 19–22.

RETTIG, MICHAEL D., and ROBERT LYNN CANADY   "The Effects of Block Scheduling," *School Administrator*, Vol. 56, No. 3, March 1999, pp. 14–20.

REYES, PEDRO, and DONALD J. MCCARTY   "Factors Related to the Power of Lower Participants in Educational Organizations: Multiple Perspectives," *Sociological Focus*, Vol. 23, No. 1, February 1990, pp. 17–30.

REYNOLDS, ARTHUR J.   "Comparing Measures of Parental Involvement and Their Effects on Academic Achievement," *Early Childhood Research Quarterly*, Vol. 7, No. 3, September 1993, pp. 441–62.

REYNOLDS, ARTHUR J. "Early Schooling of Children at Risk," *American Educational Research Journal*, Vol. 28, No. 2, Summer 1991, pp. 392–422.

RHOADES, GARY, and SHEILA SLAUGHTER "Professors, Administrators, and Patents: The Negotiation of Technology Transfer," *Sociology of Education*, Vol. 64, April 1991, pp. 65–77.

RICHARDSON, B. "More Power to the Tribes," *The New York Times*, July 7, 1993, p. A11.

RICHMOND-ABBOTT, MARIE *Masculine and Feminine: Gender Roles over the Life Cycle*, 2nd ed. (New York: McGraw-Hill, 1992).

RIEHL, CAROLYN, GARY NATRIELLO, and AARON M. PALLAS "Losing Track: The Dynamics of Student Assignment Processes in High School," paper presented at American Sociological Association meeting, Pittsburgh, Pa., August 1992.

RIORDAN, CORNELIUS *Girls and Boys in School: Together or Separate?* (New York: Teachers College Press, 1990).

RIORDAN, CORNELIUS "Single- and Mixed-Gender Colleges for Women: Education and Occupational Outcomes," *Review of Higher Education*, Vol. 15, No. 3, Spring 1992.

ROBERTS, TERRY, and LAURA BILLINGS *The Paideia Classroom: Teaching for Understanding* (Larchmont, N.Y.: Eye on Education, 1999).

ROBINSON, JEAN C. "Stumbling on Two Legs: Education and Reform in China," *Comparative Education Review*, Vol. 35, No. 1, 1991, pp. 177–89.

RODERICK, MELISSA "Grade Retention and School Dropout: Investigating the Association." *American Educational Research Journal*, Vol. 31, No. 4, Winter 1994, pp. 729–59.

RODERICK, MELISSA "Grade Retention and School Dropout: Policy Debate and Research Questions," *Phi Delta Kappan Research Bulletin*, Vol. 15, No. 8, December 1995, pp. 1–6.

RODRIGUEZ, L. J. *Always Running: La Vida Loca: Gang Days in L.A.* (New York: Simon & Schuster, 1993).

ROGERS, DAVID *110 Livingston Street: Politics and Bureaucracy in the New York City School System* (New York : Vintage Books, 1969).

ROSE, LOWELL C., and ALEX M. GALLUP, "The 31st Annual Phi Delta Kappan/Gallup Poll of the Public's Attitudes Toward the Public Schools," *Phi Delta Kappan*, September 1999, pp. 41–56.

ROSENBAUM, JAMES E., and AMY BINDER "Do Employers Really Need More Educated Youths?" *Sociology of Education*, Vol. 73, No. 1, January 1997, pp. 68–85.

ROSENBAUM, JAMES E., ET AL. "Gatekeeping in an Era of More Open Gates: High School Counselors' View of Their Influence on Students' College Plans," *American Journal of Education*, Vol. 104, No. 4, August 1996, pp. 257–79.

ROSENHOLTZ, SUSAN J., and CARL SIMPSON "Workplace Conditions and the Rise and Fall of Teachers' Commitment," *Sociology of Education*, Vol. 63, No. 4, October 1990, pp. 241–57.

ROSENTHAL, ROBERT, and LENORE JACOBSON *Pygmalion in the Classroom* (New York: Holt, Rinehart and Winston, 1968).

ROSENWEIG, MARK R. "Are There Increase Returns to the Intergenerational Production of Human Capital? Maternal Schooling and Child Intellectual Achievement," *Journal of Human Resources*, Vol. 29, No. 2, Spring 1994, pp. 670–93.

ROSIER, KATHERINE BROWN "Competent Parents, Complex Lives: Managing Parenthood in Poverty," *Journal of Contemporary Ethnography*, Vol. 22, No. 2, July 1993, pp. 171–204.

ROTHENBERG, PAULA S. *Race, Class and Gender in the United States*, 3rd ed. (New York: St. Martin's Press, 1995, 4th ed., 1998).

RUBIN, AMY MAGARO "Around the World, a Myriad of Issues Confront Colleges, *The Chronicle of Higher Education*, August 2, 1996, pp. A32, A34.

RUBIN, LINDA J., and SHERRY B. BORGERS "The Changing Family: Implications for Education," *Principal*, September 1991, pp. 11–12.

RUBINSON, RICHARD "Class Formation, Politics, and Institutions: Schooling in the United States," *American Journal of Sociology*, Vol. 92, No. 3, 1986, pp. 519–48.

RUMBAUT, RUBEN G. "The Crucible Within: Ethnic Identity, Self-Esteem, and Segmented Assimilation among Children of Immigrants," *International Migration Review*, Vol. 28, No. 4, 1994, pp. 748–93.

RUMBAUT, RUBEN G. "The New Immigration," *Contemporary Sociology*, Vol. 24, No. 4, July 1995, pp. 307–11.

RUMBAUT, RUBEN G. "Ties That Bind: Immigration and Immigrant Families in the United States," in Alan Booth, Ann C. Crouter, and Nancy S. Landale (eds.), *Immigration and the Family: Research and Policy on U.S. Immigrants.* (Hillsdale, N.J.: Lawrence Erlbaum Associates, 1996).

RUMBAUT, RUBEN G., and KENJI IMA "The Adaptation of Southeast Asian Refugee Youth: A Comparative Study," Office of Refugee Settlement, U.S. Department of Health and Human Services, December 1987.

RUMBERGER, RUSSELL W. "Family Influences on Dropout Behavior in One California High School," *Sociology of Education*, Vol. 63, October 1990, pp. 283–99.

RUMBERGER, RUSSELL W., and KATHARINE A. LARSON "Toward Explaining Differences in Educational Achievement Among Mexican American Language-Minority Students," *Sociology of Education*, Vol. 71, No. 1, 1998, pp. 69–92.

RUSCH, EDITH, and ELEANOR PERRY "Resistance to Change: An Alternative Story," *International Journal of Educational Reform*, Vol. 8, No. 3, July 1999, pp. 285–300.

RUSSELL, AVERY *Our Babies, Our Future* (New York: Carnegie Corporation of New York, 1994).

RUST, VAL D., AMINATA SOUMARE, OCTAVIO PESCADOR, and MEGUMI SHIBUYA "Research Strategies in Comparative Education," *Comparative Education Review*, Vol. 43, No. 1, February 1999, pp. 86–109.

RUTTER, MICHAEL, ET AL. *Fifteen Thousand Hours: Secondary Schools and Their Effects on Children* (Cambridge, Mass.: Harvard University Press, 1979).

RYAN, KATHRYN M., and JEANNE KANJORSKI, "The Enjoyment of Sexist Humor, Rape Attitudes, and Relationship Aggression in College Students," *Sex Roles: A Journal of Research*, Vol. 38, Nos. 9–10, May 1998, pp. 743–56.

SACKS, DAVID O. and PETER A. THIEL *The Diversity Myth: "Multiculturalism" and the Politics of Intolerance at Stanford* (Oakland, Calif.: Independent Institute, 1995).

SADKER, D., and M. SADKER *Failing at Fairness* (New York: Scribner's, 1994).

SADOVNIK, ALAN R., "Theories in the Sociology of Education," in Jeanne H. Ballantine and Joan Z. Spade (eds.), *Schools and Society* (Belmont, Calif.: Wadsworth, 2001).

SADOVNIK, A. R., P. W. COOKSON, and S. F. SEMEL *Exploring Education: An Introduction to the Foundations of Education* (Boston: Allyn and Bacon, 2000), Chap. 4.

SAHA, LAWRENCE "Bringing People Back In: Sociology and Educational Planning," in A. Yogev (ed.), *International Perspectives on Education and Society*, Vol. 5 (Greenwich, Conn.: JAI Press, 1996).

SAINT, WILLIAM S. "Universities in Africa: Strategies for Stabilization and Revitalization," World Bank Technical Paper No. 194 (Washingon, D.C.: The World Bank, 1992).

SAMOFF, JOEL "The Reconstruction of Schooling in Africa," *Comparative Education Review*, Vol. 37, No. 2, May 1993.

SANCHIRICO, ANDREW "The Importance of Small-Business Ownership in Chinese American Educational Achievement," *Sociology of Education*, Vol. 64, October 1991, pp. 293–304.

SANDAY, PEGGY REEVES *Fraternity Gang Rape: Sex, Brotherhood, and Privelege on Campus* (New York: New York University Press, 1990).

SANDERS, IRWIN T. "The University as a Community," in Perkins, *The University as an Organization*: A Report for The Carnegie Commission on Higher Education (New York: McGraw-Hill, 1973), p. 57.

SAUTMAN, BARRY "Politicalization, Hyperpoliticization, and Depoliticization of Chinese Education," *Comparative Education Review*, Vol. 35, No. 4, November 1991, pp. 669–89.

SAWICKY, MAX B., and ALEX MOLNAR "The Hidden Costs of Channel One" (University of Wisconsin, Milwaukee: Center for the Analysis of Commercialism in Education. School Crime and Safety, 1998), p. viii.

SAX, L. J., ASTIN, A. W., KORN, W. S., and MAHONEY, K. M. "The American Freshman: National Norms for Fall 1999" (Los Angeles: Higher Education Research Institute, 1999).

SCHEURICH, JAMES JOSEPH, and MICHAEL IMBER "Educational Reforms Can Reproduce Societal Inequalities: A Case Study," *Educational Administration Quarterly*, Vol. 27, No. 3, 1991, pp. 297–320.

SCHILLER, KATHRYN S., and DAVID STEVENSON "Sequences of Opportunities for Learning Mathematics," paper presented at American Sociological Association meetings, Pittsburgh, Pa., August 1992.

SCHMIDT, PETER "Department to Reconsider Controversial Bilingual-Ed Rules," *Education Week*, February 5, 1992, p. 21.

SCHNEIDER, BARBARA, ET AL. "Public School Choice: Some Evidence from the National Education Longitudinal Study of 1988," *Education Evaluation and Policy Analysis*, Vol. 18, No. 1, Spring 1996, pp. 19–29.

SCHNEIDER, JOE "Five Prevailing Charter Types," *School Administrator*, Vol. 56, No. 7, August 1999, pp. 29–31.

SCHOENHALS, MARK, MARTA TIENDA, and BARBARA SCHNEIDER "The Educational and Personal Consequences of Adolescent Employment," *Social Forms*, Vol. 77, No. 2, December 1998, pp. 723–61.

SCHOFIELD, JANET WARD "Review of Research on School Desegregation's Impact on Elementary and Secondary School Students," pp. 597–616 in *Handbook of Research on Multicultural Education* (New York: Macmillan, 1995).

SCHWEINHART, LAWRENCE J. "Child-Initiated Learning Activities for Young Children Living in Poverty. *ERIC Digest* (Washington, D.C.: Office of Educational Research and Improvement, October 1997).

Science Study: "Girls Need More Lab Work to Close Gender Gap," *Detroit News*, May 1, 1995, p. E2.

SCOTT, W. RICHARD, and JOHN W. MEYER *Environmental Linkages and Organizational Complexity: Public and Private Schools*, Project Report 84–A16, Institute for Research on Educational Finance and Governance (Stanford, Calif.: Stanford University, July 1984).

SCOTT-JONES, DIANE "Educational Levels of Adolescent Childbearers at First and Second Births," *American Journal of Education*, August 1991, p. 461.

SENDOR, BENJAMIN "Religious Clubs Gain 'Equal Access' to Schools," *The American School Board Journal*, September 1990, p. 15.

SEWELL, WILLIAM H., and VIMAL P. SHAH "Socioeconomic Status, Intelligence, and the Attainment of Higher Education," *Sociology of Education*, Vol. 40, 1967, pp. 1–23.

SHACHAR, HANNA "Developing New Traditions in Secondary Schools: A Working Model for Organizational and Instructional Change," *Teachers College Record*, Vol. 97, No. 4, Summer 1996, pp. 549–68.

SHAKESHAFT, CAROL "The Female World of School Administrators," *Educational Horizons*, Vol. 44, Spring 1986, pp. 117–22.

SHERMAN, MARY ANTOINETTE BROWN "The University in Modern Africa," *Journal of Higher Education*, Vol. 61, No. 4., July/August 1990, p. 363.

SHIELDS, PATRICK M., et al. "Improving Schools from the Bottom Up: From Effective Schools to Restructuring, Final Report" (Washington, D.C.: Department of Education (EDD00080), 1995).

SILBERMAN, CHARLES *Crisis in the Classroom* (New York: Random House, 1970).

SIMMONS, JOHN S. "Censorship: A Threat to Reading, Learning and Thinking" (Newark, Del.: International Reading Association, 1994).

SIMON, SIDNEY B. *Values Clarification: A Handbook of Practical Strategies for Teachers and Students* (New York: Hart, 1972).

SINE, BARBACAR "Non-Formal Education and Education Policy in Ghana and Senegal" (Paris: UNESCO, 1979).

SIZER, THEODORE R. *Horace's Compromise: The Dilemma of the American High School* (Boston: Houghton Mifflin, 1985).

SIZER, THEODORE R. *Horace's School: Redesigning the American High School* (Boston: Houghton Mifflin, 1992.)

SLABY, RONALD G. "Closing the Education Gap on TV's 'Entertainment' Violence," *The Chronicle of Higher Education*, January 5, 1994, pp. B1–B2.)

SLAVIN, ROBERT *Cooperative Learning* (New York: Longman, 1983).

SLAVIN, ROBERT "Cooperative Learning and Intergroup Relations" in James A. Banks and Cheryl A. Banks (eds.), *Handbook of Research on Multicultural Education* (New York: Macmillan, 1995).

SLAVIN, ROBERT E. "Achievement Effects of Ability Grouping in Secondary Schools: A Best-Evidence Synthesis," *Review of Educational Research*, Vol. 60, No. 3, Fall 1990, pp. 471–99.

SLEETER, CHRISTINE E., and CARL A. GRANT "Race, Class, and Gender and Abandoned Dreams," *Teachers' College Record*, Spring 1988.

SLOMCZYNSKI, KAZIMIERZ M., and TADEUSZ K. KRAUZE "The Meritocratic Relationship Between Formal Education and Occupational Status: A Cross-National Analysis," paper presented for 10th World Congress of Sociology, New Delhi, August 1986.

SMELZER, NEIL J. *Theory of Collective Behavior* (New York: Free Press, 1962).

SMITH, DARYL G. "Women's Colleges and Coed Colleges: Is There a Difference for Women?" *Journal of Higher Education*, Vol. 61, No. 2, March/April 1990.

SMITH, MARILYN E. *Television Violence and Behavior: A Research Summary* (Washington, D.C.: Office of Educational Research and Improvement, 1993).

SMITH, W. "Leadership for Educational Renewal." *Phi Delta Kappan*, Vol. 80, No. 8. 1999, pp. 602–5.

SMOCK, PAMELA J., and FRANKLIN D. WILSON "Desegregation and the Stability of White Enrollments: A School-Level Analysis, 1968–1984," *Sociology of Education*, Vol. 64, October 1991, pp. 278–92.

SNYDER, BENSON R. *The Hidden Curriculum* (New York: Alfred A. Knopf, 1971).

SNYDER, ELDON E., and ELMER SPREITZER "Social Psychological Concomitants of Adolescents' Role Identities as Scholars and Athletes: A Longitudinal Analysis," *Youth and Society*, Vol. 23, No. 4, June 1992, pp. 507–22.

Sociology of Education Newsletter, Winter 1992, comments by James E. Coleman, Caroline Hodges Persell, Karl Alexander, and Maureen T. Hallinan, pp. 4–6.

SOMMERFELD, MEG "Asked to 'Dream,' Student Beat the Odds," *Education Week*, April 8, 1992, p. 1.

SOMMERS, CHRISTINA HOFF "The War Against Boys," *The Atlantic Monthly*, May 2000, pp. 59–74.

SOWELL, T. *Race and Culture* (New York: Basic Books, 1994).

SPADE, JOAN Z. "To Group or Not to Group, Is That the Question?" final report, U.S. Department of Education, September 30, 1994.

SPADE, JOAN Z., LYNN COLUMBA, and BETH E VANFESSEN "Tracking in Mathematics and Science: Courses and Course Selection Procedures," *Sociology of Education*, Vol. 70 (1997), pp. 108–27.

SPENCER, DIANE "Tool Kit to Fix Family Illiteracy," *The Times Educational Supplement*, No. 4066, June 3, 1994, p. 5f.

STALLINGS, JANE A. "Ensuring Teaching and Learning in the 21st Century," *Educational Researcher*, Vol. 24, No. 6, August–September 1995, p. 4.

STANTON-SALAZAR, RICARDO D., and SANFORD M. DORNBUSCH "Social Capital and the Reproduction of Inequality: Information Networks Among Mexican-Origin High School Students," *Sociology of Education*, April 1995, p. 116.

"State of American Education Address: A 5–Year Report Card on American Education" (Washington, D.C.: Department of Education, February 22, 2000).

STEELE, CLAUDE M. "Race and the Schooling of Black Americans," *The Atlantic Monthly*, April 1992, pp. 68–78.

STEELMAN, LALA CARR, and BRIAN POWELL "Sponsoring the Next Generation: Parental Willingness to Pay for Higher Education," *American Journal of Sociology*, Vol. 96, No. 6, May 1991, pp. 1505–29.

STEINBERG, ADRIA "The Killing Grounds: Can Schools Help Stem the Violence?" *The Best of The Harvard Education Letter* (Cambridge, Mass.: The Harvard Education Letter, 1994).

STEPHENS, JESSICA E. "Wanted: Minority Educators for U.S. Schools," *School Business Affairs*, Vol. 65, No. 5, May 1999, pp. 37–42.

STEVENSON, DAVID L. "Deviant Students as a Collective Resource in Classroom Control," *Sociology of Education*, Vol. 64, No. 2, April 1991, pp. 127–33.

STEVENSON, DAVID L., and DAVID P. BAKER "The Family-School Relation and the Child's School Performance," *Child Development*, Vol. 58, 1987, pp. 1348–57.

STEWART, DAVID W. *Immigration and Education: The Crisis and the Opportunities* (New York: The Free Press/Macmillan, 1992).

STIRES, LLOYD "Classroom Seating Location, Student Grades, and Attitudes: Environment or Self-Selection?" *Environment and Behavior*, Vol. 12, 1980, pp. 241–54.

STITES, REGIE, and LADISLAUS SEMALI "Adult Literacy for Equality or Economic Growth? Changing Agendas for Mass Literacy in China and Tanzania," *Comparative Education Review*, Vol. 35, No. 1, February 1991, pp. 44–75.

STROMQUIST, NELLY P. "Romancing the State: Gender and Power in Education," *Comparative Education Review*, November 1995, p. 423.

SULLIVAN, PATRICIA "Is Smaller Better? Schools Move to Reduce Class Size in Grades K-3," *Our Children*, Vol. 23, No. 7, April 1998, pp. 34–35.

"Supreme Court Lets Stand Ruling Against Race-Based Scholarships at University of Maryland," *Jet*, Vol. 88, No. 5, June 12, 1995, p. 22.

Swedish Institute, Stockholm, "Child Care in Sweden," 1994.

TALAN, JAMIE "After 40 Years, Black Kids Still Lack Strong Racial Identity," *Dayton Daily News*, September 6, 1987, p. E11.

TALBERT, JOAN E. "Primary and Promise of Professional Development in the Nation's Education Reform Agenda: Sociological Views" (unpublished paper, January 1995).

TANNAN, DEBORAH   "Teachers' Classroom Strategies Should Recognize That Men and Women Use Language Differently," *The Chronicle of Higher Education*, Vol. 37, June 19, 1991, pp. B1, B2–B3.

TARIS, TOON W., and BOK, INGE A.   "Parenting Environment and Scholastic Achievement During Adolescence: A Retrospective Study," *Early Child Development and Care*, Vol. 121, July 1996, pp. 67–83.

TASHMAN, BILLY   "Hyping District 4," *The New Republic*, Vol. 207, No. 24, December 7, 1992, pp. 14–16.

TAVRIS, CAROL   "Boys Trample Girls' Turf," *Los Angeles Times*, May 7, 1990, p. B5.

TEDESCO, JUAN CARLOS   "Confronting Future Challenges: The Capacity for Anticipation," *Educational Innovation and Information*, from International Bureau of Education, No. 84, September 1995, p. 1.

"Teen Pregnancy. State and Federal Efforts to Implement Prevention Programs and Measure Their Effectiveness" (Washington, D.C.: General Accounting Office).

"Ten Years Later: Berkeley After the FSM," *Christian Century*, December 4, 1974, p. 1149.

TEPPER, CLARY A., and Kimberly Wright Cassidy   "Gender Differences in Emotional Language in Children's Picture Books," *Sex Roles: A Journal of Research*, Vol. 40, Nos. 3–4, February 1999, pp. 265–80.

THAYER, YVONNE V., and THOMAS L. SHORTT   "Block Scheduling Can Enhance School Climate," *Educational Leadership*, Vol. 56, No. 4, December-January 1998–1999, pp. 76–81.

THOMPSON, CHALMER E., and BRUCE R. FRETZ   "Predicting the Adjustment of Black Students at Predominantly White Institutions," *Journal of Higher Education*, Vol. 62, No. 4, July/August 1991, pp. 437–49.

THORNBERRY, TERENCE P., and JAMES H. BURCH II "Gang Members and Delinquent Behavior," *Juvenile Justice Bulletin*, June 1997.

THURSTON, LINDA P. and LORI NAVARRETT "A Tough Row to Hoe: Research on Education and Rural Poor Families," in *Rural Goals 2000: Building Programs that Work*. ERIC @ ED394771.

TIENE, DREW, and EVONNE WHITMORE   "TV or Not TV? That Is the Question: A Study of the Effects of Channel One," *Social Education*, February 1995, pp. 159–64.

TOCCI, CYNTHIA M., and GEORGE ENGELHARD JR.   "Achievement, Parental Support, and Gender Differences in Attitudes Toward Mathematics," *Journal of Educational Research*, Vol. 84, No. 5, May/June 1991, p. 280.

TOFFLER, ALVIN   *Future Shock* (New York: Random House, 1970).

TOPOLNICKI, DENISE M.   "Why Private Schools Are Rarely Worth the Money," *Money*, Vol. 23, No. 10, October 1994, pp. 98–112.

TORRES, CARLOS ALBERTO   "Paulo Freire as Secretary of Education in the Municipality of Sao Paulo," *Comparative Education Review*, Vol. 38, No. 2, May 1994, pp. 181–214.

TREMAIN, DONALD. *Occupational Prestige in Comparative Perspective* (New York: Academic Press, 1977).

TRENT, WILLIAM L. "Outcomes of School Desegregation: Findings from Longitudinal Research," *Journal of Negro Education*, Vol. 66, No. 3, Summer 1997, pp. 255–57.

TROW, MARTIN   "Comparative Perspectives on British and American Higher Education," paper presented at American Sociological Association meetings, Chicago, August 1987.

TROW, MARTIN   *Comparative Perspectives on British and American Higher Education* (New York: Cambridge University Press, 1993).

TURNER, BARRY *The Statesmans' Yearbook: Politics, Cultures, and Economics of the World* (New York: St. Martin's Press, 2000).

TURNER, RALPH   "Sponsored and Contest Mobility," *American Sociological Review*, Vol. 25, 1960, pp. 855–67.

ULLINE, CYNTHIA L. "The Privatization of Public Schools: Breaking the Model in Hartford, Connecticut," *Journal of Research and Development in Education*, Vol. 31, No. 3, Spring 1998, pp. 176–88.

"Under Five, and Under-Provided," *The Times Educational Supplement*, November 13, 1992, p. 19.

UNDERWOOD, KENNETH "Power to the People," *American School Board Review*, Vol. 179, No. 6, 1992, pp. 42–43.

UNESCO *The World's Women 1995* (New York; United Nations, 1995).

UNICEF "Country Statistics-Nepal" (New York: United Nations). www.unicef.org/statis/country.

UNICEF *State of the World's Children: 2000*, Table 4: Education. www.unicef.org/sowc00/stat6.

United Nations, *Human Development Report*. www.unicef.org/statis/country.

United Nations Development Program, "Development of Higher Education in Africa: The Accra Seminar, November 15–29, 1991," published 1992.

United Nations Development Program, *Human Development Report* (New York: Oxford University Press, 1993).

United Nations Development Programme, "Human Development Report, 1997" (New York: United Nations). www.unicef.org/statis/country.

U.S. Census Bureau, "Children Below Poverty Level, by Race and Hispanic Origin: 1970–1996," *Current Population Reports*, p. 60–198, No 757.

U.S. Census Bureau, "Resident Population Estimates of the United States by Sex, Race, and Hispanic Origin: April 1, 1990 to November 1, 1999 (Washington, D.C.: Population Estimates Program, Population Division, 1999).

U.S. Census Bureau, Population Division, Population Projections Program (Washington, D.C.: Government Printing Office, 2000).

U.S. Department of Commerce, Bureau of the Census, Current Population Survey, October 1993, unpublished data.

U.S. Department of Commerce, "U.S. Population, by Age, Sex, and Household, 1990" (Washington, D.C.: U.S. Bureau of the Census).

U.S. Department of Commerce, "Population Projects of the United States by Age, Sex, Race, and Hispanic Origin: 1995 to 2050" (Washington, D.C.: Economic and Statistics Administration, Bureau of Census, 1996), p. 25–1130.

U.S. Department of Commerce, *Current Population Survey* (Washington, D.C.: Bureau of the Census, 1999.

U.S. Department of Commerce, *Current Population Reports: Population Projections of the United States by Age, Sex, Race and Hispanic Origin: 1995 to 2050, P25–1130* (Washington, D.C.: Bureau of the Census, 1996).

U.S. Department of Education, *Schools That Work: Educating Disadvantaged Children* (Washington, D.C.: U.S. Department of Education, 1989).

U.S. Department of Education, *What Works? Schools Without Drugs* (Washington, D.C.: U.S. Government Printing Office, 1987).

U.S. Department of Education, "Reaching The Goals" (Washington, D.C.: National Center for Education Statistics, 1993).

U.S. Department of Justice, "School Crime Supplement to the National Crime Victimization Survey, 1989 and 1995; School Crime and Safety: 1998" (Washington, D.C.: Bureau of Justice Statistics, 1998).

U.S. Department of Justice, "Highlights of the 1998 National Youth Gang Survey" (Washington, D.C.: Office of Justice Programs, December 1999), #123.

USEEM, ELIZABETH L. "Social Class and Ability Group Placement in Mathematics in the Transition to Seventh Grade: The Role of Parental Involvement," paper presented at American Educational Research Association meetings, Boston, April 1990.

USEEM, ELIZABETH L. "Student Selection into Course Sequences in Mathematics: The Impact of Parental Involvement and School Policies," *The Journal of Research on Adolescence*, Vol. 1, No. 1, 1991.

USEEM, ELIZABETH L. *Renewing Schools: A Report on the Cluster Initiative in Philadelphia* (Philadelphia: PATHS/PRISM, Spring 1994).

VAGO, STEVEN *Social Change*, 2nd ed. (Englewood Cliffs, N.J.: Prentice Hall, 1989).

VAIL, KATHLEEN "Women at the Top," *American School Board Journal*, December 1999.

VANDELL, DEBORAH LOWE, and SHERI E. HEMBREE "Peer Social Status and Friendship: Independent Contributors to Children's Social and Academic Adjustment," *Merrill-Palmer Quarterly*, Vol. 40, No. 4, 1994, pp. 461–75.

VAUGHAN, GEORGE B. "Institutions on the Edge: America's Community Colleges," *Educational Record*, Vol. 72, No. 2, Spring 1991, pp. 30–33.

VELEZ, WILLIAM "Why Hispanic Students Fail: Factors Affecting Attrition in High Schools," in Leonard Cargan and Jeanne H. Ballantine, *Sociological Footprints*, 6th ed. (Belmont, Calif.: Wadsworth, 1994), pp. 261–67.

VELEZ, WILLIAM, and RAJSHEKHAR G. JAVALGI "Factors Affecting the Probabilities of Transferring from a Two-Year College to a Four-Year College," unpublished paper (1994).

VERDUGO, RICHARD R., and JEFFREY M. SCHNEIDER "Quality Schools, Safe Schools: A Theoretical and Empriical Discussion," *Education and Urban Society*, Vol. 31, No. 3, May 1999, pp. 286–307.

VERSTEGEN, DEBORAH A. "The New Wave of School Finance Litigation," *Phi Delta Kappan*, November 1994, pp. 243–50.

VIADERO, DEBRA "A School of Choice," *Education Week*, Vol. 15, No. 10, November 8, 1995, pp. 31–33.

VOELKI, K. E. "Academic Achievement and Expectations Among African-American Students," *Journal of Research and Development in Education*, Vol. 27, No. 1, Fall 1993, pp. 42–55.

WALDEN, TEDRA, ELIZABETH LEMERISE, and MAUREEN C. SMITH "Friendship and Popularity in Preschool Classrooms," *Early Education and Development*, Vol. 10, No. 3, July 1999, pp. 351–71.

WALKER, DAVID "Britain's Campuses Expect to Face a Rush of Students," *The Chronicle of Higher Education*, Vol. 38, No. 8, October 16, 1991, p. A51.

WALKER, DAVID "Britain's Pioneering Open University Begins Its Third Decade with a New Vice-Chancellor and Big Expansion Plans," *The Chronicle of Higher Education*, Vol. 31, June 19, 1991, pp. A25–26.

WALKER, ROBERT J. "Teaching About Television in the Classroom," *USA Today*, January 1995, pp. 66–67.

WALLER, WILLARD *The Sociology of Teaching* (New York: Wiley, 1932/1965), pp. 120–33.

WALLERSTEIN, IMMANUAL *The Modern World System* (New York: Academic Press, 1974).

WALPOLE, MARYBETH "College and Class Status: The Effect of Social Class Background on College Impact and Outcomes," paper presented at the annual meeting of the American Educational Research Association, Chicago, March 24–28, 1997.

WALSH, MARK "Justices Weigh Allowing Prayers at Graduation," *Education Week*, November 13, 1991, p. 1.

WALSH, MARK "Students at Private Schools for Blacks Post Above-Average Scores, Study Finds," *Education Week*, October 16, 1991.

WANG, MARGARET C., GENEVA D. HAERTEL, and HERBERT J. WALBERG "Models of Reform: A Comparative Guide," *Educational Leadership*, Vol. 55, No. 7, April 1998, pp. 66–71.

WANG, MIN QI, ET AL. "Family and Peer Influences on Smoking Behavior Among American Adolescents: An Age Trend," *Journal of Adolescent Health*, Vol. 16, No. 3, March 1995, pp. 200–203.

WARNER, W. LLOYD, ROBERT J. HAVIGHURST, and MARTIN R. LOEB *Who Shall Be Educated?* (New York: Harper & Row, 1944).

WARR, MARK "Parents, Peers, and Delinquency," *Social Forces*, Vol. 72, No. 1, September 1993, pp. 247–64.

WEBB, JOHN A., ET AL. "Relationship Among Social and Intrapersonal Risk, Alcohol Expectancies, and Alcohol Usage Among Early Adolescents," *Addictive Behaviors*, Vol. 18, No. 2, March–April 1993, pp. 127–34.

WEBER, MAX *The Theory of Social and Economic Organization* (ed. Talcott Parsons; trans. A. M. Henderson and Talcott Parsons) (Glencoe, Ill.: Free Press, 1947).

WEBER, MAX "The Chinese Literati," in H. H. Gerth and C. Wright Mills (eds. and trans.), *From Max Weber: Essays in Sociology* (New York: Oxford University Press, 1958), pp. 422–33.

WEBER, MAX "The Three Types of Legitimate Rule," in Amitai Etzioni (ed.), *Complex Organizations: A Sociological Reader* (New York: Holt, Rinehart and Winston, 1961).

WEHLING, CINDY "The Crack Kids Are Coming," *Principal*, May 1991.

WEILER, JEANNE "Recent Changes in School Desegregation," ERIC/CUE Digest Number 133, April 1998.

WEISTART, JOHN "Title IX and Intercollegiate Sports: Equal Opportunity?" *The Brookings Review*, Vol. 16, No. 4, Fall 1998, pp. 39–43.

WELCH, ANTHONY "Knowledge and Legitimation in Comparative Education," *Comparative Education Review*, Vol. 35, No. 3, 1991, pp. 508–31.

WELKER, ROBERT "Educating Homeless Children," *School Intervention Report*, August/September 1990, pp. 1–2.

WELLS, AMY STUART, ALEJANDRA LOPEZ, JANELLE SCOTT, and JENNIFER JILLISON HOLME "Charter Schools as Postmodern Paradox: Rethinking Social Stratification in an Age of Deregulated School Choice," *Harvard Educational Review*, Vol. 69, No. 2, Summer 1999, pp. 172–204.

WEXLER, PHILIP, WARREN CRICHLOW, JUNE KERN, and REBECCA MARTUSEWICZ *Becoming Somebody: Toward a Social Psychology of School* (Washington, D.C.: Falmer Press, 1992).

"What Matters Most: Teaching for America's Future" (New York: Report of the National Commission on Teacher and America's Future, 1996). p. 54.

"What We Know About Science Teaching and Learning" (Washington, D.C.: Council for Educational Developmental and Research, 1993).

WHITAKER, JOSEPH *Whitaker Almanac* (London: J. Whitaker & Sons Ltd., 1996, 1999, 2000).

WHITE, BURTON L. "Early Childhood Education: A Candid Appraisal," *Principal*, May 1991, pp. 9–11.

"The Widening Gap in Higher Education," *The Chronicle of Higher Education*, June 14, 1996, p. A10+.

WILKINSON, DORIS Y. "The American University and the Rhetoric of Neoconservatism," *Contemporary Sociology*, Vol. 20, No. 4, 1991.

WILLIAMS, EDITH "Paternal Involvement, Maternal Employment, and Adolescents' Academic Achievement: An 11–Year Follow-Up," *American Journal of Orthopsychiatry*, Vol. 63, No. 2, April 1993, pp. 306–12.

WILLIAMS, ROBIN *American Society: A Sociological Interpretation* (New York: Alfred A. Knopf, 1970).

WILLIAMSON, BILL *Education, Social Structure and Development* (London: Macmillan, 1979).

WILLIS, PAUL *Learning to Labor: How Working Class Kids Get Working Class Jobs* (New York: Columbia University Press, 1977).

WILLIS, PAUL "The Class Significance of School Counterculture," in June Purvis and Margaret Hales (eds.), *Achievement and Inequality in Education* (London: Routledge, 1983).

WILSON, FRANKLIN D. "The Impact of School Desegregation Programs on White Public School Enrollment, 1968–1976," *Sociology of Education*, Vol. 58, July 1985, pp. 137–53.

WILSON, KENNETH L., and JANET P. BOLDIZAR "Gender Segregation in Higher Education: Effects of Aspirations, Mathematics Achievement, and Income," *Sociology of Education*, Vol. 63, No. 1, January 1990, pp. 62–74.

WILSON, WILLIAM JULIUS *The Truly Disadvantaged: The Inner City, the Underclass, and Public Policy* (Chicago: The University of Chicago Press, 1987).

WINKLER, KAREN J. "Researcher's Examination of California's Poor Latino Population Prompts Debate over the Traditional Definitions of the Underclass," *The Chronicle of Higher Education*, October 10, 1990, p. A5.

WONG, SANDRA L. "Evaluating the Content of Textbooks: Public Interests and Professional Authority," *Sociology of Education*, Vol. 64, January 1991, pp. 11–18.

WOODHALL, MAUREEN "Sharing Costs of Higher Education: An International Analysis," *Educational Record*, Fall 1991, p. 30.

WOODS, PETER (ed.) *Pupil Strategies: Explorations in the Sociology of the School* (London: Croom Helm, 1980).

The World Bank, *World Development Report 1990: Poverty* (Oxford: Oxford University Press, 1990).

"The World's Women, 1995" (Washington, D.C.: Population Reference Bureau).

YOGEV, ABREHAMG, and HANNA AVALON "Vocational Education and Social Reproduction: Students' Allocation to Curricular Program in Israeli Vocational High Schools," paper presented at American Sociological Association meetings, Chicago, August 1987.

YOUNG, MICHAEL F. D. (ed.) *Knowledge and Control* (West Drayton, Middlesex, England: Collier Macmillan, 1971).

YOUNG, ROBERT E. *A Critical Theory of Education: Habermas and Our Children's Future* (New York: Teachers College Press, 1990).

ZALTMAN, GERALD, and ROBERT DUNCAN *Strategies for Planned Change* (New York: Wiley, 1977).

ZHOU, XUEGUANG, PHYLLIS MOEN, and NANCY BRANDON TUMA "Educational Stratification in Urban China 1949–94," *Sociology of Education*, Vol. 71, No. 3, July 1998, pp. 199–222.

ZIRKEL, PERRY A. "The 'N' Word," *Phi Delta Kappan*, Vol. 80, No. 9, May 1999, pp. 713–14.

ZUNIGA, ROBIN ETTER "The Road to College: Educational Progress by Race and Ethnicity," study sponsored by the Western Interstate Commission for Higher Education and The College Board (Boulder, Colo.: Wiche Publications, 1991).

Index